Journal
#1 Ch- 1, 2 &5
#2 Ch-34, 6
#3 Ch-appendix
#4 - Ch. 10
#5 - Ch- 7,8,9

Issues and Ethics
in the Helping Professions

● **Gerald Corey**
California State University, Fullerton
Diplomate in Counseling Psychology,
American Board of Professional Psychology

● **Marianne Schneider Corey**
Private Practice

● **Patrick Callanan**
Private Practice

Brooks/Cole Publishing Company
Pacific Grove, California

 A CLAIREMONT BOOK

Brooks/Cole Publishing Company
A Division of Wadsworth, Inc.

Printed in the United States of America

10 9 8 7 6 5 4 3 2

Library of Congress Cataloging-in-Publication Data

Corey, Gerald.
    Issues and ethics in the helping professions / Gerald Corey,
Marianne Schneider Corey, Patrick Callanan. — 4th ed.
        p.   cm.
    Includes bibliographical references and index.
    ISBN 0-534-18762-5 :
    1. Psychotherapists—Professional ethics.   2. Counselors-
-Professional ethics.   I. Corey, Marianne Schneider, [date]
II. Callanan, Patrick.   III. Title.
    RC455.2.E8C66   1992
174′.2—dc20   91-37997
                                                        CIP

Sponsoring Editor: Claire Verduin
Editorial Associate: Gay C. Bond
Production Coordinator: Fiorella Ljunggren
Manuscript Editor: William Waller
Permissions Editor: Carline Haga
Interior and Cover Design: Sharon L. Kinghan
Cover Photo: © Mel Pollinger–Fran Heyl Associates
Typesetting: Bookends Typesetting
Printing and Binding: Malloy Lithographing, Inc.

Dedicated to
the legion of friends, colleagues, and students
who opened our eyes to the complexities and
subtleties of ethical thinking and practice

● **Gerald Corey** is a professor of human services and counseling at California State University at Fullerton and was the coordinator of the university's Human Services Program from 1983 to 1991. A licensed psychologist, he received his doctorate in counseling from the University of Southern California. He is a Diplomate in Counseling Psychology, American Board of Professional Psychology, and is a National Certified Counselor. He is a Fellow of the American Psychological Association (Counseling Psychology) and a Fellow of the Association for Specialists in Group Work. In 1991 he received the Outstanding Professor of the Year Award from California State University at Fullerton. In 1986 the Association for Religious and Value Issues in Counseling presented him with an Award in the Field of Professional Ethics.

Jerry teaches courses in professional ethics on both the undergraduate and the graduate levels, as well as offering courses in group process, the theory and practice of counseling, and practicum in group leadership. With his colleagues he has conducted workshops in the United States, Mexico, China, and Europe, with a special focus on training in group counseling and ethics; he often presents workshops and is a guest lecturer at various universities. With his wife, Marianne, and other colleagues, he offers weeklong residential personal-growth groups and residential training and supervision workshops each summer in Idyllwild, California.

Along with Barbara Herlihy, Jerry recently co-authored *Dual Relationships in Counseling*. Other recent books he has authored or co-authored (all published by Brooks/Cole Publishing Company) are:

- *Becoming a Helper,* Second Edition (1993)
- *Group Techniques,* Second Edition (1992)
- *Groups: Process and Practice,* Fourth Edition (1992)
- *Case Approach to Counseling and Psychotherapy,* Third Edition (1991)
- *Theory and Practice of Counseling and Psychotherapy,* Fourth Edition (and *Manual*) (1991)
- *I Never Knew I Had a Choice,* Fourth Edition (1990)
- *Theory and Practice of Group Counseling,* Third Edition (and *Manual*) (1990)

● **Marianne Schneider Corey**   is a licensed marriage and family therapist in Idyllwild, California, and is a National Certified Counselor. She received her master's degree in marriage, family, and child counseling from Chapman College. She is a Fellow of the Association for Specialists in Group Work; is a Clinical Member of the American Association for Marriage and Family Therapy; and holds memberships in the California Association of Marriage and Family Therapists, the American Association for Counseling and Development, the Association for Religious and Value Issues in Counseling, and the National Organization for Human Service Education.

Marianne's professional interests include counseling individuals and couples and leading therapeutic groups and training groups for mental-health professionals. She also trains and supervises student leaders in a group-counseling class and co-leads weeklong residential growth groups at California State University at Fullerton. With her colleagues she has conducted professional workshops in the United States, Mexico, China, and Europe. She received an Award for Contributions to the Field of Professional Ethics from the Association for Religious and Value Issues in Counseling in 1986.

Marianne has co-authored the following books (all published by Brooks/Cole Publishing Company):

- *Becoming a Helper,* Second Edition (1993)
- *Group Techniques,* Second Edition (1992)
- *Groups: Process and Practice,* Fourth Edition (1992)
- *I Never Knew I Had a Choice,* Fourth Edition (1990)

She has also co-authored several articles in the *Journal for Specialists in Group Work.*

Marianne and Jerry have been married since 1964. They have two adult daughters, Cindy and Heidi, and have made their home in the mountain community of Idyllwild, California. Marianne grew up in Germany and has kept in close contact with her family in that country.

● **Patrick Callanan** is a licensed marriage and family therapist in private practice in Santa Ana, California, and is a National Certified Counselor. He graduated with a bachelor's degree in human services from California State University at Fullerton in 1973 and then received his master's degree in professional psychology from United States International University in 1976. In his private practice he works with individuals, couples, families, and groups.

Patrick is a part-time faculty member in the Human Services Program at California State University at Fullerton, where he regularly teaches the internship course. He also offers his time each year to the university to assist in training and supervising group leaders and to co-lead weeklong residential growth groups. He is a consultant for mental-health practitioners and presents workshops and training groups at conventions and for professional organizations. He is a member of the California Association of Marriage and Family Therapists, the Association for Specialists in Group Work, and the American Association for Counseling and Development. He received an Award for Contributions to the Field of Professional Ethics from the Association for Religious and Value Issues in Counseling in 1986.

Patrick has co-authored several articles in the *Journal for Specialists in Group Work,* as well as the following book (published by Brooks/Cole Publishing Company):

• *Group Techniques,* Second Edition (1992)

Preface

Issues and Ethics in the Helping Professions is written for both graduate and undergraduate students in the helping professions. It is suitable for courses involving human-services delivery, including counseling and social work. It can be used as a core textbook in courses such as practicum, fieldwork, internship, and ethical and professional issues or as a supplementary text in courses dealing with skills or theory. Because the issues we discuss are likely to be encountered throughout one's professional career, we have tried to use language and concepts that will be meaningful both to students doing their fieldwork and to professionals interested in improving their skills through continuing-education seminars or independent reading.

In this book we attempt to involve readers in learning to deal with the professional and ethical issues that most affect the actual practice of counseling and related helping professions. To this end we raise the following questions: How do the therapist's values and life experiences affect the therapeutic process? What are the rights and responsibilities of both the client and the helper? As professionals, how can we determine our level of competence? How can we provide quality services for culturally diverse populations? What are some major ethical issues facing practitioners in marital and family therapy? in group work? in community agencies? in private practice?

Our goal is both to provide a body of information and to teach readers a process of dealing with the basic issues they will face throughout their careers. For most of the issues we raise, we present a number of viewpoints to stimulate discussion and reflection. We also present our views, when appropriate, to challenge readers to formulate their own positions.

To assist in this process, we cite the ethical codes of various professional organizations, which offer some guidance for practice. These guidelines leave many questions unanswered, however. We believe that students and professionals alike must ultimately struggle with the issues of responsible practice, deciding how accepted ethical standards apply in the specific cases they encounter.

We have tried to make this book a personal one that will involve our readers in an active and meaningful way. To this end we have provided many opportunities to respond to our discussions and to draw on personal experiences. Each chapter begins with a self-inventory designed to help students focus on the key topics to be discussed in the chapter. Within the chapters we frequently ask readers to think about how the issues apply to them. Open-ended cases and situations are presented to stimulate thought and assist readers in formulating their own positions. We cite related literature when exploring ethical and professional issues. Suggestions for further reading are provided throughout the text.

This book combines the advantages of a textbook and a student manual. Instructors will find an abundance of material and suggested activities, surely more than can be covered in a single course. An *Instructor's Resource Manual* is available that contains suggestions for teaching an ethics course, test items, and study-guide questions.

There has been an increase in journal articles and books in the past decade dealing with ethical and professional issues in the helping professions. The responses from users of the previous editions of this book please us, because these people continue to say that studying ethics can lead to exciting and provocative classroom discussions.

This fourth edition of *Issues and Ethics in the Helping Professions* has been extensively revised and updated. It provides new topics and more comprehensive coverage than the previous editions. Some of the additions are:

- an expanded introductory chapter on models of ethical decision making
- an expanded chapter on issues in multicultural counseling
- inclusion in the Appendix of the revised codes of ethics of four professional organizations
- an increased focus on informed consent and the rights of clients
- updated coverage of guidelines for working with special populations, such as women, gays and lesbians, and ethnic minorities
- a new discussion of issues in child-abuse reporting
- discussions of landmark court cases with implications for professional practice
- updated coverage of confidentiality and privileged communication
- new material on the duty to warn and protect
- new material on the implications of the AIDS crisis for clinical practice
- additional methods of preventing malpractice suits
- new material on trends and practices in the field of counselor education and training
- increased coverage of counseling supervision
- new material on ethical issues in consultation
- more extensive coverage of dual relationships in counseling
- an updated and expanded discussion of sexual attractions and intimacies in the client/therapist relationship
- delineation of professional responsibilities and liabilities
- expanded coverage of ways of working in the community
- increased attention to legal issues
- many new case illustrations and examples

- new material on licensure and certification processes for the various mental-health disciplines
- resources to contact for information about certificates, licenses, and professional organizations
- new material on the role of peer review and peer-consultation groups in ensuring professional competency
- an updated discussion of ethical issues in group work and marital and family therapy
- an updated survey of the literature dealing with ethical and professional issues, with emphasis on recent journal articles

A note on terminology: We frequently use the terms *mental-health professional, practitioner, counselor, therapist, and helper.* We generally use these interchangeably but we have also tried to reflect the differing nomenclature of the various professions that we cover.

Acknowledgments

Our thanks to the prerevision reviewers: James Bray of Baylor College of Medicine; Phillip Lauver of the University of Arizona; Elaina Rose Lovejoy of St. Mary's College of California; Lewis B. Morgan of Villanova University; Robert Peterson of Metropolitan State University; and Holly Stadler of University of Missouri, Kansas City. These reviewers made valuable suggestions for revisions of the text.

We also thank the following people who reviewed the manuscript of the fourth edition of the book and offered valuable suggestions for improvement: A. Michael Dougherty of Western Carolina University; Barbara Herlihy of the University of Houston at Clear Lake; Beverly Palmer of California State University, Dominguez Hills; Terrence Patterson of the University of San Francisco; George T. Williams of California State University, Fullerton; and Robert E. Wubbolding of Xavier University.

We received extra help on selected chapters from several people. Theodore P. Remley, Jr., Executive Director of the American Association for Counseling and Development, reviewed Chapters 1 and 7. Thomas Clawson, Executive Director of the National Board of Certified Counselors, reviewed Chapter 7. Soraya Coley and David Ho, both of California State University, Fullerton, reviewed Chapter 14. David Ho, Allen E. Ivey of the University of Massachusetts, and Paul Pedersen of Syracuse University reviewed Chapter 10. Mary Moline of California State University, Fullerton, reviewed Chapter 12. The expertise of these chapter reviewers helped us in refining key points.

Finally, we want to express our appreciation to those people in the Brooks/Cole family who have contributed their talents to making this a better book. Claire Verduin, counseling and psychology editor, and Fiorella Ljunggren, production service manager, continue to demonstrate their special interest in all our books and provide us supportive guidance. Special recognition also goes to William Waller, the manuscript editor, who meticulously labored on these pages and who provided many helpful suggestions for improving the narrative flow of the book. We also wish to thank Katie Dutro for preparing the indexes.

Gerald Corey
Marianne Schneider Corey
Patrick Callanan

Contents

● **CHAPTER SIX**
Dual Relationships in Counseling   **139**

● **CHAPTER SEVEN**
Professional Competence and Training   **169**

● **CHAPTER EIGHT**
Issues in Supervision and Consultation   **192**

● CHAPTER NINE
Issues in Theory, Practice, and Research   212

● CHAPTER TEN
Ethical Concerns in Multicultural Counseling   238

● CHAPTER ELEVEN
Issues with Special Populations   267

● **CHAPTER TWELVE**
Ethical Issues in Marital and Family Therapy   **304**

● **CHAPTER THIRTEEN**
Ethical Issues in Group Work   **325**

CHAPTER ONE

Introduction to Professional Ethics

- The Focus of This Book
- Ethical Decision Making
- Some Suggestions for Using This Book
- Self-Assessment: An Inventory of Your Attitudes and Beliefs about Professional and Ethical Issues
- Chapter Summary
- Suggested Activities
- Suggested Readings

The Focus of This Book

The three of us have worked together for a number of years and have also practiced counseling independently. During that time we have had to confront a variety of professional and ethical issues that do not have clear-cut solutions. Exchanging ideas has helped us clarify our positions on these difficult issues, and conversations with students and colleagues have shown us that others are wrestling with similar questions. We have become convinced that students in the helping professions should think seriously about these problems before they begin practicing.

Some of the issues to which we are referring arise out of the fact that counselors, no less than clients, are *people,* with their own personalities, strengths, and shortcomings. In Chapter 2, for instance, we point out that it is impossible to separate the kind of person a counselor is from the kind of help he or she will be able to provide. Whether practitioners can form honest and caring relationships with their clients is a significant issue.

Other issues involve the nature of the therapeutic process and the helping relationship. What role do our personal values play in our counseling of others? What ethical responsibilities and rights do clients and counselors have? What theory of counseling should we choose, and how important is it to have a clear theoretical approach? How can we assess professional competence? What ethical issues are involved in training, supervision, and consultation? What considerations are involved in adapting one's counseling practice to diverse client populations? What special ethical issues are raised by marital and family therapy? by group counseling? What is the counselor's role in the community? How can practitioners determine the most ethical position given the myriad of ethical, legal, and community standards involved?

In considering these questions, we decided to write a book that would be meaningful both to experienced practitioners and to students about to embark on their professional careers. Many of the issues that are relevant to beginning professionals resurface later and take on different meanings at the various stages of one's professional development.

Just as we have found no easy answers to most of the issues that we face in our practices, we have tried not to fall into the trap of dispensing prescriptions or providing simple solutions to complex problems. Our main purpose is to give you the basis for formulating your own ethical guidelines within the broad limits of professional codes and divergent theoretical positions. We raise what we consider to be central issues, present a range of views on these issues, discuss our position, and provide you with many opportunities to refine your own thinking and actively develop your position.

You will realize while reading this book that we have certain biases and viewpoints about ethical behavior. We hope you will see these stances as *our* points of view rather than the *correct* points of view. We try to keep our viewpoints open to revision. We state our positions on issues not to sway you to adopt our views but, rather, to challenge you to devise your own position, for in the end you will be responsible for your own ethical practice.

We do not mean to imply that students are free to choose any set of ethical views merely because it "feels right." The various human-services professions have developed codes of ethics that are binding on their members. Any professional should, of course, know the ethical code of his or her specialty and should be aware of the consequences of practicing in ways that are not sanctioned by the organization. Even within the broad guidelines of ethical codes, responsible practice implies that professionals use informed, sound, and responsible judgment. Thus, professionals should consult with colleagues, keep themselves up to date through reading and continuing education, and continually examine their behavior. Codes of ethics provide general standards, but these guidelines are not sufficiently explicit to deal with every situation. It is often difficult to interpret ethical codes, and people differ over how to apply them in specific cases. Consequently, practitioners retain a significant degree of freedom and will encounter many situations that demand the exercise of sound judgment in order to further the best interests of their clients.

The issues dealt with in this text need to be reexamined periodically throughout your professional life. Even if you resolve some of these issues at the initial stage of your development as a counselor, they may take on new dimensions as you gain experience, and minor questions may become major concerns as you progress in your profession. Many students burden themselves with the expectation that they should resolve all possible issues before they are ready to begin practicing, but we see the definition and refinement of such issues as an evolutionary process that requires an open and self-critical attitude. If we have done our job well in presenting these issues, we will primarily be raising questions in your mind rather than providing you with answers. Our goal is to give you a flexible framework for working through ethical dilemmas.

Ethical Decision Making
Some Key Terms

The terms *ethics*, *values*, *morality*, *community standards*, *laws*, and *professionalism* intertwine as we deal with the issues presented in this book. Before focusing directly on ethical decision making, we need to make some distinctions among these related terms. Although *values* and *ethics* are frequently used interchangeably, the two terms are not identical. Values pertain to what is *good* and *desirable*, whereas ethics involve what is *right* and *correct* (Loewenberg & Dolgoff, 1988). *Ethics* are moral principles adopted by an individual or group to provide rules for right conduct. *Morality* involves an evaluation of actions on the basis of some broader cultural context or religious standard. Thus, conduct that is evaluated as moral in one society might well be evaluated as immoral in another society. *Community standards*, or *mores*, as one aspect of morals, vary on an interdisciplinary, a theoretical, and a geographical basis. The standard for a counselor's social contact with clients may differ from a large urban area to a rural area or between an analytic approach and a behavioral approach. Such community standards often become the ultimate *legal* criteria for determining whether practitioners are liable for damages. *Professionalism* has some relationship to ethical behavior, yet it is possible to be unprofessional and still not be unethical. For instance, showing up late for appointments with clients might be viewed as unprofessional, but it would probably not be considered unethical.

Some situations cut across all of the above perspectives. For instance, sexual intimacy between counselors and clients is considered unethical, unprofessional, immoral, and illegal. Keep the differences in the meanings of these various concepts in mind as you read.

Foundations of an Ethical Perspective

Ethical decisions in counseling are usually not easy. The issues involved are often complex and multifaceted, and they defy simplistic solutions. There are many gray areas that require decision-making skills. This process entails not only learning information about ethical standards but also learning how to define and work with a variety of difficult situations.

Law and Ethics. Ethical issues in the mental-health professions are regulated both by laws and by professional codes. Both laws and ethical codes provide guidelines, yet neither offers many exact answers. Laws and ethical codes, by their very nature, tend to be reactive, emerging from what has occurred rather than anticipating what may occur. We hope that you will not limit your behavior to obeying statutes and following ethical standards but will develop a sensitivity to doing what is best for your clients. It is very important that you acquire this ethical sense at the beginning of your professional program. The basic purpose of practicing ethically is to further the welfare of the client.

At times there may be conflicts between the law and ethical principles, and in these cases the values of the counselor come into the picture. Mappes, Robb, and Engels (1985) note that codes of ethics are designed to guide practitioners, protect clients, safeguard the autonomy of professional workers, and enhance the status of the profession. Conflicts between these codes and the law may arise in areas such as advertising, confidentiality, and clients' rights of access to their own files. A recent draft of the American Psychological Association's ethical code indicates that in cases where there are conflicts between ethics and the law, psychologists should seek to resolve the conflict in a way that complies with the law and at the same time most nearly conforms to the code (APA, 1991a). In those cases where neither the law nor an ethics code resolves an issue, therapists are advised to consider other professional and community standards and their own conscience as well. There are few conflicts between law and ethics. Law reflects the minimum standards that society will tolerate; ethics represents the ideal standards set by professionals. There are differences in minimum and maximum standards, but not necessarily conflicts.

In making ethical decisions, we must ask questions such as "Which values should I rely on? What values do I hold? How do my values affect my work with clients? Why do I hold certain values?" We agree with Tennyson and Strom (1986) that acting responsibly is an inner quality, not something imposed by authority.

One way of conceptualizing professional ethics is to contrast lower-level ethical functioning with higher-level functioning. The first level of ethical functioning, also called "mandatory ethics," is characterized by compliance with the law and with professional codes. Practitioners who comply at this level are generally safe from legal action or professional censure. At the higher level of ethical functioning, called "aspirational ethics," practitioners go further and reflect on the effects that their interventions have on the welfare of their clients. The 1991 draft of the APA ethics code addresses both mandatory ("standards") and aspirational ("principles") ethics.

When the word *unethical* is used, people too often think of gross violations of established codes. In reality, most violations of ethics probably happen quite inadvertently in counseling practice. If practitioners are not aware of the more subtle ways in which their behavior can adversely affect their clients, such behavior can go unnoticed, and the clients will suffer. For instance, a private practitioner whose practice is not flourishing may tend to prolong the therapy of his clients and may justify his actions on theoretical grounds. He is likely to ignore the fact that the prolongation of therapy is influenced by his financial situation. Or a counselor whose funding in an agency requires that she demonstrate that her work is effective may devote more attention to this justification than to the clients' goals. Practitioners can easily find themselves in an ethical quagmire based on competing role expectations; only a focus on the clients' best interests will enable them to maintain a clear ethical position.

Many ethical violations are hard to detect, and therefore ethical codes are difficult to enforce. Clients' needs are best met when practitioners monitor their own ethics. Many ethical violations can go undetected for the simple reason that only practitioners know about them. Rather than just looking at others and proclaiming "That's unethical!" we encourage you to challenge your own thinking and apply guidelines to your behavior by asking yourself "Is what I am doing in the best interests of my client?"

The Role of Professional Codes

Various professional organizations have established codes of ethics that provide broad guidelines for mental-health practitioners. Examples of such ethical standards are presented in the Appendix. At this time we encourage you to review these standards so that you can apply them to the issues we raise in the remaining chapters of this book. Some of the professional mental-health organizations in addition to the APA that have formulated codes are the National Association of Social Workers (NASW), the American Association for Counseling and Development (AACD), the American Association for Marriage and Family Therapy (AAMFT), the American Psychiatric Association (APA), the Association for Specialists in Group Work (ASGW), the National Board for Certified Counselors (NBCC), the Association for Counselor Education and Supervision (ACES), and the American School Counselor Association (ASCA).

We use the word *guidelines* in a generic sense to include ethical *standards* and *principles*. Although you will become familiar with the ethical guidelines of your specialization, you will be challenged to develop your own personal code to govern your practice. The ethical guidelines offered by most professional organizations are broad and general. Smith, McGuire, Abbott, and Blau (1991) remind us that ethical codes and guidelines are a combination of both rules and utilitarian principles, rather than precise dictates. They write that practitioners are challenged to clarify and interpret codes and to make personal judgments in applying these codes to various situations. Your own ethical awareness and problem-solving skills will determine how you translate general guidelines into your professional day-to-day behavior.

From what we have said, it is clear that ethical codes are necessary, but not sufficient, for exercising ethical responsibility. Thus, it is essential that you be aware of the limitations of such codes (Ibrahim & Arredondo, 1990; Mabe & Rollin, 1986; Mappes et al., 1985; Pedersen, 1989; Pope & Vasquez, 1991; Talbutt, 1981; Tymchuk, 1981):

- Some issues cannot be handled solely by relying on ethical codes.
- There are problems with enforcing codes; courts may decide that the provisions are not applicable. Community standards may be more salient factors.
- Conflicts sometimes emerge within ethical codes as well as among various organizations' codes.
- Ethical codes tend to be reactive rather than proactive.
- A practitioner's values may conflict with a code.
- Codes may conflict with institutional policies and practices.
- Ethical codes need to be understood within a cultural framework, and therefore they must be adapted to specific cultures.
- Because of the diverse viewpoints within any professional organization, not all of its members will agree with all of the specific standards.

Codes are not intended to be a blueprint that removes all need for the use of judgment and ethical reasoning (Welfel & Lipsitz, 1984). Pope and Vasquez (1991) agree with this view, maintaining that formal ethical principles can never be substituted for an active, deliberative, and creative approach to meeting ethical responsibilities. They remind us that ethical codes cannot be applied in a rote manner, mainly because each client's situation is unique and thus calls for a different solution. Final authority must rest with the helper in determining what is right in a particular situation. Keith-Spiegel and Koocher (1985) suggest that a final ethical judgment depends on the therapist's individual bias, experience, orientation within the discipline, personality, and personal values.

Ethical codes are partially designed to protect practitioners against charges of malpractice, for therapists who conscientiously practice in accordance with accepted professional codes have some measure of defense in case of litigation. Compliance with or violation of ethical codes of conduct may be admissible as evidence in some legal proceedings, depending on the circumstances. In a lawsuit a counselor's conduct would probably be judged in comparison with that of other professionals with similar qualifications and duties. Actually, the community standard—what professionals *actually* do—is less rigorous than ethical standards— what professionals *should* do. It is incumbent on professionals to remain aware of what others in their local area and subspecialties are doing on a practical level.

When faced with an ethical conflict, professionals tend to think in terms of formal codes of ethics and relevant legal guidelines in deciding what they *should* do (Smith et al., 1991). However, practitioners are more likely to respond to personal values and practical considerations in determining what they actually *would* do if faced with the situation.

We suggest that you devote some time to reviewing the basic similarities and differences among the ethical guidelines of various professional organizations. Knowing the general content of the codes (reprinted in the Appendix), you will be in a better position to apply established guidelines to the practical problems that we will pose throughout this book. In reading the professional codes, you should examine their assets and limitations. Identify any areas of possible disagreement you might have with a particular standard. If you decide to practice in violation of a specific code, you will surely need a rationale for your course of action. Realize also that there are consequences for violating the codes of your profession. Must you follow all the ethical codes of your profession to be considered an ethical practitioner? If you agree with and follow all the ethical codes of your profession, does this necessarily mean that you are an ethical professional?

The Development of Ethical Codes

The ethical codes of the professional organizations are not static but must be revised as new concerns arise. Thus, the first APA code of ethics was adopted in 1953. It was revised in 1959 and 1981 and amended in 1989, and at this time it is being revised and expanded (see APA, 1991a). There is a *Casebook on Ethical Principles of Psychologists* (APA, 1987), consisting of examples of how the code applies to a range of situations. The association plans to publish updated casebook information in A *Guide to Applying the APA Ethics Code* after the new code is approved.

The first AACD ethical code was adopted in 1961, and revisions were made in 1974, 1981, and 1988. The *AACD Ethical Standards Casebook* deals with how the 1988 code can be used to resolve a variety of ethical dilemmas (Herlihy & Golden, 1990).

Most of the other codes of ethics of the various professional organizations have also undergone several revisions. We have selected the AACD and APA versions to illustrate that such codes are established by a group of professionals for the purpose of protecting consumers and furthering the professional stance of the organizations. As such, these codes do not convey ultimate truth, nor do they provide ready-made answers for the ethical dilemmas that practitioners must face. Casebooks can never replace the informed judgment and goodwill of the individual counselor. They are tools that must be used wisely in making difficult decisions in complex situations. We want to emphasize again a need for a level of ethical functioning higher than merely following the letter of the law or the code. For instance, you might avoid a lawsuit or a professional censure by ignoring cultural diversity, but many of your ethnically diverse clients could suffer from your neglect. In Chapter 10 we will discuss how current codes do not take cultural concerns sufficiently into account.

Enforcement of Ethical Codes

Most of the professional organizations have ethics committees, elected or delegated bodies that oversee the conduct of members of the organization. Let us consider the APA Ethics Committee as an example. The main purposes of the committee are to educate the association's membership about ethical principles and practices and to protect the public from unethical practices. Bennett, Bryant, VandenBos, and Greenwood (1990) summarize the objectives of the committee as these: formulating ethical principles for adoption by the association; receiving and investigating complaints of unethical conduct by its members; processing and resolving complaints of professional misconduct and recommending a specific course of action in a given case; and reporting on types of complaints that are received by the committee. The committee meets regularly to process formal complaints against individual members of the association.

After the committee launches an investigation of a complaint lodged against a member, it can take various actions, some of which are dismissing the complaint on the ground that there is insufficient substance to the complaint; sanctioning the member; recommending that the member be allowed to resign from the organization; recommending that the member be dropped; and recommending a specific course of remedial action such as obtaining ongoing supervision or personal therapy. Dismissal or suspension of a member is a major sanction that professional associations can apply. If a member is dropped, the entire membership is notified in writing. Such practitioners also face the loss of their license or certificate to practice, but only if the state board conducts an independent investigation. State licensure boards have the right to prohibit the practice of one's profession and can also issue reprimands to professionals.

Models of Ethical Decision Making

Several writers have developed models for ethical decision making (Jordan & Meara, 1990; Keith-Spiegel & Koocher, 1985; Kitchener, 1984; Loewenberg & Dolgoff, 1988; Paradise & Siegelwaks, 1982; Smith et al., 1991; Stadler, 1986a; Tymchuk, 1981). Jordan and Meara (1990) point out that the teaching of professional ethics tends to focus on the application of principles to ethical dilemmas. They make a differentiation between principle ethics and virtue ethics. *Principle ethics* includes approaches that focus on the use of rational, objective, universal, and impartial principles in the analysis of ethical dilemmas. Principles typically focus on acts and choices, and they are used to facilitate the selection of socially and historically acceptable answers to the question of "What shall I do?" *Virtue ethics* focuses on the character of the counselor. Simply stated, principle ethics asks "Is this situation unethical?" whereas virtue ethics asks "Am I doing what is best for my client?" In the case of virtue ethics there is a consciousness of ethical behavior, even in the absence of an ethical dilemma.

Jordan and Meara conclude that virtue ethics is an essential component of responsible ethical training and practice. It is not a question of making ethical decisions by focusing exclusively on either principles or virtues; rather, both principles and virtues need to be considered, because both are important elements in thinking through ethical concerns. Some counselors concern themselves with avoiding a malpractice suit. Their practices are influenced by following the law and ethical codes so that they will stay out of trouble. Other counselors are more concerned with doing what is best for their clients than they are in protecting themselves. Such counselors would consider it unethical to use techniques that might not result in the greatest benefit to their clients or those in which they were not thoroughly trained, even though these techniques might not lead to a lawsuit. For example, a Gestalt therapist might refer a client to a cognitive-behavioral therapist because, in her opinion, the client might be more suited to the latter approach. Although this therapist could legally and ethically justify seeing this client, it might be more "virtuous" for her to refer the client in this instance. As Jordan and Meara write, "The ideals of professional psychology must include conscientious decision making, but they also must include virtuous deciders, who emphasize not so much what is permitted as what is preferred" (1990, p. 112).

A Critical-Evaluation Model. Kitchener (1984) describes a critical-evaluation model of ethical decision making that illustrates the role of virtues in making decisions. Her model is based on four basic moral principles: autonomy, beneficence, nonmaleficence, and justice, or fairness. After a definition of each of these four principles, we illustrate each one with a specific ethical guideline from the NASW code (1990).

Autonomy refers to the promotion of self-determination, or the freedom of clients to choose their own direction. The relevant NASW guideline is "The social worker should make every effort to foster maximum self-determination on the part of clients" (II, G).*

Beneficence refers to promoting good for others. Ideally, counseling contributes to the growth and development of the client, and whatever counselors do should be judged against this criterion. The following guideline illustrates beneficence: "The social worker should serve clients with devotion, loyalty, determination, and the maximum application of professional skill and competence" (II, F, 1).

Nonmaleficence means avoiding doing harm, which includes refraining from actions that risk hurting clients. An example of this concept is: "The social worker should not exploit relationships with clients for personal advantage" (II, F, 2).

Justice, or *fairness*, refers to providing equal treatment to all people. This standard implies that anyone—regardless of age, sex, race, ethnicity, disability, socioeconomic status, cultural background, religion, or lifestyle—is entitled to equal access to mental-health services. Applying this principle to the practice of social work involves the expectation that practitioners will promote the general welfare

*Citations are to the *Code of Ethics* of the NASW, reprinted in the Appendix.

of society: "The social worker should act to prevent and eliminate discrimination against any person or group on the basis of race, color, sex, sexual orientation, age, religion, national origin, marital status, political belief, mental or physical handicap, or any other preference or personal characteristic, condition, or status" (VI, P, 1).

Applying the ethical-decision-making model described by Kitchener and the NASW guidelines specified above is not as simple as it may seem. For example, promoting autonomy may have to be tempered if the client's culture discourages autonomous behavior. As you will see in Chapters 10 and 14, a number of writers contend that traditional mental-health services have only limited value in meeting the needs of culturally diverse populations. For instance, many members of minority groups do not make full use of the human-services agencies in their communities. In many cases, they may stop coming in for help after one meeting with a professional. We can examine this issue of the underuse of mental-health services in light of the four fundamental principles described by Kitchener:

1. *Autonomy.* Traditional helping services are based on the values of individualism, independence, self-determination, and making choices for oneself. However, many cultural groups stress a different set of values, such as interdependence and making decisions with the welfare of the family and community in mind. What are the implications of the principle of autonomy when it is applied to clients who do not place a high priority on the value of being autonomous? What are the implications of promoting autonomy for those incapable of it (for example, dependent youths)?

2. *Beneficence.* Consider a counselor who encourages a Japanese client to behave more assertively toward his father. The reality of this situation may be that the father would refuse to speak again to a son who confronted him. As this example shows, even though counselors may be operating with good intentions and may think they are being beneficent, they may not always be doing what is in the best interests of their clients. Questions that we raise are: Is it possible for counselors to harm the client unintentionally by encouraging a course of action that has negative consequences? How can counselors know what is in the best interests of their clients? How is it possible to determine if a counselor's interventions will lead to the growth and development of clients?

3. *Nonmaleficence.* Traditional diagnostic practices can be harmful to certain cultural groups. For instance, therapists can assign a diagnostic label to a client based on a pattern of behavior that they judge to be abnormal. Yet certain behaviors—such as inhibition of emotional expression, lack of assertiveness, unwillingness to engage freely in self-disclosure, or the avoidance of direct eye contact while speaking—may all be considered normal behaviors in certain cultures. If a culturally different client does not feel understood, or if a therapist gives an inappropriate diagnosis to the client, he or she may never return for any professional service. Practitioners need to develop cultural awareness and sensitivity in using assessment, diagnostic, and treatment procedures.

4. *Justice, or fairness.* Traditional mental-health services may not be based on principles that are just and fair to everyone in a culturally diverse society. If intervention strategies are not relevant to some segments of the population, justice

is being violated. How can practitioners adapt the techniques they use so that they fit the needs of diverse populations? How can new helping strategies be developed that are consistent with the world view of culturally different clients?

In Chapter 14 we will consider the ethical issues that practitioners are bound to face as they work in the community. Rather than relying exclusively on individual psychotherapy, therapists often need to function in the role of advocate, community organizer, consultant, and agent for change. This role involves rethinking their practice as a helper. It is a good idea for practitioners to reflect on what they do in light of the four principles discussed above to determine the degree to which their practice is consistent with promoting the welfare of the clients they serve.

Steps in Making Ethical Decisions.   Some of the following steps, suggested by the creators of various models of ethical decision making, may help you think through ethical problems:

• *Identify the problem, or dilemma.* Gather as much information as possible that sheds light on the situation. Clarify whether the conflict is ethical, legal, or moral or a combination of any or all of these. Remember that such dilemmas are complex, so that it is useful to look at the problem from many perspectives and to avoid simplistic solutions. Because ethical dilemmas do not have "right" or "wrong" answers, practitioners are challenged to deal with ambiguity.

• *Identify the potential issues involved.* After the information is collected, list and describe the critical issues and discard the irrelevant ones. Evaluate the rights, responsibilities, and welfare of all those who are affected by the situation. Part of the process of making ethical decisions involves identifying competing moral principles. Consider the basic moral principles of autonomy, beneficence, nonmaleficence, and justice and apply them to a particular situation. It may help to prioritize these principles and think through ways in which they can support a resolution to the dilemma. Good reasons can often be presented to support various sides of a given issue. Different ethical principles may sometimes imply contradictory courses of action.

•*Review the relevant ethical guidelines.* Ask whether the guidelines, standards, or principles of your organization offer a possible solution to the problem. Consider whether your own values and ethics are consistent with or in conflict with the relevant guidelines. If you are in disagreement with a guideline, do you have a rationale to support your position?

• *Obtain consultation.* At this point, it is generally helpful to consult with a colleague or colleagues to obtain a different perspective on the problem. Because of your involvement in the situation, you may have trouble in seeing the forest for the trees. Consultation can help you think about information or circumstances that you may have overlooked. In making ethical decisions, you must justify a course of action based on sound reasoning. Consultation with colleagues provides an opportunity to test your justification.

• *Consider possible and probable courses of action.* Brainstorming is useful at this stage of ethical decision making. By listing a wide variety of courses of action, you may come up with a possibility that is unorthodox but useful. Of course, one alternative is that no action is required. In this process of thinking about many different possibilities for action, it is helpful to discuss options with another person.

• *Enumerate the consequences of various decisions.* Ponder the implications of each course of action for the client, for others who are related to the client, and for you as the counselor. You might consider the four fundamental principles (autonomy, beneficence, nonmaleficence, and justice) as a framework for evaluating the consequences of a given course of action.

• *Decide on what appears to be the best course of action.* In making what you consider to be the best decision, consider carefully the information you have received from various sources. The more obvious the dilemma, the clearer is the course of action; the more subtle the dilemma, the more difficult the decision will be. After deciding, try not to second-guess your course of action. You may realize later that another action might have been more beneficial. But this hindsight does not invalidate the decision you made based on the information you had at the time.

Some Suggestions for Using This Book

If you're like many other students, you've probably found some textbooks difficult to relate to personally, because they seemed dry and abstract. Perhaps you found yourself reading passively just to acquire information, without being challenged to synthesize the ideas in the text with your own ideas or to formulate your own positions. We've tried to write in a way that will actively involve you. This book deals with the central professional and ethical issues that you are likely to encounter in your work with clients, and our aim is to stimulate you to form your own opinions on these issues and be able to justify them.

In writing this book we frequently imagined ourselves in conversations with our students. Whenever it seems appropriate, we state our own thinking and discuss how we arrived at the positions we hold. We think it's important to reveal our biases, convictions, and attitudes, so that you can critically evaluate our stance. On many issues we present a range of viewpoints. Our hope is that you will give constant attention to ways of integrating your own thoughts and experiences with the positions we explore, so that you will not only absorb information but also deepen your understanding.

The format of this book is therefore different from that of most traditional textbooks. This is a personal manual that can be useful to you at various stages in your professional development. The many questions and exercises interspersed in the text are intended to stimulate you to become an active reader and learner. If you take the time to do these exercises and complete the surveys and inventories, the book will become both a challenge to reflect personally on the issues and a record of your reactions to them.

You should know that we have intentionally provided an abundance of exercises in each chapter, more than can be integrated in one semester or in one course. We invite you to look over the questions and other exercises to decide which of them have the most meaning for you. At a later reading of the book you may want to consider questions or activities that you omitted on your initial reading.

We'd like to make several other specific suggestions for getting the most from this book and your course. Many of these ideas come from students who have been in our classes. In general, you'll get from this book and course whatever you're willing to invest of yourself, so it's important to clarify your goals and to think about ways of becoming actively involved. The following suggestions can help you become more active as a learner:

• *Preparation.* You can best prepare yourself to become active in your class by spending time reading and thinking about the questions we pose. Completing the exercises and responding to the questions and open-ended cases will help you focus on where you stand on controversial issues.

• *Dealing with your expectations.* Students often have unrealistic expectations of themselves. Even though they have had very little counseling experience, they may think that they should have all the right answers worked out before they begin to work with people. If you haven't had much experience in counseling clients, you can begin to become involved in the issues we discuss by thinking about situations in which friends have sought you out when they were in need of help. You can also reflect on the times when you were experiencing conflicts and needed someone to help you gain clarity. In this way you may be able to relate the material to events in your own life even if your counseling experience is limited.

• *Self-assessment.* At the end of this chapter there is a multiple-choice survey designed to help you discover your attitudes concerning most of the issues we deal with in this book. We encourage you to take this inventory before you read the book to see where you stand on these issues at this time. We also suggest that you take the inventory again after you complete the book. You can then compare your responses to see what changes have occurred in your attitudes as a result of the course and your reading of the book.

• *Pre-chapter self-inventories.* Each chapter begins with an inventory designed to stimulate your thinking about the issues that will be explored in the chapter. You may want to bring your responses to class and compare your views with those of fellow students. You may also find it useful to retake the inventory after you finish reading the chapter to see whether your views have changed.

• *Examples, cases, and questions.* Many examples in this book are drawn from actual counseling practice in various settings with different types of clients. We frequently ask you to consider how you might have worked with a given client or what you might have done in a particular counseling situation. We hope you'll take the time to think about these questions and briefly respond to them in the spaces provided.

• *End-of-chapter exercises and activities.* Each chapter ends with exercises and activities intended to help you integrate and apply what you've learned in the chapter. They include suggestions for things to do both in class and on your own, as well as ideas that you can consider alone or use for small-group discussions in class. The purpose of these aids is to make the issues come alive and to help you apply your ideas to practical situations. We think the time you devote to these end-of-chapter activities can be most useful in helping you achieve a practical grasp of the material treated in the text.

• *Selected outside reading.* Near the end of the book you'll find a reading list of additional sources you might want to consult. By developing the habit of doing some reading on issues that have meaning to you, you will gain insights that can be integrated into your own frame of reference.

As you read and think about the cases and end-of-chapter exercises and activities that we present in this book, attempt to formulate your personal ethical perspective on the issues they raise. We encourage you to use this book in any way that involves you in the issues. Focus selectively on the questions and activities that have the most meaning for you at this time, and remain open to new issues as they assume importance for you. Our hope is that by reading this book and getting involved in your ethics course, you will discover other ways in which to work through a process of making ethical decisions.

Students enrolled in ethics courses that we have taught, as well as users of previous editions of this book, have made comments such as these about how their course helped them think differently about ethical decision making:

• I was frustrated because I wasn't given answers in the course. All my answers came from within myself.
• I have learned that the line between right and wrong is not always clear or straight but is often fuzzy and blurred. I have learned not to be so quick to judge another person's ethics but to concentrate on discovering what is right for myself.
• This ethics class actually challenged me to reevaluate what I thought I believed and introduced me to some possibilities that I never would have considered before.
• The course was extremely useful in preparing me to deal with real issues.
• I learned to appreciate the reality that there are few clear-cut answers in ethics, and the course raises more questions than gives answers.
• I am beginning to realize that the field of counseling is much more complicated than most people think. It seems there are very few easy answers. Most decisions and choices are some shade of gray instead of black and white.
• I realized that there is a lot more to being an ethical counselor than memorizing the codes.
• The class discussions promoted a lot of growth and thought-provoking disagreements.
• I learned the importance of looking at my own behavior for the potential of unethical behavior, rather than focusing on the ethical practices of others.
• Rather than just memorizing facts, the course stirred me emotionally and made me think. The course helped me clarify my personal values and at the same time made me more comfortable with dealing with ambivalence and issues that have no easy answers.
• In this course I learned to pinpoint issues of concern to me and become more aware of my positions on an ethical problem.

- I was challenged to personalize the material and to develop my own ideas instead of embracing the position of others.
- I was stimulated to think about options that I hadn't considered or hadn't been aware of. Working with the cases allowed me the opportunity to try on attitudes and positions to see what I thought about them.
- The most significant things I have learned in this course are (1) the solidification of my own values, (2) an appreciation for the necessity of my own personal counseling experience, (3) a deep respect for the ethical responsibility I will have as a counselor, and (4) coming to the realization that the education I receive at this university only meets the minimum standard.

Self-Assessment: An Inventory of Your Attitudes and Beliefs about Professional and Ethical Issues

This inventory surveys your thoughts on various professional and ethical issues in the helping professions. Most of the items relate directly to topics that are explored in detail later in the book. The inventory is designed to introduce you to these issues and to stimulate your thoughts and interest. You may want to complete the inventory in more than one sitting, so that you can give each question your full concentration.

This is *not* a traditional multiple-choice test in which you must select the "one right answer." Rather, it is a survey of your basic beliefs, attitudes, and values on specific topics related to the practice of therapy. For each question, write in the letter of the response that most clearly reflects your viewpoint at this time. In many cases the answers are not mutually exclusive, and you may choose more than one response if you wish. In addition, a blank line is included for each item. You may want to use this line to provide another response more suited to your thinking or to qualify a chosen response.

Notice that there are two spaces before each item. Use the spaces on the left for your answers at the beginning of the course. At the end of the course you can retake this inventory using the spaces on the right and covering your initial answers so that you won't be influenced by how you originally responded. Then you can see how your attitudes have changed as a result of your experience in this course.

You may want to bring the completed inventory to your beginning class session so that you can compare your views with those of others in the class. Such a comparison might stimulate some debate and help get the class involved in the topics to be discussed. In choosing the issues you want to discuss in class, you might go back over the inventory and circle the numbers of those items that you felt most strongly about as you were responding. You may find it instructive to ask others how they responded to these items in particular.

___ ___ 1. The personal characteristics of counselors are
    a. not really that relevant to the counseling process.
    b. the most important variable in determining the quality of the counseling process.

     c. shaped and molded by those who teach counselors.

     d. not as important as the skills and knowledge the counselors possess.

     e. _____

__ __ 2. Which of the following do you consider to be the most important personal characteristic of a good counselor?

     a. willingness to serve as a model for clients

     b. courage

     ⓒ openness and honesty

     d. a sense of being "centered" as a person

     e. _____

__ __ 3. Concerning counselors' self-disclosure to their clients, I believe that

     a. it is essential for establishing a relationship.

     b. it is inappropriate and merely burdens the client.

     ⓒ it should be done rarely and only when the therapist feels like sharing.

     d. it is useful for counselors to reveal how they feel toward their clients in the context of the therapy sessions.

     e. _____

__ __ 4. A client/therapist relationship characterized by warmth, acceptance, caring, empathy, and respect is

     a. a necessary and sufficient condition of positive change in clients.

     ⓑ a necessary but not sufficient condition of positive change in clients.

     c. neither a necessary nor a sufficient condition of positive change in clients.

     d. _____

__ __ 5. Of the following factors, which is the most important in determining whether counseling will result in change?

     a. the kind of person the counselor is

     b. the skills and techniques the counselor uses

     c. the motivation of the client to change

     d. the theoretical orientation of the therapist

     e. _____

__ __ 6. Of the following, which do you consider to be the most important attribute of an effective therapist?

     a. knowledge of the theory of counseling and behavior

     b. skill in using techniques appropriately

     c. genuineness and openness

     d. ability to specify a treatment plan and evaluate the results

     e. _____

__ __ 7. I believe that, for those who wish to become therapists, personal psychotherapy

     a. should be required for licensure.

    b. is not an important factor in developing the capacity to work with others.

    c. should be encouraged but not required.

    d. is needed only when the therapist has serious problems.

    e. _____

___ ___ 8. I believe that, in order to help a client, a therapist

    a. must like the client personally.

    b. must be free of any personal conflicts in the area in which the client is working.

    c. needs to have experienced the same problem as the client.

    d. needs to have experienced feelings similar to those being experienced by the client.

    e. _____

___ ___ 9. In regard to the client/therapist relationship, I think that

    a. the therapist should remain objective and anonymous.

    b. the therapist should be a friend to the client.

    c. a personal relationship, but not friendship, is essential.

    d. a personal and warm relationship is not essential.

    e. _____

___ ___ 10. I should be open, honest, and transparent with my clients

    a. when I like and value them.

    b. when I have negative feelings toward them.

    c. rarely, if ever, so that I will avoid negatively influencing the client/therapist relationship.

    d. only when it intuitively feels like the right thing to do.

    e. _____

___ ___ 11. I expect that I will experience professional burnout if

    a. I get involved in too many demanding projects.

    b. I must do things in my work that aren't personally meaningful.

    c. my personal life is characterized by conflict and struggle.

    d. my clients complain a lot and fail to change for the better.

    e. _____

___ ___ 12. I think that professional burnout

    a. can be avoided if I'm involved in personal therapy while working as a professional.

    b. is inevitable and that I must learn to live with it.

    c. can be lessened if I find ways to replenish and nourish myself.

    d. may or may not occur, depending on the type of client I work with.

    e. _____

___ ___ 13. If I were an intern and were convinced that my supervisor was encouraging trainees to participate in unethical behavior in an agency setting, I would

a. first discuss the matter with the supervisor.

b. report the supervisor to the director of the agency.

c. ignore the situation for fear of negative consequences.

d. report the situation to the ethics committee of the state professional association.

e. _____

____ ____ 14. Practitioners who work with culturally diverse groups without having cross-cultural knowledge and skills

a. are violating the civil rights of their clients.

b. are probably guilty of unethical behavior.

c. should realize the need for specialized training.

d. can be said to be practicing ethically.

e. _____

____ ____ 15. If I had strong feelings, positive or negative, toward a client, I think that I would most likely

a. discuss my feelings with my client.

b. keep them to myself and hope they would eventually disappear.

c. discuss them with a supervisor or colleague.

d. accept them as natural unless they began to interfere with the counseling relationship.

e. _____

____ ____ 16. I won't feel ready to counsel others until

a. my own life is free of problems.

b. I've experienced counseling as a client.

c. I feel very confident and know that I'll be effective.

d. I've become a self-aware person and developed the ability to continually reexamine my own life and relationships.

e. _____

____ ____ 17. If a client evidenced strong feelings of attraction or dislike for me, I think that I would

a. help the client work through these feelings and understand them.

b. enjoy these feelings if they were positive.

c. refer my client to another counselor.

d. direct the sessions into less emotional areas.

e. _____

____ ____ 18. Practitioners who counsel clients whose sex, race, age, social class, or sexual orientation is different from their own

a. will most likely not understand these clients fully.

b. need to understand the differences between their clients and themselves.

c. can practice unethically if they do not consider cross-cultural factors.

       d. are probably not going to be effective with such clients because of these differences.

       e. _____

__ __ 19. When I consider being involved in the helping professions, I value most
       a. the money I expect to earn.
       b. the security I imagine I will have in the job.
       c. the knowledge that I will be intimately involved with people who are searching for a better life.
       d. the personal growth I expect to experience through my work.

       e. _____

__ __ 20. I see counseling as
       a. a process of reeducation for the client.
       b. a process whereby clients are taught new and more appropriate values to live by.
       c. a process that enables clients to make decisions regarding their own lives.
       d. a process of giving advice and setting goals for clients.

       e. _____

__ __ 21. With respect to value judgments in counseling, therapists should
       a. feel free to make value judgments about their clients' behavior.
       b. actively teach their own values when they think that clients need a different set of values.
       c. remain neutral and keep their values out of the therapeutic process.
       d. encourage clients to question their own values and decide on the quality of their own behavior.

       e. _____

__ __ 22. Counselors should
       a. teach desirable behavior and values by modeling them for clients.
       b. encourage clients to look within themselves to discover values that are meaningful to them.
       c. reinforce the dominant values of society.
       d. very delicately, if at all, challenge clients' value systems.

       e. _____

__ __ 23. In terms of appreciating and understanding the value systems of clients who are culturally different from me,
       a. I see it as my responsibility to learn about their values and not impose mine on them.
       b. I would encourage them to accept the values of the dominant culture for survival purposes.
       c. I would attempt to modify my counseling procedures to fit their cultural values.

d. I think it is imperative that I learn about the specific cultural values my clients hold.

e. _____

___ ___ 24. If a client came to me with a problem and I could see that I would not be objective because of my values, I would
   a. accept the client because of the challenge to become more tolerant of diversity.
   b. tell the client at the outset about my fears concerning our conflicting values.
   c. refer the client to someone else.
   d. attempt to influence the client to adopt my way of thinking.

e. _____

___ ___ 25. I believe that the real reason for professional licensing and certification is
   a. to provide information to the public about mental-health services.
   b. to protect the public by setting minimum levels of competence for psychological services.
   c. to upgrade the helping professions by ensuring that the highest standards of excellence are promoted.
   d. to protect the interests of various helping professions and to reduce competition.

e. _____

___ ___ 26. I would tend to refer a client to another therapist
   a. if I had a strong dislike for the client.
   b. if I didn't have much experience working with the kind of problem the client presented.
   c. if I saw my own needs and problems getting in the way of helping the client.
   d. if the client seemed to distrust me.

e. _____

___ ___ 27. My ethical position regarding the role of values in therapy is that, as a therapist, I should
   a. never impose my values on a client.
   b. expose my values, without imposing them on the client.
   c. teach my clients what I consider to be proper values.
   d. keep my values out of the counseling relationship.

e. _____

___ ___ 28. If I were to counsel lesbian and gay clients, a major concern of mine would be
   a. maintaining objectivity.
   b. not knowing and understanding enough about this lifestyle.
   c. establishing a positive therapeutic relationship.

d. pushing my own values.

e. _____

___ ___ 29. Of the following, I consider the most unethical form of therapist behavior to be

a. promoting dependence in the client.

b. becoming sexually involved with clients.

c. breaking confidentiality without a good reason to do so.

d. accepting a client who has a problem that goes beyond one's competence.

e. _____

___ ___ 30. Regarding the issue of counseling friends, I think that

a. it is seldom wise to accept a friend as a client.

b. it should be done rarely, and only if it is clear that the friendship will not interfere with the therapeutic relationship.

c. friendship and therapy should not be mixed.

d. it should be done only if it seems appropriate to both the client and the counselor.

e. _____

___ ___ 31. Regarding confidentiality, I believe that

a. it is ethical to break confidence when there is reason to believe that clients may do serious harm to themselves.

b. it is ethical to break confidence when there is reason to believe that a client will do harm to someone else.

c. it is ethical to break confidence when the parents of a client ask for certain information.

d. it is ethical to inform the authorities when a client is breaking the law.

e. _____

___ ___ 32. Therapists should terminate therapy with a client when

a. the client decides to do so and not before.

b. they judge that it is time to terminate.

c. it is clear that the client is not benefiting from the therapy.

d. the client reaches an impasse.

e. _____

___ ___ 33. A sexual relationship between a client and therapist is

a. ethical if the client initiates it.

b. ethical if the therapist decides it is in the best interests of the client.

c. ethical only when client and therapist discuss the issue and agree to the relationship.

d. never ethical.

e. _____

___ ___ 34. Concerning the issue of physically touching a client, I think that touching
   a. is unwise, because it could be misinterpreted by the client.
   b. should be done only when the therapist genuinely feels like doing it.
   c. is an important part of the therapeutic process.
   d. is ethical when the client requests it.

   e. _____

___ ___ 35. A clinical supervisor has initiated sexual relationships with former trainees (students). He maintains that, because he no longer has any professional responsibility to them, this practice is acceptable. In my view, this behavior is
   a. clearly unethical, because he is using his position to initiate contacts with former students.
   b. not unethical, because the professional relationship has ended.
   c. not unethical but is unwise and inappropriate.
   d. somewhat unethical, because the supervisory relationship is similar to the therapeutic relationship.

   e. _____

___ ___ 36. Regarding theories of counseling, I think that therapists should
   a. ignore them, since they have no practical application.
   b. select *one* theory and work within its framework.
   c. select something from most of the theories.
   d. select a theory on the basis of the client's personality and presenting problem.

   e. _____

___ ___ 37. In the practice of marital and family therapy, I think that
   a. the therapist's primary responsibility is to the welfare of the family as a unit.
   b. the therapist should focus primarily on the needs of individual members of the family.
   c. the therapist should attend to the family's needs and try to hold the amount of sacrifice by any one member to a minimum.
   d. the therapist has an ethical obligation to state his or her bias and approach at the outset.

   e. _____

___ ___ 38. On the matter of developing sexual relationships with *former* clients, my position is that
   a. it is strictly up to the people involved to make that decision.
   b. it is always unethical.
   c. it is an example of taking advantage of a client.
   d. it can be either ethical or unethical, depending on the case.

   e. _____

___ ___ 39. Regarding the issue of who should select the goals of counseling, I believe that
   a. it is primarily the therapist's responsibility to select goals.
   b. it is primarily the client's responsibility to select goals.
   c. the responsibility for selecting goals should be shared equally by the client and therapist.
   d. the question of who selects the goals depends on what kind of client is being seen.

   e. _____

___ ___ 40. Concerning the role of diagnosis in counseling, I believe that
   a. diagnosis is essential for the planning of a treatment program.
   b. diagnosis is counterproductive for therapy, since it is based on an external view of the client.
   c. diagnosis is dangerous in that it tends to label people, who then are limited by the label.
   d. whether to use diagnosis depends on one's theoretical orientation and the kind of counseling one does.

   e. _____

___ ___ 41. Concerning the place of testing in counseling, I think that
   a. tests generally interfere with the counseling process.
   b. tests can be valuable tools if they are used as adjuncts to counseling.
   c. tests are essential for people who are seriously disturbed.
   d. tests can be either used or abused in counseling.

   e. _____

___ ___ 42. Regarding the issue of psychological risks associated with participation in group therapy, my position is that
   a. clients should be informed at the outset of possible risks.
   b. these risks should be minimized by careful screening.
   c. this issue is exaggerated, since there are no real risks.
   d. careful supervision will offset some of these risks.

   e. _____

___ ___ 43. Concerning the counselor's responsibility to the community, I believe that
   a. the counselor should educate the community concerning the nature of psychological services.
   b. the counselor should attempt to change patterns that need changing.
   c. community involvement falls outside the proper scope of counseling.
   d. counselors should become involved in helping clients use the resources available in the community.

   e. _____

___ ___ 44. My view of personal counseling or psychotherapy for practitioners is that
   a. it is most desirable for beginning counselors.
   b. it is of great value for experienced counselors as well as beginning practitioners.
   c. it should be a strongly recommended component of any counselor-preparation program.
   d. it should not be necessary for most practitioners, unless they are faced with a personal crisis.

   e. _____

___ ___ 45. As an intern, if I thought my supervision was inadequate, I would
   a. talk to my supervisor about it.
   b. continue to work without complaining.
   c. seek supervision elsewhere.
   d. feel let down by the agency I worked for.

   e. _____

___ ___ 46. My view of supervision is that it is
   a. something that I could use on a permanent basis.
   b. a threat to my status as a professional.
   c. valuable to have when I reach an impasse with a client.
   d. a way for me to learn about myself and to get insights into how I work with clients.

   e. _____

___ ___ 47. When it comes to working within institutions, I believe that
   a. I must learn how to survive with dignity within a system.
   b. I must learn how to subvert the system so that I can do what I deeply believe in.
   c. the institution will stifle most of my enthusiasm and block any real change.
   d. I can't blame the institution if I'm unable to succeed in my programs.

   e. _____

___ ___ 48. If my philosophy were in conflict with that of the institution I worked for, I would
   a. seriously consider whether I could ethically remain in that position.
   b. attempt to change the policies of the institution.
   c. agree to whatever was expected of me in that system.
   d. quietly do what I wanted to do, even if I had to be devious about it.

   e. _____

___ ___ 49. In working with clients from different ethnic groups, I think it is most important to

    a. be aware of the sociopolitical forces that have affected these clients.

    b. understand how language can act as a barrier to effective cross-cultural counseling.

    c. refer these clients to some professional who shares their ethnic and cultural background.

    d. help these clients modify their views so that they will be accepted and not have to suffer rejection.

    e. _____

___ ___ 50. To be effective in counseling clients from a different culture, I think that a counselor must

    a. possess specific knowledge about the particular group he or she is counseling.

    b. be able to accurately "read" nonverbal messages.

    c. have had direct contact with this group.

    d. treat these clients no differently from clients from his or her own cultural background.

    e. _____

Chapter Summary

This introductory chapter has focused on the foundations of creating an ethical sense and has explored various perspectives on teaching the process of making ethical decisions. The central point is that professional codes of ethics are indeed essential for ethical practice but that merely knowing these codes is not enough. The challenge comes with learning how to think critically and knowing ways to apply general ethical principles to particular situations.

We encourage you to become active in your education and training. We also suggest that you try to keep an open mind about the issues you encounter during this time and throughout your professional career. An important part of this openness is a willingness to focus on yourself as a person and as a professional as well as on the questions that are more obviously related to your clients.

Suggested Activities

1. As a practitioner, how will you determine what is ethical and what is unethical? Think about how you will go about developing your guidelines for ethical practice, and make up a list of behaviors that you judge to be unethical. After you've thought through this issue by yourself, you may want to explore your approach with fellow students.

2. Look over all of the professional codes of ethics in the Appendix. What are your impressions of each of these codes? To what degree are they complete?

To what degree do they provide you with the needed guidelines for ethical practice? What are the values of such codes? What limitations do you see in them? What do the various codes have in common?

3. Assume that you were a member of a committee that was making recommendations for the professional training program in which you are now involved. What changes would you most want to make in your program? As you see it, what are its strengths and the weaknesses? After you have done this exercise, bring some of your ideas to your professor.

Note to the student. We want to remind you that we do not expect you to systematically think about and work on *every* suggested activity that we have at the end of each chapter. Our purpose is to invite you to personalize the material and develop your own positions on the issues we raise. Use your judgment in selecting those activities that you find the most challenging and meaningful.

Suggested Readings

At the end of each chapter we provide some suggestions for further reading on many of the topics we have explored. Because the frontiers of ethics are explored in professional journals, we emphasize the more recent journal articles. For the full bibliographic entry, consult the References and Reading List at the back of the book.

For a discussion of the nature of professional ethics and how guidelines for practice will affect you see Bennett et al. (1990). On conflicts between ethics and the law see Mappes et al. (1985) and the APA's ethics code (1991a). For models of ethical decision making see Jordan and Meara (1990), Keith-Spiegel and Koocher (1985), Kitchener (1984), and Loewenberg and Dolgoff (1988). For a survey on clinical ethical decision making see Smith et al. (1991). For a treatment on the ethics of teaching (the beliefs and behaviors of psychologists as educators) see Tabachnick, Keith-Spiegel, and Pope (1991). For an excellent book dealing with a variety of ethical dilemmas and cases based on the AACD's *Ethical Standards* see Herlihy and Golden (1990).

The Counselor as a Person and as a Professional

- Pre-Chapter Self-Inventory
- Introduction
- Self-Awareness and the Influence of the Therapist's Personality and Needs
- The Issue of Personal Therapy for Counselors
- Dealing with Transference and Countertransference
- Stress in the Counseling Profession
- Professional Burnout
- Chapter Summary
- Suggested Activities
- Suggested Readings

Pre-Chapter Self-Inventory

The pre-chapter self-inventories can help you identify and clarify your attitudes and beliefs about the issues to be explored in the chapter. Keep in mind that the "right" answer is the one that best expresses your thoughts at the time. We suggest that you complete the inventory before reading the chapter; then, after reading the chapter and discussing the material in class, you can retake the inventory to see whether your positions have changed in any way.

Directions: For each statement, indicate the response that most closely identifies your beliefs and attitudes. Use the following code:

5 = I *strongly agree* with this statement.
4 = I *agree* with this statement.
3 = I am *undecided* about this statement.
2 = I *disagree* with this statement.
1 = I *strongly disagree* with this statement.

____   1. Unless therapists have a high degree of self-awareness, there is a real danger that they will use their clients to satisfy their own needs.
____   2. Before therapists begin to practice, they should be free of personal problems and conflicts.
____   3. Counselors or therapists should be required to undergo their own therapy before they are licensed to practice.
____   4. Counselors who satisfy personal needs through their work are behaving unethically.
____   5. Most professionals in the counseling field face a high risk of burnout because of the demands of their jobs.
____   6. Counselors who know themselves can avoid experiencing overidentification with their clients.
____   7. Strong feelings about a client are a sign that the counselor needs further therapy.
____   8. Feelings of anxiety in a beginning counselor indicate unsuitability for the counseling profession.
____   9. A competent counselor can work with any client.
____ 10. I fear that I'll have difficulty challenging my clients.
____ 11. A professional counselor will avoid both getting involved socially with clients and counseling friends.
____ 12. A major fear of mine is that I'll make mistakes and seriously hurt a client.
____ 13. Real therapy does not occur unless a transference relationship is developed.
____ 14. As a counselor, I think it is important to adapt my therapeutic techniques and approaches to the cultural backgrounds of my clients.
____ 15. An experienced and competent counselor should not need either periodic or ongoing personal psychotherapy.

Introduction

A primary issue in the helping professions is the role of the counselor *as a person* in the therapeutic relationship. Because counselors are asking clients to look honestly at themselves and to choose how they want to change, counselors must open their own lives to the same scrutiny. They should repeatedly ask themselves questions like these: "What makes me think I have a right to counsel anyone else? What do I personally have to offer others who are struggling to find their way? Am I doing in my own life what I urge others to do?"

Counselors and psychotherapists usually acquire an extensive theoretical and practical knowledge as a basis for their practice. But to every therapeutic session they also bring their human qualities and their life experiences. Professionals can be well versed in psychological theory and can learn diagnostic and interviewing skills and still be ineffective as helpers. It seems obvious to us that if counselors are to promote growth and change in their clients, they must be willing to promote growth in their own lives by exploring their own choices and decisions. This willingness to live in accordance with what they teach and thus to be positive models for their clients is what makes counselors "therapeutic persons." If counselors are stagnant themselves, if they are not open to growth, and if they resist making choices, it is doubtful that they can inspire clients to do otherwise in their lives. Therapists present an ethical problem when they are unable to carry out this modeling role, which is critical in encouraging clients to change.

It is difficult to talk about the counselor *as a professional* without considering these personal qualities. A counselor's beliefs, personal attributes, and ways of living inevitably influence the way he or she functions as a professional. Some of the issues we address, however, are specifically related to the counselor's professional identity. Although these professional issues are dealt with throughout this book, in this chapter we take up problems that are closely linked to the counselor's personal life: self-awareness and the influence of the counselor's personality and needs, dealing with transference and countertransference, handling job stress, and preventing burnout.

Self-Awareness and the Influence of the Therapist's Personality and Needs

We have already mentioned the personal responsibility of counselors to be committed to awareness of their own lives. Moreover, without a high level of self-awareness, counselors will obstruct the progress of their clients. The focus of the therapy will shift from meeting the client's needs to meeting the needs of the therapist. Consequently, practitioners should be aware of their own needs, areas of "unfinished business," personal conflicts, defenses, and vulnerabilities and of how these may intrude on their work with their clients. In this section we consider some specific areas that we think counselors need to examine, such as their self-doubts and personal needs.

Exploring Self-Doubts and Fears

Students in counselor-education programs sometimes bring up fears, resistances, perfectionistic strivings, and other personal concerns. For example, many students express their anxiety over the prospect of facing clients. They ask themselves: "What will my clients want? Will I be able to give them what they want? What will I say, and how will I say it? Will they want to come back? If they do, what will I do then?" It is possible to become so anxiety-ridden that an intern or a practitioner is not able to pay attention to the client. Another concern of many students and practitioners is their expectation that they must be the perfect helpers. They often burden themselves with the belief that they cannot afford to be less than perfect, lest they make a mistake, which would have dire consequences for both their clients and themselves. These become ethical concerns when they are dealt with in a manner that reduces the effectiveness of the helper.

At this point, take the time to review the list of statements below to determine if these are things you might say. The questionnaire is drawn from statements we frequently hear in practicum and internship courses; they represent a sampling of the issues faced by those who begin to counsel others. Apply these statements to yourself, and decide to what degree you see them as your concerns. If a statement is more true than false for you, place a "T" in front of it; if it is more false than true for you, place an "F":

___ I'm afraid I'll make mistakes.

___ My clients will really suffer because of my blunders and my failure to know what to do.

___ I have real doubts about my ability to help people in a crisis situation.

___ I demand perfection of myself, and I constantly feel I should know more than I do.

___ I would feel threatened by silences in counseling situations.

___ It's important to me to know that my clients are making steady improvement.

___ It would be difficult for me to deal with demanding clients.

___ I expect to have trouble working with clients who are not motivated to change or who are required to come to me for counseling.

___ I have trouble deciding how much of the responsibility for the direction of a counseling session is mine and how much is my client's.

___ I think that I should be successful with all my clients.

___ I expect to have trouble in being myself and trusting my intuition when I'm counseling.

___ I'm afraid to express feelings of anger to a client.

___ I worry that my clients will see that I'm a beginner and wonder if I'm competent.

___ I'm concerned about looking and acting like an ethical professional.

___ Sometimes I'm concerned about how honest I should be with clients.

___ I'm concerned about how much of my personal reactions and my private life I should reveal in counseling sessions.

___ I tend to worry about whether I'm making the proper intervention.

___ I sometimes worry that I may overidentify with my client's problems to the extent that they become *my* problems.

___ During a counseling session I would frequently find myself wanting to give advice.

___ I'm afraid that I might say or do something that would greatly disturb a client.

___ I'm concerned about counseling clients whose values are different from my own.

___ I would be apprehensive about whether my clients liked and approved of me and whether they would want to come back.

___ I'm concerned about being mechanical in any counseling, as though I were following a book.

Now go back and select the issues that represent your greatest concerns. You can then begin to challenge some of the assumptions behind these statements.

Personal Needs of Counselors

One critical question that counselors can ask themselves is "What do I personally get from doing counseling?" There are many answers to this question. Many therapists experience excitement and a deep sense of satisfaction from being with people who are struggling to achieve self-understanding and who are willing to experience pain as they seek a better life. Some counselors enjoy the feeling of being instrumental in others' changes; others appreciate the depth and honesty of the therapeutic relationship. Still others value the opportunity to question their own lives as they work with their clients. Therapeutic encounters in many ways serve as mirrors in which therapists can see their own lives reflected. As a result, therapy can become a catalyst for change in the therapist as much as in the client.

Therapeutic progress can be blocked, however, when therapists use their clients, perhaps unconsciously, to fulfill their own needs. Out of a need to nurture others or to feel powerful, for example, people sometimes feel that they know how others should live. The tendency to give advice and try to direct another's life can be especially harmful in a therapist, because it leads to excessive dependence on the part of clients and only perpetuates their tendency to look outside themselves for answers. Therapists who need to feel powerful or important may begin to think that they are indispensable to their clients or, worse still, *make* themselves so.

The goals of therapy can also suffer when therapists who have a strong need for approval focus on trying to win the acceptance, admiration, respect, and even awe of their clients. Some therapists may be primarily motivated by a need to receive confirmation from their clients of their value as persons and as professionals. It is within their power as therapists to control the sessions in such a way that these needs are continually reinforced. Because clients often feel a need to please their therapists, they can easily encourage counselors who crave reinforcement of their sense of worth.

One of the goals of therapy, as we see it, is to teach the *process* of problem solving, not just to solve problems. When clients have learned the process, they have less and less need of their therapists. Therapists who tell clients what to do or use the sessions to buttress their own sense of self-worth diminish the autonomy of their clients and invite increased dependence in the future.

When therapists are not sufficiently aware of their own needs, they may abuse the power they have in the therapeutic situation. Some counselors gain a sense of power by assuming the role of directing others toward solutions instead of encouraging them to seek alternatives for themselves. A solution-oriented approach to counseling may also spring from the therapist's need to feel a sense of achievement and accomplishment. Some therapists feel ill at ease if their clients fail to make instant progress; consequently, they may either push their clients to make decisions prematurely or even make decisions for them. This tendency can be encouraged even more by clients who express gratitude for this kind of "help."

Of course, therapists *do* have their own personal needs, but these needs don't have to assume priority or get in the way of clients' growth. Most people who enter the helping professions do want to nurture others, and they do need to know that they are being instrumental in helping others to change. In this sense, they need to hear from clients that they are a significant force in their lives. In order to keep these needs from interfering with the progress of their clients, therapists should be clearly aware of the danger of working primarily to be appreciated by others instead of working toward the best interests of their clients. If they are open enough to recognize this potential danger, the chances are that they will not fall into using their clients to meet their own needs.

As Kottler (1986) has written, in the practice of psychotherapy our personal and professional roles can complement each other. Our knowledge and skills are equally useful with clients, friends, or family. Also, our life experiences, both joys and sorrows, provide the background for what we do in our therapeutic sessions with clients.

It's hard to find fault with therapists who find excitement in their work. The rewards of practicing psychotherapy are many, but one of the most significant is the joy of seeing clients move from being victims to assuming control over their lives. Therapists can achieve this reward only if they avoid abusing their influence and maintain a keen awareness of their role as facilitators of others' growth. As you consider your own needs and their influence on your work as a therapist, you might ask yourself the following questions:

- How can I know when I'm working for the client's benefit and when I'm working for my own benefit?
- How much might I depend on clients to tell me how good I am as a person or as a therapist? Am I able to appreciate myself, or do I depend primarily on others to validate my worth and the value of my work?
- How can I deal with feelings of inadequacy, particularly if I seem to be getting nowhere with a client?

Unresolved Personal Conflicts

We have suggested that the personal needs of a therapist can interfere with the therapeutic process, to the detriment of the client, if the therapist is unaware of their impact on his or her work. The same is true for personal problems and unresolved conflicts. This is not to say that therapists must resolve all their personal difficulties before they begin to counsel others; such a requirement would eliminate almost everybody from the field. In fact, it's possible that a counselor who rarely struggles or experiences anxiety may have real difficulty in relating to a client who feels desperate or caught in a hopeless conflict. Moreover, if therapists flee from anxiety-provoking questions in their own lives, they probably won't be able to effectively encourage clients to face such questions. The important point is that counselors can and should be *aware* of their biases, their areas of denial, and the issues they find particularly hard to deal with in their own lives.

To illustrate, suppose that you're experiencing a rough time in your life. You feel stuck with unresolved anger and frustration. Your home life is tense, and you're wrestling with some pivotal decisions about how you want to spend the rest of your life. Perhaps you're having problems with your clients or your spouse. You may be caught between fears of loneliness and a desire to be on your own, or between your fear of and need for close relationships. Can you counsel others effectively while you're struggling with your own uncertainty?

To us, the critical point isn't *whether* you happen to be struggling with personal questions but *how* you're struggling with them. Do you see your part in creating your own problems? Are you aware of your alternatives for action? Do you recognize and try to deal with your problems, or do you invest a lot of energy in denying their existence? Do you find yourself generally blaming others for your problems? Are you willing to consult with a therapist, or do you tell yourself that you can handle it, even when it becomes obvious that you're not doing so? In short, are you willing to do in your own life what you encourage your clients to do?

If you're not working on being aware of your own conflicts, you'll be in a poor position to pay attention to the ways in which your personal life influences your work with clients, especially if some of their problem areas are also problem areas for you. For example, suppose a client is trying to deal with feelings of hopelessness and despair. How can you intensively explore these feelings if, in your own life, you're busily engaged in cheering everybody up? If hopelessness is an issue you don't want to face personally, you'll probably steer the client away from exploring it. As another example, consider a client who wants to explore her feelings about homosexuality. Can you facilitate this exploration if you are homophobic? If you feel discomfort in talking about homosexual feelings and experiences and don't want to have to deal with your discomfort, can you stay with your client emotionally when she brings up this topic?

Since you'll have difficulty staying with a client in an area that you're reluctant or fearful to deal with, consider what present unfinished business in your own life might affect you as a counselor. What unresolved conflicts are you aware of, and how might these conflicts influence the way you counsel others?

○ ***The case of Rollo***.   Rollo is an intern completing his clinical hours for licensure. He came from a family where both parents abused alcohol. The clinic specializes in the treatment of children from abusive homes. Rollo finds himself easily moved to tears as he works with the children. At times he becomes extremely angry at the parents of these children, and he often broods obsessively about the children's plight. He typically devotes extra time beyond the scheduled activities, and he often feels overextended. He finds difficulty in saying no to his clients, and his personal life is increasingly suffering as a result of this involvement. He looks tired, and it comes to the attention of his supervisor that he frequently seems stressed and short-tempered with other staff members. In their supervision hour, Rollo retorts that the agency is not doing enough for the children. He proceeds to tell his supervisor how much he is affected by them and how he is continually trying to come up with ways to help them. After listening to Rollo, his supervisor suggests that he consider personal therapy to further explore his own unresolved childhood issues.

- What, if anything, do you see as being unethical in Rollo's behavior? Is he necessarily depriving his clients of adequate help by the manner in which he involves himself with them? At what point do you see the dividing line between being helpful and unhelpful? How would Rollo determine when his own personal involvement was counterproductive?
- Do you agree with the supervisor's suggestion of personal therapy? Why or why not?
- Do you think that Rollo's supervisor should advise him to discontinue working with these children until he has resolved his personal issues?
- What possible unresolved conflicts are you aware of in your life that might get in your way of helping certain clients through their difficulties? If you are moved to tears by your clients, does that imply that you have unresolved conflicts? Does anger directed toward abusive parents mean that you have unresolved conflicts with your parents?

The Issue of Personal Therapy for Counselors

Throughout this chapter we have stressed the importance of counselors' self-awareness. A closely related issue is whether those who wish to become counselors should themselves undergo psychotherapy and whether continuing or periodic personal therapy is valuable for practicing therapists. We are not speaking of therapy for remediation of deep conflicts but of therapeutic experiences aimed at increasing awareness of oneself in the world. There are many ways to accomplish this goal: individual therapy, group counseling, consultation with colleagues, continuing education (especially of an experiential nature), and reading. Other, less formal, avenues to personal growth are reflecting on and evaluating the meaning of one's work and life, remaining open to the reactions of significant people in one's life, enjoying music and the arts, traveling, experiencing different cultures, being outdoors, meditating, engaging in spiritual activities, enjoying physical exercise, and spending time with friends and family.

Therapy during Training

There are several reasons why potential counselors should be encouraged to experience their own therapy. First, those who expect to counsel others should know what the experience of being a client is really like. We don't assume that most potential therapists are "sick" and in need of being "cured," but then we don't make that assumption about most clients, either. Many clients are attracted to counseling because they want to explore the quality of their lives and the alternatives open to them. Potential counselors can approach therapy in much the same way. Therapy can help you take an honest look at your motivations in becoming a helper. It can help you explore how your needs influence your actions, how you use power in your life, what your values are, and whether you have a need to persuade others to be like you.

When students are engaged in practicum, fieldwork, and internship experiences and the accompanying individual and group supervision sessions, the following issues tend to surface:

- a need to "fix," or straighten out, people
- a desire to take away all pain from clients
- a need to have all the answers and to be perfect
- a need to be recognized and appreciated
- a tendency to assume too much responsibility for the changes of clients
- a fear of doing harm, however inadvertently

As students begin to practice counseling, for example, they may become aware that they are taking on a professional role that resembles the role they played in their family. They may recognize a need to preserve peace by becoming the caretaker of others. During their childhood they may have assumed adult roles with their own parents by trying to take care of them. Now, as adults, they may continue to take on most of the responsibility for the changes their clients make. When students become aware of concerns such as these, they may discover in therapy the painful memories and past experiences that are often associated with these personal issues. In the process, they can experience firsthand what their clients experience in therapy. If counseling students do not experience this process of internal searching, it is unlikely that they will be able to facilitate an in-depth exploration by their clients. If they have not traveled a path, how can they serve as a guide for others?

Another reason for undergoing therapy is that most of us have blind spots and unfinished business that may interfere with our effectiveness as therapists. Most of us have areas in our lives that aren't fully developed and that keep us from being as effective as we can be, both as persons and as counselors. Although it is not necessary for counselors to have fully resolved all of their personal problems, they at least need to be aware of the nature of such problems and the ways in which they may affect their professional work. Personal therapy is one way of coming to grips with your dynamics as well as working through unresolved conflicts. The lack of personal therapy may become an ethical issue if it diminishes your effectiveness as a counselor.

Ideally, we'd like to see potential counselors undergo a combination of individual and group therapy, because the two types complement each other. Individual therapy provides the opportunity to look at oneself in some depth. Many counselors will experience a reopening of old psychic wounds as they engage in intensive work with their clients. For example, their therapeutic work may bring to the surface guilt feelings that need to be resolved. If they are in private therapy at the same time as they are doing their internship, they can productively bring such problems to their sessions.

Group therapy, on the other hand, provides counselors with the opportunity to get feedback from others. It allows them to become increasingly aware of their personal style and gives them a chance to experiment with new behavior in the group setting. It also allows them to generalize their experiences and realize that they are not alone in what they think and feel. The reactions you receive from others can help you learn about personal attributes that could be either strengths or limitations in your work as a counselor.

Many training programs in counselor education recognize the value of having students involved in personal-awareness groups with their peers. A group can be set up specifically for the exploration of personal concerns, or such exploration can be made an integral part of training and supervision groups. Whatever the format, students will benefit most if they are willing to focus on themselves personally and not merely on their "cases." Unfortunately, some beginning counselors tend to focus primarily on client dynamics. Their group learning would be more meaningful if they were open to exploring such questions as "How am I feeling about my own value as a counselor? Do I like my relationship with my client? What reactions are being evoked in me as I work with this client?" By becoming personally invested in the therapeutic process, students can use their training program as a real opportunity for expanding their own awareness.

It is important for teachers and supervisors to clarify the fine line between training and therapy, in the same way that fieldwork agencies must maintain the distinction between training and service. Although these areas overlap, it is clear that the emphasis for students should be on training in both academic and clinical settings, and it is the educator's and supervisor's responsibility to maintain that emphasis.

Fouad, Hains, and Davis (1990) investigated the factors involved in whether counseling students endorsed therapy as a requirement for graduation from their program. The researchers found that 66% of the students believed that counseling should be a required part of the curriculum. The results showed that 65% had sought counseling before taking counseling classes and that 85% were satisfied or very satisfied with their counseling. The results also indicated that students who endorsed the counseling requirements were more likely to have had previous therapy and to have personal concerns they wanted to explore in counseling. The results of the study suggest that counseling students recognize that they do have personal concerns that can be dealt with in therapy and that unresolved personal issues may interfere with their effectiveness as counselors. From anecdotal evidence it appears that programs differ widely in fostering self-awareness. The authors of this study recommend that graduate programs facilitate trainees' self-awareness by providing them with opportunities to explore their personal concerns and by encouraging them to enter counseling.

The ethical codes of some professional organizations caution against requiring personal therapy for trainees. The codes emphasize the right of students and trainees to make informed decisions about disclosing personal matters. For example, both the AACD and the APA imply that mixing personal counseling with education constitutes what is known as a "dual relationship," which can be unethical if the counselor is in a position to evaluate the student. In the section on preparation standards for counseling students, the AACD's *Ethical Standards* (1988) specify that "forms of learning focusing on self-understanding or growth are voluntary, or if required as part of the educational program, are made known to prospective students prior to enrolling." Another standard stipulates that students should be provided with "clear and equally acceptable alternatives for self-understanding or growth experiences." Although we accept the notion that students have a right to know about a counseling requirement before enrolling in a program, we do not think that counselor-education programs have an obligation "to provide alternatives to growth experiences without prejudice or penalty," and we wonder what these alternatives could be. We believe that the drawbacks mentioned by the AACD are outweighed by the potential benefits to future clients of having students undergo counseling. And we are puzzled why prospective counselors would be reluctant to "taste the medicine" that they may be eager to dispense to others.

Faculty members in some programs do offer individual and group counseling for students. In one study 72% of the faculty reported having seen students for short-term personal counseling, and 56% of the educators maintained that it would be ethical to counsel students if the students were not in their classes at the time (Roberts, Murrell, Thomas, & Claxton, 1982). Some argue that a student is at a disadvantage in receiving personal therapy from supervisors or faculty members, because they exert power over the student in the form of grading and evaluation. If professors conduct self-awareness groups that are mandatory for trainees, students may be reluctant to disclose their personal lives. In Chapter 8 we will address the ethics of this type of dual relationship in more detail. For now, we want to mention that there are both practical and ethical reasons for assigning self-awareness groups to professionals who do not have any evaluative role in the program. For example, practitioners from the community might be hired by a counselor-training program to conduct such groups, or students might take advantage of either individual or group counseling from a community agency or a private practitioner.

○ *The case of a required personal-growth group.* Leona is a psychologist in private practice who is hired by the director of a graduate program in counseling psychology. She assumes that the students have been informed that they will be required to attend her personal-growth class, and she is given the impression that the students are eagerly looking forward to it. When she encounters the students at the first class, however, she meets with resistance. They express resentment that they were not told that they would be expected to participate in a personal group, and they say they have not really given their consent. They are attending out of fear that there would be negative consequences if they did not.

- If you had been a student in this program, what might your reactions have been?
- Were there any ethical violations in the way in which this group experience was set up?
- Is it ever ethical to mandate self-exploration experiences?
- If you were the director of the program, how might you handle the situation?
- The students knew from their orientation and the university's literature that this graduate program included some form of self-exploration. Was this disclosure sufficient for ethical purposes?
- If you were Leona, what would you do in this situation? How would you deal with the students' objections?

Therapy for Practitioners

Experienced practitioners can profit from a program that will challenge them to reexamine their beliefs and behaviors, especially as these pertain to their effectiveness in working with clients. Truly committed professionals engage in a lifelong self-examination as a means of remaining self-aware and genuine.

To what extent do practicing professionals make use of therapeutic resources? Deutsch (1985) found that 47% of therapists had entered therapy for relationship problems and that 27% had cited depression. In another study, which involved a random sample of 2,000 members of the AACD, Neukrug and Williams (undated) found that 80% had been in some form of therapy and that 67% had been in individual counseling. A large percentage of counselors had entered therapy before their professional training, and many of them had not continued with therapy following training.

Guy and Liaboe (1986b) report a puzzling silence among mental-health professionals concerning the need for periodic or ongoing therapy. They conclude that the majority of psychotherapists appear to resist entering personal therapy, even during times of distress when it may be both useful and appropriate. In a national survey of psychotherapists to examine their use of personal psychotherapy before and after entering professional practice, Guy, Stark, and Poelstra (1988) found that 18% of the respondents had never received any form of personal psychotherapy; 23% had not received individual therapy. The researchers contend that personal therapy is largely underused by the very providers of this service.

Elsewhere, Guy and Liaboe (1986a) suggest that a periodic course of psychotherapy may improve therapists' personal relationships and general well-being. They note some of the negative consequences that conducting therapy can have on therapists' interpersonal functioning: decreased emotional investment in their family, a reduction in their circle of friends, a tendency to socialize less with friends, and a tendency to become aloof and emotionally distant with friends and family. They offer ways to cope with the strains of professional practice:

> Becoming involved in nonpsychological activities, spending time with friends outside the profession, pursuing teaching or research opportunities in addition to psychotherapeutic practice, enrolling in classes outside of one's specialty, taking extended and regular vacations or sabbaticals, pursuing ongoing supervision and consultation, and undergoing personal individual or marital psychotherapy are a few possible steps to help avoid these negative consequences [p. 113].

Guy and Liaboe maintain that both professional organizations and licensing and certification boards are ethically obligated to take an active role in monitoring professionals in the field. Such bodies should encourage, if not require, periodic supervision, consultation, or psychotherapy for practitioners. Along with required continuing education and periodic peer review, these measures can be instrumental in reducing or eliminating the potential negative consequences of practicing psychotherapy.

Clark (1986) reviewed seven empirical studies exploring the question "Can therapists who have undergone psychotherapy be shown to be more effective with clients than colleagues who have not received such treatment?" The review revealed:

- Only one of the studies showed a slight and insignificant trend supporting the assumption that personal therapy would improve the therapist's performance.
- Five studies found no relationship between client outcomes and whether the therapist had experienced therapy.
- One study of student therapists found that therapy could be detrimental to client outcomes.

Clark concludes that further research is needed to clarify this important training issue. Apparently, this question has stimulated considerably more discussion than it has research. Clark suggests that future research should control for the level of experience of the therapist, the motivation of the therapist for entering therapy, and the point in the practitioner's career when personal therapy occurs.

If it is assumed that therapists themselves are their most important therapeutic instruments, their own vitality as persons and as professionals is crucial to their work. We would encourage practitioners to pay attention to what they are giving to their work and getting from it. If they are not committed to doing for themselves what they are teaching their clients, they may be unable to inspire clients to act in self-directed and responsible ways. It is ethically imperative for counselors to take care of themselves and to heal themselves.

○ ***The case of Daniel.***   Daniel has a busy private practice, and he finds relief in imbibing from a vodka bottle that he keeps in his desk drawer. During a conversation with a colleague, he opens the desk drawer and has a nip. The colleague expresses her concern for him and the potential risks involved in his behavior. He reassures her that he never gets loaded but that it helps him get through the day.

- What do you think of Daniel's habit of imbibing between sessions? Does it mean that he is abusing alcohol?
- Does his assertion that "I never get loaded" suffice to render the situation harmless?
- Is his method of stress reduction acceptable and ethical? Would you personally challenge him to seek personal therapy to deal with his stress and his use of alcohol?
- As his colleague, what ethical obligation, if any, do you have to report the matter?
- If a licensing board were to require therapy for Daniel as a condition for retaining his license, would that be an appropriate stipulation?

Therapists must be prepared to recognize and deal with their unresolved personal issues and their reactions to their clients. A high degree of self-awareness and a deep respect and concern for clients are safeguards. In the next section we explore ways in which transference and countertransference can facilitate or interfere with therapy. That discussion provides a rationale for the importance of being willing to experience one's own therapy. In addition to personal therapy, practitioners need training in dealing with feelings that both they and their clients experience.

Dealing with Transference and Countertransference

We include a discussion of *transference* and *countertransference* because of our assumption that if these factors are not attended to, the client's progress will be impeded. Therapists inevitably have to come to grips with these issues regardless of their therapeutic orientation. Although the terms *transference* and *countertransference* are derived from psychoanalytic theory, they are universally applicable to counseling and psychotherapy (Gelso & Carter, 1985). They are used to refer to the client's general reactions and orientation to the therapist and to the therapist's reactions in response. Conceptualizing transference and countertransference broadly, Gelso and Carter assume that these processes are universal and that they occur, to varying degrees, in most relationships. The therapeutic relationship intensifies the natural reactions of both client and therapist. The ways in which practitioners handle both their feelings and their clients' feelings will have a direct bearing on therapeutic outcomes. Because dealing with such feelings ineffectively is likely to block successful therapy, this matter has implications from both an ethical and a clinical perspective.

According to Deffenbacher (1985), a good cognitive-behavioral therapist works to build rapport, lessen interpersonal anxiety in the relationship, increase trust, and create a climate that invites open discussion and therapeutic work. Cognitive-behavioral therapists use themselves and the relationship with their client to achieve the aims of therapy. Yet in many cases this working alliance is insufficient to bring about change. If a client looks on a therapist as cold and distant and the therapist is unaware of or ignores this perception, therapeutic outcomes are likely to suffer. Some people in a client's life may have been cold and critical, which would certainly have an impact on the client in therapy, regardless of the therapist's orientation. This learning history would explain the client's sensitivity to the real or imagined coldness of the therapist.

Transference: The 'Unreal' Relationship in Therapy

Transference, then, refers to the process whereby clients project onto their therapist past feelings or attitudes they had toward significant people in their lives. Transference typically has its origin in early childhood, and it constitutes a repetition of past conflicts. Through this process clients' unfinished business produces a distortion in the way they perceive and react to the therapist. The feelings that they experience in transference may include love, hate, anger, ambivalence, or dependency. The essential point is that these feelings are rooted in past relationships but are now directed toward the therapist. Gelso and Carter (1985) refer to transference as the "unreal" relationship, because such projections are in error, even though the therapist's actions may serve to trigger them. Transference entails a misperception of the therapist, either positive or negative.

Watkins (1983) identifies the following five transference patterns in counseling and psychotherapy:

1. *Counselor as ideal.* The client sees the counselor as the perfect person who does everything right, without flaws. Psychoanalytically, the counselor is given an idealized image, which may be the way the client viewed his or her parents at one time. The danger here is that counselors, their egos fed, can come to believe these projections! Yet not challenging clients to work through these feelings results in infantilizing them. When clients elevate the therapist, they put themselves down. They lose themselves by trying to be just like their ideal.

2. *Counselor as seer.* Clients view the counselor as expert, all-knowing, and all-powerful. They look to the counselor for direction, based on the conviction that the counselor has all the right answers and that they themselves cannot find their own answers. Again, a danger is that the counselor may feed on this projection and give clients advice based on his or her own need to be treated as an expert. The ethical issue here is that clients are encouraged to remain dependent.

3. *Counselor as nurturer.* Some clients look to the counselor for nurturing and feeding, as a small child would. They play the helpless role, and they feel that they cannot act for themselves. They may seek touching and hugs from the therapist. A danger here is that the counselor may get lost in giving sympathy and feeling sorry for the client. The counselor may become a nurturing parent and take care of the client. In the process, the client never learns the meaning of personal responsibility.

4. *Counselor as frustrator.* The client is defensive, cautious, and guarded and is constantly testing the counselor. Such clients may want advice or simple solutions and may expect the counselor to deliver according to their desires. They may be frustrated if they don't receive such prescriptions. Counselors need to be aware that merely providing easy solutions will not help the client in the long

run, and they should be careful not to get caught in the trap of perceiving this client as fragile. Also, it is essential that counselors avoid reacting defensively to the client, a response that would further entrench the client's resistance.

5. *Counselor as nonentity.* In this form of transference the client regards the counselor as an inanimate figure without needs, desires, wishes, or problems. These clients use a barrage of words and keep their distance with these outbursts. The counselor is likely to feel overwhelmed and discounted. If counselors depend on feedback from their clients as the sole means of validation of their worth as counselors, they may have difficulty in managing cases in which this phenomenon exists.

The potential effect of transference in these examples shows how essential it is for counselors to be clearly aware of their own needs, motivations, and personal reactions. If they are unaware of their own dynamics, they will avoid important therapeutic issues instead of challenging their clients to understand and resolve the feelings they are bringing into the present from their past.

Transference is not a catch-all intended to explain every feeling that clients express toward their therapists. For example, if a client expresses anger toward you, it may be justified. If you haven't been truly present for the client, instead responding in a mechanical fashion, your client may be expressing legitimate disappointment. Similarly, if a client expresses affection toward you, these feelings may be genuine; simply dismissing them as infantile fantasies can be a way of putting distance between yourself and your client. Of course, most of us would probably be less likely to interpret positive feelings as distortions aimed at us in a symbolic fashion than we would negative feelings. It is possible, then, for therapists to err in either direction—to be too quick to explain away negative feelings or too willing to accept whatever clients tell them, particularly when they are hearing how loving, wise, perceptive, or attractive they are. In order to understand the real import of clients' expressions of feelings, therapists must actively work at being open, vulnerable, and honest with themselves. Although they should be aware of the possibility of transference, they should also be aware of the danger of discounting the genuine reactions their clients have toward them.

We will now present a series of brief, open-ended cases in which we ask you to imagine yourself as the therapist. How do you think you would respond to each client? What are your own reactions?

Your client, Shirley, seems extremely dependent on you for advice in making even minor decisions. It is clear that she does not trust herself and that she often tries to figure out what you might do in her place. She asks you personal questions about your marriage and your family life. Evidently, she has elevated you to the position of one who always makes wise choices, and she is trying to emulate you in every way. At other times she tells you that her decisions typically turn out to be poor ones. Consequently, when faced with a decision she vacillates and becomes filled with self-doubt. Although she says she realizes that you cannot give her "the" answers, she keeps asking you what you think about her decisions.

- How would you deal with Shirley? What would you say to her?
- What direction would you take in trying to understand her dependence and lack of self-trust?
- How would you respond to her questions about your private life?
- If many of your clients expressed the same thoughts as Shirley, what elements in your counseling style might you need to examine?

Marisa says she feels let down by you. She complains that you are not available and asks if you really care about her. She also says she feels that she is "just one of your caseload." She tells you that she would like to be more special to you.

- How would you deal with Marisa's expectations?
- How would you explain your position?
- How would you explore whatever might be behind her stated feelings instead of defending your position?
- Would you be inclined to tell her how she affected you?

Carl seems to treat you as an authority figure. He once said that you were always judging him and that he was reluctant to say very much because you would consider everything he said to be foolish. Although he has not confronted you directly since then, you sense many digs and other signs of hostility. On the surface, however, Carl seems to be trying very hard to please you by telling you what he thinks you want to hear. He seems convinced that you will react negatively and aggressively if he tells you what he really thinks.

- How would you respond to Carl?
- How might you deal with his indirect expressions of hostility?
- How might you encourage him to express his feelings and work through them?

Countertransference: Ethical and Clinical Implications

So far we have focused on the transference feelings of clients toward their counselors, but counselors also have emotional reactions to their clients, some of which may involve their own projections. It is not possible to deal fully here with all the possible nuances of transference and countertransference. Instead, we focus on the improper handling of these reactions in the therapeutic relationship, a situation that directly pertains to ethical practice.

Countertransference can be considered, in the broad sense, as any projections by a therapist that can potentially get in the way of helping a client. For instance, counselor anxiety, the need to be perfect, or the need to solve a client's problems might all be manifestations of countertransference. It is essential that therapists deal with these reactions in some form of supervision or consultation so that "their problem" does not become the client's problem. It may be helpful to consider the countertransference material being stirred up as a way of interpreting subtle messages from the client. The client might actually want a "cold therapist," for instance, because of a fear that more difficult material would surface if the therapist were warmer. If a therapist becomes frustrated with a client, it could be that this client, because of anxiety, wants progress to stop.

It is clear, then, that countertransference can be either a constructive or a destructive element in the therapeutic relationship. From a constructive perspective, a therapist's countertransference can illuminate some significant dynamics of a client. A client may actually be provoking reactions in a therapist by the ways in which he or she makes the therapist into a key figure from the past. The therapist who recognizes these patterns can eventually help the client change old and dysfunctional themes. Destructive countertransference occurs when a counselor's own needs or unresolved personal conflicts become entangled in the therapeutic relationship, obstructing or destroying a sense of objectivity. In this way, countertransference becomes an ethical issue.

Regardless of how self-aware and insightful counselors are, the demands of practicing therapy are great. The emotionally intense relationships that therapists develop with their clients can be expected to tap into their own unresolved conflicts. Because countertransference may be a form of identification with the client, the counselor can easily get lost in the client's world and thus be of little therapeutic value. When counselors become so concerned with meeting their own needs that they use the client for this purpose, their behavior becomes unethical.

Thus, ethical practice requires that counselors remain alert to their emotional reactions to their clients, that they attempt to understand such reactions, and that they do not meet their own needs at the expense of their clients' needs. Questions counselors might ask of themselves are "What am I feeling when I'm with this person? What am I experiencing? What do I want to say and do? What am I aware of *not* saying to the client? Do I find myself hoping the client will fail to show up? Do I find myself wanting the client to stay longer?" If countertransference is recognized by counselors, they can seek supervision as one way of sorting out their feelings.

In writing about the dynamics of countertransference, Gelso and Carter (1985) comment:

> In fact, we think that facing, and indeed inspecting, countertransference-based feelings is one of the most difficult tasks of the therapist. It requires considerable courage and a willingness to deal with one's own painful feelings for the sake of the therapeutic work. There are no easy answers to the question of how to accomplish this, but at the same time doing so is a crucial aspect of effective therapy [pp. 182–183].

Countertransference can show itself in many ways. All of the examples in the following list present an ethical issue, because the therapist's effective work is obstructed by countertransference reactions:

1. *Being overprotective with clients* can reflect a therapist's deep fears. A counselor's unresolved conflicts can lead him or her to steer clients away from those areas that open up the therapist's painful material. Such counselors may treat some clients as fragile and infantile, softening their remarks. They thus protect these clients from experiencing pain and anxiety and may thwart them in their struggle. Because the clients are not challenged to deal with their conflicts, they are likely to avoid them.

- Are you aware of reacting to certain types of people in overprotective ways? If so, what might this behavior reveal about you?
- Do you find that you are able to allow others to experience their pain, or do you have a tendency to want to take their pain away quickly?

2. *Treating clients in benign ways* may stem from a counselor's fears of their anger. To guard against this anger, the counselor creates a bland counseling atmosphere. This tactic results in exchanges that are superficial. Watkins (1985) mentions the danger of losing therapeutic distance, with the result that the client/counselor interchange degenerates into either a friendly conversation or a general "rap session."

- Do you ever find yourself saying things to guard against another's anger?
- What might you say or do if you became aware that your exchanges with a client were primarily superficial?

3. *Rejection of clients* may be based on perceiving them as needy and dependent. Yet instead of moving toward them to protect them, the counselor moves away from such clients. The counselor remains cool and aloof, keeps distant and unknown, and does not let clients get too close (Watkins, 1985).

- Are there certain types of people whom you find yourself wanting to move away from?
- What can you learn about yourself by looking at those people whom you are likely to reject?

4. *The need for constant reinforcement and approval* can be a reflection of countertransference. Just as clients may develop an excessive need to please their therapist in order to feel liked and valued, therapists may have an inordinate need to be reassured of their effectiveness. Many beginning practitioners expect instant results with their clients. When they do not see immediate positive results, they become discouraged and anxious. If a client is not getting better, they fear that the client will not like them. They engage in self-doubt and wonder about their therapeutic effectiveness.

- Do you need to have the approval of your clients? How willing are you to confront them even at the risk of being disliked?
- What is your style of confronting a client? Do you tend to confront certain kinds of clients more than others? What does this behavior tell you about yourself as a therapist?

5. *Therapists' seeing themselves in their clients* is another form of countertransference. This is not to say that feeling close to a client and identifying with that person's struggle is necessarily an instance of countertransference. However, one of the problems that many beginning therapists have is identifying with clients' problems to the point that they lose their objectivity. They become so lost in a client's world that they are unable to distinguish their own feelings. Or they may tend to see in their clients traits that they dislike in themselves. Sometimes

the particularly "difficult" client can function as a mirror for the counselor. There are many "difficult" clients, a few of whom exhibit behaviors such as extreme resistance, silence, lack of motivation, and annoying mannerisms. The very behaviors in these clients that counselors react to most strongly are often the very traits that they dislike in themselves. Thus, an overly demanding client who never seems satisfied with what his or her therapist is doing can be a reminder of the therapist's own demanding nature.

- Have you ever found yourself so much in sympathy with others that you could no longer be of help to them? What would you do if you felt this way about a client?
- From an awareness of your own dynamics, list some personal traits of clients that would be most likely to elicit overidentification on your part.

6. One of the common manifestations of countertransference is the development of *sexual or romantic feelings* between clients and therapists. Therapists can exploit the vulnerable position of their clients, whether consciously or unconsciously. Seductive behavior on the part of a client can easily lead to the adoption of a seductive style by the therapist, particularly if the therapist is unaware of his or her own dynamics and motivations. On the other hand, it's natural for therapists to be more attracted to some clients than to others, and these sexual feelings do not necessarily mean that they cannot counsel these clients effectively. More important than the mere existence of such feelings is the manner in which therapists deal with them. Feelings of attraction can be recognized and even acknowledged frankly without becoming the focus of the therapeutic relationship. The possibility that therapists' sexual feelings and needs might interfere with their work is one important reason why therapists should experience their own therapy when starting to practice and should consult another professional when they encounter difficulty because of their feelings toward certain clients. Besides being unethical and countertherapeutic, it is also illegal in many states to sexually act out with clients, a topic that we discuss in detail in Chapter 6.

- What do you think you would do if you experienced intense sexual feelings toward a client?
- How would you know if your sexual attraction to a client was countertransference or not?

7. Countertransference can also take the form of *compulsively giving advice.* A tendency to advise can easily be encouraged by clients who are prone to seek immediate answers to ease their suffering. The opportunity to give advice places therapists in a superior, all-knowing position—one that some of them can easily come to enjoy—and they may delude themselves into thinking that they *do* have answers for their clients. They may also find it difficult to be patient with their clients' struggles toward autonomous decision making. Such counselors may engage in excessive self-disclosure, especially by telling their clients how they have solved a particular problem for themselves. In doing so, the focus of therapy tends to shift from the client's struggle to the needs of the counselor. Even if a client

has asked for advice, there is every reason to question whose needs are being served when a therapist falls into advice giving.

- Do you ever find yourself giving advice? What do you think you gain from it? In what ways might the advice you give to clients represent advice that you could give yourself?
- Are there any times when advice is warranted? If so, when?

8. A *desire to develop social relationships with clients* may stem from counter-transference, especially if it is acted on while therapy is taking place. Clients occasionally let their therapist know that they would like to develop a closer relationship than is possible in the limiting environment of the office. They may, for instance, express a desire to get to know their therapist as "a regular person." Even experienced therapists must sometimes struggle with the question of whether to blend a social relationship with a therapeutic one. When this question arises, therapists should assess whose needs would be met through such a friendship and decide whether effective therapy can coexist with a social relationship. Mixing personal and professional relationships often ends up in souring the relationship, which is a topic that we examine in Chapter 6. At this point, some questions that you might ask yourself in this context are:

- If I establish social relationships with certain clients, will I be as inclined to confront them in therapy as I would be otherwise?
- Will my own needs for preserving these friendships interfere with my therapeutic activities and defeat the purpose of therapy?
- Am I sensitive to being called a "cold professional," even though I may strive to be real and straightforward in the therapeutic situation?
- Why am I inclined to form friendships with clients? Does this practice serve my own or my clients' best interests?

Stress in the Counseling Profession
Warning: Bumpy Road

Counseling is a hazardous profession, and its stresses stem both from the nature of the work and from the professional role expectations of counselors. Therapists are typically not given enough warning about the hazards of the profession they are about to enter. Many counselors-in-training look forward to a profession in which they can help others and, in return, feel a deep sense of self-satisfaction. They are not told that the commitment to self-exploration and to inspiring this search in clients is fraught with difficulties. Effective practitioners use their own life experiences and personal reactions as a way to understand their clients and as a method of working with them. As you will recall, the process of working therapeutically with people opens up the therapist's own deepest issues. The counselor, as a partner in the therapeutic journey, can be deeply affected by seeing a client's pain. The activation of painful memories resonates with the therapist's own life experiences. Unfinished business is stirred up, and old wounds are opened. In short, working with clients who are in pain often opens up therapists to their own pain, and if these countertransference issues are not recognized, they can have ethical implications. Counselors who are overburdened with stress cannot work effectively.

Many of the stressful client behaviors that we will be discussing in this section could easily be understood as countertransference issues of the therapist. When therapists assume full responsibility for a client's not making progress, for instance, they are not giving the client enough responsibility for his or her own therapy. Instead of assuming that they are to blame for the lack of progress, they should first explore the situation with the client. As a result of this exploration, they may discover that they are impeding the client's growth by too quickly assuming responsibility for such problems.

Practitioners who have a tendency to readily accept full responsibility for their clients often experience their clients' stress as their own. It is important to recognize the danger signs that indicate that stress is taking control. We need to be alert to the ways in which stress can lead to fatigue, distress, impairment, and, eventually, burnout. Some signs to look out for are irritability and emotional exhaustion, feelings of isolation, abuse of alcohol or drugs, reduced personal effectiveness, indecisiveness, compulsive work patterns, and drastic changes in behavior. Bennett, Bryant, VandenBos, and Greenwood (1990) raise the following questions that can help you assess the impact of stress on you both personally and professionally: Do you ignore your problems out of fear? Have you learned techniques for managing stress, such as time management and relaxation training? Are you able to take care of your personal needs? Are you aware of the signs and symptoms warning you that you are in trouble? Do you listen to your family, friends, and colleagues when they tell you that stress is getting the better of you? Do you consider seeking help if you find out that you are exhibiting signs of stress? Although it is not realistic to expect to eliminate the strains of daily life, you can develop practical strategies to recognize and cope with stress that is having adverse effects on you.

Sources of Stress

Deutsch (1984) and Farber (1983b) found surprisingly similar results in their surveys of therapists' perceptions of stressful client behavior. In both studies therapists reported that clients' suicidal statements were the most stressful. In the box on p. 49 are comparisons between these two studies.

Other sources of stress that therapists reported in the Deutsch study included:

- being unable to help distressed clients feel better
- seeing more than the usual number of clients
- not liking clients
- having self-doubts about the value of therapy
- having professional conflicts with colleagues

Most-Stressful Client Behaviors for Therapists

Deutsch's Findings

1. suicidal statements
2. anger toward the therapist
3. severely depressed clients
4. apathy or lack of motivation
5. client's premature termination

Farber's Findings

1. suicidal statements
2. aggression and hostility
3. premature termination of therapy
4. agitated anxiety
5. apathy and depression

- feeling isolated from other professionals
- overidentifying with clients and failing to balance empathy with appropriate professional distance
- being unable to leave client concerns behind when away from work
- feeling sexual attraction to a client
- not receiving expressions of gratitude from clients

A growing body of research suggests that many therapists experience negative effects with respect to their ability to relate meaningfully with family and friends (Guy & Liaboe, 1986a). More than half of the therapists in Farber's study (1983a, 1983b) reported that conducting therapy had decreased their emotional investment in their own family. In the area of friendships, some therapists reported that their work had hindered their ability to be genuine, spontaneous, and comfortable with friends (Farber, 1983b). Farber notes a trend for therapists to reduce their circle of friends and to socialize less during their career. One interpretation of these findings is that many therapists experience stress and negative consequences from their work.

Stress is related to irrational beliefs that many therapists hold. Practitioners with exceptionally high goals or perfectionistic strivings related to helping others often report a high level of stress. Deutsch (1984) gives the following examples of the three most stressful beliefs, all of which pertain to doing perfect work with clients:

1. "I should always work at my peak level of enthusiasm and competence."
2. "I should be able to cope with any client emergency that arises."
3. "I should be able to help every client."

The other irrational beliefs that lead to stress are: (1) "When a client does not make progress, it is my fault." (2) "I should not take off time from work when I know that a particular client needs me." (3) "My job is my life." (4) "I should be able to work with every client." (5) "I should be a model of mental health." (6) "I should be 'on call' at all times." (7) "A client's needs always come before my own." (8) "I am the most important person in my client's life." (9) "I am responsible for my client's behavior." (10) "I have the power to control my client's life."

It is interesting to note that these beliefs are related to the basic reasons why many people choose the helping professions. The needs of helpers are to be needed by others, to feel important, to have an impact on the lives of others, to have power to control others, and to be significant. When helpers are able to do these things successfully, they are likely to feel that they are making a significant difference in the lives of their clients. When they feel that they are not making a difference and are not reaching clients, stress affects them more dramatically.

Deutsch makes the point that therapists' cognitions provide clues to the experience of stress. Beliefs that create stress are those that goad the counselor to constantly produce at maximum levels, a pace that eventually leads to burnout. When therapists do not live up to unrealistically high levels of performance, they often experience frustration. When they fall short of their own idealized expectations, they view the slow progress in their clients as evidence of their failure and lack of competence. The underlying assumption that creates stress is "If I do not live up to my high expectations, I am personally incompetent and inadequate." From this vantage point the crucial factor in therapists' experience of stress is not difficult client behaviors; rather, it is the beliefs that therapists hold about their role in helping others. If they assume that they are completely responsible for the success or failure of therapy, they are burdening themselves needlessly and creating their own stress. As we have said, they are also depriving their clients of assuming their rightful share of responsibility for what they choose to do with their life. The ethical and professional question is to what degree a therapist's behavior resulting from stress has negative implications for the client's progress.

Professional Burnout

The phenomenon of professional burnout has been the topic of numerous publications and is receiving increasing attention at professional conferences and conventions. What is burnout? What are its causes? How are professionals who work in institutions particularly susceptible to losing their vitality? How does burnout contribute to an impaired practitioner, and what ethical issues are associated with this impairment? What can be done to prevent burnout? How can counselors stay alive personally and professionally?

Nature and Scope of the Problem

Burnout is a state of physical, emotional, and mental exhaustion. It is the result of repeated emotional pressures, often associated with intense involvement with people over long periods. Professionals who are burned out are characterized by physical depletion and by feelings of hopelessness and helplessness. They tend to develop negative attitudes toward themselves, others, work, and life (Pines & Aronson, with Kafry, 1981). Many people in the helping professions find that they grow tired and lose the energy and enthusiasm they once experienced in their work. They talk of feeling drained, empty, and fragmented by the pull of many different projects. Because burnout is an occupational hazard that most professional helpers face at one time or another, it is important to be prepared for it. Burnout can rob counselors of the vitality they need to be able to provide healthy modeling for their clients.

Kottler (1986) observes that therapists who tend to burn out have probably ignored the signs of their condition for months and even years. He lists a number of key symptoms: (1) when clients call to cancel an appointment, the therapist celebrates with a bit too much enthusiasm; (2) daydreaming and escapist fantasies are common; (3) there is a tendency to abuse drugs; (4) therapy sessions lose their excitement and spontaneity; (5) the therapist gets behind in paperwork and billings; (6) the therapist's social life suffers; and (7) therapists are reluctant to explore the causes and cures of their condition.

Professional helpers need to see that what they do is worthwhile; yet the nature of their profession is such that they often don't see immediate or concrete results. This lack of reinforcement can have a debilitating effect as counselors begin to wonder whether anything they do makes a difference to anyone. The danger of burnout is greater if they practice in isolation, have little interchange with fellow professionals, have demanding or disturbed clients, have few vital interests outside of work, or fail to seek an explanation of their feelings of deadness.

Susceptibility to Burnout.   Professionals who work in private practice and those who work in community agencies are both susceptible to burnout, for different reasons. Many therapists who work alone report that they get caught in the routine of seeing client after client. They find it increasingly difficult to be fully present for their clients, especially when it seems that they are dealing with the same problem over and over. After a while they may well find themselves responding almost mechanically. It may be difficult to deal with this situation if one's livelihood seems to depend on maintaining a private practice.

The problem of burnout is also critical for people working in systems or in community agencies. With the emphasis in this kind of work on giving to others, there is often not enough focus on giving to oneself. Unfortunately, some who enter the helping professions have high hopes that are never realized. If they meet with constant frustration, see almost no positive change in their clients, and encounter obstacles to meeting their goals of helping others, their hopes may eventually be replaced by the hopelessness and powerlessness that characterize many of their clients.

Counselor Impairment.   Burnout often contributes to the making of an impaired practitioner. Guy (1987) defines impairment as the "diminution or deterioration of therapeutic skills and abilities due to factors which have sufficiently impacted the personality of the therapist to result in potential incompetence" (p. 199). In a study of distressed psychologists, Thoreson, Miller, and Krauskopf (1989) found that approximately 10% of their sample had experienced frequent problems in the following categories: depression (11%), recurrent physical illness (10%), alcohol use (9%), and loneliness (8%). Their study seemed to indicate that at least a minority of psychologists experience stress levels high enough to impair their ability to function effectively as professionals.

According to Stadler (1990b), impaired counselors have lost the ability to resolve stressful events. They are not able to function professionally. Those therapists whose inner conflicts are consistently activated by client material may respond by trying to stabilize themselves rather than facilitating the growth of their clients. Clearly, impaired practitioners contribute to the suffering of their client rather than alleviating it.

Causes of Burnout

A key factor contributing to professional burnout is involvement in the lives and struggles of clients. As we mentioned in the section on stress, therapists' old wounds are opened, affecting both their personal and their professional lives and reawakening unresolved needs and problems (Farber, 1983a; Guy, 1987; Kottler & Blau, 1989).

Farber and Heifetz (1982) found that therapists had the following perceptions of the causes of burnout:

- Most practitioners (73.7%) cited "lack of therapeutic success" as the single most stressful aspect of their work.
- The majority of the therapists interviewed (54.7%) felt that burnout resulted from the nonreciprocated attentiveness, giving, and responsibility demanded by the therapeutic relationship.
- Other causes of burnout included overwork (22.2%), the general difficulty in dealing with the patients' problems (20.4%), discouragement as a function of tedious work tasks (18.5%), the tendency of therapeutic work to bring out their own personal conflicts (13%), the general passivity of counseling work (13%), and the isolation involved in therapy (11.1%).
- If they experienced stresses at home, therapists felt that they were particularly prone to transient feelings of burnout. Their own family problems lowered their threshold for the demanding work of therapy and impaired their ability to attend effectively to the needs of their clients.

The Farber and Heifetz study suggests that therapists expect their work to be difficult and even stressful but that they also expect that their efforts will be appreciated and that they will see positive results. Constant giving without the reinforcement of some measure of success apparently produces burnout. Although working conditions, such as an excessive work load and organizational politics, can create an added burden of stress for therapists who work in institutions, many therapists can accept these realities of working in the system. When therapeutic work is only minimally successful and often frustrating, however, the chances of experiencing disillusionment are particularly high. For example, therapists who work primarily with suicidal, homocidal, depressed, severely regressed, and chronically resistant clients are likely to experience burnout.

We encourage you now to look at the factors that are most likely to cause burnout in you. A common denominator in many cases of burnout is the question of *responsibility*. Counselors may feel responsible for what their clients do or don't do, they may assume too much responsibility for the direction of therapy, or they may have extremely high expectations of themselves. Does this description apply to you? In what ways could your assumption of an inordinate degree of responsibility contribute to your burnout?

There are other causes of burnout besides an excessive sense of responsibility. Consistently working with clients whom you don't like, who are unmotivated and yet demanding, or who don't appreciate or value you can cause burnout. How would working with such clients affect you? What factors might lead to your own burnout?

Ways of Preventing Burnout

Although burnout and the professional impairment associated with it have received much publicity from professional groups, it appears that many counselors have avoided or denied their existence. In a discussion of counselor impairment, Stadler (1990b) reports that we know very little about its impact on clients, we have few data on counselor impairment, and there are few professionally sponsored avenues to help burned-out counselors. She points to the ethical concerns that are raised when impaired counselors continue their professional work. Graduate training programs in the helping professions should prepare students for the disappointments they will encounter in the course of their training and in the jobs they eventually secure. Students can be prepared for both the joys and pains of the profession they are choosing. Not only can they learn about the rewards and frustrations of helping others, but they should be informed about the hazards of this profession. If students are not adequately prepared, they may be especially vulnerable to early disenchantment and high rates of burnout, for they are saddled with unrealistic expectations. There is an ethical mandate for training programs to design strategies to prevent burnout and to teach students the importance of developing healthful attitudes.

What can you do not only to prevent yourself from becoming an impaired professional but also to become committed to promoting your own wellness from a holistic perspective? Perhaps the most basic way to retain your vitality as a person and as a professional is to realize that you are not a bottomless pit and cannot give and give without replenishing yourself. Counselors often ignore signs that they are becoming depleted. They may view themselves as having unlimited capacities to give, and at the same time they may not pay attention to taking care of their own needs for nurturing, recognition, and support. However, simply recognizing that they cannot be universal givers without getting something in return is not enough to keep them alive as people and professionals. What is needed is an action plan and the commitment to carry out this plan. Learning to cope with personal and professional sources of stress generally involves making some fundamental changes in one's lifestyle. At this point, take some time to ask yourself what basic changes, if any, you are willing to make in your behavior.

Chapter Summary

One of the most basic issues in the practice of therapy and counseling is the counselor's own personality as an instrument in therapeutic practice. Counselors may possess knowledge and technical skills and still be ineffective in significantly reaching clients. The life experiences, attitudes, and caring that counselors bring to their sessions are crucial factors in the establishment of an effective therapeutic relationship. If counselors are unwilling to engage in self-exploration, it is likely that their fears, resistances, personal conflicts, and personal needs will interfere with their ability to be present for their clients. Therapists who are unaware of their personal dynamics will probably use their work primarily to satisfy their unmet needs or will steer clients away from exploring conflicts that their therapists are unwilling to acknowledge in themselves. In our view, this lack of awareness on the part of therapists is a major ethical concern. Although the harm to clients that can result from unaware therapists is often of a subtle nature, it is indeed as real as some of the more flagrant ethical violations.

Personal therapy during training and also throughout one's professional career can result in counselors who are better able to focus on the welfare of their clients. If our assumption is valid that therapists are unable to take clients on any journey that they have not been on, ongoing self-exploration is critical. By focusing on their personal development, counselor trainees and practitioners are better equipped to deal with a range of transference reactions their clients are bound to have toward them; they are also better able to detect countertransference on their part and have a basis for dealing with such reactions in a therapeutic manner. There is the potential for unethical behavior when therapists mismanage their countertransference. You may need to review your personal concerns periodically throughout your career. This honest self-appraisal is an essential quality of those who wish to be effective helpers.

Stress and the inevitable burnout that typically results from inadequately dealing with the chronic sources of stresses also raise ethical questions. How can therapists who are psychologically and physically exhausted adequately help their clients? Are counselors who have numbed themselves to human pain able to enter the world of their clients? Are impaired practitioners doing more harm than good for those who seek their assistance? Although there are no simple answers to the question of how to stay alive personally and professionally, you are challenged to find your own path to maintaining your vitality and preventing burnout.

Suggested Activities

These activities and questions are designed to help you apply your learning. Many of them can profitably be done alone or with another person; others can be done as discussion activities, either with the whole class or in small groups. We suggest that you select those that seem most significant to you and do some writing on these issues in your journal. Many of these questions are ones that prospective employers ask during job interviews. Practicing answering them can help you clarify your thinking and your positions, which in the long run could help you land a job.

1. In small groups in your class explore the issue of why you're going into a helping profession. This is a basic issue, and one that many students have trouble

putting into concrete words. What motivated you to seek this type of work? What do you think you can get for yourself? What do you see yourself as being able to do for others?

2. What personal needs of yours will be met by counseling others? To what degree might they get in the way of your work with clients? How can you recognize and meet your needs—which are a real part of you—without having them interfere with your work with others?

3. What are some of the major problems you expect to be faced with as a beginning counselor? What are some of your most pressing concerns?

4. In small groups share your own anxieties over becoming a counselor. What can you learn about yourself from a discussion of these anxieties?

5. This exercise deals with the fundamental question "Who has a right to counsel anybody?" Form small groups of perhaps three persons. Take turns briefly stating the personal and professional qualities that you can offer people. The others give feedback. Afterward, explore any self-doubts you have concerning your ethical right to counsel others.

6. What results would you look for in working with clients? How would you determine the answers to such questions as "Is the counseling doing any good? Is my intervention helping my client make the changes he or she wants to make? How effective are my techniques?"

7. Think of the type of client you might have the most difficulty working with. Then become this client in a role-playing fantasy with one other student. Your partner attempts to counsel you. After you've had a chance to be the client, change roles and become the counselor. Your partner then becomes the type of client you just role-played.

8. In subgroups explore the issue of how willing you are to disclose yourself to your clients. Discuss the guidelines you would use to determine the appropriateness of self-disclosure. What are some areas you would feel hesitant about sharing? How valuable do you think it is to share yourself in a personal way with your clients? What are some of your fears or resistances about making yourself known to your clients?

9. In subgroups discuss some possible causes of professional burnout. Then examine specific ways in which you could deal with this problem. After you've explored this issue in small groups, reconvene as a class, and make a list of the causes and solutions that your groups have come up with.

Suggested Readings

Bugental (1987) does a splendid job of addressing the importance of the personal qualities involved in the art of psychotherapy. For books that deal with the risks, challenges, and satisfactions of being a psychotherapist, see Kottler (1986, 1991) and Kottler and Blau (1989). For a textbook on the topic of personal themes of choice that apply to the counselor as a person, see Corey and Corey (1990).

For a study on trainees' attitudes toward requiring therapy as a part of a training program see Fouad et al. (1990). For therapy for practitioners see Guy and Liaboe (1986a, 1986b) and Clark (1986).

On transference see Gelso and Carter (1985), Kottler (1986), and Watkins (1983); on countertransference see Gelso and Carter (1985), Kottler (1986), Watkins (1985), Cerney (1985), and Lorion and Parron (1985).

On stress in the helping professions and therapists' personal problems see Deutsch (1984, 1985), Farber (1983a, 1983b), Guy and Liaboe (1986a, 1986b), Laliotis and Grayson (1985), Jaffe (1986), Kilburg, Nathan, and Thoreson (1986), Freudenberger (1986), and Bennett, Bryant, VandenBos, and Greenwood (1990). On causes of burnout see Farber (1983a), Farber and Heifetz (1982), Guy (1987), and Kottler and Blau (1989). On counselor impairment see Guy (1987) and Stadler (1990b). For a discussion of stress in the helping professions, stress-management techniques, and professional burnout, see Corey and Corey (1993).

CHAPTER THREE

Values and the Helping Relationship

Pre-Chapter Self-Inventory

Directions: For each statement, indicate the response that most closely identifies your beliefs and attitudes. Use the following code:

5 = I *strongly agree* with this statement.
4 = I *agree* with this statement.
3 = I am *undecided* about this statement.
2 = I *disagree* with this statement.
1 = I *strongly disagree* with this statement.

_____ 1. It is both possible and desirable for counselors to remain neutral and keep their values from influencing clients.

_____ 2. Counselors should influence clients to adopt values that seem in their opinion to be in the clients' best interests.

_____ 3. It is appropriate for counselors to express their values, as long as they don't try to impose them on clients.

_____ 4. Counselors should challenge clients to make value judgments regarding their own behavior.

_____ 5. I can work only with clients whose value systems are similar to my own.

_____ 6. Before I can effectively counsel a person, I have to decide whether our life experiences are similar enough that I'll be able to understand that person.

_____ 7. The clarification of values is a major part of the counseling process.

_____ 8. I might be inclined to subtly influence my clients to consider my values.

_____ 9. I consider it my job to challenge my clients' philosophies of life.

_____ 10. I have a clear idea of what I value and where I acquired my values.

_____ 11. I see the clarification of my own values as an ongoing process.

_____ 12. I tend to have difficulty with people who think differently from the way I do.

_____ 13. I see part of the counseling task as teaching clients a more effective way of living.

_____ 14. I see my values as the lenses through which I view the world.

_____ 15. Ultimately, I think, the choice of living or dying rests with my clients, and therefore I do not have the right to persuade them to make a different choice.

_____ 16. I have an ethical obligation to ask myself what types of clients I am unable to effectively work with and to seek referral in such cases.

_____ 17. Sometimes I think that it is ethical to impose my values on my clients, especially if I have their best interests at heart.

_____ 18. I would have no trouble in working with a man who had been referred by the court because he had molested his daughter.

_____ 19. To be helpful to a client, a counselor must accept and approve of the client's values.

_____ 20. There are no fundamental conflicts between counseling and religion, and therefore it is possible to consider religious concerns in a therapeutic relationship.

___ 21. If a client of mine subscribed to a dogmatic religion, I would be likely to challenge this person.

___ 22. If a client complained of having no meaning in life, I would be inclined to introduce a discussion of religious values as a source of finding purpose.

Introduction

The question of values permeates the therapeutic process. This chapter is intended to stimulate your thinking about your values and life experiences and the influence they will have on your counseling. We ask you to consider the possible impact
of your values on your clients, the effect that your clients' values will have on you, and the conflicts that may arise when you and your clients have different values.

Perhaps the most fundamental question we can raise is whether it is possible for therapists to keep their values out of their counseling sessions. In our view it is neither possible nor desirable for counselors to be scrupulously neutral in this respect. Although we don't see the counselor's function as persuading clients to accept a certain value system, we do think it's crucial for counselors to be clear about their own values and how they influence their work and the directions taken by their clients. We also think it's important for counselors to express their values openly when these views are relevant to the questions that come up in their sessions with clients. As Bergin (1991) writes, "It is vital to be open about values but not coercive, to be a competent professional and not a missionary for a particular belief, and at the same time to be honest enough to recognize how one's value commitments may or may not promote health" (p. 399).

Clarifying Your Values and Their Role in Your Work

When therapists disclose their values, they should clearly label them as their own. Then values can be discussed in an open and noncoercive way, which can assist clients in their exploration of their own values and the behavior that stems from these values (Patterson, 1989). We agree with Patterson that counselors need not accept or approve of their clients' values, for disagreement does not imply the rejection of clients as individuals. As he points out, however, it is the way in which counselors deal with clients' value problems that can raise ethical issues. Bergin (1991) sees the core ethical challenge as being able to use values to enhance the therapeutic process without abusing the therapist's power and exploiting the client's vulnerability:

> During treatment, therapists must make important decisions about how to enhance clients' functioning on the basis of professional values that are frequently implicit. At these decision points, therapist, client, and concerned others should collaborate in arriving at the goals toward which change is directed [p. 396].

Not everyone who practices counseling or psychotherapy would agree with these views. At one extreme, some counselors who have definite, absolute value systems believe that their job is to exert influence on clients to adopt the proper values. These counselors tend to direct their clients toward the attitudes and behaviors that *they* judge to be in their clients' best interests. At the other extreme are the counselors who are so anxious to avoid influencing their clients that they neuter themselves. They keep themselves and their values hidden so that they won't contaminate their clients' choices.

With regard to the first position, we don't view counseling as a form of indoctrination; nor do we believe that the therapist's function is to teach clients the right way to live. It's unfortunate that some well-intentioned counselors believe that their job is to help people conform to socially acceptable standards or to "straighten out" their clients. It seems arrogant to suppose that counselors know what's best for others. We question the implication that counselors have a greater wisdom than their clients and can prescribe ways of being happier. No doubt, teaching is a part of counseling, and clients do learn in both direct and indirect ways from the opinions and examples of their counselors; but this is not to say that counseling is synonymous with preaching or instruction.

On the other hand, we don't favor the opposite extreme of trying so hard to be "objective" that counselors keep their personal reactions and values hidden from their clients. Counselors who adopt this style are unlikely to do more than mechanical, routine therapy. Clients demand a lot more involvement from their therapist than mere reflection and clarification. They often want and need to know where their therapist stands in order to test their own thinking. We think that clients deserve this kind of honest involvement.

Practitioners will inevitably incorporate certain value orientations into their therapeutic approaches. As clients struggle with the choices open to them, it may be appropriate at times for the therapist to do more than merely watch them make bad decisions without interference. Bergin asserts that it is irresponsible for a therapist to fail to inform clients about alternatives: "We need to be honest and open about our views, collaborate with the client in setting goals that fit his or her needs, then step aside and allow the person to exercise autonomy and face consequences" (1991, p. 397).

The following questions may help you to begin thinking about the role of your values in your work with clients:

- Some professionals consider it unethical to influence clients in specific value directions. What do you think?
- Do you worry that openly discussing your values with certain clients might unduly influence their decision-making process?
- Is it possible for therapists to interact honestly with their clients without making value judgments? Is it desirable for therapists to avoid making such judgments?
- If you were convinced that your client was making a bad decision, would you want to influence this individual to move in a different direction?
- Do you think that it is the therapist's responsibility to inform clients about a variety of value options?

- Do you have a need to see your clients adopt your beliefs and values?
- Can you remain true to yourself and at the same time allow your clients the freedom to select their own values, even if they differ sharply from yours?
- How do you determine whether a conflict between your values and those of your client necessitates a referral to another professional?
- What specific values do you consider to be essential to the therapeutic process?
- How does honestly exposing your clients to your viewpoint differ from subtly "guiding" them to accept your values?
- To what degree do you need to have had life experiences that are similar to those of your clients? Is it possible that too much similarity in values and life experiences might result in therapy that is not challenging for the client?

If, as we have maintained, your values will significantly affect your work with clients, it is incumbent on you to clarify them and the ways in which they enter the therapeutic process. For example, counselors who have "liberal" values may find themselves working with clients who have more traditional values. If these counselors privately scoff at conventional values, can they truly respect clients who don't think as they do? Or if counselors have a strong commitment to values that they rarely question, whether these values are conventional or radical, will they be inclined to promote these values at the expense of hindering their clients' free exploration of their own attitudes and beliefs? If counselors never reexamine their own values, can they expect to provide a climate in which clients can reexamine theirs?

Whatever your own values are, there may be many instances in which they present some difficulty for you in your work with clients. In the following sections we examine some sample cases and issues that can help you clarify what you value and how your values might influence your counseling. As you read through those examples, keep the following questions in mind:

- What is my position on this issue?
- Where did I develop my views?
- Are my values open to modification?
- Have I challenged my views, and am I open to being challenged by others?
- Do I insist that the world remain the same as it was earlier in my life?
- Do I feel so deeply committed to any of my values that I'm likely to push my clients to accept them?
- How can I communicate my values to my clients without imposing those values?
- How do my own values and beliefs affect my approach to working with clients?

The Ethics of Imposing Your Values on Clients

Successful therapy involves change, and with this change often comes the shifting of one's values. Some writers believe that therapists have a role in promoting self-determination as a value for clients. Bergin (1991) compares effective therapy to good parenting:

Trust is established; guided growth is stimulated; values are conveyed in a respectful way; the person being influenced becomes stronger, more assertive, and independent; the person learns ways of clarifying and testing value choices; the influencer decreases dependency nurturance and external advice; and the person experiments with new behaviors and ideas until he or she becomes more mature and autonomous [p. 397].

A national survey found a consensus among a representative group of mental-health practitioners that certain basic values, including self-determination, were important for giving clients mentally healthy lifestyles and for guiding and evaluating the course of psychotherapy (Jensen & Bergin, 1988). These values also include developing effective strategies for coping with stress; developing the ability to give and receive affection; increasing one's ability to be sensitive to the feelings of others; becoming able to practice self-control; having a sense of purpose for living; being open, honest, and genuine; finding satisfaction in one's work; having a sense of identity and self-worth; being skilled in interpersonal relationships, sensitivity, and nurturance; being committed in marriage, family, and other relationships; having deepened self-awareness and motivation for growth; and practicing good habits of physical health. The practitioners in this survey viewed these values as universal and based their therapy on them. They considered other values as relative ones, which therapists should deal with sensitively and not impose on clients.

Even if you think it's inappropriate or unethical to impose your values on clients, you may unintentionally influence them in subtle ways to embrace your views. It will be difficult to avoid communicating your values to your clients. What you pay attention to during counseling sessions will reinforce what your clients choose to talk about. The methods you use will provide them with clues to what you value. There are no clear answers in resolving the ethical dilemma of whether to convert clients to a general set of values that you hold.

Your nonverbal behavior and body messages give clients indications of when you like or dislike what they are doing. If they feel a need to have your approval, they may respond to these cues by acting in ways that they imagine will meet with your favor instead of developing their own inner direction. Suppose, for example, that an unhappily married man knew or surmised that you really thought he was wasting good years of his life in the marriage. This client might be influenced to obtain a divorce simply because he thought you would approve. So, although you may have decided not to push clients to believe and act in ways that agree with your own values, you still need to be sensitive to the subtle messages that can be powerful influences on their behavior.

According to Tjeltveit (1986), there are ways to minimize significantly the ethically questionable conversion of others to your values. Some of these measures are informing yourself about the varieties of values held in society, being aware of your own values, presenting value options in an unbiased manner, being committed to the freedom of choice of your clients, respecting clients who have values different from yours, consulting with others when necessary, and referring clients to another counselor when necessary.

Value Conflicts: To Refer or Not to Refer

Tjeltveit (1986) suggests that referrals are appropriate when moral, religious, or political values are centrally involved in a client's presenting problems and when any of the following situations exist: the therapist's boundaries of competence have been reached, the therapist has extreme discomfort with a client's values, the therapist is unable to maintain objectivity, or the therapist has grave concerns about imposing his or her values on the client. In such cases it is appropriate to refer a client to a therapist who does not have the limitations mentioned above or who shares the client's values. Merely having a conflict of values does not necessarily require a referral, for it is possible to work through a conflict successfully.

You might ask yourself "Will I be able to work effectively with anyone who seeks counseling from me?" Some counselors believe that they can work with any client or with any problem. They may be convinced that being professional means being able to assist anyone. On the other hand, some counselors are so unsure of their abilities that they are quick to refer anyone who makes them feel uncomfortable.

Somewhere between these extremes are the cases in which your values and those of your client clash to such an extent that you question your ability to function in a helping way. Obviously, there are no easy ways to determine what to do when this happens. The burden must be on counselors to honestly assess whether their values are likely to interfere with the objectivity they need to be useful to their clients. To make such an assessment, counselors must be clear about their feelings concerning value-laden issues, they must be honest about their own limitations, and they must be honest with potential clients when they think value conflicts will interfere with the therapeutic relationship.

Consider the circumstances in which you would be inclined to refer a client to someone else because of a conflict of value systems. For each of the following, indicate the response that best fits you. Use the following code: A = I could work with this person; B = I would have difficulty working with this person; C = I could not work with this person.

_____ 1. a man with fundamentalist religious beliefs

_____ 2. a woman who claims that she is seeking a way to put Christ at the center of her life and that if she could only turn her life to Christ, she would find peace

_____ 3. a person who shows little development of a conscience, who is strictly interested in his or her own advancement, and who uses others to achieve personal aims

_____ 4. a homosexual couple hoping to work on conflicts in their relationship

_____ 5. a man who wants to leave his wife and children for the sake of sexual adventures with other women that might bring zest to his life

_____ 6. a woman who has decided to leave her husband and children in order to gain her independence but who wants to explore her fears of doing so

_____ 7. a woman who wants an abortion but wants help in confirming her decision

_____ 8. a man who is disturbed because he periodically becomes violent with his wife and has beaten her severely a number of times

_____ 9. a man who lives by extremely rigid "macho" expectations of what a man should be

_____ 10. a person who lives by logic and is convinced that feelings are confusing and should be avoided

_____ 11. a man who believes that the only way to discipline his children is through the use of corporal punishment

_____ 12. an interracial couple coming for premarital counseling

_____ 13. a husband and wife who seek counseling to discuss conflicts they are having with their adopted son, who is from a different culture

_____ 14. a lesbian couple wanting to adopt a child

_____ 15. a person whose way of life includes a consistent reliance on marijuana as a means of coping with stress

_____ 16. a man who has found a way of beating the system and getting more than his legal share of public assistance

_____ 17. a man and his wife, who is unwilling to give up her affair

_____ 18. an interracial couple wanting to adopt a child and being faced with their respective parents' opposition to the adoption

_____ 19. a client from another culture who has values very different from your own

_____ 20. clients who have values that you strongly disapprove of or goals that you do not respect

Now go back over the list, and pay particular attention to the items you marked "C." Why do you think you'd have particular difficulty in working with these people? What other people do you envision posing problems for you because of a clash of values?

Case Studies of Possible Value Conflicts

In this section we present some case studies of possible value conflicts. Try to imagine yourself working with each of these clients. How do you think your values would affect your work with them?

○ *The case of Candy.* Candy is a 14-year-old client whom you are seeing because of family conflicts. Her parents have recently divorced, and Candy is having problems coping with the breakup. Eventually, she tells you that she is having sexual relations with her boyfriend. Moreover, she tells you that she's opposed to any birth-control devices because they seem so contrived. She assures you that she won't be one to get pregnant.

What are your feelings about Candy's having sex? If you sense that her behavior is an attempt to overcome her feelings of isolation, how might you deal with it? How would you respond to her decision not to use birth-control measures? Is she a danger to herself or others?

After you've been working with Candy for a few months, she discovers that she is pregnant. Her boyfriend is also 14 and is obviously in no position to support her and a baby. She tells you that she has decided to have an abortion but feels anxious about following through on her decision. How would you respond? In the blanks put an "A" if you agree more than disagree with the statement, and put a "D" if you mainly disagree:

___ I'd encourage Candy to do whatever she wants to do.

___ I'd encourage her to consider other options besides abortion, such as adoption, keeping the child as a single parent, marrying, and so on.

___ I'd reassure her about having an abortion, telling her that thousands of women make this choice.

___ I'd consult with a supervisor or a colleague about the possible legal implications in this case.

___ I'd attempt to arrange for a family session, or at least a session with Candy and her parents, as a way to open up communication on this issue.

___ I'd encourage her to explore all the options and consequences of each of her choices.

___ I'd inform her parents, because I believe they have a right to be a part of this decision-making process.

___ I'd refer Candy to a family-planning center and encourage her to at least seek abortion counseling so that she could deal with her fears, guilt, and ambivalence pertaining to abortion as one option.

___ I'd pay particular attention to helping her clarify her value system; I'd be sensitive to her religious and moral values and the possible implications of specific choices she might make.

___ I'd refer her to another professional because of my opposition to abortion.

___ I'd tell her that I am personally opposed to (or in favor of) abortion but that I want to remain her counselor during this difficult time and will support whatever decision she makes for herself.

___ I would reprimand her and tell her that I had known this was going to happen.

Value issues.   Candy's case illustrates several thorny problems. What do you do if you feel that you cannot be objective because of your views on abortion? Do you refer Candy to someone else? If you do, might she feel that you are rejecting her because she has committed some horrible offense? If you're firmly opposed to abortion, could you support her in her decision to go ahead with it? Would you try to persuade her to have the baby because of your views on abortion?

A possible course of action would be to tell Candy about your values and how you felt they would influence your work with her. If you felt that you couldn't work effectively with her, perhaps you should ask yourself why. Why is it crucial that her decision be compatible with your values? Do you necessarily have to approve of the decisions your clients make?

Consider the possible decisions Candy might make, and ask yourself what your goals in working with her would be. What are *your* values in a case such as hers?

As can be seen in Candy's case, women are often unprepared or unwilling to have a child. When the subject of abortion arises, they may be reluctant to consider this option, either because of their value systems or because of feelings of guilt, shame, and fear. Thus, an unwanted pregnancy and its termination constitute a crisis for them. Some pregnant women may feel ambivalent and may want to explore all of their options.

Ask yourself the following additional questions about Candy's case:

- How would I react to not being allowed to explore abortion as one option for Candy?
- Do you think that it is unethical to fail to discuss with a client all of her options if this is her desire?
- What do you think about the behavior of a counselor who decides to ignore the federal prohibition and proceeds to provide abortion counseling for a client who has asked for this service? If this defiance were discovered and the agency lost its funding, what would be your reaction to the counselor's decision to explore all options?

○ *The case of Paul.*   Paul comes to a counselor with many difficulties and anxieties, one of which is his antipathy toward interracial marriage. He expresses disappointment in his daughter and in himself as a father because of her engagement to a man of another race. Paul has gone as far as threatening to write her out of his will if she marries this man. What this client does not know is that the therapist herself is a partner in an interracial marriage. The therapist discloses this fact and lets him know of her difficulties with what she perceives as his prejudices.

- How do you react to her self-disclosure? (Was it ethical for her to do so? Would it have been ethical not to do so? Explain.)
- Would a referral be in order? Why or why not?
- What are your values in this situation, and what might you do or say if you were the counselor?

Value issues.   Your views on racial issues can have an impact on your manner of counseling in certain situations. As we encouraged you to clarify your values in other areas, we suggest that you take the following inventory and then think about what your responses tell you about how your values might operate in cases pertaining to racial concerns. In the space, write an "A" if you agree more than you disagree with the statement, and put a "D" if you disagree more than you agree:

____ 1. I could effectively counsel a person of a different race.
____ 2. I'd be inclined to refer a person of a different race to a counselor of that race, since the client is bound to have more trust in a therapist of the same race.

___ 3. My approach to counseling would entail modifying my practices and techniques in working with clients who are racially and culturally different.

___ 4. Interracial marriages in this society are almost doomed to failure because of the extra pressures on them.

___ 5. Interracial marriages pose no greater strain on a relationship than do interfaith marriages.

___ 6. I have certain racial (cultural) prejudices that would affect my objectivity in working with clients of a different race (culture) from mine.

Reflect on values you hold that would influence your way of working with clients such as Paul who present interracial issues.

○ ***The case of Lupe.***   Lupe is a social worker in a community mental-health agency. Her agency is sponsoring workshops aimed at prevention of the spread of AIDS. The agency has attempted to involve the local churches in these workshops. One church withdrew its support because the workshops encouraged "safe" sexual practices, including the use of condoms, as a way of preventing AIDS. A church official contended that the use of condoms implied either homosexual behavior or promiscuous heterosexual activities, both of which are contrary to church teachings. Being a member of this church, Lupe finds herself struggling with value conflicts. She is in basic agreement with the teachings of the church, and she thinks that the official had a right to withdraw his support of these workshops, based on his beliefs and the church's position. But she is also aware that many people in the community she serves are at high risk for contracting AIDS, because of both drug usage and sexual practices. In her attempt to resolve her value conflicts she seeks out several of her colleagues, each of whom responds differently:

Colleague A says: "I would encourage you to tell your clients and others in the community that you agree with the position of the church. Then actively attempt in your workshops to change people's risky behavior. You could try to get them to give up their drug use, and you could steer them in the direction of monogamous sex practices."

Colleague B says: "I hope you will be up front with the people you come in contact with by telling them of your values and then providing them with adequate referrals so they can get information about prevention of this disease. But you do owe it to them not to steer them in the direction you think they should move."

Colleague C says: "I think it is best that you not disclose your values or let them know that you agree with the church's views. Instead, work toward changing their behavior and modifying their values indirectly. After all, in this case the end justifies the means."

Colleague D says: "More harm can come by your failure to provide necessary information. Even though your values are in sympathy with the church's position, I think that ethically you owe it to the community to teach them methods of safe sex."

Value issues.   If Lupe were to seek you out and ask for your advice, consider what you might say to her. In formulating your position, consider these questions:

- Which of her colleagues comes closest to your thinking, and why?
- With which colleague do you find yourself disagreeing the most, and why?
- Do you think that Lupe would be ethical if she did not disclose her values to her clients? Why or why not?
- Given the gravity of this situation and considering the possibility of the spread of disease, do you think that Lupe is ethically bound to provide people who are at high risk with facts and information about prevention?
- What advice would you be inclined to give Lupe, and what does this response tell you about your values in this situation?

Differences in Life Experiences and Philosophies

Many people would contend that the life experiences and value systems of counselors must be similar to those of their clients. The idea is that counselors can understand and empathize with their clients' conflicts only if they have had the same kinds of subjective experiences. Thus, an elderly person may feel that a counselor who hasn't reached this stage of life cannot hope to understand what it means to cope with loss, physical decline, loneliness, and anxiety about the future. Many people who belong to racial or ethnic minorities think it is extremely important to seek counselors of their own ethnic group, in the belief that counselors who haven't had to contend with discrimination and prejudice cannot really understand how they see the world. Similarly, many women are convinced that men's life experiences and biases prevent them from being able to understand women's needs. Homosexuals may seek gay therapists because they are convinced that heterosexual counselors lack the experience and understanding to work with them on their conflicts. Many drug addicts and alcoholics reveal failure after failure in their psychotherapy experiences with professionals who haven't experienced drug and alcohol problems.

The growth of self-help groups reflects the idea that people who have encountered and resolved certain difficulties possess unique resources for helping others like themselves. Thus, overweight people share their problems in Overeaters Anonymous. Alcoholics who have chosen to live one day at a time without drinking provide support for fellow alcoholics who are trying to quit. Many drug addicts who have entered Synanon have found that they cannot deceive former addicts with their games and that being confronted by people who once played the same games forces them to look at how they are living. Members of Recovery Incorporated find support in facing the world once they have left state mental hospitals.

To what degree do you share the view that you must have had life experiences similar to those of your clients? Do you think you need to have the same philosophy of life in order to work effectively with them? Do you think that you can be helpful to people whose experiences, values, and problems are different from yours by tuning in to their feelings and relating them to your own? Consider for a moment whether you could communicate effectively with:

- an elderly person
- a person with a strict religious background
- a person of a different race or ethnic group
- a physically handicapped person
- a delinquent or a criminal
- an alcoholic
- a person with a different sexual orientation
- an obese person

Our position is that counselors need not have experienced each of the struggles of their clients to be effective in working with them. When the counselor and the client are relating on a *feeling* level, cultural and age differences are transcended. It is possible for a relatively young counselor to work effectively with an elderly client in spite of the fact that the counselor has not yet experienced some of the problems of the older client. For example, the client may be experiencing feelings of loss, guilt, sadness, and hopelessness over a number of situations in life. The counselor still has the capacity to empathize with these feelings, for he or she can tie into different experiences that resulted in some of the same feelings. What is essential is that the counselor be sensitive to the differences in their backgrounds.

In *Counseling the Culturally Different: Theory and Practice*, D. W. Sue and D. Sue (1990) point out that many counselors are "culturally blind" in the sense that they perceive reality exclusively through the filters of their own life experiences. What is important, they contend, is for counselors to become "culturally aware"—to be able to critically evaluate their conditioned values and assumptions and the conditioning of their clients. Sue and Sue see it as imperative that counselors have a broad perspective of diverse cultural value systems. Those counselors who remain victims of their own cultural conditioning risk further oppressing minority clients.

To facilitate your reflection on whether you need to have life experiences or value systems that are similar to those of your clients, we'll present a number of situations that you might face as a counselor. In each case, assess what factors in your life would either help or hinder you in establishing a good working relationship with the client we describe:

Frances is a 60-year-old teacher who is thinking about going to law school because it's something she has wanted to do for a long time. For 30 years she has taught government and history in community colleges, and now she wants to retire early in order to take up a new profession. Frances wonders whether she has the stamina to endure long hours of study, and she is asking herself whether leaving teaching at this stage in life would be a wise move.

- What experiences have you had that could help you understand Frances's desires and conflict?

- How do you respond to a person's beginning law school at the age of 60?
- Would you be inclined to encourage Frances to take a risk, or would you favor her staying with a secure job in her situation?
- How might your answers to the preceding questions affect the way you would counsel her?

Alberto, a minority-group client, comes to a community mental-health clinic on the recommendation of one of his friends. His presenting problem is depression, chronic sleep disturbance, and the imminent threat of losing his job. During the initial session you are aware that he is extremely guarded. He discloses little about himself or how he is feeling in this situation with you. Although he will answer your questions briefly, you sense that he is withholding much information from you. As a counselor, you may assume that self-disclosure and openness to feeling enhance one's life. In working with Alberto, consider these questions:

- How sensitive are you to the client's sense of privacy? Have you considered that keeping one's thoughts and feelings to oneself might be a value in certain cultures? How might this be a survival mechanism in some cultures?
- Assume that you succeed in getting Alberto to be more self-disclosing and expressive, not only with you but also within his environment. What potential hazards can you see in terms of his reentry into his environment?
- Is it ethical to convert him to your point of view without first understanding the cultural context? Explain.
- One of your aims might be to teach Alberto to be more autonomous (to become less dependent on his parents and his extended family). How might this aim be an expression of your value system, and how might that affect your client as he attempts to deal with his family?
- How might your intervention reflect your lack of understanding of the importance of the extended family in certain cultures?
- Some might label Alberto's behavior as bordering on paranoia. How might his cautiousness be more adaptive than maladaptive?

At a community clinic Sylvia, who is 38, tells you that she is an alcoholic. During the intake interview she says: "I feel so much remorse, because I've tried to stop my drinking and haven't succeeded. I'm fine for a while, and then I begin to think that I have to be a 'perfect' wife and mother. I see all the ways in which I don't measure up—how I let my kids down, the many mistakes I've made with them, the embarrassment I've caused my husband—and then I get so down I feel compelled to take that next drink to stop my shaking and to blur my depression. I see that what I'm doing is self-destructive, but I haven't been able to stop, in spite of going to A.A."

- What experiences have you had that would help you understand what it's like for Sylvia to feel compelled to drink?
- Do you see Sylvia as having a disease? as suffering from a lack of willpower? as an irresponsible, indulgent person?
- How does the fact that Sylvia is a woman affect your view of her problem?
- What is your reaction to Sylvia's being in Alcoholics Anonymous? Do you see it as a desirable adjunct to therapy? Or do you see it as potentially working at cross purposes with your therapy? Explain.

○ ***The case of Jan.***   Jan is a physicist, born and educated in northern Europe. He has several degrees from prestigious universities. Jan's lifestyle and interests center on intellectual pursuits, and he tends to show very little affect in most situations. His wife is having an affair, and he seeks your counsel, not so much on his own initiative but because of the encouragement of colleagues who think he can use some guidance. He talks calmly about the potential breakup of his family and indicates that he has discussed the matter with his wife. In essence, he has asked her to decide the outcome. Jan is in your office to find a logical explanation for why the affair occurred, yet he does not display any strong emotional reactions to the situation. He gives no clues to how he is feeling about it.

- Would you consider Jan's cultural and educational background in dealing with his reaction to his situation?
- Would you immediately pursue the expression of feeling? Can you see yourself saying: "Cut out the intellectualizing and tell me how you feel?" Why or why not?

Commentary.   This example is used to illustrate another type of cultural difference. Although we do not deny the value of expressing one's emotional reactions to a situation such as Jan's, we would be especially sensitive to his cultural background and his conditioning. In certain cultures openly admitting having been affected by a situation such as this is equivalent to a loss of face or pride. Jan might never show the degree of emotionality that we deem appropriate, but that does not mean that he cannot express an emotional reaction. Our main point is that to push for the "norm" of "getting at feelings" could be counterproductive and potentially unethical. Although this example could apply to many American men as well, it is even more representative of Jan's cultural conditioning not to share his feelings.

You are the probation counselor for Mike, who has a history of being expelled from school. He has spent much of his life in and out of juvenile court. The customs of the gang he belongs to dictate how he lives. He's silent during most of your first session, but he does let you know that he doesn't really trust you, that he's only there because the court sent him, and that you can't possibly understand what his life is about.

- Have you had any life experiences that would qualify you to counsel Mike?
- What are your immediate reactions to him?
- Would you want to convert him to any of your values? For example, would you want to see him finish school? stop being involved in gang fights? take counseling seriously?
- If you haven't had the kinds of experiences growing up that he has had, could you still communicate effectively with him and understand his view of the world?

Luigi is a middle-aged businessman who says that he's not seeking personal counseling but rather wants advice on how to manage his teenage daughter. According to Luigi, his daughter is immature and unruly. She isn't learning self-discipline, she socializes too much and works too little, she doesn't respect her parents, and in other ways she is a disappointment and a worry to him. Luigi seems to be op-pressive rather than loving, and to him the full responsibility for the conflict in his family rests with his daughter. You surmise that he doesn't see any need to examine his own behavior or his role in contributing to the family's difficulties.

- How do you imagine you might relate to Luigi?
- Would your own values get in the way of understanding his values?
- Do you think you might want to get him to look at his own part in the family disturbances? Would you want to challenge his values as they pertain to his daughter's behavior?
- Would you accept him as a client, even if he wanted to focus on how he could change his daughter?
- Would family therapy be indicated?

You can add your own examples of clients whom you might have difficulty in counseling because of a divergence in values or life experiences. How would you deal with such clients? You could decide to refer most of them to other counselors, but you might also look at how to broaden yourself so that you could work with a wider range of personalities. If you have difficulty relating to people who think differently from the way you do, you can work on being more open to diverse viewpoints. This openness doesn't entail accepting other people's values as your own. Instead, it implies being secure enough in your own values that you aren't threatened by really listening to, and deeply understanding, people who think about life differently. It implies listening to your clients with the intent of understanding what their values are, how they arrived at them, and the mean-ing these values have for them and then communicating this acceptance. This kind of accepting attitude requires a willingness to let your clients be who they are without trying to convince them that they should see life the way you do. Achieving this acceptance of your clients can significantly broaden you as a per-son and as a professional.

Controversial Issues: Implications for Counseling

In the previous sections you have seen that differences in life experiences and values are bound to influence the interventions you make. As you counsel a variety of clients, you may find yourself struggling with how your beliefs affect the way you work with them. This is especially true in controversial cases pertaining to the right to die, religion, and sexuality. As you read this section, attempt to clarify your values in these areas and think about how your views might either enhance or interfere with your ability to establish contact with certain clients.

The Right to Die and the Issue of Suicide

In March 1990 Bruno Bettelheim stunned the psychological community when he took his own life. In an interview with Celeste Fremon (1991), Bettelheim shared some of his views on the right to take one's own life. He told Fremon that although he was not afraid of dying, he did fear suffering. As people grow older, he contended, there is a greater likelihood that they will be kept alive without a purpose. At age 86, Bettelheim was no longer able to do most of the things that brought him enjoyment and meaning, such as hiking, reading, and writing. He wrestled with the decision of whether to live or to die. Apparently, he feared what another stroke might do to him, and he felt that he was living on borrowed time. He told the interviewer that he was considering meeting with a doctor in the Netherlands who was willing to give him a lethal injection. His situation highlights the issue of a person's right to choose the manner of death, especially in the event of terminal illness.

Might there come a time in your life when there was nothing for you to live for? Imagine yourself in a rest home, growing more and more senile. You are unable to read, to carry on meaningful conversation, or to go places, and you are partially paralyzed by a series of strokes. Would you want to be kept alive at all costs, or might you want to end your life? Would you feel justified in doing so? What might stop you?

Now apply this line of thought to other situations in life. If you accept the premise that your life is yours to do with as you choose, do you believe it is permissible to commit suicide at *any* period in your life? In many ways, people who choose suicide are really saying that they want to put an end to the way they are living *now*. Suppose you felt this way even after trying various ways of making your life meaningful, including getting intensive psychotherapy. Imagine that you felt as if nothing worked, as if you always wound up in a dead-end street. Would you continue to live until natural causes took you? Would you feel justified in ending your own life if your active search had failed to bring you peace?

Perhaps thinking about conditions that might lead you to consider suicide is so unpleasant that you have never really allowed yourself to imagine such situations. If you give some thought to how this issue applies to you, however, you may feel less threatened in entering into real dialogues with individuals who are contemplating the balance sheet of their lives. If you are closed to any personal consideration of this issue, you may tend to interrupt these dialogues or cut off your clients' exploration of their feelings.

The ethical questions associated with suicide can come up in other ways as well. Consider the following example:

○ *The case of Emily.*   Emily, who is in her early 20s, is dying painfully of cancer. She expresses her wish to forego any further treatment and to take an overdose of pills to end her suffering. Her parents cling to hope, however, and in any event they deeply believe that it is always wrong to take one's own life. If her parents were coming to you for counseling, what might you say to them? Do you feel that Emily has the right to end her life? What role should your opinion play in your counseling? How might your values affect the things you say to the family?

Now assume that Emily herself comes to you, her therapist of long standing, and says: "I am dying and I have no desire to suffer. I don't want to involve you in it, but as my therapist, I would like you to know my last wishes." She tells you of her plan to take an overdose of pills, an action she sees as more humane than continuing to endure her suffering. Consider the following questions:

- What legal implications are involved here?
- Do you think you have the ethical and legal responsibility to prevent Emily from carrying out her intended course of action?
- If you were in full agreement with her wishes, how might this feeling influence your intervention?
- What do you consider to be the ethical course of action?

○ *The case of Bettina*.   Let's consider a different case involving the termination of one's life. Bettina, who is living at a boarding school, makes several suicidal overtures. Because these attempts seem to be primarily attention-getting gestures, her counselor feels manipulated and does not report them to her parents. During the last of these attempts, however, she seriously hurts herself and ends up in the hospital.

- Did the counselor take the "cry for help" too lightly?
- What are the ethical and legal implications of the counselor's deciding that the client's attempts were more manipulative than serious and therefore should be ignored?
- What can a counselor do in a situation in which he or she determines that the attempts are manipulative rather than serious?
- Assume that the counselor had told Bettina that she was going to inform the girl's parents about these suicidal attempts. Bettina had responded by saying that she would quit counseling if the counselor did so. What do you think the counselor should have done?

Issues involved in right-to-die cases.   Although the cases of Emily and Bettina are different, they do raise similar issues that are worth considering. What is your position on these issues pertaining to the right to die?

- Do counselors have the responsibility and the right to forcefully protect people from the potential harm that their own decisions may bring?
- Do helpers have an ethical right to block clients who have clearly chosen death over life? Do they have an ethical duty to respect clients' decisions?
- What are the counselors' legal obligations if clients decide to commit suicide?
- Once a therapist determines that a significant risk exists, must some action be taken? What are the consequences of failing to take steps to prevent clients from ending their lives? Do factors such as the age of the client, the client's level of competence, and the special circumstances of each case make a difference?

In his paper "Adolescence and the Right to Die," Powell (1982) discusses the issues of autonomy, competence, and paternalism as directly related to the right to die. Although Powell's article focuses on adolescents, his paper has broader implications, since the three concepts he discusses can be applied to all age levels. *Autonomy* refers to a person's independence, self-reliance, and ability to make decisions that affect his or her life. Autonomy, in turn, is based on a presumption of the person's *competence*. Competence is determined in part by the person's degree of ability to understand the potential consequences of his or her decisions. Thus, people experiencing trauma and extreme crisis and those who are actively hallucinating and clinging to false beliefs (or displaying other psychotic behaviors) are not viewed as competent to make certain critical decisions. In cases in which clients are found to be unable to direct their own lives or incompetent to make decisions of life and death, *paternalism* comes into the picture. This concept implies that the therapist (or some agent of the client) makes decisions and acts in the "best interests" of the client. Powell says he has been unable to find a clear constitutional or legal statement of a person's right to choose death. What does appear to have a constitutional basis, however, is the right to refuse treatment, even life-saving treatment. Powell cites an adolescent girl, dying from bone cancer, whose refusal of a leg operation was supported by the courts. In this case, her own wishes were considered to be crucial.

Religion

What role does religion play in your life? Does it provide you with a source of meaning? What are your views concerning established and organized religion? Has religion been a positive, negative, or neutral force in your life? Even if religious issues are not the focus of a client's concern, religious values may enter into the sessions indirectly as the client explores moral conflicts or grapples with questions of meaning in life. Do you see yourself as being able to keep your religious values out of these sessions? How do you think they will influence the way you counsel? If you're hostile to organized religions, can you empathize with clients who feel committed to the teachings of a particular church?

As you formulate your own position on the place of religious values in the practice of counseling, we suggest that you reflect on these questions: Is it appropriate to deal with religious issues in an open and forthright manner as a client's needs arise in the counseling process? Do clients have the right to explore their religious concerns in their therapy? Are therapists forcing their values on their clients when they decide what topics can be discussed?

Religious beliefs and practices affect many dimensions of human experience that are brought into counseling situations. How people handle guilt feelings, authority, and moral questions are just a few of these areas. The key issue here is whether you can understand your clients' religious beliefs if these views differ from your own. For example, you may think that a client has accepted an unnecessarily strict and authoritarian moral code. Yet you need to be able to understand what these beliefs mean to your client, whatever your own evaluation of them for yourself might be.

Suppose you have a client, Janet, who seems to be suffering from a major conflict because her church would disapprove of the way she is living. Janet experiences a great deal of guilt over what she sees as her transgressions. If you sharply disagreed with the values she accepted from her church or thought they were unrealistic, how might your views affect your counseling? Do you think you might try to persuade her that her guilt was controlling her and that she would be better off freeing herself from her religious beliefs? Why or why not?

Consider the case of Susan, who is a devout Catholic. She was married for 25 years, until her husband left her. Later, she fell in love with another man and very much wanted a relationship with him. But her moral upbringing resulted in her having guilt feelings about her involvement with another man. She sees her situation as hopeless, for there is no way in her mind to resolve an impossible situation. She might live alone for the rest of her life, and that scares her. She might marry the man, but she fears that her guilt feelings would eventually ruin the relationship.

- What are your values that pertain to this case, and how do you think they would influence your interventions?
- Would you recommend that Susan see a priest to help her resolve her guilt feelings? Explain.
- Assume that she asks you what she should do, or at least what you think about her dilemma. What would you say to her?

In this final case, assume that Jeremiah is in a group that you are leading. He calls himself a "born-again Christian" and feels that he has found peace and strength in his own life. In a sincere and caring way, Jeremiah wants to pass on to other members in the group what has become very meaningful to him. Several members respond negatively, asserting that he is pushing his values on them and that he comes across in a superior way.

- As a group leader, how would you intervene?
- What reactions do you think you'd have toward a person who held very strong religious values, and how might your reactions either inhibit or enhance your ability to work with such a person?
- If your views were very similar to this person's, what interventions might you make, and how might you react?

Sexuality

What are your values with respect to sexual behavior? Do they tend to be restrictive or permissive? What are your attitudes toward:

- the belief that sex should be reserved for marriage only
- sex as an expression of love and commitment
- casual sex
- group sex
- extramarital sex
- premarital sex
- homosexuality
- teenage sex

An important issue is whether you can counsel people who are experiencing conflict over their sexual choices if their values differ dramatically from your own. For example, if you have permissive views about sexual behavior, will you be able to respect the restrictive views of some of your clients? If you think their moral views are giving them difficulty, will you try to persuade them to adopt your views?

How will you view the guilt they may experience? Will you treat it as an undesirable emotion that they need to free themselves of? Or, if you have fairly strict sexual standards that you use as guidelines for your own life, will you tend to see the more permissive attitudes of some of your clients as a problem? Can you be supportive of choices that conflict with your own values?

○ *The case of Virginia and Tom.*   Virginia and Tom find themselves in a marital crisis when she discovers that he has been having sexual affairs with several women. These affairs have been going on for several years. Tom agrees to see a marriage counselor, and the couple come for a counseling session. Tom says that he has no intention of giving up his lifestyle, because he doesn't think the affairs are interfering in his relationship with his wife. He says that he loves his wife and that he does not want to end the marriage. His involvements with the other women are sexual in nature rather than committed love relationships. Virginia says that she would like to accept her husband's affairs but that she finds it too painful to continue living with him while knowing of his activities.

Counselor A.   This counselor has a definite bias in favor of Tom. She points out that the two seem to have a basically sound marriage, and she suggests that with some individual counseling Virginia can learn to accept and live with her husband's affairs.

- With her bias, is it ethical for this counselor to accept this couple for counseling? Should she suggest a referral to another professional?
- Is the counselor ignoring the wife's needs and values?
- Is there an ethical issue in siding with the husband?
- Would it be a better course of action for the counselor to keep her values and attitudes to herself so that she would be less likely to influence the couple's decisions?

Counselor B.   From the outset, this counselor makes it clear that she sees affairs as disruptive in any marriage. She maintains that they are typically started because of a deep dissatisfaction within the marriage. In her view affairs are symptomatic of other real conflicts. The counselor suggests that, with marital therapy, Tom and Virginia can get to the basis of their problem. She further says that she will not work with them unless Tom is willing to give up his affairs, since she is convinced that counseling will not work unless he is fully committed to doing what is needed to work on his relationship with Virginia.

- Do you see this counselor as imposing her values?
- Is this approach appropriate, since the counselor is openly stating her conditions and values from the outset?
- To what degree do you agree or disagree with this counselor's thinking and approach?

Counselor C.   This counselor tells the couple at the initial session that from her experience extramarital affairs add many strains to a marriage, that many people tend to get hurt in such situations, and that affairs do pose some problems for couples seeking counseling. However, she adds that affairs sometimes actually have positive benefits for both the wife and the husband. She says that her policy is to let the husband and wife find out for themselves what is acceptable to them. She accepts Virginia and Tom as clients and asks them to consider as many options as they can to resolve their difficulties. Counselor C asks Virginia to consider the possibility of getting involved with other men.

- Do you see this counselor as neutral or biased? Explain.
- Does it seem practical and realistic to expect the couple to make the decision by coming up with some alternatives?
- Is it ethical for the counselor to suggest that Virginia consider becoming sexually involved with other men?

Religion and Homosexuality

Before you deal with the following case of Ronald, take a few minutes to assess some of your values involving homosexuality and religion. In the blanks, put an "A" if you agree more than you disagree with the statement, and put a "D" if you disagree more than you agree.

_____ 1. My views on religion would influence my approach in working with clients who have homosexual concerns.

_____ 2. Regardless of what my values relating to homosexuality are, I think it would be important to disclose them to clients with homosexual concerns.

_____ 3. Knowing my own values, I think I'd be inclined to steer my clients in a definite direction rather than encouraging them to choose their own path.

_____ 4. From my viewpoint, I think that homosexuality should be discussed within the framework of religious and moral values.

_____ 5. To be honest, I think that I have some fears of openly discussing the issue of homosexuality with clients.

_____ 6. If a client said he saw himself as "a religious person" and also experienced guilt feelings because of a homosexual orientation, his religious convictions should be challenged in therapy.

_____ 7. I see guilt as a way of controlling people.

_____ 8. If I were working with a client who had decided on a homosexual lifestyle, I'd tend to be supportive of his or her choice.

_____ 9. Ethical practice in counseling with homosexual clients demands that at some point a referral be made to a therapist who is homosexual.

_____ 10. Homosexuals in this society are subjected to unfair discrimination, and they are an oppressed minority.

Look over your responses above, and attempt to clarify your own values pertaining to homosexuality. Do you think you can counsel objectively in this area? Would you be inclined to "push" your own values? In what ways do you think your values would influence the interventions you'd make? Consider these questions as you read the following case:

○ *The case of Ronald.*   Ronald is a 22-year-old college junior. He tells you that he wants to get into counseling with you in order to sort out conflicts that he is experiencing between his sexual feelings and his religion. Ronald sees himself as a good Christian and a believer in the Bible. He has had very little experience in dating and hasn't had any sexual relationships. He is troubled because he experiences far more intense feelings toward men than he does toward women. This is what he tells you:

> I haven't yet acted on my sexual feelings for other men, because I feel that this would be morally wrong. My religious beliefs tell me that it's very wrong for me even to have sexual desires for other men, let alone *act* on these desires! If I did have homosexual experiences, I'd feel extremely guilty. But I just don't have much interest in women, and at the same time I'm intensely interested in having a close emotional and physical relationship with a man. I'm torn by what I feel I want to experience and what my religion tells me I *ought* to do. So, I was wondering whether you think you can help me, and I'd also like to know what your views are about religion and about homosexuality.

From what you know about Ronald, would you want to accept him as a client? Do you think you could help him clarify his feelings and achieve some resolution of his conflict? What kind of answer would you give him concerning your view of homosexuality? What would you tell him about your religious values? How would your views either help or hinder him resolving his struggle?

Let's examine the responses that three different counselors might make to Ronald. As you read these responses, think about the degree to which they might represent what you might say if you were counseling him.

Counselor A.   "Well, Ronald, the answer to whether I can help you really depends on several factors. First of all, you need to know that I'm a Christian counselor, and I share many of your beliefs about religion, morality, and the Bible. I think that I could be very supportive in helping you work through some of your religious doubts. You should know that I believe my clients will find real serenity when they make Christ the center of their lives and when they live by the example He gave us. Next, you need to know that I cannot condone homosexuality, because I do believe that it is immoral. I'm not implying that you're sinful for merely having homosexual wishes, but I think it would be morally wrong for you to act on these impulses."

Do you share any of Counselor A's views? Do you see Counselor A as *imposing* or merely *exposing* his beliefs? Do you think Counselor A can work effectively with Ronald? Why or why not?

Counselor B.   "I'm not sure whether I'm the counselor for you or not. Ultimately, I think you'll need to decide whether you want to work with me. Before you decide, you should know that I think that religion is a negative influence on most people. In your case, for example, you were taught to feel guilty over your impulses. I see guilt as a way of controlling people, so, if I worked with you, I'd probably challenge some of your religious values and the source of your guilt feelings. I'd have you look carefully at where you obtained your notions of right and wrong. As far as your homosexual feelings are concerned, I'd want to explore the relationship you had with your father and mother, and I'd challenge you to look at your motivations in not making more contact with women. Is it because you're afraid of them? Do you have enough experience with either sex to know whether you want to be homosexual or heterosexual?"

What do you agree or disagree with in Counselor B's thinking? Do you think this counselor will impose her views on Ronald? Or do you think that Counselor B's values will challenge him to decide what *he* values?

Counselor C.   "Ronald, your sexual preference really doesn't affect me one way or the other. I'd want you to decide to do what *you* think is right for you. For instance, if you decide on a homosexual lifestyle, I'd be supportive, and I'd want to help you work through any problems that might arise as a result of your choice. Your religious views also don't affect me one way or the other. I realize that your religion is a part of you, and we could work on how your teachings might cause you difficulty in living the way you want to. I really don't see why it's important that I tell you my personal values, because they won't be entering into our relationship that much, and I wouldn't want them to influence you. I want you to choose whatever way is right for you, and I'll support whatever that is."

Do you see Counselor C as being neutral, passive, or accepting and nonjudgmental? Do you think Counselor C can keep his values out of the therapeutic relationship? What do you agree or disagree with in Counselor C's approach?

After thinking about the three different approaches we've considered, how do you think you would respond to Ronald? Would you have any reservations about accepting him as a client? Would you be able to accept his choice of homosexuality if that was what he wanted? Would you prefer that he not make this choice? Would you be more concerned about his religious struggles than about his sexual orientation? Take a moment now to write down the essence of what you might want to say to him about the direction your work with him would take.*

Chapter Summary

In this chapter we've looked at a variety of value-laden counseling situations and issues. Of course, you'll encounter many other value questions in your work. Our intent has been to focus your attention on the ways in which your values and those of your clients will affect your counseling relationships.

The central theme is the importance of being clear about what *you* value and how that affects your work with a client. Counselors cannot be neutral in the area of values and should frankly acknowledge those values related to questions

*The ethical issue of how a therapist's values pertaining to gay men and lesbians affect the course of therapy will be considered in more detail in Chapter 11.

that clients are struggling with. It takes honesty and courage to recognize how your values affect the way you counsel, and it takes wisdom to determine when you cannot work with a client because of a clash of values. These questions have no ready-made or universally appropriate answers. They demand ongoing introspection and discussions with supervisors or colleagues to determine how to make the optimal use of your values.

Suggested Activities

1. Have a panel discussion on the topic "Is it possible for counselors to remain neutral with respect to their clients' values?" The panel can also discuss different ways in which counselors' values may affect the counseling process.

2. Invite several practicing counselors to talk to your class on the role of values in counseling. Each of these counselors can have a different theoretical orientation. For example, you might ask a behavior therapist and a humanistic therapist to talk to your class at the same time on the role of values.

3. For a week or so keep a record of your principal activities. Then look over your record and, on the basis of what you do and how you use your time, list your values reflected in your record in order of their priority. How do you think these values might influence the way you counsel others?

4. In class, do the following exercise in pairs: First, discuss counseling situations that might be difficult for each of you because of a conflict of values. For example, one student might anticipate difficulty in working with clients who have fundamentalist religious beliefs. Then choose one of these situations to role-play, with one student playing the part of a client and the other playing the part of the counselor. The client brings up some problem that involves the troublesome value area. It is important for you and your partner to really get into the particular frame of reference being role-played and to feel the part as much as possible.

5. As a variation of the preceding exercise, you can assume the role of a client whose values you have difficulty identifying with. For instance, if you think you'd have trouble counseling a woman who wanted an abortion, become this client and bring her problem to another student, who plays the part of a counselor.

6. For this exercise, work in small groups. Discuss the life experiences you've had that you think will enable you to effectively counsel others. You might also talk about *limitations* in your life experiences that might hinder your understanding of certain clients.

7. Interview some practicing counselors about their experiences with values in the counseling process. You could ask such questions as "What are some kinds of clients that you've had difficulty working with because of your value system? How do you think your values influence the way you counsel? How are your clients affected by your values? What are some of the main value issues that clients bring into the counseling process?"

8. Do this exercise in pairs. One student plays a counselor; the other plays a client. The counselor actively tries to convert the client to some value or point of view that the counselor holds. The job of the counselor is to try to persuade the client to do what the counselor thinks would be best for the client. This exercise can give you a feel for what it's like to persuade a person to adopt your point of view and what it's like to be subjected to persuasion. Then the two students can switch roles.

9. This exercise can also be done in pairs. Each person interviews the other on the following issue: What are some of your central values and beliefs, and how do you think they will inhibit or facilitate the work you will do as a counselor?

Suggested Readings

For a discussion of goals and values in psychotherapy see Patterson (1985b, 1989). For a personal exploration of values pertaining to topics such as marriage and the family, sex-role identity, work and leisure, meaning in life, death and loss, love and intimacy, and sexuality, see Corey and Corey (1990). For a discussion of a survey of the mental-health values of professional therapists, see Jensen and Bergin (1988). For an exploration of the need to include education about values and religious issues in the training of clinicians, see Bergin (1991).

Client Rights and Confidentiality

Pre-Chapter Self-Inventory

Directions: For each statement, indicate the response that most closely identifies your beliefs and attitudes. Use the following code:

5 = I *strongly agree* with this statement.
4 = I *agree* with this statement.
3 = I am *undecided* about this statement.
2 = I *disagree* with this statement.
1 = I *strongly disagree* with this statement.

_____ 1. If there is a conflict between a legal and an ethical standard, a therapist
must follow the law.

_____ 2. Practitioners who do not use written consent forms are being unethical.

_____ 3. In order to practice ethically, therapists must become familiar with the
laws related to their profession.

_____ 4. Clients in therapy should have access to their files.

_____ 5. Clients should be made aware of their rights at the outset of a diagnostic
or therapeutic relationship.

_____ 6. It is unethical for counselors to alter their fee structure once it has been
established.

_____ 7. Ethical practice demands that therapists develop procedures to ensure
that clients are in a position to make informed choices.

_____ 8. Therapists have the responsibility to learn about community resources
and alternatives to therapy and to present these alternatives to their
clients.

_____ 9. Before entering therapy, clients should be made aware of the purposes,
goals, techniques, policies, and procedures involved.

_____ 10. Therapists have an ethical responsibility to discuss a possible termination date with clients during the initial session(s) and then to review this
matter with them periodically.

_____ 11. Involuntary commitment is a violation of human rights, even in those
cases where clients are unable to be responsible for themselves or their
actions.

_____ 12. Mental patients in institutions should be consulted about the treatment
they might receive.

_____ 13. Clients should be informed at the initial counseling session of the limits
of confidentiality.

_____ 14. There are no situations in which I would disclose without a client's permission what the client had told me.

_____ 15. Absolute confidentiality is necessary if effective psychotherapy is to take
place.

_____ 16. A therapist should be aware of any client dependence, because it is
counterproductive in therapy.

_____ 17. Mystification of the client/therapist relationship tends to increase
client dependence and decrease clients' ability to assert their rights in
therapy.

____ 18. A good therapist gets involved in the client's case without becoming personally invested in a specific outcome.

____ 19. A therapeutic relationship should be maintained only as long as it is clear that the client is benefiting.

____ 20. Much of therapy is really the "purchase of friendship."

____ 21. It is primarily the therapist's responsibility to determine the appropriate time for termination of therapy.

____ 22. I will make my clients aware of both the benefits and risks associated with counseling before we begin a professional relationship.

____ 23. I will keep detailed clinical notes on my clients, and it will often be therapeutic to share these notes with my clients.

____ 24. I can easily make clients worse by attaching labels to them as a part of therapy.

____ 25. I worry about what to tell my clients about confidentiality.

Introduction

Counselors who hope to practice in an ethical and legal manner cannot take the rights of clients for granted. In this chapter we deal with ways of educating clients about their rights and responsibilities as partners in the therapeutic process. We give special attention to the need to ensure that clients give their informed consent to therapy, and we examine the ethical and legal issues that arise when therapists fail to provide for such consent.

We also take a look at the ways in which clients' dependence and therapists' manipulation of them can present ethical issues. Clients have a right to expect that therapy will increase their chances of functioning independently. If they are manipulated by their therapists, then they hardly have a basis for acting autonomously.

Perhaps the central right of clients is the guarantee that their disclosures in therapy sessions will be respected. As you will see, however, you cannot legally make a blanket promise to your clients that *everything* they talk about will *always* remain confidential. It becomes critical that you become aware of the ethical and legal ramifications of confidentiality. You need to inform your clients from the outset of therapy of those circumstances that limit confidentiality. Because issues pertaining to confidentiality are rarely clear-cut, we present a number of cases to help you develop ethical-decision-making skills in problematic situations.

Part of ethical practice is talking with clients about their rights. Depending on the setting and the situation, this discussion can involve such questions as the circumstances that may affect the client's decision to enter the therapeutic relationship, the responsibilities of the therapist toward the client, the possibility of involuntary hospitalization, the possibility of being forced to submit to certain types of medical and psychological treatment, matters of privacy and confidentiality, and the possible outcomes and limitations of therapy.

Frequently, clients don't realize that they have rights. Because they are vulnerable and sometimes desperate for help, they may unquestioningly accept whatever their therapist says or does. There may be an aura about the therapeutic process, and clients may have an exaggerated confidence in the therapist. It is much like the trust that many patients have in their physician. For most clients the therapeutic situation is a new one, so they are unclear about what is expected of them and what they should expect from the therapist. For these reasons it is the therapist's responsibility to protect clients' rights and teach them about these rights. The ethical codes of most professional organizations require that clients be given adequate information to make informed choices about entering and continuing the client/therapist relationship. (See the accompanying box.) By helping clients accept their rights and responsibilities, the practitioner is encouraging them to develop a healthy sense of autonomy and personal power.

The Rights of Clients and Informed Consent: Some Ethical Codes

American Psychological Association (1989):

- "Psychologists fully inform consumers as to the purpose and nature of an evaluative, treatment, educational or training procedure, and they freely acknowledge that clients, students, or participants in research have freedom of choice with regard to participation."

National Association of Social Workers (1990):

- "The social worker should make every effort to foster maximum self-determination on the part of clients."
- "The social worker should provide clients with accurate and complete information regarding the extent and nature of the services available to them."
- "The social worker should apprise clients of their risks, rights, opportunities, and obligations associated with social service to them."

American Association for Counseling and Development (1988):

- "The member must inform the client of the purposes, goals, techniques, rules of procedure, and limitations that may affect the relationship at or before the time that the counseling relationship is entered. When working with minors or persons who are unable to give consent, the member protects these clients' best interests."

The Client's Right to Give Informed Consent

One of the best ways of protecting the rights of clients is to develop procedures to help them make informed choices. Informed consent involves the right of clients to be informed about their therapy and to make autonomous decisions pertaining to it. This process of providing clients with the information they need to become active participants in the therapeutic relationship begins with the intake interview and continues throughout counseling. Informed consent entails a balance between telling clients too much and telling them too little. Although most professionals agree on the ethical principle that it is crucial to provide clients with information about the therapeutic relationship, how to do so in practice is much more difficult to ascertain.

On the one hand, it is a mistake to overwhelm clients with too much detailed information at once. On the other hand, it is a mistake to withhold important information that clients need if they are to make wise choices about their therapeutic program. *What* and *how much* is told to clients is determined in part by the clientele. Surely, any unusual practices should be clarified and discussed. It helps to consider informed consent as an ongoing process, especially during the initial stages of counseling, and not something that must be completed at the intake session.

Professionals have a responsibility to their clients to make a reasonable disclosure of all significant facts, the nature of their procedures, and some of the more probable consequences and difficulties. Regardless of their capacity to understand, all clients have the right to have treatment explained to them. To the extent that counselors do not provide information about the counseling process, they are promoting paternalism. Bednar, Bednar, Lambert, and Waite (1991) assert that it is essential for clients to understand the treatment and to give their consent voluntarily and that it is the responsibility of professionals to assess clients' level of understanding and to protect their free choice. Professionals need to avoid subtly coercing clients to cooperate with a therapy program to which they are not freely consenting. Generally, informed consent requires the client to be competent, to have knowledge of what will occur, and to be in treatment voluntarily (Bennett, Bryant, VandenBos, & Greenwood, 1990).

Legal Aspects of Informed Consent

Legal issues of violating the rights of clients are raised when a practitioner fails to provide them with adequate information that may affect their welfare. Bray, Shepherd, and Hays (1985) specify two types of liability for practitioners who fail to obtain informed consent. One is negligence or malpractice. The failure to make a complete disclosure of possible risks or of deviations from standard professional practice may result in a judgment of negligent practice. The second liability is breach of contract. If therapists guarantee that a certain treatment will "cure" a person and it does not, they are liable to be sued.

According to Bednar and his colleagues (1991), informed consent as a relatively new and developing legal doctrine is rooted in the law's growing recognition of the importance of self-determination. They report that the informed-consent doctrine is gradually becoming a standard part of mental-health practices. Legally, there are three elements to adequate informed consent: capacity, comprehension of information, and voluntariness (Bray et al., 1985). *Capacity* means that the client has the ability to make rational decisions. When this capacity is lacking, a parent or guardian is typically responsible for giving consent. *Comprehension of information* means that therapists must give clients information in a clear way and check to see that they understand it. To give valid consent, clients must have adequate information about a particular procedure and its possible consequences. The information must include the benefits and risks, possible adverse effects, the risk of foregoing treatment, and alternate procedures that are available. *Voluntariness* means that the person giving consent is acting freely in the decision-making process. It implies that the professional and the client discuss the nature of the problem and possible treatments for it. The therapist should explain to competent clients, who have not been ordered by the court to undergo evaluation or treatment, that they are free to withdraw their consent at any time for any reason (Bennett et al., 1990).

Educating Clients about Informed Consent

It is a good practice for therapists to encourage clients' questions about evaluation or treatment to offer useful information as the counseling process progresses. Some questions that therapists should answer at the outset of the counseling relationship are:

- What are the goals of the therapeutic program?
- What services will the counselor provide?
- What behavior is expected of the client?
- What are the risks and benefits of therapeutic procedures?
- What are the qualifications of the practitioner?
- What are the financial considerations?
- How long is the therapy expected to last?
- What are the limitations of confidentiality?
- In what cases does the counselor have mandatory reporting requirements?

The draft of the APA's ethics code (1991a) specifies that therapists clarify their role and discuss with clients any questions they have about the therapeutic process:

- "Psychologists discuss with clients or patients as early as is feasible in the therapeutic relationship appropriate issues such as the nature and anticipated course of therapy, fees, and confidentiality."
- "Psychologists make reasonable efforts to answer patients' questions, to avoid apparent misunderstanding about therapy, and to avoid creating unrealistic expectations in patients."

The process of educating clients about their rights might well begin with having them sign informed-consent forms, but we think that clients should continue to be involved as fully as possible at every stage of their therapy. From our perspective, the more that clients know about how therapy works, the more they will benefit from the therapeutic experience.

The Use of Informed-Consent Forms.   In a study of the use, content, and readability of informed-consent forms for treatment, Handelsman, Kemper, Kesson-Craig, McLain, and Johnsrud (1986) found that only 29% of psychologists in private practice reported using such forms. The major reason given for not using them was a preference for oral agreements. Most forms dealt mainly with financial arrangements. The authors assert that practitioners seemed to be attempting to avoid malpractice suits with the forms but were not meeting the ethical requirements of informed consent. Some of the conclusions of Handelsman and his colleagues are as follows:

- Practitioners who do not use consent forms are not necessarily derelict in their duty.
- Clinicians who do use consent forms are not necessarily doing all they need to do.
- Therapists need to evaluate both the ability of their clients to understand the forms used and the kind of information that clients should have in order to make informed choices about their therapy.

A number of writers on this subject suggest using written contracts. It is important that both the client and the therapist have the option to revise the therapeutic contract. Bennett and his colleagues (1990) recommend that practitioners record the nature of the consent, either by having the client sign a form or by including in the client's file a report of what was told to the client about the therapeutic process. They suggest that a consent form could include some of the following information: date of discussion regarding consent; name of the practitioner and the client; a statement affirming that the client understood what was explained to him or her; a statement of the client's right to withdraw from treatment; likely benefits and inherent risks associated with therapy; a description of the kind of treatment that will be provided; issues of confidentiality, privilege, and their limits; and the signature of the client. Consent forms are best viewed as merely one aspect of the ongoing dialogue between the therapist and client about the therapeutic process and its consequences (Bednar et al., 1991). Handelsman and Galvin (1988) have proposed a form that presents the clients with a list of questions that they are entitled to ask their therapist. Some of these questions deal with the nature of treatment, alternatives to therapy, financial arrangements, scheduling of appointments, and confidentiality and its limits. Handelsman and Galvin contend that their written format has several advantages over narrative forms. It preserves clients' right to refuse information, it is readable, and it fosters discussion between the therapist and client about the nature of therapy. In conclusion, it is clinically, ethically, and legally sound practice to provide clients with some type of informed-consent form at the beginning of therapy.

Two Cases for Discussion.   We have emphasized the importance of the therapist's role in teaching clients about informed consent and encouraging clients' questions about the therapeutic process. With this general concept in mind, put yourself in the therapist's place in each of the following cases. Identify what you consider to be the main ethical issues in each case, and think about your stance if you were faced with these concerns.

○ *A case of second thoughts.*   At the initial interview the therapist, Dottie, does not provide an informed-consent form and touches only briefly on the process of therapy. In discussing confidentiality, she implies that whatever is said in the office will stay in the office. Three months into the therapy, the client exhibits some suicidal ideation. Dottie has recently attended a conference in which malpractice was discussed and worries that she may have been remiss in not providing her client with adequate information about her services, including confidentiality and its limitations. She hastily reproduces an informed-consent document that she received at the conference, and she then asks her client to sign the form at the next session. This procedure seems to evoke confusion in the client, and he makes no further mention of suicide. After five more sessions, he calls in to cancel an appointment and does not schedule another appointment. Dottie does not pursue the case further.

- What are the ethical and legal implications of the therapist's practice? Do you think she was remiss in not providing an informed-consent document at the first session?
- Did Dottie exacerbate the problem by introducing the document after therapy had already been under way for three months?
- If you had been in Dottie's shoes, what might you have done instead of introducing a written document at that juncture?
- Would you have contacted this client after he canceled? Was it unethical for Dottie to ignore the situation by not following up on his case?

○ **A case of rigid conditions.**   During the initial interview Simone asks the counselor how long she might need to be in therapy. He tells her the process will take a minimum of two years of weekly sessions. She expresses dismay at such a lengthy process. The counselor says that this is the way he works and that if she is not willing to commit herself to this process, she should find another therapist.

- Did the counselor take care of the need for informed consent?
- Did he have an ethical and a professional obligation to explain his rationale for requiring two years of therapy?
- Should the therapist have been willing to explore alternatives to his approach to therapy?

The Content of Informed Consent

There is a danger of becoming overly legalistic with clients, and there is no assurance that practitioners won't be involved in a lawsuit even if they do obtain written informed consent. Rather than focusing on legal documents, it is a good idea to develop informed-consent procedures that will increase clients' understanding about the counseling process and will forestall dissatisfaction and, therefore, legal action (Deardorff, Cross, & Hupprich, 1984). We now look in more detail at some of the topics about which clients should be informed.

The Therapeutic Process.   Although it may be difficult to give clients a detailed description of what happens in therapy, some general ideas can be explored. We support the practice of letting clients know that counseling might open up levels of awareness that could cause pain and anxiety. Clients who want long-term counseling need to know that they may experience changes that could produce disruptions and turmoil in their lives. Some clients may choose to settle for a limited knowledge of themselves rather than risking this kind of disruption. We believe that a frank discussion of the chances for change and its personal and financial costs is an appropriate way to spend some of the initial sessions. Clients should have a knowledge of the procedures and goals of therapy, especially if any unusual or experimental approaches or techniques are to be employed. It is their right to refuse to participate in certain therapeutic techniques.

Background of the Therapist.   The matter of therapists' developing professional disclosure statements will be covered in Chapter 7. Such a statement is an excellent way to help clients decide whether they should make use of the practitioner's service. Therapists should provide clients with a description of their training and education, their credentials, any specialized skills, their theoretical orientation, and the types of clients and types of problems that they are best trained to deal with. If the counseling will be done by an intern or a paraprofessional, the clients should know this. Likewise, if the provider will be working with a supervisor, this fact should be made known. Such a clear description of the practitioner's qualifications, coupled with a willingness to answer any questions about the process, reduces the unrealistic expectations of clients about therapy. It also reduces the chances of malpractice actions.

Costs Involved in Therapy.   Milton Berger (1982) lists as part of a "patient's bill of rights" the right to a reasonable financial arrangement. According to Berger, this right entails several therapist responsibilities, some of which are:

- providing information regarding all fees by the end of the initial session, including the arrangements for a payment schedule
- avoiding exploitation of clients by prolonging therapy needlessly or convincing them to undergo unnecessary diagnostic or treatment procedures
- making clients aware of insurance reimbursement and taking whatever steps are necessary to help them collect payments from a third party
- not springing unexpected costs on the client

Matters of finance are delicate, and if they are handled poorly, they can easily result in a strained relationship between the client and therapist. Thus, the manner in which fees are dealt with has much to do with the tone of the therapeutic partnership. It also says a great deal about the therapist's attitude toward clients.

The Length of Therapy and Termination.   Many agencies have a policy of limiting the number of sessions that a client can have. If this is the case, clients need to be informed at the outset that they cannot receive long-term therapy. Also, clients have the right to expect a referral so that they can continue exploring whatever concerns initially brought them to therapy.

Some therapists make it a practice to discuss with their clients an approximate length for the therapeutic process. They may make this matter part of a written or verbal contract during the initial session(s). Other therapists maintain on theoretical grounds that because the problems that brought the client into therapy are typically complex and long-standing, therapy will necessarily be long-term. These therapists may be unwilling to talk during the initial phase about the length of treatment, simply because of their conviction that individual differences among clients make such a prediction impossible.

Regardless of the therapist's theoretical orientation, clients have a right to expect that their therapy will end when they have realized the maximum benefits from it or have obtained what they were seeking when they entered it. We think that the issue of termination needs to be openly explored by the therapist and client and that the decision to terminate ultimately rests with the client.

Kramer (1990) reminds us that termination may do more than signal the end of therapy, for it can be a new beginning for clients. We agree with Kramer's contention that when termination issues are ignored or mishandled, the whole of therapy is jeopardized. In his view, termination is one of the most crucial phases of therapy, yet it is also the least understood and complex of all aspects of therapy. He finds a lack of consensus with regard to every aspect of termination, including the criteria for ending therapy. Furthermore, there are few theoretical and practical guidelines for practitioners to follow as they assist their clients in working through these issues. It is clear that responsible practitioners should discuss this phase of therapy with clients at critical junctures in the therapeutic process.

Consultation with Colleagues.   Student counselors generally meet regularly with their supervisors and fellow students to discuss their progress and any problems they are encountering in their work. It is a good policy for counselors to inform their clients that they are meeting with others and may be talking with them about some of the sessions. Clients can be reassured that their identities will not necessarily be disclosed, and they can be informed of the reasons for these meetings with supervisors and others. Even though it is ethical for counselors to discuss their cases with other counselors, it is wise to routinely let clients know about this possibility. Clients will then have less reason to feel that the trust they are putting in their counselors is being violated. Counselors can explain that these discussions may well focus on what *they* are doing and feeling as counselors, rather than on their clients as "cases."

Interruptions in Therapy.   Most ethical codes specify that therapists should consider the welfare of their clients when it is necessary to interrupt the therapeutic process. For example, a NASW (1990) guideline states: "The social worker who anticipates the termination or interruption of service to clients should notify clients promptly and seek the transfer, referral, or continuation of service in relation to the clients' needs and preferences." It is a good practice to explain to clients from the outset the possibilities of both expected and unexpected interruptions in therapy and how they will be dealt with. A therapist's absence might seem like abandonment to some clients, especially if the absence is poorly handled. As much as possible, therapists should make plans for any interruptions in therapy, such as vacations or long-term absences. Clients need information about the therapist's method of handling emergencies. When practitioners know they will be on vacation, ethical practice entails providing the name and telephone number of another therapist in case of need. Of course, therapists should obtain clients' written consent to provide information to their substitutes (Bennett et al., 1990).

Clients' Right of Access to Their Files.   An area of potential conflict between ethics and the law pertains to the right of clients to have access to their files and records. This matter is not directly addressed by the ethical codes of counselors, psychologists, social workers, and family therapists. Conflict may arise if therapists are reluctant to share their notes, including the diagnosis, with their clients. Some therapists operate on the assumption that their clients are not sophisticated enough to understand their diagnosis and the clinical notes; they may think that more harm than benefit could result from disclosing such information to their clients. Remley (1990) maintains that clients have a legal right to inspect and obtain copies of records kept on their behalf by professionals. Remley advises therapists who believe that it may be harmful to a client to share the clinical records to attempt to convince the client that he or she should not demand the records. Rather than automatically providing clients access to what is written in their files, some therapists give an explanation of the client's diagnosis and the general trend of what kind of information they are recording.

Giving clients access to their files seems to be consistent with the consumer-rights movement, which is having an impact on the fields of mental health, counseling, rehabilitation, and education. One way of reducing the growing trend toward malpractice suits and other legal problems in these professions is to allow patients to see their medical records, even while hospitalized.

○ *A case of keeping clinical notes*.   Noah is a therapist in private practice who primarily sees relatively well-functioning clients. He considers keeping records to be basically irrelevant to the therapeutic process for his clients. As he puts it: "In all that a client says to me in one hour, what do I write down? And for what purpose? If I were seeing high-risk clients, I would certainly keep notes. Or if I were a psychoanalyst, where everything a client said matters, then I'd keep notes." One of his clients, Sue, who watched a television talk show in which clients' rights were discussed, asks to see her file, saying "I would like to see what you've written about me."

- What do you think of Noah's philosophy on note taking and record keeping? Do you consider it unethical, and if so, why?
- Taking into consideration the kind of clientele that this therapist sees, is his behavior justified? If you disagree, what criteria would you use in determining what material should be recorded?
- What if a legal issue arises during or after Sue's treatment? How would documenting each session help or not help both the client and the counselor?
- Assume that some of Noah's clients move to another state, where they see new therapists. Does the absence of notes to be transferred to the new therapists have ethical implications? Is this lack putting a burden and expense on the clients in having to cover old ground?

Rights Pertaining to Diagnostic Labeling.   One of the major obstacles to the open sharing of files with clients is the need to give clients a diagnostic classification as a requirement for receiving third-party reimbursement for psychological services. Many clients are not informed that they will be so labeled, what those labels are, or that the labels and other confidential material will be given to insurance companies. Clients also do not have control over who can receive this information, nor are they informed of their right not to be labeled (Mappes, Robb, & Engels, 1985).

Greenhut (1991) contends that therapists often make clients worse by attaching labels to them. She believes that therapy sometimes becomes exploitation of the already exploited. In treating incest survivors, rape victims, and those who have been physically abused, for example, therapists can further oppress these victims by assigning them labels such as "co-dependent," "narcissistic," "eating-disordered," and "chronically depressed." Greenhut urges that therapists encourage their clients to act on the basis of what they believe is best for themselves and, thus, to move beyond their labels. On the other hand, it is important for therapists to have assessment skills and to know that clients' behaviors can fit patterns or categories that can assist in the development of a treatment plan. The dangers are in viewing a client entirely in terms of a diagnostic label or in viewing a disorder as being static, with the end result that the client is left with the notion of being labeled forever.

We agree with Smith's position (1981) that one of the basic rights of a client is the freedom to choose whether to be coded and classified by a psychologist or psychiatrist. He urges that the psychologist obtain the consent of clients when they are diagnosed for the purposes of insurance reimbursement. An open discussion with clients about their condition is one way to demystify the client/therapist relationship. It is essential to maintain the client's confidentiality and right to informed consent when it is necessary to deal with insurance companies (Bennett et al., 1990). We endorse the maximum possible openness with clients about our procedures, so that they can become active and informed agents in their own therapy rather than believe that we have magical healing powers.

The Nature and Purpose of Confidentiality.   Clients should be educated about confidentiality, privileged communication, and privacy (which we discuss later in this chapter). It is clear that the effectiveness of the client/counselor relationship is built on a foundation of trust. If clients do not trust their therapist, it is not likely that they will engage in significant self-disclosure and self-exploration. Trust depends largely on the degree to which clients feel sure that what they share in therapy will be kept confidential. As you will see later in this chapter, confidentiality is not an absolute, for there are certain circumstances that demand that a therapist disclose what was said by a client in a private therapy session or relinquish counseling records.

Tape-Recording or Videotaping of Sessions.   Many agencies require recording of counseling interviews for training or supervision purposes. Clients have a right to be informed about this procedure at the initial session, and it is important that they understand why the recordings are made, how they will be used, who will have access to them, and how they will be stored. Therapists often make recordings because they can benefit from listening to them or from having colleagues listen to their interactions with clients and give them feedback. An example of an ethical standard on this issue is "The social worker should obtain informed consent from clients before taping, recording, or permitting third party observation of their activities" (NASW, 1990). Frequently, clients are happy to give their consent if they are approached in an honest way. Clients, too, may want to listen to a taped session during the week to help them remember what went on or to evaluate what is happening in their sessions.

Personal Relationships and Informed Consent.   When supervisees, students, employees, colleagues, close friends, or relatives approach a therapist about initiating a therapeutic relationship, it is essential that the therapist discuss with these prospective clients the problems that may be associated with what are known as "dual relationships," which form when a professional assumes more than one role. Most ethical codes caution against dual relationships and point to the need to avoid the exploitation of clients out of the therapist's need, the misuse of power, and situations involving conflict of interests. For example, psychiatrists are cautioned to monitor their practices so as to avoid exploiting the client: "The patient may place his/her trust in his/her psychiatrist knowing that the psychiatrist's ethics and professional responsibilities preclude him/her gratifying his/her own needs by exploiting the patient" (American Psychiatric Association, 1989). Clients have a right to expect that their therapist will be primarily concerned with their welfare, which implies maintaining some degree of "therapeutic distance." It also implies that therapists will be aware of their own countertransference feelings, so that they do not unnecessarily complicate the therapy process.

Benefits and Risks of Treatment.   Clients should have some information about both the possible benefits and the risks associated with a treatment program. Because clients are largely responsible for the outcomes of therapy, it is a good policy to emphasize their responsibility. Clients need to know that no promises can be made about specific outcomes. Bednar and his colleagues (1991) comment that until more is known about risks, it is wise for practitioners to make every attempt to note negative reactions and begin to devise strategies for assisting clients in making more informed choices about their treatment.

Alternatives to Traditional Therapy.   According to the ethics codes of some professional organizations, clients need to know about alternative helping systems. Therefore, it is a good practice for therapists to learn about community resources so that they can present these alternatives to a client. The following are some examples of alternatives to psychotherapy: self-help programs, stress-management, programs for personal-effectiveness training, peer self-help groups, bibliotherapy, twelve-step programs, support groups, and crisis-intervention centers.

This information about therapy and its alternatives can be presented in writing, through an audio tape or videotape, or during an intake session. An open discussion of therapy and its alternatives may, of course, lead some clients to choose sources of help other than therapy. Given the state of psychotherapy research, however, it is difficult to discuss the advantages of alternative treatments and make recommendations (Bednar et al., 1991). For practitioners who make a living providing therapy, asking their clients to consider alternative treatments can produce financial anxiety. On the other hand, openly discussing therapy and its alternatives is likely to reinforce many clients' decisions to continue therapy. Clients have a right to know about alternative therapeutic modalities (such as different theoretical orientations and medication) that are known to be effective with particular clients and conditions.

Client Dependence as an Ethical Issue

Clients have a right to expect that psychotherapy will enable them to move toward increased change and autonomy. Certainly, a therapist who fosters clients' dependence rather than their autonomy is thwarting their progress. Clients frequently experience a period of dependence on therapy or on their therapist. This temporary dependence isn't necessarily a bad thing, nor does it take away from their autonomy. Some clients have exaggerated the importance of being independent. They see the need to consult a professional as a sign of weakness. When these people do allow themselves to need others, their dependence isn't necessarily unethical.

An ethical issue does arise, however, when counselors *encourage* dependence on the part of a client. They may do so for any number of reasons. Counselor interns need clients, and sometimes they may keep clients coming to counseling longer than is necessary because they will look bad if they "lose" a client. Some therapists in private practice may fail to challenge clients who show up and pay regularly, even though they appear to be getting nowhere. Some therapists foster dependence in their clients in subtle ways out of a need to feel important. When clients play a helpless role and ask for answers, these counselors may readily tell them what to do. Dependent clients can begin to view their therapists as all-knowing and all-wise; therapists who have a need to be perceived in this way may act in ways that will keep their clients immature and dependent.

Stensrud and Stensrud (1981) observe that counseling can be hazardous to health, for it can teach people to be powerless instead of teaching them to trust themselves. They describe powerlessness as a "learned state of generalized helplessness in which clients (a) believe they are unable to have an impact on their environment, and (b) need some external force to intercede on their behalf" (p. 300). These authors note that clients can develop a self-fulfilling prophecy, whereby their expectation of powerlessness feeds into their experience of being powerless. Stensrud and Stensrud urge that clients participate actively in the entire therapy process. They also caution that because people often produce the behavior that is expected of them, if therapists relate to clients in ways that tell them that they are not responsible for themselves, these clients are being taught to feel dependent and helpless.

Like many of the other ethical issues discussed in this chapter, the issue of encouraging dependence in clients is often not clear-cut in practice. Because our main purpose here is to stimulate you to think of possible ways in which you might be fostering dependence or independence in your clients, we'll present a couple of illustrative cases and ask you to respond to them.

Marcia is single and almost ready to graduate from college. She tells you that she has ambivalent feelings about graduating, because she feels that she will be expected to get a job and live on her own. This prospect frightens her, and she doesn't want to leave the security she has found as a college student. As she puts it, she doubts that she can "make it in the real world." Marcia doesn't trust her own decisions, because when she does make choices, the result, in her eyes, is disastrous. Her style is to plead with you to advise her whether she should date, apply for a job, leave home, go on to graduate school, and so forth. Typically, she gets angry with you because you aren't being directive enough for her. She feels that you have more knowledge than she does and should therefore give her more guidance. "Why am I coming here if you won't tell me what to do?" she asks. "If I could make decent decisions on my own, I wouldn't need to come here in the first place!"

- How do you imagine you'd feel if Marcia were your client?
- How might you respond to her continual prodding for answers?
- How do you imagine you'd feel about her statement that you weren't doing your job and that you weren't being directive enough?
- What steps would you take to challenge her?
- In what ways do you think it would be possible for you to tie into her dependency needs and foster her dependence on you for direction, instead of freeing her from you?

Ron, a young counselor, encourages his clients to call him at home whenever they need to. He frequently lets sessions run overtime, lends money to clients when they're "down and out," devotes many more hours to his job than he is expected to, and overtaxes himself by taking on an unrealistically large caseload. He says that he lives for his work and that it gives him a sense of being a valuable person. The more he can do for people, the better he feels.

- In what ways could Ron's style be keeping his clients dependent on him?
- What could he be getting from being so "helpful"? What do you imagine his life would be like if there were no clients who needed him?
- If you were Ron's colleague and he came to you to talk about how "burned out" he felt because he was "giving so much," what would you say to him?
- Can you identify with him in any ways? Do you see yourself as potentially needing your clients more than they need you?

Delaying Termination as a Form of Fostering Client Dependence

In spite of the fact that most professional codes have guidelines that call for termination whenever further therapy will not bring significant gains, some therapists do have difficulty in letting go of their clients. They run the risk of unethical conduct because of either financial or emotional needs. On the financial issue, we contend that ethical practitioners continually examine whether they are resistant to termination because it would mean a decline in income. Obviously, termination cannot be mandated by ethical codes alone but rests on the honesty and goodwill of the therapist. We agree with Kramer's position (1990) that more than any other phase of therapy, the ending demands that therapists examine and understand their own needs and feelings. Therapists are challenged to confront their own dependence and anxieties honestly. Kramer emphasizes the therapist's role in enabling clients to understand and accept the termination process: "A general philosophy that is respectful of patients and sees them as autonomous, proactive, and self-directive is essential if the therapist is to facilitate healthy, productive endings" (1990, p. 3). In our view the ultimate sign of an effective therapist is the ability to help clients reach the stage of autonomy, where they no longer need a therapist.

The AACD *Ethical Standards* (1988) have this guideline:

> If the member determines an inability to be of professional assistance to the client, the member must either avoid initiating the counseling relationship or immediately terminate that relationship. In either event, the member must suggest appropriate alternatives. (The member must be knowledgeable about referral resources so that a satisfactory referral can be initiated.) In the event the client declines the suggested referral, the member is not obligated to continue the relationship.

The AACD guideline raises several questions:

- What criteria can you use to determine whether your client is benefiting from the therapeutic relationship?
- What do you do if a client feels that he or she is benefiting from therapy but you don't see any signs of progress?
- What do you do if you're convinced that your client is coming to you seeking friendship and not really for the purpose of changing?

Situations to Consider

Put yourself, as a therapist, in each of the following situations. Ask yourself what you would do, and why, if you were confronted with the problem described.

After five sessions your client, George, asks: "Do you think I'm making any headway toward solving my problems? Do I seem any different to you now than I did five weeks ago?" Before you give him your impressions, you ask him to answer his own questions. He replies: "Well, I'm not sure whether coming here is doing that much good. I suppose I expected resolutions to my problems before now, but I still feel anxious and depressed much of the time. It feels good to come here, and I usually continue thinking after our sessions about what we discussed, but I'm not coming any closer to decisions. Sometimes I feel certain this is helping me, and at other times I wonder whether I'm just fooling myself."

- What criteria can you employ to help you and your client assess the value of counseling for him?
- Does the fact that George continues to think about his session during the rest of the week show that he is probably getting something from counseling? Why or why not?

- Does it sound as if he has unrealistic expectations about finding neat solutions and making important decisions too quickly? Is he merely impatient with the process?

Joanne has been coming regularly to counseling for some time. When you ask her what she thinks she is getting from her therapy, she answers: "This is really helping. I like to talk and have somebody listen to me. I often feel as if you're the only friend I have and the only one who really cares about me. I suppose I really don't do that much outside, and I know I'm not changing that much, but I feel good when I'm here."

- If it became clear to you that Joanne wasn't willing to do much to change her life and wanted to continue counseling only because she liked having you listen to her, do you think you'd be willing to continue working with her? Why or why not? Would you say that she is benefiting from the relationship with you? If so, how?
- Is it ethical to continue the counseling if her main goal is the "purchase of friendship"? Why or why not?
- Would it be ethical to terminate her therapy without exploring her need to see you?
- If you thought that she was using her relationship with you to remain secure and dependent but that she believed she was benefiting from the relationship, what might you do? How do you imagine you'd feel if you continued to see her even though you were convinced that she wasn't changing?

Manipulation versus Collaboration

If psychotherapy is a process that teaches people how to be honest with themselves, it is of the utmost importance for therapists to be honest with their clients. Unfortunately, there are many ways for therapists to deceive or manipulate clients, often under the guise of being helpful and concerned. Therapists who have plans for what they want their clients to do or to be and who keep these plans hidden are manipulative. Other therapists may attempt to control their relationships with their clients by keeping therapy a mysterious process and maintaining a rigid "professional stance" that excludes the client as a partner. Therapy thus becomes a matter of the therapist's *doing* therapy on an unquestioning client.

To offset the danger of manipulating clients toward ends that they have not chosen, some approaches give clients an active role in deciding what happens to them in the therapeutic relationship. As you will see in Chapter 9, many therapists use a contract containing specific goals and the criteria for evaluating when these goals have been met. Proponents say that a contract emphasizes the partnership of client and therapist.

Sidney Jourard contrasts manipulation with dialogue. He sees psychotherapy as "an invitation to authenticity" in which the therapist's role is to be an exemplar. Therapists can foster their clients' honesty and invite them to drop their pretenses only by dropping their own defenses and meeting their clients in an honest manner. According to Jourard (1968), "the psychotherapist is the teacher in the therapeutic dance, and the patient follows the leader" (pp. 64–65). One of the best ways for therapists to demonstrate their goodwill is by avoiding manipulation and being open, trusting, and thus vulnerable to their clients. If counselors manipulate their clients, they can expect manipulation in return; if they are open, however, their clients may be open as well. As Jourard says:

> If I want [a client] to be maximally open, but I keep myself fully closed off, peeking at him through chinks in my own armor, trying to manipulate him from a distance, then in due time he will discover that I am not in that same mode; and he will then put his armor back on and peer at me through chinks in it, and he will try to manipulate me [1968, p. 64].

Manipulation can work in subtle ways. Consider the degree to which you think the behavior of the therapists in the following example is manipulative and unethical.

○   *The case of Josephine*.   Among Clyde's patients is Josephine, a middle-aged widow. She has been seeing him for three years on a regular basis because of her loneliness and depression. Much of the dialogue of the sessions is now social in nature. Josephine continually tells Clyde how she enjoys the sessions and how meaningful they are to her. She has connections with a professional sports franchise and has been able to obtain choice tickets for him. At times he lets it be known when he needs tickets for specific events.

- Is it unethical for Clyde to continue to see Josephine when the sessions are primarily social?
- Is it ethical to continue to accept the tickets?
- Could this arrangement be construed as a manipulation of the therapeutic relationship?
- Would mere enjoyment of the sessions warrant their continuation?

Involuntary Commitment and Human Rights

The practice of involuntary commitment of people to mental institutions raises difficult professional, ethical, and legal issues. Practitioners must know their own state's laws in this area and must be very familiar with community resources before taking measures leading to involuntary hospitalization. Good practice involves consulting with professional colleagues to determine the length and type of treatment (Austin, Moline, & Williams, 1990). The focus of this discussion is not on specific legal provisions but, rather, on the ethical aspects of involuntary commitment.

Under the social policy of "deinstitutionalization," which has gained popularity over the past 25 years, involuntary commitment is sought only after less restrictive alternatives have failed. The main purpose of involuntary hospitalization is to secure treatment for clients, rather than to punish them. As it applies to mental-health practices, the legal doctrine of using the "least restrictive alternative" requires that treatment be no more harsh, hazardous, or intrusive than necessary to achieve therapeutic aims and to protect clients and others from physical harm (Bednar et al., 1991).

Professionals are sometimes confronted with the responsibility of assessing the need to commit clients who pose a serious danger either to themselves or to others. The growing trend is for courts to recognize the therapist's duty to commit such clients. Under most state laws, involuntary civil commitment is based on the following criteria: mental illness, dangerousness to self or others, grave disability, refusal to consent, treatability, incapacity to decide on treatment, and compliance with the "least restrictive" criterion (Bednar et al., 1991).

Bennett and his colleagues (1990) offer specific recommendations pertaining to the commitment process, some of which are:

- Be familiar with your state laws and regulations pertaining to both voluntary and involuntary commitment.
- If you notice that a client's condition is deteriorating, consider consulting with colleagues.
- Carefully consider what you hope to obtain in recommending commitment. Assess the degree to which your client is a danger to self or others.
- Before deciding on a course leading to commitment, consider other options. Also, consider the advisability of referring your client to another professional for evaluation or treatment.
- Ask yourself how commitment might affect the client's attitude toward you as a therapist and toward therapy in general.
- If hospitalization is involuntary, know the procedural steps that must be followed under your state laws.
- Make certain that you can offer reasons for commitment.

Making a decision to commit a client is a serious matter that has implications for you, your client, and members of the client's family. It is essential that you obtain consultation if there is any doubt about the proper course to follow. You need to raise many questions about the appropriateness of choosing commitment over other alternatives. Some writers emphasize practices such as conducting ongoing psychiatric and psychosocial assessments and documenting all examinations and consultations in the client's record. Practitioners are advised to protect themselves from liability associated with involuntary hospitalization by documenting all the steps they take in making their decision (Austin et al., 1990; Bednar et al., 1991).

Imagine yourself in the following situation: You're employed as a counselor at a state mental hospital. The ward on which you work is overcrowded, and there aren't enough professionals on the staff to provide for much more than custodial services. You observe patients who seem to be psychologically deteriorating, and the unattractive surroundings reinforce the attitude of hopelessness that is so prevalent among the patients. You become aware that the rights of patients are often ignored, and you see many of the hospital's practices as destructive. When patients are given medication, for instance, there is rarely a consistent evaluation of the effects of the drug treatment and of whether it should be continued. Moreover, you recognize that some of the people who have been hospitalized against their will really don't belong there, yet institutional procedures and policies make it difficult for them to be released or placed in a more appropriate agency. Finally, although some members of the staff are both competent and dedicated, others who hold positions of power are incompetent.

What do you think you might do if you were involved in this situation? What do you see as your responsibility, and what actions might you take? Check as many of the following statements as you think appropriate:

____ Because I couldn't change the people in power, I'd merely do what I could to treat the patients with care and dignity.

____ I'd bring the matter to public attention by writing to newspapers and talking with television reporters.

____ I'd attempt to rectify the situation by talking to the top administrators and telling them what I had observed.

____ I'd form a support group of my peers for collective action.

____ I'd keep my views to myself, because the problem is too vast and complex for me to do anything about it.

____ I'd encourage the patients to revolt and demand their rights.

____ I'd directly confront the people who I thought were incompetent or who were violating the rights of patients and attempt to change them.

____ I'd spruce up the environment.

Confidentiality, Privileged Communication, and Privacy

An important obligation of practitioners in the various mental-health professions is to maintain the confidentiality of their relationships with their clients. This obligation is not absolute, however, and practitioners need to develop a sense of professional ethics for determining when the confidentiality of the relationship should be broken. It also behooves them to become familiar with the legal protection afforded the privileged communications of their clients, as well as the limits of this protection.

Definition of Terms

Confidentiality, privileged communication, and privacy are related concepts, but there are important distinctions among them.

Confidentiality.   Confidentiality entails the ethical and legal responsibility of mental-health professionals to safeguard clients from unauthorized disclosures of information given in the therapeutic relationship. It implies that when clients reveal private information, the professional must not disclose this information except for the reasons for which it was intended (Austin et al., 1990). There are limitations to the promise of confidentiality. Court decisions, for example, have underscored the therapist's duty to warn and protect others, even if it means breaking confidentiality (see Chapter 5).

The draft of the APA ethics code specifies the following pertaining to disclosures of confidential information:

> Psychologists disclose confidential information only as required by law, or where permitted by law, for a valid purpose such as: (1) to provide needed professional services to the patient or client, (2) to obtain appropriate professional consultations, (3) to protect the patient or client or others from harm, or (4) to obtain payment for services, in which instance, disclosure is limited to the minimum that is necessary to achieve the purpose [1991a].

Privileged Communication.   Privileged communication is a *legal* concept protecting the right of clients to withhold testimony in a court proceeding (Leslie, 1991b). In order for client communication to be privileged, it is essential that a state statute specifically identify the communication between the professional and the client as privileged (Remley, 1991). Privileged-communication laws ensure that clients' disclosures of personal and sensitive information will be protected from exposure by therapists in legal proceedings (Baird & Rupert, 1987). This privilege belongs to the client and is designed for the client's protection, rather than for the protection of the professional. If a client waives this privilege, therefore, the professional has no legal grounds for withholding the information. Professionals are obligated to disclose information when the client requests it, but only the information that is specifically requested and only to the individuals or agencies that are specified by the client (Hopkins & Anderson, 1990). Some other relationships that are protected in various jurisdictions in the United States include those between attorneys and clients, marital partners, physicians and patients, psychotherapists and clients, priests and penitents, accountants and clients, and nurses and patients.

Knapp and VandeCreek (1985) contend that the greatest threat to the integrity of privileged communication comes from the fact that various mental-health professions are excluded from these laws. Many professionals practice counseling and psychotherapy: psychologists, social workers, psychiatrists, marriage and family therapists, mental-health counselors, and pastoral counselors. But the privilege exists only for clients of professionals specifically enumerated in the statutes. In most states the definition of the terms *psychologist, psychiatrist,* or *social worker* in the statutes determines which mental-health professionals are included.

Leslie (1991b) cites recent court decisions that address issues pertaining to psychotherapist/client privilege:

- Legislatures have decided that a greater public good results from protecting client communications than from making client disclosures fully discoverable in a legal proceeding. It is important to consider privileged communication in context. There must be a balance between the person's right to privacy and society's need for information.
- The privileges granted by legislatures are not absolute; there are many circumstances in which the client's privilege will not be upheld and courts will order records to be released.

- If practitioners are not covered by the privilege, because they are not specifically listed in a statute, the client's rights are compromised because evidence that might otherwise be withheld may now be ordered admissible by the court.
- There are differences among the states with respect to privileged-communication legislation. Therapists need to know the laws of their state and also know how to handle subpoenas for client records, because improper handling of a subpoena can result in liability to the therapist and harm to the client.

Because psychotherapist/client privilege is a legal concept, there are certain circumstances under which information *must* be provided by the therapist:

- when the therapist is acting in a court-appointed capacity—for example, to conduct a psychological examination or to serve as an expert witness in a child-custody case (Remley, 1991)
- when the therapist makes an assessment of a foreseeable risk of suicide (Bednar et al., 1991)
- when the client initiates a lawsuit against the therapist, such as for malpractice (Denkowski & Denkowski, 1982; Leslie, 1991b)
- in any civil action when the client introduces mental conditions as a claim or defense (Denkowski & Denkowski, 1982)
- when the client is under the age of 16 and the therapist believes that the child is the victim of a crime—for example, incest, child molestation, rape, or child abuse (Everstine et al. 1980)
- when the therapist determines that the client is in need of hospitalization for a mental or psychological disorder (Austin et al., 1990; Bednar et al., 1991)
- when information is mandated by a court (Leslie, 1991b; Remley, 1991)
- when clients reveal their intention to commit a crime or when they can be accurately assessed as dangerous to society or dangerous to themselves (Austin et al., 1990; Bednar et al., 1991; Hopkins & Anderson, 1990; Schutz, 1982)

Generally speaking, the legal concept of privileged communication does not apply to group counseling. Members of a counseling group can assume that they could be asked to testify in court concerning certain information revealed in the course of a group session, unless there is a statutory exception. Similarly, couples therapy and family therapy are not subject to privileged-communication statutes in many states. No clear judicial trend has emerged for communications that are made in the presence of third persons. It is best for therapists to assume that such communications are not privileged. Therapists should inform their clients of the ethical need for confidentiality and the lack of legal privilege concerning disclosures made in the presence of third persons (Hopkins & Anderson, 1990; VandeCreek, Knapp, & Herzog, 1988). However, a few states have statutes that specifically ensure privacy in group therapy, couples therapy, and family therapy. For example, social worker/client privilege statutes exist in California, Colorado, Idaho, Kansas, Louisiana, Maryland, New York, Oklahoma, and Virginia when third parties are present if these persons are instrumental in the treatment (VandeCreek et al., 1988).

From the foregoing discussion it should be clear that privileged communication between therapist and client is *not* an absolute matter. There are exceptions to privilege, and therapists are legally bound to comply with the exceptions stated above.

Privacy.   Siegel (1979) defines privacy as "the freedom of individuals to choose for themselves the time and the circumstances under which and the extent to which their beliefs, behavior, and opinions are to be shared [with] or withheld from others" (p. 251). Stadler (1990a) describes privacy as the "right of persons to choose what others may know about them and under what circumstances" (p. 102). In discussing some basic issues pertaining to privacy, Everstine and his colleagues (1980) raise the following questions:

- To what extent should beliefs and attitudes be protected from manipulation or scrutiny by others?
- How can it be decided who may intrude on privacy and in what circumstances privacy must be maintained?
- Assuming that privacy has been violated, what can be done to ameliorate the situation?
- Do people have a right to waive their privacy, even when their best interests might be threatened?

Practitioners need to exercise caution with regard to the privacy of their clients. It is easy to invade a client's privacy unintentionally. Examples of some of the most pressing situations in which privacy is an issue include an employer's access to an applicant's or an employee's psychological tests, parents' access to their child's school records and health records, and a third-party payer's access to information about a client's diagnosis and prognosis.

Most of the professional codes of ethics contain guidelines for safeguarding a client's right to privacy. An example of such a standard is the draft of the APA ethics code: "In order to minimize intrusions on privacy, psychologists include in records of psychological services, and in written and oral reports, consultations, and the like, only information germane to the purpose for which the communication is made" (1991a).

One other area where privacy is an issue involves practitioners who also teach courses, offer workshops, write books and journal articles, and give lectures. If these practitioners use examples from their clinical practice, it is of the utmost importance that they take measures to adequately disguise their clients' identities. We think it is a good practice for them to inform their clients that they are likely to use some of their clinical experience in their writing and in giving lectures. One relevant guideline on this issue of privacy is given by the APA draft ethics code: "Psychologists do not disclose confidential, personally identifiable information obtained during the course of professional work, in their writings, lectures, or other public media, unless that patient, client, or subject has consented in writing" (1991a).

Two Case Illustrations of Confidentiality and Privacy

There are often subtle dimensions to maintaining the confidentiality and privacy of clients, as the two following cases show.

An Illustration of a Small-Town Private Practice.*

I practiced for many years as a marriage and family therapist in a small community. This situation presented a set of ethical considerations involving safeguarding the privacy of clients. First, it was important that I choose an office that afforded privacy to clients as they entered and left. I had considered leasing a space in a small professional building in the center of town. But I quickly discovered that people would be uncomfortable in making themselves that visible while they were seeking psychological help. A home office, which was remote from the center of the village, worked out well. However, I had to carefully schedule clients by allowing ample time between sessions so that clients who might know each other would not meet in the office. Whenever an office is located within the therapist's home, it is essential that a professional atmosphere be provided. Clients have a right to expect privacy and should not have to deal with intrusions by the therapist's family members.

I discussed with my clients the unique variables pertaining to confidentiality in a small community. For instance, I informed them that I would not discuss professional concerns with them should we meet at the grocery store or the post office. I also respected their preferences regarding such interactions away from the office. Knowing that they were aware that I saw many people from the town, I reassured them that I would not talk with anyone about who my clients were, even when I might be directly asked. Another example of protecting my clients' privacy pertained to the manner of depositing checks at the local bank. Since the bank employees knew my profession, it would have been easy for them to identify my clients. Again, I talked with my clients about their preferences. If they had any discomfort about my depositing their checks in the local bank, I arranged to have them deposited elsewhere. My clients had an opportunity to talk with me about any of their concerns over seeking counseling in a small community.

Now consider the following questions:

- What other ethical issues do you think apply to practicing in a small community?
- Can you apply any of the principles illustrated in this example to having a private practice in a large city or working in a community mental-health center?
- Is there room for flexibility in setting guidelines regarding social relationships and outside business contacts with clients in a small community?

A Case of Confidentiality and Privacy in a School Setting.

Donna discussed with us some of the difficulties she encountered when she shifted her career from private practice to counseling in an elementary school. She was particularly surprised by the differences between private practice and school counseling with respect to confidentiality issues. She remarked that she was constantly fielding questions from teachers such as "Whom do you have in that counseling group?"

*This case is presented from the perspective of Marianne Corey.

"How is Johnny doing?" "It's no wonder this girl has problems. Have you met her parents?" Although Donna talked to the teachers about the importance of maintaining a safe, confidential environment for students in counseling situations, she would still receive questions from them about students, some of whom were not in their classes.

In addition to the questions from teachers, Donna found that she had to deal with inquiries from school secretaries and other staff members, some of whom seemed to know everything that was going on in the school. They would ask her probing questions about students, which she, of course, was not willing to answer. For example, although she would not tell a secretary whom she was counseling, a teacher might have told the secretary that she was seeing one of his students. One secretary asked her: "Why are you working with Jimmy Smith? He doesn't have as many problems as some of the other students!"

Donna observed that principals and parents also asked for specific information about the students she was seeing. She learned the importance of talking to all who were concerned about the importance of privacy. If she had not exercised care, it would have been easy for her to say more than would have been wise to teachers, staff members, and parents. She also learned how critical it was to talk about matters of confidentiality and privacy in simple language with the schoolchildren whom she counseled.

Laws regarding confidentiality differ in some states with regard to school counseling. In California, for instance, psychotherapists are normally required to demonstrate that attempts have been made to contact the parents of children who are younger than 16, whereas school counselors are not required to do so. Given this information, consider that you were in a similar situation as an elementary school counselor, and address these questions:

- If you were asked some of the questions that were posed to Donna, how would you respond? How might you protect the privacy of the students and at the same time avoid alienating the teachers and staff members?
- How might you explain the meaning of confidentiality and privacy to teachers? staff members? parents? administrators? the children?

Ethical and Legal Ramifications of Confidentiality

The ethics of confidentiality rest on the premise that clients in counseling are involved in a deeply personal relationship and have a right to expect that what they discuss will be kept private. The compelling justification for confidentiality is that it is necessary to encourage clients to develop the trust needed for full disclosure and for the other work involved in therapy. Surely no genuine therapy can occur unless clients trust that what they say is confidential. Professionals therefore have an obligation to discuss with clients the circumstances that might affect the confidential relationship.

When it does become necessary to break confidentiality, it is a good practice to inform the client of the intention to take this action and also to invite the client to participate in the process. This step may preserve the therapeutic relationship and create the opportunity to resolve the issue between the individuals concerned (Mappes et al., 1985). For example, most states have statutes that require professionals who suspect any form of child abuse to report it to the appropriate agencies. Professionals who do report suspected child abuse are immune from prosecution for breaching confidentiality in these cases. When therapists find that they have to report actions such as incest, they can still work toward enlisting the cooperation of the client, and they can be instrumental in securing help for both the child and the parent.

The Limits of Confidentiality.　When we discussed informed consent, we mentioned that confidentiality was not absolute. But the circumstances under which confidentiality cannot be maintained are not clearly defined by accepted ethical standards, and therapists must exercise their own professional judgment. When assuring their clients that what they reveal will ordinarily be kept confidential, therapists should point out that they have obligations to others besides their clients. For instance, they are bound to act in such a way as to protect others from harm. The AACD's ethical guidelines state: "When the client's condition indicates that there is clear and imminent danger to the client or others, the member must take reasonable personal action or inform responsible authorities. Consultation with other professionals must be used where possible" (1988).

All the other major professional organizations have also taken the position that practitioners must reveal certain information when there is clear and imminent danger to an individual or to society. Consistent with these professional guidelines from the professions is the following specific exception to the right of privileged communication and confidentiality, as created by the California Legislature:

> There is no privilege under this article if the psychotherapist has reasonable cause to believe that the patient is in such mental or emotional condition as to be dangerous to himself or to the person or property of another and disclosure of the communication is necessary to prevent the threatened danger [cited in Leslie, 1991b, p. 15].

It is the responsibility of therapists to clarify the ethical and legal restrictions on confidentiality. There are three general exceptions to the legal and ethical requirement that therapists keep client confidentiality: (1) cases in which clients pose a danger to themselves or others, (2) cases in which clients request that their records be released to themselves or a third party, and (3) cases in which a court orders a counselor to make records available (Remley, 1990).

The limitations of confidentiality may be greater in some settings and agencies than in others. If clients are informed about the conditions under which confidentiality may be compromised, they are in a better position to decide whether to enter counseling. If they are involved in involuntary counseling, they can decide what they will disclose in their sessions. Pope and Vasquez (1991) note that clients have a right to understand in advance the circumstances under which therapists are required or allowed to communicate information about the client to third parties. They contend that unless clients understand this information, their consent to treatment is not genuinely informed.

Miller and Thelen (1986) conducted a survey to assess the public's knowledge and beliefs about the confidentiality of therapeutic communications. The majority of the respondents (69%) believed that everything discussed with a professional therapist would be held strictly confidential. Further, most of the respondents (74%) thought that there should be no exceptions to maintaining confidential disclosures. The vast majority of respondents (96%) wanted information about confidentiality. Many of them (46%) wanted to be told of the exceptions to confidentiality before the first session, whereas others (29%) preferred discussions at various points throughout the therapeutic process. Miller and Thelen concluded that most of the respondents perceived confidentiality as an all-encompassing mandate for therapists. The authors point out that there was apparently a huge gap between what clients expected and standard therapeutic practice with regard to maintaining confidentiality.

Practitioners tend to assume that clients' expectations of confidentiality are an important factor in their being able to trust the therapist and reveal personally significant material. Muehleman, Pickens, and Robinson (1985) designed a study to explore the impact on clients of discussing the limits of confidentiality. Strikingly, they found very little evidence that providing detailed information about the limits of confidentiality actually inhibited clients' disclosures. Based on their findings, the authors recommended that practitioners provide accurate, impartial, and comprehensive information to their clients.

In a survey of clinicians' practices, Baird and Rupert (1987) found little evidence of standard procedures for informing clients about confidentiality. They report that psychologists were moving toward informing clients at the outset of therapy about the limitations of confidentiality. However, half of the respondents in their survey either said nothing at all about confidentiality to their clients or indicated that everything would be kept confidential. The respondents welcomed ethical guidelines and legal decisions that would aid them in dealing with confidentiality issues. Over 70% of the respondents favored an ethical guideline that clients be informed before starting therapy of the limits of confidentiality. Baird and Rupert concluded that the advantages of thoroughly informing clients about these limits might outweigh any potential disadvantages in terms of inhibited discourse.

Guidelines for Practitioners.   Sheeley and Herlihy (1986) suggest that confidentiality, privileged communication, and privacy need to be viewed within the broad context of both society's values and the individual's interests. They offer the following guidelines as ways in which counselors can meet their obligations to confidentiality:

- Difficulties in the client/counselor relationship can be resolved by working within a spirit of confidence.
- Clients need to be informed that even in cases where privileged communication does exist by statute, there are circumstances in which practitioners are ethically or legally obliged to breach confidence—for example, when clients present a danger to themselves or others, when they lack capacity (minors or the infirm), when they themselves request it, or when a court requests it.

- Practitioners need to know whether their clients' communications are privileged under state statute and, if a statute exists, what exceptions it specifies. Even when these statutes exist, they do not represent absolute guarantees. Counselors should not assume that an existing statute or their license will exempt them from testifying in court.
- Counselors would do well to maintain strict adherence to the confidentiality provisions in the ethical codes of their professional organization.
- Physical settings should be selected that allow for privacy of communications.
- It is important to ask clients to sign waiver forms before counselors disclose information to third parties.
- Counselors should be aware that courts generally do not consider privileged those communications made in the presence of a third party.

Faced with conflicting standards in certain situations, counselors are challenged to learn to live with ambiguity over what the legal or ethical course of action is.

Confidentiality: Cases to Consider

To assist you in considering the practical issues involved in confidentiality we present a case study involving drug use. We describe the actions of the counselor and ask you to evaluate her handling of the situation. Then we offer some brief open-ended situations dealing with confidentiality.

○ ***The case of Larry.*** Larry is 14 years old when he is sent to a family-guidance clinic by his parents. He is seen by a counselor who has nine years of counseling experience. At the first session the counselor sees Larry and his parents together. She tells the parents in his presence that what she and Larry discuss will be confidential and that she will not feel free to disclose information acquired through the sessions without his permission. The parents seem to understand that confidentiality is necessary in order for trust to develop between their son and his counselor.

Larry is reluctant at first to come in for counseling, but eventually he begins to open up. As the sessions go on, he tells the counselor that he is "heavily into drugs." Larry's parents know that he was using drugs at one time, but he has told them that he is no longer using them. The counselor listens to anecdote after anecdote about Larry's use of dangerous drugs, about how "I get loaded" at school every day, and about a few brushes with death when he was under the influence of drugs. Finally, she tells the client that she does not want the responsibility of knowing he is experimenting with dangerous drugs and that she will not agree to continue the counseling relationship unless he stops using them. At this stage she agrees not to inform his parents, on condition that he quit using drugs, but she does tell him that she will be talking with one of her colleagues about the situation.

Larry apparently stops using drugs for several weeks. However, one night while he is under the influence of PCP, he has a serious automobile accident. As a result of the accident he becomes paralyzed for life. Larry's parents angrily assert that they had had a legal right to be informed that he was unstable to the point of committing such an act, and they file suit against both the counselor and the agency.

1. What is your general impression of the way Larry's counselor handled the case?
2. Do you think the counselor acted in a responsible way toward (a) herself? (b) the client? (c) the parents? (d) the agency?
3. Suppose you had been Larry's counselor and had been convinced that he was likely to hurt himself or others because of his drug use and his emotionally unstable condition. Would you have informed his parents, even though doing so would probably have ended your counseling relationship with him? Why or why not?
4. Which of the following courses of action might you have taken if you had been Larry's counselor? Check as many as you think are appropriate:

___ stating during the initial session the legal limits on you as a therapist
___ consulting with the director of the agency
___ referring Larry for psychological testing to determine the degree of his emotional disturbance
___ referring him to a psychiatrist for treatment
___ continuing to see him without any stipulations
___ insisting on a session with his parents as a condition of continuing counseling
___ informing the police or other authorities
___ requesting supervision and consultation from the agency
___ documenting your decisional process with a survey of pertinent research

5. Discuss in class other specific courses of action you might have pursued.

O   ***Three short cases***.   The following cases deal with ethical and legal aspects of confidentiality. What do you think you would do in each of these situations?

You're a student counselor. For your internship you're working with college students on campus. Your intern group meets with a supervisor each week to discuss your cases. One day, while you're having lunch in the campus cafeteria with three other interns, they begin to discuss their cases in detail, even mentioning names of clients. They joke about some of the clients they're seeing, while nearby are other students who may be able to overhear this conversation. What would you do in this situation?

___ I would tell the other interns to stop talking about their clients where other students could overhear them, and I would say that I thought they were behaving unprofessionally.
___ I would bring the matter up in our next practicum meeting with the supervisor.
___ I wouldn't do anything, since the students who could overhear the conversation would most likely not be that interested in what was being said.
___ I wouldn't do anything, because it's natural to discuss cases and make jokes to relieve one's own tensions.

_____ I would encourage them to stop talking and to continue their discussion in a private place.

You're leading a counseling group on a high school campus. The members have voluntarily joined the group. In one of the sessions several of the students discuss the drug traffic on their campus, and two of them reveal that they sell marijuana and various pills to their friends. You discuss this matter with them, and they claim that there is nothing wrong with using these drugs. They argue that most of the students on campus use drugs, that no one has been harmed, and that there isn't any difference between using drugs (which they know is illegal) and relying on alcohol (which many of them see their parents doing). What would you do in this situation?

_____ Because their actions are illegal, I'd report them to the police.

_____ I'd do nothing, because their drug use doesn't seem to be a problem for them, and I wouldn't want to jeopardize their trust in me.

_____ I would report the *situation* to the school authorities while keeping the identities of the students confidential.

_____ I would let the students know that I planned to inform the school authorities of their actions and their names.

_____ I wouldn't take the matter seriously, because the laws relating to drugs are unfair.

_____ I would explore with the students their reasons for making this disclosure.

You're counseling children in an elementary school. Barbara is referred to you by her teacher because she is becoming increasingly withdrawn. After several sessions Barbara tells you that she is afraid that her father might kill her and that he frequently beats her as a punishment. Until now she has lied about obvious bruises on her body, claiming that she fell off her bicycle and hurt herself. She shows you welts on her arms and back but tells you not to say anything to anyone because her father has threatened a worse beating if she tells anyone. What would you do in this situation?

_____ I would respect Barbara's wishes and not tell anyone what I knew.

_____ I would report the situation to the principal and the school nurse.

_____ I would immediately go home with Barbara and talk to her parents.

_____ I would take Barbara home with me for a time.

_____ I would report the matter to the police.

_____ I would ask Barbara why she was telling me about the beatings if she didn't want me to reveal them to anyone else.

_____ I would tell her that I had a legal obligation to make this situation known to the authorities but that I would work with her and not leave her alone in her fears.

Chapter Summary

All the ethical codes of mental-health organizations specify the centrality of informed consent. One of the best guarantees of protecting the rights of clients is for the therapists to develop procedures that will aid their clients in making informed choices. We have seen that, legally, informed consent entails the client's ability to act freely in making rational decisions. The process of informed consent includes providing information about the nature of therapy as well as the rights and responsibilities of both the therapist and the client. A basic challenge therapists face is to provide accurate and sufficient information to clients yet at the same time not overwhelm them with too much information too soon. Thus, informed consent can best be viewed as an ongoing process during the early course of therapy that is aimed at increasing the range of choices and responsibility of the client as an active therapeutic partner.

Confidentiality in therapy has both ethical and legal aspects that demand careful consideration. The purpose of confidentiality is to protect clients from unauthorized disclosures by professionals. Generally, therapists have a moral, ethical, legal, and professional obligation not to breach confidentiality without the client's knowledge and authorization unless it is in the client's interest to do so or unless the law requires disclosure of certain information. It is essential that clients learn about the limitations of confidentiality. Related to confidentiality is privileged communication, which is a legal concept. It refers to the rights of clients not to have their disclosures used in court without their consent. If clients waive their privilege, however, the professional does not have grounds for withholding the information. The privilege belongs not to the therapist but to clients for their protection. In most states the statutes determine which mental-health professionals are included under the privileged-communication concept. Therapists can be held legally responsible for violating a client's right to confidentiality. Many therapists are under the mistaken assumption that if their clients do not have privileged communication by statute, the responsibilities for confidentiality are less or do not exist. Therapists have an obligation to maintain the privacy of their clients' communications except in compelling circumstances.

Suggested Activities

1. As a class project form small groups, and create an informed-consent document. What does your group think clients must be told either before therapy begins or during the first few sessions? How might you implement your informed-consent procedures?

2. Working in small groups in class, explore the topic of the rights clients have in counseling. One person in each group can serve as a recorder. When the groups reconvene for a general class meeting, the recorders for the various groups share their lists of clients' rights on a three-point scale: "extremely important," "important," and "somewhat important." What rights can your class agree on as the most important?

3. Select some of the open-ended cases presented in this chapter to role-play with a fellow student. One of you chooses a client you feel you can identify with, and the other becomes the counselor. Conduct a counseling interview. Afterward, talk about how each of you felt during the interview, and discuss alternative courses of action that could have been taken.

4. Providing clients with access to their files and records seems to be in line with the consumer-rights movement, which is having an impact on the human-services professions. What are your own thoughts on providing your clients with this information? What information would you want to share with your clients? In what ways might you go about providing them with this information? What might you do if there were a conflict between your views and the policies of the agency that employed you?

5. As a class project several students can investigate the laws of your state pertaining to confidentiality and privileged communication and then present their findings to the class. What kinds of mental-health providers in your state can offer their clients privileged communication? What are the exceptions to this privilege? Under what circumstances are you legally required to breach confidentiality? Regarding confidentiality in counseling minors, what state laws should you know?

6. In small groups discuss specific circumstances in which you would break confidentiality, and see whether you can agree on some general guidelines. When your class reconvenes for a general meeting, the results of the small groups can be discussed.

7. Discuss some ways in which you can prepare clients for issues pertaining to confidentiality. How can you teach them about the purposes of confidentiality and the legal restrictions on it? Examine how you would do this in various situations, such as school, group work, marital and family counseling, and counseling with minors.

8. In a class debate, one side can take the position that absolute confidentiality is necessary to promote full client disclosure. The other side can argue for a limited confidentiality that still promotes effective therapy.

Suggested Readings

For a discussion of the role of informed consent in psychotherapy consult the following sources: Bennett et al. (1990), Austin et al. (1990), Bray et al. (1985), Handelsman et al. (1986), Mappes et al. (1985), and Bednar et al. (1991). For a description of an informed-consent document designed to foster discussion between the therapist and the client about the therapeutic process, see Handelsman and Galvin (1988). On the topic of the legal and clinical issues pertaining to involuntary commitment, see Austin et al. (1990), and Bednar et al. (1991).

On the clinical management of confidentiality see Baird and Rupert (1987) and Austin et al. (1990). For a survey assessing the public's knowledge and beliefs about confidentiality see Miller and Thelen (1986) and Muehleman et al. (1985). On privileged-communication laws for therapists see Knapp and VandeCreek (1985), Leslie (1991b), and VandeCreek et al. (1988).

For guidelines for practitioners on confidentiality, privileged communication, and privacy see Sheeley and Herlihy (1986). For a discussion of legal and ethical issues pertaining to counseling records see Remley (1990); for guidance on preparing for courtroom appearances see Remley (1991). For a comprehensive discussion of confidentiality see Stadler (1990a).

Professional Responsibilities and Liabilities

Pre-Chapter Self-Inventory

Directions: For each statement, indicate the response that most closely identifies your beliefs and attitudes. Use the following code:

5 = I *strongly agree* with this statement.
4 = I *agree* with this statement.
3 = I am *undecided* about this statement.
2 = I *disagree* with this statement.
1 = I *strongly disagree* with this statement.

____ 1. If I were working with a client whom I had assessed as potentially
dangerous to another person, I would see it as my duty to warn the possible victim.

____ 2. Once I make an assessment that one of my clients is suicidal or at a
high risk of carrying out self-destructive acts, it is my ethical obligation
to take action.

____ 3. Counselors should make it more difficult for suicidal clients to reject
responsibility for deliberately taking their own life.

____ 4. If a suicidal client does not want my help or actively rejects it, I would
be inclined to leave the person alone.

____ 5. Personally, the potential of a malpractice suit concerns me greatly and
makes me want to practice conservatively.

____ 6. I should think about specific ways to protect myself from malpractice
suits.

____ 7. To avoid a malpractice suit, I need to have superior knowledge, skills,
and judgment.

____ 8. Malpractice claims arise only against dishonorable practitioners.

____ 9. At this point in my career I feel quite clear about my professional
responsibilities.

____ 10. If I follow the ethical code of my profession, I should have few conflicts
or difficulties in carrying out my professional responsibilities to my clients
and to those who are related to my clients.

____ 11. I often feel that laws and codes restrict my talents to function effectively as a professional.

Introduction

As we said in the last chapter, on the rights of clients, it is not realistic from an
ethical or legal viewpoint to make a blanket promise to clients that *everything*
they talk about will *always* remain confidential. Landmark court cases have shed
new light on the therapist's duty to violate confidentiality in some cases in order
to warn and protect both clients and others who may be directly affected. As
a professional, for example, you have both ethical and legal responsibilities to
protect innocent people who might be injured by a dangerous client. You also
have the responsibility to assess and intervene effectively with clients who are

likely to try to take their own life. To help you think about your position in deal-ing with potentially dangerous clients or suicidal clients, we will offer guidelines and case illustrations.

As you saw in the previous chapter, the more one considers some of the legal ramifications of confidentiality, the clearer it becomes that most matters are not neatly defined. Even if therapists have become familiar with local and state laws that govern their profession, this legal knowledge alone is not enough to enable them to make sound decisions. Each case is unique, there are various and sometimes conflicting ways to interpret a law, and professional judgment always plays a significant role in resolving cases.

At a conference we attended dealing with ethical and legal issues in counsel-ing, the participants expressed their anxiety over problems raised by potentially violent clients. Most of the counselors said they feared lawsuits and were con-cerned about what "exercising sound professional judgment" really meant. In discussing the tone of this conference, the three of us became concerned that some counselors were primarily worried about protecting themselves and not about the welfare of their clients. We agree with Bednar, Bednar, Lambert, and Waite (1991) that the exaggerated fears and misconceptions associated with a lawsuit in high-risk clinical situations rarely bring out the best qualities in practitioners.

As a counselor you will surely want to protect yourself legally. Yet we hope that you won't allow this necessity to immobilize you and inhibit your profes-sional effectiveness. While minimizing unnecessary risks, you need to realize that counseling is a risky venture. Although you should be familiar with the laws that govern privileged communications and should know what you can and cannot do legally, you should not become so involved in legality that you cease being sensitive to the ethical and clinical implications of what you do in your practice. It is certainly possible to get entangled in statutes and codes of ethics in such a way as to limit yourself. Realize that ethical codes and laws are designed not to limit your talent but to guide you in attaining the highest standards of practice.

The Duty to Warn and Protect

Mental-health professionals, spurred by the courts, have come to realize that they have a double professional responsibility: to protect other people from poten-tially dangerous clients and to protect clients from themselves. In this section we look first at therapists' responsibility to warn and protect potential victims and then at the problems posed by suicidal clients.

The Duty to Protect Potential Victims

After analyzing the legal literature, Bednar and his colleagues (1991) conclude that practitioners need to integrate legal and professional issues into their clinical practices in such a manner that care of clients is not compromised. They main-tain that counselors must exercise the ordinary skill and care of a reasonable professional in (1) identifying those clients who are likely to do physical harm to third parties, (2) protecting third parties from those clients judged potentially dangerous, and (3) treating those clients who are dangerous. These authors recommend that practitioners "take reasonable precautions in *record keeping* and collegial *consultations* that will most dramatically reduce the chances of successful malpractice suits" (Bednar et al., 1991, p. 59). It is, in fact, this standard of what a *reasonable* professional in the community would do under similar circumstances that often determines professional liability in a malpractice suit.

As created by the courts, the responsibility to protect the public from dangerous acts of violent clients entails liability for civil damages when practitioners neglect this duty by (1) failing to diagnose or predict dangerousness, (2) failing to warn potential victims of violent behavior, (3) failing to commit dangerous individuals, and (4) prematurely discharging dangerous clients from a hospital (APA, 1985). The first two of these legally prescribed duties are illustrated in the case of *Tarasoff v. Board of Regents of the University of California*, which has been the subject of extensive analysis in the psychological literature. The other two duties are set forth in additional landmark court cases.

The Tarasoff Case.   In August 1969 Prosenjit Poddar, who was a voluntary outpatient at the student health service on the Berkeley campus of the university, was in counseling with a psychologist named Moore. Poddar had confided to Moore his intention to kill an unnamed woman (who was readily identifiable as Tatiana Tarasoff) when she returned from an extended trip in Brazil. In consultation with other university counselors, Moore made the assessment that Poddar was dangerous and should be committed to a mental hospital for observation. Moore later called the campus police and told them of the death threat and of his conclusion that Poddar was dangerous. The campus officers did take Poddar into custody for questioning, but they later released him when he gave evidence of being "rational" and promised to stay away from Tarasoff. He was never confined to a treatment facility. Moore followed up his call with a formal letter requesting the assistance of the chief of the campus police. Later, Moore's supervisor asked that the letter be returned, ordered that the letter and Moore's case notes be destroyed, and asked that no further action be taken in the case. It should be noted that Tarasoff and her family were never made aware of this potential threat.

Shortly after Tarasoff's return from Brazil, Poddar killed her. Her parents filed suit against the Board of Regents and employees of the university for having failed to notify the intended victim of the threat. A lower court dismissed the suit in 1974, the parents appealed, and the California Supreme Court ruled in favor of the parents in 1976, holding that a failure to warn an intended victim was professionally irresponsible. The court's ruling requires that therapists breach confidentiality in cases where the general welfare and safety of others are involved. Since this was a California case, courts in other states are not bound to decide a similar case in the same way.

Under the *Tarasoff* decision the therapist must first accurately diagnose the client's tendency to behave in dangerous ways toward others. This first duty is judged by the standards of professional negligence. In this case the therapist did not fail in this duty. He even took an additional step of requesting that the dangerous person be detained by the campus police. But the court held that simply notifying the police was insufficient to protect the identifiable victim (Laughran & Bakken, 1984).

In the first ruling, in 1974, the lower court indicated a "duty to warn." This duty was expanded by the California Supreme Court into a "duty to protect." Practitioners now have a duty to protect third parties from dangerous clients. The *Tarasoff* decision made it clear that client confidentiality can be readily compromised; indeed, "the right of clients to privacy ends where the public peril begins" (cited in Fulero, 1988).

Issues of the welfare of the individual client are balanced against the concerns for the welfare of society. As Bednar and his colleagues (1991) indicate, the mental-health professional is a double agent. Therapists have ethical and legal responsibilities to their clients, and they also have legal obligations to society. These dual responsibilities sometimes conflict, and they can create ambiguity in the therapeutic relationship. A number of state courts have not ruled on applications of *Tarasoff*, and thus practitioners remain in a state of uncertainty about the nature of their duty to protect or to warn (Fulero, 1988).

In their assessment of *"Tarasoff*: Five Years Later,"* Knapp and VandeCreek (1982) make the point that variations in state laws make the procedures involved in the "duty to warn" a difficult matter. In the *Tarasoff* case the identity of the victim was known. However, therapists are often concerned about their legal responsibility when the identity of the intended victim is unknown. What are the therapist's obligations in cases of generalized statements of hostility? What is the responsibility of the therapist to predict future violence? In their recommendations to therapists Knapp and VandeCreek (1982) write: "Psychotherapists need only follow reasonable standards in predicting violence. Psychotherapists are not liable for the failure to warn when the propensity toward violence is unknown or would be unknown by other psychotherapists using ordinary skill" (pp. 514–515).

Their point is that therapists should not become intimidated by every idle fantasy, for every impulsive threat is not evidence of imminent danger. In their opinion recent behavioral acts can best predict future violence. In addition to warning potential victims, Knapp and VandeCreek suggest, practitioners should consider other alternatives that could diffuse the danger and, at the same time, satisfy their legal duty. They recommend seeking consultation with other professionals who have expertise in dealing with potentially violent people, and also documenting the steps taken.

In his assessment of *"Tarasoff*: Ten Years Later,"* Fulero (1988) suggests that the issues raised by the decision are likely to continue generating litigation, legislation, and controversy for some time to come. To clarify the soundness of their professional practices, it is suggested that clinicians seek consultation. As mentioned earlier, therapists are not liable for a negative outcome unless their actions fall below the expected standard of care. Fulero recommends that therapists keep abreast of the current statutes and case law in their states and acquire knowledge in assessing and dealing with dangerousness.

The Bradley Case.   A second case illustrates the duty not to negligently release a dangerous client. In *Bradley Center* v. *Wessner* the patient, Wessner, had been voluntarily admitted to a facility for psychiatric care. Wessner was upset over his wife's extramarital affair. He had repeatedly threatened to kill her and her lover and had even admitted to a therapist that he was carrying a weapon in his car for that purpose. He was given an unrestricted weekend pass so that he could visit his children, who were living with his wife. He met his wife and her lover in the home and proceeded to shoot and kill both of them. The children filed a wrongful death suit, alleging that the psychiatric center had breached a duty to exercise control over Wessner. The Georgia Supreme Court ruled that a physician has a duty to take reasonable care to prevent a potentially dangerous patient from inflicting harm (Laughran & Bakken, 1984).

The Jablonski Case.   A third legal ruling underscores the duty to commit a dangerous individual. The intended victim's knowledge of a threat does not relieve therapists of the duty to protect, according to the decision in *Jablonski* v. *United States*. Meghan Jablonski filed suit for the wrongful death of her mother, Melinda Kimball, who was murdered by Philip Jablonski, the man with whom she had been living. Earlier, Philip Jablonski had agreed to a psychiatric examination at a hospital. The physicians determined that there was no emergency and thus no basis for involuntary commitment. Kimball later again accompanied Jablonski to the hospital and expressed fears for her own safety. She was told by a doctor that "you should consider staying away from him." Again, the doctors concluded that there was no basis for involuntary hospitalization and released him. Shortly thereafter Jablonski killed Kimball.

The Ninth U.S. Circuit Court of Appeals found that failure to obtain Jablonski's prior medical history constituted malpractice. The essence of *Jablonski* is a negligent failure to commit (Laughran & Bakken, 1984).

The Hedlund Case.   The decision in *Hedlund* v. *Superior Court* extends the duty to warn to anyone who might be near the intended victim and who might also be in danger. LaNita Wilson and Stephen Wilson had received psychotherapy from a psychological assistant, Bonnie Hedlund. During treatment Stephen Wilson told the therapist that he intended to harm LaNita Wilson. He later did assault her, in the presence of her child. The allegation was that the child had sustained "serious emotional injury and psychological trauma."

In keeping with the *Tarasoff* decision, the California Supreme Court held (1) that a therapist has a duty first to exercise a "reasonable degree of skill, knowledge, and care ordinarily possessed and exercised by members [of that professional specialty] under similar circumstances" in making a prediction about the chances of a client's acting dangerously to others and (2) that therapists must "exercise reasonable care to protect the foreseeable victim of that danger." One way to protect the victim is by giving a warning of peril. The court held that breach of such a duty with respect to third persons constitutes "professional negligence" (Laughran & Bakken, 1984).

In the *Hedlund* case the duty to warn of potentially dangerous conduct applied to the mother, not to her child, against whom no threats had been made. However, the duty to exercise reasonable care could have been fulfilled by warning the mother that she and her child might be in danger.

Guidelines for Dealing with Dangerous Clients.   Stimulated mainly by the *Tarasoff* ruling, most counseling centers have developed guidelines regarding the duty to warn and protect when the welfare of others is at stake. These guidelines generally specify how to deal with emotionally disturbed individuals, violent behavior, threats, suicidal possibilities, and other circumstances in which counselors may be legally and ethically required to breach confidentiality.

The question raised by these documents is "What are the responsibilities of counselors to their clients or to others when, in the professional judgment of the counselor, there is a high degree of probability that a client will seriously harm another person or destroy property?" Many counselors find it difficult to predict when clients pose a serious threat to others. Clients are encouraged to engage in open dialogue in therapeutic relationships; believing that what they say is confidential, they may express feelings or thoughts about doing physical harm to others. Generally, these are expressions of feelings, and relatively few of these threats are actually carried out. Counselors should therefore *not* be expected to routinely reveal all threats, for such a policy of disclosure could seriously disrupt clients' relationships with their therapists or with the persons who are "threatened." Counselors have the obligation not to disclose confidential material unless such disclosures are necessary to prevent harm to clients or to others.

What is expected of counselors is that they exercise reasonable professional judgment and apply practices that are commonly accepted by professionals in their specialty. If they determine that clients pose a serious danger of violence to others, they are obliged to exercise reasonable care to protect the would-be victims.

Cases to Consider.   It is often difficult to ascertain a client's intent to harm others. As you think about these following cases, ask yourself how you would assess the degree to which Marvin and Kevin are potentially dangerous. What would you do if you were the therapist in each case?

○ *The case of Marvin.*   Marvin has been seeing Robin, his counselor, for several months. One day he comes to the therapy session somewhat drunk and very angry. He has just found out that a close friend is having an affair with his wife. He is deeply wounded over this incident. He is also highly agitated and even talks about killing the friend who betrayed him. As he puts it, "I'm so damn mad I feel like getting my gun and shooting him." Marvin experiences a great deal of catharsis in this session. Robin does everything she can to defuse his rage and to stabilize him before the session ends. The session continues for about two hours (instead of the usual hour), and she asks him to call her a couple of times each day to check in. Before he leaves, she contracts with him that he will not go over to this man's house and that he will not act out his urges. Because she knows him well and thinks that basically he is not a violent person, she decides to let him leave the session without discussing legal imperatives in this type of case. He follows through and calls her every day. When he comes to the session the following week, he admits to still being in a great deal of pain over his discovery, but he no longer feels violent. As he puts it, "I'm not going to land in jail because of this jerk!" He tells Robin how helpful the last session was in allowing him to get a lot off his chest.

- Do you think that Robin followed the ethical and legal course of action in this case?
- Did she fulfill her responsibilities by making sure that Marvin called her twice a day?
- Some would say that she should have broken confidentiality and warned the intended victim. What might have been the consequences for Marvin's therapy had she followed this course?
- What criteria could a therapist use to determine whether the situation is dangerous enough to warn a potential victim? What is the fine line between overreacting and failing to respond appropriately in this kind of case?
- Knowing what you do about the case, what actions might you have taken? Why? If Robin had sought you out for consultation in this case immediately after the session at which Marvin talked about wanting to kill his friend, what would you have told her?

○ *The case of Kevin.*   You're working with a young man Kevin, who you think is potentially violent. During his sessions with you Kevin talks about his impulses to hurt others and himself, and he describes times when he has seriously beaten his girlfriend. He tells you that she is afraid to leave him because she thinks he'll beat her even more savagely. He later tells you that sometimes he gets so angry that he comes very close to killing her. You believe that he is very likely to seriously harm and possibly even kill the young woman. Which of the following would you do?

____ I would notify Kevin's girlfriend that she might be in grave danger.
____ I would notify the police or other authorities.
____ I would keep Kevin's threats to myself, because I couldn't be sure that he would act on them.
____ I would seek a second opinion from a colleague.
____ I would inform my director or supervisor.
____ I would refer Kevin to another therapist.
____ I would arrange to have him hospitalized.

What else might you do?

The Duty to Protect Suicidal Clients

Many therapists inform their clients that they have an ethical and legal obligation to break confidentiality when they have good reason to suspect suicidal behavior. Even if clients argue that they can do what they want with their life, including taking it, therapists do have a duty to protect suicidal clients. In the preceding discussion we emphasized the therapist's obligation to protect others, but these principles apply also to the client. The crux of the issue is knowing when to take a client's hints seriously enough to report the condition. Certainly not every mention of the possibility of taking one's own life justifies extraordinary measures.

The evaluation and management of suicidal risk is a source of great stress for most therapists. It brings to the surface many of the troublesome issues that clinical practitioners must face, such as their degree of influence, competence, level of involvement with a client, responsibility, legal obligations, and ability to make life-or-death decisions. Szasz (1986) has noted that failure to prevent suicide is now one of the leading reasons for successful malpractice suits against mental-health professionals and institutions.

Guidelines for Assessing Suicidal Behavior.

Although it is not possible to prevent every suicide, it is possible to recognize the existence of common crises that may precipitate a suicide attempt and reach out to people who are experiencing these crises. Counselors must take the "cry for help" seriously and have the necessary knowledge and skills to intervene once they make an assessment that a client is suicidal (Fujimura, Weis, & Cochran, 1985). The following guidelines are important factors to consider in making the evaluation of suicidal risk. Although this is a partial list, it does give some idea about what to be alert for in making an assessment (Fujimura et al., 1985; Pope, 1985b).

- Direct verbal warnings must be taken seriously, as they are one of the most useful single predictors of a suicide.
- The therapist should pay attention to previous suicide attempts, as these are the best single predictor of lethality. Up to 80% of suicides were preceded by a prior attempt.
- One common characteristic of all suicide victims is depression. Sleep disruption, which can intensify depression, is a key sign. For people with clinical depression the suicide rate is about 20 times greater than that of the general population.
- A sense of hopelessness seems to be closely associated with suicidal intentions. Individuals may feel helpless, desperate, and worthless.
- Definitiveness of a plan is an indicator. The more definite the plan, the more serious is the situation. Suicidal individuals should be asked to talk about their plans. They should be asked to explore their suicidal fantasies.
- Clients who have a history of severe alcohol or drug abuse are at greater risk than the general population. Between one-fourth and one-third of all suicides are associated with alcohol as a contributing factor.
- Giving prized possessions away, finalizing business affairs, or revising wills may be critical signs.
- The suicide rate for men is about three times greater than that for women. The rate rises rapidly for men until the age of 35.
- Living alone tends to increase the risk of suicide. Single individuals are twice as likely as married people to commit suicide.

- Unemployment increases the risk for suicide.
- A history of previous psychiatric treatment or hospitalization is a pertinent factor. Clients who have been hospitalized for emotional disorders are more likely to be inclined to suicide.
- Clients who do not have resource and support systems available are more at risk. A person's refusal to use these systems signifies a cutting off of communication and makes the intent more serious.

The Case for Suicide Prevention.   Suicidal individuals are often hoping that somebody will listen to their cry. Many of these clients are struggling with short-term crises, and if they can be given help in learning to cope with the immediate problem, their potential for suicide can be greatly reduced.

Therapists have the responsibility to prevent suicide if they can reasonably anticipate it. Once it is determined that a client is at risk, professionals are legally required to break confidentiality and to take appropriate action. Failure to take action can result in the therapist's being held liable. There have been successful lawsuits against therapists who did not follow standard procedures to protect a client's life (Austin, Moline, & Williams, 1990). Liability generally arises when counselors fail to act in such a way as to prevent the suicide or do something that might contribute to it.

Once the therapist makes the assessment of foreseeable risk, what are some possible courses of action? What are some ethical and legal options to consider? How can professionals take appropriate steps to demonstrate that a reasonable attempt is being made to control the suicidal client? The following are recommendations for managing suicidal behavior (see Austin et al., 1990; Bednar et al., 1991; Bennett, Bryant, VandenBos, & Greenwood, 1990; Bonger, 1991; Fujimura et al., 1985; Pope, 1985b; Pope & Vasquez, 1991; Schutz, 1982):

- Know your personal limits; recognize the stresses involved in working with suicidal clients and the toll that they take on you personally.
- Screen your clients for suicidal risk during the early phase of therapy.
- Explore any fantasies that clients may have about suicide.
- Work with the suicidal client to create a supportive environment.
- Bargain with the client or attempt to secure a promise that he or she will not try to commit suicide.
- Periodically collaborate with colleagues and ask for their views regarding the client's condition; realize that even for experienced practitioners, two perspectives are better than one.
- Consider asking the client to check into a hospital.
- Keep up to date on the clinical literature on the assessment and management of suicidal behavior patterns.
- Specify your availability to your clients; let them know how they can contact you during your absences.
- Obtain training for suicide prevention and for crisis-intervention methods. Keep up to date with current research, theory, and practice.

- Recognize the importance of knowing how, when, and where to appropriately refer clients whose concerns are beyond the boundary of your competence. Know your professional limits.
- Be aware of the hospitals where you can make referrals. Know the procedures for both voluntary and involuntary hospitalization of suicidal clients. If the client is assessed as being suicidal and unable to control self-destructive impulses, psychiatric hospitalization becomes the most logical course of action. A commitment procedure may be called for as a way of protecting the client.
- When considering hospitalization, weigh the benefits, the drawbacks, and the possible effects. If the client does enter a hospital, pay particular attention to the increased risk of suicide immediately after discharge.
- Become familiar with the legal standards as they affect this area of practice.
- If suicidal issues arise, consult an attorney with expertise in this area.
- Be clear and firm with the client, and do not allow yourself to be manipulated by threats. Also, give clear messages to the client. The literature reveals the dangers of using techniques such as paradoxical intention with suicidal clients.
- Especially in crisis counseling, make an assessment of your clients for suicidal risk during the early phase of therapy, and keep alert to this issue during the course of therapy.
- For services that take place within a clinic or agency setting, ensure that clear and appropriate lines of responsibility are explicit and are fully understood by everyone.
- Work with clients so that dangerous instruments are not within easy access. If the client possesses any weapons, make sure that they are in the hands of a third party.
- Consider increasing the frequency of the counseling sessions.
- Work with the client's strengths and desires to remain alive.
- Attempt to communicate realistic hopes.
- Develop a therapeutic contract with suicidal clients. If a client says that when life gets too unbearable, he or she will commit suicide, the therapist can firmly point out that the client is probably sabotaging their work together. Many therapists call a client in crisis at appointed times or encourage the client to call them in the event of serious loss of hope.
- Be willing to communicate your caring. Suicidal people sometimes interpret the unwillingness of others to listen as a sign that they do not care. People may be driven to suicide by an avoidance of the topic on the part of the listener. Remember that caring entails some specific actions and setting of limits on your part.
- Do not make yourself the only person responsible for the decisions and actions of your clients. Take your share of professional responsibility, but do not accept all of the responsibility. Your clients must share in the responsibility of their ultimate decisions. Also, in working with clients in crisis, attempt to develop a supportive network of family and friends to help them face their struggles. Of course, let your clients know that you are trying to create a social-support system, and enlist their help in building this resource of caring people.

- Let the client know that you will be seeking consultation and discussing possible courses of action. It is a good idea to document in writing the steps you take in crisis cases, for documentation may be necessary to demonstrate that you did use sound professional judgment and acted within acceptable legal and ethical parameters.
- Remember that clients are ultimately responsible for their actions and that there is only so much that you can reasonably do to prevent self-destructive actions. Even if you take specific steps to lessen the chances of your clients' committing suicide, they can still take this ultimate step at some time.

The Case against Suicide Prevention.   Now that we have looked at the case for suicide prevention, we explore another point of view. Szasz (1986) challenges the perspective that mental-health professionals have an absolute professional duty to try to prevent suicide. He presents the thesis that suicide is an act of a moral agent who is ultimately responsible, and he opposes coercive methods of preventing suicide, such as forced hospitalization. Szasz argues that by attempting to prevent suicide, mental-health practitioners often ally themselves with the police power of the state and resort to coercion, therefore identifying themselves as foes of individual liberty and responsibility. In taking this course of action, professionals assume the burden of responsibility of keeping clients alive, depriving their clients of their rightful share of accountability for their own actions. It is the client's responsibility to choose to live or to die. According to Szasz, if clients seek professional help for their suicidal tendencies, the helper has an ethical obligation—and in some cases a legal obligation—to provide the help being sought. On the other hand, Szasz argues, if clients do not seek such help and actively reject it, the professional's duty is either to persuade them to accept help or to leave them alone. He puts the core of his argument as follows:

> Because I value individual liberty highly and am convinced that liberty and responsibility are indivisible, I want to enlarge the scope of liberty and responsibility. In the present instance, this means opposing policies of suicide prevention that minimize the responsibility of individuals for killing themselves and supporting policies that maximize their responsibility for doing so. In other words, we should make it more difficult for suicidal persons to reject responsibility for deliberately taking their own lives and for mental health professionals to assume responsibility for keeping such persons alive [1986, p. 810].

It should be noted that Szasz is not claiming that suicide is always good or a morally legitimate option; rather, his key point is that the power of the state should not be used to either prohibit or prevent people from taking their own life. The right to suicide implies that we must abstain from empowering agents of the state to coercively prevent it.

Your Stance on Suicide Prevention.   You will recall that in Chapter 3 we explored the issue of the right to die. Your own value system will have a lot to do with the actions you would be likely to take. Considering the arguments for and against suicide prevention, what is your stance on this complex issue? Where do you stand with respect to your ethical obligations to recognize, evaluate, and intervene with potentially suicidal clients? To what degree do you agree with the guidelines listed earlier? Which are the ones that make the most sense to you? Do you take a contrary position on at least some cases of suicide? How do you justify your position? To what extent do you agree or disagree with the contention of Szasz that current policies of suicide prevention displace responsibility from the client to the therapist and that this needlessly undermines the ethic of self-responsibility?

After clarifying your own values underlying the professional's role in assessing and preventing suicide, reflect on the following cases of clients who are contemplating suicide. If they were your clients, what actions would you take?

○ **The case of Rupe.**   Rupe, a 16-year-old high school student, is being seen by a therapist at the request of his parents. His school work has dropped off, he has become withdrawn socially, and he has expressed to his parents that he has thought of suicide, even though he has not made a specific plan. After the therapist has seen Rupe for several weeks of individual counseling, his concerned parents call and ask how he is doing. They wonder whether they should be concerned about possible suicide attempts. Rupe's parents tell the therapist that they want to respect confidentiality and are not interested in detailed disclosures but that they want to find out if they have cause for worry. Without going into details, the counselor reassures them that they don't need to worry.

- Is the therapist's behavior ethical? Would it make a difference if Rupe were 25 years old?
- Does the therapist have an ethical obligation to inform Rupe of the conversation with his parents?
- If the parents were to insist on having more information, does the therapist have an obligation to say more?
- If the therapist is to provide details to the parents, does he have an obligation to inform Rupe before talking with his parents?
- Other than doing what the therapist did, do you see other courses of action?
- If Rupe was indeed suicidal, what ethical and legal obligations would the therapist have toward the parents?

○ **The case of Emmanuel.**   Emmanuel is a middle-aged widower who complains of emptiness in life, loneliness, depression, and a loss of the will to live any longer. He has been in individual therapy for seven months with a clinical psychologist in private practice. Using psychodiagnostic procedures, both objective tests and projective techniques, she has determined that he has serious depressive tendencies and is potentially self-destructive. Emmanuel came to her for therapy as a final attempt to find some meaning that would show him that his life had significance. In their sessions he explores in depth the history of his failures, the isolation he feels, the meaninglessness of his life, and his bouts with feelings of worthlessness and depression. With her encouragement he experiments with new ways of behaving in the hope that he will find reasons to go on living. Finally, after seven months of searching, he decides that he wants to take his own life. He tells his therapist that he is convinced he has been deluding himself in thinking that anything in his life will change for the better and that he feels good about finally summoning the courage to end his life. He informs her that he will not be seeing her again.

The therapist expresses her concern that Emmanuel is very capable of taking his life at this time because so far he has not been able to see any light at the end of the tunnel. She acknowledges that the decision to commit suicide is not a sudden one, for they have discussed this wish for several sessions, but she lets him know that she wants him to give therapy more of a chance. He replies that he is truly grateful to her for helping him to find his answer within himself and that at least he can end his life with dignity in his own eyes. He says firmly that he doesn't want her to attempt to obstruct his plans in any way. She asks that he postpone his decision for at least a week and return to discuss the matter more fully. He tells her he isn't certain whether he will keep this appointment, but he agrees to consider it.

The therapist does nothing further. During the following week she hears from a friend that Emmanuel has committed suicide by taking an overdose of sleeping pills.

1. What do you think of the way the therapist dealt with her client?
2. What is your view of suicide?
3. What might you have done differently if you had been Emmanuel's therapist?
4. How do you think that your viewpoint regarding suicide influenced your answer to the preceding question?
5. Which of the following courses of action might you have pursued if you had been Emmanuel's counselor?
   ___ committing him to a state hospital for observation, even against his will, for 48 hours
   ___ consulting with another professional as soon as he began to discuss suicide as an option
   ___ respecting his choice of suicide, even if you didn't agree with it
   ___ informing the police and reporting the seriousness of his threat
   ___ informing members of his family of his intentions, even though he didn't want you to
   ___ bargaining with him in every way possible in an effort to persuade him to keep on trying to find some meaning in life
6. Discuss in class any other steps you might have taken in this case.

Malpractice Liability in the Helping Professions

How vulnerable are mental-health professionals to malpractice actions? What are some practical safeguards against being involved in such a lawsuit? In this section we examine these questions. It is easy to become swept up in a tide of anxiety over the possibility of being sued for negligence, but such fear is certainly not likely to bring out the best in practitioners. Instead, we hope that our discussion of malpractice will lead to an increased awareness of the range of professional responsibilities and of ways to lessen the chances of being accused of negligent practices.

What Is Malpractice?

Malpractice is the failure to render professional services or to exercise the degree of skill that is ordinarily expected of other professionals in a similar situation. Malpractice is a legal concept involving negligence that results in injury or loss to the client. Thus, professional negligence consists of departing from usual practice or not exercising due care in fulfilling one's responsibilities.

Practitioners are expected to abide by legal standards and adhere to the ethical codes of their profession in providing care to their clients. Unless they take due care and act in good faith, they are liable to a civil suit for failing to perform their duties as provided by law. The primary problem in a negligence suit is determining which standards of care apply to determine whether a counselor has breached a duty to a client. Counselors are judged according to the standards that are commonly accepted by the profession in their region (Hopkins & Anderson, 1990). Practitioners need not be superior, but they are expected to possess and exercise the knowledge, skill, and judgment common to other members of their profession (Bednar et al., 1991; VandeCreek et al., 1987; Woody, 1984). Practitioners should try to maintain a reasonable view of the realities involved in dealing with high-risk clients:

> As professionals, we are expected to be clairvoyant only on rare and unreasonable occasions. We are usually held accountable only for failure to exercise the ordinary skill and expertise that can be expected from similarly trained professionals. Any of our beliefs that imply that more can be expected of us, or that it is against the law to make mistakes or have unfavorable client outcomes, only enhance the fear that deters quality clinical care [Bednar et al., 1991, p. 18].

The description below of the elements of malpractice is adapted from the views of several writers (Austin et al., 1990; Bednar et al., 1991; Bennett et al., 1990). To succeed in a malpractice claim, the following four elements of malpractice must be present: (1) a professional relationship between the therapist and the client must have existed; (2) the therapist must have acted in a negligent or improper manner or must have failed to provide services that are considered "standard practice in the community"; (3) the client must have suffered harm or injury, which must be demonstrated; and (4) there must be a causal relationship between the practitioner's negligence or breach of duty and the damage or injury claimed by the client. The burden of proof that harm actually took place is the client's. The plaintiff must demonstrate that all four elements applied in his or her situation:

1. *Duty.* For malpractice to occur, it is necessary to demonstrate that a professional relationship was established and that the therapist owed a duty of care to the client.
2. *Breach of duty.* After the plaintiff proves that a professional relationship did exist, he or she must show that the duty was breached, or that the practitioner failed to provide the appropriate standard of care. The breach of duty may involve either actions taken by the therapist or the failure to take certain precautions.
3. *Injury.* Plaintiffs must prove that they were harmed in some way, either physically or psychologically, and that actual injuries were sustained. Examples of such injuries include wrongful death (suicide), loss (divorce), and pain and suffering.
4. *Causation.* Plaintiffs must demonstrate that the professional's breach of duty was the direct cause of the injury they suffered. The test in this case lies in proving that the harm would not have occurred if it were not for the practitioner's actions or failure to act.

In the case of suicide, for example, two factors determine a practitioner's malpractice liability: forseeability and reasonable care. Most important is *foreseeability*, which involves assessing the level of risk. Failing to conduct a comprehensive risk assessment and to document this assessment would be a major error on the therapist's part. Practitioners need to demonstrate that their judgments were based on observed data and that these judgments were reasonable. The second factor in liability is whether *reasonable care* was provided. Once an assessment of risk is made, it is important to document that appropriate precautions were taken to prevent a client's suicide.

Causes of Malpractice Suits

Violations of confidentiality and sexual misconduct have received the greatest attention in the literature as grounds for malpractice suits. In order to be liable in the first case, psychotherapists must have violated client confidentiality under circumstances outside the legitimate exceptions mandated by ethical guidelines or by state laws. As we said in the last chapter, these exceptions include cases in which clients pose a threat to themselves or others or lack capacity and cases in which a court orders a disclosure.

According to the American Psychological Association Insurance Trust, which is the major carrier for practicing psychologists, sexual relationships between client and therapist represent the greatest cost to the APA insurance program. Although the actual number of claims is relatively small, such cases account for 45% of the professional-liability payments made for the last ten years and 20% of the total reported claims. As a way of reducing the impact that this type of unethical practice has on the insurance premiums charged to all psychologists, the APA insurance carrier has placed a $25,000 cap on payments for damages when sexual misconduct is alleged in a lawsuit.

A review of the literature reveals the following to be other frequent causes of malpractice actions against human-service professionals: nonsexual dual relationships; a countersuit over fee collection; undue influence; abandonment; failure to treat properly; negligence; the improper death of a client or other person; failure to supervise properly; misrepresenting one's professional training and skills; failure to respect the client's integrity and privacy; breach of confidentiality or privacy; failure to exercise reasonable care in cases of suicide; failure to protect others from a violent client; failure to refer a client when it becomes clear that the person needs intervention that is beyond the worker's level of competence; faulty termination; failure to consult; faulty diagnosis; improper methods of collecting fees; defamation (libel and slander); violation of legal regulations; loss of child custody or visitation; violation of civil rights (such as illegal search of a school locker); unethical research practices; striking a client as a part of the treatment; providing birth-control and abortion information to minors (as opposed to making appropriate referrals for such help); prescribing and administering drugs inappropriately; breaching of a contract with a client; the failure to keep adequate records; and the failure to provide for informed consent (Austin et al., 1990; Bednar et al., 1991; Bennett et al., 1990; Hopkins & Anderson, 1990; Pope & Vasquez, 1991; Reaves, 1986; Van Hoose & Kottler, 1985; Woody, 1988; Woody & Associates, 1984).

In some recent cases counselors have been held liable for damages after they gave poor advice. If clients rely on the advice given by a professional and suffer damages as a result, they can initiate a civil action. Thus, professional health-care providers should work only with those clients and deliver only those services that are within the realm of their competence.

Ways to Protect Yourself from Malpractice Suits

One of the best ways to protect yourself from becoming embroiled in a malpractice action is to restrict your practice to clients for whom you are prepared by virtue of your education, training, and experience. Pope and Vasquez (1991) point out cases in which practitioners functioning within their legitimate specialty have tried to work with specific populations or to use specific techniques that exceed the boundaries of their competence. Some research suggests that about 25% of psychologists admit providing services outside of their area of competence, at least occasionally (Pope, Tabachnick, & Keith-Spiegel, 1987). Another precaution against a malpractice suit is personal and professional honesty and openness with clients. Although you may not always be able to make the "right choice" in every situation, it is crucial that you know your limitations and remain open to seeking consultation in difficult cases.

Here are some additional safeguards against malpractice accusations:

- Clearly define your fees at the outset of therapy. If it is your practice to increase your fees periodically, tell clients that fees are subject to change with notice. Some practitioners avoid raising fees for current clients.
- Take steps to maintain your competence, even if this is not required by state laws (Bennett et al., 1990).

- Carefully document a client's treatment plan. Records might include notes on symptoms, diagnosis, and treatment; documents verifying informed consent and relevant consultations; and a copy of the therapeutic contract (Austin et al., 1990; Remley, 1990).
- Maintain adequate business records. In case of a suit, if you admit that you don't keep records, you will probably be perceived as unprofessional. How detailed you make your clinical notes is a matter of preference (Austin et al., 1990; Remley, 1990).
- Recognize your professional and legal responsibility to preserve the confidentiality of your clients' records. Know the circumstances when you might be required to disclose counseling records: (1) when clients are a danger to themselves or others, (2) when clients request that records be released, and (3) when a court orders the disclosure of records (Remley, 1990).
- Keep clients' records for five to seven years. Such records include homicide or suicide attempts or threats, written treatment plans, and clients' failure to follow major suggestions (Austin et al., 1990).
- Report any case of suspected child abuse as required by law.
- Avoid involvement in searches of students (Hopkins & Anderson, 1990). When school counselors take on monitoring and policing duties or become guardians of school lockers, they open themselves to the risk of invading the students' privacy.
- Do not barter services. Such exchanges are likely to lead to resentment on both your part and your clients'.
- Avoid sexual relationships with either current or former clients and with current supervisees and students.
- A dual relationship may occur whenever you interact with a client in more than one capacity (such as therapist and business partner or therapist and teacher). Be aware of your position of power, and avoid even the appearance of conflict of interest. Before engaging in any dual relationship, talk with your client about the possible repercussions of such a relationship and the dangers to both of you of unfulfilled expectations and lack of objectivity (Bennett et al., 1990; Herlihy & Corey, 1992).
- Absences on your part may appear to a client to be abandonment. Although you cannot always prevent this perception, you can ameliorate it (Bennett et al., 1990; Pope & Vasquez, 1991). Because you can be sued for abandonment, make sure that you provide coverage for emergencies when you are going away. Consider an answering service so that you can be reached in times of crisis.
- Consult with colleagues when you are in doubt. Because the legal standard is based on the practices of fellow professionals, the more consensus you have, the better chance you have of prevailing in a suit. Record these case consultations in the client's file.
- Before consulting with others about a specific client, obtain consent from the client for the release of information. However, some state laws allow emergency consultation without the client's consent (Austin et al., 1990; Bennett et al., 1990).

- In cases where you have limited experience or encounter cultural barriers, consult with a colleague experienced in treating this population and, if necessary, refer the client (Bennett et al., 1990).
- Make use of informed-consent procedures, and use contracts to clarify your professional relationships with clients. Realize that there is a wide variation in age of consent, depending on what the client is consenting to. Present information to your clients in clear language.
- In describing a treatment approach, explain its risks and benefits, as well as possible alternatives, in sufficient detail to ensure that the client understands the procedures (Bennett et al., 1990).
- In accepting or making referrals, carry out your responsibility to obtain or transfer information pertaining to a client (Austin et al., 1990).
- Learn how to assess and intervene in cases in which clients pose a danger to themselves or others. Knowing the danger signs of suicidal clients is the first step toward prevention.
- If you make a professional determination that a client is dangerous, take the necessary steps to protect the client or others from harm (Austin et al., 1990; Bednar et al., 1991; Remley, 1991; VandeCreek et al., 1987).
- It is risky to accept gifts from your clients. Although you can be friendly and personal with clients, your relationships should be primarily professional.
- In counseling minors, be aware of sources to whom you can send them when they seek specific information about birth-control methods or abortion.
- Become aware of local and state laws that limit your practice, as well as the policies of an agency you may work for. Keep up to date with legal and ethical changes by becoming actively involved in professional organizations.
- Be open in communications with clients, and take an interest in their welfare (Van Hoose & Kottler, 1985).
- Treat your clients with respect by attending carefully to your language and your behavior. This practice generally leads to good relationships and reduces the likelihood of a malpractice action.
- Avoid undue influence over clients (such as imposing your values or making decisions for clients). Recognize that it is possible for you to unintentionally influence a client in an inappropriate way (Bennett et al., 1990).
- Have a theoretical orientation and a rationale for employing techniques as a guide in your practice.
- Create reasonable expectations about what psychotherapy can and cannot do. It is especially important to test innovative therapeutic approaches before they are used with the general public (Schutz, 1982).
- Have adequate professional-liability insurance.

In their very helpful book, *Professional Liability and Risk Management*, Bennett and his colleagues (1990) emphasize the importance of anticipating and recognizing potential problem areas and then guarding against those behaviors that might harm the client. They remind practitioners of their ethical and legal obligations and suggest risk-management procedures. They urge clinicians to assess their own practices and to keep up to date on legal, ethical, and community standards affecting their profession and their client population.

Malpractice claims are not reserved exclusively for the dishonorable practitioner but may also be filed against honorable practitioners who make themselves legally vulnerable through their actions or inactions. The best way to avoid being sued is to know the rules and follow them. Sometimes, however, the therapeutic relationship is negatively affected when therapists develop too many forms of self-protection. Clients may infer from these attempts that the counselor is not to be trusted. In turn, they may be reluctant to engage in the self-disclosure that is so important for successful therapy.

Course of Action in a Malpractice Suit

Even though you practice prudently and follow most of the guidelines we have given, there is still a chance that you may be sued. An increasing number of mental-health professionals find themselves involved in court proceedings (Remley, 1991). In the event that you are sued, consider some of the recommendations given by Bennett and his associates (1990):

- Treat the lawsuit seriously, even if it represents a client's attempt to punish or control you.
- Do not attempt to resolve the matter with the client, because anything you do might be used against you in the litigation.
- Become familiar with your liability policy, such as the limits of coverage and procedures that the company will use.
- If a client threatens to sue you or if you receive a subpoena notifying you of a lawsuit, contact your insurance company immediately.
- Never destroy or alter files or reports pertinent to the client's case.
- In consultation with your attorney, prepare summaries of any pertinent events about the case that you can use.
- Do not discuss the case with anyone other than your attorney. Avoid making self-incriminating statements to the client or to his or her attorney.
- Determine the nature of support available to you from professional associations to which you belong.
- Do not continue a professional relationship with a client who is bringing a suit against you.

If you face going to court, you must have some basic knowledge and take steps to prepare yourself for your appearance. A helpful resource for understanding legal matters pertaining to mental-health practices and for preparing for court is Remley's monograph (1991).

Legal Liability in an Ethical Perspective

Even though malpractice is not an ethical issue, it overlaps with ethical concerns. It may be that practitioners' increased interest in ethics stems largely from the potential for malpractice actions. Legal issues give substance and direction to the evolution of ethical issues.

The public's use of the legal system for resolving grievances against mental-health professionals is increasing. Private practitioners are becoming more vulnerable and are likely to find themselves involved in more litigation than in the past. It is a good idea to consult an attorney about questionable matters. Furthermore, it is at least wise, if not essential, to have professional-liability insurance. This change toward increased litigation can have a positive effect, for it can stimulate professionals to offer higher quality service. But there is also a negative side: rising use of the legal system can lead to excessive caution by therapists because of their concern about being sued.

In spite of the increase in malpractice litigation, a survey has found that few practitioners have serious concerns about being sued (Wilbert & Fulero, 1988). The researchers report that the fear of being sued has provided incentives to adopt appropriate professional practices. They conclude that "a careful practitioner who follows the prescribed guidelines for proper professional practice and who refrains from sexual improprieties appears to run a very small risk of malpractice litigation" (p. 382).

This brief discussion of malpractice is not aimed at making you overcautious. Rather, we hope that this entire chapter has helped to familiarize you with legal and ethical standards that can guide your practice. Although no professional is expected to be perfect, it is beneficial for practitioners to evaluate what they are doing and why they are practicing as they are.

Chapter Summary

A major focus of this chapter has been the scope of professionals' responsibilities. Besides their duties to the client, therapists also have responsibilities to their agency, to their profession, to the community, to the members of their clients' families, and to themselves. Ethical dilemmas arise when there are conflicts of responsibilities—for instance, when the agency's expectations conflict with the concerns or wishes of clients. Members of the helping professions need to know and observe the ethical code of their professional organization and need to make sound judgments that are within the parameters of acceptable practice. We have encouraged you to think about specific ethical issues and to develop a sense of professional ethics and knowledge of state laws so that your judgment will be based on more than what "feels right."

Court decisions have provided an expanded perspective on the therapist's duty to protect the public. As a result of the *Tarasoff* case, for instance, therapists are now becoming aware of their responsibility to the potential victims of a client's violent behavior. This duty spans interventions from warnings to threatened individuals to involuntary commitment of clients. Therapists are vulnerable to malpractice action when they demonstrate negligent failure to diagnose dangerousness, negligent failure to warn a known victim once such a diagnosis has been made, negligent failure to commit a dangerous person, or negligent failure to keep a dangerous client committed.

Therapists also have a duty to protect clients who are likely to injure or kill themselves. This responsibility implies that practitioners develop skills in making accurate assessments of potentially suicidal persons. Once they diagnose a client as a danger to himself or herself, they are responsible for preventing suicide by acting in professionally acceptable ways. A dissenting opinion on this issue is that of Szasz (1986), who challenges the assumption that therapists should be held accountable for a client's decision to die. He believes that suicide is an ultimate right and responsibility of the client and that it is unethical for therapists to employ coercive measures aimed at preventing it.

Associated with professional responsibilities are professional liabilities. If practitioners ignore legal and ethical standards or if their conduct is below the expected standard of care, they incur the risk of being sued. Practitioners who fail to keep adequate records of their procedures are therefore opening themselves to liability. It is realistic to be concerned about strategies to avoid malpractice actions, and there are a number of ways to greatly lessen the chance of a suit. But practitioners should not become so preoccupied with making mistakes that they render themselves ineffective as clinicians.

Suggested Activities

1. In small groups discuss the cases and guidelines presented in this chapter on the duty to protect potential victims from violent clients. If you found yourself faced with a potentially dangerous client, what specific steps might you take to carry out this duty? Elect a recorder in each group, and when the class reconvenes, share your ideas.

2. Structure a class debate around the arguments for and against suicide prevention. Failure to prevent suicide is one of the main grounds for successful malpractice suits against mental-health professionals and institutions (Szasz, 1986). Consider debating a specific case of a client who is terminally ill with AIDS and decides that he wants to end his life because of his suffering and because there is no hope of getting better. Divide the class into teams for an exchange on the therapist's responsibility to prevent his suicide.

3. Consider inviting an attorney who is familiar with the legal aspects of counseling practice to address your class. Possible questions for consideration are: What are the legal rights of clients in therapy? Legally, what are the main responsibilities of therapists? What are some of the best ways to become familiar with laws pertaining to counselors? What are the grounds for lawsuits, and how can counselors best protect themselves from being sued? What are some key areas in which therapists have a duty to warn and a duty to protect? What are some future projections concerning the link between the law and ethical counseling practices?

4. Interview practicing counselors about some of their most pressing ethical concerns in carrying out their responsibilities. How have they dealt with some of

these ethical issues? What are some of their legal considerations? What are their concerns, if any, about malpractice suits?

5. Review the cases and situations presented in this chapter, and role-play some of them in dyads or in small groups. By actually experiencing these situations, you may be able to clarify some of your thoughts. If you role-play in your small group, the other members can give you valuable feedback on how they experienced you as a client or as a counselor.

6. Read some of the recent literature on malpractice and on how to reduce the chances of being sued. Students can research different aspects of malpractice and bring the findings to class for a general discussion.

7. In small groups discuss your own concerns about professional liability. How worried are you about being sued someday? What can you do to lessen the chances of being accused of not having practiced according to acceptable standards?

Suggested Readings

For discussions of the duty to warn and protect, landmark court cases, and guidelines for dealing with dangerous clients, see Laughran and Bakken (1984), Fulero (1988), Knapp, VandeCreek, and Herzog (1986), APA (1985), Bednar et al. (1991), and Austin et al. (1990). For a discussion of confidentiality and the duty to warn see Fischer and Sorenson (1991).

See Bednar et al. (1991) for a comprehensive treatment of legal and clinical duties in these areas: dangerousness, suicidal clients, informed consent, and involuntary civil commitment. On malpractice risks in treating dangerous patients see VandeCreek et al. (1987).

For guidelines on the assessment of suicidal behavior see Fujimura et al. (1985), Pope (1985b), Ray and Johnson (1983), Bednar et al. (1991), Berman and Jobes (1991), Bonger (1991), Austin et al. (1990), and Bennett et al. (1990). On the clinical and legal standards of care for suicidal patients see Bonger (1991). On assessment and intervention strategies in the area of adolescent suicide see Berman and Jobes (1991). For a provocative discussion of the case against suicide prevention see Szasz (1986). For a study on how client suicide affects practitioners see Chemtob, Bauer, Hamada, Pelowski, and Muraoka (1989).

For an overview of the law and ethics of counseling, protecting client confidences, and avoiding civil liability see Hopkins and Anderson (1990). See Austin et al. (1990) for a review of court cases and implications for therapists in these areas: records, confidentiality, privacy, defamation of character, failure to warn and protect, failure to take precautions against suicide, sexual misconduct, injury from nontraditional therapy, inadequate termination or abandonment, informed consent, illegal detainment, wrongful release, undue influence, and negligent supervision. For a treatment of the subject of laws pertaining to school counseling, psychology, and social workers, see Fischer & Sorenson (1991). On preparing for court appearances see Remley (1991).

For treatments of professional liability and malpractice see Austin et al. (1990), Bennett et al. (1990), Bednar et al. (1991), Woody & Associates (1984), Woody (1988), Van Hoose and Kottler (1985), Hopkins and Anderson (1990), Deardorff, Cross, and Hupprich (1984), Schutz (1982), DePauw (1986), Knapp (1980), Wright (1981), and Reaves (1986).

Dual Relationships in Counseling

Pre-Chapter Self-Inventory

Directions: For each statement, indicate the response that most closely identifies your beliefs and attitudes. Use the following code:

5 = I *strongly agree* with this statement.
4 = I *agree* with this statement.
3 = I am *undecided* about this statement.
2 = I *disagree* with this statement.
1 = I *strongly disagree* with this statement.

_____ 1. A good therapist gets involved in the client's case without getting involved with the client emotionally.

_____ 2. Touching, whether erotic or not, is best avoided in counseling, because it can easily be misunderstood by the client.

_____ 3. Therapists who touch clients of only one sex are guilty of sexist practice.

_____ 4. Although it may be unwise to form social relationships with clients while they are in counseling, there should be no ethical or professional prohibition against social relationships *after* counseling ends.

_____ 5. If I were a truly ethical professional, I would never be sexually attracted to a client.

_____ 6. If I were counseling a client who was sexually attracted to me, I might refer this client to another counselor.

_____ 7. I might be inclined to barter my therapeutic services for goods if my clients could not afford my fees.

_____ 8. If a client initiated the possibility of exchanging services in lieu of payment, I would consider bartering as an option.

_____ 9. Sexual involvement with a client is never ethical, even after therapy has ended.

_____ 10. I think that topics such as nonerotic touching, dealing with sexual attractions, and sexual dilemmas should be addressed throughout the counselor's training program.

_____ 11. Unethical behavior is anything that results in harm to the client.

_____ 12. If another professional were doing something I considered to be unethical, I would report him or her to the state licensing agency.

_____ 13. I should always be thinking about ways to lessen the chances of unethical behavior on my part.

_____ 14. Following the ethical codes of my profession implies that I will avoid unethical behavior.

_____ 15. It is inappropriate for a professional organization to have the power to sanction its members for unethical conduct.

_____ 16. Dual relationships are almost always problematic and therefore should be considered unethical.

_____ 17. Because dual relationships are so widespread, they should not be considered as either inappropriate or unethical in all circumstances but should be decided on a case-by-case basis.

_____ 18. I would have no trouble accepting a close friend as a client if we had a clear understanding of how our personal relationship could be separated from our professional one.

_____ 19. As long as my client felt comfortable with developing a social relationship with me once therapy was over, I would have little difficulty in forming such a relationship.

_____ 20. I think that my course work, training, and supervision have prepared me to deal with dual-relationship issues.

Introduction

Ethical problems are often raised when counselors blend their professional relationship with a client with another kind of relationship. Dual relationships, which can take many forms, have been called a violation of ethical, legal, and clinical standards (Pope, 1985a). In these situations a professional relationship is potentially impaired because of a combining of incompatible roles. A few examples of dual relationships, as described by Keith-Spiegel and Koocher (1985), are combining the roles of teacher and therapist (which we discussed in Chapter 2), bartering therapy for goods or services, providing therapy to a relative or a friend's relative, socializing outside therapy sessions, becoming emotionally or sexually involved with a client or former client, and combining the roles of supervisor and therapist (which we will discuss in Chapter 8).

The underlying theme of this chapter is the need for therapists to be honest and self-searching in determining the impact of their behavior on clients. Although some of the issues and cases we present may seem clear-cut to you, others may not be so cut-and-dried. In ambiguous cases it becomes a personal challenge to make an honest appraisal of your behavior and its effect on clients. Resolving the ethical dilemmas we pose requires personal and professional maturity and a willingness to continue to question one's own motivations. A key question is: Whose needs are being met, the therapist's or the clients? To us, behavior is unethical when it reflects a lack of awareness or concern about the impact of the behavior on clients. For some counselors it may take the form of placing their personal needs above the needs of their clients. Therapists who engage in more than one role with clients may be trying to meet their own financial, social, or emotional needs.

A good deal of this chapter deals with sexual relationships in therapy. We include a discussion of recent books and articles to give you a view of how the helping professions are dealing with this problem. And we examine the more subtle aspects of sexuality in therapy, including erotic attractions and the misuse of power.

Dual Relationships in Perspective

There has been increasing concern over dual relationships as an ethical issue. During the 1980s sexual relationships received considerable attention in the professional literature. It is clear that such relationships with clients are unethical, and all of the major professional ethics codes have specific prohibitions against them. However, nonsexual relationships have also been arousing increased interest (see Herlihy & Corey, 1992).

There is a wide range of viewpoints on dual relationships. If you are intent on being a conscientious professional and try to clarify your position on this issue, you will encounter conflicting advice. Some writers focus on the problems inherent in dual relationships. Pope (1985a) and Pope and Vasquez (1991), for instance, contend that such relationships tend to impair the therapist's judgment, that there is a potential for conflicts of interest, that there is a danger of exploiting the client because the professional occupies the more powerful position, and that boundaries become blurred and distort the professional nature of therapeutic relationships. Pope and Vasquez detail the rationalizations that therapists often use to justify, trivialize, and discount their practices of engaging in more than one role with clients. Some of these justifications include blocking out of awareness the potential for serious harm; focusing on the beneficial aspects of such relationships; asserting that these practices are widely prevalent, that they are inevitable and unavoidable, and that they reflect tradition; and emphasizing the right of clients to enter into relationships of their choice. According to Pope and Vasquez, skillful rationalization is an attempt to evade the professional responsibility of designing acceptable alternative approaches.

Other writers take a more moderate view and see the entire discussion of dual relationships as subtle and complex, defying simplistic solutions or absolute answers. After reviewing the literature on dual relationships, Herlihy and Corey (1992) suggest that they are inherent in the work of all helping professionals, regardless of their work setting or client population. Although the ethical codes of most professions caution against engaging in dual relationships, not all such relationships can be avoided (Keith-Spiegel & Koocher, 1985). They are not necessarily harmful, and there may be some beneficial aspects. For example, "mentoring" involves the blending of roles, yet both mentors and learners can certainly benefit from this relationship.

Herlihy and Corey conclude that there is no clear consensus regarding nonsexual relationships in counseling. It is the responsibility of practitioners to monitor themselves and to examine their motivations for engaging in such relationships. The decision whether to enter dual relationships should be based on what clients need rather than on protection of professionals from censure. In rural areas, for instance, mental-health practitioners may have to blend several professional roles and functions. They may find it more difficult to maintain clear boundaries than do those who work in a large city, and they may attend the same church or community functions as the clients they serve. In an isolated area a priest or a minister may seek counseling for a personal crisis from the only counselor in the town, who also happens to be a parishioner.

In the same vein, Kitchener and Harding (1990) contend that dual relationships range from those that are potentially seriously harmful to those that have little potential for harm. They maintain that even in cases where there is a low risk of damage, practitioners have an obligation to evaluate the risk and act responsibly:

Only after concluding that the risks of harm are small should they engage in relationships that have dual expectations. They should never enter in such relationships when the potential for harm is high unless there are strong offsetting, ethical benefits for the consumer and the risks are clearly discussed" [p. 153].

Herlihy and Corey (1992) indicate that when there is the potential for negative consequences, it is the responsibility of professionals to design safeguards to reduce the potential for harm. Some of these measures aimed at minimizing the risks inherent in dual relationships are:

- securing the informed consent of clients and discussing with them both the potential risks and benefits of dual relationships
- remaining willing to talk with clients about any unforeseen problems and conflicts that may arise
- consulting with other professionals as a means of resolving any dilemmas
- seeking supervision when dual relationships become particularly problematic or when the risk for harm is high
- documenting any dual relationships in clinical case notes and examining one's motivations for being involved in such relationships

We agree that dual relationships are not always unethical. But we challenge you to think about certain relationships that could place you in professional jeopardy. Rather than unequivocally condemning bartering of therapy for goods or services, for example, we ask you to reflect on how such an arrangement could complicate the therapeutic relationship.

Bartering for Professional Services

The practice of bartering psychotherapy for either goods or services has the potential for conflicts. When clients are unable to afford therapy, they may offer a bartering arrangement. Thus, a mechanic might exchange his or her work on a therapist's car for counseling sessions. If a client were expected to provide several hours of work on the therapist's car in exchange for a therapy session, this client might become resentful over the perceived imbalance of the exchange, especially if much more time were required for the repairs than for the session. The therapist might resent the client if his or her car were not repaired properly, and the client might suffer because of this resentment.

Problems of another sort can occur with this form of dual relationship, especially when clients clean house for the therapist, perform secretarial services, or do other personal work. Clients can easily be put in a bind when they are in a position to learn personal material about their therapists. In one of our case examples in this section, we have a massage therapist proposing an exchange of massages for her therapy sessions. The other case involves a proposal for the client to baby-sit for the therapist's children. Certainly, many problems can arise from these exchanges for both the therapist and the clients.

Ethical Standards

Most professional codes do not have a specific standard on bartering. The draft of the APA ethics code (1991a) includes a standard that discourages bartering as a general rule but also delineates circumstances when psychologists might become involved in such an arrangement:

> Psychologists ordinarily refrain from accepting goods, services, or other non-cash remuneration from patients or clients in return for psychological services because such arrangements create inherent potential [*sic*] for conflicts, exploitation, and distortion of the relationship. A psychologist may participate in bartering only if (1) the patient or client requests this method of payment, (2) unusual circumstances make it the only feasible option, (3) it is not clinically contraindicated, and (4) the relationship is not exploitative. When the client or patient is providing services as barter, the time required of them must be equitable.

We agree with the general tone of this standard, although we propose that it is more a matter of the financial value of the time, rather than the actual amount of time, that needs to be considered. In some cultures or in certain communities, bartering is an accepted practice. However, before bartering is entered into, it is essential that both parties talk about the arrangement, gain a clear understanding of the exchange, and come to an agreement. It is also important that they discuss the potential problems that might develop. Alternatives might also be looked at, such as using a sliding scale to determine fees. Bartering is an example of a dual relationship that we think allows some room for practitioners to use their professional judgment and to consider the cultural context in which they practice.

Two Case Examples

Consider the cases that we present below, and apply the APA's guideline and the principles that we have discussed to your analysis. What ethical issues are involved in each case? What potential problems do you see emerging from these cases? What alternatives to bartering can you think of?

○ ***The case of Barbara.***   Barbara is 20 years old and has been in therapy with Sidney for over a year. She has developed respect and fondness for her therapist, whom she sees as a father figure. She tells him that she is thinking of discontinuing therapy because she has lost her job and simply has no way of paying for the sessions. She is obviously upset over the prospect of ending the relationship, but she sees no alternative. Sidney informs her that he is willing to continue her therapy even if she is unable to pay. He suggests that as an exchange of services she can become the baby-sitter for his three children. She gratefully accepts this offer.

After a few months, however, Barbara finds that the situation is becoming difficult for her. Eventually, she writes a note to Sidney telling him that she cannot handle her reactions to his wife and their children. It makes her think of all the things she missed in her own family. She writes that she has found this subject difficult to bring up in her sessions, so she is planning to quit both her services and her therapy.

- What mistakes, if any, do you think that Sidney made?
- How would you have dealt with this situation? What might you have done differently?
- Do you think that it was unethical for the therapist to suggest that Barbara do baby-sitting for him? In doing so, to what degree did he take into consideration the nature of the transference relationship?

○ ***The case of Isle.*** Isle is a massage therapist in her community. Her services are sought by many professionals, including Gerard, a local psychologist. In the course of a massage session, she confides in him that she is experiencing difficulties in her marriage. She would like to discuss with him the possibility of exchanging their professional services. She proposes that in return for marital therapy she will give him massage treatments. An equitable arrangement based on their fee structure can be worked out, she says, and they will save some money on taxes as well. Assume that Gerard makes any one of the following responses:

Response A: "That's fine with me, Isle. It sounds like a good proposal. Neither one of us will suffer financially because of it, and we can each benefit from our expertise."

Response B: "Well, Isle, I feel OK about the exchange, except I have concerns about the dual relationship."

Response C: "Even though our relationship is nonsexual, Isle, I do feel squeamish about seeing you as a client in marital therapy. I certainly could refer you to a competent marital therapist."

- What do you think about each of the responses given by Gerard?
- What are your thoughts about Isle's proposal? What are the ethical implications in this case? List the possible ethical violations in this case.
- If you were in this situation, how would you deal with Isle?

Pope and Vasquez (1991) point out a particular problem with exchanging services:

> The therapist who is treating a patient in exchange for some services may find himself or herself manipulating or otherwise influencing the patient to provide better services or might become so critical of the patient's seemingly poor services that the therapeutic process becomes destructive for the patient [p. 116].

To what degree do you think this statement fits these two cases? What implications do you see?

Social Relationships with Clients

Do social relationships with clients necessarily interfere with therapeutic relationships? Some would say no, contending that counselors and clients are able to handle such a relationship as long as the priorities are clear. They see social contacts as particularly appropriate with clients who are not deeply disturbed and who are seeking personal growth. Some peer counselors, for example, maintain that friendships before or during counseling are actually positive factors in establishing trust.

Other counselors take the position that counseling and friendship should not be mixed. They argue that attempting to manage a social and professional relationship simultaneously can negatively affect the therapeutic process, the friendship, or both. Some of the reasons for discouraging the practice of accepting friends as clients or of becoming socially involved with clients are that (1) counselors may not be as confrontive with clients they know socially; (2) counselors' own needs to be liked and accepted may lead them to be less challenging, lest the friendship or social relationship be jeopardized; (3) counselors' own needs may be enmeshed with those of their clients to the point that objectivity is lost; and (4) counselors are in a more powerful position than clients, and the possibility of exploiting clients becomes more likely when the relationship takes on social dimensions. Woody argues that "therapists should never socialize with clients or engage in any other form of dual relationship" (1988, p. 184).

In a survey of dual relationships between therapist and client (Borys & Pope, 1989), psychologists, psychiatrists, and social workers rated the following practices as being "never ethical":

- accepting a client's invitation to a special occasion (6.3%)
- becoming friends with a client after termination (14.8%)
- inviting clients to an office or clinic open house (26.6%)
- going out to eat with a client after a session (43.2%)
- inviting a client to a personal party or social event (63.5%)

In a study on the beliefs and behaviors of therapists (Pope, Tabachnick, & Keith-Spiegel, 1987), 42.1% of respondents said that they never became friends with a *former* client, and 6.4% considered the behavior unethical. Regarding inviting clients to a party or social event, 82.9% said they had never engaged in the behavior, and 50% viewed this behavior as unethical.

It is our view that the blending of social and personal relationships is not a closed issue that can be resolved with a dogmatic answer. We question the assumption that social involvement with a client other than in the office implies an unwillingness to challenge the client and automatically makes the therapist less objective. Although the possibility exists that therapists may be less confrontive because of their fear of losing the relationship, we do not think that all forms of out-of-office contacts necessarily preclude honest and effective confrontation. Counselors need to be aware of their own motivations, as well as the motivations of their prospective clients, and they must objectively assess the impact a social relationship might have on the client/therapist relationship. This issue can take several forms. To illustrate, we'll ask you to respond to a specific case.

You are an intern in a college counseling center, and one of your clients says to you: "I really like working with you, but I hate coming over here to this cold and impersonal office. I always feel weird waiting in the lobby as if I were a 'case' or something. Why can't we meet outside on the lawn? Better yet, we could get away from campus and meet in the park nearby. I'd feel more natural and uninhibited in a more informal setting."

- Would you agree to meet your client outside the office?
- Would your decision depend on how much you liked or were attracted to your client? Would your client's age and sex have much to do with your decision?

Later, your client invites you to a party and lets you know that it would mean a lot if you were to come. Your client says: "I'd really like to get to know you on a personal basis, because I'm being so deeply personal in here. I really like you, and I'd like more time with you than the hour we have each week."

- What are your immediate reactions? Assuming that you like your client and would like to go to the party, do you think it would be wise to attend? What would your decision be, and what would you say to your client? How would you support your decision?
- What effect do you think meeting your client on a social basis would have on the therapeutic process?

One of the reviewers of this book takes the position that social relationships with clients are *never* appropriate. The reviewer argues that counselors make themselves vulnerable legally if they enter into such relationships. Ethically, there is the problem that therapists are not so superhuman that they can manage dual relationships that demand different responses.

Certainly, there are problems when professional and social relationships are blended. Such arrangements demand a great deal of honesty and self-awareness on the part of the therapist. They also take a high degree of maturity on the client's part. It is possible that when clear boundaries are not maintained, both the professional and the social relationship can sour. It is important to consider the client's ability (or inability) to keep the two relationships separate. Clients may well become inhibited during the therapy hour out of fear of alienating their therapist. They may fear losing the respect of a therapist with whom they have a friendship. They may censor their disclosures so that they do not threaten this social relationship.

Your stance on the issue of socializing with clients will be influenced by a number of factors. There are many types of socializing, ranging from dating a client to merely attending a social function organized by a client. There are differences between a social involvement initiated by a client and one instigated by a therapist. Another factor to consider is whether the social contact is ongoing as opposed to occasional. Also important is the degree of intimacy involved. Is the contact one that is public, or does it involve a private setting? For instance, there is a difference between meeting a client for coffee and having a candlelight dinner. In thinking through your own position, you will need to consider the nature of the social function, the nature of your client's problem, the client population, the setting where you work, the kind of therapy being employed, and your theoretical approach. If you are psychoanalytically oriented, you are likely to adopt clear boundaries and will be concerned about polluting the transference relationship should you blend any form of socializing with the therapy. If you are a behavior therapist helping a client stop smoking, it may be possible to have social contact at some point. In weighing the various issues raised, what are your thoughts on this matter from both the client's and the therapist's perspective?

Sexual Attractions in the Client/Therapist Relationship

In a pioneering study, "Sexual Attraction to Clients: The Human Therapist and the (Sometimes) Inhuman Training System," Pope, Keith-Spiegel, and Tabachnick (1986) develop the theme that there has been a lack of systematic research into the sexual attraction of therapists to their clients. This silence gives the impression that therapists are incapable of being sexually attracted to those they serve or that the phenomenon is a regrettable aberration limited to the few who sexually act out with clients. Many therapists feel that if they do experience sexual attractions toward clients, they are guilty of therapeutic errors. The authors of this study provide clear evidence that attraction to clients is a prevalent experience among both male and female therapists. The authors investigated questions such as the following: What is the frequency of sexual attraction to clients by therapists? Do therapists feel guilty or uncomfortable when they have such attractions? Do they tend to tell their clients about their attractions? Do they consult with colleagues? Do therapists believe that their graduate training provided adequate education on attraction to clients?

Pope and his colleagues studied 585 respondents. Only 77 reported never having been attracted to any client. The vast majority (82%) reported that they had never seriously considered actual sexual involvement with a client. An even larger majority (93.5%) reported never having had sexual relations with their clients. Therapists gave a number of reasons for having refrained from acting out their attractions to clients, including a need to uphold professional values, a concern about the welfare of the client, and a desire to follow personal values. Although fears of negative consequences were mentioned, they were less frequent than values pertaining to client welfare. Most respondents (69%) believed that sexual attractions to clients were useful or beneficial, at least in some instances, to the therapy. With respect to the client's being aware of the therapist's attraction, 71% believed that the client was probably not aware. Most therapists (81%) believed that the attraction had been mutual. Over half (55%) indicated that they had received no education on the subject of sexual attraction to clients in their graduate training and internships. Twenty-four percent had received "very little," 12% had received "some," and 9% thought that they had received adequate preparation in dealing with sexual attraction to clients. Those who had had some graduate training in this area were more likely to have sought consultation (66%) than were those with no such training.

Another study on the beliefs and behaviors of psychologists as therapists shed light on the topic of sexual attractions in therapy (Pope et al., 1987). In this study only 9.2% of the respondents said they had never been "sexually attracted to a client"; 11.2% of them considered this behavior unethical. With respect to "engaging in sexual fantasy about a client," 27% said they had never engaged in this behavior; and 18.9% considered this behavior unethical. With respect to telling a client "I'm sexually attracted to you," 78.5% said they had never done so; 51.5% considered this behavior unethical.

Dealing with Sexual Feelings toward a Client

There is a distinction between finding a client sexually attractive and being preoccupied with this attraction. Bennett, Bryant, VandenBos, and Greenwood (1990) offer suggestions on how therapists can deal with powerful attractions to clients:

- Explore the reasons why you are attracted to a client. Ask if there is something about this person that meets one of your needs.
- Seek out an experienced colleague who might be able to help you decide on a course of action.
- Seek personal counseling, if necessary, to help you resolve your feelings about this client and to uncover the issues in your life that you may not be dealing with.
- If you are unable to resolve your feelings appropriately, terminate the professional relationship, and refer the client to another therapist.

Consider these guidelines, and imagine yourself becoming attracted to one of your clients. You're aware that your client has sexual feelings toward you and would be willing to become involved with you. Your own feelings are growing in intensity, and you often have difficulty paying attention during sessions because of your fantasies.

1. Would you interpret this situation in any of the following ways?
   - This is a sure sign of the beginning of countertransference.
   - My feelings are acceptable and can easily be hidden from the client.
   - This is something to be discussed immediately with the client, with a strong recommendation for referral.
   - My own needs have become more important than my client's needs.
   - I need to consult with a colleague.
   - I have serious problems.
2. What do you think about the appropriateness of each of the following courses of action when you are sexually attracted to a client?
   - I could ignore my feelings for the client and my client's feelings toward me and focus on other aspects of the relationship.
   - I could tell my client of my feelings of attraction, discontinue the professional relationship, and then begin a personal relationship.
   - I could openly express my feelings toward my client by saying: "I'm glad you find me an attractive person, and I'm strongly attracted to you as well. But this relationship is not about our attraction for each other, and I'm sure that's not why you came here."
   - If there were no change in the intensity of my feelings toward my client, I could arrange for a referral to another therapist.
   - I could consult with a colleague or seek professional supervision.

Which of the above courses of action would you take, and why? Can you think of another direction in which you might proceed? Why would you choose this direction?

○ ***The case of Diana.***   Diana's husband, a police officer, was killed in the line of duty, leaving her with three young children. She seeks professional help from Clint and works through her grief, in the process uncovering some deep-rooted abandonment issues pertaining to other areas in her life. After three years of therapy, she and Clint discuss termination. During this final stage of therapy she confesses to him that she is finding it increasingly difficult to think of not seeing him anymore. She has grown fond of him, she finds herself constantly thinking about him, and she wonders if they could continue to see each other socially, maybe even romantically. At first he is taken aback. But he also realizes that throughout the course of therapy he has come to admire and respect her, and he discloses his fondness for her. He explains to her that because of their professional relationship, he is bound by ethical guidelines not to become involved with his clients socially or romantically. He proposes to her that they not see each other for a year but that if their feelings persist, he will then consider initiating a personal relationship. Diana expresses her disappointment at the year's delay but agrees to the stipulation rather than have no hopes at all. They warmly embrace, and Diana leaves the office.

• What are your thoughts about Clint's way of handling the situation? Do you see any possible ethical violations in how the case evolved?
• Do you see any therapeutic issues that he did not explore?
• If he had been attracted to Diana but had withheld this information for therapeutic reasons, would you consider that to be ethical behavior? Why or why not?
• What if he had had no feelings of attraction or desire to continue any sort of relationship but had said what he did to avoid a difficult ending? How ethical would that be? If you were in such a situation and did not want to pursue the relationship, how might you deal with Diana?
• What are your reactions to their warm embrace at the end?

Sexual Relationships: Ethical and Legal Issues

The issue of erotic contact in therapy is not simply a matter of whether to have sexual intercourse with a client. Even if you decide intellectually that you wouldn't engage in such intimacies, it's important to realize that the relationship between therapist and client can involve varying degrees of sexuality. Therapists may have sexual fantasies, they may behave seductively with their clients, they may influence clients to focus on romantic or sexual feelings toward them, or they may engage in physical contact that is primarily intended to arouse or satisfy their sexual desires. Their behavior is clearly sexual in nature and can have much the same effect as direct sexual involvement would have. Sexual overtones can easily distort the therapeutic relationship and become the real focus of the sessions. It is crucial that practitioners learn to accept their sexual feelings and consciously decide how to deal with them in therapy.

During the past decade a number of studies have documented the harm that sexual relationships with clients can cause. As you will see in Chapter 8, there has also been considerable writing on the damage done to students and supervisees when educators and supervisors enter into sexual relationships with them. Later in this section we discuss the negative effects on clients that typically occur when the client/therapist relationship becomes sexualized.

The Scope of the Problem

Sexual misconduct is considered to be one of the most serious of all ethical violations for a therapist, and as we said in Chapter 5, it is also the leading cause of malpractice suits. The journal *The California Therapist* carries a section on disciplinary actions in each issue. A cursory review of this section generally reveals that most therapists who are subject to disciplinary actions by both the Board of Behavioral Science Examiners and the Board of Psychology have been charged with sexual misconduct. In the May/June 1991 issue, for example, the following three charges against therapists are reported:

- A licensed clinical social worker was accused of "unprofessional conduct, gross negligence or incompetence in that respondent created a dual and personal relationship by sleeping in the same bed with a patient after therapy. Respondent further created a dual relationship by providing therapy to the client's child patients" (p. 33).
- A licensed marriage, family, and child counselor was charged with "alleged sexual misconduct with a client, gross negligence, incompetence, intentionally or recklessly causing physical or emotional harm to a client, and dishonest, corrupt or fraudulent acts. Respondent had previously been disciplined by the board for sexual misconduct with a client" (p. 34).
- A licensed psychologist was charged with "sexual misconduct with clients [and] gross negligence—social relationships with clients" (p. 35).

Not only do clients who are the victims of sexual misconduct suffer dire consequences, but those therapists who engage in sexual intimacies with clients (or former clients) risk negative consequences for themselves, both personally and professionally. They may be the target of a lawsuit, be convicted of a felony, have their license revoked, be expelled from professional organizations, lose their insurance coverage, and lose their job (Vasquez & Kitchener, 1988). They may also be placed on probation, be required to undergo their own psychotherapy, be closely monitored if they are allowed to resume their practice, and be required to obtain supervised practice.

Holroyd and Brodsky (1977) report the results of a nationwide survey of 500 male and 500 female licensed psychologists, all Ph.D.s, that was conducted to assess their attitudes and practices with respect to erotic and nonerotic contact with clients. The return rate was 70%, and the findings include these:

- Erotic contact and intercourse were almost always between male therapists and female clients.
- Therapists who crossed the sexual boundary once were likely to do so again. Of those who reported intercourse with patients, 80% had repeated it.
- Of the male therapists, 5.5% reported having had sexual intercourse with clients; for female therapists the figure was 0.6%
- Seventy percent of male therapists and 88% of female therapists took the position that erotic contact was never beneficial to clients.

Most of the psychologists responding strongly disapproved of erotic contact in therapy and contended that it should never occur in a professional relationship. They took the position that such contact was totally inappropriate and was an exploitation of the relationship by the therapist. Erotic contact with clients was thus viewed as unprofessional, unethical, and antitherapeutic.

A Continuum of Sexual Contact with Clients

Coleman and Schaefer (1986) write that sexual abuse of clients by counselors can best be considered along a continuum ranging from psychological abuse to covert and overt abuse: (1) In *psychological abuse* the client is put in the position of becoming the emotional caretaker of the counselor's needs. Therapists may meet their own needs for intimacy through the client, reverse roles with the client, or self-disclose without aiding the client. (2) In *covert abuse* the counselor's boundary confusion with the client becomes more pronounced as he or she displays behaviors with intended sexual connotations. The result is a further intrusion into the client's intimacy boundaries. Common forms of this level of abuse include sexual hugs, professional voyeurism, sexual gazes, overattention to the client's dress and appearance, and seductiveness through dress and gestures. (3) At the far end of the continuum are overt forms of sexual misconduct. This category includes the most clearly recognized forms of counselor abuse: sexual remarks, passionate kissing, fondling, sexual intercourse, oral or anal sex, and sexual penetration with objects.

Ethical Standards on Sexual Intimacy

Virtually all of the professional organizations now have a specific statement condemning sexual intimacies in the client/therapist relationship, as can be seen in this summary of relevant codes. It is clear from the statements of the major mental-health organizations that these principles go beyond merely condemning sexual relationships with clients.

Sexual Relations in Therapy: Summary of Codes of Ethics

American Association for Counseling and Development (1988):

- "The member will avoid any type of sexual intimacies with clients. Sexual intimacies with clients are unethical."

(continued)

American Psychiatric Association (1989):

- "The necessary intensity of the therapeutic relationship may tend to activate sexual and other needs and fantasies on the part of both patient and therapist, while weakening the objectivity necessary for control. Sexual activity with a patient is unethical. Sexual involvement with one's former patients generally exploits emotions deriving from treatment and therefore almost always is unethical."

American Association for Marriage and Family Therapy (1991):

- "Sexual intimacy with clients is prohibited. Sexual intimacy with former clients for two years following the termination of therapy is prohibited."

National Association of Social Workers (1990):

- "The social worker should under no circumstances engage in sexual activities with clients."

American Psychoanalytic Association (1983):

- "Sexual relationships between analyst and patient are antithetical to treatment and unacceptable under any circumstances. Any sexual activity with a patient constitutes a violation of this principle of ethics."

American Psychological Association (1991a):

- "Psychologists do not engage in sexual intimacies with current patients or clients."
- "Psychologists do not accept as patients or clients persons with whom they have previously engaged in sexual intimacies."
- "In no case may a psychologist engage in sexual intimacies with a former psychotherapy patient or client within one year after cessation or termination of professional services."

Harmful Effects of Sexual Intimacy on Clients

Bouhoutsos, Holroyd, Lerman, Forer, and Greenberg (1983) suggest that when sexual intercourse begins, therapy as a helping process ends. When sex is involved in a therapeutic relationship, the therapist loses control of the course of therapy. The researchers concluded that sexual contact was especially disruptive if it began early in the relationship and if it had been initiated by the therapist. Ninety percent of 559 clients in their study who became sexually involved with their therapists were adversely affected. This harm ranged from mistrust of opposite-sex relationships to hospitalization and, in some cases, suicide. Other effects of sexual intimacies on clients' emotional, social, and sexual adjustment included negative feelings about the experience, a negative impact on their personality, and a deterioration of their sexual relationship with their primary partner. The authors contend that the harmfulness of sexual contact in therapy validates the ethical codes barring such conduct and provides a rationale for enacting legislation prohibiting it.

Commenting on the study by Bouhoutsos and her colleagues, Coleman and Schaefer (1986) describe other negative outcomes such as depression and other emotional disturbances, impaired social adjustment, and substance abuse. Many clients found that their primary relationships deteriorated. Even though these clients felt that their emotional problems had increased, they also found it more difficult to seek out further therapy because of their previous negative experience.

According to Coleman and Schaefer, the psychological and covert forms of abuse may be more damaging than overt abuse. In cases involving overt actions there is no question about the ethical violation, and clients often feel justified in considering themselves abused. With either psychological or covert abuse, however, clients are likely to feel more confusion, guilt, and shame.

Research conducted by Holroyd and Bouhoutsos (1985) suggests that the estimate that 90% of involved clients were harmed may even be low. This study found that therapists who reported that clients had not been harmed admitted a greater prevalence of sexual intimacy with their clients than did therapists in the population at large. Thus, biased reporting may be a significant factor in the estimate that 10% of clients were unharmed.

Pope (1988) describes a syndrome that is associated with sexual contact between therapist and client. The syndrome bears a striking relationship to the rape syndrome, the battered-spouse syndrome, and the responses to child abuse. Some of the aspects of the therapist/client syndrome are ambivalence, guilt, emptiness and isolation, sexual confusion, an impaired ability to trust, identity and role confusion, emotional liability, suppressed rage, increased suicidal risk, and cognitive dysfunction. After his extensive survey of the research on the harmful consequences of sexual intimacies with clients, Pope (1988) concludes that awareness of this problem can help professionals avoid the temptation to act out sexual attractions to clients. This awareness can challenge the mental-health professions to create effective measures to ensure that clients are protected from exploitive therapists, and it can help other professionals recognize and respond therapeutically to victims who have experienced distress over this abuse.

The Committee on Women in Psychology of the APA (1989) asserts that sexual relationships between therapists and clients are never the fault of the client, that such relationships are never appropriate or helpful in therapy, and that therapists can never be excused for sexual misconduct. This committee contends that sexual contact destroys the objectivity that is necessary for effective therapeutic relationships and that it damages not only clients' trust in the therapist but also their trust in other people, including other therapists. Although the negative impact may be apparent almost immediately, it often does not become evident until later. Clients typically feel taken advantage of and may discount the value of any part of their therapy. They may become embittered and angry, and they may terminate therapy with psychological scars. The problem is compounded if they are deterred from initiating therapy with anyone else because of their traumatic experience.

Legal Sanctions against Sexual Violators

Clients have sued therapists who engaged in sex with them. Psychologists found guilty of malpractice have been given sanctions, have been expelled from the APA, have had their license revoked or suspended by the state, and have been ordered to undergo therapy to resolve their problems. Austin, Moline, and Williams (1990) reviewed relevant court cases and came to the conclusion that therapists who had engaged in sex with their clients had few arguments they could use in court. Courts have rejected claims of consent by clients, mainly because of the vulnerability of clients and the power of the transference relationship.

Some states have legal sanctions in cases of sexual misconduct in the therapeutic relationship. Sexual intimacy with a client is considered a felony in the states of Colorado, Wisconsin, and Minnesota (Pope, 1988). In 1984 the Minnesota Legislature created a task force on sexual exploitation by psychotherapists after numerous complaints by victims. In Minnesota it is a felony to have sexual contact with a client during the therapy session, and in certain cases the counselor may be found guilty of sexual misconduct even if the contact occurred outside the session. Client consent cannot be used as a defense (Coleman & Schaefer, 1986).

A California law makes it a criminal offense to have sexual contact with a client. An offender is charged with a misdemeanor on the first offense; second and following offenses may be a misdemeanor or a felony. Offenders are subject to being fined and/or sentenced to county jail or state prison for up to one year. This California law applies to two situations: (1) the therapist has sexual contact with a client during therapy, and (2) the therapist ends therapy for the purpose of beginning a sexual relationship with the client (California Department of Consumer Affairs, undated).

Other states have passed legislation making it considerably easier to remove licenses in situations involving sexual misconduct. In those states it is no longer necessary to prove that damage has resulted from sexual intimacy with a therapist; rather, the only question is whether the sexual intimacy occurred (Holroyd & Bouhoutsos, 1985). These laws state that the ultimate ethical and legal burden of responsibility to avoid sexual relationships rests squarely on the licensed professional. Consistent with such laws is the position of Coleman and Schaefer (1986) that the counselor must take responsibility for setting appropriate sexual boundaries for the client, communicate these boundaries, and keep the relationship a professional rather than a personal one. It is clear that professionals cannot argue that the client seduced them. Even if clients behave in seductive ways, it is clearly the professional's responsibility to maintain the appropriate boundaries.

Ethical Sanctions

There are definite procedures for filing and processing ethical complaints against psychologists, and such complaints are dealt with by the state professional associations and by the APA's Committee on Scientific and Professional Ethics and Conduct. Sanders and Keith-Spiegel (1980) present a summary of an investigation of a psychologist who was accused of becoming sexually involved with his female client after two years of therapy. The psychologist promptly terminated the therapeutic relationship, according to the client, yet no attempt was made to resolve the therapeutic issues remaining. The sexual relationship continued for about a year, on a weekly basis, until it was finally cut off by the client because of her guilt and disgust over the situation. The psychologist made two attempts to resume the affair, but the client refused to become involved.

Although the psychologist at first flatly denied the client's charges, he eventually admitted that they were true. He also said that he loved his client, that he was struggling with a midlife crisis, and that he was having severe marital problems. He added that he was willing to seek personal therapy to work on his problems.

In this case the state psychological association voted to monitor the psychologist's personal therapy and have his practice reviewed for one year. In his hearing before the APA's ethics committee he gave a progress report on his personal therapy and attempted to convince the committee members that the insights he had gained would preclude the recurrence of this sort of ethical violation in the future. The committee offered a stipulated resignation from the APA for five years, after which he might reapply if no further ethical violations had been brought to the association.

In thinking about this case, attempt to answer these questions:

- Do you think that this psychologist should have been allowed to continue his professional practice? Why or why not?
- If you had been a member of the ethics committee that reviewed this case, what action would you have recommended?
- If the psychologist was aware that he had fallen in love with his client and wanted to become sexually involved with her (yet had not done so), what ethical course of action could he have taken? Is termination of the professional relationship enough?

Assisting Victims in the Complaint Process

In spite of the fact that the number of complaints of sexual misconduct against therapists has risen dramatically, women still report great reluctance in filing complaints for disciplinary action against their therapists, educators, and supervisors (Gottlieb, 1990; Hotelling, 1991; Howard, 1991; Riger, 1991). Many clients do not know that sexual contact between counselors and clients is unethical and illegal. They are often unaware that they can file a complaint, and they frequently do not know the avenues available to them to address sexual misconduct. Hotelling (1988) describes ethical, legal, and administrative options for individuals who have been victims of professional misconduct. Clients can file an ethical complaint with a professional association or with the therapist's licensing board. Another option is to lodge a complaint with the counselor's employer. There are also legal alternatives: civil suits or criminal actions. A malpractice suit on civil grounds seeks compensatory damages for the client for the cost of treatment and for the suffering involved. Each option has both advantages and disadvantages, and it is ultimately up to clients to decide what is best for them. However, it is an obligation of the profession to take steps to increase public awareness about the nature and extent of sexual misconduct and also to educate the public about possible courses of action.

In his article on assisting victims in the complaint process, Gottlieb (1990) describes the institutional barriers within the profession that lead women to feel intimidated and deterred by the complaint procedures. He suggests the need for establishing an organizational structure to help them. Howard (1991) also focuses on the need for written policies and consistent, accessible grievance procedures for addressing sexual violations. Asserting that the profession has an obligation to do more than merely process ethical complaints, Gottlieb encourages the creation of a Committee for Complaint Assistance within each state or provincial professional association. The main goal of the committee is to reach out to clients, students, and trainees who have been abused by professionals. Another function would be to educate the public and the profession about the problem.

Sexual Relationships with Former Clients

What are the ethics of beginning a sexual relationship once therapy has ended? In the absence of clear guidelines, according to Coleman and Schaefer (1986), counselors must make their own ethical decisions. The authors add that sentiment seems to be building that such contact is an ethical violation. Gutheil (1989) asserts that many professionals wrongly operate on the assumption that sexual relationships are permissible if a client's therapy has ended or if there is a termination with a referral. Gutheil emphasizes the principle that to avoid a possible legal or ethical conflict, practitioners should not establish a social or sexual relationship with either a present or a past client.

In general agreement with Gutheil are Sell, Gottlieb, and Schoenfeld (1986), who contend that it is ethically questionable to assume that the therapeutic relationship ends at a finite point and that a social or sexual relationship with a former client is then permissible. State licensing boards and ethics committees have tended to rule against psychologists who use the defense that the professional relationship had ended. Sell and his colleagues believe that the only realistic way to deal with the problem is to prohibit posttreatment sexual relations altogether. They take a position that they recognize as being controversial and one that leaves no room for compromise: "We contend that sexual relationships with former clients are exploitive and unethical if they follow any therapeutic relationship, regardless of the elapsed time" (p. 507).

Although all states specifically prohibit sexual intimacies with clients, some have gone further and are requiring a waiting period after termination. Licensed counselors in Texas and California are prohibited from having sexual relationships with clients for two years after counseling has ended (Herlihy & Corey, 1992). In Florida it is illegal for a therapist to have sex with a former client no matter how long it has been since the therapy ended (Bates & Brodsky, 1989). Woody (1988) suggests that individuals who have been clients should always be considered clients. He cites the rule of the Florida Board of Psychological Examiners: "For purposes of determining the existence of sexual misconduct . . . , the psychologist-client relationship is deemed to continue in perpetuity" (pp. 183–184). If there are grounds to believe that treatment was ended in order to give the appearance of compliance with the ethical proscription against sexual intimacies between client and therapist, ethics committees will find that there has been a clear violation (Gottlieb, 1990). Data gathered by Sell and his colleagues (1986) contradict the premise that once the professional relationship ends, social and romantic relationships are permissible.

In a national survey of APA members, Akamatsu (1988) found that 44.7% of the respondents believed that intimate relationships with former clients were highly unethical, 23.9% felt that they were somewhat unethical, and 22.9% rated them as "neither ethical nor unethical." This study identified factors that should be taken into account in determining the ethics of intimate relationships with former clients: the length of time since termination, transference issues, the length of the therapy, the nature of the therapy, the nature of the termination, the client's degree of freedom of choice, any exploitation of the client, the client's mental health, and any harm to the client.

Although the mental-health professions have not completely resolved the question of whether sexual relationships with former clients are ever acceptable, there appears to be a trend toward prohibiting this behavior. The revised ethical code of the American Psychiatric Association (1989) adds this element: "Sexual involvement with one's former patients generally exploits emotions deriving from treatment and therefore almost always is unethical." The AAMFT has a more specific clause, which includes a prohibition of sexual involvement with former clients for two years after the termination of a therapy relationship. The draft ethics code of the APA (1991a) states: "Psychologists do not engage in sexual intimacies with former psychotherapy patients or clients except in the most unusual circumstances. The psychologist who engages in such activity bears the burden of demonstrating that there has been no exploitation." Another clause states that therapists are not allowed, in any case, to engage in sexual intimacies with a former client for at least one year after therapy ends. At this time, the AACD and the NASW have not taken a definite position with respect to romantic relationships with former clients.

Bennett and his colleagues (1990) offer several suggestions to those considering initiating a relationship with a former clients:

- Be aware that developing a personal relationship with a former client is illegal in some jurisdictions and that therapists have been sued for malpractice for engaging in this practice.
- Reflect on the reasons for termination. If you, the client, or both of you experienced an attraction before ending therapy, was the professional relationship terminated for an appropriate reason or so that a sexual relationship could develop?
- Ask yourself about the potential benefits and risks of developing a personal relationship with a former client. Will there be effects on other family members?
- Before initiating such a relationship, consider discussing the matter with a colleague.

At this point, reflect on your own stand on the controversial issue of forming sexual relationships once therapy has ended. Consider these questions in clarifying your position:

- Do you think that counselors should be free to formulate their own practices about developing a sexual relationship with former clients?
- Does the length and quality of the therapeutic relationship have a bearing on the ethics involved in such a personal relationship? If a client was in therapy for several years and struggled with an intense transference relationship with her therapist, for example, would it be ethical for them to establish a personal relationship two years after her therapy had ended? If a client saw her counselor for only six sessions to learn how to cope with stress, would it be ethical for them to get involved personally two years after her final session?
- Do you think that sexual relationships with former clients are unethical, regardless of the elapsed time or regardless of the type of therapy? Do you see any exceptions that might justify developing intimate relationships with former clients?
- What guidelines can you come up with to determine the ethics of personal relationships with former clients?

Educating Counselor Trainees to Deal with Sexual Dilemmas

As you can see from the previous discussion, sexual intimacy in the therapeutic relationship has harmful effects on the client and the therapist (Bates & Brodsky, 1989; Bouhoutsos et al., 1983; Brodsky, 1986; Pope, 1988, 1990b; Pope & Bouhoutsos, 1986). Although counselor/client sexual contact is one of the most common ethical violations, most training programs spend little or no time addressing the prohibition. Nor do these programs devote much time to dealing with sexual attraction to clients (Pope, 1987; Pope et al., 1986; Rodolfa, Kitzrow, Vohra, & Wilson, 1990; Vasquez, 1988). Moreover, little attention has been given to the ethical aspects of nonerotic physical contact (Holub & Lee, 1990) (see the next section).

In their discussion of ways to reduce sexual misconduct, Stake and Oliver (1991) indicate that a multifaceted approach is needed, including changes in legal codes, consumer education, and training for therapists. They suggest that the best approach is encouraging training programs to include the topic of sexual misconduct as a basic component of ethics education and also providing continuing education for therapists.

We think that training programs have a responsibility to help students identify and openly discuss their concerns pertaining to the resolving of sexual dilemmas in counseling practice. Prevention of sexual misconduct is a better path than remediation. Gutheil (1989), for example, suggests that students should receive explicit instruction on the ethical, legal, and clinical issues pertaining to sexual abuses. Holub and Lee (1990) recommend that these issues be addressed in clinical supervision, in ethics seminars, in continuing-education programs, in in-service training, and formally by ethics committees. They also recommend that trainees experience personal therapy as a way to better clarify their own needs and motivations.

Rodolfa and his colleagues (1990) describe training seminars on sexual dilemmas. Small groups typically explore cases such as these:

- A therapist feels sexually attracted to a client.
- A supervisor and a supervisee are mutually attracted to each other.
- A therapist feels attracted to a former client.
- During an intake session, a client reports a sexual involvement with a previous therapist.

Some of the topics that are generally covered during the seminar are these:

- an overview of sexual dilemmas and the distinction between having sexual feelings and acting on them
- dealing with attractions between client and therapist and preparing trainees to respond in ethical and therapeutic ways
- interventions after clients have been sexually involved with another therapist
- intervening with a therapist who is sexually attracted to a client or sexually involved with a client
- attraction between supervisees and supervisors
- feelings during sex therapy and sexual assessments

These seminars encourage interns to work through some of the complex issues involved. The aim is to assist them to think flexibly and develop options that satisfy professional responsibilities and adhere to ethical standards. Most therapists will encounter sexual dilemmas during their careers, and some formal training in this area is vital.

Vasquez (1988) addresses specific strategies for preventing counselor/client sexual contact. These strategies include providing students with knowledge, conducting experiential activities that promote their self-awareness, and encouraging a climate that enhances the development of ethical values and behavior. With respect to their *knowledge*, students need to learn about the legal and professional consequences of sexual misconduct. They especially need to know about the deleterious consequences for clients. *Experiential activities* are particularly useful in dealing with issues such as touching in counseling, maintaining proper boundaries, and managing sexual feelings. Role-playing situations can heighten a trainee's sensitivity to the complexity of relationship issues. Vasquez also underscores the place of modeling of ethical behavior by faculty members and clinical supervisors. In addition, educational programs need to provide a *safe environment* where students can acknowledge and explore matters such as sexual attraction and learn how to respond ethically.

Herlihy and Corey (1992) focus on the responsibility of training programs to help students identify and openly discuss their concerns about sexual temptations. Ignoring this subject in training sends a message to students that the subject should not be talked about and probably inhibits their willingness to seek consultation when they encounter sexual dilemmas in their practice.

A Special Case: Nonerotic Physical Contact with Clients

Although we contend that acting on sexual feelings and engaging in erotic contact with clients is unethical, we do think that *nonerotic* contact is often appropriate and can have significant therapeutic value. It is important to stress this point, because some counselors perceive a taboo against touching clients. Therapists may hold back when they feel like touching their clients affectionately or compassionately. They may feel that touching can be misinterpreted as sexual or exploitative; they may be afraid of their impulses or feelings toward clients; they may be afraid of intimacy; or they may believe that to express closeness physically is unprofessional. With the current attention being given to sexual harassment and lawsuits over sexual misconduct in professional relationships, some counselors are likely to decide that it is not worth the risk of touching clients at all, lest their intentions be misinterpreted. Although touching does not necessarily constitute a dual relationship, we include this discussion here because certain kinds of touching can lead to dual relationships. A therapist's touch can be a genuine expression of caring, or it can be done primarily to gratify the therapist's own needs.

There are two sides to the issue of touching, for some studies support it and others do not. After reviewing both the research and clinical data, Willison and Masson (1986) found some indication that touching could be therapeutic when used appropriately. They also found little evidence of any negative effects of appropriate touching. (By appropriate touching they mean nonsexual contact aimed at fostering therapeutic progress and serving the client's needs.) Some clinicians, however, oppose any form of physical contact between counselors and clients, on the grounds that it can promote dependency, can interfere with the transference relationship, can be misread by clients, and can become sexualized.

Although research into the use of touching in therapy has produced mixed findings, there do appear to be some therapeutic benefits to nonerotic physical contact. In writing about a men's therapy group, Rabinowitz (1991) cites research findings indicating that appropriate touching can foster self-exploration, increase verbal interaction, increase the client's perception of the expertness of the counselor, and produce more positive attitudes toward the counseling process.

There is also evidence that most psychologists do not consider it unethical to hug a client or a student. In one study only 13.4% of the therapists reported that they had never hugged a client and only 4.6% viewed hugging a client as unethical (Pope et al., 1987). In another study, 28.4% of educators said that they had never hugged a student and 5.6% of them viewed such behavior as unethical (Tabachnick et al., 1991). Of course, hugging clients or students can be sexual or nonsexual, and the two participants may interpret the hug differently.

Holub and Lee (1990) maintain that there are instances in which good therapists who are concerned with the best interests of distressed clients choose to reach out with the healing power of touching. But they add this caution: "It should not be done unthinkingly or without considering the therapist's motives and the client's possible reaction" (p. 117). Stake and Oliver (1991) remind us that therapists may not accurately and objectively judge the erotic side of their behavior.

In their discussion, Holub and Lee assert that the decision to touch or not to touch clients involves more than considering its effectiveness in helping clients or engaging them in therapy. They maintain that this decision should also include deliberating over the correctness, motivations, and interpretations of the touching. The power differential between the therapist and client needs to be considered. The authors add that touching elicits different feelings in men than it does in women. The practice of male therapists' touching only female clients might be interpreted as sexist or at least as poor judgment.

Holroyd and Brodsky (1980) explored the question "Does touching patients lead to sexual intercourse?" Their results indicate that respondents who admitted having had sexual intercourse with their clients more often advocated and participated in nonerotic contact with opposite-sex clients but not with clients of the same sex. Also, male therapists who had had intercourse with clients were likely to have used and to advocate affectionate touching with women but not with men, even though the men might have initiated contact. Based on the data from questionnaires received from 347 male therapists and 310 female therapists, the authors came to the following conclusions:

- Touching that does not lead to intercourse is associated with older and more experienced therapists.
- It is the practice of restricting touching to opposite-sex clients, not touching itself, that is related to intercourse.

Holroyd and Brodsky observe that it is difficult to determine where "nonerotic hugging, kissing, and affectionate touching" leave off and "erotic contact" begins. They also suggest that any therapeutic technique that is reserved for one gender can be suspected of being sexist. They conclude: "The use of nonerotic touching as a mode of psychotherapeutic treatment requires further research. Moreover, the sexist implications of differential touching of male and female patients appear to be an important professional and ethical issue" (1980, p. 810).

Rabinowitz (1991) describes some therapeutic values of embracing in a men's group. He points out that it may be safer for a hug to occur in group therapy rather than in individual counseling because there are witnesses to the context of the touching, leaving less room for misinterpretation. However, counselors are still responsible for being sensitive to each member of the group and for avoiding meeting their own needs at the expense of the members. Rabinowitz adds: "Despite the cultural taboo for men to engage in physical touching, the act of embracing another man, in the context of the therapy group, does seem to encourage the expression of deeper feelings and lessen the isolation men often feel in our competitive society" (p. 576).

Bennett and his colleagues suggest that if touching is consistently and actively used in therapy, it is wise to explain this practice to clients and their families, if appropriate, before therapy begins. They recommend that practitioners consider how clients are likely to react to touching and that they ask themselves questions such as:

- How well do I know the client?
- Is the client ready to be touched?
- Could the touch be misinterpreted by the client (or the client's family) as a sexual overtone?
- Is touching appropriate in this circumstance?

In our view, touching should be a spontaneous and honest expression of the therapist's feelings. We think it is unwise for therapists to touch clients if this behavior is not congruent with what they feel. A nongenuine touch will be detected by clients and could erode their trust in the relationship. Counselors need to be sensitive to when touching could be counterproductive. There are times when touching clients can distract them from what they are feeling. There are also times when a touch that is given at the right moment can convey far more empathy than words can. Thus, therapists need to be aware of their own motives and to be honest with themselves about the meaning of physical contact. They also need to be sensitive to factors such as the client's readiness for physical closeness, the client's cultural understanding of touching, the client's reaction, the impact such contact is likely to have on the client, and the level of trust that they have built with the client.

Think about your position on the ethical implications of the practice of touching as a part of the client/therapist relationship by answering these questions:

- What criteria could you use to determine whether touching your clients was therapeutic or countertherapeutic?
- Do you think that some clients may never be ready to engage in touching in therapy?
- How could you honestly answer the question "Are my own needs being met at the expense of my client's needs?" What might you do if you hugged a client whom you felt needed this kind of physical support and the client suggested that you were meeting your own needs?
- To what degree do you think your professional training has prepared you to determine when touching is appropriate and therapeutic?
- What factors do you need to consider in determining the appropriateness of touching clients? (Examples are age, gender, the type of client, the nature of the client's problem, and the setting in which the therapy occurs.)
- Do you agree or disagree with the conclusions of Holroyd and Brodsky concerning the sexist implications of differential touching of male and female clients?
- Imagine your first session with a same-sex client who is crying and in a state of crisis. Might you be inclined to touch this person? Would it make a difference if the client asked you to hold him or her? Would it make a difference if this client were of the opposite sex?
- If you are favorably inclined toward the practice of touching clients, are you likely to restrict this practice to opposite-sex clients? to same-sex clients? to attractive clients of either sex? Explain.

○ ***The case of Ida***. Tu Chee is a warm and kindly counselor who routinely embraces his clients, both male and female. One of his clients, Ida, has had a lonely life, has had no success in maintaining relationships with men, is now approaching her 40th birthday, and has come to him because she is afraid that she will be alone forever. She misreads his friendly manner of greeting and assumes that he is giving her a personal message. At the end of one session when he gives his usual embrace, she clings to him and does not let go right away. Looking at him, she says: "This is special, and I look forward to this time all week long. I so much need to be touched." He is surprised and embarrassed. He explains to her that she has misunderstood his gesture, that this is the way he is with all of his clients, and that he is truly sorry if he has misled her. She is crestfallen and abruptly leaves the office. She cancels her next appointment.

- What are your thoughts on the counselor's manner of touching his clients?
- Was he guilty of insensitivity in not picking up Ida's reactions to him at an earlier point?
- If he explained to all of his clients that his touching was part of his style, would that be acceptable?
- Was the manner in which he dealt with Ida's clinging to him ethically sound?
- What obligations, if any, do you think he had when she canceled her appointment?

Dealing with Unethical Behavior in Dual Relationships

In our classes and workshops many students have raised the question "What should I do when I know of other therapists who are engaging in unethical behavior?" To sharpen your thinking on this question, reflect for a few moments on the possibility of your being involved in the following situations:

- You are aware that a clinical supervisor has made it a practice to have sexual relationships with several of her supervisees. Some of these students are friends of yours, and they tell you that they felt pressure to comply, since they were in a vulnerable position. What would you do?
- You know a student intern who initiates social relationships with his clients. He says that his clients are consenting adults, and he argues that by dating them, he actually gets to know them better, which helps him in his role as a therapist. What would you do?
- Several of your friends tell you that a counseling professor makes it a practice to date former students. When colleagues confronted him in the past, he maintained that all of these students were adults, that none of them were his students when he dated them, and that what he did in his private life was strictly his own business. What is your view of his behavior? If his behavior were not known to his colleagues, would you report him? Why or why not?
- You have heard unsettling reports from several clients about another therapist in an agency where you work. They say that he touches them frequently and that he behaves seductively. When you confront this therapist, he becomes defensive, telling you that he is not hung up on touching and that he likes to express his feelings spontaneously. What would you say to him? If you felt you were not getting through to him, what might you do next?

- Imagine yourself as a student in a training program. One of your professors makes several inappropriate and unwelcome advances to you. How might you react? What would you do?

You may wonder whether it is your place to judge the practices of colleagues or other practitioners whom you know. Even if you are convinced that the situation involves clear ethical violations, you may be in doubt about the best way to deal with it. Should you first discuss the matter with the person? Assuming that you do and that the person becomes defensive, should you take any other action, or simply drop the matter? When would a violation be serious enough that you would feel obligated to bring it to the attention of an appropriate local, state, or national committee on professional ethics?

Most professional organizations have specific ethical standards that clearly place the responsibility for confronting recognized violations squarely on members of their profession. Further, to ignore an ethical violation is considered a violation in itself. (See the accompanying box.)

Unethical Behavior by Colleagues: Ethical Codes

American Psychological Association (1989):

- "When psychologists know of an ethical violation by another psychologist, and it seems appropriate, they informally attempt to resolve the issue by bringing the behavior to the attention of the psychologist. If the misconduct is of a minor nature and/or appears to be due to lack of sensitivity, knowledge, or experience, such an informal solution is usually appropriate. Such informal corrective efforts are made with sensitivity to any rights to confidentiality involved. If the violation does not seem amenable to an informal solution, or is of a more serious nature, psychologists bring it to the attention of the appropriate local, state, and/or national committee on professional ethics and conduct."

American Association for Counseling and Development (1988):

- "Ethical behavior among professional associates, both members and nonmembers, must be expected at all times. When information is possessed that raises doubt as to the ethical behavior of colleagues, whether Association members or not, the member must take action to attempt to rectify such a condition. Such action shall use the institution's channels first and then use procedures established by the Association."

In a survey of APA-approved clinical training programs, graduate students were asked what they *should* do in a hypothetical situation in which a friend and colleague had violated APA ethical principles, and then what they *would* do (Bernard & Jara, 1986). Approximately half of these students said they would not live up to their own interpretation of what the ethical codes required of them as professionals. Bernard and Jara contend that the problem in training professionals is not how to communicate ethical codes to students but, rather, how to motivate them to apply their knowledge of ethical standards: "Psychologists need to carefully examine this question and to arrive at ways to reorder priorities so that their responsibility to monitor their own practices is taken more seriously" (1986, p. 315).

Generally, the best way to proceed when you have concerns about the behavior of colleagues is to tell them directly. Then, depending on the nature of the complaint and the outcome of the discussion, reporting a colleague to a professional board would be one of several options open to you.

It is sometimes easier to see the faults in others and to judge their behavior than to examine one's own behavior. You can make a commitment to continually reflect on what you are doing personally and professionally. Being your own judge is more realistic and valuable than being someone else's judge. This book aims to provide a catalyst for such self-inquiry.

Chapter Summary

Sexual relationships with clients are an obvious detriment to their welfare. However, it is important that you not overlook some of the more subtle and perhaps insidious behaviors of the therapist that may in the long run cause as much damage to clients.

As you have seen, it is unwise, unprofessional, unethical, and in many states illegal to become sexually involved with clients. This is not to say that as a counselor you aren't also human or that you will never have strong feelings of attraction toward certain clients. You are probably imposing an unnecessary burden on yourself if you believe that you shouldn't have such feelings for clients or if you try to convince yourself that you shouldn't have more feeling toward one client than toward another. What is important is how you decide to deal with these feelings as they affect the therapeutic relationship. Referral to another therapist isn't necessarily the best solution, unless it becomes clear that you can no longer be effective with a certain client. Instead, you may recognize a need for consultation or, at the very least, for an honest dialogue with your colleagues. It may also be appropriate to have a frank discussion with the client, explaining that the decision not to act on one's sexual feelings is based on a commitment to the primacy of the therapeutic relationship.

Becoming a therapist doesn't make you perfect or superhuman. You'll make some mistakes. What we want to stress is the importance of reflecting on what you're doing and on whose needs are primary. A willingness to be honest with yourself in your self-examination is your greatest asset in becoming an ethical practitioner.

Suggested Activities

1. There is an increased interest in both the ethical and legal aspects of dual relationships. Investigate this topic as it applies to the area of your special professional interests. Look for any trends, special problems, and alternatives in your area of specialization. Once you have gathered some materials and ideas, consider presenting your findings in class.

2. Some say that dual relationships are inevitable, pervasive, and unavoidable and have the potential to be either beneficial or harmful. Form two teams and debate the core issues. Have one team focus on the potential benefits of dual relationships and argue that they cannot be dealt with by simple legislative or ethical mandates. Have the other team argue the case that dual relationships are unethical because they have the potential for bringing harm to clients and that there are other and better alternatives.

3. Write a brief journal article on your position on dual relationships in counseling. Take some small aspect of the problem, and then develop a definite position on the issue and present your own views. Consider submitting this article to one of the professional journals. If your article is accepted, you are already on the road to professional writing! If your article is rejected, you have had the experience of writing a position paper and actually going through the process of submission and review. Consider doing this project jointly with one of your professors. (That way, if the article is rejected, you can always blame the professor.)

4. What are your views about forming social relationships with clients during the time they're in counseling with you? after they complete counseling?

5. What guidelines would you employ to determine whether nonerotic touching was therapeutic or countertherapeutic? Would the population you work with make a difference? Would the work setting make a difference? How comfortable are you in both receiving and giving touching? What are your ethical concerns about touching?

6. Take some time to review the ethical codes listed in the Appendix as they apply to two areas: (a) dual relationships in general and (b) sexual intimacies with present or former clients. Have several students team up to analyze different ethical codes, make a brief presentation to the class, and then lead a discussion on the codes' value.

7. Review the discussion on sexual relationships with former clients. Form two teams, and debate the issue of whether sexual and romantic relationships with former clients should be allowed after a specific length of time.

8. What unethical behaviors by your colleagues do you think you would report, if any? How might you proceed if you knew of the unethical practice of a colleague?

9. Take some of the cases in this chapter, and form small groups to explore the core issues involved. Role-play the cases, and then discuss the implications. Acting out the part of the therapist and the client is bound to enliven the discussion and also to give you a different perspective on the case. Feel free to embellish on the details given in the cases.

10. Divide the class into a number of small groups, and brainstorm one case other than the ones we have presented in this chapter. The case should illustrate some ethical dilemma in the general area of dual relationships. Come up with titles for your case, creative names for the therapist and the client, and interesting points that will make the case a good discussion tool. Each group can act out its case in class and lead a general discussion.

Suggested Readings

For a discussion of dual relationships see Kitchener and Harding (1990), Borys and Pope (1989), Pope (1985a), Stadler (1986b), and Keith-Spiegel and Koocher (1985). For a legal view of dual relationships see Leslie (1989b). On the issue of sexual attraction to clients see Pope et al. (1986), Claiborn (1985), and Ponzo (1985). On the role of touching in therapy see Rabinowitz (1991), Willison and Masson (1986), and Holroyd and Brodsky (1977, 1980). For a discussion of the ethical concerns associated with the use of nonerotic physical contact, see Holub and Lee (1990).

For a discussion of gender dilemmas in sexual-harassment policies and procedures, see Riger (1991).

For a book dealing with the subject of dual relationships in counseling from a comprehensive perspective see Herlihy and Corey (1992). Although this book has one chapter devoted to sexual relationships, the focus is on nonsexual relationships in counselor preparation and in areas such as private practice, school counseling, rehabilitation counseling, group counseling, and consultation.

An excellent first-person account from a victim's perspective on the subject of sexual intimacy in the therapeutic relationship is Bates and Brodsky (1989). The book also deals with topics such as therapists at risk, patients at risks, the legal process in dealing with sexual misconduct, and training and rehabilitation of impaired therapists. Two other pioneering books on sexual intimacy in therapy are (1) Pope and Bouhoutsos (1986), which explores issues such as risks for therapists, vulnerabilities of clients, consequences of therapist/client sexual involvement, specific techniques and principles of the subsequent therapy undertaken by the client with another therapist, filing of complaints, legal proceedings, and prevention of sexual involvement; and (2) Edelwich, with Brodsky (1982), which deals with issues such as seduction, power, opportunity and vulnerability, self-interest, morality, relationships among staff colleagues, legal considerations, and malpractice actions.

The topic of sexual harassment is well covered in the following journal articles: Hotelling (1991), Howard (1991), and Lee and Heppner (1991). A female counseling student's experience of sexual harassment is reported well in Anonymous (1991).

For journal articles on issues of sexual intimacy in the client/therapist relationship see Bouhoutsos et al. (1983), Coleman and Schaefer (1986), Glaser and Thorpe (1986), Holroyd (1983), Holroyd and Bouhoutsos (1985), Holroyd and Brodsky (1977, 1980), Pope, Schover, and Levenson (1980), Gutheil (1989), Vinson (1989), Stake and Oliver (1991), Pope (1988), Schoener and Gonsiorek (1988), Vasquez (1988), Hotelling (1988), Fitzgerald and Nutt (1986), and Robinson and Reid (1985). For a discussion of the ethics of social and romantic relationships with present or former clients see Gottlieb, Sell, and Schoenfeld (1988) and Sell et al. (1986). For a national survey of attitudes and behavior among practitioners on intimate relationships with former clients, see Akamatsu (1988). Brodsky (1986) contains an excellent chapter on sexual intimacy with an exploitation of clients. For a discussion of therapist-client sex as sexual abuse see Pope (1990b).

Professional Competence and Training

Pre-Chapter Self-Inventory

Directions: For each statement, indicate the response that most closely identifies your beliefs and attitudes. Use the following code:

5 = I *strongly agree* with this statement.
4 = I *agree* with this statement.
3 = I am *undecided* about this statement.
2 = I *disagree* with this statement.
1 = I *strongly disagree* with this statement.

___ 1. Counselors are ethically bound to refer clients to other therapists when working with them is beyond their professional training.

___ 2. Ultimately, practitioners must create their own ethical standards.

___ 3. Possession of a license or certificate from a state board of examiners shows that a person has therapeutic skills and is competent to practice psychotherapy.

___ 4. Professional licensing protects the public by setting minimum standards of preparation for those who are licensed.

___ 5. The present processes of licensing and certification encourage the self-serving interests of the groups in control instead of protecting the public from incompetent practice.

___ 6. Continuing education should be a requirement for renewal of a license to practice psychotherapy.

___ 7. Health-care professionals should be required to demonstrate continuing competency in their field as a prerequisite for renewal of their licenses.

___ 8. Institutions that train counselors should select trainees on the basis of both their academic record and the degree to which they possess the personal characteristics of effective therapists (as determined by current research findings).

___ 9. I think that the arguments *for* licensing counselors and therapists outweigh the arguments against licensing.

___ 10. Peer review, or the analysis and judging of a professional's practice by other practitioners, provides a high degree of assurance to consumers that they will receive competent services.

___ 11. A major problem of the peer-review process is the difficulty in determining the qualifications of the reviewer.

___ 12. I think that candidates applying for a training program have a right to know the criteria for selecting trainees.

___ 13. Once students are admitted, a graduate training program is ethically obliged to continue to assess them to determine their suitability to complete the requirements.

___ 14. Trainees who display rigid and dogmatic views about human behavior should not be allowed to continue in a training program.

___ 15. It is unethical for a program to train practitioners in only one therapeutic orientation if it does not provide an unbiased overview of other theoretical systems.

____ 16. The process of licensing and certification tends to pit the professional specializations against one another.

____ 17. Peer-consultation groups are useful for counselors at all levels of experience.

____ 18. If a peer-consultation group were available to me at this time, I would certainly join it.

____ 19. It is unethical for counselors to practice without continuing their education.

____ 20. For myself, I might not seek out workshops, seminars, courses, and other postgraduate learning activities if continuing education were not required as a stipulation for maintaining my practice.

Introduction*

This chapter focuses on the ethical and legal aspects of professional competence and the education and training of mental-health professionals. We also deal with the topic of professional licensing, certification, and approaches to continuing education. The roles of peer review and peer-group supervision are examined as ways of ensuring competence.

Ability is not an easy matter for practitioners to assess. In order to maintain their competence, they must keep up to date on the new developments in their specialty. They also need to sharpen their skills and find ways to meet the needs of new populations. Areas such as eating disorders, sexual abuse, substance abuse, and AIDS all present challenges that demand that practitioners do more than boast of what they learned in their training programs. Continuing education is essential.

In this chapter we examine professional certification and licensure as a measure of ability. You will see that these measures have certain limitations in assessing competence.

The topic of training is given special attention because there are ethical implications to how counselors are trained. Indeed, there are ethical considerations in admission and screening procedures in graduate programs. One key issue is the role of training programs in safeguarding the public when it becomes clear that a trainee has problems that are likely to interfere with professional functioning.

Therapist Competence: Ethical and Legal Aspects

This section examines what therapist competence is, how we can assess it, and what some of its ethical and legal dimensions are. We pose such questions as these: What ethical standards do the various mental-health professions have regarding competence? What ethical issues are involved in the training of therapists?

*We want to acknowledge Theodore Remley, Executive Director of the AACD, and Tom Clawson, Director of the NBCC, for their review of this chapter and for their comments.

To what degree is professional licensing an accurate and valid measure of competence? What are the ethical responsibilities of therapists to continue to upgrade their knowledge and skills?

Perspectives on Competence

We begin this discussion of competence with an overview of specific guidelines from various professional associations. They are summarized in the accompanying box.

Professional Codes of Ethics on Competence

American Association for Marriage and Family Therapy (1991):

- "Marriage and family therapists do not diagnose, treat, or advise on problems outside the recognized boundaries of their competence."

American Psychological Association (1989):

- "Psychologists recognize the boundaries of their competence and the limitations of their techniques. They only provide services and only use techniques for which they are qualified by training and experience."

National Association of Social Workers (1990):

- "The social worker should accept responsibility or employment only on the basis of existing competence or the intention to acquire the necessary competence."
- "The social worker should not misrepresent professional qualifications, education, experience, or affiliations."

American Association for Counseling and Development (1988):

- "Members recognize the boundaries of competence and provide only those services and use only those techniques for which they are qualified by training or experience. Members should only accept those positions for which they are professionally qualified."

National Board for Certified Counselors (1989):

- "Certified counselors recognize their limitations and provide services or only use techniques for which they are qualified by training and/or experience. Certified counselors recognize the need, and seek continuing education, to assure competent services."
- "When certified counselors determine an inability to be of professional assistance to a potential or existing client, they must, respectively, not initiate the counseling relationship or immediately terminate the relationship. In either event, the certified counselor must suggest appropriate alternatives. Certified counselors must be knowledgeable about referral resources so that a satisfactory referral can be initiated. In the event that the client declines a suggested referral, the certified counselor is not obligated to continue the relationship."

American Psychiatric Association (1989):

- "A psychiatrist who regularly practices outside of his/her area of professional competence should be considered unethical. Determination of professional competence should be made by peer review boards or other appropriate bodies."

The guidelines leave several questions unanswered. What are the boundaries of one's competence, and how do professionals know when they have exceeded them? How can they determine whether they should accept a client if they lack the experience or training they would like to have? These questions become more complex when we consider what criteria to use in evaluating competence. Many people who complete a doctoral program lack the skills or knowledge needed to carry out certain therapeutic tasks. Obviously, degrees alone don't confer the ability to perform any and all psychological services.

You also need to assess how far you can safely go with clients and when you should refer them to other specialists. Similarly, it's important to learn when to consult another professional if you haven't had extensive experience in working with a certain problem. If you were to refer all the clients with whom you encountered difficulties, you'd probably have few clients. Keep in mind that many beginning counselors have doubts about their general level of competence; in fact, it's not at all unusual for highly experienced therapists to wonder seriously at times whether they have the personal and professional abilities needed to work with some of their clients. Thus, difficulty in working with some clients doesn't by itself imply incompetence.

One way to develop or upgrade your skills is to work with colleagues or professionals who have more experience in certain areas than you do. You can also learn new skills by going to conferences and conventions, by taking additional courses in areas you don't know well, and by participating in workshops that combine didactic work with supervised practice. The feedback you receive can give you an additional resource for evaluating your readiness to undertake certain therapeutic tasks.

Making Referrals

It is crucial for professionals to know the boundaries of their own competence and to refer clients to other professionals when working with them is beyond their professional training or when personal factors would interfere with a fruitful working relationship. After counseling with a client for a few sessions, for example, you may determine that he or she needs more intensive therapy than you're qualified to offer. Even if you have the skills to undertake long-term psychotherapy, the agency you work for may, as a matter of policy, permit only short-term counseling. Or you and a client may decide that, for whatever reason, your relationship isn't productive. The client may want to continue working with another person rather than discontinue counseling. As we discussed in Chapter 3, there may be times when the discrepancy or conflict between your values and those of a client necessitates a referral. For these and other reasons you will need to develop a framework for evaluating *when* to refer a client, and you'll need to learn *how* to make this referral in such a manner that your client will be open to accepting your suggestion.

To make the art of referral more concrete, consider the following exchange between a client and her counselor. Helen is 45 years old and has seen a counselor at a community mental-health center for six sessions. She suffers from periods of deep depression and frequently talks about how hard it is to wake up to a new day. In other respects it is very difficult for her to express what she feels. Most of the time she sits silently during the session.

The counselor decides that Helen's problems warrant long-term therapy that he doesn't feel competent to provide. In addition, the center has a policy of referring clients who need long-term treatment to therapists in private practice. The counselor therefore approaches Helen with the suggestion of a referral:

Counselor: Helen, during your intake session I let you know that we're generally expected to limit the number of our sessions to six visits. Since today is our sixth session, I'd like to discuss the matter of referring you to another therapist.

Helen: Well, you said the agency *generally* limits the number of visits to six, but what about exceptions? I mean, after all, I feel as if I've just started with you, and I really don't want to begin all over again with someone I don't know or trust.

Counselor: I can understand that, but you may not have to begin all over again. I could meet with the therapist you'd be continuing with to talk about what we've done these past weeks.

Helen: I still don't like the idea at all. I don't know whether I'll see another person if you won't continue with me. Why won't you let me stay with you?

Counselor: Well, there are a couple of reasons. I really think you need more intensive therapy than I'm trained to offer you, and, as I've explained, I'm expected to do only short-term counseling.

Helen: Intensive therapy! Do you think I'm *that* sick?

Counselor: It's not a question of being sick, but I *am* concerned about your prolonged depressions, and we've talked about my concerns over your suicidal fantasies. I'd just feel much better if you were to see someone who's trained to work with depression.

Helen: *You'd* feel better, but *I* sure wouldn't! The more you talk, the more I feel crazy—as though you don't want to touch me with a ten-foot pole. You make me feel as if I'm ready for a mental hospital.

Counselor: I wish I could make you understand that it isn't a matter of thinking you're crazy; it's a matter of being concerned about many of the things you've talked about with me. I want you to be able to work with someone who has more training and experience than I do, so that you can get the help you need.

Helen: I think you've worked with me just fine, and I don't want to be shoved around from shrink to shrink! If you won't let me come back, then I'll just forget counseling.

This exchange reflects a common problem. What do you think of the way Helen's counselor approached his client? Can you see anything you would have done differently? If you were Helen's counselor, would you agree to continue seeing her if she refused to be referred to someone else?

If you didn't want Helen to discontinue counseling, a number of alternatives would be open to you. You could agree to see her for another six sessions, provided that your director or supervisor approved. You could let her know that you would feel a need for consultation and close supervision if you were to continue seeing her. Also, you could say that although this might not be the appropriate time for a referral, you would want to work toward a referral eventually. Perhaps you could obtain Helen's consent to have another therapist sit in on one of your sessions so that you could consult with him or her. There may be a chance that Helen would eventually agree to begin therapy with this person. What other possibilities can you envision? What would be the consequences if you refused to see Helen or could not obtain approval to see her?

Ethical Issues in the Training of Therapists

Training is obviously a basic component of mental-health practitioners' competence. In his article "Ethical Issues in the Training of Psychotherapists," Grayson (1982) asks four key questions: (1) How do we select whom to train? (2) What should we teach? (3) What are the best ways of training? (4) What should be the criteria for certification? Our discussion of the central ethical and professional issues in training is organized around these questions and also addresses the process of accrediting a preparation program.

How Do We Select Whom to Train?

A core ethical and professional issue involves formulating policies and procedures for selecting appropriate candidates for a training program. Some questions that can be raised are:

- Should the selection of trainees be based solely on traditional academic standards, or should it take into account the latest findings on the personal characteristics of effective therapists?
- To what degree is a candidate for training open to learning and to considering new perspectives?
- Does the candidate have problems that are likely to interfere with training and with the practice of psychotherapy?
- What are some ways to increase applications to programs by underrepresented groups?
- Whom do we select to work with which populations?

We think that training programs have an ethical responsibility to establish clear selection criteria, and certainly candidates have a right to know the nature of these criteria at the time they are applying. Although factors such as grade-point averages, scores on the Graduate Record Examination, and letters of recommendation are often considered in the selection process, relying on these measures alone does not provide a comprehensive picture of a candidate. Many programs ask candidates to write a detailed essay that includes their reasons for wanting to be in the program, their professional goals, an assessment of their personal assets and liabilities, and life experiences that might be useful in their work as a counselor. It is a good idea to conduct group interviews with candidates. A number of programs have both faculty members and graduate students on the reviewing committee. If many sources are considered and if more than one person makes the decision about whom to select for training, there is less likelihood that people will be screened out on the basis of some personal whim. In addition, we favor periodic reviews at various junctures in the program to determine whether trainees should be retained. Ideally, trainees will engage in self-examination to decide for themselves whether they are "right" for the program and the program is suitable for them. We are uncomfortable with a judgment such as "You'll *never* be a counselor." Our belief is that people can change for the better and that if shortcomings are sensitively pointed out to trainees, they can often correct them.

How to encourage members of various minority groups to apply to graduate programs in the mental-health professions is a current issue. Data on the ethnic distribution of counseling doctorates show that most students in the programs are Caucasians, with African Americans and Hispanics severely underrepresented. Thus, it appears that efforts to redress racial and ethnic imbalances in training programs have not been effective (Zimpfer & DeTrude, 1990).

○ *The case of Leo.*   Julius is on a review committee in a graduate counseling program. Leo has taken several introductory courses in the program, and he has just completed an ethics course with Julius. It is clear to this professor that Leo displays a rigid and dogmatic approach to human problems, particularly in areas such as interracial marriage, gay and lesbian lifestyles, and abortion. In the course of the semester, it did not seem that he was either willing or able to modify his thinking. When he was challenged by other students in the class about his views, he argued that certain behaviors were simply "never proper" and that it was the task of the counselor to point this out. In meeting with the committee charged with determining whether candidates should be advanced in the program, Julius expresses his strong concern about retaining Leo in the program. His colleagues share this concern, and Leo is denied advancement.

- What concerns, if any, do you have about the manner in which this case was handled? Were any of Leo's rights violated?
- Was it clear to him that when he expressed his ideas in his classes, they could be held against him? Is there an ethical issue in that situation?
- How could the committee determine so early in the program that Leo would not change his ideas in the course of his education?
- Were any other avenues open in dealing with him short of disqualifying him from the program?
- If his values reflected his minority cultural background, would that make a difference? Would the committee be culturally insensitive for rejecting him from the program?
- What if Leo said that when he eventually obtained his license, he intended to work exclusively with people from his cultural and religious background? Should he be denied the opportunity to pursue a degree in counseling if his career goal was to work with a specific population that shared his views and values?
- Using the criteria seemingly espoused by this selection committee, would a minister from a fundamentalist background who was attempting to get a master's degree in counseling be rejected?

- If you were on the committee, how would you handle candidates who exhibited racism, homophobia, and absolutist thinking?

What Should Be Taught?

Lazarus (1990) writes that "most graduate programs socialize their students into delimited schools of thought" (p. 351). In his lectures to professional audiences, he often warns of the limitations of rigidly following a particular theory and then stretching clients to fit its preconceptions, rather than adapting the techniques that flow from a theory to fit the unique needs of each client. He argues that a multimodal, systematic, technically eclectic model can point the way to a genuinely scientific approach to the training of therapists. Thus, training programs would do well to offer students a wide range of therapeutic techniques and strategies that can be applied to the diverse problems of a diverse clientele.

On this same issue, Grayson (1982) does not think that all specialty training should be abolished, but he does take the position that it is unethical to train practitioners in only one therapeutic orientation (without also providing unbiased introductions to other systems). Thus, there is merit in an analytically trained therapist's learning about alternative systems such as behavior therapy. By the same token, a behavior therapist should be able to recognize the role of transference and countertransference in the therapeutic process. Therapists should learn when a particular approach is contraindicated, especially if it is their own specialty.

It is our view that students should be exposed to the major contemporary counseling theories and that they should be able to have a rationale for the therapeutic techniques they employ. In Chapter 9 we discuss the ethical issues of practicing without any clear sense of how one's theoretical orientation guides practice. (For an overview of the contemporary counseling theories see Corey, 1991b.)

In deciding what to teach, certain questions are worth considering:

- Is the curriculum based on a monocultural or a multicultural set of assumptions?
- Is there a universal definition of mental health, or is mental health culturally defined?
- Should therapy help clients adjust to their culture? Or should it encourage them to find ways of constructively changing their culture?
- Does the curriculum give central attention to the ethics of professional practice? Is it ethical to leave out training in ethics? Is it enough to hope that ethical issues will be addressed through the supervision process alone?
- What is the proper balance between academic course work and supervised clinical experience?
- What core knowledge should be taught in counselor-education programs?

In addressing the issue of required learning for counselors, we can look to the standards formulated originally by the ACES in 1973, which have evolved into the standards of the Council for Accreditation of Counseling and Related

Educational Programs (CACREP). Later, the NBCC built on these standards for designing its certification examination for professional counselors. The purpose of the National Counselor Examination is to assess a professional's knowledge of basic counseling information and skills, regardless of the counselor's individual specialization (NBCC, 1989). The board has identified the following eight areas as basic to the practice of counseling:

1. *Human growth and development.* Counselors should have a broad understanding of normal and abnormal development and behavior, personality theory, and change over the life span.
2. *Social and cultural foundations.* Factors such as gender, ethnicity, lifestyle diversity, poverty, and other cultural and environmental variables provide a broad understanding of societal changes and trends, social mores and interaction patterns, multiculturalism and pluralism, and societal concerns.
3. *The helping relationship.* The philosophic bases of the helping process provide a framework for acquiring both basic and advanced skills of counseling and consulting.
4. *Group dynamics and group counseling.* This area includes counseling theories applied to group work, group-leadership styles, and group-counseling techniques and methods.
5. *Lifestyle and career development.* Students should acquire a framework for understanding the theory and practice of career development, leisure education and counseling, and lifestyle and career decision making.
6. *Appraisal of individuals.* This area pertains to knowledge and skills in the selection, administration, interpretation, and application of objective and projective tests and other methods of assessment. It also provides an understanding of group and individual educational and psychometric theories.
7. *Research and evaluation.* Counselors should have an understanding of research methods, program evaluation, and needs assessment and skills in the evaluation of individual and group counseling and psychotherapy. This area also includes ethical and legal considerations in research.
8. *Professional orientation.* The final element is a broad understanding of professional roles and functions, ethical and legal standards, and the governance and credentialing structures of the counseling profession.

Most state credentialing boards for counselors adhere to curricular requirements similar to these. In addition to these eight core areas, counselor-education programs must include *environmental studies* (knowledge and skills pertaining to various settings), *specialized studies* (the application of procedures to specific populations), and *clinical instruction* as part of students' training. The clinical-instruction component includes mastering a range of counseling skills through supervised laboratory, practicum, and internship experiences.

How Can We Best Train?

Programs geared to educating and training counselors should be built on the foundation of the natural talents and abilities of the students. Ideally, as we have said, programs teach people the knowledge and skills they need to work effectively with diverse populations. In addition, students need a core set of attitudes and values that are congruent with carrying out their role as helping professionals.

In his provocative article "Can Psychotherapists Transcend the Shackles of Their Training and Superstitions?" Lazarus (1990) contends that formal education and training in psychological diagnosis and treatment often undermine the natural talents and skills of trainees. In illustrating his point, he describes a friend who was "an absolute natural when it came to understanding people and showing genuine warmth, wisdom, and empathy" (p. 352). When Lazarus brought his own problems to his friend, he found the experience to be "amazingly therapeutic." After his friend obtained a Ph.D. in psychology, however, Lazarus was able to receive only "a string of platitudes and labels." He maintains that as his friend took courses in assessment, diagnosis, and treatment, his natural talents were destroyed. Of course, Lazarus does not believe that training *necessarily* erodes one's natural talent, but he does warn that "one of the main shackles under which many therapists labor comes from the almost endless list of proscriptions that they are handed" (p. 353). We would hope that the way we educate and train students will help them acquire and hone their skills and will not instill in them a list of do's and don'ts. Critical in this regard is what students learn from the modeling of faculty members in the program.

In one graduate counseling program, conflict among faculty members was obvious, and no attempts were made to address it. At times, students were drawn into these rivalries by being expected to side with a particular faculty member. There was a high degree of professional competition as well as a general lack of respect among colleagues. This lack of cohesiveness resulted in a high rate of faculty turnover.

- What problems would you encounter if you found yourself in this kind of program? How would you deal with them?
- What are your reactions to a student who says: "I don't care what they do. I just want to get my degree and get out of here"?
- If you were concerned about the ethics of this program as a student, what actions would be open to you besides quitting?

What Should Be the Criteria for Certification or Graduation?

A key question is whether personality factors such as openness or rigidity are made part of the criteria for certification or whether meeting academic requirements is the sole criterion. The training institution has an ethical responsibility to screen candidates so that the public will be protected from incompetent practitioners. Programs clearly have a dual responsibility: to honor their commitment to the students they admit and also to the future consumers who will be served by those who graduate. Just as the criteria for selecting applicants to a program should be clear, the criteria for successful completion need to be spelled out as objectively as possible.

Donigian (1991) takes the provocative position that the consumer's trust in the profession is violated if counselors are not psychologically prepared for the challenges they will confront as they undertake their work. He suggests that preparation programs take the responsibility for evaluating students' emotional and psychological readiness to become practitioners. Certainly there are ethical ramifications to the practice of denying students graduation from a program without due cause and without prior notification so that they have had opportunities to rectify any shortcomings. If faculty groups assume the role of examining and evaluating both the academic and personal fitness of students to graduate, the question ought to be raised "Who evaluates and examines the examiners?"

Assume that several advanced students approach the dean of their graduate school to express their concern about the seeming discrepancies between what they are experiencing in their internships and supervised sessions and what they are being taught in their counseling classes. They complain that their professors live in an ivory tower, and they point out that not one of their professors is a counseling practitioner. The dean replies that all of the faculty members are properly credentialed. Although they are not seeing clients, they have had practical experience in the past.

- If a program stresses the rights of clients, is it important for counselor educators to have current hands-on experience with clients?
- Every program evaluates students and their suitability for the counseling profession. Is it equally as important to evaluate the evaluators and their suitability to make such assessments?

For licensing and certification in areas such as clinical social work, clinical or counseling psychology, rehabilitation counseling, mental-health counseling, and marriage and family therapy, most states have established specific requirements of supervised practice beyond the receipt of a master's or doctor's degree. We now turn our attention to the issues involved in the accreditation of preparation programs.

Accreditation: How to Assess a Training Program

Accreditation refers to a professional group's passing judgment on a preparation program. Each specialty has its own accreditation policies and procedures.

• The CACREP was established in 1981 by the AACD as a free-standing accreditation group. About 70 counselor-education programs are accredited by the council. They offer master's level training in mental-health, community, school, and marriage and family counseling and also in counselor education and supervision on the doctoral level (Brooks & Gerstein, 1990; personal communication, Thomas Clawson, July 17, 1991). Only accredited universities are eligible to offer these programs. In most states, licenses may be granted only to those with degrees from accredited universities.

• The APA has a Committee on Accreditation of doctoral programs in clinical, counseling, and school psychology. It accredits programs only at the doctoral level. There are APA-accredited internships for doctoral training. Each year the *American Psychologist* publishes a list of accredited programs.

• The AAMFT has a Commission on Accreditation of training programs throughout the United States and Canada and certifies graduates and postdegree clinical-training centers in marital and family therapy after a program is carefully reviewed. Recognition of this commission in 1978 by the U.S. Office of Education "defined unequivocally marital and family therapy as a separate and distinct field of study" (Everett, 1990, p. 500). Individuals seeking professional status in marital and family therapy may earn a graduate degree from a university or obtain professional preparation at a center offering specialized training (Goldenberg & Goldenberg, 1991). In Chapter 12 there is a further discussion of the requirements that practitioners need to fulfill before they are accepted as clinical members of the AAMFT.

• The NASW has standards for the accreditation of social-work programs. In 1960 it created the Academy of Certified Social Workers (ACSW), which established certification for self-directed social-work practitioners. The NASW now has a new credential: qualified clinical social worker, with specific educational and experience requirements (Garcia, 1990).

Professional Licensing and Credentialing

This section focuses on some of the basic assumptions of the practice of licensing; its relationship to competence, arguments for and against licensing and certification for mental-health professionals, professional jealousy and turf battles, the values of professional collaboration, and professional disclosure as an adjunct to the legal regulation of practice.

Purposes of Legislative Regulation of Practice

Although licensing and certification differ in their purposes, they have some features in common. Both require applicants to meet specific requirements in terms of education and training and acceptance from practicing professionals. Both also generally rely on tests to determine those applicants who have met the standards and who deserve to be granted a credential. Fretz and Mills (1980) define licensure as "the statutory process by which an agency of government, usually a state, grants permission to a person meeting predetermined qualifications to engage in a given occupation and/or use a particular title and to perform specified functions" (p. 7). Certification, in contrast, refers to a voluntary attempt by a group such as the NBCC to promote a professional identity.

Licensure and certification assure the public that the practitioners have completed minimum educational programs, have had a certain number of hours of supervised training, and have gone through some type of evaluation and screening. Licenses and certifications do not, and probably cannot, ensure that practitioners will competently *do* what their credentials permit them to do. The main advantages of licensure and certification are the protection of the public from grossly unqualified and untrained practitioners and the formal representation to the public that the practitioners are part of an established profession.

Legislation has been enacted over the years to protect the public from unqualified persons who call themselves psychologists, counselors, social workers, and marriage and family therapists (see Cummings, 1990; Everett, 1990; Garcia, 1990). Below are some defining characteristics and trends in each of these mental-health fields:

- Psychology was the first nonmedical mental-health profession to seek state licensure and certification and to accomplish this in all states by 1977. It laid the foundation for other mental-health professions, such as social work, marital and family therapy, and counseling (Cummings, 1990).
- Social-work licensing laws vary from state to state. Some states regulate a broad spectrum of practitioners, whereas others limit their regulation to clinical social workers who practice psychotherapy. Of the 49 states with some type of legal regulation, 29 have licensing statutes, and 11 have registration statutes (Garcia, 1990).
- Counselor licensure, certification, or registration laws have been enacted in 34 states, and they continue to have a profound impact on the development of the professional identity of counselors. This legislation has specified appropriate activities and roles for professional counselors or mental-health counselors and has contributed to protecting the public from unqualified individuals (Gerstein & Brooks, 1990; personal communication, Thomas Clawson, July 17, 1991).
- Competence in the evolving field of marital and family therapy is reflected in the integration of theoretical knowledge, clinical-assessment skills, and applied techniques acquired through educational and supervisory experiences. With the leadership provided by the AAMFT, marital and family therapists have been struggling for recognition of their professional identity and independence within the broader mental-health community. Legislation recognizing marital and family therapy exists in California, Florida, Nevada, and Utah (Everett, 1990).

Most licenses and credentials are generic; that is, they usually don't specify the clients or problems that practitioners are competent to work with, nor do they specify the techniques that they are competent to use. A licensed psychologist may possess the expertise needed to work with adults yet lack the ability to work with children. The same person may be qualified to do individual psychotherapy yet have neither the experience nor the skills required for family counseling or group therapy. Most licensing regulations do specify that licensees are to engage only in those therapeutic tasks for which they have adequate training, but it is up to the licensee to put this rule into practice. Such a broad definition of practice also applies to many other professions.

Arguments for and against Professional Licensing and Credentialing

Four main arguments have been put forth in favor of legislation to regulate the delivery of mental-health services. The first assumption is that the public is protected by setting minimum standards of service and holding professionals accountable if they do not measure up. This argument contends that the consumer would be harmed by the absence of such standards, because incompetent practitioners can cause long-term negative consequences. Secondly, the regulation of practitioners is designed to protect the public from its ignorance about mental-health services. This argument rests on the assumption that the consumer who needs psychological services typically does not know how to choose an appropriate practitioner or how to judge the quality of services received. Most people do not know the basic differences between a licensed psychologist, a psychiatrist, a licensed clinical social worker, a licensed marital and family therapist, and a licensed professional counselor. Third, because insurance companies frequently reimburse clients for the services of licensed practitioners, licensing means that more people can afford mental-health care. Finally, there is the view that licensing allows the profession to define for itself what it will and will not do. In fact, there is the perception that licensure itself enhances the profession and is a sign of maturity.

In summary, the essence of the argument for licensure is the contention that the consumer's welfare is better safeguarded with legal regulation than without it. Challengers to this assumption often maintain that licensing is designed to create and preserve a "union shop" and that it works more as a self-serving measure that creates monopolistic helping professions than as a protection for the public from misrepresentation and incompetence (Davis, 1981).

Some are skeptical when it comes to setting up criteria for regulating mental-health practitioners. Carl Rogers (1980) has maintained that as soon as criteria are set up for certification, the profession inevitably becomes frozen in a past image. He notes that there are as many *certified* charlatans as there are uncertified practitioners. Another drawback to licensing, from his viewpoint, is that professionalism builds up a rigid bureaucracy (pp. 243–248). According to the executive director of the NBCC, licensure is a threat if the profession does not maintain a strong voice. (Thomas Clawson, personal communication, July 17, 1991). If licensure becomes the chief professional identity, then legislators, not professionals, are defining the profession.

In our view, the process of licensing often contributes to professional specializations' pitting themselves against one another. Instead of fostering a collaborative spirit between licensed clinical social workers and licensed marriage and family counselors or between licensed psychologists and licensed professional counselors, the licensing process of each group tends to promote working in isolation. In the next section we address how turf battles are partially created by the process of licensure and certification.

Turf Battles or Interprofessional Collaboration?

The process of certification, licensure, credentialing, or registration can promote a sense of professional identity. It can also be the basis for professional jealousy over turf and can lead to restrictive regulation that is motivated by competition for access to the marketplace. How has interprofessional bickering manifested itself? According to Cummings (1990), professional psychology has struggled with the psychiatric profession to retain its turf in the areas of hospital privileges, licensure to prescribe drugs, and inclusion in Medicare. Cummings asserts that a major contribution of psychology to the other mental-health professions was designing and implementing the freedom-of-choice amendments to state insurance codes. Psychology has also recently made great strides in expanding mental-health services to the elderly and residents of rural areas through revision of Medicare regulations.

Just as psychology has struggled with psychiatry for turf, clinical psychologists often contend that their scientific discipline makes them preeminent over other disciplines (Cummings, 1990). They have opposed the licensing efforts of social workers, mental-health counselors, counselors, and marital and family therapists. Some writers warn about the dangers of competition to the welfare of the client; they contend that such fighting among professions can lead to an eroding of the quality of services and that those who stand to suffer the most are the consumers (Garcia, 1990; Ivey & Rigazio-DiGilio, 1991). Brooks and Gerstein (1990) also decry the competition within and among the various professional fields, and they urge the various helping professions to join forces and collaborate. They add that interprofessional bickering must cease if mental-health professionals, their associations, and the respective licensing boards are to achieve their goal of delivering the best services possible. The more that money (in the form of third-party insurance payments) is a factor, the more vigorous the "ideological" turf battles are bound to become. Surely there is room for collaboration in the public interest.

Professional Disclosure as an Adjunct to Licensing and Certification

The idea of a model based on competence as an option to licensing and certification practices is proposed by Bernstein and Lecomte (1981). They contend that the nature of the regulatory process (rather than regulation itself) is what should be challenged. Their proposal includes a number of specific ways to assess competence. One way is to review candidates who apply for entry-level licenses on a range of factors that have a demonstrable relationship to positive client outcomes. Further, those who earn a license would be required to continue to demonstrate competent performance at regular intervals as a condition for renewal. As a part of their competence-based alternative to current practices, Bernstein and Lecomte call for licensed practitioners to file a *professional-disclosure statement*, updated annually, with the state licensing board. It would include information for clients about the practitioner's academic and professional background. In addition to providing basic information, each practitioner might include a philosophy of counseling, the proposed length of treatment, anticipated outcomes, and a fee schedule. This would provide clients with the data necessary for making intelligent decisions regarding the use of a particular practitioner's services.

Although we do not think that professional disclosure is a realistic alternative to legal regulation, we do agree that it is an excellent supplement to the current licensure and certification process. It does have certain limitations: How can consumers be sure that they are getting accurate information from a practitioner? If therapists are expected to provide a comprehensive disclosure to clients, what is to prevent them from exaggerating or misrepresenting their qualifications?

We applaud the trend toward expecting professionals to demonstrate that they are indeed accomplishing what they say they are doing. Accountability procedures are part of the current debate over licensure and the continued demonstration of competence. Examples of the trend toward accountability in practice are the attention given to consumer rights, attempts to provide for informed consent, efforts to demystify the therapeutic process, descriptions of the nature of the client/therapist relationship through contracts that guide the process, and the efforts to educate the public about psychotherapy and related services. Before proceeding to the next section, consider these questions:

- What are your views on alternatives to licensing?
- What are your thoughts about professional disclosure as a supplementary procedure for those who are licensed or credentialed?
- Some states have enacted "sunset legislation" requiring professionals to reconvince the legislature periodically that their profession needs to be regulated to protect the public. The assumption is that licensing procedures have become too rigid and restrictive and that bureaucratic factors have contributed to excluding many competent practitioners from legally practicing (while creating a restricted guild based on the survival of those with licenses). Do you think that sunset legislation is a workable solution to the problems associated with licensure and certification? What might you want to say if you were on a committee that had the task of evaluating and modifying existing licensing regulations?
- What would you think of requiring that those who serve on examining boards also be examined to determine their level of knowledge and skills? If the examiners were unable to measure up to an acceptable level of competence, would you support suspending their licenses?
- What do you think the likely consequences would be if all professional licensing laws were eliminated? What would the results be for the various mental-health professions? What might the consequences be for the public?

We have presented this overview as an illustration of some of the controversies surrounding licensure and certification. We encourage you to write to the appropriate agency in your state to find out the specific requirements for licensing or certification of social workers, counselors, psychologists, marriage and family counselors, and other types of mental-health professionals. The specific requirements for the same category of licensure vary considerably from state to state. If you are seeking a professional license, you should keep informed of the changing requirements.

The Appendix lists general information about professional groups. You can ask the appropriate organizations about specific requirements for certification.

Continuing Education and Demonstration of Competence

Most professional organizations support efforts to make continuing education a mandatory condition of relicensing. In the past, people could obtain licenses to practice professionally and then act as though there were no need to obtain further education. We question how ethical it is to neglect keeping abreast of developments. In any event, the trend now is to encourage professionals to engage in ongoing education and training in their specializations.

It should be noted that one of the weak points of mandatory continuing education is that it cannot require intellectual and emotional involvement. A practitioner's résumé may look impressive in terms of knowledge acquired, but the amount of this knowledge that is absorbed and is integrated into practice may be much less than a piece of paper indicates.

Many professional organizations have voluntary programs. All clinical members of the AAMFT, for example, are encouraged to complete 150 hours of continuing education every three years. The association regards the program, known as Continuing Education in Family Therapy, as a part of an ongoing process of professional development with the goal of maintaining high-quality services to consumers. National Certified Counselors, in order to be recertified, must complete at least 100 contact hours of approved continuing education or be re-examined; they must show evidence of continuing professional practice, and they must adhere to the NBCC Code of Ethics in their practice.

The Role of Peer Review and Peer Support

Peer review is an organized system by which practitioners within a profession assess one another's services. This approach is gaining in popularity. It provides some assurance to consumers that they will receive competent services. In addition to providing peer review, colleagues can challenge practitioners to adopt a fresh perspective on problems they encounter in their practice. In one survey it was found that psychologists rated informal exchanges among colleagues as the most effective resource for promoting effective and ethical practice (Pope, Tabachnick, & Keith-Spiegel, 1987). Such networks were perceived as more valuable in fostering ethical practice than laws, committees, research, continuing education, or professional codes of ethics.

Peer Review as a Way to Ensure Quality.   Regarded as a means rather than an end in itself, peer review has as its ultimate goals not only determining whether a practitioner's professional activity is adequate but also ensuring that future services will be acceptable. Peer review continues a tradition of self-regulation. A possible drawback of the peer-review model is implied in these questions we raise: Who determines the qualifications of the peer reviewer? What criteria should be used to determine the effectiveness of counseling practice?

Peer-Consultation Groups.   Borders (1991) described the value of structured peer groups that foster the development of skills, conceptual growth, participation, instructive feedback, and self-monitoring. Borders maintains that peer-supervision groups are useful for counselors at all levels of experience. For trainees, peer groups offer a supportive atmosphere and help them learn that they are not alone with their concerns. For counselors in practice, they provide an opportunity for continued professional growth.

Greenburg, Lewis, and Johnson (1985) describe peer-consultation groups as an important means for helping private practitioners improve their therapeutic effectiveness and counter the loneliness that is associated with this endeavor. In private practice there is no built-in provision for sharing problems, and peer-consultation groups can provide a source of support and new perspectives. Following is a summary of the key points of their article. The goals of peer-consultation groups are to provide mutual support and help in dealing with problematic cases and various sources of stress in private practice; to provide a source of objectivity in dealing with countertransference issues; and to share information about referral resources, therapeutic procedures, research, and professional meetings. Such groups function best when they advise rather than censure. The content of peer-consultation group sessions also includes ethical issues; professional issues, such as third-party payments; legal decisions that affect the professional; fees; political issues; problems pertaining to private practice; and burnout. At group meetings, which in one case were four hours long once a month, leadership is a shared function, and the agenda is flexible and determined by the needs of the members.

A national survey of psychologists in private practice revealed that 23% of the sample belonged to a peer-consultation group and that 24% had belonged in the past (Lewis, Greenburg, & Hatch, 1988). Of those not in a group, 61% said they would join if one were available. Private practitioners in one group reported that their peers provided suggestions for working with difficult clients, offered consultation on ethical and legal issues, and were helpful to them in dealing with feelings of isolation and burnout. In general, their findings showed a high degree of satisfaction with membership.

Borders (1991) believes that peer-supervision groups are valuable resources for counselors throughout their professional career:

> The structured peer group approach provides the procedure and tasks needed for groups to capitalize on the benefits of peer feedback. The approach also offers counselors methods and skills they can adapt for consultative supervision with other counselors in their work settings and for self-supervision. By using approaches such as this one, counselors can actively contribute to their own professional development and that of their colleagues [p. 251].

Peer-consultation groups can also function as an informal and voluntary form of review in which individual cases and ethical and professional issues are examined (Lewis et al., 1988). These groups provide additional safeguards to consumers and a greater measure of accountability, which governmental agencies often require. Furthermore, being a part of a peer-consultation group offers reassurance to private practitioners who are concerned about malpractice litigation.

Clarifying Your Views on Maintaining Competence

Apply the principles of supervision and the development of competence as an ongoing process to the following case of a therapist who believes that competence can be attained once and for all.

○ *The case of Conrad.*   Dr. Conrad Hadenuf has been a licensed psychologist for 20 years and has always maintained a busy practice. He sees a wide variety of clients. As a condition of license renewal, he is required to attend a 15-hour retraining program on substance abuse. He is indignant. "I have a Ph.D., I have 3000 hours of supervised experience, and I have years of experience with all sorts of problems," he says. "This is just a money-making gimmick for those who want to generate workshops!" Knowing that he has no choice if he wants to retain his license, Conrad grudgingly attends the workshop, sits in the back of the room, takes no notes, takes longer breaks than scheduled, and leaves as soon as the certificates of attendance are available.

- What are your reactions to Conrad's resistance? Is his rationale for not wanting to participate in the workshop justified?
- Even though he says he has no desire to deal with substance abuse, can he realistically say that he will never be confronted with clients with drug-abuse problems?
- How do you view mandated continuing education as a condition for license renewal?
- Are practitioners being ethically responsible to their clients if they never expose themselves to upgrading their knowledge and skills?

Applying the Discussion to Yourself.   We hope that you have thought about ways to maintain and enhance your competence. Use the following questions as a way to clarify your thinking on the issues that we have raised, giving special attention to identifying your own strategy for remaining professionally competent:

- What effects on individual practitioners do you think the trend toward increased accountability is likely to have? How might this trend affect you?
- Do you think it is ethical to continue practicing if you do not continue your education? Why or why not?
- What are some advantages and disadvantages to using continuing-education programs solely as the basis for renewing a license? Is continuing education enough? Explain.
- What are your reactions to competence examinations (oral and written) for entry-level applicants and as a basis for license renewal? What kinds of exams might be useful?
- Should evidence of continuing education be required (or simply strongly recommended) as a basis for recertification or relicensure? If you support mandatory continuing education, who do you think should determine the nature of this education? What standards should be used in making this judgment?
- Can you think of both advantages and disadvantages to basing license renewal strictly on peer-review procedures?
- What are some potential difficulties with the peer-review model? For instance, who would decide on the criteria for assessment?
- Assume that the peers who reviewed you had been chosen because they had a similar orientation to counseling (behavioral). Would they be assessing your competence or your fidelity to the tenets of the particular school? If the peers

who reviewed your work had a different theoretical orientation from yours (psychoanalytic), how competent would they be to assess you within the framework of your practice?

• What are your thoughts about a peer-consultation group for yourself? If you would like to be involved in such a group, how might you take the initiative to form one?

• What kinds of continuing education would you want for yourself? Through what means do you think you can best acquire new skills and keep abreast of advances in your field?

Concluding Commentary.   Before closing this discussion of competence, we want to mention the danger of rarely allowing yourself to experience any self-doubt and being convinced that you can handle any therapeutic situation. There are therapists who feel this way. They tell themselves they have it made and attend conventions to show off how much they know and impress their colleagues with their competence. Sidney Jourard (1968) warns about this delusion that one has nothing new to learn. He maintains that exciting workshops or contact with challenging colleagues can keep therapists growing. He urges professionals to find colleagues whom they can trust, so that they can avoid becoming "smug, pompous, fat-bottomed and convinced that they have *the* word." Such colleagues, he writes, can "prod one out of such smug pomposity, and invite one back to the task" (p. 69).

We support the view that supervision is a useful tool throughout one's career. Along with Jourard, we also see the development of competence as an ongoing process, not a goal that counselors ever finally attain. This process involves a willingness to continually question whether you're doing your work as well as you might and to search for ways of becoming a more effective person and therapist.

Chapter Summary

Clients' welfare is directly affected by ethical issues in the training of therapists, the debate over whether professional licensure and credentialing are adequate signs of competence, the role of peer review and peer-consultation groups in ensuring professional competence, and the importance of continuing one's education.

After completing a graduate program, counselors must acquire new knowledge and skills throughout their professional career. This is particularly true for those practitioners who wish to develop a specialty area dealing with certain client populations or problems. In addition to continuing-education activities, peer-consultation groups are useful routes to maintaining professional competence.

A core ethical and professional issue in training involves the question of how to develop policies and procedures for selecting the candidates who are best suited for the various mental-health professions. The challenge is to adopt criteria for choosing people who have the life experiences that will enable them to understand the diverse range of clients with whom they will work. The personal characteristics of trainees, such as attitudes and beliefs, are critical in deciding whom to admit to training programs.

Other important issues are the effectiveness of professional licensing and credentialing as a sign of an individual's competence and accreditation as a way to assess the worth of a training program. The issues are complex, yet the goal is to focus licensure and certification more on protecting consumers than on protecting professional specializations. We would like to see a move toward increased collaboration among the various mental-health professions, rather than the isolation that is too often created by turf battles and professional jealousies.

Suggested Activities

1. Invite several practicing counselors to talk to your class about the ethical and legal issues they encounter in their work. You might have a panel of practitioners who work in several different settings and with different kinds of clients.
2. In small groups explore the topic of when and how you might make a referral. Role-play a referral, with one student playing the client and another the counselor. After a few minutes the "client" and the other students can give the "counselor" feedback on how he or she handled the situation.
3. In small groups explore what you think the criteria should be for determining whether a therapist is competent. Let a student role-play an "incompetent" therapist and defend himself or herself. Make up a list of specific criteria, and share it with the rest of the class. Are you able as a class to come up with some common criteria?
4. Several students can look up the requirements for licensure or certification of the major mental-health specializations in your state. What are some of the common elements? Present your findings to the class.
5. Work out a proposal for a continuing-education program. In small groups, develop a realistic model of ensuring competency for professionals once they have been granted a license. What kind of design most appeals to you? A peer-review model? Competency examinations? Taking courses? Other ideas?
6. Assume that you are applying for a job or writing a résumé to use in private practice. Write up your own professional-disclosure statement in a page or two. Another suggestion is to bring your disclosure statements to class and have fellow students review what you've written. They can then interview you, and you can get some practice in talking with "prospective clients." This exercise can help you clarify your own positions and give you valuable practice for job interviews.
7. As a class project several students can form a committee to investigate some of the major local and state laws that apply to the practice of psychotherapy. You might want to ask mental-health professionals what major conflicts they have experienced between the law and their professional practice.
8. Form a panel to discuss procedures for selecting appropriate applicants for your training program. Your task as a group is to identify specific criteria for candidates. Consider questions such as the following: In addition to grade-point averages, scores on the Graduate Record Examination, and letters of recommendation, what other criteria might you establish? What life experiences

would your group look for? What personal qualities are essential? What attitudes, values, and beliefs would be congruent with becoming a counseling professional? What personal characteristics, if any, would you use as a basis for rejecting an applicant? What process should the program use in making selections? Would you recommend individual interviews? interviews conducted in small groups?

9. Assume that you are a graduate student who is part of the interviewing team for applicants for your training program. Identify six questions to pose to all applicants. What are you hoping to learn about the applicants from your questions?

10. Interview professors or practitioners in schools, agencies, or work settings that interest you. Ask them what they most remember about their training program. What features were most useful for them? What training do they wish they had had more of, and what would they like to have had less of? How adequately do they think their graduate program prepared them for the work they are now doing? What continuing-education experiences do they most value?

11. Form a small group for role-playing a licensing board that will interview candidates for a professional license. Meet out of class for the time it takes to draw up a list of questions to pose to the "practitioners" who will be examined by your group. Several students in the class can volunteer to sit for the interview.

12. Consider the advantages of forming a peer-support group within one of your own classes. Several of you could make a commitment to meet to explore ways to get the most from your training and education. The group could also study together and exchange ideas for future opportunities.

Suggested Readings

On ethical issues in the training of therapists see Grayson (1982). For an interesting discussion of ways in which graduate programs socialize their students into schools of thought, see Lazarus (1990). For a discussion of the licensing process as it is applied to social workers, see Garcia (1990); to marriage and family therapists, see Everett (1990); to psychologists, see Cummings (1990). For a discussion of licensure and certification see Gerstein and Brooks (1990). For a discussion of the dangers of competition and turf battles among the professions, see Garcia (1990), Ivey and Rigazio-DiGilio (1991), and Brooks and Gerstein (1990). On the topic of peer-consultation groups see Borders (1991), Greenburg et al. (1985), and Lewis et al. (1988).

CHAPTER EIGHT

Issues in Supervision and Consultation

Pre-Chapter Self-Inventory

Directions: For each statement, indicate the response that most closely identifies your beliefs and attitudes. Use the following code:

5 = I *strongly agree* with this statement.
4 = I *agree* with this statement.
3 = I am *undecided* about this statement.
2 = I *disagree* with this statement.
1 = I *strongly disagree* with this statement.

_____ 1. Ethical guidelines are needed to govern the conduct of counselors' supervisors in order to protect the client, the supervisor, and the supervisee.

_____ 2. Supervisors should be held legally accountable for the actions of the trainees they supervise.

_____ 3. Supervisors have the responsibility to monitor and assess a trainee's performance in a consistent and careful manner.

_____ 4. I think that working under supervision is one of the most important components in my development as a competent practitioner.

_____ 5. Supervisors must be sure that trainees fully inform clients about the limits of confidentiality.

_____ 6. I think that the focus of supervision should be on my progress as a practitioner, rather than on the client's problems.

_____ 7. Ideally, supervisory sessions should not be aimed at providing therapy for the trainee.

_____ 8. It is clearly unethical for counselor educators to date their students or other students who are involved in the training program.

_____ 9. It is acceptable for a supervisor or educator to date former students, once they have completed the program.

_____ 10. Supervisees and trainees should have a right to know what is expected of them and how they will be evaluated, as well as a right to periodic feedback and evaluation from supervisors so that they have a basis for improving their clinical skills.

_____ 11. I consider it unethical for counseling supervisors to operate in multiple roles such as mentor, adviser, teacher, and evaluator.

_____ 12. Ethically, supervisors need to clarify their roles and to be aware of potential problems that can develop when boundaries become blurred.

_____ 13. It is unethical for supervisors or counselor educators to provide therapy to a current student or supervisee.

_____ 14. It is essential that consultants subscribe to ethical standards to ensure that their services are competent and that the consumer receives professional service.

_____ 15. Consultants are obligated to determine with certainty who the consultee is.

_____ 16. Before initiating a contract, consultants may ethically investigate the goals of the agency to determine whether they can support them.

____ 17. When consultants become aware of value clashes that cannot be resolved, ethical practice dictates that they decline to negotiate a contract.

____ 18. Consultants need to make an ethical determination whether they are sufficiently trained to offer the services they contract to perform.

____ 19. In consulting it is almost impossible to avoid dual relationships, because the work involves blending teaching skills and counseling skills as needed in the situation.

____ 20. Ethical practice requires that consultants inform their consultees about the goals and process of consultation, the limits to confidentiality, the voluntary nature of consultation, the potential benefits, and any potential risks.

Introduction

Supervision is an integral part of the training of helping professionals and is one of the ways in which they can acquire the competence needed to fulfill their professional responsibilities. As we mentioned in the last chapter, professional competence is not something that can be attained once and for all. Remaining competent in one's field demands not only continuing education but also a willingness to obtain periodic supervision when one faces ethical dilemmas. By consulting experts in a particular field, practitioners show responsibility in obtaining the necessary assistance to provide the highest quality of care for clients. As practitioners, we can never know all that we might like to know, nor can we attain all the skills required to effectively intervene with all client populations or all types of problems. This is where the processes of supervision and consultation come into play.

Counselors are often expected to function in the roles of both supervisor and consultant. To carry out these roles ethically and effectively, they must have the proper training in both areas. Merely acquiring skills as a counselor does not necessarily give them the knowledge and skills to adequately supervise trainees or to advise other helping professionals. This chapter explores dilemmas frequently encountered in supervision and consultation and provides some guidelines for ethical and legal practice in these areas.

Ethical and Legal Issues in Clinical Supervision

The relationship between the clinical supervisor and the trainee (or student of psychotherapy) is of critical importance in the development of competent and responsible therapists. If we take into consideration the dependent position of the trainee and the similarities between the supervisory relationship and the therapeutic relationship, the need for guidelines describing the rights of trainees and the responsibilities of supervisors becomes obvious. Although specific guidelines for ethical behavior between a supervisor and trainee have not been delineated in all of the ethical codes of the various professional associations, the

ACES has developed "Standards for Counseling Supervisors" (1990), which consist of eleven core areas of knowledge, competencies, and personal traits that characterize effective supervisors.

In their discussion of ethical and legal considerations for counseling supervisors, Borders and Leddick (1987) list the following themes of which supervisors need to be cognizant: informed consent, due process, dual relationships, evaluation, confidentiality, and legal liability. As they say, supervisors are challenged with choosing whether to adhere to minimal requirements or to aspire to the highest ethical principles. Because most unethical behavior remains undetected by the legal establishment, ethical standards must be inforced by the profession. Harrar, VandeCreek, and Knapp (1990) distinguish between the ethical and legal aspects of clinical supervision. The *ethical issues* are supervisors' qualifications, their duties and responsibilities, dual relationships, the consent of trainees' clients, and third-party payments. The legal issues involve direct and vicarious liability, confidentiality and the supervisor's duty to protect, and standards of care. Sherry (1991) also discusses ethical issues in supervision: responsibility, the welfare of clients and supervisees, confidentiality, competence, moral and legal standards, and professional relationships.

The Supervisor's Roles and Responsibilities

Supervisors are ultimately responsible, both ethically and legally, for the actions of their trainees. Therefore, they are cautioned not to supervise more trainees than they can responsibly manage at one time. They must check on the trainees' progress and be familiar with their caseloads. Just as practitioners keep case records on the progress of their clients, supervisors should maintain records pertaining to their work (Harrar et al., 1990). The trainee has the right to know about training objectives, assessment procedures, and evaluation criteria. Supervisees have a right to know what is expected of them and how they will be evaluated. It is the responsibility of supervisors to inform trainees about these matters at the beginning of supervision (ACES, 1990; Cormier & Bernard, 1982; Pope & Vasquez, 1991).

Trainees have a legal right to periodic feedback and evaluation so that they have a basis for improving their clinical skills (Cormier & Bernard, 1982). Supervision is perhaps the most important component in the development of a competent practitioner. It is within the context of supervision that trainees begin to develop a sense of professional identity and to examine their own beliefs and attitudes regarding clients and therapy.

Counseling or clinical supervisors have a position of influence with their supervisees, in that they operate in multiple roles as a teacher, evaluator, counselor, model, mentor, and advisor. According to Sherry (1991), there are three main reasons why supervisors are ethically vulnerable: (1) the power differential between the participants, (2) the "therapylike" quality of the supervisory relationship, and (3) the conflicting roles of the supervisor and supervisee. He points to the multiple roles that supervisors are expected to play. Although the requirements of these roles overlap in some cases, they may also conflict. Supervisors are faced with the responsibility of protecting the welfare of the client, the supervisee, the public and the profession. Sherry maintains that the client's welfare comes first, followed by that of the supervisee. He also reminds us that because supervision is like therapy in some ways, there is a risk of harm to both the client and the supervisee from a supervisor's blurred objectivity, impaired judgment, or exploitation.

Supervisors are responsible for ensuring compliance with relevant legal, ethical, and professional standards for clinical practice (ACES, 1990). They can demonstrate these standards through the behavior they model in the supervisory relationship.

Methods, Techniques, and Styles of Supervision.

The ACES standards (1990) require that supervisors demonstrate a conceptual knowledge of supervisory methods and techniques and that they be skilled in using this knowledge to promote the development of trainees. They specify ways in which clinical supervisors can promote counselor development:

- stating the purposes of supervision and explaining the procedures to be used
- negotiating mutual decisions about the educational needs of the counselor-in-training
- performing the role of teacher, counselor, or consultant as they are appropriate
- clarifying the supervisory role
- integrating knowledge of supervision with their own interpersonal style
- interacting with counselor trainees in a manner that facilitates their self-exploration and problem-solving ability

It is our assumption that the most important tool in the supervisory process is the kind of person the supervisor is. We think that the methods and techniques supervisors use are less important than their ability to establish an effective and collaborative working relationship with supervisees. In much the same way that effective therapists create a climate in which clients can explore their conflicts, supervisors need to establish a collaborative relationship that encourages trainees to reflect on what they are doing. Fogel (1990), who considers herself a "rebellious supervisor," makes an urgent plea to teach trainees the value of doubting and of creative innovation:

> My whole purpose in supervision has been to create such a safe environment that the trainee can function in his/her own style and feel cherished enough to ask for help when the going gets rough. We can then reflect, explore options, and discover together the process which feels suited to the trainee's present psychic state and skills [p. 6].

Because supervisees are at different stages in their professional development, they require different types of supervision. Overholser (1991) points out that an important element in the supervisory process is balancing a directive style and a permissive one. A supervisor's task is to strive for an optimal level of challenge, in order to promote autonomy, without overwhelming the supervisee. Although supervisees may need more direction when they begin their training, it is a good idea to foster a reflective and questioning approach that leads to self-initiated discovery. Overholser applies the Socratic method to supervision. This method assumes that trainees achieve more insight when they discover a relationship on their own than when it is explained to them. Therefore, the Socratic supervisor functions more as a catalyst for exploration than as a lecturer and helps trainees realize that the answers lie within themselves.

Focus on the Supervisory Process.   When we supervise, we focus on the dynamics between ourselves and our trainees. Our style of supervision can be grasped by the questions we explore: "What is going on with you? How are you reacting to your clients? How is your behavior affecting them? Which clients bring out your own resistances? How are your values manifested by the way you interact with your clients?"

We do not look merely at the cases that trainees bring to the supervisory sessions; rather, we focus on the interpersonal and intrapersonal variables. Although we see supervision as a separate process from psychotherapy and do not attempt to make training sessions into therapy sessions, we think that the supervisory process can be therapeutic and growth-producing.

The proper focus of supervision must also include the ways in which individual differences can influence the process. The ACES guidelines (1990) call for the counseling supervisor to demonstrate knowledge of individual differences with respect to gender, race, ethnicity, culture, and age and to understand the importance of these characteristics in supervisory relationships. Stoltenberg and Delworth (1987) believe that any model of supervision must be judged partly on how it treats the development of women and ethnic minorities. They recommend that supervisors be knowledgeable of possible gender and ethnic differences and explore these factors in the supervisory process. They have observed instances in which supervisors were deficient in their understanding of how individual differences influenced both the therapist/client relationship and the supervisor/supervisee relationship. Certainly, supervisors have an ethical responsibility to become aware of the complexities of a multicultural society, which will be addressed in Chapter 10.

Legal Aspects of Supervision

Three legal considerations in the supervisory relationship are informed consent, confidentiality and its limits, and the concept of liability. First, supervisors must see that trainees provide the information to clients that they need to make informed choices. This requirement implies that clients be made fully aware that the counselor they are seeing is a trainee, that he or she is meeting on a regular basis for supervisory sessions, that the client's case may be discussed in group-supervision meetings with other trainees, and that sessions may be taped or observed. As Borders and Leddick (1987) indicate, by virtue of supervision, supervisors have a relationship with the client whom a trainee is counseling. Therefore, it is necessary that the client be informed of that relationship in all details.

Second, supervisors have a legal and ethical obligation to respect the confidentiality of client communications. There may be certain exceptions, however, such as cases when the supervisor determines that the client is potentially dangerous to himself or herself or to others. Supervisors must make sure that clients are fully informed about the limits of confidentiality, including those situations in which supervisors have a duty to warn or a duty to protect.

Third, supervisors ultimately bear legal responsibility for the welfare of those clients who are counseled by their trainees. Cormier and Bernard (1982) assert that supervisors must be familiar with each case of every supervisee in order to avoid being negilgent. This requirement may not be practical, in the sense that supervisors cannot be cognizant of all details of every case. But they should at least know the direction in which the cases are being taken. Also, university training programs have a responsibility to clients to make some kind of formal assessment of each trainee before allowing the person to counsel clients. Harrar and his colleagues (1990) indicate that supervisors bear both direct liability and vicarious liability. *Direct liability* can be incurred if supervisors are derelict in the supervision of their trainees, if they give trainees inappropriate advice about treatment, or if they give tasks to trainees that exceed their competence. *Vicarious liability* pertains to the responsibilities that supervisors have because of the actions of their supervisees. From both a legal and ethical standpoint, trainees should not assume final responsibility for clients; rather, their supervisors must carry the decision-making responsibility and liability.

Dual Relationships and the Supervisory Process

The ACES standards (1990) imply that counseling supervisors possess the personal and professional maturity to play multiple roles. Ethically, supervisors need to clarify their roles and to be aware of potential problems that can develop when boundaries become blurred. As Herlihy and Corey (1992) point out, unless the nature of the supervisory relationship is clearly defined, both the supervisor and the supervisee may find themselves in a difficult situation at some point in their relationship. There is the potential that the supervisor's objectivity will be impaired and that the supervisee will not be able to make maximum use of the process. If the relationship evolves into a romantic one, the entire supervisory process becomes confounded, with the supervisee likely to feel exploited sooner or later.

Sexual Intimacies during Professional Training

As in the case of sexual relations between therapists and clients (which was explored in Chapter 6), sex in the supervisory relationship can result in an abuse of power because of the difference in status between supervisees and supervisors. Further, there is the matter of poor modeling for trainees for their future relationships with clients.

In a study of the beliefs and behaviors of psychologists as educators (Tabachnick, Keith-Spiegel, & Pope, 1991), only 23.9% of the educators said they had never been "sexually attracted to a student"; 15.4% of them considered this behavior unethical. With respect to "engaging in sexual fantasies about students"

39.8% said they had never engaged in this behavior; 20% considered this behavior unethical. With respect to telling a student "I'm sexually attracted to you," 92.7% said they had never done so; 68.9% considered this behavior unethical.

In the draft of the APA ethics code (1991a) the nature of exploitative relationships is specified in the following two standards:

1. "Psychologists do not exploit, sexually or otherwise, their professional relationships with current students, supervisees, employees, research participants, or other persons over whom they have significant supervisory or other authority."
2. "Sexual relationships with current students or direct supervisees are so likely to be exploitative that they are always unethical."

Supervisory relationships have qualities in common with the instructor/ student and the therapist/client relationships. Bartell and Rubin (1990) make the point that students, clients, and supervisees trust that the relationship will operate in their best interests. They conceptualize the supervisor/supervisee relationship as both a human and a professional one. Although sexual involvement may enhance a human relationship, it does so at the expense of professional relationships such as supervisory ones. It is clear that sexual harassment, sexual involvement, and sexual discrimination are violations of professional relationships.

Bartell and Rubin emphasize the supervisor's responsibility to create an ethical climate for self-exploration. It is essential that supervisees believe that they can explore difficult topics, such as sexual feelings for clients, without having to fear that the discussion will be perceived by the supervisor as an invitation to some kind of sexual involvement (Pope, Keith-Spiegel, & Tabachnick, 1986).

Glaser and Thorpe (1986) conducted an anonymous survey of 464 female members of the APA's Division 12 (Clinical Psychology). It examined (1) the women's experiences during graduate training of sexual intimacy with and sexual advances from psychology educators and (2) their past and current perceptions and evaluations of these experiences in terms of coercion, ethicality, and impact on the professional working relationship. Glaser and Thorpe found that sexual contact was quite prevalent between graduate students and supervisors or educators. The overall rate was 17%; among recent doctoral graduates it was 22%; and among students divorcing or separating during graduate training the rate was 34%. Of those individuals who reported sexual contact, only 28% perceived some degree of coercion at the time of contact. As they looked back, however, 51% saw some degree of coercion. Similarly, 36% saw an ethical problem at the time of contact, but in retrospect, 55% saw an ethical problem. Interestingly, only 12% of the respondants received graduate training on the issue of sexual intimacies between educators and students, while 67% of them reported having received training about sex between therapists and clients.

This study revealed that the judgments of the majority of the respondents were very negative: over 95% of them evaluated such contact as unethical, coercive, and harmful to the working relationship to a considerable degree. Sexual advances were reported by 31% and were judged by most to be overwhelmingly negative. Almost all judged sexual contact between an educator and a student during a working relationship to be highly unethical.

The core ethical issue is the difference in power or status between teacher and student. Because of the vulnerable position of supervisees when a supervisor makes a sexual proposition, many would argue that the supervisees are not in a position to give free consent. The developmental level of supervisees may also be related to their vulnerability to sexual contact with a supervisor (Bartell & Rubin, 1990). When supervisees first begin counseling, they are typically naive and uninformed with respect to the complexities of therapy. They frequently regard their supervisors as experts, and thus, they have a dependence on their supervisors that may make it difficult to resist sexual advances. Supervisees may disclose personal concerns and intense emotions during supervision, much as they might in a therapeutic situation. The openness of supervisees and the trust they place in their supervisors can be exploited by supervisors who satisfy their own psychological needs at the expense of their supervisees.

Consider the following assumptions: sexual relationships between graduate students and their professors or supervisors *cannot* be equated with relationships between a client and a therapist because:

- Students are not emotionally unstable and are not seeking therapy.
- Students in the counseling field who purport to teach responsibility to clients later in their profession must themselves be responsible for what they do and cannot blame others for "what was done to them."

What is your evaluation of these assumptions? What are your views on the ethical and professional implications of sexual intimacies between students and faculty members?

Assume that you are a trainee and that your clinical supervisor consistently harasses you sexually, along with touching you in questionable ways. During your individual supervision sessions the supervisor makes many comments with double meanings. The supervisor frequently looks at you in flirtatious ways. From what your supervisor says and does, you get the distinct impression that your evaluations will be more favorable if you engage in "playing the game." What course of action might you take in such a situation? Is there a difference between sexual harassment and consensual sexual relationships, or are all sexual advances in unequal power relationships really a form of sexual harassment?

○ ***The case of George.***   George meets weekly with his professor, Amy, for individual supervision. With only three weeks remaining in the semester, George hesitantly confesses to having a strong attraction to Amy and says he finds it difficult to maintain professional distance with her. Amy discloses that she, too, feels an attraction. But she is sensitive to the professional boundaries governing their relationship, and she tells him it would be inappropriate for them to have any other relationship until the semester ends. She lets him know that she would be open to further discussion about a dating relationship at that point. She says that even though he will still be in the program, she will no longer have a supervisory role with him, nor will she be evaluating his status in the program.

- What ethical implications do you see in this situation? List them and say why you see them as ethical concerns.

- Do you think that Amy handled her attraction to George in the best way possible? Would it have been better for her to wait until the semester was over before she acknowledged her feelings of attraction? Would that have been ethical?
- If you were a colleague of Amy's and heard about this situation from another student, what would you do, if anything?
- Is the fact that Amy will no longer be supervising George sufficient to eliminate the imbalance of power in the relationship? Do you think that it would be appropriate for them to date each other while he is still a student in the program? after he graduates?

Ethical Issues in Combining Supervision and Counseling

Besides inappropriate sexual contact between faculty supervisors and students, there are other dual relationships related to one's professional training. We now consider the issue of supervisors who also provide counseling for their supervisees. In a national survey on dual relationships 75% of the respondents said that providing therapy to a current student or supervisee was either "never ethical" or "ethical under rare conditions" (Borys & Pope, 1989). In the literature on supervision, there seems to be basic agreement that the process should concentrate on the supervisee's professional development rather than on personal concerns and that supervision and counseling have different purposes. However, there is a lack of consensus and clarity about the degree to which supervisors can ethically deal with the personal issues of supervisees (Herlihy & Corey, 1992).

Wise, Lowery, and Silverglade (1989) contend that supervision cannot provide supervisees with the kinds of personal-growth experiences that are afforded through personal counseling. They assert: "Ethical concerns, as well as differences between supervision and counseling, lead to the conclusion that personal counseling as a component of counselor training should be offered by professionals other than the supervisor or counselor education faculty member" (p. 328).

Whiston and Emerson (1989) also explore the ethical issues involved in a supervisor's blending of supervising and counseling. Contending that combining these roles often presents serious conflicts, they propose a model of supervision that incorporates an examination of personal problems that are causing an impasse in a trainee's counseling work. They contend that after the supervisor identifies personal issues that could impede a trainee's performance, it is the trainee's responsibility to resolve them. They think that by limiting the focus of supervision to the professional development of trainees, there is less of a chance that dual-relationship conflicts will emerge.

If supervisees become aware of personal problems for which therapy may be useful, they should consult a separate therapist to avoid the dual-relationship problem (Pope & Vasquez, 1991). We agree that it is a supervisor's responsibility to help trainees identify how their personal dynamics are likely to influence their professional work but that it is not the supervisor's proper role to counsel them.

○ *The case of Greta.* Ken is a practicing therapist as well as a part-time super-visor in a counseling program. One of his supervisees, Greta, finds herself in a personal crisis after she learns that her mother has been diagnosed with inoperable cancer. Much of her internship placement involves working with hospice patients. In tears, she approaches Ken and lets him know that she feels unable to con-tinue doing this work. He is impressed with her therapeutic skills and thinks that it would be most unfortunate for her to interrupt her education at this point. He also assumes that he can more expeditiously deal with her personal crisis because of their trusting relationship. For the next four supervision sessions, he focuses exclusively on her personal problems. As a result of his help, she recovers her stability and is able to continue working with the hospice patients, with no apparent adverse affects for either them or for her.

- Given Greta's crisis, was Ken justified in blending the roles of supervisor and counselor? If it was clear that her personal crisis was affecting her ability to function therapeutically with her clients, was his assuming the role of counselor for only four sessions acceptable? Does the fact that his interventions worked in just four sessions ethically justify the action he took?
- What ethical issues, if any, would you see if Ken had recommended that Greta temporarily discontinue her field placement and enter therapy with him in his private practice?
- If he recommended that she see another therapist for her personal therapy but she refused on the ground that he knew her best and that she would like him as her therapist, would that make his acceptance ethical?
- What alternatives do you see for dealing with this situation both ethically and effectively?
- Do you think that it is ever appropriate for supervisors to blend the roles of supervisor and therapist? Why or why not?

Educators Who Counsel Students

Stadler (1986b) contends that the dual-relationship standard of ethical conduct can and should be used to establish limits on the methods used to train counselors. On the issue of educators' serving as counselors for their students, Stadler con-cludes that there are many negative repercussions that can sour student/faculty relationships. These consequences are summarized in the accompanying box.

There is no clear answer to the ethical question raised by counselor educators who provide counseling for their students. As we mentioned in Chapter 2, many professional programs strongly recommend, if not require, a personal therapeutic experience. Some programs expect students to undergo individual therapy for a time, and other programs provide a growth-group experience. At the very least, students have a right to know of these requirements before they make a commit-ment to begin a program. Further, we think that students should generally be allowed to decide what type of therapeutic experience is most appropriate for them. The practice of faculty members' providing counseling for students for a fee is highly questionable.

Negative Effects of Dual Relationships

- *Effects on the student.* Students' autonomy may be compromised if they fear that an academic evaluation will be influenced by information divulged during counseling. Further, students who seek counseling from a faculty member are likely to assume that dual relationships are ethical and may go on to engage in them as a professional.
- *Effects on other students.* Assuming that students are aware that dual relationships in most cases violate ethical standards, they may lose respect for the educator, for the graduate program, and for a profession that appears to support unethical behavior. Further, resentment may build up among those who have not been singled out for what may appear to be a privileged relationship with a faculty member.
- *Effects on other faculty members.* Fellow educators can be placed in the difficult position of having either to confront their colleague or to condone this behavior.
- *Effects on the counseling profession.* Ethical violations are especially detrimental when violators are those responsible for the education of beginning professionals.
- *Effects on the educator.* Faculty members who violate an ethical standard by engaging in dual relationships may find themselves obtaining information in therapy that could have a bearing on academic decisions.

Some situations are not so clear-cut, however. Once students complete a program, for example, what are the ethics of a psychology professor's taking them on as clients? Can it still be argued that the prior role as educator might negatively affect the current role as therapist? If the former student and the professor/therapist agree that there are no problems, is a therapeutic relationship ethically justified? To clarify your position on this issue, reflect on the case that follows.

○ ***The case of Brent.*** A psychology professor, Hilda, teaches counseling classes, supervises interns, and also provides individual therapy at the university counseling center. One of her graduate students, Brent, approaches her with a request for personal counseling. Even though she tells him of her concern over combining roles, he is persuasive and adds that he trusts her and sees no problem in being both her student and her counselee. He also informs her that he will be in her internship class next semester.

- Would Hilda be acting unethically if she accepted Brent as a client, given his feelings about the matter?
- Would you see any difference if he approached her for counseling after he had completed the course with her?
- Would the situation take on a different ethical dimension if the professor had a private practice? Is the matter partly one of the professor's charging a fee for her service?
- Assume that Hilda was leading a therapy group during the semester and that Brent wanted to join the group. Do you think that being a client in a group is different from being an individual client? Would it be unethical for her to accept him into the group? Would it be unethical for her to reject him on

the ground that he was a student, especially if she believed that the group would benefit him?

- Do you think that the lack of availability of other resources in the area should make a difference in whether to accept him as a client?

Questions to Consider

What is your position on the ethical and legal issues raised in this section? Specifically, take a stand on the following situations:

- Your supervisor does not provide what you consider to be adequate supervision. You are left mainly on your own with a difficult caseload. The staff members where you work all are overloaded, and when you do get time with a supervisor, the person feels burdened with many responsibilities. Thus, you do not get enough time to discuss your cases. What would you be inclined to do?
- You have a conflict with your supervisor over the most ethical way to deal with a client. What would you do?
- You are aware that a clinical supervisor with whom you are scheduled to work has a reputation of becoming sexually involved with supervisees. What action, if any, would you take?
- You do not get adequate feedback on your performance as a trainee. At the end of the semester your supervisor gives you a negative evaluation. What ethical and legal issues are involved? What might you do or say?
- Do you think it is unethical for a supervisor to initiate social or sexual relationships with trainees after they have graduated (and when the supervisor has no professional obligations to the trainee)? Explain your position.
- If during the course of your supervision you became aware that personal problems were interfering with your ability to work effectively with clients, what would you be inclined to do? If you trusted your supervisor, would you feel that it might be appropriate to discuss your personal concerns?
- What are the main problems with dual relationships in supervision? Can you think of ways to avoid problems that might arise from certain dual relationships? Do you think that all such relationships in supervision should be avoided entirely?
- What possible benefits, if any, do you see when supervisors combine a multiplicity of roles such as teacher, mentor, counselor, consultant, evaluator, and supervisor? Can you think of ways to maximize potential benefits and also to decrease the potential for harm from such dual relationships?

Ethical and Professional Issues in Consultation

Consultation is emerging into a specialized professional process, and it is being carried out by many different groups in diverse work settings (Kurpius, 1986). Consultants often work with individuals and small groups in schools, agencies, and businesses. Consultation often involves sharing of expertise with others in the helping professions so that they can better serve their own clients. This process is aimed at helping people to work more effectively on the individual, group, organizational, or community level. Consultants assist consultees with immediate problems and also try to improve their ability to solve future problems.

After surveying the literature, Dougherty (1990) found general agreement on the common characteristics of consultation:

- Consultants help practitioners better serve their own clients.
- Participation in the consultation process should be voluntary by all the parties involved.
- Consultees have the freedom to decide what they will do with the suggestions and recommendations of the consultant.
- The relationship between the consultee and the consultant, at its best, is a collaboration of peers who are equal in power.
- Consultation is a temporary process aimed at helping consultees move toward autonomy and independence.
- Consultation is primarily aimed at problems with work or caretaking as opposed to personal concerns (such as the consultee's marital discord or depression). For example, consultants might provide training workshops for counselors and social workers in an agency. The focus of consultation could be on learning to recognize and deal effectively with job-related stress that can easily interfere with one's professional functions.

Ethical Standards for Consultants

It is essential that consultants have a set of ethical standards to ensure that the consumer receives professional service. One of the ethical issues in consulting involves the potential for an imbalanced power relationship. The consultant has certain skills or abilities that the consultee desires. This situation can place the consultant in a powerful position, and there is a high potential for abuse (Tokunaga, 1984). Practitioners who function as consultants come from many disciplines, and thus there are few ethical guidelines that encompass this diversity. Consultants need to rely on their own professional organizations for general rules. Because the role of consulting within a counseling framework is so complex and because ethical codes are lacking, many qualified professionals often do not know how to deal with ethical dilemmas they face. Such dilemmas are particularly serious because of the potentially large number of people who are indirectly affected by a consultant's ethical principles and decisions. With these problems in mind, Gallessich (1982) asserts that a code of ethics for consultants is urgently needed to protect the public. Other writers agree with the need for guidelines for consultants, yet they argue that the responsibility for ethical and professional behavior ultimately rests with the consultant (Dougherty, 1990; Robinson & Gross, 1985; Tokunaga, 1984; Wubbolding, 1991).

Wubbolding (1991) mentions several pitfalls facing consultants and offers some useful guidelines for responsible practice:

- Consultants need to identify their real client, for the expectations of the manager and of the participants are frequently quite different.
- The cultural context in which consultation occurs is important. In Asian cultures, for example, consultants may be expected to assume a more directive role in their dealings with consultees.
- Creating a job for oneself is a pitfall that a consultant needs to monitor. The goal is to help people acquire skills that will lead to independence, rather than to create a niche for the consultant.
- Even though the optimal consultant/consultee relationship is an equal one, the potential for dual relationships exists; these can be problematic from both a business and a professional perspective.

The following suggested ethical guidelines, which can contribute to consultants' professionalism, are adapted from a variety of sources. We are indebted to Dougherty's excellent chapter on ethical, professional, and legal issues in consultation (1990) and his article on ethical issues in elementary school consultation (in press). Our discussion also incorporates some of the code of ethics that Gallessich (1982) has proposed. And we are including guidelines provided by Robinson and Gross (1985) and by the AACD's *Ethical Standards* (1988).

Dougherty (1990) has described five ethical and professional issues that pertain to consultation in the human-services professions: values, competence and training, the consultation relationship, the rights of consultees and their clients, and consultation in groups. We draw on Dougherty's example of elementary school consulting to illustrate how these ethical guidelines can be applied to a particular work setting.

Value Issues in Consulting.   The consultant's values raise a number of ethical concerns. A consultant who is biased against special education, for example, might persuade parents to not allow their child to make use of services that could be beneficial. Some school counselors might err on the other side, being hesitant to express their own values lest they sway the consultee.

Before initiating a contract, consultants should investigate the goals of the organization to determine whether they can support them. When consultants become aware of value differences that cannot be resolved, ethical practice dictates refusing to negotiate a contract. This approach prevents arriving at an insoluble value conflict in the middle of the consulting contract. Because of a difference between the values of the consultant and the consultee, referral is sometimes in order.

Competence and Training in Consultation.   Consultants need to determine if they have adequate education and training to perform the services for which they intend to contract. Furthermore, they are ethically bound to assume the responsibility for keeping abreast of the theoretical and technical developments in their field. The codes of ethics of the AACD (1988) and the APA (1989) make reference to consultants' delivering only those services that they are competent to perform. Consultants should also present their professional qualifications so as to avoid misrepresenting themselves. They can maintain a high level of professionalism by continuing their education, by attending professional conferences, by consulting with more experienced colleagues, and by obtaining the relevant credentials or licenses for the profession in which they expect to serve as a consultant. It is also essential that consultants know and appreciate the boundaries of their competence, which implies knowing when to decline a position and when to refer. Consultants must be reasonably certain that the organization employing them has the resources to give the kind of help that its clients need and that referral resources are available.

Consultants need to be aware of personal problems (such as burnout, rigid beliefs about the target populations, or substance abuse) that interfere with their effective functioning, and they should not practice when such conditions would impair their services. Ideally, they will meet their personal needs outside the consulting relationship and avoid using clients for that purpose. If their personal problems or biases affect their performance as a consultant, they will consider terminating their services and making a referral.

Relationship Issues in Consulting.   The consultee's interests and needs are paramount. The consulting relationship is based on an understanding and agreement between the consultant and the consultee on what the problem is, the goals for change, and the predicted outcomes of the interventions selected (AACD, 1988). Consultants should establish a clear contract with well-defined limits, respect their contract, and communicate its terms to all who are participating in consulting activities. Any changes in the contract are made only through explicit agreement with staff members and the administration.

From an ethical perspective, consultants need to be aware of the dangers of establishing dual relationships, such as acting as a counselor. If it becomes evident that a consultee needs personal counseling, then the appropriate course is to refer the consultee for appropriate professional help. For instance, school counselors should avoid discussing the personal concerns of a teacher or an administrator during consultation with that person. Ethical practice dictates that they monitor their interventions so that they avoid situations such as creating dependency or otherwise misusing their power.

An ethical consultant places top priority on the consultee's freedom of choice. Consultants have a responsibility to protect the freedom of consultees by declining to be involved in activities that require discussion of highly personal issues. They should not attempt to coerce people to do what they do not want to do. Consultants assist clients in moving toward self-direction and growth; they do not become a decision maker for the client (AACD, 1988).

Rights of Consultees.   Two central issues involving the rights of consultees are confidentiality and informed consent. Just as in any professional relationship, absolute confidentiality cannot be guaranteed in the consultation relationship. The matter of who will have access to the consultant's findings should be established before gathering data. Consultants should remind staff members and administrators of the limits of confidentiality as established during contract negotiations. Certain information that is given confidentially may be useful when it is presented anonymously to an administrator.

Consultants who work in schools may need to break confidentiality when there is abusive behavior on a consultee's part, such as a teacher's consistent violation of a school's policy regarding corporal punishment.

Ethical practice implies that consultants inform their consultees about the goals and process of consultation, the limits to confidentiality, the voluntary nature of consultation, the potential benefits, and any potential risks. As was mentioned in Chapter 4, informed consent is not exclusively accomplished at the outset of a relationship but is best achieved through a continuing discussion of relevant issues. Consultants should put themselves in the place of their consultees and ask themselves what they would want to know. For example, teachers should know if the consultant is keeping a list of those who seek consultation and should be told who has access to that list.

Issues in Consulting in Groups.   Consultation is increasingly being done between a consultant and a group of consultees. The ethical guidelines for group work that are discussed in Chapter 13 apply here to the process of consulting in groups. Certainly those who participate in consultation in groups have a right to know what will be expected of them. Matters such as self-disclosure, privacy, the boundary between work-related concerns and personal concerns, and the limits of confidentiality are all particularly important.

Three Case Examples of Consulting

○ *A case of possible conflict of interest.*   The principal of a school hires Lynn, a psychologist in private practice, to conduct a communications workshop focusing on improving interpersonal relationships between the faculty and the administration. The workshop is a two-day intensive group experience involving all teachers and the three administrators in the school. They are encouraged to openly express their concerns and difficulties, and to focus on possible strategies for improving working conditions. The workshop seems to go well.

The following week, the principal calls Lynn and asks for a meeting. The principal agrees that the workshop seemed successful and says she would be interested in Lynn's assessment of the key faculty members whom she needs to play closer attention to. She would like to know more about the natural leaders and the potential troublemakers. Lynn is asked to go through the list of teachers and make an assessment of each person's potential to be troublesome or helpful.

- What ethical issues, if any, are involved in this case?
- Since the principal attended the workshop and basically heard everything, would it be permissible for Lynn to give her professional assessment of each person?
- The consultation contract was between the principal and Lynn. What rights, if any, does that fact give the principal?
- Because the teachers are being professionally assessed on the basis of their participation in the workshop, what were their rights regarding knowing in advance that this kind of assessment would be made and that it would be given to the principal?

- Does informed consent require that all participants know exactly how the information they offer will be used?

○ *A case of a consultant's dual relationship.*   An airline-management group is concerned about the loss of working hours because of on-the-job stress. Delilah is hired to provide stress-management skills to solve the problem. The contract calls for her to teach specific strategies such as relaxation, diet, exercise, aerobics, and visualization, with the stated goal of reducing stress and improving efficiency. In the process of teaching employees how to cope with stress, she discovers that many outside personal problems are contributing to their stress. She decides to alter her strategy to include several hours of group counseling to address the personal problems of the participants. In addition, she gives the participants three sources of referral for further professional help.

- Can a consultant unilaterally change the provisions of a contract?
- Is it ethical for Delilah to ignore the personal problems that are contributing to inefficiency on the job, because this information was not available to her when the contract was designed?
- Does management have any rights to insist on the contract being strictly adhered to, since it contends that personal problems are best dealt with separately and financed by the employees or their insurance company?
- Is Delilah now involved in a dual relationship as consultant and counselor, and is her holding of group sessions unethical?

○ *A case of a hidden agenda in consulting.*   A state-funded agency employs a team of consultants to conduct human-relations training and staff development. Over time, these consultants earn a reputation for effectively working with the lower-level staff. The director of the agency expresses to the consultants a desire to "work on" key members of the upper-level staff, who are considered particularly troublesome to the agency. The stipulation is that the focus on these key members is not to be disclosed; rather, the impression to be given is that the team is working to improve the overall efficiency to the staff.

- If the consultants accept this contract as it is written, are they being unethical?
- If this hidden agenda is indeed successfully carried out, overall efficiency is also enhanced, and the entire agency benefits, did the end justify the means?
- Assume that a hidden agenda becomes evident to you during the course of a consulting workshop you are giving. What would be the ethical thing to do? Would you disclose to the members that you suspect a hidden agenda? Would you confront the director who had hired you?

Chapter Summary

Supervision and consultation are two roles that counselors are often asked to assume. It is clear that special training is needed to effectively perform the many functions required in these activities. Some of the key ethical issues associated with supervision and consultation involve carrying out professional roles and responsibilities, maintaining clear boundaries between roles, and avoiding the problems created by dual relationships.

Supervision is one way in which trainees learn how to apply their knowledge and skills to particular clinical situations. It is essential that supervisees receive regular feedback so that they have a basis for honing their skills. Effective supervision deals with the professional as a person and as a practitioner. It is not enough to focus on the trainee's skills, for the supervisory relationship is a personal process. Thus, the supervisee's dynamics are equally important in this process.

Consultation is a growing professional specialization that can be carried out with individuals and in small groups with diverse client populations in various work settings. Consultants help human-services workers deliver services to their clients more effectively. Thus, they focus on work-related concerns. Ethical and professional issues pertaining to consultation can be broken down into these areas: values, competence and training, the consulting relationship, the rights of consultees, and consulting in groups.

Suggested Activities

1. Role-play a situation that involves a supervisor's asking supervisees to get involved in therapy situations that are beyond the scope of their training and experience. One student in class can play the role of a persuasive supervisor who thinks that students will learn best by "jumping into the water and learning how to swim—or sink." The supervisor can ask trainees to work with a family, lead a therapy group alone, or work with abused children. After the role playing, discuss the ethical and clinical issues involved, with a focus on ways to deal with inadequate supervision.

2. Set up another role-playing situation. In this case, the supervisor is difficult to reach and rarely keeps his or her appointments with the supervisees. One student can role-play the inaccessible supervisor, and several others can assume the role of students who need to meet with their supervisor to discuss their difficult cases.

3. Investigate some of the community agencies in your area to learn what supervision they offer to interns and to newly hired practitioners. Several students can form a panel to share the results.

4. Form an ethics committee in class to review the following cases dealing with supervision:
   • A supervisor has made sexual offers to several supervisees.
   • A supervisor is accepting supervisees as clients in his or her private practice.
   • A supervisor makes it a practice to date former students in the program.
   The ethics committee can present its case in class with appropriate courses of action for each problem area. The others in the class can interact with the committee by providing alternative viewpoints.

5. Interview a consultant to discover how this person was trained and what professional activities he or she typically performs. It would be useful for various students to interview consultants in different settings, such as businesses,

public schools, agencies, and private practice. Ask the consultants to share some of the ethical dilemmas that they have faced in their work. How did they deal with them?

6. Design a role-playing situation that involves consultation. At least one student assumes the role of consultant. A number of students can play the role of consultees who are seeking help from the consultant. Again, think of diverse settings to add some variety. Afterward, discuss the process involved.

7. Interview several clinical supervisors to determine what they consider to be some of the most pressing ethical and legal issues in the supervisory relationship. Some questions you might ask supervisors are: What are the rights of trainees? What are the main responsibilities of supervisors? To what degree should supervisors be held accountable for the welfare of the clients who are counseled by their trainees? What kind of specialized training have they had in supervision? Who is the proper focus of supervision—the client? the trainee? What are some common problems faced by supervisors in effectively carrying out their duties?

8. Assume that you are in a field placement as a counselor in a community agency. The administrators tell you that they do not want you to inform your clients that you are a student intern. They explain that your clients might feel that they were getting second-class service if they found out that you were in training. What would you say and do if you found yourself as an intern in this situation? Would it be ethical to follow this directive and not inform your clients that you were a trainee and that you were receiving supervision? Do you agree or disagree with the rationale of the administrators? Might you accept the internship assignment under the terms outlined if you could not find any other field placements?

Suggested Readings

On the liability of supervisors see Harrar et al. (1990). On ethical issues in the conduct of supervision see Sherry (1991). On ethical issues in supervising counseling practitioners see Kurpius, Gibson, Lewis, and Corbet (1991). For a discussion of dual relationships in supervision and consulting, see Herlihy and Corey (1992). On the issue of sexual contact in the supervisory relationship see Bartell and Rubin (1990). On ethical concerns of counselor educators, see Roberts, Murrell, Thomas, and Claxton (1982), Glaser and Thorpe (1986), Pope, Levenson, and Schover (1979), and Pope, Schover, and Levenson (1980). On dual relationships in counselor education see Stadler (1986b) and Herlihy and Corey (1992). On the ethical issues in combining supervision and counseling see Wise et al. (1989) and Whiston and Emerson (1989).

On ethical issues in consultation see Dougherty (1990), Tokunaga (1984), Robinson and Gross (1985), Wubbolding (1991), and Gallessich (1982).

CHAPTER NINE

Issues in Theory, Practice, and Research

Pre-Chapter Self-Inventory

Directions: For each statement, indicate the response that most closely identifies your beliefs and attitudes. Use the following code:

5 = I *strongly agree* with this statement.
4 = I *agree* with this statement.
3 = I am *undecided* about this statement.
2 = I *disagree* with this statement.
1 = I *strongly disagree* with this statement.

___ 1. I should adhere to a definite theory of counseling.

___ 2. I would rather combine insights and techniques derived from various theoretical approaches to counseling than base my practice on a single model.

___ 3. People are basically capable of and responsible for changing their behaviors.

___ 4. What happens in counseling sessions is more my responsibility than it is my client's.

___ 5. I would find it difficult to work for an agency if I were expected to perform functions that I didn't see as appropriate to counseling.

___ 6. I have the power to define my own role and professional identity as a counselor.

___ 7. Clients should always select the goals of counseling.

___ 8. I'd be willing to work with clients who didn't seem to have any clear goals or reasons for seeking counseling.

___ 9. A diagnosis is helpful, if not essential, when a client begins counseling.

___ 10. The drawbacks associated with diagnosis in counseling outweigh the values.

___ 11. Testing can be a very useful adjunct to counseling.

___ 12. I think the medical model of mental health can be fruitfully applied in counseling and psychotherapy.

___ 13. There is a real danger that counseling techniques can be used to keep the therapist hidden as a person.

___ 14. Skill in using a variety of techniques is one of the most important qualities of a therapist.

___ 15. Theories of counseling can limit counselors by encouraging them to pay attention only to behavior that fits their particular theory.

___ 16. Counselors should develop and modify their own theory of counseling as they practice.

___ 17. In my view of human nature, people are responsible both for creating and for solving their problems.

___ 18. Although I do not see people as responsible for creating their problems, I do see them as responsible for finding ways to deal effectively with these problems.

___ 19. It can be unethical for practitioners to fail to do some type of assessment and diagnosis, especially with "high-risk" (suicidal or dangerous) patients.

_____ 20. In assessment and diagnosis it is critical to take cultural factors into consideration if the therapist hopes to gather accurate data and come up with a valid perspective on a client.

Introduction

Professional counselors should be able to conceptualize *what* they are doing in their counseling sessions and *why* they are doing it. Too often practitioners are unable to explain why they use certain counseling procedures. When you meet a new client, for example, what guidelines should you use in structuring your first interview? What do you want to accomplish at this initial session? Rank in order of importance the following factors that you would be interested in knowing about your client:

- the presenting problem (the reason the client is seeking counseling)
- the client's style of coping with demands, stresses, and conflicts
- early experiences as a child, particularly in relation to parents and siblings
- ego strength
- functional strengths and weaknesses
- history of successes and failures
- developmental history
- the client's struggle with current choices
- goals and agenda for counseling
- current support system
- motivation to change
- level of reality testing

What interventions might you make during your initial session in getting to know your client? How would you structure your future sessions? Consider the following questions, and briefly write your responses:

- Would you begin with a detailed case history? Why or why not?
- Do you consider diagnosis a necessary prerequisite to counseling? Why or why not?
- Are tests important as a prerequisite to counseling? Would you decide whether to test, or would you allow your client to make this decision?
- How much would you structure the session to obtain current information about your client's life? How much would you want to know about the client's past?
- Would you do most of the talking? Why or why not?
- Who would set the goals of therapy? Who would be primarily responsible for what was discussed? Why?
- Who would take the greater responsibility for *directing* the initial session? Would you ask many questions? Would you encourage your client to structure the session?
- Would you develop contracts with your clients specifying what they could expect from you, what they wanted from counseling, and what they were willing to do to meet their goals? Why or why not?

- Would you be inclined to use directive, action-oriented techniques, such as homework assignments? Why or why not?
- What aspects of the client's life would you stress?

In this chapter we focus on how your theoretical positions and biases influence your actual practice. Ideally, theory should help you make sense of what you do in your counseling sessions. Since your answers to the preceding questions depend on your view of personality and of counseling, looking at how you responded to these questions is one way to begin clarifying your theoretical approach. Another way of thinking about this issue is to imagine a client asking you to explain your view of counseling in clear and simple terms. Would you be able to tell your client what you most hoped to accomplish and how you would go about it? Ethical practice is grounded in a solid theoretical and research base. Thus, practitioners who operate in a theoretical vacuum, with little or no interest in the practical applications of psychotherapeutic research, may be engaging in ethically questionable behavior.

You might consider how open you are to challenging your theoretical stance and how this openness or lack of it might influence the therapeutic outcome for your clients. Think about how your theoretical viewpoint influences your stand on questions such as these: What are some goals for counseling? What is the proper place of diagnosis and testing in the counseling process? What techniques are most appropriate in reaching certain goals of counseling? In your assessment and treatment of clients, how do you make provisions for cultural diversity? What is the place of research in counseling practice? In what ways are issues pertaining to theory, practice, and research interrelated?

Developing a Counseling Stance

Developing a counseling stance is more complicated than merely accepting the tenets of a given theory. We believe that the theoretical approach you use to guide your practice is an expression of your uniqueness as a person and an outgrowth of your life experience. Further, your counseling stance must be appropriate for the type of counseling you do and the unique needs of your clients.

We believe that a theoretical approach becomes more useful and meaningful after you've taken a critical look at the *theorist* who developed it as well as its key concepts, since a theory of counseling is often an expression of the personality of the theorist. Blindly following any single theory, however, can lead you to ignore some of the insights that your life opens up to you. This is our bias, of course, and many would contend that providing effective therapy depends on following a given theory.

A major consideration in developing or evaluating a theory is the degree to which that perspective helps you understand what you're doing. Does your framework provide a broad base for working with diverse clients in different ways, or does it restrict your vision and cause you to ignore variables that don't fit the theory? If you are a "true believer" of one theory, there's a danger of forcing your clients to conform to your expectations. It's important, therefore, to evaluate what you are emphasizing in your counseling work. The following questions may help you make this evaluation:

- Where did you acquire your theory? Did you incorporate many of the views of your instructors or training supervisors? Has one theory intrigued you to the point that it is the sole basis for your orientation?
- Do you embrace a particular theory because it is a justification of your own lifestyle, experiences, and values? For instance, do you adopt a theory that stresses an active, didactic role for the therapist because you see yourself as "straightening out" your clients? What does your approach stress, and why does it appeal to you?
- To what degree does your theory challenge your own previous frame of reference? Does it cause you to test your hypotheses, beliefs, and assumptions? Does it encourage you to think of alternatives? To what degree does your theory reinforce your present world view? Does it force you to extend your thinking, or does it merely support your biases?
- How do you see your own life experiences as an influence in your counseling style? In what ways have your life experiences caused you to modify your theoretical viewpoint?
- What are the ethical implications of a counselor's practicing without a theoretical orientation? Does ethical practice demand having a rationale for the interventions you make?

Your assumptions about the nature of counseling and the nature of people have a direct impact on your manner of practice. The goals that you think are important in therapy, the techniques and methods you employ to reach these goals, the way in which you see the division of responsibility in the client/therapist relationship, your view of your role and functions as a counselor, and your view of the place of diagnosis and testing in the therapeutic process—these are largely determined by your theoretical orientation.

Practicing counseling without an explicit theoretical rationale is somewhat like flying a plane without a map and without instruments. We do not see a theoretical orientation (or a counseling stance) as a rigid structure that prescribes the specific steps of what to do in a counseling situation but, rather, a set of general guidelines that counselors can use to make sense of what they are doing.

The Division of Responsibility in Therapy

We've observed that many beginning counselors tend to deprive their clients of their rightful responsibility for their experience in therapy, because they anxiously take so much of this responsibility on themselves. If clients don't progress fast enough, these counselors may blame themselves for not knowing enough, not having the necessary skill and experience, or not being sensitive or caring enough. They may worry constantly about their adequacy as counselors and transmit their anxiety to their clients. *If only* they were better therapists, their clients would be changing in more positive directions. This may be true, of course, but overly anxious counselors frequently fail to see the role their clients play in the outcome of their own therapy, whether for better or for worse.

We believe that counselors do well to bring up the question of responsibility during the initial sessions, so that clients can begin to think about their part in their own therapy. One way of clarifying the sharing of responsibility in a therapeutic relationship is a contract. A contract is based on a negotiation between the client and the therapist to define the therapeutic relationship. It encourages the client and the therapist to specify the goals of the therapy and the methods likely to be employed in obtaining these goals. Other aspects of a contract include the length and frequency of sessions, the duration of therapy, the cost and method of payment, provisions for the renegotiation of the contract, any factors limiting confidentiality, the extent of responsibility for each partner, and ways of determining the effectiveness of the therapeutic relationship.

We see therapy as a joint venture of the client and the therapist. Both have serious responsibilities for the direction of therapy, and this issue needs to be clarified during the initial stages of counseling. In our view counselors who typically decide what to discuss and are overdirective run the risk of perpetuating their clients' dependence. We'd like to see clients encouraged from the start to assume as much responsibility as they can. Even directive therapies such as transactional analysis, behavior therapy, rational-emotive therapy, and reality therapy stress client-initiated contracts and homework assignments as ways in which clients can fulfill their commitment to change. These devices help to keep the focus of responsibility on the clients by challenging them to decide what *they* want from therapy and what *they* are willing to do to get what they want.

As you consider the range of viewpoints on the division of responsibility in therapy, think about your own position on this issue. What do you see as your responsibility, both to your client and to yourself? What do you expect from your client? Do you burden yourself with the total responsibility for what happens in therapy?

○ *The case of Ivan.*   Ivan is a member of a weekly group. At the 16th meeting he unexpectedly tells the group that he has often thought of suicide. He has never developed a detailed plan, but suicide is weighing heavily on his mind, and it frightens him. Consider three possible responses that a group leader could make to Ivan:

Counselor A: "Ivan, this is news to me! I'm very willing to work with you on your suicidal ideation, but I hold you responsible for your life. If you choose to kill yourself, that is your responsibility. If you choose to challenge yourself and live, that, too, is your responsibility. I refuse to burden myself with the responsibility of your life."

Counselor B: "Ivan, this really surprises me! If I'd known this, I wouldn't have put you in the group. I'd like to switch you from group treatment to individual treatment twice a week. Furthermore, I'll check in with you by telephone every day, and I'd like you to call me at any time if you become frightened by your impulses. Perhaps later on, when you have worked through this problem, you may be able to be in a group again."

Counselor C: "This is a surprise. I'd like you to tell me more about what's going on in your life now. Perhaps you can address the members in the group and give each person a reason why life isn't worth living. This will give you an opportunity to explore at a deeper level the meaning of your suicidal thinking." At the end of the session, the therapist adds: "Ivan, you are ultimately responsible for your life, but I'd like to make myself available to you to explore and understand what you are experiencing. I think you could also use this group as a tool to help you in this struggle."

In reviewing these three approaches, consider your own stand:

- Which approach are you most likely to take, and why?
- Imagine yourself as Ivan. Which of these approaches would you find most helpful? least helpful? Why?
- How can this case help you formulate your own ideas about the division of responsibility in counseling?

Deciding on the Goals of Counseling

Aimless therapy is unlikely to be effective, yet too often practitioners fail to devote enough time to thinking about the goals they have for their clients and the goals clients have for themselves. In this section we discuss possible aims of therapy, how they are determined, and who should determine them. Counselors' answers to these questions are directly related to their theoretical orientations.

In considering therapeutic goals it is important to keep in mind the cultural determinants of therapy. The aims of therapy are specific to a particular culture's definition of psychological health. Levine and Padilla (1980) note that the goals for therapy in any culture can range from removal of symptoms to attitude change, behavior change, insight, improved relations with others, social effectiveness, personal adjustment, and preventive health. They give an example of Morita therapy, a popular treatment in Japan that involves discussion of the concepts of Zen Buddhism. This therapy directs the person toward an Eastern conception of mental health based on an inner-directed life acquired through peace and meditation. The experiential therapies, on the other hand, have the goal of helping people move in the direction of becoming self-actualizing and autonomous, which is typically a goal of Western cultures.

Most counseling approaches agree that effective counseling does not result when the therapist imposes goals; rather, goals should be set by the client and the therapist working together. However, some therapists believe that they know what is best for their clients and try to persuade their clients to accept certain goals. Others are convinced that the specific aims of counseling ought to be determined entirely by their clients.

Of course, the issue of who sets the goals of counseling must be seen in the light of the theory you operate from, the type of counseling you offer, the setting in which you work, and the nature of your clientele. If you work in crisis intervention, your goals are likely to be short-term and practical, and you may be very directive. If you're working with children in a school, you may combine educational and therapeutic goals. As a counselor with elderly people in an institution, you may stress survival skills and ways of relating to others on their ward. What your goals are and how actively involved your client will be in determining them depend to a great extent on the type of counseling you provide and the type of client you see.

Diagnosis as a Professional Issue

The main purpose of the diagnostic approach is to allow the therapist to plan treatments tailored to the special needs of the client. There are different kinds of diagnosis. *Medical diagnosis* is the process of examining physical symptoms, inferring causes of physical disorders or diseases, providing a category that fits the pattern of a disease, and prescribing an appropriate treatment. *Psychodiagnosis* (or *psychological diagnosis*) is a general term covering the process of identifying an emotional or behavioral problem and making a statement about the current status of a client. This process also includes the identification of the possible causes of the person's emotional, psychological, and behavioral difficulties, and it entails suggesting the appropriate therapy techniques to deal effectively with the identified problem and estimating the chances for a successful resolution. *Differential diagnosis* is the process of distinguishing one form of disease or psychological disorder from another by determining which of two (or more) diseases or disorders with similar symptoms the person is suffering from. The third edition of the American Psychiatric Association's (1987) *Diagnostic and Statistical Manual of Mental Disorders* (DSM-III-R) is the standard reference for pathology.

Whether diagnosis should be part of psychotherapy is a controversial issue. Some mental-health professionals see diagnosis as an essential step in any treatment plan, but others view it as an inappropriate application of the medical model of mental health to counseling and therapy. Even though you may not yet have had to face the practical question of whether to diagnose a client, you will probably need to come to terms with this issue at some point in your work. In this section we briefly review some of the arguments for and against the use of diagnosis in therapy and ask you to consider how valuable diagnosis is from your viewpoint.

Arguments for Psychodiagnosis

Practitioners who favor the use of diagnostic procedures in therapy generally argue that such procedures enable the therapist to acquire sufficient knowledge about the client's past and present behavior to develop an appropriate plan of treatment. This approach stems from the medical model of mental health, according to which different underlying causal factors produce different types of disorders.

Psychoanalytically oriented therapists favor psychodiagnosis, since this form of therapy was patterned after the medical model of mental health and stresses the understanding of past situations that have contributed to a dysfunction. Some psychological-assessment devices used in psychodiagnosis involve projective techniques that rest on psychoanalytic concepts.

For different reasons, practitioners with a behavioristic orientation also favor a diagnostic stance, inasmuch as they emphasize specific treatment programs. Although they may not follow the medical model, these practitioners value observation and other objective means of appraising both a client's specific symptoms and the factors that have led up to the client's malfunctioning. Such an appraisal, they would argue, enables them to use the techniques that are appropriate for a particular disorder and to evaluate the effectiveness of the treatment program.

Brammer, Shostrom, and Abrego (1989) see diagnosis as being broader than simply labeling clients with some category from the DSM-III-R. They argue in favor of diagnosis as a general descriptive statement identifying a client's style of functioning. Such information can motivate clients to change their behavior. They contend that practitioners must make some decisions, do some therapeutic planning, and be alert for signs of pathology in order to avoid serious mistakes in therapy. They propose that a therapist "simultaneously understand diagnostically and understand therapeutically" (p. 148). In favoring this broad type of diagnostic process, which involves developing hunches, Brammer and his colleagues caution against accepting a narrow and rigid diagnostic approach.

Arguments against Psychodiagnosis

Although many professionals see diagnosis as an essential component of psychotherapy, there are as many critics who view it as unnecessary or harmful. Generally, existential or relationship-oriented therapists fall into this group. Their arguments against diagnosis include the following:

- Diagnosis is typically done by an expert observing a person's behavior and experience from an external viewpoint, without reference to what they mean to the client.
- Diagnostic categories can rob people of their uniqueness.
- Diagnosis can lead people to accept self-fulfilling prophecies or to despair over their condition.
- Diagnosis can narrow therapists' vision by encouraging them to look for behavior that fits a certain disease category.
- The best vantage point for understanding another person is through his or her subjective world, not through a general system of classification.
- Many potential dangers are implicit in the process of reducing human beings to diagnostic categories.

Many psychologists and some psychiatrists have objected to the use of diagnosis in therapy. Rogers (1942, 1951, 1961) has consistently maintained that diagnosis is detrimental to counseling because it tends to pull clients away from an internal and subjective way of experiencing themselves and to foster an objective and external conception *about* them. The result may be to increase tendencies toward dependence and cause clients to act as if the responsibility for changing their behavior rested with the expert and not with themselves. Of course, client-centered therapy is grounded on the belief that clients are in the best position to understand and resolve their personal difficulties. Rogers (1951) maintains that "when the client perceives the locus of judgment and responsibility as clearly resting in the hands of the clinician, he is, in our judgment, further from therapeutic progress than when he came in" (p. 223).

Our Position on Psychodiagnosis

We believe that diagnosis, broadly construed, is a legitimate part of the therapeutic process. The kind of diagnosis we have in mind is the result of a joint effort by the client and the therapist. Both should be involved in discovering the nature of the client's difficulty, a process that commences with the initial sessions and continues until therapy is terminated. Even practitioners who oppose conventional diagnostic procedures and terminology need to raise such questions as:

- What is going on in this client's life at this time?
- What are the client's resources for change?
- What does the client want from therapy, and how can it best be achieved?
- What should be the focus of the sessions?
- What factors are contributing to the client's problems, and what can be done to alleviate them?
- What are the prospects for meaningful change?

The counselor and the client can discuss each of these questions as a part of the therapeutic process. Counselors will develop hypotheses about their clients, and they can talk about these conjectures with them. Diagnosis does not have to be a matter of categorizing clients; rather, counselors can describe behavior and think about its meaning. In this way, instead of being done mechanically and technically by an expert, diagnosis becomes a process of thinking *about* the client *with* the client.

From our perspective, diagnosis should be associated with treatment, and it should help the practitioner conceptualize a case. Ethical dilemmas are often created when diagnosis is done strictly for insurance purposes, which often entails arbitrarily assigning a client a diagnostic classification. As we have seen earlier, many practitioners use diagnosis for a variety of reasons other than thinking about the dynamics of a client and an appropriate treatment plan.

It is clear that diagnosis raises critical ethical and legal issues. One of the reviewers of this book contends that many counselors engage in diagnostic practices that could be considered unethical, illegal, or both. Because some therapists reject the diagnostic system, for example, they give every client the same diagnosis. Other practitioners diagnose without a proper understanding of the categories and the DSM-III-R system.

If therapists do not understand how to work within a diagnostic framework, it is likely that they will develop inappropriate treatment plans. Unless practitioners have a full diagnostic picture of their clients, they cannot be certain that they are ethically providing the most appropriate treatment. For example, unless a practitioner knows that a client has had a manic episode, he or she may proceed incorrectly by treating depression alone. We also think it is an ethical (and sometimes legal) obligation of therapists to screen clients for life-threatening problems such as organic disorders, schizophrenia, manic-depression, and suicidal types of depression. Students need to learn the clinical skills necessary to do this type of screening, which is a form of diagnostic thinking.

If practitioners view the DSM-III-R manual as a bible, however, they can bring harm to their clients by making them fit into neatly defined diagnostic categories. Sometimes practitioners begin to treat their clients in restrictive ways because they have diagnosed them on the basis of a pattern of symptoms. Therapists can actually behave toward clients in ways that make it very difficult for them to change. Furthermore, it is essential that practitioners who use the DSM-III-R be trained in its use. This training implies learning more than diagnostic categories; it involves knowing personality theory and seeing how it relates to therapeutic practice. Unless practitioners are adequately trained in diagnosis, there is a danger that they will assign a "mental disorder" inappropriately to a client.

Practical Issues in Diagnosis

Those who support the traditional forms of diagnosis agree that present classification systems have limitations and that some of the problems mentioned by the critics of diagnosis do exist. Rather than abandoning diagnostic classifications altogether, however, they favor updating diagnostic manuals to reflect improvements in diagnosis and treatment procedures.

Another important issue is whether clients should know their diagnosis and have access to all the information concerning themselves that their therapists have. Some practitioners contend that they should decide how much information to reveal to their clients. Others believe that it is unethical to keep pertinent information from their clients. Can you think of situations in which you would not be willing to share your hunches or information about a client with that client?

A further practical concern is that many insurance companies that pay for psychological services require a diagnosis. Presumably, clients who consult a therapist regarding problems that don't fit a standard category are not to be reimbursed for their psychotherapy. These insurance carriers take the position that psychotherapy is treatment for specific mental or emotional disorders; consequently, if a therapist doesn't write down a specific diagnosis, the client's insurance may not cover his or her expenses.

We think that Smith (1981) goes to the heart of the controversy over the traditional diagnostic system when he addresses informed-consent procedures. He points out that, while unprecedented attention is being given to informed decisions by clients regarding treatment plans and expectations, most practitioners remain virtually silent on clients' rights to be informed about diagnostic classifications for the purpose of securing third-party payments. Smith contends that psychologists are compromising their integrity and sacrificing the dignity of their clients for economic gain by using the DSM system without the informed consent of the client. He argues for psychologists to make a bold gesture to declare to their clients whether they are advocates or opponents of the mental-illness model. They will have taken another commendable step when they begin to lobby with other mental-health professionals to persuade legislative bodies to enact laws to protect consumers from the wholesale abuse of diagnostic codes and classifications.

Two Cases on Diagnostic Practices

O *The case of a hurried diagnosis.*   Irma has just accepted her first position as a counselor in a community agency. An agency policy requires her to conduct an intake interview with each client, to determine a diagnosis, and to establish a treatment plan—all in the first session. After three weeks, she lets a colleague know that she is troubled by this requirement. Her colleague reassures her that what she is doing is acceptable and that the agency's aim is to satisfy insurance companies. Irma does not feel reassured and cannot justify making an assessment in so short a time.

- Do you share Irma's concerns? Are there ethical difficulties with this agency's policies?
- Is it ever justified to provide a person with a diagnosis mainly for the purpose of obtaining third-party payment? How can you ethically satisfy the demands of insurance companies that a psychiatric disorder be identified and treated?
- If Irma retains her convictions, is she ethically obliged to discontinue her employment at this agency? What other alternatives, if any, do you see for her situation?
- In the course of a client's treatment, when the original diagnosis becomes obsolete, would you continue to use that diagnosis simply because your client wishes to see you?

O *The case of Bob.*   Bob displays symptoms of anxiety and lethargy. After 12 weeks of treatment, Felicity, a Gestalt therapist, realizes that her client has all the symptoms of a major depression and that he is showing no improvement. She is inclined to double the number of weekly sessions in order to accelerate her client's progress.

- What do you think of Felicity's plan? Is it justified?
- Should she have done a more thorough assessment earlier in the treatment? Might the results have indicated alternative treatments?
- Is Felicity obligated to inform Bob of the option of antidepressant medication? Is she obliged to refer him if he so desires?
- Do you see any other ethical issues in this case?

Questions on Diagnosis

What is your position on diagnosis? The following questions may help you formulate such a position:

- After reviewing the arguments for and against psychodiagnosis, what position do you tend to support? Why?
- Some contend that clients have a right to know their diagnoses on the ground of informed consent, whereas others maintain that clients should not be told their diagnoses because of the dangers of their living up to a self-fulfilling prophecy. What is your thinking on this matter?
- Smith (1981) asserts that practitioners should take a stand against classification and coding for the purpose of third-party payments unless clients know of their diagnoses and agree to provide this information to insurance companies. Do you see an ethical issue in this practice? Do you agree or disagree that therapists who do not accept the medical model, yet who provide diagnoses for reasons of third-party payments, are compromising their integrity? What options are open to them?
- What ethical and professional issues can you raise pertaining to diagnosis? In your view what is the most critical issue?

The Issue of Using Tests in Counseling

At some point in your career you may need to decide on the place that testing will occupy in your counseling. This section focuses on when and how you would use tests in your work with clients. As is true of diagnosis, the proper use of testing in counseling and therapy is the subject of some debate. Generally, those therapeutic approaches that emphasize an objective view of counseling are inclined to use testing procedures as tools to acquire information about clients or as resources that clients themselves can use to help them in their decision making. The client-centered and existential approaches tend to view testing in much the same way that they view diagnosis—as an external frame of reference that is of little use in counseling situations.

Ethical Considerations in Using Tests

We think that the core issue is not whether you will use tests as an adjunct to counseling but rather under what circumstances and for what purposes. Many tests can be used for counseling purposes, including measures of aptitude, ability, achievement, intelligence, values and attitudes, vocational interests, and personality characteristics. Unfortunately, tests have often been misused. They may be given routinely to unwilling clients, given without providing feedback to clients, used for the wrong purposes, or given by unqualified testers. The following questions will help you think about the circumstances under which you might want to use tests for counseling purposes:

• What do you know about the tests you may use? It is important for counselors to be familiar with any tests they use and to have taken these tests themselves. They should know the purpose of each test and how well it measures what it purports to measure. Sometimes mental-health workers find themselves expected to give and interpret tests as a basic function of their job. If they have not had adequate training in this area, they are in an ethical bind. In-service training and continuing-education programs are ways of gaining competence in using psychological-assessment devices. The AACD (1988) offers this guideline on this matter: "Different tests demand different levels of competence for administration, scoring, and interpretation. Members must recognize the limits of their competence and perform only those functions for which they are prepared." The draft of the APA ethics code (1991a) stresses the importance of competence in assessment: "Psychologists who develop, administer, score, interpret, or use psychological assessment techniques and instruments do so in a manner consistent with professional standards and for appropriate purposes."

• How much involvement should clients have in the selection of tests? Should counselors assume the responsibility, or should clients decide whether they want to take certain tests?

• Do you know why you want to use a particular test? Does your agency require that you administer certain tests? Are you giving tests because they will help you understand a client better? Do you administer tests mainly when clients request them? Whatever your reasons, you should be able to state them clearly.

• When clients request testing, do you explore their reasons? Some clients may think that a test will provide them with answers in making important decisions. There are even those who expect tests to make decisions *for* them. Clients need to be aware that tests are merely tools that can provide useful information about themselves, which they can proceed to explore in their counseling sessions. They also need to know clearly what the tests are designed for. These points are particularly relevant in testing culturally diverse populations. In a discussion of the uses of assessment in cross-cultural situations, Lonner and Ibrahim (1989) assert:

> Ultimately, it is the cross-cultural counselor who will have to decide what to assess, when and by which method to assess it, and how to weigh the risks involved against the possible benefits. Nothing will ever replace the counselor's careful consideration of what is best for the client [p. 324].

• How do you integrate test results into the counseling sessions? In general, it's best to give test *results*, not simply test *scores*. In other words, you should explore with your clients the meaning the results have for them. However, just as clients need to be involved in the selection of tests, they also should be involved in their interpretation. In this connection you will need to evaluate your clients' readiness to receive and accept certain information, and you will need to be sensitive to the ways in which they respond to the test results. The interpretation and discussion of test data should be understandable and relevant to the needs of ethnically and culturally diverse client populations (APA, 1991b).

• Are you concerned about maintaining the confidentiality of test results? Results may be handled in different ways, depending on the purpose and type of each test. Nevertheless, your clients need to feel that they can trust you and that test results will neither be used against them nor revealed to people who have no right to this information.

• Are you critical in evaluating tests? Too often mistakes are made because counselors have blind faith in tests. You should know the limitations of the tests you use, and you should keep in mind that a test can be useful and valid in one situation but inappropriate in another. On this point, the APA guidelines for working with diverse populations (1991b) caution psychologists to consider the validity of a given test and to interpret test data in the context of the cultural and linguistic characteristics of the individual being tested. It is also important to be aware of the reference population of the test and to recognize the possible limitations of such an instrument with other populations.

The AACD (1988) has developed a number of specific standards governing the ethical use of tests in counseling. People taking a test should know what it is intended to discover, how it relates to their situation, and how the results will be used. Test results should be placed in proper perspective and read in the context of other relevant factors. Furthermore, in interpreting tests it is essential for counselors to recognize the effects of socioeconomic, ethnic, linguistic, and cultural factors that might affect scores. The AACD warns counselors to proceed with caution in testing minorities if the norm group on which the instrument was standardized did not include the minority population. It is also important to be aware that minority clients might react to testing with suspicion if tests have been used to discriminate against them in schools and employment. To minimize such negative reactions, it is a good practice to explore a minority-group member's views and feelings about testing and to work with the client in resolving attitudes that are likely to affect the outcome of a test.

There are also ethical implications in the use of computers as an assessment tool in counseling. The AACD *Ethical Standards* (1988) now address nine ethical issues associated with computers: (1) broadening the concept of counseling records to include the storage of electronic data; (2) the potential misuse of computer-maintained client data; (3) possible client misconceptions of the validity of computer-generated data; (4) the need for counselor interventions in cases where clients make use of computers—for example, in testing; (5) the potential negative impact on minority groups of computer applications; (6) the development of self-help computer software; (7) the need to train counselors to use computers for interpreting tests; (8) the accuracy of computer-assisted test scoring; and (9) the validity of computer test interpretations (see Sampson, 1990).

The draft of the APA ethics code (1991a) identifies guidelines for assessment, diagnosis, and psychological evaluation. It deals with topics such as competence in assessment, test construction, appropriate use of assessments, testing special populations, scoring and interpreting tests, explaining assessment results, and maintaining test security.

Perhaps the most basic ethical guideline for using tests is to keep in mind the primary purpose for which they were designed: to provide objective and descriptive measures that can be used by clients in making better decisions. Further, a wide range of appraisal techniques, including both test and nontest data, should be used in providing clients with useful information. And it is wise to remember that tests are tools that should be used in the service of clients, not against clients.

The Use of Techniques in Counseling and Therapy

Your view of the use of techniques in counseling and therapy is closely related to your theoretical model. The issue of techniques includes such questions as *what* techniques, procedures, or intervention methods you would use and *when* and *why* you would use them. Some counselors are very eager to learn new techniques, treating them almost as if they were a bag of tricks. Others, out of anxiety over not knowing what to do in a given counseling situation, may try technique after technique in helter-skelter fashion. However, counselors should have a rationale for using particular methods of intervention, and we question the benefit to the client of an overreliance on technique.

It can be illuminating to see yourself working with a client on videotape or to listen to a session you've tape-recorded. Instead of focusing your attention on what your client said or did, you can monitor your own responses and get some general sense of how you related to your client. We suggest that you review your sessions with several clients in this way, paying attention to questions such as the following:

- Do you ask many questions? If so, are the questions mainly to get information, or are they open-ended ones designed to challenge your client? Do you raise questions merely because you don't know what else to do and hope that your questions will keep things moving?
- Do you tend to give advice and work quickly toward solutions? Or do you allow your client to explore feelings in depth instead of focusing on solutions to problems?
- How much direction do you give to the sessions? Who typically structures the sessions?
- How much support and reassurance do you give? Do you allow your clients to fully express what they're feeling before you offer support? Do your attempts to give support tend to cut them off from what they're feeling?
- Do you challenge your clients when you think they need it? Do your interventions get them to think about what they're saying on a deeper level?
- Who does most of the talking? Do you hear yourself as preaching or persuading? Are you responsive to what your client is saying?
- How often do you clarify what you hear? Do you check whether you're hearing what your client means to express?
- Do you reflect back to your clients what you hear them saying? If so, is your reflection done mechanically, or does it encourage a deeper self-exploration?
- Do you interpret much, telling your clients what you think certain behaviors mean? Or do you leave it to them to discover what their behavior means from their own perspectives?
- Do you use techniques primarily to get clients moving, or do you wait until they express some feelings and then use a technique geared to helping them experience their feelings on a more intense level?
- Do you use techniques that "feel right" for you and that you're comfortable using? Have you experienced these techniques yourself as a client?

- Are the procedures you use drawn from one counseling approach? Or do you borrow techniques from various approaches and use them when they seem appropriate?
- When you use a particular technique, does it seem mechanical to you? Or do you feel that your techniques are appropriate and unforced?
- How do your clients generally respond to the techniques you use? Do they react negatively to any of your counseling methods?

Monitoring your own work in light of these questions can help you discover your counseling style, ask yourself why you're making the interventions you make, and evaluate the impact these counseling procedures have on your clients. This willingness to reflect on the effects your interventions have on clients is of the utmost importance.

We believe that the purpose of techniques is to facilitate movement in a counseling session and that your counseling techniques really cannot be separated from your personality and your relationship with your client. When counselors fall into a pattern of mechanically employing techniques, they become technicians and are not responding to the particular individuals they're counseling. You can lessen the chances of falling into a mechanical style by deliberately paying attention to the ways you tend to use techniques. Particular techniques may be better suited to some therapists' personalities and styles of counseling than to others'. At times you may try a technique that you've observed someone else using very skillfully, only to find that it fails for you. In essence, your techniques should fit your counseling style, and you should feel comfortable and real in using them.

Ethical Issues in Psychotherapeutic Research

As can be seen, most of the questions that we have raised in this chapter have a direct relationship on one's therapeutic approach. Matters such as the use of specialized techniques, the balance of responsibility in the client/therapist relationship, the functions of the therapist, and the goals of treatment are tied to one's theory. Surely one critical ethical question is: Does a given psychotherapeutic approach or technique work? Failing to at least attempt to base one's practice on the findings of research is tantamount to asking consumers to simply trust that practitioners know what they are doing.

Although the ethical implications of conducting research in counseling and psychotherapy are vast, we do want to address a few selected ethical issues and encourage you to think about your responsibilities in this area. Some of the questions that we encourage you to keep open are:

- In conducting research in a counseling setting, must the participants always give informed consent? Can you think of situations in which it might be justified *not* to obtain informed consent for the sake of a better research design?
- Is it ever ethical to use deception in psychological research? Is deception justified if the subjects are given the accurate details after the research study is completed?

- Can practitioners be considered ethical if they practice without conducting any research on the techniques they use or without having them empirically validated?

Ethics and Research: Some Situations

Considering the vast number of studies on psychotherapeutic research, there is little discussion in the literature of ethical problems in designing and conducting studies. Yet there are critical ethical issues in this field that deserve the careful attention of investigators (Imber et al., 1986). In this section we consider some of these issues, including informed consent, using deception in psychological research, withholding of treatment, the use of placebos, research with training and personal-growth groups, and cross-cultural considerations in research.

Situations Involving Informed Consent.   Informed consent is defined as the participant's assent to being involved in a research study after having received full information about the procedures and their associated risks and benefits. The basic elements of informed consent include competence, voluntarism, full information, and comprehension (Imber et al., 1986).

Competence refers to the legal capacity of the subject to give consent. Ethical issues here pertain to subjects who are not able to make decisions. *Voluntarism* means that subjects are allowed to make their decision about whether to participate in a study without being pressured. It is essential that clients understand that they may refuse to participate in a study and that they will still be eligible for alternative services. They should also know that, even if they do consent to participate, they are still free to withdraw or drop out without penalty and with the provision of appropriate referrals. *Full information* implies that potential subjects are fully advised of the potential risks and benefits involved in participation. Full information about research is a contradiction in terms, however, because research designs require a withholding of certain information. In general, potential research subjects have a right to know what is going to happen to them in the study, what risks they are facing and whether their personal rights are jeopardized, and what safeguards will be taken. *Comprehension* means that consent forms are written in language that can be understood by most people.

Informed consent is important for a variety of reasons (Lindsey, 1984): it protects people's autonomy, because it allows them to make decisions about matters that directly concern them; it guarantees that the participants will be exposed to certain risks only if they agree to them; it decreases the possibility of an adverse public reaction to experimenting with human subjects; and it helps researchers scrutinize their designs for inherent risks. The researcher might be guided by the question "What would clients who are interested in their own welfare need to know before making a decision?" With these points in mind consider the following situation to determine the ethics of the researcher's behavior.

○ *A case of informed consent.*   Hannah is committed to designing research procedures to evaluate the process and outcome of her treatment programs. She is convinced that in order to obtain valid data she must keep the research participants ignorant in many respects. Thus, she thinks that it is important that the clients she sees be unaware that they are being studied and be unaware of the hypotheses under investigation. Although she agrees that some ethical issues may be raised by her failing to inform her clients, she thinks that good research designs call for such procedures. She does not want to influence her clients and thus bias the results of her study, so she chooses to keep information from them. She contends that her practices are justified because there are no negative consequences or risks involved with her research. She further contends that if she is able to refine her therapeutic techniques through her research efforts with her clients, both they and future clients will be the beneficiaries.

- What are your thoughts about Hannah's ethics and the rationale she gives for not obtaining informed consent?
- Assume that she was interested in studying the effects of therapists' reinforcement of statements by clients during sessions. Do you think that if the clients knew she was using certain procedures and studying certain behaviors, it would bias the results?
- If the values of the research seem to be greater than the risks involved to participants, do you think that the researcher is justified in not obtaining the informed consent of the subjects?

Commentary.   Although some of Hannah's contentions have some merit, we think that the ends are not justified by the means she employs in this case. Further, although she might be justified in withholding some of the details of her research studies (or the hypotheses under investigation), it seems unethical for her to fail even to mention to her clients that she is actually doing research with them as a part of her therapeutic approach. Since her clients are investing themselves both emotionally and financially in their therapy, they have the right to be informed about procedures that are likely to affect them. They further have the right to agree or refuse to be a part of her study. Her approach does not give them that right.

Situations Involving Deception.   Baumrind (1985) defines intentional deception as "withholding information in order to obtain participation that the participant might otherwise decline, using deceptive instructions and confederate manipulations in laboratory research, and employing concealment and staged manipulations in field settings" (p. 165). The case against deception in psychological research has been strongly made. The arguments against deception are that it violates the individual's right to voluntarily choose to participate, abuses the trusting relationship between experimenter and subject, contributes to deception as a societal value, is contrary to the professional roles of educator or scientist, and will eventually erode the trust in the profession of psychology (Adair, Dushenko, & Lindsay, 1985). Baumrind has argued that the use of intentional deception is unethical, imprudent, and unwarranted scientifically. With these points in mind, consider the following situation and determine whether deception is justified.

○ **A case of deception.**   Gerard, a family therapist, routinely videotapes his initial session with families without their knowledge. Hc does so on the ground that he wants to have a basis for comparing the family's behavior at the outset with their behavior at the final session. He assumes that if the family members knew they were being videotaped at the initial session, they would behave in self-conscious and fearful ways. At this stage in the therapy he does not think that they could handle the fact of being taped. Yet he likes to have *them* be able to look at themselves on videotape at their final session, at which time he tells them that he taped their initial session. He also explains to them his reasons for not having informed them.

- Since Gerard eventually does tell families that they were taped at the initial session, do you think that he is guilty of deception? Explain.
- To what degree do you think that the practice of taping clients without their knowledge affects the trust level in the therapeutic relationship? Are the possible benefits of this practice worth the potential risks to the practitioner's reputation?

Commentary.   We think that the therapist's policy of videotaping clients without their knowledge and consent is unethical. Most of the professional codes of the national organizations explicitly state that such a practice is to be avoided. Because the therapeutic relationship is built on goodwill and trust, we oppose any practices that are likely to jeopardize the trust that clients have toward the helping professionals. Deception cuts to the core of the helping professions, and it fosters distrust among the public toward the profession.

Situations Involving Withholding of Treatment.   Is it ethical to withhold treatment from a particular group so that it can be used as a control group? Consider this situation:

○ **A case of withholding treatment.**   Hope works with depressive psychotics in a state mental hospital. In the interest of refining therapeutic interventions that will help depressed clients, she combines therapy and research procedures. Specifically, she employs cognitive-behavioral approaches in a given ward. Her research design specifies treatment techniques for a particular group of patients, and she carefully monitors their rate of improvement as a part of the treatment program. Hope says that she believes in the value of cognitive-behavioral approaches for depressive patients, yet she feels a professional and ethical obligation to empirically validate her treatment strategies. For her to know whether the treatment procedures alone are responsible for changes in the patients' behaviors, she deems it essential to have a comparable group of patients that does not receive the treatment. When she is challenged on the ethics of withholding treatment that she believes to be potent from a particular group of patients on the ward, she justifies her practice on the ground that she is working within the dictates of sound research procedures.

- Some researchers contend that they are necessarily caught in ethical dilemmas if they want to use a control group. Do you see an apparent contradiction between the demands of sound research methodology and sound ethical practice?
- Do you think Hope was acting ethically in withholding treatment so that she could test her therapeutic procedures? Would it be better for her to simply forget any attempts at empirical validation of her procedures and devote her efforts to treating as many patients as she can? Would it be ethical for her to use procedures that are untested?

○ *A modification of the case.*   In a second case Hope uses placebo controls. That is, rather than merely denying treatment to a group or keeping members on a waiting list, she meets with a control group whose members think they are receiving therapy but actually are not receiving standard treatment. In short, the group is led to believe that it is benefiting from therapy.

- What are the ethics of using placebos in counseling and clinical research?
- Does the placebo approach by its very nature constitute deception of patients? Can you think of any situations that justify the use of this approach?

Situations Involving Research with Training and Personal-Growth Groups.   In many graduate programs it is common for trainees in counseling internships to participate in personal-growth groups. Sometimes these groups are integrated with training or supervision groups in which the interns are encouraged to explore their own personal issues that arise in conjunction with their placements in the field.

○ *A case of research with trainees.*   A professor, Wesley, makes it a practice to conduct research on the process and outcomes of the personal-growth groups he leads for counselor trainees. To begin with, all the students in his graduate counseling program are required to attend the sessions of a personal-growth group for a full academic year. In addition to leading these growth groups for trainees, he also teaches theory courses and supervises students in writing master's theses and doctoral dissertations. His primary theoretical orientation is Gestalt therapy, with emphasis on other experiential and role-playing techniques. He expects the students to come to the sessions and be willing to work on personal concerns. These personal concerns often pertain to issues that arise as a result of problems they encounter with difficult client situations in their internship. At the beginning of the group Wesley asks students to take psychological tests that assess traits such as openness, dogmatism, degree of self-acceptance, level of self-esteem, and other dimensions of personality that he deems to be related to one's ability to counsel others. He again administers these same devices at the end of the year so that he has a comparison. During the year he asks a group of experts to observe his trainees in the group sessions at various points. This is done so that outsiders can assess the level of growth of individuals at different points as well as get a sense of the progress of the group as a whole.

As a part of informed consent Wesley tells the trainees what he is attempting to evaluate during the year, and he discusses fully with them the rationale for using outsiders to observe the group. He also promises the students that he will meet with them individually at any time during the semester if they want to discuss any personal issues. He also meets with them individually at the end of the group to discuss changes in scores on the psychological tests. As a way to correct for his bias in the investigation he submits his research design to a university committee. The function of this committee is to review his design for any ethical considerations and to give him suggestions for improving his study.

- Do you think it is ethical for a program to require student attendance at personal-growth groups? And is it ethical for the leader of such a group to also have these same students in academic classes and to evaluate and supervise them?
- What ethical steps, if any, do you commend Wesley for?
- What research practices, if any, would you say are ethically questionable?
- Do you think that it is ethically sound to have observers as a part of the design? The students know about these outsiders, but the observers will be a part of the process even if some students do not like the idea. Do you see pressure being exerted? If so, is it justified in this case?
- What recommendations can you make for improving Wesley's research design as well as improving the quality of the learning experience for the students?

A Cross-Cultural Perspective on Research

Although research is considered basic to the development of theory, cultural factors are often neglected in both research and theory. This neglect led Triandis and Brislin (1984) to question the universality of psychological theories and to argue instead for the cultural relativity of these theories. The assumptions of psychotherapeutic studies of minority groups must include the minority culture's view of mental health, self-disclosure, privacy, and social interactions. Ibrahim and Arredondo (1986) emphasize that attending to cultural issues in research is not only ethical behavior but also good scientific practice.

As we will see in the following chapter, some have criticized both the AACD's *Ethical Standards* (1988) and the APA's *Ethical Principles* (1989) on the ground that they are not responsive and relevant to the pragmatic research needs of racial and ethnic minorities. In a critique of these two ethical codes, Casas and Thompson (1991) contend that the philosophical premises underlying them are narrow in scope. They assert that the codes reflect the individually oriented values of the majority culture and fail to take into account the rich diversity of world views and values held by other cultures. Casas and Thompson propose an alternative set of philosophical premises for research:

- Researchers need to expand traditional counseling studies to embrace an action-oriented approach that directly addresses psychosocial problems.
- Fieldwork studies could challenge the researcher to work directly in the community to solve real-life problems.

- Researchers should consider meeting with leaders of minority communities to identify and assign priorities to those research projects that the members of the communities perceive as needing immediate attention.
- Researchers would do well to develop ways to recruit and retain racial and ethnic minority students who can be used as research assistants.
- Researchers should work to ensure that their efforts result in tangible benefits to the targeted minority community. Research findings can best be used to actively influence public policy that will bring both short-term and long-term benefits to that community.

Casas and Thompson favor more altruistic, group-centered, community-oriented, and action-driven philosophies. Their recommendations suggest how such changes could be translated into research benefits for minority communities.

The draft of the APA's *Guidelines for Providers of Psychological Services to Ethnic, Linguistic, and Culturally Diverse Populations* (1991b) calls for a conceptual framework that will enable service providers to organize and accurately assess the value and utility of current and future research involving diverse ethnic and cultural populations. These guidelines include an exploration of several research issues:

- the impact of ethnic and racial similarity in the counseling process
- minority groups' use of mental-health services
- the relative effectiveness of directive styles of therapy and nondirective styles
- the role of cultural values in treatment
- appropriate counseling models
- competence in skills for working with specific ethnic populations

In a discussion of new approaches to cultural diversity, Lee (1991b) contends that research evidence must guide counseling. Based on reviews of what has been accomplished in research into cross-cultural counseling, he proposes that the following three areas be the targets of future research:

1. New process and outcome research needs to be conducted in the area of multicultural counseling. Evaluation of culturally responsive methods must be made an integral part of practice in various settings.
2. Research needs to be conducted on normal human development from a cross-cultural perspective. New studies might focus on coping skills among diverse groups of people.
3. Empirical data on intragroup differences would be most useful. Differences within the same groups due to factors such as level of ethnic identity, level of acculturation, and socioeconomic status are possible areas for further research.

Inventory of Your Position on Research

As a way of concluding this discussion, we suggest that you clarify your own thinking on the matter of balancing scientific rigor with ethical rigor. If you agree more than you disagree with the following statements, place an "A" in the space; if you disagree more than you agree, place a "D" in the space. After you've finished the inventory, we suggest that you discuss some of your answers with fellow students.

_____ 1. To use therapeutic techniques or interventions that lack a sufficient research base is irresponsible and unethical.

_____ 2. Deception is sometimes a necessary evil in psychological research.

_____ 3. The failure to obtain the informed consent of participants in research is always unethical.

_____ 4. If a research study contains any risks to the participants, its design should be changed, for by its very nature it is unethical.

_____ 5. The use of placebo groups can be justified, for if these controls are not used, practitioners will have difficulty in evaluating the efficacy of the intervention they use.

_____ 6. I think that researchers will ultimately get the best results if they are open and honest about the research design with the participants in the study.

_____ 7. In cases where "debriefing" of the subjects is used after deception has been a part of the study, the practice can be justified.

_____ 8. Practitioners should use no techniques that have not been empirically shown to be of value.

_____ 9. If we are concerned about producing sound research studies of therapy, we must be willing to tolerate some ethical violations.

_____ 10. It is ethical to justify research in educational settings solely on the basis of the potential benefits of the research itself.

Chapter Summary

Issues in theory, practice, and research are necessarily interrelated. From an ethical perspective, therapists need to anchor their practices to both theory and research. Without a theoretical foundation, practitioners are left with little rationale for formulation of therapeutic goals and for developing techniques to accomplish these goals. Practitioners are sometimes impatient when it comes to articulating a theory that guides practice. Some are riveted to concrete techniques to deal with every conceivable problem clients may present. However, a good theory is highly practical, for theoretical concepts help clinicians understand what they are doing. Just as clinicians sometimes have little use for theory, some do not see the practical applications of research. Without understanding how to translate current research findings into their practices, therapists have little basis for deciding what techniques to use with different clients. Thus, an appreciation of how theory and research can enhance how therapists function may result in ethical and effective practice.

We do not advocate that you subscribe to one established theory, because you can find ways to draw on therapeutic techniques from many theoretical approaches. We hope you will develop clear views pertaining to these questions: How does change come about? What is the nature of human nature? How does the therapeutic relationship lead to change? What is the role of diagnosis and assessment as a prelude to designing a treatment plan? When might tests be useful in the counseling process? How can research help practitioners determine the degree to which a therapy program is working? Ideally, practitioners' theoretical orientation will serve as a basis for reflecting on matters such as goals in counseling, the division of responsibility between the client and the counselor in meeting these goals, and techniques that are most appropriate with specific clients in resolving a variety of problems.

Suggested Activities

1. Do this exercise in dyads. Describe your theoretical stance, and tell your partner how you view human nature. How will this view determine the way you counsel?
2. How do you determine for yourself the proper division of responsibility in counseling? How might you avoid assuming responsibility that you think belongs to your client? How might you ensure that you will accept your own share of responsibility?
3. If you were applying for a job as a counselor and were asked, "What are the most important goals you have for your clients?" how would you respond?
4. In class, debate the role of diagnosis in therapy. One person makes a case *for* diagnosis as a valuable part of the therapeutic process, and the other person argues *against* the use of diagnosis. Or have a class discussion on trends in diagnosis, its uses and abuses, and its purpose and value.
5. Suppose that a client came to you and asked you to administer a battery of interest, ability, and vocational tests. How would you respond? What questions would you ask the client before agreeing to arrange for the testing?
6. What is your position on the use of techniques in counseling? When do you think they are appropriate? How can you determine for yourself whether you're using techniques as gimmicks to allay your anxiety or as extensions of your personal style as a counselor?
7. Interview at least one practicing therapist in order to discuss how theoretical orientation affects his or her practice. Ask the practitioner the kinds of questions that were raised in this chapter. Bring the results of your interview to class.
8. Suppose that you were applying for a job in a community mental-health center and that the following questions were asked of you during the interview: "Many of our clients represent a range of diverse cultural and ethnic backgrounds. To what degree do you think you will be able to form positive therapeutic relationships with clients who are culturally different from you? How do you think your own acculturation will influence the way you counsel ethnically and culturally diverse clients? Can you think of any factors that might get in the way of forming trusting relationships with these clients?"
9. In dyads, one person can take the position that a thorough assessment (diagnosis) is not necessary with a majority of clients in outpatient counseling. The

other person can argue that without a thorough assessment of each client, it is not ethically possible to proceed with an appropriate treatment plan.

Suggested Readings

For readings about theoretical perspectives on counseling and therapy see Corey (1991b) and Corsini and Wedding (1989). On the question "Are all psychotherapies eqivalent?" see Stiles, Shapiro, and Elliott (1986). On broadening the ethical standards pertaining to assessment and testing in multicultural situations see Ibrahim and Arredondo (1986, 1990) and Ibrahim (1986). On testing and other assessment methods in cross-cultural counseling see Lonner and Ibrahim (1989). For a racial-minority perspective on research, see Casas and Thompson (1991). For a treatment of the research implications of working with culturally diverse populations see Lee (1991b); see also APA (1991b) for the draft of *Guidelines for Providers of Psychological Services to Ethnic, Linguistic, and Culturally Diverse Populations.* For a discussion of ethical issues in research on psychotherapy, see Garfield (1987). For a discussion of empirical studies of ethical issues in research see Stanley, Sieber, and Melton (1987).

CHAPTER TEN

Ethical Concerns in Multicultural Counseling

Pre-Chapter Self-Inventory

Directions: For each statement, indicate the response that most closely identifies your beliefs and attitudes. Use the following code:

5 = I *strongly agree* with this statement.
4 = I *agree* with this statement.
3 = I am *undecided* about this statement.
2 = I *disagree* with this statement.
1 = I *strongly disagree* with this statement.

____   1. Therapists who are well-trained, sensitive, and self-aware and who do not impose their values can be considered effective cross-cultural counselors.

____   2. To counsel effectively, I must be of the same ethnic background as my client.

____   3. As a condition for state licensure, counselors should be able to demonstrate knowledge and competence in multicultural counseling.

____   4. I must challenge cultural stereotypes when they become obvious in counseling situations.

____   5. Contemporary counseling theories apply to all cultural populations.

____   6. A sensitive cross-cultural counselor is a spokesperson for the particular culture from which the client comes.

____   7. As a counselor I will be able to examine my behavior and attitudes to determine the degree to which cultural bias might influence the interventions I make with clients.

____   8. There is a need for special guidelines for counseling members of minority groups.

____   9. Counselors must take into account the ethnic and cultural differences between them and their clients.

____   10. The primary function of majority-group counselors is to alert their clients to the choices available to them in the mainstream culture.

____   11. An effective counselor facilitates the assimilation of the minority client into society.

____   12. Ethical practice demands that counselors become familiar with the various value systems of diverse cultural groups.

____   13. I would have no trouble working with someone from a culture very different from mine, because we would be more alike than different.

____   14. If I just listen to my clients, I will know all I need to know about their cultural background.

____   15. Client resistance is typically encountered in multicultural counseling and must be eradicated before changes can take place.

____   16. The ability to observe and work with nonverbal communication is an important aspect of effective cross-cultural counseling.

____   17. Establishing a trusting relationship is more difficult when the counselor and the client come from different cultures.

___ 18. Unless practitioners have been educated about cultural differences, they cannot determine whether they are competent to work with diverse populations.

___ 19. As a condition for licensure, all counselors should have specialized training and supervised experience in multicultural counseling.

___ 20. At this point in my educational career I feel well prepared to counsel culturally diverse client populations.

Introduction*

One of the major challenges facing counseling professionals is understanding the complex role that cultural diversity plays in their work. In a sense, all counseling interventions are multicultural. Clients and counselors bring to their relationship attitudes, values, and behaviors that can vary widely. One mistake is to deny the importance of these cultural variables in counseling; another is to overemphasize such cultural differences to the extent that practitioners lose their naturalness and fail to make contact with their clients.

This chapter focuses on the ethical implications of a multicultural perspective in the helping professions. So that the terms that we use in this chapter will have a precise meaning, we begin this chapter with definitions in the accompanying box. We then introduce you to the need for a multicultural emphasis and suggest ways to avoid cultural tunnel vision and expand your consciousness. The ethical codes of the AACD and the APA are critiqued from a multicultural perspective. We focus on how your cultural values and your assumptions are likely to influence the manner in which you practice. We also consider what it means to be a culturally skilled counselor and deal with the training of multicultural counselors. This chapter is not a comprehensive treatment of all the ramifications of multicultural counseling, for the field is complex and is developing rapidly. Also, we do not treat separate ethnic groups, except by way of providing examples of some groups. We encourage you to go further by consulting some of the suggested readings at the end of the chapter.

The Need for a Multicultural Emphasis

There is a trend in the counseling profession to face the reality of cultural diversity. Because cultural diversity is a fact of life in today's "global village," counselors can no longer afford to ignore the issue of culture.

*We would like to thank the following people, who reviewed this chapter and provided us with useful comments: David Ho, of California State University at Fullerton; Allen Ivey, of the University of Massachusetts; and Paul Pedersen, of Syracuse University.

Key Terms

It is helpful to define some of the terms that we will be using in this chapter: *ethnicity, culture, minority group, cross-cultural counseling, multicultural, ethnic-sensitive practice,* and the *culturally encapsulated counselor.*

Ethnicity is a sense of identity that stems from common ancestry, nationality, religion, and race. An ethnic group shares a unique social and cultural heritage passed on from generation to generation. Ethnicity provides cohesion and strength. It is a powerful unifying force that offers a sense of belonging and sharing based on commonality (Axelson, 1985; Lum, 1992, pp. 42–43).

The word *culture* can be interpreted broadly, for it can be associated with a racial or ethnic group as well as with gender, religion, economic status, nationality, physical capacity or handicap, or affectional or sexual orientation (Ivey, 1990). Pedersen (1988, 1991) describes culture as including *demographic* variables such as age, gender, and place of residence; *status* variables such as social, educational, and economic background; formal and informal *affiliations*; and the *ethnographic* variables of nationality, ethnicity, language, and religion. Culture can be conceptualized as the values, beliefs, and practices that are frequently shared by groups identified by these variables (Lopez et al., 1989). Considering culture from this broad perspective is particularly important in preparing counselors to deal with the complex differences among clients (Pedersen, 1991). A more restricted definition of culture as it is used within the context of multicultural counseling in America refers to the developmental needs of racial and ethnic groups of non-European origin (Lee, 1991a).

Minority group has come to refer to a category of people who have typically been discriminated against or subjected to unequal treatment and oppression by society, largely because of their group membership. These groups have been characterized as subordinate, dominated, and powerless. Although the term *minority* has traditionally referred to national, racial, linguistic, and religious groups, it now also applies to women, people with a gay or lesbian lifestyle, the aged, the physically handicapped, and the behaviorally deviant (Atkinson, Morten, & Sue, 1989; Lum, 1992).

Cross-cultural counseling refers to any counseling relationship in which the participants are from different cultures (Atkinson et al., 1989).

Multicultural is a generic term that we tend to use rather than *cross-cultural, transcultural,* or *intercultural.* It more accurately reflects the complexity of culture and avoids any implied comparison. The multicultural perspective in human-service education takes into consideration the specific values, beliefs, and actions conditioned by a client's ethnicity, gender, religion, socioeconomic status, political views, lifestyle, geographic region, and historical experiences with the dominant culture (Wright, Coley, & Corey, 1989). It seeks to provide a conceptual framework that recognizes the complex diversity of a pluralistic society, while at the same time suggesting bridges of shared concern that bind culturally different individuals to one another (Pedersen, 1991).

Ethnic-sensitive practice focuses on the present-day influences in the daily activities of minority groups. Going beyond the concerns of the individual, this type of practice addresses the consequences of racism, poverty, and discrimination on the group; it aims to change those institutions that perpetuate these conditions (Devore, 1985).

The *culturally encapsulated counselor,* a concept introduced by Wrenn (1962, 1985), is characterized by:

- defining reality according to one set of cultural assumptions
- showing insensitivity to cultural variations among individuals
- accepting unreasoned assumptions without proof and without regard to rationality
- failing to evaluate other viewpoints and making little attempt to accommodate the behavior of others

(continued)

(continued)

The encapsulated counselor is trapped in one way of thinking that resists adaptation and rejects alternatives (Pedersen, 1991). According to Ho, this concept of encapsulation can also apply to "cross-cultural" counselors; they, too, may be bound by their own narrow perspective (personal communication, June 27, 1991). The culture-bound counselor as an *unintentional racist* is described by Ridley (1989) and elaborated on by Pedersen (in press). Counselors who presume that they are free of any traces of racism seriously underestimate the impact of their own socialization. The exploitation that is part of racism is not always intentional. Indeed, this form of racism emerges as an unintentional action by well-meaning and caring professionals who believe that they are fair. Whether racism is intentional or unintentional, it continues to be dangerous and harmful. Pedersen believes that the key to changing unintentional racism lies in the willingness of practitioners to examine the underlying assumptions. *Racism* is a term used broadly to apply to discrimination against any minority. It can be defined as "any behavior or pattern of behavior that systematically tends to deny access to opportunities or privilege to one social group while perpetuating privilege to members of another group" (Ridley, 1989, p. 60). Racism can operate on both an individual and an institutional basis.

Note about names: There is some concern about how to refer appropriately to certain racial and ethnic groups. Preferred names tend to change. For instance, some alternate names for one group are Hispanic, Latino (Latina), Mexican American, or Chicana (Chicano). Realizing that there is no one "right" designation to fit any group, practitioners can show sensitivity to the fact that a name is important; they can ask a client how he or she would like to be identified.

The Problem of Cultural Tunnel Vision

A faculty member overheard one of our students inquiring about possibilities for a fieldwork placement in a community agency. The student made a remark to the effect that "I don't want a placement where I'll have to work with poor people or minority groups." The faculty member, who teaches our multicultural course, was aghast. This brief statement revealed much about the student's attitudes and beliefs about both people and the helping professions. If we want students to become more culturally aware, we should encourage them to seek out people who are different from them.

We have found that many students from the majority culture come into training with cultural tunnel vision. They have had limited cultural experiences, and in many cases they see it as their purpose to teach their clients about their view of the world. At times, these helpers from the majority group have expressed the attitude, explicitly or implicitly, that racial and ethnic minorities are unresponsive to professional psychological intervention because of their lack of motivation to change or their "resistance" to seeking professional help. Lorion and Parron (1985) contend that mental-health professionals need to appreciate and be prepared to respond to the needs of minority groups whose social, psychological, and behavioral disorders are accentuated by realities such as economic hardship, racism, discrimination, and environmental stress. Counselors may have difficulty in identifying with clients who feel a sense of powerlessness. These clients may be slow to form trusting relationships with counselors who possess greater power than they do. Many clients have come to distrust those who are associated with the establishment or with social-service agencies, because they fear oppression and unequal treatment by those whom they perceive as possessors of the power. Helpers from all cultural groups need to honestly examine their own expectations and attitudes about the helping process. Most counselors are culture-bound to some extent, and it takes a concerted effort to monitor one's biases so that they do not impede the formation of helping relationships. Later in this chapter we look at some of these assumptions underlying the helping process.

D. W. Sue and D. Sue (1990) are convinced that the field of clinical and counseling psychology has failed to meet the particular mental-health needs of ethnic minorities. They note the evidence that minority-group members often encounter problems such as immigrant status, poverty, cultural racism, prejudice, and discrimination. In addition, many tend to underutilize traditional mental-health services. Some findings reveal that half of minority clients terminate counseling after only one contact with a therapist. Sue and Sue suggest that a basic reason for underutilization of services and early termination is the biased nature of the services themselves: "The services offered are frequently antagonistic or inappropriate to the life experiences of the culturally different client; they lack sensitivity and understanding, and they are oppressive and discriminating toward minority clients" (p. 7). From an ethical perspective, Sue and Sue maintain that mental-health professionals have a moral and professional responsibility to (1) become aware of and deal with the biases, stereotypes, and assumptions that undergird their practice; (2) become aware of the culturally different client's values and world view; and (3) develop appropriate intervention strategies that take into account the social, cultural, historical, and environmental influences of culturally different clients.

There are other ways to interpret the underutilization of traditional psychotherapeutic services by minority clients. It may not be a Hispanic person's style to seek professional help quickly when faced with a problem. For example, consider Marco's experience of being torn between marrying a person selected by his parents and marrying a woman of his choice. He might first look for a solution within himself through contemplation. If he was still unable to resolve his dilemma, he might seek assistance from a family member. Then he might look to some of his friends for advice and support in making the best decision. If all of these approaches did not result in a satisfactory resolution of his problem, he might then turn to a professional for help. The fact that he did not seek professional services sooner might have had nothing to do with his resistance or with insensitivity on the part of professionals; he might have been following a route that was congruent with his cultural background.

Some argue that clients who make use of these professional resources may lose their cultural values in the process. As an example, Wood and Mallinckrodt (1990) recommend culturally sensitive assertiveness training for minority clients. But therapists who provide such training must be certain that gaining these interpersonal skills is a value shared by the client and not a goal imposed by the therapist. Culturally encapsulated counselors tend to mistakenly assume that a lack of assertiveness is a sign of dysfunctional behavior that should be changed. Merely labeling a behavior dysfunctional reflects a particular value orientation. Practitioners need to consider whether passivity is a problem from their clients' perspective and whether assertiveness is a useful behavior that their clients hope to acquire. As Wood and Mallinckrodt point out, there might be a conflict between clients' cultural values and what is in their best interests. Counselors can initiate a dialogue about these issues with clients. "This openness and respect will help to ensure that the therapist will become, not another medium of cultural domination and discrimination, but rather the client's ally in more effective coping" (p. 10). Ideally, therapists will not merely tolerate the reality of cultural complexity but will also welcome and celebrate this complexity.

As we noted in the previous chapter, the APA (1991b) has drafted *Guidelines for Providers of Psychological Services to Ethnic, Linguistic, and Culturally Diverse Populations*. One of the provisions of this document is that regardless of their ethnic or racial background, service providers need to become aware of how their own culture, life experiences, attitudes, values, and biases have influenced them. Additionally, they are challenged to go beyond their cultural encapsulation by correcting any of their prejudices and biases. Practitioners can ask themselves "Is it appropriate for me to view these clients any differently than I would if they were from my own ethnic or cultural group?" The APA's guidelines also call practitioners to respect the roles of family members and community structures, hierarchies, values, and beliefs that are an integral part of the client's culture. They suggest that providers identify resources in the family and the larger community and use them in delivering culturally sensitive services. For example, an entire Native American family may come to a clinic to provide support for an individual in distress. It is well for providers to know that many of the healing practices found in Native American communities are centered in the family and community.

In writing about Chinese-American cultural values and their impact on the counseling process, D. Sue and D. W. Sue (1991) have identified several core traditional Chinese values. Filial piety is a significant value in Chinese-American families. Emphasis is given to the obedience owed to parents as well as to respect and honor for them. Self-determination and independence are valued less than family bonds and unity. Family communication patterns are based on cultural tradition and emphasize appropriate roles and status. There is generally considerable stress on academic achievement and career development. Individuals are taught to suppress strong emotions outside of the family. Counselors who do not understand or accept these values are likely to make the mistake of encouraging Chinese-American clients to change in directions that are not in harmony with their values.

Cultural sensitivity is not limited to one group but applies to all cultures. There is no sanctuary from cultural bias. All counselors must be vigilant in avoiding an ethnocentric use of their own group as the standard by which to assess appropriate behavior. Thus, African-American counselors need to be aware of their possible prejudices toward the Caucasian culture as much as white counselors must be sensitive to any biased attitudes toward clients from the black culture. Indeed, African-American counselors also need to be clear about how their own cultural experiences and views are likely to influence their work with black clients. There can be even greater differences within the same cultural group than there are between different cultural groups.

Learning to Deal with Cultural Pluralism

Herr (1991) encourages counselors to take steps to deal effectively with cultural diversity and pluralism. He raises some excellent questions:

- How can counselors complement theories and practices that arise from Western approaches with those that arise from Eastern and other approaches?
- How can counselors become more familiar with the world views that different cultures reinforce?
- How can counselors help people of different cultures learn about majority norms, which are useful in some situations, without replacing their cultural pride and perspectives?
- How can counselors help majority clients face their own conscious and unconscious racism and sexism? How can counselors help their clients learn about and from nonmajority cultures?
- How can minority counselors become aware of their own unconscious racism and sexism? How can they become less culturally encapsulated?
- What are some ways to provide cross-cultural counseling when the socialization of the client and the counselor are significantly different?

It may be more important for counselors to develop a process of learning rather than simply to acquire knowledge about cultural diversity. Students can best do this if they force themselves to think differently by immersing themselves in practical experiences.

In writing about the training of counselors, Herr holds that "all mental health counselors must be . . . equipped with the skills necessary to engage in cross-cultural counseling as defined in ethnic, racial, and socioeconomic terms" (1991, p. 18). Lee maintains that "culturally responsive counseling strategies and techniques must be predicated on an understanding of cultural dynamics and their crucial role in fostering optimal mental health" (1991a, p. 13). Pedersen, Fukuyama, and Heath challenge counselors to pay attention to the salient cultural variables in counseling relationships: "We may choose to ignore cultural variables in counseling. However, the multicultural dynamics of counselors and clients will continue to shape the delivery of counseling services with or without our cooperation" (1989, p. 42).

Ethical Codes in Multicultural Counseling

Most of the professional codes mention the practitioner's responsibility to recognize the special needs of diverse client populations. For example, the *Ethical Standards* of the AACD (1988) specify that counselors must guard the individual rights and personal dignity of the client through an awareness of the negative impact of both racial and sexual stereotyping and discrimination. The APA draft code (1991a) encourages psychologists to be responsive to human differences:

- "To the extent relevant to their professional activities, psychologists strive to be sensitive to differences among people, such as those associated with age, gender, race, ethnicity, national origin, religion, sexual orientation, disability, or socioeconomic status."
- "Where these differences may significantly affect psychologists' work concerning particular individuals or groups, psychologists obtain the training, experience, or supervision necessary to ensure the competence of their services."

The Limitations of Existing Codes

Pedersen (1989) contends that the APA *Ethical Principles* (1989) are culturally encapsulated and that multicultural ethical guidelines for psychology are still lacking. He thinks that although it may not be possible to develop "culture-free" or "culture-fair" ethical codes, the goal might be to establish guidelines like those for the culturally sensitive interpretation of test data. He makes the following key points:

- To the extent that codes are based on stereotyped values from the dominant culture's perspective, they need to be revised so that the interests of minority groups are taken into account.
- To the extent that these codes are grounded in a single standard of normal and ethical behavior, they require revision to incorporate a variety of culturally defined alternatives.
- To the extent that the codes are "technique oriented," they need to be made applicable to a wide range of multicultural situations.

The AACD ethical code also has some distinct limitations with reference to cultural issues. Ibrahim and Arredondo (1990) offer suggestions for expanding the *Ethical Standards* of the AACD (1988) to more fully address the needs of diverse cultural groups. They note that although many minority groups do share similarities with the mainstream culture, they also have unique belief systems, values, assumptions, coping strategies, and lifestyles that do not reflect majority values and assumptions. They underscore the point that it is unethical for professionals to remain monocultural and still practice in this society. In agreement with this point of view are Casas and Thompson (1991), who maintain that both the APA and AACD codes have serious shortcomings in dealing with racial and ethnic differences. They describe deficiencies in prescribing behavior for all major professional activities, including research, training, and delivery of services.

Although the ethical codes of most of the helping professions have been recently revised, the main criticism is that they are grounded in a narrow set of assumptions that reflects the prevailing individualistic values of the majority culture and fails to take into account the contributions of minority groups (LaFromboise & Foster, 1989). As we have noted, the APA's Board of Ethnic

Minority Affairs established a task force that has produced a draft of guidelines for services to minority populations (APA, 1991b). These guidelines are designed for, but not limited to, the following populations: Native Americans, Alaska natives, Asian Americans, Pacific Islanders, African Americans, and Hispanics. In our opinion, this draft effectively addresses many of the criticisms cited above and represents progress.

Toward Ethical Multicultural Practice

Some writers assert that the prevailing theories of counseling and therapy are based on a middle-class, Euro-American, highly individualistic, and ethnocentric ethic (Ivey, 1990; D. W. Sue & D. Sue, 1990). Therapeutic practices often reflect instances of racism, sexism, and other forms of prejudice. Sue and Sue (1990) contend that this ethnocentric bias has been destructive to the natural help-giving networks of minority communities. They suggest that helpers need to expand their perception of mental-health practices to include support systems such as the family, friends, community, self-help programs, and occupational networks.

Counselors may misunderstand clients who are of a different sex, race, age, social class, or sexual orientation from them. If they do not integrate these cross-cultural factors into their practice, they are infringing on the client's cultural autonomy and basic human rights and lessening the chances of establishing an effective therapeutic relationship. The failure to address these factors constitutes unethical practice (Cayleff, 1986; Ivey, 1990).

Case Examples for Discussion.   Consider the following cases as illustrations of issues that we have been exploring.

○ ***The case of Lee.***   Stacy, a majority counselor, is on the staff of a university counseling center. A Vietnamese student, Lee, is assigned to her because of academic difficulties. She observes that he is slow and deliberate in his conversational style. She immediately signs him up for a class in English as a second language. In the course of their conversations, he discloses that his father is directing him toward a career in medicine, for which he thinks he is not suited. Stacy gives him a homework assignment to confront his father and tell him that he no longer wants to pursue medicine and that he is instead going to follow a direction that appeals to him.

- Was the fact that Lee spoke slowly and deliberately an indication that he was deficient in English? Was the counselor insensitive in recommending an ESL class so hastily?
- Did the therapist's actions reveal a respect for the roles of family members, hierarchies, values, and beliefs within the client's structure?
- Was Stacy too quick in making her assessments, considering that Lee was sent to the counseling center? Would it have made a difference if he had come voluntarily for guidance?
- How would you have handled this situation?

○ ***The case of Cynthia.*** An Asian counselor, Ling, has recently set up a private practice in a culturally mixed, upper-middle-class neighborhood. A white housewife, Cynthia, seeks him out for counseling. She is depressed, feels that life has little meaning, and feels enslaved by the needs of her husband and small children. When Ling asks about any recent events that could be contributing to her depression, she tells him that she has discussed with her husband her desire to return to school and pursue a career of her choosing. She let her husband know that she felt stifled and needed to pursue her own interests. Her husband's response was to threaten a divorce if she followed through with her plans. She then consulted with her pastor, who counseled her by pointing out her obligations to her family. Ling is aware of his own cultural biases, which include a strong commitment to family and to the role of the man as the head of the household. Although he shows empathy for Cynthia's struggle, he directs her toward considering postponing her own aspirations until her children have grown up. She agrees to put her own agenda on the back burner because she feels guilty about asserting her own needs, and she is also fearful of being left alone. Ling then works with her to find other ways to add zest to her life that would not involve such a radical impact on the family.

- Do you see any evidence of bias or unethical behavior in Ling's approach to this case?
- List some of the potential gender, age, and cultural issues in this case. How might you have addressed each of them?
- Even though Cynthia was inclined to take the pastor's advice to stay with her family, could or should the therapist have explored more with her the lack of meaning in her life? Was it unethical not to do so?
- Could Ling have acted any differently and still have been true to himself and his own cultural values?
- Would the approach and the issues involved have been any different if Cynthia had been from a traditional Asian family in the community?
- Because Ling had different family values from Cynthia's, should he have referred her to another professional?
- If Ling had approached you for consultation, what advice might you have given him?
- Given what you know about your values, how might you have worked with Cynthia if she had been your client?

At this point we suggest that you review the professional codes of ethics found in the Appendix to determine for yourself the degree to which they take cultural and racial dimensions into account. From a multicultural perspective, what are their shortcomings? To what degree do you think that most of them are culturally encapsulated? What revisions and additions can you think of as a basis for mental-health practitioners to function ethically in today's multicultural world?

Cultural Values and Assumptions in Therapy

In this section we explore the difference between Western and Eastern assumptions about therapy, examine the importance of the counselor's values in multicultural therapy, and discuss the need for therapists to challenge stereotypical beliefs.

Western versus Eastern Values

Ho (1985) has described the value assumptions of various approaches and has called for a creative synthesis of Western and Eastern values. The categories *Eastern* and *Western* are not geographic terms but represent social, political, and cultural orientations. When we speak of the Eastern and Western worlds, moreover, we are not implying a complete distinction between the two. It is not a matter of all Easterners thinking alike and all Westerners thinking alike.

Contemporary theories of therapy and therapeutic practices are grounded in Western assumptions. Yet most of the world is not like mainstream U.S. culture. Saeki and Borow (1985) discuss some contrasts between the Eastern and Western systems. Western culture emphasizes choice, the uniqueness of the individual, self-assertion, and the strengthening of the ego. Therapeutic goals include improving assertive coping by changing the environment, changing one's other coping behaviors, and learning to manage stress. This position advocates ways of changing objective reality to improve one's way of life. By contrast, Eastern views stress interdependence, underplay individuality, and emphasize the losing of oneself in the totality of the cosmos. The Asian counseling perspective, for example, typically mirrors the life values associated with inner enlightenment and acceptance of one's environment.

Being oriented toward change is part of the Westernized approach. In many Eastern countries people have little chance—or inclination—to move out of their cultural context. Therapeutic approaches in China and in Japan rely much more on resources within the community. There is more of a social framework than a focus on the development of the individual. Applying the Western model of therapy to the Chinese culture does not work. Likewise, this model has major limitations when it is applied to minority groups such as Asian Americans, Hispanics, Native Americans, and blacks. Seeking professional psychological help is not a typical option for many minority groups. In fact, in most non-Western cultures informal groups of friends and relatives provide a supportive network. Informal counseling consists of the spontaneous outreach of caring people to others in need (Brammer, 1985).

According to Ho, Asians underuse professional therapy. Although they may seek formal therapy, they do so when other informal sources of help have not worked. Ho proposes a creative synthesis of collectivism and individualism, whereby it is possible to draw from both worlds. Agreeing with Ho are Saeki and Borow (1985), who believe that the aims of treatment in both worlds are linked to striving for the good life as defined in the respective dominant cultures: "Eastern and Western systems both address the nature and control of intrapersonal conflict but do so in different ways" (p. 225). In the accompanying table we describe general characteristics that, according to Ho, differentiate these two perspectives.

A Comparison of the Western and Eastern Systems

West	East
Values	
Primacy of individual	Primacy of relationship
Democratic orientation	Authoritarian orientation
Nuclear family structure	Extended family structure
Emphasis on youth	Emphasis on maturity
Independence	Interdependence
Assertiveness	Compliance
Nonconformity	Conformity
Competition	Cooperation
Conflict	Harmony
Freedom	Security
Guiding Principles for Action	
Fulfillment of individual needs	Achievement of collective goals
Individual responsibility	Collective responsibility
Behavior Orientation	
Expression of feelings	Control of feelings
Uniqueness of individual	Uniformity
Self-actualization	Collective actualization
Time Orientation	
Future orientation	Traditionalism
Innovation	Conservatism
Ethical Orientation	
Morality anchored in person	Morality linked to relationships

○   ***The case of two immigrants.***   An Asian immigrant couple come to a marriage counselor in a small midwestern American city with concerns for the future of their marriage. The husband is quiet and controlled; the wife cries often but says little.

Dan, their counselor, has just completed a workshop in cross-cultural counseling. He is immediately conscious of their silence and is determined to respect this behavior. He is aware that in Oriental cultures the wife typically defers to the husband. So he decides to be careful in prompting the wife to speak lest he be guilty of a cultural faux pas. The result is that Dan becomes silent and feels stifled and useless to them as a counselor.

- How would you proceed to work with this couple?
- Even though the problem of marital discord seems straightforward, what are some of the potential cultural issues that Dan may need to consider?
- What would you do or not do with this couple?

Cultural Contradictions.   According to Ho (1985), there is a basic contradiction between the traditional moralistic and authoritarian orientation of Eastern perspectives and the psychological and therapeutic orientation of Western approaches. He contends that to follow the Western orientation in the East would lead eventually to a head-on collision with entrenched traditional values. These cultural contradictions often apply in multicultural counseling situations in the United States, especially when white counselors function within the framework of the model we have just described. Likewise, a minority counselor working with a majority client from mainstream society would surely falter if he or she did not give sufficient consideration to cultural variables.

Ho contends that research is needed on clients' belief systems, on perceptions of psychological services, and on the effectiveness of treatment in cross-cultural counseling. He also maintains that Western approaches need to examine their underlying value assumptions. Indeed, we want to stress that all approaches should examine the basic assumptions that influence practice.

A Creative Synthesis of Individualism and Collectivism.   Can Western approaches be transplanted? Are Asian and Western systems of psychotherapy mutually exclusive because of contrasting philosophical bases? The challenge, according to Ho (1985), is to find a way to integrate elements of collectivism and individualism after exploring these issues with the client and letting the client decide. This synthesis entails the collective actualization of individuals-in-society and, at the same time, the actualization of the individual.

Patterson (1985b) criticizes the conclusion of many writers that the methods of Western therapeutic approaches are not appropriate in Eastern cultures. He also contends that the two cultures must move toward each other. "Eastern cultures must change in the direction of greater concern for individual personal development. Western culture must move in the direction of greater concern for the influence of the individual upon others and . . . of cooperation in fostering personal development in others" (p. 188).

The Counselor's Values

It is crucial that counselors be aware of their values and be willing to examine the potential impact of these values on clients with different cultural experiences. In addition, counselors must resist making value judgments of clients who are culturally different. They need to understand and accept clients who have a different set of assumptions about life, and they need to avoid imposing their world view.

Before you read the next section, reflect on the two case examples and on the questions that follow as a way of examining some of your own assumptions about the helping process as applied to culturally different clients:

○ *The case of Mac.*   Mac, a white, middle-class psychologist, is very vocal in his denunciation of "all this cross-cultural stuff." He sees it as more trendy than useful. "I do not impose my values. I do not tell clients what to do. I listen, and if I need to know something, I ask. How am I to know whether a Japanese-American client is more American than Japanese or vice versa unless I ask him? My motto is that the client will tell you all you need to know."

- What stereotypical beliefs and assumptions do you hold?
- Do you focus mainly on the weakness of values different from your own?
- Do you assume that all your clients will be ready to engage in self-disclosure? What interventions might you make, assuming that the client's hesitancy to disclose is cultural rather than a sign of resistance?
- To what extent do you value assertiveness? Is this a value that you expect most of your clients to acquire? How might you react to clients who are culturally conditioned not to be assertive?
- What assumptions about culture and the helping relationship do you have that may either help or hinder you in establishing effective therapeutic relationships with culturally diverse clients?
- What do you think of the view of Patterson (1985b), who argues that it is not necessary, or desirable, to design new approaches for counseling clients from other cultures, because universal human values provide the common goal and methods of counselors in all cultures?

○ ***The case of Claudine.***   Claudine, a white counselor, takes over as director of a clinic that has a large percentage of Oriental immigrants as clients. At a staff meeting she sums up her philosophy of counseling in this fashion: "People come to counseling to begin change or because they are already in the process of change. Our purpose is to challenge them to change. This holds true whether the client is white, Oriental, or some other minority. If the clients are slow to speak, our job is to challenge them to speak, because the majority in American culture deals with problems through talking. Silence may be a mark of the Oriental culture, but it does not work in this culture, and the sooner they learn this, the better for them."

- To what degree, if any, do you think Claudine has "tunnel vision"?
- Do you detect any signs of cultural bias?
- To what degree do you agree or disagree with Claudine, and why?

Challenging Stereotypical Beliefs

Counselors may think they are not biased, yet they may hold some stereotypical beliefs that could well affect their practice. Examples are: "Failure to change stems from a lack of motivation." "People have choices, and it is up to them to change their life." Counselors who make such assumptions are ignoring that some people do not have a wide range of choices because of environmental factors beyond their control. Another assumption is that "talk therapy" works best, ignoring the fact that many cultures rely more on nonverbal expression.

Assumptions about Self-Disclosure.   Another assumption is that clients will be ready to talk about their intimate personal issues. This assumption ignores that in some cultures such self-disclosure is taboo and that some European ethnic groups stress keeping problems "in the family." Ridley (1984, 1989) asserts that individual verbal therapies often place the black client in a paradoxical situation.

Although self-disclosure is typically considered essential for maximizing therapeutic outcomes, complex personal, interpersonal, and social factors affect the black client's willingness to be open. In this light, the goals of most traditional "talking" therapies appear to be incompatible with the tendencies of many black clients. According to Ridley, this is the therapeutic paradox. Asian Americans who seek therapy are frequently described as the "most repressed of all clients" (D. W. Sue & D. Sue, 1985). Such clients may in fact be holding true to their cultural background. Disagreeing with this view are those who say that the inability to self-disclose is something to be overcome, not accepted. Patterson (1985b) contends that if this obstacle cannot be overcome, the client is unable to participate in the therapeutic relationship. Unless clients are willing to verbalize and communicate their thoughts, feelings, attitudes, and perceptions, he argues, there is no basis for empathic understanding by the therapist.

○ ***The case of Lily.***   Lily, a licensed counselor, has come to work in a family-life center that deals with many immigrant families. She often becomes impatient over the slow pace of her clients' disclosures. It is sometimes like squeezing blood from the proverbial turnip. Lily decides to teach her clients by modeling for them. With one of her reticent couples she says: "My husband and I have many fights and disagreements. We express our feelings openly and clear the air. In fact, several years ago my husband had an affair, which put our relationship into a turmoil. I believe it was my ability to vent my anger and express my hurt that allowed me to work through this terrible event."

- What do you think of Lily's self-disclosure? Would such a disclosure be helpful to you if your were her client?
- Might you be inclined to make a similar type of disclosure to your clients? Why or why not?
- What possible positive or negative outcomes might occur after such a disclosure?
- Is it a culturally sensitive thing to do with those who have not known such candor in their own experience?

Assumptions about Assertiveness.   Most counselors assume that clients are better off if they can behave in assertive ways, such as telling people directly what they think and what they want. In fact, much of therapy consists of teaching clients the skills to take an active stance toward life. Sue and Sue (1985) report a widespread view that Asian Americans are nonassertive and passive. They contend, however, that this assumption has not been supported by research. These authors do stress that traditional counseling practices may act as barriers to effective cross-cultural helping, and they call for culturally appropriate intervention strategies, or culture-specific methods, that are congruent with the value orientation of Asian-American clients.

Assumptions about Self-Actualization and Trusting Relationships.   Another assumption made by mental-health professionals is that it is important for the individual to become a fully functioning person. A counselor may often focus on what is good for the individual and neglect the impact of the individual's change on the significant people in that person's life or the impact of those significant people on the client. It is not a question of individual versus group but, rather, a creative synthesis between these two dimensions.

Patterson (1985b) again has another point of view. For him, the purpose and goal of counseling is to help people who are hampered in their personal development to become more self-actualizing. He maintains that for personality change to occur in the direction of self-actualization, three core conditions of the therapeutic relationship are necessary. These conditions—empathic understanding, respect, and therapeutic genuineness—are viewed as essential in cross-cultural counseling, since the striving for self-actualization is assumed to be common to all cultures.

Another assumption pertains to the development of a trusting relationship. Mainstream Americans tend to form quick relationships and to talk easily about their personal lives. This characteristic is reflected in our counseling approaches. We expect clients to come to therapy open and willing to explore personal issues with a counselor who is a total stranger. Among many cultures it takes a long time to develop such a relationship. Many Asian Americans, Hispanics, and Native Americans have been brought up not to speak until spoken to, especially when they are with the elderly and authority figures (D. W. Sue, 1981a). Counselors may interpret the client's hesitancy to speak as resistance when it is only a sign of respect.

Assumptions about Nonverbal Behavior.   Many cultural expressions are subject to misinterpretation, including personal space, eye contact, handshaking, dress, formality of greeting, perspective on time, and so forth. Mainstream Americans frequently feel uncomfortable with periods of silence, and so they tend to fill the air with words. In some cultures silence may be a sign of respect and politeness rather than a lack of a desire to continue to speak. Certain cultures, such as the Japanese, place value on indirectness and nonverbal communication. As Henkin (1985) has observed, the Western counselor, whose confrontational style involves direct eye contact, physical gestures, and probing personal questions, may be seen as offensively intrusive by Japanese-American clients and by clients from many other cultures. There is a need for counselor sensitivity to the different meanings of nonverbal behaviors.

Western counselors are often systematically trained in attending skills, which include keeping an open posture, maintaining good eye contact, and leaning toward the client (Egan, 1990). Although these behaviors are aimed at creating a positive therapeutic relationship, individuals from certain ethnic groups may have difficulty in responding positively or understanding the intent of such posturing. In American culture eye contact is considered a sign of attentiveness and presence, and a lack thereof is viewed as being evasive. Devore (1985) cautions that Asians and Native Americans may view direct eye contact as a lack of respect. Thus, it is a mistake to prematurely label clients as "resistive" or "pathological" if they avoid eye contact and do not respond to the invitation of the attending behavior. In some cultures lack of eye contact may even be a sign of respect and good manners. In writing about Native Americans, Attneave (1985) indicates that direct eye-to-eye gaze generally indicates aggressiveness; in cross-gender encounters it usually means sexual aggressiveness.

It should be clear that there are no universal meanings of nonverbal behaviors. Thus, it is essential for counselors to acquire sensitivity to cultural differences in order to reduce the probability of miscommunication, misdiagnosis, and misinterpretation of behavior (Wolfgang, 1985, p. 100).

Assumptions about Directness.   Western therapeutic approaches prize directness. Yet some cultures see it as a sign of rudeness and as something to be avoided. The counselor could assume that a lack of directness is evidence of pathology or at least a sign of lack of assertiveness, rather than a sign of respect. Although getting to the point immediately is a prized value in the dominant American culture, certain other cultures could see this type of behavior as inappropriate. Clients from other cultures might be seen as wanting to avoid dealing with their problems.

○   *The case of Miguel.*   Miguel, a Mexican American born in the United States, has completed his Ph.D. and is working at a community clinic in family therapy. In his training he has learned of the concept of triangulation, or the tendency of two persons who are in conflict to involve a third person in their emotional system in order to reduce the stress (see Brown & Christensen, 1986). Miguel is on the watch for evidence of this tendency. While he is counseling a Mexican-American family, the father says to his son, "Your mother wants you to show her more respect than you do and to obey her more." Miguel says to the mother: "Do you always allow your husband to speak for you? Can you say this directly to your son yourself, rather than speaking through your husband?" The room falls silent, and there is great discomfort.

Was Miguel culturally sensitive with his statement? How would you have handled this situation differently, especially if you saw "triangulation" as leading to family pathology?

A Personal Illustration.   A few years ago Marianne Corey and Jerry Corey conducted a training workshop with counselors from a Latin-American country. Marianne was accused by a male participant of being too direct and assertive. He said that he had difficulties with Marianne's active leadership style and indicated that it was her place to defer to Jerry by letting him take the lead. Recognizing and respecting our cultural differences, we were able to arrive at a mutual understanding of different values.

Jerry had difficulty with the tardiness of the participants and had to accept the fact that we could not follow a rigid time schedule. Typically we have thought that, if people were late or missed a session, group cohesion would be difficult to maintain. Because the issue was openly discussed in this situation, however, the problem did not arise. We quickly learned that we had to adapt ourselves to their view of time. To insist on interpreting such behavior as resistance would have been to ignore the cultural context.

Matching Client and Counselor

Does the counselor have to share the cultural background of the client to be effective? This is a difficult question to answer, and the research in this area is inconclusive. Some argue that successful interracial counseling is highly improbable because of the cultural and racial barriers involved. Others argue that well-trained and sensitive counselors may be able to establish effective therapeutic relationships with their culturally different clients. One of the pitfalls associated with multiculturalism is that some helping professionals may give up in exasperation when they ask "How can I really be effective with a client whose cultural background is different from mine?" Lee and Richardson (1991b) warn about the danger when counselors become overly self-conscious about their ability to work with diverse client populations. If counselors become too analytical about what they say and do, they will not be themselves but will respond using some external set of expectations.

D. W. Sue and D. Sue (1990) maintain that counselors who are afraid to face the differences between themselves and their clients, who refuse to accept the reality of these differences, who perceive such differences as problematic, or who are uncomfortable in working out these differences are bound to fail. They add:

> Counselors who are willing to address cultural differences directly are those who do not perceive them as impediments. Instead, counselors who view these differences as positive attributes will most likely meet and resolve the challenges that arise in cross-cultural counseling. Such an individual is a "culturally skilled counselor" [p. 172].

We agree that counselors can work with clients who differ from them in gender, race, culture, socioeconomic background, age, or lifestyle. But our position is tempered by certain reservations and conditions. First, counselors need to have training in multicultural perspectives, both academic and experiential. Second, as in any other counseling situation, it is important that the client and counselor agree to develop a working therapeutic relationship. Third, counselors are advised to be flexible in applying theories to specific situations. The counselor who has an open stance has a greater likelihood of success than someone who rigidly adheres to a single theoretical system. We support Ridley's (1989) contention that skillful counselors are able to focus on correct treatment goals and to employ a wide range of therapeutic techniques appropriately to specific presenting problems. Ridley believes that flexibility in using therapeutic techniques is probably the most important factor in effectively treating minority clients.

Fourth, the counselor should be open to being challenged and tested in order to earn trust and credibility. In multicultural counseling there is a greater likelihood that clients will exhibit suspicion and distrust. Consider the situation of a African American client and a white counselor. Some African Americans may tend to perceive whites as potential enemies unless proved otherwise. They may use many defenses as survival strategies to prevent whites from knowing their true feelings. A black client who has had to experience discrimination and pain at the hands of the majority society may not easily trust a representative of that dominant culture, no matter how sensitive and skillful the counselor may be. White counselors are often perceived as symbols of the establishment, and the minority client is likely to project past experiences onto the present situation. Even though the white counselor has admirable motives, the client may distrust the counselor simply because he or she is white. Counselors who see themselves as culturally skilled and sensitive may have a difficult time withstanding this kind of testing. If they become excessively defensive in such situations, they will probably lose the client. Clients may feel that they would have to reject their own culture to accept the counselor's values or solutions. To minority clients it may seem that a professional who is not part of the solution to their problem is really part of the problem.

Fifth, it becomes even more important in multicultural counseling situations that counselors be aware of their value system, of potential stereotyping, and of any traces of prejudice. Earlier we described those culture-bound counselors who are unintentional racists. Counselors who view themselves as being totally free of all prejudices are seriously underestimating the impact of their own socialization. In some ways, such counselors can be more dangerous than those who are more open with their prejudices. According to Pedersen (in press), unintentional racists must be challenged either to become intentional racists or to modify their racist attitudes and behaviors. The key to changing unintentional racism lies in examining basic assumptions. Examples of two forms of covert racism that Ridley (1989) identifies are color blindness and color consciousness. The counselor who says "When I look at you, I see a person, not a black person" may encounter mistrust from clients who have difficulty believing that. This counselor's color blindness is an illusion based on the faulty assumption that the minority client is simply another client. Likewise, a counselor is not likely to earn credibility by saying "If you were not black, you wouldn't have the problem you're facing." This is probably a case of color consciousness, which is an illusion based on the erroneous assumption that all of the client's problems come from being a member of an ethnic minority. For a thought-provoking analysis of the role of racism in counseling practice, we suggest a reading of Ridley (1989).

We suggest that you pause here to think about these questions:

- What is your position on whether the counselor needs to share the cultural background of the client to be effective?
- If you were to encounter considerable "testing" from a minority client, how do you think you would react? What are some ways in which you could work therapeutically, rather than being defensive?
- What experiences have you had with discrimination? How do you think your own experiences could either help or hinder you in working with clients who have been discriminated against?

It may be difficult for minority clients to discuss their anger over prejudice with a counselor who is empathetic to the point of condescension. Smith (1985a) writes that the life concerns of African American women are both similar to and different from those of mainstream women, and she cautions counselors not to overgeneralize. On this issue Jones (1985) makes the point that a therapist's self-knowledge is at least as important as cultural understanding in effectively treating the African American client. Jones concedes that culture and race do play a key role but adds that they should not be overplayed to the extent that they blur the unique individuality of the client.

Finally, counselors need to be aware of their reactions to unusual behavior. The definition of abnormal behavior has a cultural bias. When counselors observe such unusual behavior, it is essential to examine it within the minority client's cultural context. Thus, minority clients may be suspicious and may declare that people are out to get them. They may not be suffering from clinical paranoia but, indeed, be reacting to the realities of an environment in which they have suffered oppression and prejudice.

In the case that follows consider this well-intentioned counselor's lack of sensitivity to the needs of minority clients. As you read the case, think about ways in which you could increase your own sensitivity to individuals from cultural groups different from your own.

○ *The case of John.*   John, who comes from a lower-middle-class neighborhood in an eastern city, has struggled to get a college degree and has finally attained a master's degree in counseling. He has moved to the West Coast, proud of his accomplishments, yet he considers himself sensitive to his own background and to those who struggle with similar problems. He has been hired to work in a clinic in a neighborhood with a large minority population.

At the clinic John starts a group for troubled adolescents. His goals for this group are as follows: (1) to instill pride in his group members so that they will see that their present environment is an obstacle to be overcome, not to suffer with; (2) to increase self-esteem in his group members and to challenge them to fight the negativism they may encounter in their home environments; (3) to teach them to minimize their differences in terms of the larger community (for example, he points out how some of their idioms and ways of speaking separate them from the majority and reinforce differences and stereotypes); and (4) to teach them how one can overcome obstacles and achieve a graduate degree with minimal help from one's environment. He tells them, not in an arrogant way, "If I can do it, you can do it too."

John does not work very closely with the other staff members. He views them as being more interested in politics and red tape and as actually giving very little energy to working in the community. He has little to do with the families of the adolescents, because he sees them as being too willing to accept handouts and welfare and not very interested in being self-sufficient and independent. He tells his group members: "What you have at home with your families has obviously not worked for you. What you have in this group is the opportunity to change and to have that change appreciated."

- Do you see John as possessing the competencies necessary to qualify as a cross-cultural counselor? Why or why not?
- Does he demonstrate an understanding of the unique needs of this minority group? If so, how?

- What, if any, cultural prejudices does he exhibit in the way he deals with his group members? What prejudices, if any, do his goals for his adolescent group imply?
- What effect might it have had on his goals if he had become familiar with the environment of his group?
- What potential risks has John exposed his group members to after the group is finished?
- What difficulties do you anticipate he might encounter because of his attitude toward his colleagues in the clinic? Do you think he might be open to criticism from the parents? Explain.
- What stereotyping might he be doing in terms of his attitudes toward the parents of his adolescents?
- What reactions do you have to the manner in which he set up group goals?

Commentary. John is an illustration of the well-intentioned counselor who demonstrates an almost complete lack of sensitivity to the particular needs of this minority community. We disagree with his axiom that simply because he could obtain a graduate degree (against difficult odds), anybody could have the same success. John made no attempt to become aware of the unique struggles or values of his clients. An obvious oversight is that he failed to include the adolescents in the development of goals that would guide their group. He stereotyped in a very indirect, but powerful, fashion the parents of his group members. He imposed majority values in terms of language and upward mobility. He set up potential conflicts between his members and their families by the way he downplayed and labeled their families' value systems.

The point we wish to make is that even though this may be an extreme example of a well-intentioned, but nevertheless insensitive, counselor, John's attitude typifies the mentality of many of those who come from the majority community to work with the minority community. This counselor's own struggles to achieve his goals did not necessarily make him competent to deal with another's life situation. The counselor entering the minority community has at least as much to learn as to teach, and if any real work is to be done, it must be accomplished on a cooperative basis.

Multicultural Training of Counselors

It is the consensus of writers in the field that the theories and practices of counseling need to be adapted to this multicultural perspective (Herr, 1991; Ivey, 1990; Ivey & Rigazio DiGilio, 1991; Katz, 1985; Lee, 1991a, 1991b; Pedersen, 1985a; Smith, 1985b; D. W. Sue & D. Sue, 1990; Wrenn, 1985). Thus, it is essential for counselors to learn the skills that will enable them to function effectively and ethically in a multicultural society. Although many training programs appear to be making efforts to instill cultural awareness in students, it seems that some programs have been slow to integrate these concerns into the curriculum

(LaFromboise & Foster, 1989). Both minority and majority students need cross-cultural training to work effectively with clients who differ from them. One example of the commitment to training counseling students to work within the framework of cultural diversity are the standards established by the Council for Accreditation of Counseling and Related Educational Programs (CACREP). They require programs to provide curricular and experiential offerings in multicultural and pluralistic trends (Ivey & Rigazio-DiGilio, 1991).

Future professionals need to be prepared to work with clients from all backgrounds. This guideline is consistent with the recommendations of the Association for Counselor Education and Supervision, which is a division of the AACD. According to the ACES (1990), trainees should study ethnic groups, subcultures, the changing roles of women, sexism, urban and rural societies, cultural mores, and differing life patterns. The standards call for supervised practicum experiences that include people from the environments in which the trainee is preparing to work. Counseling supervisors are expected to demonstrate knowledge of individual differences with respect to gender, race, ethnicity, culture, and age.

Ivey and Rigazio-DiGilio (1991) challenge the helping professions to develop culture-specific and gender-specific counseling methods that will offer a framework for assessing and treating a variety of individual, group, family, and community developmental blocks. They write that the time is ripe for integrating multiculturalism, gender awareness, and developmental concerns into training programs.

Cultural awareness is not an either/or matter. Instead, cultural sensitivity can best be considered from a developmental perspective ranging from extreme unawareness of cultural issues to a heightened awareness of the role that cultural factors play in the counseling process. In writing about the developmental process that student therapists go through in becoming culturally sensitive, Lopez and his colleagues (1989) propose the following four stages:

1. An unawareness of cultural issues appears to be the initial stage in the development of cultural sensitivity. At this stage counseling students do not understand or appreciate the role that clients' cultural background plays in their functioning.
2. During the second stage there is a heightened cultural awareness that includes recognizing that group differences and culture-specific issues are crucial to effective counseling. This increased awareness can lead students to recognize their lack of the knowledge and training necessary to work effectively with certain client populations. At this time they often feel unprepared to work with culturally different clients.
3. Eventually, counseling students may become overly vigilant in identifying cultural factors and confused in determining the cultural significance of the client's actions. Thus, they may become overburdened with having to focus on cultural concerns, which can actually detract from their ability to be present in counseling sessions.
4. In the last developmental phase counseling students show a more sophisticated view of cultural issues and have acquired a synthesis that results in cultural

sensitivity. This knowledge tends to reduce the stereotypes, misunderstandings, faulty assumptions, and prejudices that often interfere with effective counseling. Students are able to entertain cultural hypotheses and carefully test them before accepting cultural explanations. There is an increased likelihood that they will understand the role of culture in a given client's functioning.

Lopez and his associates point out that cultural sensitivity is not a static accomplishment by counselors but a continuing therapeutic challenge. It can be increased by the willingness of both students and clinicians to continue sharing their questions, thoughts, and feelings about cultural issues with supervisors, colleagues, and clients.

Characteristics of the Culturally Skilled Counselor

D. W. Sue and D. Sue (1990) provide a concise view of the characteristics of culturally skilled counselors. First, such therapists are actively examining their assumptions about human behavior, values, biases, ethnocentric attitudes, and personal limitations. Second, they are actively attempting to understand the world views of their clients. This effort does not imply that they need to accept these views as their own, but they are able to work with other perspectives in a nonjudgmental manner. Rather than being encapsulated, they welcome diverse value orientations and diverse assumptions about human behavior. Third, they are committed to developing and practicing appropriate, relevant, and sensitive interventions in working with diverse clients. Culturally skilled counselors are truly eclectic in that they use skills, methods, and goals that are appropriate to the experiences and lifestyles of the culturally different. Sue and Sue conclude that counselors who are willing to address cultural differences directly do not view such differences as problematic.

Mental-health services can be delivered best if practitioners genuinely believe that their clients are basically psychologically healthy and are experiencing normal developmental struggles. Lee (1991b) contends that counseling services are enhanced when helpers recognize the cultural dynamics of their clients and have learned how to incorporate naturally occurring support systems into a range of interventions. For Lee, culturally responsive counseling is predicated on making full use of indigenous sources of helping.

The APA draft guidelines (1991b) call for service providers to seek out educational and training experiences to enhance their understanding of the cultural, social, psychological, political, economic, and historical dimensions that are specific to the particular ethnic group being served. Furthermore, when counselors do not possess the knowledge and training to work appropriately and effectively with a given ethnic group, they are urged to seek consultation with appropriate experts or make an appropriate referral, if necessary.

D. W. Sue and his associates (1982) developed minimal cross-cultural counseling competencies to be incorporated into training programs. The characteristics described in the accompanying box are based on an adaptation of their position paper, on other sources (Pedersen, 1985a, 1988; Pedersen, Draguns, Lonner, &

Trimble, 1989), and on the characteristics of the culturally skilled counselor as summarized by D. W. Sue and D. Sue (1990).

Essential Attributes of Culturally Skilled Counselors

1. *Beliefs and attitudes of culturally skilled counselors*
   - They are aware of their own values, beliefs, attitudes, feelings, and biases and of how they are likely to affect minority clients. They monitor their functioning through consultation, supervision, and continuing education.
   - They can appreciate diverse cultures, and they feel comfortable with differences between themselves and their clients in terms of race and beliefs. Rather than being ethnocentric and maintaining that their cultural heritage is superior, they are able to value and accept cultural differences.
   - They believe that there can be a unique integration of different value systems that can contribute to both therapist and client growth.
   - They are aware of their limitations and are not threatened by the prospect of referring a minority client to a member of his or her own race or culture, when necessary.
2. *Knowledge of culturally skilled counselors*
   - They understand the sociopolitical system's operation in the United States with respect to its treatment of minorities.
   - They are aware of institutional barriers that prevent minorities from making full use of psychological services in the community.
   - They understand how the value assumptions of the major theories of counseling may interact with the values of different cultural groups.
   - They are aware of culture-specific (or indigenous) methods of helping.
   - They possess specific knowledge about the particular group they are working with.
3. *Skills of culturally skilled counselors*
   - They are able to use counseling methods and goals that are consistent with the life experiences and cultural value systems of different minority groups.
   - They are able to modify and adapt conventional approaches to counseling and psychotherapy in order to accommodate cultural differences.
   - They are able to send and receive both verbal and nonverbal messages accurately and appropriately.
   - They are able to employ institutional intervention skills on behalf of their clients when necessary or appropriate.
   - They are able to make out-of-office interventions when necessary by assuming the role of consultant and agent for change.
   - They recognize their limitations and are able to anticipate their impact on the culturally different client.

Consider this situation: During a counseling staff meeting that you are attending, a white female colleague says to the group: "Based on my years of counseling experience, I've found that I'm 'color-blind.' It doesn't make any difference in my counseling if the client is yellow, red, black, or white. I still do the same things with the same results. This whole business of minority counseling is a camouflage for the real issues. Some counselors just don't have it!"

- To what degree do you agree or disagree with her statements?
- What might you have been thinking and feeling in this situation?
- How might you have responded to this counselor?

Our Views on Multicultural Training

We believe that a self-exploratory class should be required to help counseling students identify their cultural and ethnic blind spots. This course would ideally be required for all trainees in the mental-health professions and would be taught by someone with experience in multicultural issues. It is an ethical obligation of counselor educators to identify, and perhaps even screen out of such a program, those students who exhibit and maintain rigid notions of the way people ought to live, regardless of their cultural background. In addition to this introductory course, we would like to see at least one course dealing exclusively with multicultural issues and minority groups. Because there are an increasing number of articles and books on minority groups, students should have this literature available to them.

It is also extremely important that this multicultural perspective be integrated throughout the rest of the curriculum. The teaching of theories and techniques of counseling, for example, can emphasize how such concepts and strategies can be adapted to the special needs of diverse client populations and how some theories may be quite inappropriate for culturally different clients. Wherever possible, representatives of these diverse cultures can speak directly to the students. These representatives can also address social, economic, and culture-specific factors that may affect mental-health treatment. In addition, we support Lee's proposal for comprehensive and ongoing professional-development experiences related to multicultural counseling (1991b). It is essential that all counselors have training in learning how to account for salient cultural dynamics in the therapeutic process.

The integration of multiculturalism and gender awareness can certainly be a thread running through relevant formal courses. In addition, there could be at least one required internship in which trainees have multicultural experiences. Ideally, the supervisor at this agency will be well-versed in the cultural variables of that particular setting and also be skilled in cross-cultural understanding. Further, trainees should have access to both individual and group supervision on campus from a faculty member. Students can be encouraged to select supervised field placements and internships that will challenge them to work on gender issues, cultural concerns, developmental issues, and lifestyle differences. They will not learn to become effective multicultural counselors by working exclusively with clients with whom they are comfortable and who are "like them" (Corey, 1991a). We agree with Lee's statement that there is a limit to how much can be learned about cultural diversity from courses and workshops (1991b). Lee maintains that more can be learned by going out into the community and interacting with diverse groups of people who face a myriad of problems. Through well-selected internship experiences, trainees will not only expand their own consciousness but will also increase their knowledge of diverse groups and will have a basis for acquiring intervention skills. S. Sue and his colleagues (1985) contend that understanding the culture of clients is necessary, but not sufficient, in effectively counseling ethnic-minority clients. Although they value didactic methods of acquiring knowledge, they emphasize the value of actual work in ethnic communities and work with a large number of clients.

Finally, we would highly recommend that trainees open themselves through reading and travel to people in other cultures. Students can also make use of films and videotapes and can attend seminars and workshops that focus on multicultural issues in the helping professions. Any experiences that will sensitize students to a broad range of life experiences and cultural values will contribute to their effectiveness as counselors.

As a way of getting the most from your training, we encourage you to accept your limitations and to be patient with yourself as you expand your vision of how your culture continues to influence the person you are today. It is not helpful to overwhelm yourself with all that you do not know or to feel guilty over your limitations or parochial views. You will not become more effective in multicultural counseling by expecting that you must be completely knowledgeable about the cultural backgrounds of all your clients, by thinking that you should have a complete repertoire of skills, or by demanding perfection. Instead, recognize and appreciate your efforts toward becoming a more effective person and counselor.

Chapter Summary

A number of writers have urged over the last decade that counselors learn about their own culture and become aware of how their experiences affect the way they work with others who are culturally different. By being ignorant of the values and attitudes of clients who are of a different race, age, sex, social class, or culture, therapists open themelves up to criticism. Imposing one's own vision of the world on clients not only leads to negative therapeutic outcomes but also constitutes unethical practice.

We are all limited by our cultural and ethnic experiences. But we can increase our awareness by direct contact with a variety of ethnic and cultural groups, by reading, by special course work, and by in-service professional workshops. It is essential that our practices be appropriate for the clients with whom we work. This entails modifying our theories and techniques to clients' unique needs and not rigidly applying interventions in the same manner to all clients. We encourage you to carefully examine your assumptions, attitudes, and values so that you can determine how they could influence your practice.

Suggested Activities

1. Select two or three cultures or races different from your own. What attitudes and beliefs about these cultures did you hold while growing up? How have your attitudes changed, if at all, and what contributed to the changes?

2. What values do you owe primarily to your culture? With the passing of time have any of your values changed, and, if so, how? How might these values influence the way you work with clients who are culturally different from you?

3. What cross-cultural life experiences have you had? Did you learn anything about your potential prejudices? What prejudices, if any, did you feel directed at you? You might bring your experiences to class. Also, we suggest that you interview other students or faculty members who identify themselves as ethnically or culturally different from you. What might they teach you about differences that you as a counselor would need to take into consideration in order to work more effectively with them?

4. Invite speakers to class to talk about cross-cultural factors as they relate to values. Speakers representing special concerns of various ethnic groups can address the topic of certain values unique to their group and can discuss the implications of these values for counseling.

5. To what degree have your courses and field experience contributed to your ability to work effectively with people from other cultures? What training experiences would you like to have to better prepare you for multicultural counseling?

6. Divide into groups of three in your class. One person becomes a minority client. A second person assumes the counselor role. And the third person acts as an alter ego for the client, as the anticounselor. You might have the minority client be somewhat reluctant to speak. The counselor can deal with this silence by treating it as a form of resistance, using typical therapeutic strategies. During this time the anticounselor expresses the cultural meaning of the silence. Now, devise a way to deal with silence from this frame of reference, without using traditional therapeutic techniques.

7. Assume that you were asked this question: "Minorities are often put under strong pressure to give up their beliefs and ways in favor of adopting the ideals and customs of the dominant culture. What do you think your approach would be in working with clients who feel such pressure? How might you work with clients who see their own ethnicity or cultural heritage as a handicap that is to be overcome?

Suggested Readings

Lee and Richardson (1991a) have edited an excellent text on multicultural issues in counseling, with some particularly useful articles on the impact of culture on mental-health interventions. Some of these articles cover the problems and pitfalls of multicultural counseling (Lee and Richardson, 1991b); the role of cultural dynamics in multicultural counseling (Lee, 1991a); and the implications of cultural diversity for counselor training and research (Lee, 1991b). One of the basic publications in the area of multicultural counseling is Pedersen, Draguns, Lonner, and Trimble (1989). For an excellent reference book that reviews the history, assumptions, theories, present status, future directions, and specializations within the field of cross-cultural counseling and therapy, see Pedersen (1985a). Atkinson and his colleagues (1989) have pulled together a very useful collection of articles on the topic of counseling American minorities. The textbook on counseling the culturally different by D. W. Sue and D. Sue (1990) is comprehensive, well-written, and current. For an excellent treatment of counseling diverse populations (racial and ethnic minority groups, single parents, older persons, gay and lesbian populations, people with physical disabilities, and women reentering the workplace), see Vacc, Wittmer, and De Vaney (1988). On the subject of ethics in multicultural counseling, see LaFromboise and Foster (1989).

For a treatment of ways of becoming aware of multicultural assumptions and of developing the knowledge and skills essential for multicultural practice, see Pedersen (1988). For a textbook that presents a life-span perspective on multicultural counseling, see Baruth and Manning (1991). On the need for culturally sensitive assertiveness training for minority clients, see Wood and Mallinckrodt (1990). For a discussion of the challenges of the counseling profession in dealing with cultural diversity and pluralism, see Herr (1991) and Ivey and Rigazio-DiGilio (1991). For a description of the stages that students go through in becoming culturally sensitive, see Lopez et al. (1989). On dilemmas and choices in cross-cultural counseling, see Draguns (1989) On racism in counseling see Ridley (1989). On the role of client and counselor variables in multicultural counseling see Pedersen, Fukuyama, and Heath (1989).

For an excellent presentation of current concerns in multicultural counseling see the special issue entitled "Multiculturalism as a Fourth Force in Counseling" in the *Journal of Counseling and Development* (vol. 70, no. 1, September/October 1991). There are 35 articles dealing with areas such as the conceptual framework, education and training, research opportunities, and direct service delivery. Examples of articles that are particularly relevant to the topics covered in this chapter are:

- a redefinition of multicultural counseling
- multicultural gender issues
- sensitizing counselors and educators to multicultural issues
- a model for cultural-diversity training
- reflections on a multicultural internship experience
- toward training for competence in multicultural counselor education
- evaluating the impact of multicultural counseling training
- racism as a disease
- the nature of prejudice revisited

Issues with Special Populations

Pre-Chapter Self-Inventory

Directions: For each statement, indicate the response that most closely identifies your beliefs and attitudes. Use the following code:

5 = I *strongly agree* with this statement.
4 = I *agree* with this statement.
3 = I am *undecided* about this statement.
2 = I *disagree* with this statement.
1 = I *strongly disagree* with this statement.

_____ 1. Gay and lesbian clients are best served by gay and lesbian counselors.

_____ 2. As a condition for licensure, counselors should have some specialized training in counseling lesbian and gay clients.

_____ 3. A therapist who is lesbian is unlikely to be effective in counseling heterosexual women.

_____ 4. It is the therapist's job to discourage the transmission of myths associated with gay and lesbian lifestyles and to be prepared to substitute reality for mythology.

_____ 5. As a counselor, I see it as my ethical responsibility to learn about referral resources for gay and lesbian clients and to make appropriate referrals if I do not have the knowledge and skills to work effectively with this population.

_____ 6. Mental-health professionals have an ethical and moral obligation to address lesbian and gay issues in an affirmative manner and to take the necessary steps to eliminate all forms of oppression.

_____ 7. I think I would have difficulty in counseling a lesbian couple who wanted support in adopting a child.

_____ 8. Therapists with very traditional values are unlikely to be effective in counseling women.

_____ 9. It is appropriate for therapists who work with children and adolescents to serve as their advocates in certain legal situations.

_____ 10. When a child is in psychotherapy, the therapist has an ethical and legal obligation to provide the parents with any information about the child that they request.

_____ 11. Minors should be allowed to seek psychological guidance regarding pregnancy and abortion counseling without parental consent or knowledge.

_____ 12. As a helping professional, I have the responsibility to report suspected child abuse, regardless of when it occurred.

_____ 13. The reporting laws pertaining to child abuse sometimes have the effect of preventing therapy for the abuser.

_____ 14. I question the effectiveness of requiring a therapist to report all child abuse, because this decision should be left to the judgment of the therapist.

_____ 15. In order to protect children from abuse, strict laws must be enacted, and professionals must be penalized for failing to report abuses.

___ 16. When it comes to protecting children from child abuse, there are times when what is legal may not always be ethical.

___ 17. I think that the AIDS crisis has definite implications for all those who practice psychotherapy.

___ 18. If my client is HIV-positive, I have a duty to warn all of the person's identifiable sexual partners.

___ 19. In counseling HIV-positive clients, I would be inclined to maintain confidentiality on the ground that failing to do so would erode their trust.

___ 20. If an HIV-positive client of mine refused to disclose his infection to his partner, I would explore his reasons for not doing so.

Introduction

This chapter deals with ethical, legal, and clinical issues pertaining to several special populations. It is not possible to do justice to the many special populations that practitioners will serve. But we have selected a few of these groups of clients and explored some of their key concerns. This chapter is an extension of the previous chapter, dealing with cultural diversity. Many of the same principles that we established for multicultural counseling also apply to counseling homosexuals, children and adolescents, women, or clients with AIDS. These special populations have something in common with racial or ethnic minority groups: their needs have generally been denied by society, they have all been faced with discrimination and oppression, and the mental-health professions are being challenged to develop intervention strategies that are meaningful to them. Special training is needed to equip therapists with the knowledge and skills to work with special populations. This chapter addresses the importance of acquiring this knowledge base and learning how to deal sensitively with diversity.

Ethical Issues in Counseling Gay and Lesbian Clients

Working with lesbians and gay men often presents a challenge to those who hold traditional values. Even counselors who intellectually accept gay lifestyles may reject them emotionally. Counselors who have negative reactions to homosexuals are likely to impose their own values. Buhrke and Douce (1991) remind mental-health professionals that they have an ethical and moral obligation to address lesbian and gay issues in an affirmative manner. It is their professional responsibility to take the steps necessary to eliminate all forms of oppression. The ethics codes of both the AACD and the APA clearly state that discrimination on the basis of minority status—be it race, ethnicity, gender, or sexual orientation—is unethical and unacceptable. If the profession is serious about meeting this guideline, it will need to train students to provide sensitive treatment of gays and lesbians (Buhrke & Douce, 1991). We highlight this topic because it illustrates not only the ethical problems involved in imposing values but also the problems of working with clients who have had different life experiences.

A professor of psychology, in a discussion of homosexuality, made the following comment:

> I believe that heterosexuality is the only normal sexual orientation. Helping people is possible by educating and teaching them to be normal. The mainstream of most cultures considers homosexuality a deviation. Some believe that most homosexuals were forced to be, because they learned homosexuality in an age when they weren't mature.

If a professor holds this view, it is easy to see that education about sexual orientations is badly needed. Professional helpers who have such attitudes would find it very difficult to be objective or to allow their clients to make their own choices.

The American Psychiatric Association, in 1973, and the American Psychological Association, in 1975, stopped calling homosexuality a form of mental illness. Along with these changes came the assumption that therapeutic practices would be modified to reflect a view of homosexuality as an alternative lifestyle. Furthermore, after decades of discrimination against gay people by the mental-health system, there has been a trend toward treating the *problems* of homosexuals rather than their sexual orientation (Fassinger, 1991b).

Ritter and O'Neill (1989) write that although more clinicians are counseling gay and lesbian clients, a number of practitioners still view them as needing to be cured. They propose that counselors develop therapeutic strategies that "can assist gay men and lesbian women in freeing their souls of the negativity and death-dealing emotions that may be preventing them from proceeding along their spiritual journeys" (p. 12).

Before counselors can change their therapeutic strategies, they must change their attitudes toward lesbians and gays and acquire a body of knowledge about community resources for such clients. Unless they become conscious of their own faulty assumptions and homophobia, they may project their misconceptions about homosexuality and their fears onto their clients. Therapists must confront their personal prejudices, myths, fears, and stereotypes regarding homosexuality. As a part of the process of expanding their self-awareness, they need to acquire specialized knowledge about gay people in general and about the meaning of a gay identity to particular individuals (Sobocinski, 1990). They also need to find ways to continue to educate themselves about gay identity development and management and about affirmative counseling models (Shannon & Woods, 1991).

In an empirical study designed to examine common psychosocial assumptions pertaining to lesbian mothers, Falk (1989) found that discrimination had persisted in court decisions denying them petitions for custody of their children. The courts often assume that lesbians are emotionally unstable or unable to perform a maternal role. They also assume that children with lesbian mothers are more likely to be emotionally harmed, that they will be subject to molestation, that their role development will be negatively affected, or that they will themselves become homosexual. Falk concludes that "no research has identified significant differences between lesbian mothers and their heterosexual counterparts or the children raised by these groups. Researchers have been unable to establish empirically that detriment results to children from being raised by lesbian mothers"

(p. 946). It is assumptions and misconceptions such as these that need to be critically examined by practitioners so that such beliefs do not interfere with their ability to provide effective service for gay people. In addition to being aware of their assumptions and beliefs, counselors must learn the special counseling emphases and needs of gay clients.

We agree with Herek's (1989) suggestions about the need for community education as a way to lessen the incidents of hate crimes against lesbians and gay men. Some elements in his proposal for this educational program are as follows:

- Federal, state, and local funds should be granted for programs to reduce prejudice against all minority groups, including the gay population.
- Elementary and secondary schools should design programs to foster a tolerance of diversity. To do this, it is essential that school personnel receive explicit training in sensitivity to lesbian and gay issues.
- College and university personnel should recognize antigay bias and act against it. These institutions should include sexual orientation in their antidiscrimination policies.

Herek concludes: "Through our research, teaching, advocacy, and practice, psychologists can confront the menace of hate crimes and the bigotry that feeds them" (p. 954).

The APA's Task Force on Bias in Psychotherapy with Lesbians and Gay Men conducted a survey of 2,544 licensed psychologists to identify their attitudes pertaining to homosexuals (Youngstrom, 1991a). Almost 95 percent of the psychologists reported that they had treated at least one lesbian or gay man. One of the purposes of the survey was to identify examples of both good and poor therapeutic practices with this population. The task force identified 25 themes that revealed biased, inadequate, or inappropriate practices and 20 themes indicating exemplary practices. Some examples of biased practices, which may be unethical, are:

- automatically attributing a client's problems to his or her sexual orientation
- discouraging lesbian or gay clients from having or adopting a child
- expressing attitudes or beliefs that trivialize or demean gay and lesbian individuals or their experience
- showing insensitivity to the impact of prejudice and discrimination on gay and lesbian parents and their children
- providing or teaching inaccurate or biased information about lesbians and gay men

Exemplary practices included the following:

- not attempting to change the sexual orientation of a client without evidence that the client desires this change
- recognizing that gay and lesbian people can live happy and fulfilled lives
- recognizing the importance of educating professionals, students, supervisees, and others about gay and lesbian issues and attempting to counter bias and misinformation
- recognizing the ways in which societal prejudices and discrimination create problems for clients and dealing with these concerns in therapy

At a recent APA annual convention several presentations dealt with the ethical and sociopolitical dimensions of gay and lesbian lifestyles. One example of these programs was a symposium entitled "Beyond Stigma: Lesbian and Gay Policy Issues in the 1990s." A panel of five participants addressed concerns related to family life, school life, the struggle for civil rights, job discrimination, and the future of AIDS politics. As the panel addressed the political challenges facing gays and lesbians in the 1990s, it was clear that psychologists need to deal with a number of ethical issues if they hope to reach this population.

Specialized Training

One key issue is whether it is ethical to counsel gay and lesbian clients without having received specialized training with this population. Buhrke and Douce (1991) suggest ways in which gay and lesbian concerns might be integrated into both the academic courses and the internship experience in a counseling program. Slater (1988) makes the point that myths surrounding homosexuality continue to abound. She sees it as the therapist's job to discourage such myths and to substitute reality. These myths and misconceptions tend to perpetuate the illness model and lead to discrimination, rejection, and even attacks on homosexuals. Slater concludes that it is essential that therapists who work with gays have a knowledge of developmental theories, that they be relatively free of homophobia, and that they be knowledgeable about gay lifestyles. Being a gay-affirming therapist implies understanding and accepting homosexuality as an acceptable, rather than inferior, lifestyle. Fassinger (1991b) contends that "we should deliberately create a gay affirmative approach that validates a gay sexual orientation, recognizes the oppression faced by gay people, and actively helps them overcome its external and internal effects" (p. 170). It is clear that practitioners need to critically examine any misconceptions they hold about gay men and lesbians and to obtain specialized training in working with gay clients.

Although counselors may choose not to work with a gay and lesbian population, they may not always know the sexual orientation of their clients. This issue may not surface until the therapeutic relationship develops, with serious conflicts for both the client and the counselor. Even though counselors may not specialize in gay and lesbian counseling, it is essential that they be clear about where they stand in regard to major issues pertaining to homosexuals. It is also essential that they be direct and honest about their views with clients who want to explore concerns pertaining to sexual orientation.

One way for counselors to increase their awareness of ethical and therapeutic considerations in working with gay and lesbian clients is to take advantage of the continuing-education workshops that are available as part of many national, regional, state, and local professional organizations. For the past few years, for example, the AACD has offered a daylong professional development institute on counseling with gay and lesbian clients. Participants learn about referral resources and specific interventions and strategies that are appropriate for gay and lesbian clients.

Special Needs of Gay and Lesbian Clients

Gay and lesbian clients have special counseling needs. Like any other minority group, they are subjected to discrimination, prejudice, and oppression. This discrimination manifests itself when gay people seek employment or a place of residence. For instance, the U.S. Department of Defense does not permit openly homosexual individuals to serve in the military. A special issue that lesbians and gay men often bring to counseling is the struggle between concealing their identity and "coming out." Dealing with family members is also of special importance to gay couples. They may want to be honest with their parents, yet they may fear hurting them or receiving negative reactions from them. With the reality of the AIDS crisis, gay men often face the loss of friends who are dying. Not only do they need to deal with death and loss, but they may want to explore their fears of becoming infected. Counselors who work with gay men need to be able to talk with their clients about safe-sex practices. In short, counselors need to listen carefully to their clients and be willing to explore whatever concerns they bring to the counseling relationship.

On the topic of the special needs of gay men and lesbians, Sobocinski (1990) contends that it is not the therapist's task to "make" clients either gay or straight. Instead, he underscores that the ethical course of action entails "providing an opportunity for those youth who are dealing with issues of sexual orientation to begin to work through these questions so that they might become the unique individuals that they in truth are already" (p. 246).

○ ***The case of a lesbian couple.***   Myrna seeks relationship counseling, saying that she and her partner are having communication problems. They have a number of conflicts that they both want to work out. Myrna clearly states that she is involved in a lesbian relationship and that her lifestyle is not an issue she wants to explore. She indicates that they are comfortable with their sexual preferences but need help in learning how to communicate more effectively.

Counselor A.   This counselor agrees to see Myrna and her partner, and during the first session he suggests that they ought to examine their homosexuality. He says he finds it hard to believe that their nontraditional lifestyle is not a contributing factor to their present difficulties.

• Do you agree or disagree with the stance of Counselor A?
• Since Myrna made it clear over the telephone that she and her partner did not want to explore the issue of being lesbian, was the counselor's intervention appropriate? Explain.

Counselor B.   This counselor agrees to see the couple. During the initial session he realizes that he has strong negative reactions toward them. These reactions are so much in the foreground that they interfere with his effectively working with the couple's presenting problem. He tells the two women about his difficulties and reactions and suggests a referral. He lets them know that he had hoped he could be objective enough to work with them but that this is not the case.

- Was this counselor's behavior ethical?
- Given his negative reactions, should he have continued seeing the couple?
- Would this in itself have been unethical?
- What would be more damaging to the clients—referring them or continuing to see them?
- Is it ethical for Counselor B to charge the couple for this session? Explain your point of view.

Counselor C. This counselor agrees to see the two women and work with them much as she would with a heterosexual couple. The counselor adds that if at any time the uniqueness of their relationship causes difficulties, it would be up to them to bring this up as an issue. She lets them know that if they are comfortable with their lifestyle, she has no need to explore it. What are your reactions to this counselor's approach?

In reviewing the approaches of these three counselors, think about which approach would be closest to yours. In clarifying your thinking on the issue of counseling gay and lesbian clients, reflect on the following questions:

- Therapists often find that the presenting problem that clients bring to a session is not their major problem. Does it show the therapist's values to assume that a couple's homosexuality might be the real problem? Do you see the counselor as justified in bringing up homosexuality as a therapeutic issue?
- What are the ethical implications of a heterosexually oriented therapist's working with homosexual couples?
- Is it an appropriate function of counselors to attempt to sway people toward a lifestyle deemed "acceptable" by the counselor? Is it the counselor's role to make life decisions for clients, or should the counselor challenge clients to make their own decisions?
- What attitudes on the part of therapists are necessary for them to be instrumental in helping gay men and lesbians accept their orientations?
- Can a counselor who is not comfortable with his or her own sexuality possibly be effective in assisting homosexual clients to accept their identities?

Counseling Gay Parents and Their Children

You might become involved in counseling a gay parent, a child of a gay parent, or a heterosexual former spouse of a gay parent who is fighting for custody over their children. At this point imagine yourself first in a counseling situation with a lesbian mother who consults you because of concerns about the effects on her son of her sexual orientation. Now imagine yourself counseling a daughter of a gay father who struggles over being teased at school because her friends know about this situation. And now imagine counseling the former spouse of the lesbian mother, who tells you that he wants to get custody of the children and is capable of providing a more normal home environment for them. What values do you hold that might make it difficult to counsel any of these clients? What values do you possess that might facilitate building a relationship with your client in each of these situations?

Cramer (1986) acknowledges that a gay parent seeking custody, continuation of parental rights, or visitation privileges is typically at a disadvantage from a legal perspective. He reviews research in three areas that tend to be the focus of legal concerns. Following are the three concerns usually raised, along with Cramer's responses, based on studies:

1. The first concern is whether a child reared by a gay parent will grow up to be gay. The research tends to contradict the notion that gay parents rear gay children—or disturbed children—to any greater extent than do heterosexual parents.
2. The second concern is that a gay parent will sexually abuse a child of the same sex or reject a child of the opposite sex. There is no evidence to support either of these assertions.
3. The third concern is that a child of a gay parent will suffer from peer pressure and rejection. Cramer does find this an area of concern, especially when children reach adolescence and are sensitive to comments about their parent's sexuality.

○ *The case of a counselor who has a gay son.*   Ruby is counseling Henry, who expresses extremely hostile feelings toward homosexuals and toward people who have contracted AIDS. Henry is not coming to counseling to work on his feelings about gay people; rather, his primary goal is to work out his feelings of resentment over his wife, who left him. In one session he makes derogatory comments about gay people. He strongly feels that all of them are deviant and that it serves them right if they do get AIDS. Ruby's son is gay, and Henry's prejudice affects her emotionally. She is taken aback by her client's comments, and she finds that his views are getting in her way as she attempts to work with him. Her self-dialogue has taken the following turns:

- "Maybe I should tell Henry how he is affecting me and let him know I have a son who's gay. If I don't, I'm not sure I can continue to work with him."
- "I think I'll express my hurt and anger to a colleague, but I surely won't tell Henry how he's affecting me. Nor will I let him know I'm having a hard time working with him."
- "Henry's disclosures get in the way of my caring for him. Perhaps I should tell him I'm bothered deeply by his prejudice but not let him know that I have a gay son."
- "Because of my own countertransference, it may be best that I refer him without telling him the reason I'm having trouble with him."
- "Maybe I should just put my own feelings on a shelf and try to work with him on reducing his prejudice and negative reactions toward gays."

If Ruby came to you as a colleague and wanted to talk about her reactions and the course she should take with Henry, what are some things you might say to her? In reflecting on what you might tell her, consider these issues:

- Is it ethical for her to work on a goal that her client has not brought up?
- To what degree would you encourage her to be self-disclosing with Henry? What do you think she should reveal of herself to him? And what do you think she should not disclose? Why?
- Do you think there are ethical issues if Ruby continues to see Henry but decides not to deal with him on the matter of how she is affected by him?

Evaluating Your Ability to Counsel Gay and Lesbian Clients

Consider your own values, and evaluate your capacity for objectivity. Might you try to reorient a gay client, depending on your value orientation? If so, in what direction would you steer your client? In what cases would you recommend a referral, and why? What ethical issues do you see in imposing your values on your client? What do you consider to be the major issue for you in counseling gay and lesbian clients? If homosexuality is an alternative lifestyle and not a disease, why is specialized training in the area required to work effectively with this population? Do you think you should have specialized training for each client you accept? If your church taught that homosexuality was sinful and not to be condoned under any circumstances, could you work with a gay or lesbian client? What ethical obligations to refer, if any, do you have if you are convinced that you cannot be objective or helpful in working with homosexuals? How might you develop a referral network and use it for special client populations?

Counseling Women: A Special Case?*

Although we are devoting a section to counseling women, we do not mean to imply that gender issues pertain only to them. Men are also victims of stereotyping and countertransference by therapists. Much of what we say about women in this section can be applied to men in a general way. Our reason for focusing on women is the overwhelming evidence of discrimination against them in our culture. The literature conveys the underlying message that men should be sensitive to women and vice versa. Yet some female therapists are as biased toward their female clients as some men are toward women. Both female and male therapists need to be aware of their values and beliefs about gender. You will remember that in the previous chapter we spoke about the importance of counselors' being aware of how their culture has influenced their personality. We think that the ways in which people perceive gender likewise have a lot to do with their surrounding culture.

*We want to acknowledge the suggestions for this section from Barbara McDowell, director of the Women's Center at California State University, Fullerton, and Michelle Naden, of Loma Linda University.

Effective communication between therapists and their clients is often undermined by stereotypical views about how women and men think, feel, and behave. Counselors need to be alert to particular issues with which women and men struggle and the ways in which their own views about gender might restrict autonomy in their female clients. Cayleff (1986) writes that true autonomy for women may require distinguishing their own beliefs from society's traditional view of their tendency to please and accommodate others. Her perspective stresses the importance of a therapeutic relationship that avoids paternalism, pays attention to the complexity of relationships in women's lives, and supports women's movement toward autonomy. She makes the point that counseling women by encourging them to comply with traditional sex-role expectations in their personal and professional lives can violate their autonomy and harm their welfare.

The task of counseling professionals is to help both women and men explore and challenge the stereotyped expectations that they behave in certain limited ways. Men may need assistance in learning new ways to take responsibility for their own emotional lives in spite of the tug toward relying on women's strength when it comes to emotions. Women may need assistance in overcoming internal barriers to autonomy and in raising their self-esteem and overcoming dependency.

Learning to make autonomous choices does not mean that women have to deny their needs for connection, and choosing to take care of oneself does not imply being unconcerned about others. Similarly, for men, learning to be more relational and sharing one's inner life does not mean a loss of independence and strength. Autonomy sets the stage for healthy relating in a loving relationship. M.C. McBride writes: "As counselors, we need to encourage our female clients to choose to define themselves rather than be defined by others, to choose self-mastery rather than live up to the expectations of others, and to give themselves as much or more than they give to others" (1990, p. 25). Although we are in basic agreement with McBride, we think that it is not the therapist's role to impose any set of values on women. Instead, the therapist can best function in the interests of female clients by challenging them to examine any self-contradictions. The therapist's task is to help clients decide who and what they want to be, not what the therapist thinks they should be. For example, a woman might choose to be a homemaker and mother. Some clinicians might be uncomfortable in supporting traditional roles for women for fear of perpetuating stereotypes and being labeled sexist. The point is that a woman does have choices and that her choices need to be supported by her therapist.

Gender Roles and Stereotypes

Good, Gilbert, and Scher (1990) discuss the value of integrating knowledge about the impact of gender into the practice of counseling women and men. They advocate the use of "gender-aware therapy" in working with couples and families. Gender-aware therapy is aimed at helping clients understand how societal conceptions of gender often limit their thinking, feeling, and behaving.

According to Hare-Mustin (1980), therapists who work with couples and families need to clarify their own values pertaining to traditional and nontraditional family arrangements and should also be open in divulging these values. She further contends that therapists should be prepared to explain to the family their views on issues such as sex-role requirements and the distribution of power between spouses and between parents and children. If such explanations are given, the clients know from the outset what views are likely to influence the course of their therapy.

In writing about feminist therapy, Gilbert (1980) summarizes the viewpoints of writers who question the usefulness of traditional therapeutic approaches that focus exclusively on how people learn cultural and social values and that aim to maintain the status quo. She points out that U.S. society's ideology has called for women to accommodate to a set of discriminatory role behaviors and sex-typed personality characteristics. She criticizes many of the traditional approaches as encouraging women to comply with these expectations. In their place, she recommends several research priorities in the area of feminist therapy. DeVoe (1990) argues that feminist therapy should not be restricted to women and contends that the time is long overdue for its principles and values to permeate the counseling relationship.

Counselors who work with couples and families can practice more ethically if they are aware of the history and impact of gender stereotyping as it is reflected in the socialization process in families. Effective practitioners must continually evaluate their own beliefs about appropriate family roles and responsibilities, child-rearing practices, multiple roles, and nontraditional vocations for women and men. Counselors also must have the knowledge to help their clients explore educational, vocational, and emotional goals that they previously deemed unreachable. The principles of gender-aware therapy have relevance for counselors as they help clients identify and work through gender concepts that have limited them. Some of these principles, which are elaborated by Good and his colleagues (1990) include the following:

- Counselors need to understand clients' difficulties from a gender perspective and make that awareness an integral part of their practice.
- Problems in counseling are best explored by understanding that the personal and political dimensions cannot be isolated from each other.
- Counselors are challenged to seek actively to change gender injustices that both women and men experience. In counseling a dual-career couple, for example, it is a mistake to assume that the woman will make child care her priority instead of her career. Likewise, counselors are making a mistake if they assume that the man in a dual-career relationship would never seriously consider being the primary caretaker of his children.

Margolin (1982) has given a number of recommendations on how to be a nonsexist family therapist and how to use the therapeutic process to challenge the oppressive consequences of stereotyped roles and expectations in the family. One recommendation is that family therapists examine their own behavior for unwitting comments and questions that imply that the wife and husband should perform specific roles and hold a specific status. For example, a therapist can show bias in subtle and nonverbal ways, such as looking at the wife when talking about rearing children or addressing the husband when talking about decisions that need to be made. Further, Margolin contends that family therapists are particularly vulnerable to the following biases: (1) assuming that remaining married would be the best choice for a woman, (2) demonstrating less interest in a woman's career than in a man's career, (3) encouraging couples to accept the belief that child rearing is solely the responsibility of the mother, (4) showing a different reaction to a wife's affair than to a husband's, and (5) giving more importance to satisfying the husband's needs than to satisfying the wife's needs. She raises two important questions dealing with the ethics of doing therapy with couples and families:

1. How does the therapist respond when members of the family seem to agree that they want to work toward goals that (from the therapist's vantage point) are sexist in nature?
2. To what extent does the therapist accept the family's definition of sex-role identities rather than trying to challenge and eventually change these attitudes?

Brown (1990) makes the point that a clinician's own countertransference responses to gender issues affect the assessment process, which further influences the way therapy is conducted. Some of her guidelines in incorporating gender concerns into assessment and therapy include inquiring into the meaning of femininity or masculinity for the client and guarding against the inappropriate imposition of gender-stereotyped values regarding healthy functioning. Including gender issues in the assessment process increases the chances of an unbiased assessment.

In light of the foregoing discussion, we present several open-ended cases for you to consider. What are your values pertaining to gender, and how do these values influence your perception of these cases? How do you think your values might affect your manner of counseling in each case?

○ *The case of Marge and Fred.* Marge and Fred come to marriage counseling to work on the stress that they are experiencing in rearing their two adolescent sons. The couple direct the focus toward what their sons are doing and not doing. In the course of therapy it develops that both have full-time jobs outside of the home. In addition, Marge has assumed another full-time job—mother and homemaker—but her husband flatly refuses to share any domestic responsibilities. Marge never questions her dual career and very much feels that this is her station in life. Neither Marge nor Fred shows much interest in exploring the possibility that they have uncritically adopted cultural stereotypes pertaining to what women and men "should" be. Instead, they tend to draw the attention during their sessions to getting advice on how to handle the problems with their sons.

- Is it ethical for the therapist to focus simply on the expressed concerns of Marge and Fred, or is there a responsibility at least to challenge them to look at how they have defined themselves and their relationship through assumptions about sex roles?

- If you were counseling this couple, what might you do? What are your values, and how do you think they would influence the interventions you might make in this case?
- What would you do with their presenting problem, their trouble with their sons? What else might the behavior of the sons imply?

As you think about this case and the following one, ask yourself how your values regarding traditional wives and mothers might affect your relationship with clients like Marge and Melody.

○ **The case of Melody.**   Melody, 38, is married and has returned to college to obtain a teaching credential. During the intake session she tells you that she is going through a lot of turmoil and is contemplating some major changes in her life. She has met a man who shares her interest and enthusiasm for school as well as many other aspects of her life. She is considering leaving her husband and children to pursue her own interests for a change.

The following statements represent some possible responses that counselors might have to Melody, whether or not they actually voiced them to her. Which of these statements can you see yourself making to Melody? Which of them represent reactions you might have but would keep from her?

- "This is just a phase you're going through. It happens to a lot of women who return to college. Maybe you should slow down and think about it."
- "You'll never forgive yourself for leaving your children."
- "You may have regrets later on if you leave your children in such an impulsive fashion."
- "I really think that what you're doing is terrific. You have a lot of courage. Many women in your position would be afraid to do what you're thinking about doing. Don't let anybody stop you."
- "I hate to see you divorce without having some marriage counseling first to determine whether that's what you both want."
- "Maybe you ought to look at the prospects of living alone for a while. The idea of moving out of a relationship with your husband and right into a new relationship with another man concerns me."

If Melody were your client, which of your own values might influence your counseling with her? For example, what do you think of divorce? Would you want her to use divorce only as a last resort? How much do you value keeping her family intact?

○ **The case of Naomi.**   The White family (consisting of wife, husband, four children, and the wife's parents) has been involved in family therapy for several months. During one of the sessions, Naomi (the wife) expresses the desire to return to college to pursue a degree in law. This wish causes a tremendous resistance on the part of every other member of her family. The husband says that he wants her to continue to be involved in his professional life and that, although he admires her ambitions, he simply feels that it would put too much strain on the entire family. Naomi's parents are shocked by their daughter's desire, viewing it as selfish, and they urge her to put the family's welfare first. The children express their desires for a full-time mother. Naomi feels great pressure from all sides, yet she seems committed to following through her professional plans. She is aware of the sacrifices that would be associated with her studies, but she is asking for everyone in the family to make adjustments so that she can accomplish some goals that are important to her. She is convinced that her plans would not be detrimental to the family's welfare. The therapist shows an obvious bias by giving no support to Naomi's aspirations and by not asking the family to consider making any basic adjustments. Although the therapist does not openly say that she should give up her plans, his interventions have the result of reinforcing the family's resistance.

- Do you think that this therapist is guilty of furthering sex-role stereotypes? With his interventions, is he showing his interest in the well-being of the entire family?
- Are there any other ethical issues in this case? If so, what are they?
- Being aware of your own bias regarding sex roles, how would you work with this family?
- Assume that the therapist had an obvious bias in favor of Naomi's plans and even pushed the family to learn to accept her right to an independent life. Do you see any ethical issue in this approach? Is it unavoidable for a therapist to take sides?

Special Guidelines for Counseling Women

To deal with the problem of gender-biased therapy, the APA and the AAMFT have devoted special attention to the oppression of women, including gender-role stereotyping in therapeutic practice. In the following chapter, which deals with ethics in marital and family therapy, we will feature the AAMFT ethical codes dealing with gender concerns.

The APA approved the "Principles Concerning the Counseling/Psychotherapy of Women" as an official policy statement for the Division of Counseling Psychology. These principles are presented in the accompanying box. (See Fitzgerald and Nutt, 1986, for a discussion of the background and rationale for each principle as well as suggestions for carrying them out.)

Specialized Training in Women's Issues

Lewis (1985) makes the assumption that to achieve the goal of ethical and responsible counseling, practitioners need specialized training in the psychology of women as a first step. Adequate training would involve systematic and comprehensive information on historical perspectives, personality-development theory, and counseling theory applicable to women. Nonsexist research methods and personal exploration of gender bias would be an integral part of such training. There are several approaches to the inclusion of gender in APA-approved and

Principles Concerning the Counseling and Psychotherapy of Women

Counselors and therapists:

1. Are knowledgeable about women, particularly with regard to biological, psychological, and social issues that have impact on women in general or on particular groups of women in our society.
2. Are aware that the assumptions and precepts of theories relevant to their practice may apply differently to men and women. They are aware of those theories and models that proscribe or limit the potential of women clients, as well as those that may have particular usefulness for women clients.
3. Continue to explore issues related to women, including the special problems of female subgroups, throughout their professional careers.
4. Recognize and are aware of all forms of oppression and how these interact with sexism.
5. Are knowledgeable and aware of verbal and nonverbal process variables (particularly with regard to power in the relationship) as these affect women in therapy so that counselor/client interactions are not adversely affected. The need for shared responsibility between clients and counselors is acknowledged and implemented.
6. Have the capability of utilizing skills that are particularly facilitative to women in general and to particular subgroups of women.
7. Put no preconceived limitations on the direction or nature of potential changes or goals in counseling for women.
8. Are sensitive to circumstances in which it is more desirable for a woman client to be seen by a female or male therapist.
9. Use nonsexist language in counseling, supervision, teaching, and journal publications.
10. Do not engage in sexual activity with their women clients under any circumstances.
11. Are aware of and continually review their own values and biases and the effects of these on their women clients. Therapists understand the effects of sex-role socialization on their own development and functioning and the consequent values and attitudes they hold for themselves and others. They recognize that behaviors and roles need not be sex based.
12. Are aware of how their personal functioning may influence their effectiveness in counseling with women clients. They monitor their functioning through consultation, supervision, or therapy so that it does not adversely affect their work with women clients.
13. Support the elimination of sex bias toward institutions and individuals.

Adapted from "Principles Concerning the Counseling/Psychotherapy of Women" by the American Psychological Association, Division of Counseling Psychology, 1986, *The Counseling Psychologist, 14*(1), 180–216. (See Fitzgerald and Nutt, 1986.) Copyright 1986 by the American Psychological Association. Reprinted by permission of Sage Publications, Inc.

AAMFT-approved doctoral programs, including requiring formal courses or integrating these issues into other courses in the program. As you saw in the previous chapter, multicultural issues and sensitivity to cultural diversity can best be accomplished by a genuine integration of cultural content throughout the curriculum. Likewise, gender concerns are probably best addressed in all relevant courses, rather than restricting a discussion of gender to one specialized course.

Lewis (1985) designed a study to explore the ways in which APA-approved training programs in counseling psychology had begun to pay systematic attention to the psychology of women. Her study revealed that the topics most likely to be included in courses or programs included feminist theory, professional identity, eating disorders, sense of self, sexual identity and sexuality, violence against women, depression, stereotyping, and therapist/client gender dyads. She found that the implementation of an earlier version of the APA's principles had been incomplete and inconsistent and concluded that there was little to suggest that training programs were producing more sensitive and better informed graduates than they had before the principles were published.

In his recommendations for training gender-sensitive counselors, DeVoe (1990) emphasizes that feminist therapy is not only a method that is taught but also a new way of thinking to be practiced daily. He points out that teaching counselors this new way of life involves removing sexism and abuses of power from therapeutic and supervisory practices.

Separate Guidelines: A New Form of Sexism?

Many of the writers we have cited contend that specialized knowledge, skills, and attitudes are needed for effectively working with women clients. We should point out that other writers are opposed to such separate principles on the ground that they are a new form of sexism. One of these writers is Spiegel (1979), who was among a group of women's advocates who attempted to institute changes in response to the growing evidence that female clients were at a marked disadvantage in counseling and therapy when compared with men. She rejects the premise that counseling women is sufficiently different from counseling men to warrant a separate set of standards of practice. According to Spiegel, separate standards merely change the form of sexism in therapy rather than alleviating it. Her position is that there is a need to reduce sexism in counseling but that this can best be accomplished within a single set of standards that applies to all practitioners:

> With regard to values, sexism follows when a double standard exists. Thus I am opposed to developing a separate set of values, no matter how optimal and generally applicable they may appear to be, if they are enforced only for those who choose to work with women clients. Since nonsexist values are the basis for all good therapy, a single set of standards should be adopted for all counselors/ therapists [p. 50].

We think that Spiegel's case is well worth considering. Our position is that women are one of the groups that have not been treated justly by the mental-health profession. We agree that women have many times been expected to adjust to the traditional values of society and to accept their roles with a minimum of disruption of the status quo. Thus, we agree with the spirit of the principles and recommendations for counseling various subgroups of women. However, we do not agree that women can receive effective counseling only from other women. In general, it is a mistake to assume that specialization is the only effective way to proceed. We question the assumption that gay and lesbian clients can be genuinely understood and helped only by gay and lesbian counselors, that the concerns of certain ethnic or cultural groups can be addressed meaningfully only by counselors of that particular group, or that religious clients necessarily ought to seek out a counselor with the same beliefs.

What is essential is that counselors understand the feelings, values, life ex-periences, and concerns of whatever population they accept as clients. Therefore, to effectively counsel a woman contemplating an abortion, the counselor need not have faced the same issue, but he or she must have the capacity to under-stand the values, struggles, and feelings of the client. We think that ethical prac-tice requires that counselors determine *with whom* and *in what circumstances* they are unable to be effective and that they then make an appropriate referral. Further, we agree with Spiegel's contention that work with subgroups may re-quire specialized knowledge, skills, and attitudes but that what have been iden-tified as "women's issues" should be within the province of all effective counselors. Spiegel presents the case of a hypothetical black, Protestant, married, professional woman who is a mother of three children. Which set of qualifications would her counselor need to have? Some would argue that only a black female counselor is appropriate to help her deal with racial and sexual issues. Some would say that her religious upbringing during childhood is critical and that the counselor must have shared the same Christian views and experiences. Some would urge her to seek a counselor with expertise in women's issues, since some of her conflicts may deal with the multiple roles of wife, mother, and professional woman. Our position is that well-trained counselors (who are aware of their values and do not impose them) should be able to work with all of her concerns.

Ethical and Legal Issues in Counseling Children and Adolescents

Consistent with the increasing concern over children's rights in general, more attention is being paid to such issues as the minor's right of informed consent. There are legal and ethical trends toward granting greater rights to children and adolescents in these areas (Glenn, 1980). According to Koocher (1976), ethical standards in counseling with minors deserve attention, because often "the stan-dards of professional associations do not specifically address children as a unique subset of the population" (p. 3). Some of the legal and ethical questions faced by therapists who work with children and adolescents are: Can minors consent to treatment without parental consent? Can minors consent to treatment without parental knowledge? To what degree should minors be allowed to participate in setting the goals of therapy and in providing consent to undergo it? What are the limits of confidentiality in counseling with minors? What does informed con-sent consist of in working with minors? In this section we consider some of these questions and focus on the rights of children when they are clients.

The Right to Treatment

In most states parental consent is legally required for minors to enter into a rela-tionship with health-care professionals. There are exceptions to this general rule; some state statutes grant adolescents the right to seek counseling about birth control, abortion, substance abuse, and other crisis concerns. An example is a

Virginia law of 1979 that is the broadest statute in the country on the rights of children and adolescents to consent to therapy. This law implies that "mature minors" should be able to consent to psychotherapy independently on grounds of personal privacy and liberty (Melton, 1981b). More specifically, a minor is deemed an adult for the purposes of consenting to:

1. health services needed to determine the presence of or to treat venereal disease or any infections or contagious disease that the State Board of Health requires to be reported
2. health services required for birth control, pregnancy, or family planning
3. health services needed for outpatient care, treatment, or rehabilitation for substance abuse
4. health services needed for outpatient care, treatment, or rehabilitation for mental or emotional illness

In keeping with this law, counselors in Virginia have the duty to keep information in the above areas confidential, even from parents. This duty challenges the commonly accepted premise that before counselors accept a minor as a client, they are required to inform the parents and obtain their consent (Swanson, 1983).

Like Virginia, California provides for certain exceptions. Minors who have reached the age of 12 may consent to mental-health treatment if certain conditions are met: the minors must be mature enough to participate intelligently in mental-health treatment on an outpatient basis (in the opinion of the therapist), *and* they must present a danger of serious physical or mental harm to themselves or others *or* have been the alleged victims of incest or child abuse. Minors who meet the above stipulations may consent to receive outpatient mental-health services from sources such as licensed marriage and family counselors, licensed clinical social workers, licensed psychologists, or any governmental agency or community crisis center with qualified practitioners (Board of Medical Quality Assurance, 1980).

The justification for allowing children and adolescents to seek treatment without parental consent is that they might not obtain this needed treatment in some circumstances without such a right. There is some evidence that adolescents who seek help when given independent access might not have done so without the guarantee of privacy (Melton, 1981a). This is especially true in cases where the presenting problems involve family conflict, psychological or physical abuse, drug or alcohol abuse, and pregnancy or abortion counseling.

Counselors who are faced with the issue of when to accept minors as clients without parental consent must consider various factors. What is the competence level of the minor? What are the potential risks and consequences if treatment is denied? What are the chances that the minor will not seek help or will not be able to secure parental permission for needed help? How serious is the problem? What are the laws pertaining to providing therapy for minors without parental consent? Melton recommends to practitioners who must make decisions about accepting minors without parental consent that they seek legal advice about the relevant statutes in their state. He also advises them to consult with other professionals in weighing the ethical issues involved in each case.

Informed Consent of Minors

Therapists who work with children and adolescents have ethical responsibilities to provide information that will help minors become active participants in their treatment. On this matter the guideline provided by the APA (1989) is as follows: "When working with minors or other persons who are unable to give voluntary, informed consent, psychologists take special care to protect these persons' best interests."

Allowing children and adolescents to consent to therapy may have the benefit of increasing their participation in decision making about treatment when they enter *with* parental consent (Melton, 1981b). It is a good policy to provide children with treatment alternatives and enlist their participation in defining goals for their therapy. There are both ethical and therapeutic reasons for involving minors in their treatment. By giving them the maximum degree of autonomy within the therapeutic relationship, the therapist demonstrates respect for them. Also, it is likely that therapeutic change is promoted by informing children about the process and enlisting their involvement in it. On this issue Melton (1981a) concludes: "Available research suggests that involvement of children in treatment planning increases the efficacy of treatment and that the presumption of incompetence to consent to treatment may be invalid for many adolescents" (p. 246).

In cases where children do not have the capacity to give full, unpressured consent, some writers have recommended that there be an advocate to examine and protect their interests, especially when they are reluctant to participate in therapy (Koocher, 1976). This advocate should be a person other than the parent or the therapist. If children lack the background to weigh risks and benefits and if they cannot give complete informed consent, therapists should still attempt to provide some understanding of the therapy process. If formal consent cannot be obtained, then even partial understanding is better than proceeding with therapy without any attempt to explain the goals and procedures of the process (Margolin, 1982).

At this point we suggest that you think about some of the legal and ethical considerations in providing therapy for minors.

- Some argue that it is the right of parents to know about matters that pertain to their adolescent daughters and sons. They assert, for example, that parents have a right to be involved in decisions about abortion. What is your position?
- There are those who argue for the rights of minors to seek therapy without parental knowledge or consent, on the ground that needed treatment might not be given to them otherwise. When, if at all, do you think that you would counsel a minor without parental knowledge and consent?
- What are your thoughts on the kinds of information that should be provided to children and adolescents before they enter a therapeutic relationship?
- Do you think that therapists who do not provide minors with the information necessary to make informed choices are acting unethically? Why or why not?
- Glenn (1980) suggests that the child therapist should be able to function as the advocate of the child in certain legal situations and that he or she should be able to function as a social, political, and legal agent for change. What are your reactions to this viewpoint?

Counseling Reluctant Children and Adolescents.   Taylor, Adelman, and Kaser-Boyd (1985) contend that most children and adolescents seen in psychotherapy are referred by others and that many (79%) manifest significant reluctance and dissatisfaction toward therapy. The most significant negative impact of this reluctance is seen in the large number of minors who either refuse to consent to therapy or who drop out. The authors' findings suggest that reluctance among minors with regard to entering and staying in therapy is often a problem and that given the opportunity to do so, a significant number will decline to participate. This study revealed that the initial reluctance of a few did give way to positive attitudes once they had engaged in counseling, but the majority remained negative toward the experience. The study also showed that a large number of youngsters had insufficient information about the positive features of therapy and felt that the choice of entering therapy had been made for them. Rather than "resistance," this reluctance to become involved in the treatment process can be interpreted as a rational and reactive effort to cope and avoid or as the result of failure to establish a clear and mutually agreeable contract.

One interpretation of the finding that many minors have negative perceptions of therapy is that these reactions are often based on previous experiences. Some young people simply resent not having a choice about entering a therapeutic relationship. Adolescents often resist therapy because they become the "identified patient" and the focus is on changing them. These adolescents are frequently aware that they are only a *part* of the problem in the family unit. Although many minors indicate a desire to participate in treatment decisions, few are given the opportunity to become involved in a systematic way. The message here is that resistance to therapy can at least be minimized if therapists are willing to openly and nondefensively explore the reasons behind this resistance.

○ *The Case of Frank.*   Consider Frank's situation in light of the discussion above. He was expelled from high school for getting explosively angry at a teacher, who, according to Frank, had humiliated him in front of his class. Frank was told that he would not be readmitted to school unless he sought professional help. His mother called a therapist and explained the situation to her, and the therapist agreed to see him. Although Frank was uncomfortable and embarrassed over having to see a therapist, he was nevertheless willing to talk. He told the therapist that he knew he had done wrong by lashing out angrily at the teacher but that he had provoked him. He said that although he was usually good about keeping his feelings inside, this time he had "just lost it."

After a few sessions the therapist made a determination that there were many problems in Frank's family, that he lived with an extreme amount of stress, and that to work effectively with him it would be essential to see the entire family. Indeed, he did have a problem, but he was not *the* problem. He was covering up many family secrets, including a verbally abusive stepfather and an alcoholic mother. Hesitantly, he agreed that it would be a good idea to have the entire family come in for therapy. When the therapist contacted the family, the other members totally rejected the idea of family therapy. The mother asserted that the problem was with Frank and that the therapist should concentrate her efforts on him. A few days before his next scheduled appointment his mother called to cancel, saying that they had put him on independent study and that he therefore no longer required counseling.

Commentary.   One of the ethical problems in this case was the treatment of the individual as opposed to the treatment of the family. There was an alcoholism problem within the family. Frank's expulsion from school was more a symptom of the family dysfunction than of his own disturbance. Indeed he did need to learn anger management, as both the school and the mother contended, yet there was more going on within this family that needed pressing attention. In this case it might have been best for the therapist to stick to her initial convictions of family therapy as the treatment of choice. If the parents would not agree to this, she could have made a referral to another therapist who would be willing to see Frank in individual counseling.

Reflect on these questions:

- What are the ethical responsibilities of the therapist?
- Should Frank be seen as a condition of returning to school?
- What other strategies could the therapist have used?
- What would you have done differently, and why?
- Should the therapist have seen Frank and the teacher?
- Did the family interfere with Frank's right to treatment by being uncooperative?
- Should the therapist have encouraged him to continue his therapy even if his family refused to undergo treatment?

Specialized Training for Counseling Children and Adolescents

An important ethical and professional issue is the necessity of obtaining adequate training to counsel children and adolescents effectively. As we noted in Chapter 7 in a discussion of therapist competence, the ethical codes of the major professional organizations specify that it is unethical to practice in areas for which one has not been trained. Many human-service professionals have been trained and supervised in "verbal therapies." Yet there are distinct limitations in applying these therapeutic interventions to children. Practitioners who want to counsel children may have to acquire supervised clinical experience in methods such as play therapy, art and music therapy, and recreational therapy. These practitioners also must have a knowledge of developmental issues pertaining to the population with which they intend to work. They need to become familiar with laws relating to minors, to be aware of the limits of their competence, and to know when and how to make appropriate referrals. It is essential to know about community referral resources, such as the Child Protective Services.

Counselors working with children and adolescents also must have training in dealing with special issues, such as confidentiality. For example, therapists cannot guarantee minors blanket confidentiality. If the parents or guardians of minors request some information about the progress of the counseling, the therapist is expected to provide some feedback. It is essential that areas that either will or will not be disclosed to parents or guardians be discussed at the outset of therapy with both the child or adolescent and the parent or guardian. If this matter of confidentiality is not clearly explored with all parties involved, it is almost certain that problems will emerge later in the course of therapy. In addressing confidentiality as it applies to children and adolescents, Hendrix (1991) writes that there are times when alternatives to absolute confidentiality must be applied. He maintains that counselors would do well always to seek voluntary, informed consent, even when working with children under the age of 14. In the case of adolescents, the consensus of writers and judges appears to be that they have the same confidentiality rights as adults.

Child Abuse: Ethical and Legal Issues

As a mental-health practitioner, you have professional responsibilities and liabilities associated with protecting children (and, in many states, the elderly) from abusive treatment. You have an ethical and legal obligation to report suspected child abuse or neglect, which implies that you know how to assess signs of abuse. In many states licensed professionals are required to take continuing-education workshops in the assessment and reporting of child abuse as a stipulation for renewal of their licenses. Once you suspect child abuse, you are expected to know the procedures for making an appropriate report. All states require the reporting of child abuse or neglect if it results in physical injury. Youngstrom (1991b) notes that such mandatory-reporting laws differ from state to state. In Pennsylvania, for example, therapists are required to file a report if the client is a child who appears to be the victim of abuse. If the client is the abuser, however, the mandatory-reporting law does not apply. In New York, therapists must report abuse whether they learn about the situation from the child in therapy, the abuser who is in therapy, or a relative. In 1989 Maryland changed its law, which now requires therapists to report both present and past cases of child abuse that have been revealed by adult clients in therapy. Obviously, it is essential that you check periodically with the appropriate state agencies to keep abreast of the laws in your state.

In 1974 Congress enacted the National Child Abuse Prevention and Treatment Act (PL 93-247), which defines child abuse and neglect as follows:

> Physical or mental injury, sexual abuse or exploitation, negligent treatment, or maltreatment of a child under the age of eighteen or the age specified by the child protection law of the state in question, by a person who is responsible for the child's welfare, under circumstances which indicate that the child's health or welfare is harmed or threatened thereby.

Child abuse includes physical abuse or neglect, sexual abuse, and emotional maltreatment. On the basis of existing information, national estimates indicate that over 1 million American children are being subjected to abuse and neglect at any given time. Furthermore, it is generally accepted that abuse and neglect are leading causes of childhood deaths (Crime Prevention Center, 1988).

Depending on the nature of your professional specialty, you have certain responsibilities in the areas of prevention, intervention, and treatment of victims of abuse. One way of carrying out your professional responsibilities is to become familiar with the public child-welfare services in your community. In many communities there is a network of child-abuse prevention and intervention services available. Knowing about these resources and knowing how to make appropriate referrals is a major responsibility. Your state may have a handbook for practitioners that summarizes pertinent information about child abuse. For example, the Crime Prevention Center of the California Office of the Attorney General has produced a *Child Abuse Prevention Handbook* (1988). It deals with topics such as the nature of child abuse, information about child abusers, laws pertaining to child abuse, professional responsibilities, prevention strategies, intervention methods, and treatment approaches.

The Obligation to Report Child Abuse

Whether you work with children or adults in your practice, you are expected to know how to assess potential abuse and then to report it in a timely fashion. Privileged communication does not apply in cases of child abuse and neglect. If children disclose that they are being abused or neglected, the professional is required to report the situation. If adults reveal in a therapy session that they are abusing or have abused their children, the matter must generally be reported. As we have said, each state statute that mandates reporting specifies the procedures to be followed. If you have reason to suspect abuse or neglect, the law requires you to report the situation under penalty of fines and imprisonment. You can be sued for monetary damages if you fail to report. Increasingly, states are enacting laws that impose liability for those professionals who fail to report abuse or neglect. Every state provides immunity by law from a civil suit that may arise from the reporting of suspected child abuse and neglect. Thus, counselors who act in good faith are immune (Fischer & Sorenson, 1991).

How effective are state laws in inducing professionals to report suspected child abuse? What situational factors and clinical experiences influence therapists' decisions to report? There is evidence that many professionals do not adhere to mandatory reporting laws. In a study to assess psychologists' decisions to report suspected child abuse, Kalichman and Craig (1991) found that the age of the child, the child's behavior during a clinical interview, and the type of abuse influenced their decisions. These investigators cite studies suggesting that clinicians may decide not to report because of concerns about the potential negative effect that reporting may have on therapy. Their review of the research indicates that clinicians are hesitant to report unless they are fairly certain that abuse is occurring. They conclude:

> There is a need for reviewing definitions in child abuse statutes, particularly with respect to what constitutes suspicion to warrant a report. Reporting laws appear to be sufficiently vague to allow clinicians flexibility in their decisions, and yet penalize them for failure to report as a result of clinical judgment. For clinicians to be effective in protecting children, mandatory reporting laws will require either greater definitional clarity or more allowance for the application of clinical judgment in the determination of reporting, or both [p. 89].

Although you are likely to accept your professional responsibility in protecting innocent children from physical and emotional mistreatment, you may have difficulty in determining how far to go in making a report. In some cases you may be unclear about how to reconcile your ethical responsibilities with your legal obligations. You may feel that you have been placed in the predicament of either behaving unethically (by reporting and thus damaging the therapy relationship) or ignoring the legal mandate to report all cases of suspected child abuse. At other times you may not be certain when you need to report an incident. You may have concerns about reporting adult clients who admit having abused a child years ago or who were abused as minors themselves. The laws of some states now require therapists to report disclosures by adult clients about child sexual abuse that occurred years before treatment.

It is important for clinicians to develop a clear position regarding child-abuse assessment and reporting. This is not to imply that every case is clear-cut but that therapists must maintain a clinical stance and not assume an investigative one. It is helpful to remember that when therapists reasonably suspect that abuse has occurred, they are obliged to report it. Investigation is a matter for child-protection and law-enforcement officials to pursue.

A newspaper article (Roan, 1991) cites a report questioning the effectiveness of mandated reporting of all child abuse. It reflects the concerns of a growing number of therapists who are dissatisfied with reporting laws that in effect punish (more than treat) the client. The director of the law and psychiatry institute at the University of Massachusetts Medical School, Paul Applebaum, is quoted as follows:

> There are situations where people are in danger, and the ethical thing to do is to protect someone in danger. But where the problem comes up is when you've got statutes that require reporting of past episodes of abuse, which may have occurred years before, and where children are now much older or out of the house and unlikely to be victimized again. It leaves the therapists wondering what the purpose [of the law] is.

The article suggests taking into account the fact that abusers voluntarily step forward and ask for help. If the authorities intervene in a punitive way that would require either the abuser to leave the home or the child to be removed, many offenders are not likely to seek treatment. Youngstrom (1991b) indicates that mandatory reporting appears to discourage the honest disclosure of child abuse by adults who are in therapy. It also appears to deter unidentified potential clients who are abusers (or have engaged in child abuse in the past) from entering treatment. Thus, therapists are deprived of opportunities to change abusive behavior, which also means that many children may continue to be abused unnecessarily.

This section is not intended to be a comprehensive discussion of child abuse but, rather, to focus on some ethical and legal responsibilities of those in the helping professions. As a way of clarifying your ethical stance in dealing with the duty to protect children (and the elderly) from abuse, consider these questions:

- Can you think of a rationale for excluding therapists from mandatory-reporting laws if their clients (abusers) voluntarily seek treatment?

- Some question the effectiveness of laws that require reporting all child abuse, regardless of when it occurred. What are your thoughts about such laws? Do they always serve to protect children from abuse?
- Can you think of ways in which you could file a report on an adult abuser and continue working with the client therapeutically?
- What struggles, if any, have you encountered with respect to following the laws regarding reporting child abuse?
- Do you think that by following the law in all cases, you are also following an ethical course? Do you see any potential conflicts between doing what is legal and what is ethical? If so, what are they?
- Can you envision situations in which by encouraging the client to participate in reporting abuse, the therapist has actually enhanced the therapeutic relationship?
- If an adult perpetrator admits having abused a child, reporting the situation could obviously engender distrust and result in the client's terminating therapy. What are your thoughts about a therapist who argues that keeping such clients in therapy is the best way to help them work through their problems, even if it means failing to report the matter to authorities? Do you think that therapists should have some flexibility in deciding when it would be best to make a report? What policies might be in the best interests of the abused child?
- An alternative to mandatory reporting is for therapists to document a clinical plan that adequately addresses the well-being of children or the elderly who are abused, as well as the treatment of the perpetrator (reported in Youngstrom, 1991b). What are your thoughts about this alternative? What other alternatives can you think of to mandatory reporting of all cases of child or elderly abuse?

Two Cases of Child Abuse

We present the following two cases to help you clarify your position with respect to situations involving child abuse. In the first case, ask yourself how far you should go in reporting suspected abuse. Does the fact that you have reported a matter to the officials end your ethical and legal responsibilities? In the second case, look for ways to differentiate between what is ethical and legal practice. Ask yourself what you would be inclined to do if you saw a conflict between ethics and the law.

○ *The case of a school counselor.*   Martina, a high school counselor, has reason to believe that one of her students is being physically abused. As part of the abuse, critical medication is being withheld from the student. Marina reports the incident to Child Protective Services and gives all the information she has to the caseworker. She follows up the phone conversation with the caseworker with a written report. A week later, the student tells her that nothing has been done.

- Has Martina adequately fulfilled her responsibility by making the report? Does she have a responsibility to report the agency for not having taken action?
- If the agency does not take appropriate action, is it Martina's role to take other measures?

- Would it be ethical for her to take matters into her own hands and to call for a family session or make a house call, especially if the student requests it?
- Does she have an obligation to inform the administration? Does the school have a responsibility to see that action is taken?

○ *The case of a daughter's abuse.*   One night, in a rare moment of intoxication, a father stumbles into his 12-year-old daughter's bedroom and briefly fondles her. The daughter's cries bring her mother into the room, and the incident does not go further. Later, the father does not recall the incident. There has been no previous history of molestation. During therapy the family is able to talk openly about the incident and is working through the pain that resulted. The family is adamant that this situation should not be reported to social services. The therapist knows that the statute in her state clearly specifies that she is required to report this incident, even if it had happened in the past and no further incidents had occurred. What follows are a few glimpses of the inner dialogue of the therapist as she attempts to decide whether to report the incident. Think about your reactions to each course of action that occurs to the helper.

- "There are many hazards involved if I don't report this incident. If this family ever broke up, the mother or daughter could sue me for having failed to report what happened. I would be obeying the law and protecting myself totally by reporting it, and I could justify my actions by citing the requirement of the law."
- "But this is a one-time incident. The father was intoxicated, and the situation did not progress beyond the fondling stage. The daughter was traumatized by the incident, but she seems to be able to talk about it in the family now. If I just obey the law, my actions may be more detrimental to the family at this time than beneficial."
- "But the law is there for a reason. It appears that a child has been abused— that is no minor incident—and there was trauma for some time afterward."
- "What is the most ethical thing to do? I would be following the law by reporting it, but is that the most ethical course in this case? Is it the best thing for this family now, especially since none of the members wants it reported? My ethical sense tells me that my interventions should always be in the best interests of all three members of this family."
- "I'm required to report only if I suspect or believe that abuse has occurred. Some could argue that no abuse has taken place, which is what the parents seem to indicate by their behavior."
- "The family is now in therapy with me. If I do make a report, the family might terminate therapy. Is reporting this situation worth risking that chance?"
- "Child-protective agencies are often overburdened, and only the most serious cases may be given attention. Because no abuse is presently going on, I wonder if this case will be followed up. Will it be worth risking the progress that has been made with this family?"
- "As an alternative to reporting this matter to the authorities, I could document a clinical plan of action that addresses therapeutic interventions with the father and also the well-being of the others. This course of action might be the best way to meet my legal and ethical obligations in this particular case."

- "Before I act, perhaps I should consult an attorney for advice on how to proceed."
- "I need to call Child Protective Services to find out what I must do."
- "I could call the Board of Ethics of my professional organization and get some advice on how to proceed."
- "I don't know what action to take. Maybe I should consult with a colleague."

Discussion.   This case illustrates some of the difficulties a counselor can find herself in when her inner ethical sense conflicts with the law or an ethical code. This counselor must struggle with herself to determine whether she will follow her clinical intuitions by doing what she thinks is in the best interests of this family or whether she will do what is required by the law. If she simply reported this case, she would be acting on the lower level of ethical functioning. Her actions would be characterized by compliance with the law and adherence to the ethical code of her profession. If the therapist called the ethics committee of her professional organization or a colleague, she would be acting on a slightly higher level of ethical functioning because of her willingness to consult. Consulting colleagues is always recommended in cases such as the one described. The consultation process would help from a legal perspective, because if other professionals agreed with her course of action, she would have a good chance of demonstrating that she had acted in good faith and that she had met the professional standards of her peers. In addition, consulting colleagues would provide her with one or more different perspectives on a difficult case. Perhaps the therapist is acting on the highest level of ethical functioning in examining all the factors and special circumstances of this family before acting. She is struggling to act appropriately, not just to protect herself, and is truly concerned with the best interests of everyone in the family. The welfare of the family members does not require her to violate the law, but it does require her to think beyond merely obeying the law. It would be good for her to keep in mind that although she has the obligation to report a situation, it is not her task to conclude whether abuse has actually taken place. Also, it is not her role to get involved in the actual investigation. It may still be possible for her to continue her therapeutic relationship with the family even if she decides to make a report. If this therapist approached you for consultation, what suggestions would you give her? What are your views about this case?

Issues Pertaining to the AIDS Crisis

AIDS affects a large population with diverse demographics and will continue to gain prominence as a public-health and social issue. All mental-health practitioners will inevitably come in contact with people who have AIDS, with people who have tested positive as carriers of the virus, or with people who are close to these victims. Ethically, counselors need to be aware of the many issues that have emerged from the AIDS epidemic. They need to learn about the problem and to keep up-to-date with the latest research and clinical issues in order to educate those with whom they come in contact. In addition, it is essential that they explore their attitudes, values, biases, misconceptions, and fears about working with AIDS patients and those who have tested positive. Hoffman (1991b), who describes approaches to training mental-health counselors to respond to the AIDS crisis, begins with the premise that all counselors will eventually work in some capacity with people who are affected by it. Some practitioners will provide direct services to clients with the disease or their loved ones. They may also provide indirect services aimed at education and prevention.

We think you have an ethical obligation to be knowledgeable about the disease, so that you can ask the right questions. You can start by reading about AIDS-related issues and by attending a workshop on the subject, such as the one described by Hoffman (1991b). You can also contact one of the clinics being started all over the country, which are useful resources for treatment and referrals. In many communities groups of volunteers have been organized to work with AIDS clients.

Morrison (1989) cautions therapists to carefully consider their own ethical position regarding the duty to treat HIV-positive clients and people with AIDS. She challenges them to confront any biases toward gay men and intravenous drug users before they become involved in these therapeutic situations. One study revealed that the psychologists and social workers who were sampled consistently held negative and biased views toward HIV-infected people and those with AIDS (Crawford, Humfleet, Ribordy, Ho, & Vickers, 1991). The respondents indicated that people with AIDS were more responsible for their illness, less deserving of compassion, and more dangerous to society than people who had leukemia. The mental-health professionals in the survey consistently indicated that they did not want to provide service to clients with AIDS. Clearly, if counselors perceive people with the disease negatively, there is little hope that they will be able to offer services to this new client population.

People who come to counselors because they have discovered that they are carriers of the AIDS virus are likely to be highly anxious. Those who have tested positive (and those who have contracted AIDS) are usually in need of short-term help. They need to find a system to support them through the troubled times they will endure. They live with the anxiety of wondering whether they will come down with this incurable disease. Most of them also struggle with the stigma attached to AIDS. They live in fear not only of developing a life-threatening disease but also of being discovered and thus being rejected by society and by friends and loved ones. In addition to feeling different and stigmatized, they typically have a great deal of anger, which is likely to be directed toward others, especially those who have given them the virus. Those at risk are often angry at health professionals as well. Do you think you could deal with the anger that such clients might direct toward you? Do you see yourself as being able to help them work through these feelings?

Because such clients are particularly vulnerable to ostracism and discrimination, it is critical that professionals obtain their informed consent and educate them about their rights and responsibilities. Therapists need to be very clear in their own mind about the limits of confidentiality, matters of reporting, and their duty to warn and to protect third parties, and they need to communicate their professional responsibilities to their clients from the outset. If therapists decide that they cannot provide competent services to HIV-infected people, it is ethically appropriate that they refer such people to professionals who can provide assistance. We recommend that you review the discussion in Chapter 5 of the therapist's duty to warn and protect as it is applied to people who have AIDS or are HIV-positive.

You may easily be confronted with situations similar to those presented in the case examples in this section. As a counselor you may indeed work with clients who are HIV-positive. You might accept a client and establish a therapeutic relationship, only to find out months later that this person had recently tested positive. If this were the case, would it be ethical to terminate the professional relationship and make a referral? Would the ethical course be to become informed so that you could provide competent help? What would be in the best interests of your client? If you are counseling HIV-positive individuals, do you have a duty to both your clients and to their sexual partners? Do you have a responsibility to warn and protect third parties in cases of those who are infected? We hope that as you think about these questions, you will consider your ethical responsibilities to respond to this population before you encounter possible difficult situations.

Case Examples Involving AIDS

The three cases that follow are designed to help you clarify your positions on the ethical dimensions of counseling clients who have AIDS or are HIV-positive.

○ *The case of Al and Wilma.*   Al and Wilma are seeing Sarina for marital counseling. After a number of sessions Wilma requests an individual session, in which she discloses that she has tested HIV-positive as a result of several extramarital alliances. Sarina finds herself in a real dilemma: she has concerns for the welfare of the couple, but she is also concerned about Wilma's painful predicament, especially because Wilma has a sincere desire to make her marriage work. Part of Sarina's quandary is that she did not tell the couple her policy about handling confidentiality for private sessions.

- Does Sarina have a duty to warn Al? Why or why not?
- Would such a duty supersede any implied confidentiality of the private session?
- What are some of the potential ethical violations in the manner in which Sarina handled this case?
- Would it be more therapeutic for the therapist to persuade Wilma to disclose her condition to Al, rather than the therapist's taking the responsibility for this disclosure?
- If Wilma refused to inform her husband, should Sarina discontinue therapy with the couple? If she were to discontinue working with them, how might she ethically explain her decision?
- If she felt obligated to continue therapy with the couple, how would she handle the secret, and what would be the ethical implications of her practices?

- Are there factors in this situation that would compel her to treat Wilma's secret differently from other major secrets in couple's therapy?

○ *The case of Paddy.*   Paddy has been seeing a counselor for several months to deal with his depression. He comes to one session in a state of extreme anxiety. He has been married for 15 years and on a recent business trip had a homosexual experience with a male prostitute. He is now worried that he may have contracted the AIDS virus, but he refuses to be tested, for he is terrified of confirming his worst fear. The counselor encourages him to challenge his fears and be tested. He also encourages him to discuss this matter with his wife. Paddy steadfastly refuses to consider either of the counselor's suggestions. When the counselor asks Paddy what he wants from him, he replies that he wants to be reassured that he is merely overreacting. He also would like to get over feeling depressed most of the time.

- What are the ethical dilemmas in this case?
- Are there any legal ramifications?
- How would you work with Paddy? Would you try to convince him to be tested, and would this be ethical? Would you try to persuade him to tell his wife, and would your persuasion be ethical?
- What kind of referral might you make? What if Paddy refused a referral you suggested but insisted on continuing to see you?
- How would you help him achieve his stated goal for seeing you? Do you have enough information to accomplish that goal?
- What values of yours might come into play in dealing with this situation?
- What if Paddy consented to being tested and was found to be HIV-positive but still refused to disclose this fact to his wife, with whom he intended to continue marital relations? What ethical and legal concerns would now come into play? How would you proceed with this new information?

○ *The case of Hershel.*   Hershel is a vice-president in a large company. He is married and has young children. Hershel's job necessitates transcontinental travel several times a year. During these trips he spends time with a lover. On his last trip she confided that one of the men that she had recently been sexually involved with had received an HIV-positive diagnosis. Hershel is panic stricken and seeks the help of a counselor, Blanche, who immediately recommends that he be tested. He follows her recommendation, and his test results are negative. He is elated and now sees no reason to continue therapy. Blanche makes no attempt to persuade him to explore other issues in this case. She has no expertise in the treatment of AIDS clients and lacks essential knowledge pertaining to the latest AIDS research.

- Blanche appeared to take the ethical course in suggesting that Hershel be tested for AIDS, but was one test sufficient? What else needed to be done?
- Given this therapist's level of knowledge about AIDS, should she have referred Hershel?

- Although he was symptom-free and may not have transmitted the virus to his wife, there is a chance that he could be carrying the virus and that symptoms might not develop until years later. Given these facts, do you think that he presented a clear and imminent danger to his wife or to other sexual partners?
- Did the therapist have a duty to warn his wife of the potential life-threatening situation in which she was involved?
- Did the therapist have a duty to notify the authorities, and if so, which authorities?
- If Hershel had disclosed to Blanche that he and his wife were planning on having more children, how might that have affected the complexity of this case?
- Did Blanche have an obligation to persuade him to discontinue his potentially threatening lifestyle?
- Did she have an obligation to get him to discuss the matter with his wife, because her health might also be at risk?
- If he had come to see you, what course of action would you have taken?

Ethical and Legal Considerations in AIDS-Related Cases

In the past few years much has been written about the conditions under which confidentiality might be breached in AIDS-related therapy situations. To date, no courts have applied the duty to warn to cases involving HIV infection (Hoffman, 1991a). Therefore, it may be necessary to wait for some future landmark court decisions to get clearer directions on the nature of the therapist's responsibility in protecting sexual partners of HIV-positive clients. At this time, practitioners have few ethical or legal guidelines about when or how to inform a potential victim of the threat of HIV transmission.

In Chapter 5 we discussed principles involving situations where therapists have a duty to warn and to protect innocent victims. The literature reveals some attempts at applying the *Tarasoff* decision to AIDS-related cases (Cohen, 1990; Gray & Harding, 1988; Hoffman, 1991a; Knapp & VandeCreek, 1990; Lamb, Clark, Drumheller, Frizzell, & Surrey, 1989; Melton, 1988, 1991; Morrison, 1989; Totten, Lamb, & Reeder, 1990).

Melton (1988) believes that the core ethical and legal issue is the duty to protect third parties from HIV infection by a client, with minimal violation of the client's privacy. The ethical obligations of therapists to their clients and to third parties are also addressed by Cohen (1990). Posey (1988) explores confidentiality as it pertains to AIDS support groups and concludes that their goal "is to assist each person in the process of developing a style for dealing responsibly with the AIDS-related condition by caring for oneself and others" (p. 227). Gray and Harding (1988) discuss the limits of confidentiality with clients who have contracted HIV, review current legal and ethical practices, emphasize ways to increase the client's responsibility for informing sexual partners, and recommend that therapists take action to protect third parties if the HIV-positive client refuses to do so. In response to the article by Gray and Harding, Kain (1988) focuses more on the client's needs as opposed to protecting others. Kain argues that the role of the therapist is not that of a reporter; rather, it is to help HIV-positive clients address issues such as rejection, abandonment, loneliness, homophobia, and infidelity. If clients will not disclose their HIV status to their partners, Kain prefers exploring with them their reasons for refusing to do so.

Knapp and VandeCreek (1990) point out that breaking confidentiality with HIV-positive clients goes against the grain of most therapists. Furthermore, the duty to protect would extend only to identifiable sexual or needle-sharing partners. Most casual partners would not be easy to identify. Before the duty to protect can be invoked, the danger must be foreseeable. These authors express concern that the duty to protect could turn into a "morality watch" whereby even the remote threat of transmitting the virus could be used as an excuse to reveal extramarital affairs or intravenous drug usage. A therapist should strongly encourage HIV-infected clients to inform their partner of their infectious status, and if they refuse to do so, it is the therapist's responsibility to inform a client's partner of the risk of infection. Knapp and VandeCreek emphasize the need for statutory protection for therapists who breach confidentiality in these cases.

In an investigation of the implications of the *Tarasoff* case as it pertains to confidentiality in AIDS-related psychotherapy, Totten and her colleagues (1990) found that some clinicians used the criteria of degree of dangerousness and identifiability of a third party in determining when to break confidentiality. These researchers found that dangerousness appeared to be a more relevant factor than identifiability of a victim. Those clinicians who had had professional contact with AIDS clients were less likely to favor breaking confidentiality than those practitioners who had not had such contact. Melton (1991) suggests that protection of confidentiality is sometimes necessary for successful treatment or valid research, especially if harm is not likely to result to the individuals involved or to society. A question he poses is "When is the harm to society (including harm to specific third parties) resulting from protection of clients' confidentiality likely to exceed the harm that may result from a breach of confidentiality?" (p. 562).

Lamb and his associates (1989) used *Tarasoff* as a framework for examining decisions about breaking confidentiality and protecting third parties. The authors identify four key issues in handling confidentiality in AIDS-related therapy cases: (1) the existence of a special client/therapist relationship and the professional duty to treat, (2) the assessment of dangerousness, (3) the determining of an identifiable victim, and (4) the carrying out of appropriate action:

1. *Special relationship.* Evidence supports the conclusion that the special client/therapist relationship entails the practitioner's responsibility for the safety of the client and also of other parties whom the therapist knows to be threatened by the client.
2. *Assessment of dangerousness.* The degree of dangerousness of a client who has tested HIV-positive depends on several factors: (a) the client's medical diagnosis, (b) the extent to which the person engages in high-risk behaviors, and (c) the use of safer sex techniques aimed at reducing the chances of transmission of the virus.

3. *Identifiable victim.* AIDS and HIV-positive clients may have been sexually in-volved with many people in the past and may now have multiple sexual part-ners. This matter is complicated by the fact that the virus can remain dor-mant for years. Who are the potential victims? How should the therapist decide whom to inform?

4. *Therapist's action.* The implications of *Tarasoff* are that therapists have the duty to both warn and protect third parties who are threatened by a client. But there has been no ruling on applying this doctrine to HIV-positive clients. Even if a therapist uses the *Tarasoff* doctrine as a framework for making deci-sions, it is not clear how protection might be accomplished.

Noting that there is a trend away from absolute confidentiality in the therapeutic relationship, Lamb and his colleagues identify specific areas of pro-fessional responsibility and present guidelines for clinicians who are struggling with value conflicts and ethical dilemmas in this area. Some of the ways in which professionals can fulfill their responsibilities are listed below:

- Therapists can learn updated information on the medical aspects of AIDS, including means of transmitting the virus.
- Practitioners can seek training for intervening in the crises facing HIV-positive clients and those with AIDS.
- Therapists need to be aware of their own attitudes, biases, and prejudices as they relate to individuals who are at a higher risk of becoming infected.
- Clinicians need to be in a position to educate clients. Regardless of their cur-rent AIDS status, clients should be informed and encouraged to adopt safer sex practices in order to reduce risks.
- It is essential that therapists be familiar with the laws of their state pertaining to any form of sexually transmitted disease.
- Early in the course of therapy, the limits of confidentiality need to be clarified and discussed.

In summary, dealing responsibly with the dilemmas posed in this section demands an awareness of the ethical, legal, and clinical issues involved in work-ing with clients with AIDS and AIDS-related disorders. There are no simple solu-tions to the many complex issues that practitioners may face and, as Melton (1991) points out, there may not even be any satisfactory solutions. As we have been stressing throughout this book, consulting with colleagues is an excellent prac-tice that can help you make appropriate decisions.

Chapter Summary

As we mentioned in Chapter 3, it takes honesty and courage to recognize how your values affect the way you counsel, and it takes wisdom to determine when you cannot work with a client because of a clash of values. These virtues are particularly needed in counseling lesbians and gay men. Often these clients do not enter counseling for the purpose of changing their sexual orientation but to explore their own acceptance of their identity and to deal with reactions from others. We have emphasized the need for special training to impart the knowledge and skills for working with gay and lesbian clients. Actually, this principle of specific training also applies to the other populations we have discussed in this chapter: women, children, and clients with AIDS.

It is essential for therapists to be aware of any sex-role bias and to challenge their own stereotypical views. A number of writers have proposed specialized training in women's issues, given the fact that many therapists are male and many clients are female. Regardless of your gender, you need to monitor your bias about sex roles so that you do not impose your perspectives on clients.

The particular considerations involved in counseling children and adolescents also demand specialized training. One of the challenges of working with minors is to create a trusting climate while being candid about the limitations of confidentiality. Another is to keep abreast of the referral resources in the community. A gray area in counseling involves deciding on the best way to work with perpetrators of child abuse.

There are no clear legal decisions at this time with regard to the issue of reporting HIV-positive clients who are not willing to inform their partner about their status. In making ethical decisions in situations involving HIV-positive clients, it is always wise to seek help from colleagues. What is most important is that you educate yourself about AIDS so that you are in a position to provide accurate information to your clients. It is also essential that you come to terms with your own views and attitudes about situations involving AIDS.

Suggested Activities

1. Debate the ethical and legal requirements of therapists to break confidentiality in cases of known or suspected child abuse. One team can argue in favor of granting therapists an exemption from reporting abuse when clients have presented themselves voluntarily for treatment. Another team can argue for mandatory reporting of all child-abuse incidents.
2. Every state has now enacted dual-faceted laws that (a) mandate that certain professionals must report suspected child abuse and (b) create an organization to investigate such reports and intervene when necessary. Depending on the state's specific requirements, professionals have specific procedures to follow in cases of suspected child abuse (McWhirter & Okey, 1990). Several students can investigate the legal requirements for reporting child abuse in their state and can bring a summary to class. They can also gather information about assessing abuse and about using resources available within the community.
3. Several students can investigate ethical and legal issues pertaining to psychotherapy with children and adolescents and bring the findings to class. Some topics to consider: What are the rights of children in treatment? What legal considerations are involved in therapy with minors? What obligations does the therapist have toward the parents of these children? Should parental consent always be required?

4. Review the special guidelines for counseling women. Which guidelines do you particularly like? Which ones might you disagree with? Are there any guidelines that you would like to add? Discussion groups can explore the advantages and disadvantages of a set of special guidelines for therapists. Do you think there should also be special guidelines for female therapists who work with men? A subgroup could be assigned the task of devising special guidelines for counseling men.

5. In the section on counseling women, there are several cases for discussion. As a class activity some students can volunteer to play various roles in the cases and enact the key issues. For instance, in the cases of Marge and Melody, who perform traditional roles in the family, different students could assume the roles of each of the family members. Different students can role-play the therapist to demonstrate various ways of working with the same situation.

6. There are also cases dealing with a therapist's ethical and legal duty to warn and protect the sexual partners of HIV-positive individuals. One student can play the role of an infected client who refuses to tell his partner. Several students can show how they would approach this client in different ways. A small group of students can form a panel and discuss various alternatives for dealing with these dilemmas.

7. A few students can form a panel in class to serve as expert consultants. A student can identify an ethical dilemma and use this consulting group as a sounding board. The consultants have the task of providing as many appropriate alternatives as possible to each student who approaches them. The dilemmas can be in areas such as working with gay men and lesbians, counseling adolescents, dealing with the concerns of people with AIDS, and counseling women. The objective is to provide discussion material and to brainstorm various ways of dealing with ethical dilemmas.

Suggested Readings

For a primer on gay and lesbian issues from the perspective of counseling psychology, consult the April 1991 special issue of *The Counseling Psychologist* (vol. 19, no. 2), entitled "Counseling Lesbian Women and Gay Men." This journal includes a variety of excellent articles that deal with the unique issues and concerns facing lesbians (Browning, Reynolds, & Dworkin, 1991); the unique issues that confront gay male clients (Shannon & Woods, 1991); an overview of salient issues and challenges in counseling lesbians and gay men (Fassinger, 1991b); and training issues for counseling homosexual clients (Buhrke & Douce, 1991). For a discussion of ethical principles in the counseling of gay and lesbian adolescents, consult Sobocinski (1990); for a discussion of the spiritual journey of gay and lesbian individuals, see Ritter and O'Neill (1989). An excellent recent book is *Coming Out Within: Stages of Spiritual Awakening for Lesbians and Gay Men* (O'Neill & Ritter, 1992).

Five articles in the public forum section of the September 1991 issue of *American Psychologist* (vol. 46, no. 9) deal with gay and lesbian issues:

1. removing the stigma
2. furthering lesbian and gay male civil rights
3. avoiding heterosexual bias in psychological research
4. avoiding heterosexual bias in language
5. a survey of psychologists' attitudes toward lesbian and gay clients

For a discussion of issues pertaining to counseling women, see Cayleff (1986), Wyman and McLaughlin (1979), Fitzgerald and Nutt (1986), Lewis (1985), Spiegel (1979), and Downing and Roush (1985). For a discussion of feminist perspectives on counseling practice, see DeVoe (1990); Good et al. (1990); and M. C. McBride (1990). On taking account of gender issues in the assessment process, see Brown (1990). For gender-role stereotypes and the effect on psychotherapy, see Mintz and O'Neil (1990). For future trends with respect to gender and counseling, see Scher and Good (1990a). For training recommendations on working with gender differences, see McGowen and Hart (1990). On gender dilemmas see Sheinberg and Penn (1991). For placing gender issues at the heart of graduate programs in marital and family therapy, see Storm (1991). For a discussion of empowerment in counseling, see McWhirter (1991). For a feminist response to empowerment see Bowen, Bahrick, and Enns (1991). For therapist gender bias see Barak and Fisher (1989).

For a discussion of child abuse, including reporting laws, see *Child Abuse Prevention Handbook,* by the Crime Prevention Center, California Office of the Attorney General (1988). On ethical conflicts in cases of suspected child abuse, see McWhirter & Okey (1990). For a study of the clinical and situational factors that influence professionals' decisions to report suspected child abuse, see Kalichman and Craig (1991).

For a discussion of ethical and legal issues pertaining to AIDS see Melton (1988, 1991); Morrison (1989); Cohen (1990); Totten et al. (1990); Knapp and VandeCreek (1990); Gray and Harding (1988); Kain (1988); and Hoffman (1991a). On the stigmatization of AIDS patients by mental-health professionals see Crawford et al. (1991). Consult the October 1991 special issue of *The Counseling Psychologist* (vol. 19, no. 4) for a series of articles on counseling the HIV-infected client.

Ethical Issues in Marital and Family Therapy

- Pre-Chapter Self-Inventory
- Introduction
- Ethical Standards in Marital and Family Therapy
- Contemporary Professional Issues
- Values in Marital and Family Therapy
- Responsibilities of Marital and Family Therapists
- Confidentiality in Marital and Family Therapy
- Informed Consent in Marital and Family Therapy
- Chapter Summary
- Suggested Activities
- Suggested Readings

Pre-Chapter Self-Inventory

Directions: For each statement, indicate the response that most closely identifies your beliefs and attitudes. Use the following code:

5 = I *strongly agree* with this statement.
4 = I *agree* with this statement.
3 = I am *undecided* about this statement.
2 = I *disagree* with this statement.
1 = I *strongly disagree* with this statement.

___ 1. A person who comes from a troubled family is generally a poor candidate
to become a good family therapist.

___ 2. I would never divulge in a family session any secrets given to me privately
by one of the members.

___ 3. In practicing marriage counseling, I would see my clients only in con-
joint therapy.

___ 4. Counselors have an ethical responsibility to encourage spouses to leave
partners who are physically or psychologically abusive.

___ 5. I would not be willing to work with a couple in marital therapy if I knew
that one of them had had an affair unbeknownst to the other.

___ 6. It is ethical for family therapists to use pressure and even coercion to
get a reluctant client to participate in family therapy.

___ 7. Therapists who feel justified in imposing their own values on a couple
or a family can potentially do considerable harm.

___ 8. In couples or family therapy I would explain my policies about confidentiality at the first session.

___ 9. Most family therapists, consciously or unconsciously, proselytize for
maintaining a family way of life.

___ 10. There are ethical problems in treating only one member of a family.

___ 11. I would be willing to work with a single member of a family and eventually attempt to bring the entire family into therapy.

___ 12. Before accepting a family for treatment, I would obtain supervised training in working with families.

___ 13. Before working with families, I need to explore issues in my own family
of origin.

___ 14. Skill in using family-therapy techniques is far more important to success in this area than knowing my own personal dynamics.

___ 15. I favor requiring continuing education in the field of marital and family
therapy as a condition for renewal of a license in this area.

Introduction

There has been a rapid increase in the development of theories and techniques
of marital and family therapy. The field has evolved and grown dramatically and
is emerging as a major component in the national health-care-delivery system

(Everett, 1990). As of this writing a coalition of major professional associations is drafting for DSM-IV a proposed diagnostic category for families and couples. Recent surveys of counselor-preparation programs in the United States (see Hollis & Wantz, 1990) have found that marriage and family courses are ranked high among those most frequently added to these programs. (Other courses that have frequently been added include those dealing with substance abuse, legal and ethical issues, multicultural counseling, and consultation.) One of the trends projected by Hollis and Wantz is a continued interest in developing marriage and family components in counseling programs.

Much of the practice of marital and family therapy rests on the foundation of systems theory. This theory views psychological problems as arising from within the individual's present environment and the intergenerational family system. Symptoms are believed to be an expression of a dysfunction within the system that is often passed across numerous generations. We should note, however, that other theoretical frameworks also guide the practice of family therapy (Horne & Passmore, 1991): Satir's interactional/communicational approach, Bowen's intergenerational theory, structural family therapy, strategic therapy, object-relations family therapy, Gestalt family therapy, person-centered therapy, Adlerian therapy, rational-emotive family therapy, reality therapy, social-behavior-modification family therapy, cognitive family therapy, and integrative family therapy.

Goldenberg and Goldenberg (1991) urge therapists to view all behavior, including the symptoms expressed by the individual, within the context of the family and society. Thus, the family system is a unit for achieving change. The Goldenbergs add that a systems orientation does not preclude dealing with the individual but does broaden the traditional emphasis on addressing the roles that individuals play in the family. The systems perspective views the family as a functioning entity that is more than the sum of its members. The family provides the context for understanding how individuals behave. Actions by any individual member influence all the other members, and their reactions have a reciprocal effect on the individual. For instance, an acting-out child may be expressing deep conflicts between the mother and the father and may actually be expressing the pain for an entire family. Family therapists therefore often work with individuals, the couple, parents and children, several siblings together, the nuclear family, the family of origin, and social networks to get a better understanding of patterns that affect the entire system and to develop strategies for change (Everett, 1990).

Although the traditional approaches to treating the individual have merit, there are advantages to broadening one's perspective by considering clients as members of their family, community, and society. A theoretical understanding of families as social systems, direct experience in working with families, and careful supervision are the core components in an effective training program for family therapists (Goldenberg & Goldenberg, 1991). Many contemporary marital and family therapists base their clinical practice on a foundation of systems theory, using a broad range of therapy techniques drawn from various other theoretical approaches. This integration has made possible the emergence of graduate education and formal curricula in marital and family therapy (Everett, 1990). Many master's programs in counseling now offer a specialization in relationship counseling or marital and family therapy. In addition, there has been an increased focus on ethical, legal, and professional issues that are unique to a systems perspective.

Many of the ethical issues that we have already discussed take on special significance when therapists work with more than one client. Most graduate programs in marital and family therapy now require a separate course in ethics and the law pertaining to this specialization. Some specific areas of ethical concern for family therapists that we will discuss in this chapter include therapist responsibility, confidentiality, client privilege, informed consent and the right to refuse treatment, therapist values, and training and supervision (Margolin, 1982). The professional practice of marital and family therapy is regulated by state laws, ethical codes, peer review, continuing education, and consultation (Goldenberg & Goldenberg, 1991). We will focus particularly on the code of ethics developed by the AAMFT (1991).

The role of the family therapist's values cannot be overstressed. Values pertaining to marriage, the preservation of the family, divorce, traditional and non-traditional lifestyles, sex roles and the division of responsibility in the family, child rearing, and extramarital affairs can all influence the therapist's interventions. Counselors who feel justified in imposing their own values on a couple or a family can do considerable harm. This chapter also focuses on certain other responsibilities of marital and family therapists, such as the responsibility to consult and to give courtroom testimony in custody cases.

Ethical Standards in Marital and Family Therapy

The *AAMFT Code of Ethics* (1991) provides a framework for many of the ethical issues that we will consider in this chapter. The code covers eight areas. A statement of each of these main principles follows, along with a brief commentary and questions. (Consult the Appendix for the complete code.)

1. *Responsibility to clients.* "Marriage and family therapists advance the welfare of families and individuals. They respect the rights of those persons seeking their assistance, and make reasonable efforts to ensure that their services are used appropriately." More specifically, marriage and family therapists do not refuse their professional services to individuals because of their race, sex, religion, or nationality; enter into dual relationships with clients; exploit clients; develop sexual relationships with a client's partner; continue counseling once clients are no longer benefiting; or abandon or neglect clients without making reasonable arrangements for the continuation of their treatment. Also, sexual intimacy is prohibited for a two-year period after termination of therapy.

As the focus of therapy shifts from the individual to the family system, a new set of ethical questions is raised: Whose interests should the family therapist serve? To whom and for whom does the therapist have primary loyalty and responsibility? The identified patient? The separate family members as individuals? The family as a whole? The primary goal of family therapists has changed over the years from simply maintaining marital units to maximizing individual fulfillment within mutually satisfying marriages (Patten, Barnett, & Houlihan, 1991). By agreeing to become involved in family therapy, however, members can generally be expected to place a higher priority on the goals of therapy than on their own personal goals, and they may also have to relinquish a sense of privacy and confidentiality (Goldenberg & Goldenberg, 1991). Other questions can also be raised: Should the therapist work with one client and then eventually attempt to bring the entire family into therapy? What is the proper course in cases involving reluctant children and adolescents? Later we consider these and other issues pertaining to the responsibilities of marital and family therapists.

2. *Confidentiality.* "Marriage and family therapists have unique confidentiality concerns because the client in a therapeutic relationship may be more than one person. Therapists respect and guard confidences of each individual client." This principle implies that marriage and family therapists do not disclose what they have learned through the professional relationship, except (1) when mandated by law, such as in cases of physical or psychological child abuse, incest, child neglect, and abuse of the elderly; (2) when it is necessary to protect clients from harming themselves or to prevent a clear and immediate danger to others; (3) when the family therapist is a defendant in a civil, criminal, or disciplinary action arising from the therapy; and (4) when a waiver has previously been obtained in writing. If therapists use any material from their practice in teaching, lecturing, and writing, they take care to preserve the anonymity of their clients.

As we discuss later, confidentiality assumes unique significance in the practice of marital and family therapy. This issue arises within the family itself, in deciding how to deal with secrets. Incest, extramarital affairs, or physical or psychological abuse of a wife or children may be involved. Should the therapist attempt to have families reveal all their secrets? What are the pros and cons of revealing a family secret when some members are likely to suffer from extreme anxiety if it is disclosed? Family therapists have different perspectives on maintaining confidentiality. Some treat all information they receive from a family member just as if the person were in individual therapy. Others refuse to see any member of the family separately, on the ground that doing so fosters unproductive alliances and promotes the keeping of secrets. And others tell family members that they will exercise their own judgment about what to disclose from an individual session in a marital or family session.

3. *Professional competence and integrity.* "Marriage and family therapists maintain high standards of professional competence and integrity." This principle implies that therapists seek professional help when their own personal problems are likely to negatively affect their professional work or impair their clinical judgment. It also implies that they keep abreast of developments in the field through continuing education and clinical experiences. It is considered unethical for practitioners to exceed the bounds of their competence and experience in assessing and treating marital or family problems. A single course or two in a graduate counseling program is hardly adequate preparation for functioning ethically and effectively as a counselor with couples or families. Some questions that can be productively explored are: How can therapists know when their own personal problems are indeed likely to hamper their professional work? What are some ways

in which therapists can best maintain their level of competence? How can therapists use their values in a constructive fashion?

4. *Responsibility to students, employees, and supervisees.* "Marriage and family therapists do not exploit the trust and dependency of students, employees, and supervisees." The code cautions practitioners to avoid dual relationships, which are likely to impair clinical judgment. Examples of nonsexual dual relationships include the provision of therapy to students, employees, or supervisees. Practitioners are advised against forming business or close personal relationships with students, employees, or supervisees. Sexual harassment and sexual intimacies with students, employees, and supervisees are prohibited.

Ryder and Hepworth (1990) suggest that the dual-relationship prohibition is undesirable because of the complex nature of such relationships. Not only are dual relationships virtually impossible to eliminate, they contend, but even if it were possible, it would be a bad idea. Ryder and Hepworth are against making these complex relationships overly simple by legislation. Instead, they recommend that training and supervision include preparing students to deal with such complexity as well as teaching them how to deal with issues such as exploitation and power. They point out that a good supervisory relationship might well be characterized by ambiguity and contradiction and would be a good place to teach students how to manage their own complex relationships. At this point you might consider these questions: What are your views about nonsexual dual relationships? Do you agree with the AAMFT guideline that cautions against forming dual relationships? Are they inevitable? Are there potential benefits as well as potential risks to such relationships? How might these issues be best addressed as a part of a student's training program?

5. *Responsibility to research participants.* "Investigators respect the dignity and protect the welfare of participants in research and are aware of federal and state laws and regulations and professional standards governing the conduct of research." This standard implies that those doing research carefully consider the ethical aspects of any research proposal. They make use of informed-consent procedures, and they explain to participants what is involved in any research project. At times, might there be a conflict between research purposes and therapeutic purposes? If so, how would you resolve it? What are some cross-cultural considerations in doing research in this area? Can marital and family therapists who do not conduct research be considered ethical? What obstacles do you see to doing research in this area?

6. *Responsibility to the profession.* "Marriage and family therapists respect the rights and responsibilities of professional colleagues and participate in activities which advance the goals of the profession." Ethical practice implies measures of accountability to professional standards. It is expected that marriage and family therapists will contribute time to the betterment of society, including donating services. What would you say about the ethics of those marital and family therapists who do not contribute any of their professional time without a fee? What do you see as your ethical obligation to advance the goals of your profession? What activities do you participate in (or expect to participate in) for professional advancement?

7. *Fees.* "Marriage and family therapists make financial arrangements with clients, third party payors, and supervisees that are reasonably understandable and conform to accepted professional practices." This principle makes explicit that marriage and family therapists do not accept payment for making referrals and do not exploit clients financially for services. They are truthful in representing facts to clients and to third parties regarding any services rendered. Ethical practice dictates a disclosure of fee policies at the onset of therapy. What steps would you take to inform your clients about your fee policies? What are some examples of your fee policies? Would you charge for missed appointments? What would you say about the ethics of a practitioner who charged a fee for making a referral to another professional? What are some ways in which clients can be exploited financially?

8. *Advertising.* "Marriage and family therapists engage in appropriate informational activities, including those that enable laypersons to choose professional services on an informed basis." Ethical practice dictates that practitioners accurately represent their competence, education, training, and experience in marital and family therapy. Professional standards are used in announcing services. Therapists do not advertise themselves as specialists (for example, in sex therapy) without being able to support this claim by virtue of their education, training, and supervised experience. How would you propose to advertise your services? How might you promote yourself as a marital and family practitioner?

Ethical Problems for Family Therapists

Green and Hansen (1989) investigated the self-reported responses of family therapists to a variety of ethical dilemmas. The results were very similar to those found in a previous study (see Green & Hansen, 1986). Below is a listing in rank order of the ethical problems most often experienced by family therapists:

1. treating the entire family
2. having values different from those of the family
3. treating the entire family after one member leaves
4. professional development activities
5. imposing therapist values—feminist
6. manipulating the family for therapeutic benefit
7. payment for services
8. decisions on marital status
9. reporting child abuse
10. supervision of trainees
11. balancing family and individual needs
12. consultation with other professionals
13. informed consent
14. testifying
15. working for an unethical organization
16. sharing research results

In their review of the literature on ethical problems facing family therapists, Green and Hansen (1986) concluded that, although the AAMFT ethical code was helpful, it was not sufficient as a guide. A more recent review of the literature reveals that several themes are frequently encountered by practitioners: engaging nonattenders, maintaining confidentiality, understanding therapist values and biases, and terminating therapy (Patten et al., 1991). There does not appear to be a great outpouring of new research in the area of ethics in marital and family therapy. Most of the references are to studies in the 1970s and 1980s. Given the fact that marital and family therapy is a growing profession, we think that there should also be an increased interest in research and writing on the ethical dimensions of this specialization.

Contemporary Professional Issues

In this section we identify a few of the current professional issues in the practice of marital and family therapy. These include the personal, academic, and experiential qualifications necessary to practice in the field.

Personal Characteristics of the Therapist

A debate surrounds the issue of the preparation of marital and family therapists. According to Humphrey (1983), of all the professional issues in marital therapy the least studied and most controversial one is what personal qualities are associated with an effective therapist. He contends that who a trainee is as a person is of crucial significance. If candidates have good personal qualities, he maintains, they can be provided with the knowledge and skills to make them effective professionals. But in his view, power-hungry or judgmental people will never make good counselors.

Educational Requirements

Competence in marital and family therapy involves integrating theoretical knowledge, abilities in clinical assessment, and treatment techniques, which are acquired through both educational and supervisory experiences (Everett, 1990). The AAMFT has developed minimum academic standards for marital and family therapists. Candidates are expected to demonstrate that they have successfully completed a graduate program from an accredited institution, with a minimum of a master's degree. To become a *clinical member* of the AAMFT, individuals must also have successfully completed appropriate graduate course work in the areas of family systems, family therapy, human development, research, and ethical and professional issues; a supervised practicum in marital and family therapy; and two years of postdegree clinical work involving 200 hours of supervision on 1,000 hours of work with marriage and family cases.

Training, Supervision, and Clinical Experience.   We agree with a number of writers who give primary emphasis to the quality of supervised practice and clinical experience in the training of marital and family therapists. Above all, therapists need to be skilled and sensitive clinicians. Mere knowledge of theories is of limited practical value if the therapists are not able to use themselves as persons con-

structively in sessions with couples and families (Humphrey, 1983). Academic knowledge comes alive in supervised practicum and internship, and trainees learn how to use and sharpen their intervention skills.

Training in marital and family therapy is a legal and professional issue as well as an ethical concern. If counselors are seeing families as part of their work, and if their program did not adequately prepare them for competence in intervening with families, they are vulnerable to a malpractice suit for practicing outside of the boundaries of their competence. Those practitioners who did not receive specialized training in their program need to involve themselves in postgraduate in-service training or special workshops.

Most graduate programs employ both didactic and experiential methods and supervised practice. Didactic methods include classroom lectures, readings, demonstrations, films and videotapes of family-therapy sessions, role playing, and discussion. Clinical experience with families is of limited value without regularly scheduled supervisory sessions. Live supervision can be conducted by a supervisor who watches the sessions behind a one-way mirror and who offers useful feedback and consultation to the trainee (Goldenberg & Goldenberg, 1991). Family-therapy trainees can also profit from the practice of co-therapy, which provides trainees with opportunities to work closely with a supervisor or a colleague. A great deal of the supervision can take place immediately after and between the sessions.

Experiential methods include both personal therapy and working with one's own family of origin. A rationale for personal therapeutic experiences is that they enable trainees to increase their awareness of transference and counter-transference. The AAMFT recommends such therapy. A rationale for exploring the family of origin is that it enables trainees to relate more effectively to the families they will meet in their clinical practice. (For a discussion of our perspectives on the value of this type of therapeutic experience for any type of therapist, review our discussion in Chapter 2.)

Concerning the objectives of professional training, Goldenberg and Goldenberg (1991) assert that firsthand clinical contact with families is the most important component. It is through these encounters, under close supervision, that trainees develop their own style of interacting with families. The Goldenbergs emphasize the need for students to work therapeutically with a variety of families from different ethnic and socioeconomic backgrounds that have various presenting problems. A program offering both comprehensive course work and clinical supervision provides the ideal learning situation.

Continuing Education. Obtaining a graduate degree in marital and family therapy does not end the need for education (see our discussion in Chapter 7). New theories and techniques of family intervention emerge, along with topical professional issues. Furthermore, legislative and judicial decisions have a major impact. Therapists who are not aware of these changes will not be able to provide the highest quality of professional service.

Marital and family therapists could benefit from continuing education in dealing with culturally diverse families and in understanding how gender roles play a vital role in family dynamics. According to Brown (1990), of all the factors that can inform the process of psychological assessment, gender issues are among the most neglected. She writes that the issues of gender membership, gender roles, and gender-related influences on certain life events are rarely included in the core curriculum. These concerns could be profitably explored in continuing-education workshops for family therapists.

Family Therapy versus Individual Therapy: A Case to Consider

Ludwig is a counselor whose education and training have been exclusively in individual and group dynamics. He is presented with a client, Ella, whose difficulties indicate that much of her problem lies not just with her but with her entire family system. This realization comes to Ludwig after more than a dozen sessions with her, and he has already established a strong working relationship with his client. Because he has no experience in family therapy, he ponders what to do. He thinks of referring Ella to a colleague who is well trained in family therapy, but he realizes that doing so could have a detrimental effect on her. One of her problems has been a sense of abandonment by her parents. He wants to avoid giving her the impression that he, too, is abandoning her. He decides to stay with her and work with her individually. Much of the time is spent trying to understand the dynamics of the family members who are not present.

- Do you agree with Ludwig's clinical decision? Do you agree with his rationale?
- Even though he was practicing within the framework of his orientation and training, was he underestimating the limitations of that framework when part of Ella's problem was due to the family as a system? Was that ethical practice?
- Even though he was not trained as a family therapist, what if he had decided to see the entire family and to attempt to do family therapy for the benefit of his client? Would that have been ethical?
- What if he had been trained in family systems but, when he suggested family sessions to Ella, she refused? What would you do if faced with such a dilemma?
- Assume that Ludwig decided to see each family member individually for the purpose of learning how each viewed the family system. In the process he discovered a great discrepancy between Ella's description of the family and what the other family members said, and he became convinced that his client was either misreading the family or was not presenting an accurate description of her problem. What is your opinion of how he should then proceed? Do you consider his strategy a good one? What theoretical rationale would you give for such a strategy? Was it an ethical thing to do?

Values in Marital and Family Therapy

In Chapter 3 we explored the impact of the therapist's values on the goals and direction of the therapeutic process. Values take on special significance in the counseling of couples and families. Goldenberg and Goldenberg (1991) write that a family therapist's value orientation typically includes a respect for the institution of marriage and for stability in family life, the importance of using child-rearing methods that fit the needs of each child, the desire to transmit the family's cultural values to the next generation, and the belief that a family is necessary for maintaining psychological health. They point to the need for family therapists to examine their attitudes and values (toward divorce, extramarital affairs, and sex roles in the family). It is crucial for therapists to understand how they might be biased against an individual or family whose views differ radically from their own. The Goldenbergs assert that "most family therapists—deliberately or unwittingly, consciously or unconsciously—proselytize for maintaining a family way of life, which may be inappropriate or worse for a particular warring couple" (p. 310).

The value system of therapists has a crucial influence on their formulation and definition of the problems they see in a family, the goals and plans for therapy, and the direction the therapy takes. We want to emphasize again that we do not see it as the function of any therapist to make decisions for clients. Family therapists should not decide for the members of a family how they should change. From our perspective, the role of the therapist is to help family members see more clearly what they are doing, to help them make an honest evaluation of how well their present patterns are working for them, and to help and encourage them to make necessary changes.

In this section we invite you to think about your own values and to reflect on the impact that they are likely to have on the interventions you make with couples and families. To assist you in formulating your personal position on these issues, we provide a couple of cases to consider and raise value-laden issues that could effect the course of therapy.

○ **The case of Sharon.**   Suppose you have a 25-year-old client, Sharon, who says, "I'm never going to get married, because I think marriage is a drag! I don't want kids, and I don't want to stay with one person forever." What follows are the inner dialogues of three therapists regarding her case.

Therapist A.   "What a spoiled and selfish brat. What a tough cookie. It's a good thing she's not going to get married, because she'd kill some poor guy. I wonder why she's in therapy. She doesn't sound like a good candidate."

Therapist B.   "Oh, the poor thing. She must have had some very painful experiences growing up. She must have had a terrible relationship with her father that prevents her from forming healthy relationships now. But she's such a beautiful woman, and she'd make a fine wife and mother. If I can only get to the bottom of her pain and nurture her inner child, I know she'll be able to overcome her bad experiences."

Therapist C.   "Well, she doesn't have to be married. Mental health doesn't necessarily require that one be married. I certainly would want to communicate to her that remaining single is an acceptable lifestyle. But I'd like to explore with her how she went about making this decision. I want to ensure that this is clearly what she wants to do and that it's not mainly a reaction to some painful situation in her life."

- What is your reaction to Sharon's statement?
- What is your reaction to each of the therapist's responses to her? What implied value is each therapist expressing?
- Why would you want to challenge (or accept) Sharon's decision?
- In what ways do you think you might work with Sharon differently from the three therapists? If you don't feel comfortable with a commitment to marriage and a family yourself, do you think you could be objective enough to help her explore some of the possibilities she might be overlooking?

○ *The case of Frank and Judy.*   During the past few years Frank and Judy have experienced many conflicts in their marriage. Although they have made attempts to resolve their problems by themselves, they have finally decided to seek the help of a professional marriage counselor. Even though they have been thinking about divorce with increasing frequency, they still have some hope that they can achieve a satisfactory marriage.

We will present the approaches of three marriage counselors, each holding a different set of values pertaining to marriage and the family. As you read these responses, think about the degree to which they represent what you might say and do if you were counseling this couple.

Counselor A.   At the first session this counselor states his belief in the preservation of marriage and the family. He feels that many couples take the easy way out by divorcing too quickly in the face of difficulty. He says that he sees most couples as having unrealistically high expectations of what constitutes a "happy marriage." The counselor lets it be known that his experience continues to teach him that divorce rarely solves any problems but instead creates new problems that are often worse. The counselor urges Frank and Judy to consider the welfare of their three dependent children. He tells the couple of his bias toward the saving of the marriage so that they can make an informed choice about initiating counseling with him.

- What are your personal reactions toward the orientation of this counselor?
- Is it ethical for him to state his bias so obviously?
- What if he were to keep his bias and values hidden from the couple and accept them into therapy? Do you see any possibility that he could work objectively with this couple? Explain.

Counselor B.   This counselor has been married three times herself. Although she believes in the institution, she is quick to maintain that far too many couples stay in their marriages and suffer unnecessarily. She explores with Judy and Frank the conflicts that they bring to the sessions. The counselor's interventions are leading them in the direction of divorce as the desired course of action, especially after they express this as an option. She suggests a trial separation and states her willingness to counsel them individually, with some joint sessions. When Frank brings up his guilt and reluctance to divorce because of the welfare of the children, the counselor confronts him with the harm that is being done to them by a destructive marriage. She tells him that it is too much of a burden to put on the children to keep the family together at any price.

- Do you see any ethical issues in this case? Is this counselor exposing or imposing her values?
- Do you think that she should be a marriage counselor, given her bias and her background of three divorces?
- What interventions made by the counselor do you agree with? What are your areas of disagreement?

Counselor C. This counselor believes that it is not her place to bring her values pertaining to the family into the sessions. She is fully aware of her biases regarding marriage and divorce, but she does not impose them or expose them in all cases. Her primary interest is to help Frank and Judy discover what is best for them as individuals and as a couple. She sees it as unethical to push her clients toward a definite course of action, and she lets them know that her job is to help them be honest with themselves.

- What are your reactions to this counselor's approach?
- Do you see it as possible for a counselor to keep his or her values out of the therapy process in a case such as this?

Commentary. The preceding case illustrates that the value system of the counselor determines the direction that counseling will take. The counselor who is dedicated to the mission of preserving marriage and family life is bound to function differently from the counselor who puts prime value on the welfare of an individual family member. What might be best for a given person might not necessarily be in the best interests of the entire family. It is essential, therefore, for counselors who work with couples and families to be aware of how their values influence the goals and procedures of therapy. We take the position that ethical practice challenges clients to clarify their own values and to choose a course of action that is best for them.

Responsibilities of Marital and Family Therapists

Margolin (1982) argues persuasively that difficult ethical questions confronted in individual therapy become even more complicated when a number of family members are seen together. She observes that the dilemma with multiple clients is that in some instances an intervention that serves one person's best interests could burden another family member or even be countertherapeutic. Under the family-systems model, for example, therapists do not focus on their responsibility to the individual but on the family as a system. Such therapists avoid becoming agents of any one family member, because they believe that all family members contribute to the problems of the whole family. It should be clear that therapists are ethically expected to declare the nature of their commitments to each member of the family.

Therapist responsibilities are also a crucial issue in couple counseling or marriage counseling. This is especially true when the partners do not have a common purpose for seeking counseling. An interesting question is raised when one person wants divorce counseling and the other is coming to the sessions under the expectation of saving the marriage or improving the relationship. In such a situation, who is the primary client? How do therapists carry out their ethical responsibilities when the two persons in the relationship have differing expectations?

In addition to clinical and ethical considerations, Margolin mentions legal provisions that can decide when the welfare of an individual takes precedence over that of a relationship. A clear example of a therapist's legal obligations is a case of child neglect or child abuse. The law requires family therapists to inform authorities if they suspect such abuse or become aware of it during the course of therapy. Even though reporting this situation may have negative consequences for the therapist's relationships with some members of the family, the therapist's ethical and legal responsibility is to help the threatened or injured person. It is clear that in some situations interventions to help an individual become more important than the goals of the family as a system, and clients should be informed of these situations during the initial session.

Morrison, Layton, and Newman (1982) agree with Margolin's position that family therapists may face more ethical conflicts than most other therapists. They write that family therapists sometimes face accusations that they are the agents of the parents against the children, the children against the parents, or of one parent against the other. In addition to these problems, we also take up in this section the family therapist's responsibility to know when to seek consultation, the responsibility to use power wisely, and the responsibility to testify in the courtroom.

The Responsibility to Consult

At times marriage and family therapists must struggle over the issue of when to consult with another professional. This is especially true of situations in which a person (or couple or family) is already involved in a professional relationship with a therapist and seeks the counsel of another therapist. What course of action would you take if a husband sought you out for private counseling while he and his wife were also seeing another therapist for marriage counseling? Would it be ethical to enter into a professional relationship with this man without the knowledge and consent of the other professional? What might you do or say if the husband told you that the reason for initiating contact with you was to get another opinion and perspective on his marital situation and that he did not see any point in contacting the other professional?

○ *An open-ended case.*   In this situation a couple is seeing the same therapist for marriage counseling. The husband decides to quit the joint sessions and begins private sessions with another therapist. The wife remains in individual therapy with the original therapist. In the course of individual therapy the husband comes to realize that he does not want to terminate the marriage after all. He persuades his wife to come with him for a joint session with *his* therapist to pursue the possibility of keeping the marriage intact.

- What are the ethical obligations of the husband's therapist? Does he have the responsibility of consulting with the wife's therapist?
- Do the two therapists need to get permission of their clients to consult with each other?
- Would it be ethical for the husband's therapist to do marital therapy with the couple, ignoring the work being done by the wife's therapist?

The Responsibility to Use Power Wisely

The therapist's use of power is a critical issue in family therapy. Although power is a vital component in any therapeutic relationship and of itself is not a negative force, there are dangers when power is used to keep clients dependent. If power is misused, clients may attribute to the therapist a magical ability to "cure" their troubles. They may thus be discouraged from looking within and tapping their own resources to bring about constructive change. O'Shea and Jessee (1982) note that a position of power and influence is seen by most marital and family therapists as particularly important in working with couples and families. They write: "The therapist's process of establishing rapport and joining with family members requires deciphering the communications and cracking the role of the family's meaning pattern. This enables the therapist to recognize, intervene, and assign new meaning to, and ultimately change, destructive interactional patterns in the family" (p. 5). They conclude that for family therapists to be effective, they need to be influential. Systems therapists gain this influence by being active and directive during the early phases of therapy.

Minuchin (1974) and his colleagues work with the structural aspects of the family system toward the goal of changing it so that it will no longer support a dysfunction. The structural approach focuses on how the family organizes itself, on how its members communicate, and on how dysfunctional patterns develop. Because structural family therapy requires the therapist to take a highly active role in the therapeutic process, it raises some critical ethical issues. Does this approach impose the therapist's value system on the family? Should the primary responsibility for change within the family rest with the therapist or the family? According to Minuchin, the goal of structural family therapy is to modify the present, not to explore and interpret the past. To accomplish this aim, family therapists join the system and then use themselves to transform it. Minuchin writes that the family system is organized around certain functions of its members, such as support, nurturing, control, and socializing. The therapist's responsibility is clear: "Hence, the therapist joins the family not to educate or socialize it, but rather to repair or modify the family's own functioning so that it can better perform these tasks" (1974, p. 14).

Structural family therapy does emphasize the power of the therapist, and this power is viewed as a major variable in bringing about therapeutic change. In Minuchin's words: "Change is seen as occurring through the process of the therapist's affiliation with the family and his restructuring of the family in a carefully planned way, so as to transform dysfunctional transactional patterns" (p. 91).

Fieldsteel (1982) notes that the ethical issues raised by the structural approach involve recognizing the possible differences between the value system of the therapist and that of the family. She identifies the danger of the therapist's assuming an inordinate share of the responsibility for change in family systems. Fieldsteel questions the ethicality of a therapist's encouraging clients to accept his or her perceptions as truth while at the same time the clients suspend their own perceptions by placing more trust in the therapist than in themselves. She also points out that some therapists assume that by virtue of their professional expertise they have the right to impose a new set of beliefs and values on the family. We agree with her position that family therapists should be aware of their clients' tendencies to attribute inordinate powers to them. Power and influence are inherent in family therapy. Thus, family therapists have the obligation to continually examine the ways in which they might misuse personal power, for doing so can keep families dependent.

Responsibilities in the Courtroom

It is essential to have a basic understanding of the law as it relates to families. The legal areas in which family therapists need to be knowledgeable include malpractice and legal liability, courtroom testimony, divorce and child custody, and lawyer/therapist relationships (Brown & Christensen, 1986). Confidentiality is limited when family therapists are called on to give expert testimony, which occurs in child-custody cases. If a family therapist is asked to make an evaluation in a custody case, an ethical issue arises as to the criteria for such an evaluation. Is the child evaluated independently of the family system or as a part of it? Some therapists assert that an evaluation independent of the family system is inaccurate and misleading. They argue that this evaluation must take into account power struggles, triangles, coalitions, alliances, and family boundaries (Brown & Christensen, 1986, p. 284). Often a consultation with an expert in family assessment is appropriate. This is especially important if the therapist is unfamiliar with making assessments for legal purposes. A related issue pertains to the need for skill in assessing children when evaluations about individual functioning are made.

A helpful monograph, *Preparing for Court Appearances* (Remley, 1991), underscores the need for therapists who are drawn into court proceedings to seek advice from an attorney. Remley points out that legal advice may be expensive but that failure to get it can prove more costly in the long run. Because an increasing number of mental-health professionals are finding themselves involved in court testimony, he encourages counselors to think ahead. He writes, for example, that counselors should not allow themselves to be forced into giving expert testimony if they are not prepared to function as an expert witness.

Confidentiality in Marital and Family Therapy

Therapists have differing views on the role of confidentiality in working with families. One view is that therapists should not divulge in a family session any information given to them by individuals in private sessions. In the case of marriage counseling, some practitioners are willing to see each spouse for individual sessions. Information given to them by one spouse is kept confidential. Other therapists, however, reserve the right to bring up certain issues in a joint session, even if one person mentioned the issue in a private session.

Some therapists who work with entire families go further. They have a policy of refusing to keep information secret that was shared individually. Their view is that secrets are counterproductive for open family therapy. Therefore, "hidden agendas" are seen as material that should be brought out into the open during a family session. Still another view is that therapists should inform their clients that any information given to them during private sessions will be divulged as they see fit in accordance with the greatest benefit for the couple or family. These therapists reserve the right to use their professional judgment about whether to maintain individual confidences. In our opinion this latter approach is the most flexible, in that it avoids putting the counselor in the awkward position of having to either divulge secrets or keep secrets at the expense of the welfare of the family. As Margolin (1982) notes, therapists who have not promised confidentiality have more options and thus must carefully consider the therapeutic ramifications of their actions.

What is absolutely essential to ethical practice is that each marital and family therapist make his or her stand on confidentiality clear to each family member from the outset of therapy. In this way each family member can decide whether to participate in therapy and can then decide how much to disclose to the therapist. For example, a husband might disclose less in a private session if he knew that the therapist was assuming the right to bring these disclosures out in joint sessions.

○ *A case of therapist quandary.* A husband is involved in one-to-one therapy to resolve a number of personal conflicts, of which the state of his marriage is only one. Later, his wife comes in for some joint sessions. In their joint sessions much time is spent on how betrayed the wife feels over having discovered that her husband had an affair in the past. She is angry and hurt but has agreed to remain in the marriage and to come to these therapy sessions as long as the husband agrees not to resume the past affair or to initiate new ones. Reluctantly, the husband agrees to her demands. The therapist does not explicitly state her views about confidentiality, yet the husband assumes that she will keep to herself what she hears in both the wife's private sessions and his private sessions. During one of the joint sessions the therapist does state her bias that if they are interested in working on their relationship, then maintaining or initiating an affair is counterproductive. She says it is her strong preference that if they both want to work on improving their marriage, they agree not to have extramarital affairs.

In a later individual session the husband tells the therapist that he has begun a new affair. He brings this up privately with his therapist because he feels some guilt over not having lived up to the agreement. But he maintains that the affair is not negatively influencing his relationship with his wife and has helped him to tolerate many of the difficulties that he has been experiencing in his marriage. He also asks that the therapist not mention this in a joint session, for he fears that his wife will leave him if she finds out that he is involved with another woman.

Think about these questions in taking your position on the ethical course of action:

- Since the therapist has not explicitly stated her view of confidentiality, is it ethical for her to bring up this matter in a joint session?
- How does the therapist handle her conviction regarding affairs in light of the fact that the husband tells her that it is actually enhancing, not interfering with, the marriage?
- Does she attempt to persuade the husband to give up the affair? Does she persuade the client to bring up this matter himself in a joint session? Is the therapist colluding with the husband against the wife by not bringing up this matter?
- Do you think that she could have avoided getting herself into this dilemma? If so, how?
- Does the therapist discontinue therapy with this couple because of her strong bias? If she does suggest termination and referral to another professional, might not this be tantamount to admitting to the wife that the husband is having an affair? What might the therapist say if the wife is upset over the suggestion of a referral and wants to know the reasons?

Informed Consent in Marital and Family Therapy

In Chapter 4 we examined the issue of informed consent and clients' rights within the framework of individual therapy. As Margolin (1982) notes, informed consent and the right to refuse treatment are also critical ethical issues in the practice of marital and family therapy. Before each individual agrees to participate in family therapy, it is essential that the counselor provide information about the purpose of therapy, typical procedures, the risks of negative outcomes, the possible benefits, the fee structure, the limits of confidentiality, the rights and responsibilities of clients, the option that a family member can withdraw at any time, and what can be expected from the therapist. When therapists take the time to obtain informed consent from everyone, they convey the message that no one member is the "crazy person" who is the source of all the family's problems.

Most family therapists consider it essential that all members of the family participate. This bias raises ethical questions about exerting pressure on an individual to participate, even if that person is strongly against being involved. Although coercion of a reluctant person is generally viewed as unethical, many therapists strongly suggest to this person that he or she give a session or two a try to determine what potential value there might be in family therapy. Some resistance can arise from a family member's feeling that he or she will be "ganged up on" and will be the focus of the sessions. In several sessions this resistance can be lessened and perhaps even eliminated if the therapist does not allow the family to use one member as a scapegoat. Although getting the informed consent of each member of the family is ideal from an ethical point of view, actually carrying out this practice may be difficult.

Patten and her colleagues (1991) and Haas and Alexander (1981) question the controversial strategy of withholding services until all participants are engaged in therapy. Haas and Alexander contend that the therapist who requires all members to be a part of therapy may be cooperating with the most resistant family member in keeping the more willing members from beginning or continuing therapy as a family. If an individual does not want to participate in family therapy, the therapist needs to explore other options for working with the family.

Protecting children's rights is typically made easier by treating the whole family, according to Haas and Alexander. They note that parents retain the legal authority to consent to their children's treatment and to know what is occurring in individual therapy. This problem obviously does not arise in family therapy, because the parents are involved. The issue of informed consent needs to be open for family discussion. Haas and Alexander recommend that family therapists establish ground rules for dealing with matters such as family secrets and the privacy of individual members. If these rules are made a part of the informed-consent procedure at the initial session(s), issues of confidentiality are less likely to become a problem as therapy progresses. A survey of therapists' attitudes suggests a trend toward the increased involvement of adolescents in these informed-consent procedures (Beeman & Scott, 1991).

Hare-Mustin (1980) observes that family therapy may be dangerous to one's health. Because it gives priority to the good of the entire family, it may not be in the best interests of individual family members. Further, by being required to participate in therapy, the members may have to subordinate their own goals and give up limited confidentiality. Hare-Mustin suggests that ethical practice demands minimizing these risks for individual members. This can be done by encouraging them to question the goals of therapy, so that they can understand how their own needs relate to the family's goals. Also, it is the therapist's responsibility to open for discussion the subject of how one member's goals are incompatible with family goals or perhaps even unacceptable to other members.

The implications of informed consent for family therapists and systems-oriented therapists are also discussed by Bray, Shepherd, and Hays (1985). These writers encourage therapists to tell prospective clients that they are looking beyond treating a specific and diagnosed problem to a broader view of the clients' health. Clients have a right to know that the family system will be the focus of the therapeutic process and to know about the practical implications of this theoretical perspective. Bray and his colleagues suggest that professionals have the responsibility to disclose to their clients the nature of the procedures they will use, the more probable consequences of these procedures, alternative treatments, and the risks of therapy. However, they do not see it as realistic to discuss every possible risk. They suggest that a risk should be disclosed when the client might find it important in deciding whether to consent to therapy. Further, family members should be encouraged to ask questions about therapy, and it is good to inform them that they are always free to withdraw their consent and terminate treatment at any point.

Chapter Summary

The field of marital and family therapy is rapidly expanding and developing. With an expansion in educational programs being offered comes the need for specialized training and experience. A thorough discussion of ethical issues must be a part of all such programs. A few of these issues are determining who is the primary client, dealing with confidentiality, providing informed consent, using and misusing power and control, counseling with minors, and exploring the role of values in family therapy.

The job of the therapist is to help the family or couple sort through their own values and not to influence them to conform to the therapist's value system. Likewise, a key ethical issue is the impact of the therapist's life experiences on his or her ability to practice effectively and objectively. For instance, if family therapists are bogged down by their own unfinished business with their family of origin or unresolved conflicts in their current family, it is not likely that they will be able to be a therapeutic agent for other families. Therapists who are using their work as a way to fulfill their needs or who have intense countertransference reactions toward particular family members may be blocking a family's progress. The ethical issues are clear in these cases.

As is true regarding all ethical issues, there is a significant relationship between sound ethical and clinical decision making. Family therapists may sometimes experience confusion, for example, regarding the ethical aspects of deciding who will attend family sessions. It is obvious, however, that such decisions cannot be made without a solid foundation in clinical theory and methodology. With increased knowledge and practical experience, therapists can make these ethical decisions with greater certainty. Being open to periodic supervision, seeking consultation when necessary, and being willing to participate in one's own therapy are some ways in which marital and family therapists can refine their clinical skills.

Suggested Activities

1. In the practice of marital and family therapy informed consent is especially important. As a class-discussion topic explore some of these issues: What are the ethical implications of insisting that all members of a family participate in family therapy? What kind of information should a family therapist present from the outset to all those involved? Are there any ethical conflicts in focusing on the welfare of the entire family rather than on what might be in the best interests for an individual?

2. As a project you can investigate the status of regulating professional practice in marital and family therapy in your state. What are the academic and training requirements, if any, for certification or licensure in this field?

3. Small groups might focus on what they consider to be the major ethical problem facing marital and family therapists. Consider issues such as confidentiality, enforced therapy involving all family members, qualifications of effective family therapists, imposing the values of the therapist on a family, and practicing beyond one's competence.

4. Consider designing a project in which you study your own family of origin. Interview as many relatives as you can. Look for patterns in your own relationships, including problems you currently struggle with, that stem from your family of origin. What advantages do you see in studying your own family as one way to prepare yourself for working with families?

5. Suppose that you were participating on a board to establish standards—personal, academic, training, and experiential—for family therapists. What would you see as being minimum requirements to prepare a trainee to work with families? What would your ideal training program for marital and family therapists look like?

Suggested Readings

For ethical considerations in marital and family therapy see Margolin (1982), Hare-Mustin (1980), and Patten et al. (1991). For studies on ethical dilemmas most often faced by family therapists see Green and Hansen (1986, 1989). For two excellent textbooks on family therapy see Goldenberg and Goldenberg (1991) and Nichols and Schwartz (1991). For a discussion of dual relationships in marital and family therapy see Ryder and Hepworth (1990). On competence issues and for a discussion of training standards in marital and family therapy see Everett (1990). For training issues in marital and family therapy see Goldenberg and Goldenberg (1991) and Humphrey (1983). For a review of the literature on ethics in marital and family therapy see Patten et al. (1991). For a discussion of courtroom procedures applicable to marital and family therapists see Remley (1991).

CHAPTER THIRTEEN

Ethical Issues in Group Work

Pre-Chapter Self-Inventory

Directions: For each statement, indicate the response that most closely identifies your beliefs and attitudes. Use the following code:

5 = I *strongly agree* with this statement.
4 = I *agree* with this statement.
3 = I am *undecided* about this statement.
2 = I *disagree* with this statement.
1 = I *strongly disagree* with this statement.

_____ 1. A group leader's actual behavior in a group is more important than his or her theoretical approach.

_____ 2. Ethical practice requires that prospective group members be carefully screened and selected.

_____ 3. It's important to prepare members so that they can derive the maximum benefit from the group.

_____ 4. Requiring people to participate in a therapy group raises ethical issues.

_____ 5. It is unethical to allow a group to exert pressure on one of its members.

_____ 6. Confidentiality is less important in groups than it is in individual therapy.

_____ 7. Socializing among group members is almost always undesirable, since it interferes with the functioning of the group.

_____ 8. Ethical practice requires making some provision for evaluating the outcomes of a group.

_____ 9. A group leader has a responsibility to devise ways of minimizing any psychological risks associated with participation in the group.

_____ 10. People are not competent to be group leaders until they have completed a structured program of education and training approved by one of the major mental-health professions.

_____ 11. It is unethical for counselor educators to lead groups of their students in training.

_____ 12. Verbal abuse and subsequent emotional casualties are more likely to occur in groups than in individual counseling.

_____ 13. Adequate training is sufficient in and of itself to prepare one for effective co-leading of groups.

_____ 14. It is the group leader's responsibility to make prospective members aware of their rights and responsibilities and to demystify the process of a group.

_____ 15. Group members should know that they have the right to leave the group at any time.

_____ 16. Before people enter a group, it is the leader's responsibility to discuss with them the personal risks involved, especially potential life changes, and help them explore their readiness to face these risks.

_____ 17. It is a sound practice to provide written ethical guidelines to group members in advance and discuss them in the first meeting.

_____ 18. Group therapists who do not keep the content of group sessions confidential are legally and ethically liable, and they can be sued for breach of confidence.

___ 19. Under certain circumstances it may be ethical for a group leader to tape a group session without the prior knowledge and consent of the members, *if* the leader tells the members at the end of the session that they were taped.

___ 20. It is unethical for group leaders to employ a technique unless they are thoroughly trained in its use or under the supervision of an expert familiar with it.

___ 21. Ethical practice demands that leaders inform members about any research activities that might be a part of the group.

___ 22. Confrontation in groups is almost always destructive and generally inhibits the formation of trust and cohesion.

___ 23. A group leader has a responsibility to teach members how to translate what they've learned in the group to their outside lives.

___ 24. A leader has a responsibility to ask potential members who are already being counseled to consult with their therapist before joining the group.

___ 25. One way of minimizing psychological risks to group participants is to negotiate contracts with the members.

Introduction

We are giving group work special attention, as we did with marital and family therapy, because it raises unique ethical concerns. Practitioners who work with groups face a variety of situations that differ from those encountered in individual therapy. Groups have been increasing in popularity, and in many agencies and institutions they are the primary form of therapy. They are also considered the most cost-effective. Along with this increased use of groups, there has been a rising ethical awareness. For instance, the ASGW developed its first set of ethical guidelines for group counselors in 1980; these were fully revised and expanded in 1989. In a special issue of the *Journal for Specialists in Group Work*, Forester-Miller (1990a) notes:

> We have come a long way in the past decade in continuing to explore and contest the ethical issues in group work. It is important, however, to remember that the ethical challenge is an ongoing process, that we must continue to question and evaluate ourselves. Once we become complacent, we become stagnant and cease to grow as professionals and will be less effective as counselors [p. 66].

Our illustrations of important ethical considerations are drawn from a broad spectrum of groups, including therapy groups, personal-growth groups, educational groups, structured groups, and different types of counseling groups. Obviously, these groups differ with respect to their member population, purpose, focus, and procedures, as well as in the level of training required for their leaders. Although these distinctions are important, the issues we discuss are common to most groups. This chapter is structured around the *Ethical Guidelines for Group Counselors,* as developed and approved by the ASGW (1989). These guidelines complement the broader standards of the AACD (1988). Among the topics we discuss are the training of group leaders, the ethical issues surrounding group membership, confidentiality in groups, and possible abuses of group techniques.

Training and Supervision of Group Leaders
Professional Training Standards*

The ASGW (1991) has extensively revised and expanded its *Professional Standards for the Training of Group Workers*. The revised standards provide that all professional counselors should possess basic *knowledge* and basic *skills* in group work. These core competencies are the foundation on which specialized training in group work is built. The standards also contain a set of guidelines for integrating the new provisions with CACREP accreditation standards.

A few examples of group leaders' basic *areas of knowledge* are identifying one's strengths, weaknesses, and values; being able to describe the characteristics associated with the typical stages in a group's development; being able to describe the facilitative and debilitative roles and behaviors of group members; knowing the therapeutic factors at work in a group; understanding the importance of group and member evaluation; and being aware of the ethical issues special to group work.

Examples of *skill competencies* include being able to open and close group sessions, modeling appropriate behavior for group members, engaging in appropriate self-disclosure in the group, giving and receiving feedback, helping members attribute meaning to their experience, helping them integrate and apply their learning, and demonstrating the ability to apply the ASGW ethical standards in group practice.

At a minimum, a counselor-training program should include one group course, which should be structured to help students acquire these basic knowledge and skill competencies. The ASGW standards state that these group skills are best mastered through supervised practice, which should include observation and participation in a group experience. Although they set a minimum of 10 hours of supervised practice, they recommend 20 hours.

Once counselor trainees have mastered these core knowledge and skills domains, they can acquire training in group-work specializations in one or more of these four areas: (1) task/work groups, (2) guidance/psychoeducational groups, (3) counseling/interpersonal-problem-solving groups, and (4) psychotherapy/personality-reconstruction groups. The standards detail specific knowledge and skill competencies for these specialties and also specify the recommended number of hours of supervised training for each.

The training for *task/work groups* involves courses in the broad area of organizational development and management. It also includes course work in

*Adapted from Professional Standards for the Training of Group Workers, adopted April 20, 1991, and reproduced by permission from *Together: Association for Specialists in Group Work, 20* (Fall 1991), 9–14. The ASGW is a division of the American Association for Counseling and Development, 5999 Stevenson Avenue, Alexandria, VA 22304.

consultation. A minimum of 30 hours of supervised experience in leading or co-leading a task/work group is required.

The specialist training for *guidance/psychoeducation groups* involves course work in the broad area of community psychology, health promotion, marketing, consultation, and curriculum design. This speciality requires an additional 30 hours of supervised experience in leading or co-leading a guidance group in field practice.

The training for *counseling/interpersonal-problem-solving groups* should ideally include as much course work in group counseling as possible, with at least one course beyond the generalist level. There is a minimum of 45 hours of supervised experience in leading or co-leading a counseling group.

The specialist training for *psychotherapy groups* consists of courses taken in the area of abnormal psychology, psychopathology, and diagnostic assessment to assure capabilities in working with more disturbed populations. There is a minimum of 45 hours of supervised experience in working with therapy groups.

The guidelines for integrating the ASGW standards with the CACREP accreditation standards call for supervised clinical experience that should be obtained in both practicum and internship programs. For the master's practicum, at least 15 hours should be spent in supervised leadership or co-leadership in a group-work specialty as outlined by the ASGW. For the internship in a master's degree program, at least 90 hours should be spent in supervised group leadership. For a doctoral internship at least 450 hours (of the 1200 hours stipulated) should be spent in supervised clinical work with groups. The current trend in training group workers focuses on supervised experiences. Certainly, the mere completion of one graduate course in group theory and practice does not equip one to lead groups competently. Both direct participation as a member of planned and supervised small groups and clinical experience in leading various groups under careful supervision are needed to equip leaders with the skills to meet the challenges of group work.

Our Views on Training

We do not think that professional codes, legislative mandates, and institutional policies alone will ensure professional group leadership. Students in group-leadership training need to confront the typical dilemmas they will face in practice and learn ways to clarify their views on these issues. This can best be done by including ethics in the trainees' academic program as well as discussing ethical issues that grow out of the students' experiences in practicum, internship, and fieldwork. We have found that one effective way to teach ethical decision making is presenting trainees with case vignettes of typical problems that occur in group situations and encouraging discussion of the ethical issues and pertinent guidelines. We tell both students and professionals who attend our workshops that they will not have the answers to many of the dilemmas they encounter in practice, because ethical decision making is an ongoing process that takes on new forms and increased meaning as the practitioner gains experience. What is critical is that group leaders develop a receptivity to self-examination and to questioning the professionalism of their group practice.

We highly recommend at least three experiences as adjuncts to a training program for group workers: (1) personal (private) psychotherapy; (2) experience in group therapy, group counseling, or a personal-growth group; and (3) participation in a supervision and training group.

Personal Psychotherapy. We agree with Yalom (1985) that extensive self-exploration is necessary if trainees are to perceive countertransference feelings, recognize blind spots and biases, and use their personal attributes effectively in groups. Although videotaping, working with a co-leader, and supervision all are excellent sources of feedback, Yalom maintains that personal therapy is usually necessary for fuller understanding and correction. We think that group leaders should demonstrate the courage and willingness to do for themselves what they expect members in their groups to do: expand their awareness of self and the effect of that self on others.

Self-Exploration Groups. As an adjunct to formal course work and internship training, participation in a therapeutic group can be extremely valuable. In addition to helping interns resolve personal conflicts and develop increased self-understanding, a personal-growth group can be a powerful teaching tool. One of the best ways to learn how to assist group members in their struggles is to work yourself as a member of a group. Yalom (1985) strongly recommends a group experience for trainees. Some of the benefits, he suggests, are experiencing the power of a group, learning what self-disclosure is about, coming to appreciate the difficulties involved in self-sharing, learning on an emotional level what one knows intellectually, and becoming aware of one's dependence on the leader's power and knowledge. He cites surveys indicating that 60% to 70% of group-therapy training programs offer some type of personal-group experience. About half of these programs offer an optional group, and the other half, a mandatory group.

Participation in a Training and Supervisory Group. We have found that workshops help group trainees develop the skills necessary for effective intervention. Also, the interns can learn a great deal about their response to criticism, their competitiveness, their need for approval, their concerns over being competent, and their power struggles. In working with both university students learning about group approaches and with professionals who want to upgrade their skills, we have found an intensive weekend workshop to be effective and dynamic. After a segment in which the participants lead their group, we intervene by giving feedback and by promoting a discussion by the entire group. By the end of the weekend each participant has led the group at least twice (for an hour each time) under direct supervision (Corey & Corey, 1986).

A particularly controversial ethical issue in the preparation of group counselors pertains to the practice of combining experiential and didactic methods. Counselor educators who teach group courses do not appear to agree on the goals for combining therapeutic and training groups or on how students can best be evaluated (Forester-Miller & Duncan, 1990). The use of the experiential group as an adjunct to training graduate students in group counseling has become the focus of increasing criticism among counselor educators because of the existence of dual relationships and their potential for unethical practice, such as invasion of privacy, conflict of interest, and abuses of power (Merta & Sisson, 1991). Those who teach group courses often function in multiple roles as group facilitator, instructor, evaluator, and supervisor. Although the blending of these roles does present potential ethical problems, the literature reveals that various strategies are being employed in the preparation of group counselors. It is essential that faculty members who teach group courses monitor their practices by keeping the purpose of the training group clearly in mind. The two separate domains of training group and therapy group can be clarified by reflecting and by discussing relevant issues with colleagues.

In their article examining the ethical dilemma surrounding the use of experiential groups in training group counselors, Merta and Sisson (1991) conclude that counselor educators need to consider the needs of the students, the program, and the profession. Although they contend that experiential groups are an indispensable component in training, they also offer the following eight recommendations for ethical practice in the preparation of group workers.

1. Training programs should be surveyed nationally to determine how experiential groups are being used.
2. The opinions of current trainees in group counseling can be useful in making ethical decisions.
3. Although it is not appropriate that experiential groups become therapy groups, such groups need not be restricted to mere role-playing exercises.
4. Because experiential groups are essential to the preparation of effective group counselors, participating in them should not be voluntary, nor should alternatives be provided for those who do not wish to become involved in these groups.
5. It is preferable to have advanced students or practitioners from outside the department as leaders of experiential groups, rather than the course instructor or other faculty members in the department.
6. Students have a right to expect feedback regarding their performance in the experiential group.
7. Instructors who teach group courses should meet with those who facilitate experiential groups for the purpose of discussing student progress in the group.
8. Before enrolling in a program, students should be fully advised of the requirement of participating in an experiential group that encourages self-disclosure and personal exploration.

For a more detailed discussion of dual-relationship controversies in the preparation of group counselors, see Herlihy and Corey, 1992.

As you consider the training of group leaders, answer these questions for yourself:

• Who is qualified to lead groups? What are the criteria for determining the competence of group leaders?
• What do you think of the training in clinical practice suggested in the ASGW's *Professional Standards for the Training of Group Workers?*

- What are some differences between a training group and a therapy group? What are some potential problems in attempting to combine these groups in preparing group leaders? Can you think of safeguards to minimize the potential risks of combining experiential and didactic methods?
- Does ethical practice demand that group leaders receive some form of personal therapy? Should this be group therapy or experience in a personal-growth group? How important are continuing education and training once one has completed a professional program?
- What are your reactions to the suggestions we offered for the training of group workers?

Co-Leadership

If you should decide to lead groups, you'll probably work with a co-leader at some time. We think there are many advantages to the co-leader model. The group can benefit from the insights and feedback of two leaders. The leaders can complement and balance each other. They can grow by discussing what goes on in the group and by observing each other's style, and together they can evaluate what has gone on in the group and plan for future sessions. Also, co-leaders can share the burden. While one leader is working with a particular member, the other can be paying attention to others in the group.

The choice of a co-leader is crucial. A group can suffer if its leaders are not working together toward a common goal. If much of the leaders' energy is directed at competing with each other or at some other power struggle or hidden agenda, there is little chance that the group will be effective.

We think that the selection of a co-leader should involve more than attraction and liking. Each of the leaders should be secure enough that the group won't have to suffer as one or both of them try to "prove" themselves. We surely don't think it's essential that co-leaders always agree or share the same perceptions or interpretations; in fact, a group can be given vitality if co-leaders feel trusting enough to express their differences of opinion. Mutual respect and the ability to establish a relationship based on trust, cooperation, and support are most important. Also, each person should be autonomous and have his or her own style yet be able to work with the other leader as a team.

In our view it's essential for co-leaders to spend some time together immediately following a group session to assess what has happened. Similarly, we believe that they should meet at least briefly before each session to talk about anything that might affect their functioning in the group.

At this point we ask you to draw up your own guidelines for selecting a co-leader:

- What are the qualities you'd look for in a co-leader?
- What kind of person would you *not* want to lead with?
- If you found that you and your co-leader clashed on many issues and approached groups very differently, what do you think you'd do?

- What ethical implications are involved when a great deal of time during the sessions is taken up with power struggles and conflicts between the co-leaders?
- In what ways could you be most helpful to your co-leader?

Ethical Issues in Group Membership
Recruitment and Informed Consent

How can group leaders make potential members aware of the services they are providing? What information do clients have a right to expect before they decide to attend a group? The ASGW ethical guidelines (1989) clarify the group leader's responsibility for providing information about services to prospective clients: "Group counselors adequately prepare prospective or new group members by providing as much information about the existing or proposed group as necessary" (guideline 1).*

People have a right to know what they are getting into before they make a commitment to become a part of any group. Informed consent requires that leaders make the members aware of their rights (as well as their responsibilities) as group participants.

○ *A case of informed consent.*   A group leader operates on the assumption that giving members information about her groups will ultimately be counter-productive. She does not tell them about the nature of the group process, the procedures she may use, or the best ways to get the maximum benefit from the group. She is concerned that members would focus on meeting her expectations. She does not emphasize defining goals and believes that members' uncertainty about what they want from the group will be good material to explore as part of the group process.

- Is this leader behaving unethically in not providing members with information about the goals of the group or the procedures she may use?
- What are some of the potential dangers of providing too much information about a group before members enroll?
- What are some ways in which members can be given information about the purpose of techniques in general, without defeating the purpose of these techniques?
- What information do you think a member should have before deciding whether to participate in a group?

Screening and Selection of Group Members

Group leaders are faced with the difficult task of determining who should be included in a group and who should not. Are groups appropriate for all people?

*From *Ethical Guidelines for Group Counselors,* by the Association for Specialists in Group Work. Copyright 1989 by the American Association for Counseling and Development. This and all other quotations from the same source are reprinted by permission.

To put the question in another way, is it appropriate for *this* person to become a participant in *this* type of group, with *this* leader, at *this* time?

Assuming that not everyone will benefit from a group experience—and that some people will be psychologically harmed by certain group experiences—is it unethical to fail to screen prospective group candidates? Many group leaders do not screen participants, for various reasons. Some practitioners are theoretically opposed to the notion of using screening as a way of determining who is suitable for a group, and some maintain that they simply do not have the time to carry out effective screening. Others take the position that ethical practice demands the careful screening and preparation of all candidates.

Yalom (1985) argues that unless careful selection criteria are employed, group-therapy clients may end up discouraged and may not be helped. He maintains that it is easier to identify the people who should be excluded from group therapy than those who should be included. Citing clinical studies, he lists the following as poor candidates for a heterogeneous outpatient intensive-therapy group: brain-damaged people, paranoid individuals, hypochondriacs, those who are addicted to drugs or alcohol, acute psychotics, and sociopaths. In terms of criteria for inclusion, he contends that the client's level of motivation to work is the most important variable. From his perspective, groups are useful for people who have problems in the interpersonal domain, such as loneliness, inability to make or maintain intimate contacts, feelings of unlovability, fears of being assertive, and dependency issues. Clients who lack meaning in life, who suffer from diffuse anxiety, who are searching for an identity, who fear success, and who are compulsive workers might also profit from a group experience.

The *Ethical Guidelines for Group Counselors* (ASGW, 1989) provide:

> The group counselor screens prospective group members (when appropriate to their theoretical orientation). Insofar as possible, the counselor selects group members whose needs and goals are compatible with the goals of the group, who will not impede the group process, and whose well-being will not be jeopardized by the group experience. An orientation to the group is included during the screening process [guideline 2].

Are practitioners who meet their groups without screening or orienting the members behaving unethically? We think that one alternative is to use the initial session for screening and informed consent. Screening is most effective when the leader interviews the members and the members also have an opportunity to interview the leader. While prospective group members are being screened, they should be deciding whether they want to work with a particular leader and whether the group in question is suitable for them. Group candidates should not passively allow the matter to be decided for them by an expert. Practitioners should welcome the opportunity to respond to any questions or concerns that prospective members have, and they should actively encourage them to raise questions about matters that will affect their participation.

In our own approach to screening we've often found it difficult to predict who will benefit from a group experience. We realize that pregroup screening interviews are like any other interview in that people tend to say what they think the interviewer expects. Those who are interviewed for a group often feel that they must sell themselves or that they are being evaluated and judged. Perhaps these feelings can be lessened somewhat if leaders emphasize that these interviews are really designed as a two-way process in which leaders and prospective members can decide together whether a particular group, with a particular leader, at a particular time is in the best interests of all concerned. Although we do have difficulty in predicting who will benefit from a group, we have found screening interviews most helpful in excluding some people who we believed would probably have left the group with negative feelings or would have drained the group of the energy necessary for productive work.

It often happens that both the prospective member and the group leader are unsure whether a particular group is indicated for that person. For this reason, in a group that will be meeting a number of times, the first few sessions can be considered exploratory. Members can be encouraged to come to the first session or two and then consider whether the group is what they're looking for. In this way leaders encourage a self-selection process that gives members the responsibility of deciding what is right for them. Actually experiencing the group for a time enables members to make an informed decision about participation. If then, after a few sessions, either the leader or a particular member has any reservations, a private meeting to explore these concerns can be arranged.

Preparing Group Participants

To what extent are group counselors responsible for teaching participants to benefit from their group experience? Many practitioners do very little to prepare members systematically for a group. In fact, we know of some group workers who are opposed to systematic preparation on the ground that it would inhibit a group's spontaneity and autonomy. Others take the position that members must be given some structuring in order to derive the maximum gains. As we saw in the previous sections, the ASGW's ethical guidelines (1989) emphasize the importance of preparation and orientation.

Yalom (1985) advocates exploring group members' misconceptions and expectations, predicting early problems, and providing a conceptual framework that includes guidelines for effective group behavior. He views this preparatory process as more than the dissemination of information. He contends that it reinforces the therapist's respect for the client, demonstrates that therapy is a collaborative venture, and shows that the therapist is willing to share his or her knowledge with the client. This cognitive approach to preparation has the goals of providing a rational explanation of the group process, clarifying how members are expected to behave, and raising expectations about what the group can accomplish.

In our training workshops we have seen much resistance that can be attributed to ignorance of group process and a misunderstanding of goals. Our preparation procedures apply to all types of groups, with some modifications. At both the screening session and the initial group meeting, we explore the members' expectations, clarify goals and objectives, discuss procedural details, explore the possible risks and values of group participation, and discuss guidelines for getting the most from a group experience (G. Corey, M. Corey, Callanan, & Russell, 1992, pp. 38–55; M. Corey & G. Corey, 1992, pp. 77–96). As part of member preparation we include a discussion of the values and limitations of groups, the psychological risks involved in group participation, and ways of minimizing these risks. We also allow time for dealing with misconceptions that people have about groups and for exploring any fears or resistances the members may have. In most of our groups members do have certain fears about what they will experience, and until we acknowledge these fears and talk about them, very little productive work can occur. Further, we ask members to spend time before they come to the group defining for themselves what they most want to achieve. To make their goals more concrete, we usually ask them to develop a contract that entails areas of concern on which they're willing to work in the group. We also ask them to do some reading and to write about their goals and about the significant turning points in their lives.

At this point, we ask you to write down a few things you might do to prepare people for a group. What is your position on the ethical aspects of omitting such preparation? What do you think would occur if you did little in the way of preparing group members?

Voluntary and Involuntary Participation

Should group membership always be voluntary? Are there situations in which it is ethical to require or coerce people to participate in a group? What problems are involved in mandatory group participation? How is informed consent especially critical in groups where attendance is mandatory?

The ASGW's guideline (1989) is "Group counselors inform members whether participation is voluntary or involuntary" (guideline 4). A subguideline is "With involuntary groups, every attempt is made to enlist the cooperation of the members and their continuance in the group on a voluntary basis."

Involuntary Clients. When group participation is mandatory, much effort needs to be directed toward fully informing members of the nature and goals of the group, procedures to be used, the rights of members to decline certain activities, the limits of confidentiality, and what effect their level of participation in the group will have on critical decisions about them outside of the group. An example will help make our point. The three of us provide in-service training workshops for staff members who lead involuntary groups at a state mental hospital. Groups are the basic treatment for "those incompetent to stand trial," "sociopathic criminals," and "mentally disordered sex offenders." One of the factors involved in determining patients' release from the hospital and return to the community is their cooperation in the treatment program, which includes participation in regular group-therapy sessions. If patients do not show up for a group, they are likely to have their "hall cards" taken from them, which means that they are restricted to their wards. In such cases where attendance at group sessions is mandatory, informed consent implies that leaders explore with members, during an orientation session, what the group will be about. Thus, members will understand clearly what their rights and responsibilities are.

The Freedom to Leave a Group.   Once members make a commitment to be a part of a group, do they have the right to leave at any time they choose? The ASGW's position on this issue is that provisions should be made to help a group member terminate in an effective way. Procedures for leaving a group are explained to all members during the initial session. Ideally, the leader and the member cooperate to determine whether a group experience is proving to be productive or counterproductive for each individual. Corey, Corey, Callanan, and Russell (1992) take the position that clients have a responsibility to the leader and other members to explain why they want to leave. There are several reasons for this policy. It can be deleterious to members to leave without having been able to discuss what they considered threatening or negative in the experience. Further, it is unfortunate for members to leave a group because of a misunderstanding about some feedback they have received. Such a termination can be harmful to group cohesion, for the members who remain may think that they caused a particular member's departure. We tell our members that they have an obligation to attend all sessions and to inform us and the group should they decide to withdraw. If members even consider withdrawing, we encourage them to bring this up for exploration in a session. We do not think it is ethical to use undue pressure to keep these members, and we are alert to other members' pressuring a person to stay. In the case that follows, consider the ethical issues involved in mandated group therapy, the failure to give members enough information to make decisions, and the use of pressure.

○ *A case of a mandatory group.*   In a prison group an inexperienced leader senses that little progress is being made. In an attempt to lessen the members' resistance, she tells them that she does not want anybody to be part of the group who is not willing to participate freely in the sessions. She neglects to inform them that their refusal to attend group sessions will be documented and will be a factor in the decision about their release. Thus, the members are operating under the assumption that they have freedom of choice, yet they have not been given the information they need to make a real choice.

- Does this leader's desire for an effective group justify her practice? Explain.
- Do you think that members can benefit from a group experience even if they are required to attend? Why or why not?
- What strategy might this leader have used to foster more effective group participation while still giving the patients true freedom of choice?

Psychological Risks

The fact that groups can be powerful catalysts for personal change means that they are also risky. Although we don't think groups should be free of risks, ethical practice demands that group practitioners at least inform prospective participants of the potential hazards involved in the group experience. Group leaders have an ethical responsibility to take precautionary measures to reduce unnecessary psychological risks. However, merely informing participants does not absolve leaders of all responsibility. Certain safeguards can be taken during the course of a group to avoid disastrous outcomes. In this section we list some of the risks that participants should know about (M. Corey & G. Corey, 1992):

- Members may experience major disruptions in their lives as a result of their work in the group.
- Group participants are often encouraged to "let it all hang out." In this quest for complete self-revelation, privacy is sometimes invaded.
- A related risk is group pressure. The participants' right not to explore certain issues or to stop at a certain point should be respected. Also, members should not be coerced into participating in an exercise.
- Scapegoating is another potential hazard in groups. Unchallenged projection and blaming can have dire effects on the target.
- Confrontation can be used or misused in groups. Harmful attacks on others should not be permitted under the guise of "sharing."
- Even though a counselor may continue to stress the necessity not to discuss with outsiders what goes on in the group, there is no guarantee that all members will respect the confidential nature of their exchanges.
- People have occasionally been physically injured in groups as a result of engaging in physical techniques. Group counselors who introduce such techniques should have enough experience and training to understand the process and possible consequences of such work.

One way of minimizing psychological risks in groups is to use a contract, in which leaders specify what their responsibilities are and members specify their commitment to the group by declaring what they're willing to do. If members and leaders operate under a contract that clarifies expectations, there is less chance for members to be exploited or damaged by a group experience.

Of course, a contract approach is not the only way to reduce potential risks, nor is it sufficient in itself to do so. One of the most important safeguards is the leader's training in group processes. Group counselors have the major responsibility for preventing needless harm to members, and to fulfill this role, they need to have a clear grasp of the boundaries of their competence. Leaders should conduct only those types of groups for which they have been sufficiently prepared. A counselor may be trained to lead a personal-growth or consciousness-raising group but be ill-prepared to embark on a therapy group. Sometimes people who have attended a few intensive groups become excited about doing this type of group as leaders, even though they have had little or no training or supervision. They soon find that they are in over their head and are unable to cope with what emerges in the group. Working with an experienced co-leader is one good way to learn and also a way of reducing potential risks.

Confidentiality in Groups

The ethical, legal, and professional aspects of confidentiality (discussed in Chapter 4) have a different application in group situations. Are members of a group under the same ethical and legal obligations as the group leader not to disclose the identities of other members or the content of what was shared in the group? The legal concept of privileged communication generally does not apply in a group setting, unless there has been a statutory exception. Therefore, group workers have the responsibility of informing the members about the ethical need for confidentiality and also the absence of legal privilege concerning what is shared in a group (Hopkins & Anderson, 1990). A few states have statutes that specifically ensure privacy in group, marital, and family therapy. These states grant privileged communications when third parties are present if the persons are instrumental in treatment, which is true of group therapy (VandeCreek, Knapp, & Herzog, 1988). From an *ethical* perspective members have an obligation to respect the communications of others in the group. For a more detailed review of the ethical dimensions of confidentiality in groups, see M. Corey and G. Corey (1992).

How to Encourage Confidentiality

Although most writers on ethical issues in group work make the point that confidentiality cannot be guaranteed, most of them also talk about the importance of teaching the members to avoid breaking confidences. Confidentiality in group situations is difficult to enforce. Because members cannot assume that anything they say or hear in the group will remain confidential, they should be able to make an informed choice about how much to reveal.

It is our position that leaders need periodically to reaffirm to group members the importance of not discussing with outsiders what has occurred in the group. In our own groups we talk with each prospective member about the necessity of maintaining confidentiality in order to establish the trust and cohesion required if participants are to reveal themselves in significant ways. We discuss this point during the screening interviews, again during the pregroup or initial meetings, at times during the course of a group when it seems appropriate, and again at termination. Because the three of us have conducted intensive residential groups in which as many as 16 participants live together for an entire week, we have been concerned about maintaining the confidential character of the group. It has been our experience that most people in our groups do not maliciously attempt to hurt others by talking with people outside the group about specific members. However, it's tempting for members to share their experience with other people, and in so doing they sometimes make inappropriate disclosures. This is particularly true of participants in intensive groups, in which participants are likely to be asked many questions when they return home. Because of this tendency to want to share with outsiders, we repeatedly caution participants in any type of group about how easily and unintentionally the confidentiality of the group can be compromised.

If you were to lead any type of group, which of the following measures might you take to ensure confidentiality? Check any of the statements that apply:

___ I'd repeatedly mention the importance of confidentiality.
___ I'd require group members to sign a statement saying that they would maintain the confidential character of the group.

___ I'd let members know that they would be asked to leave the group if they violated confidentiality.

___ I'd have a document describing the dimensions of confidentiality to which all the members could refer.

___ With the permission and knowledge of the members, I'd tape-record all the sessions.

___ I'd say very little about confidentiality and leave it up to the group members to decide how they would deal with the issue.

Exceptions to Confidentiality

The ASGW (1989) specifies that group counselors have a responsibility to define clearly what confidentiality means, explain its importance, and inform members of the difficulties involved in enforcing it. Although counselors are expected to stress the importance of confidentiality and set a norm, they are also expected to inform members about its limits. "When a group member's condition indicates that there is clear and imminent danger to the member, others, or physical property, the group counselor takes reasonable personal action and/or informs responsible authorities" (guideline 3a).

Uses and Abuses of Group Techniques

Group techniques can be used to facilitate the movement of a group and to deepen and intensify certain feelings. We think leaders should have a clear rationale for using each technique. This is an area in which theory can be a useful guide for practice.

Techniques can also be abused or used in unethical ways. Some of the ways in which leaders can employ techniques unethically are:

• using techniques with which they are unfamiliar
• using techniques to serve their own hidden agendas or to enhance their power
• using techniques whose sole purpose is to create an intensive atmosphere because of the leader's need for catharsis
• using techniques to pressure members or in the other ways rob them of dignity or the respect of others

Following are guidelines that we use in our practice to avoid abusing techniques in a group:

• There should be a therapeutic purpose and grounding in some theoretical framework.
• The client's self-exploration and self-understanding should be fostered.
• Techniques are devised for each unique client situation, and they assist the client in experimenting with some form of new behavior.
• Leaders should modify their techniques so that they are suitable for the client's cultural and ethnic background.

- Techniques are not used to cover up the leader's incompetence; rather, they are used to enhance the group process.
- Techniques are introduced in a timely and sensitive manner, and they are abandoned if they are not working.
- The tone of a leader is consistently invitational, in that members are given the freedom either to participate in or to skip a given experiment.
- It is important that leaders use techniques about which they have some knowledge and that they be aware of the potential impact of these techniques.

Although it is unrealistic to expect that leaders will always know exactly what will result from an intervention, they should know how to cope with unexpected outcomes. For example, guided fantasies into times of loneliness as a child or physical exercises designed to release anger can lead to intense emotional experiences. If leaders use such techniques, they must be ready to deal with any emotional release.

It is essential that group counselors become aware of the potential for encouraging catharsis to fulfill their own needs. The ASGW (1989) cautions leaders that their personal and professional needs are not to be met at the members' expense. Some leaders may enjoy seeing people express anger because they would like to be able to do so themselves, and so they unethically push members to get into contact with angry feelings by developing techniques to bring out such feelings and to focus the group on anger. The point is not that these are not legitimate feelings, for surely most members are at times angry. The issue is that anger was dealt with at the behest of the leader, not the members. This question ought to be raised frequently: "Whose needs are primary, and whose needs are being met—the members' or the leader's?"

Therapist Competence

The ASGW's basic principle is that "group counselors do not attempt any technique unless trained in its use or under supervision by a counselor familiar with the intervention" (guideline 10). How can leaders determine whether they are competent to use a certain technique? Although some leaders who have received training in the use of a technique may hesitate to use it (out of fear of making a mistake), other overly confident leaders without training may not have any reservations about trying out new techniques. It is useful if leaders have experienced these techniques as members of a group and have a clear rationale for using them. The guideline is "Group counselors are able to articulate a theoretical orientation that guides their practice, and they are able to provide a rationale for their interventions" (guideline 10a).

○ *A case of an inexperienced leader.* An inexperienced group leader has recently graduated from a master's degree program in counseling. As a part of his job as a community mental-health counselor, he organizes a weekly two-hour group. He realizes that his training in group approaches is limited, so he decides to attend a weekend workshop on body therapy. He does some intensive personal work himself at the workshop, and he comes away impressed with the power of what he has witnessed. He is eager to meet his group on Tuesday evening so that he can try out some of these body-oriented techniques designed to "open the feelings." (He has not been trained in these techniques in graduate school, nor is he receiving any direct supervision in the group that he is leading.)

At the next session of the group a member says "I feel choked up with pain and anger, and I don't know how to deal with my feelings." The leader intervenes by having the member lie down, while he pushes on the client's abdomen and encourages her to scream, kick, shout, and release all the feelings that she's been keeping locked up inside of her. The client becomes pale and her breathing becomes shallow and fast. She describes tingling sensations in her arms, a numbness, and a tight mouth, and she says that she is scared and cannot breathe. The leader encourages her to stay with it and get out all those pent-up feelings that are choking her up. At the same time others in the group seem frightened, and some are angry with the leader for pushing the client.

- Do you think that most leaders would be competent to use body-oriented techniques after one weekend workshop?
- Was this leader's behavior inappropriate, unethical, or both? If the leader had had a qualified supervisor at the session, would your answer be different?
- How can a conscientious group leader determine when he or she is adequately trained in the use of a technique?
- Do you agree with the ASGW guideline that group counselors should not use "any technique unless trained in its use or under supervision by a counselor familiar with the intervention?" Why or why not?

Unfinished Business

Another major issue pertaining to the use of group techniques relates to providing immediate help for any group member who shows extreme distress during or at the end of a group session, especially if techniques were used to elicit intense emotions. Although some "unfinished business" promotes growth, there is an ethical issue in the use of a technique that incites strong emotional reactions if the client is abandoned at the end of a session because time has run out. Leaders must take care to allow enough time to deal adequately with the reactions that were stimulated in a session. Techniques should not be introduced in a session when there is not enough time to work through the feelings that might result or in a setting where there is no privacy or where the physical setup would make it harmful to employ certain techniques.

Our position on the ethical use of techniques is that group leaders need to learn about potential adverse effects. One way for group leaders to learn is by taking part in group therapy themselves. By being a group member and first experiencing a range of techniques, they can develop a healthy respect for using techniques appropriately to meet the client's needs, not to enhance the therapist's ego. In our training workshops for group leaders we encourage spontaneity and inventiveness in the use of techniques, but we also stress the importance of striking a balance between creativity and irresponsible bravado.

In our opinion the reputation of group work has suffered from the actions of irresponsible practitioners, mostly those who use techniques randomly without a clear rationale. If the group leader has a sound academic background, has had extensive supervised group experience, has experienced his or her own therapy or personal-growth experience, and has a basic respect for clients, he or she is not likely to abuse techniques (Corey, Corey, Callanan, & Russell, 1992).

Issues Concerning Termination

The termination phase of a group provides an opportunity for members to clarify the meaning of their experience, to consolidate the gains they've made, and to make decisions about the new behaviors they want to carry away from the group and apply to their everyday lives. The following professional issues and questions are involved in the termination of a group:

- What responsibilities do group leaders have for assisting participants to develop a conceptual framework that will make sense of, integrate, and consolidate what they've learned in their group?
- To what degree is it the leader's responsibility to ensure that members aren't left with excessive unfinished business at the end of the group?
- How can group leaders help participants translate what they've learned as a result of the group into their daily lives? Should leaders assume that this translation will occur automatically, or must they prepare members for generalizing their learning?

As a stage in the life of the group, termination has its own meaning and significance. Yalom (1985) observes that therapy-group members tend to avoid the difficult work of terminating by ignoring or denying their concerns about it; therefore, it is the leader's task to keep them focused on the ending of their group. His view is that termination is an integral part of the therapeutic process, which if properly understood and managed can be a major force in promoting and maintaining change. In addition, therapists need to look at their feelings about the termination process, for they sometimes unnecessarily delay a member's termination because of their own perfectionistic expectations or their lack of faith in their clients' ability to function effectively without the group.

Follow-Up and Evaluation

What kind of follow-up should be provided after the termination of any group? What professional obligation does the group leader have to systematically evaluate the outcomes of a group? How can leaders help members evaluate the effectiveness of their group experience?

Follow-up group sessions are useful to the members and the group counselor as well. Both short-term follow-up (after one month) and long-term follow-up (after three months to a year) can be an invaluable measure of accountability. Because the members know that they will be coming together to evaluate their progress toward their goals, they are more willing to work actively at making changes. Participants can develop contracts during the final sessions involving actions to be taken between the termination and the follow-up session (or sessions). These sessions are valuable not only because they offer the leader an opportunity to evaluate the effectiveness of the group but also because they provide members with the opportunity to gain a more realistic assessment of the group's impact. Members have a chance to express and work through their reactions to the group experience, and they can report on the degree to which they have fulfilled their contracts since they left the group. They also have a chance to receive additional feedback and reinforcement from the other members.

Follow-up group sessions provide an opportunity to evaluate both the process and the outcomes of a group experience. The ethical guidelines of the ASGW encourage counselors to "make every attempt to engage in ongoing assessment and to design follow-up procedures for their groups" (guideline 14). More specifically, group counselors need to assist members in assessing their own progress, evaluate the group's experience throughout its life, and monitor their style of modeling in the group.

Other Ethical Guidelines for Group Work

In this section we list some other ethical guidelines as developed by the ASGW (1989) and briefly comment on these issues.

Experimentation and Research

"Group members are informed by the group counselor of unusual or experimental procedures that might be expected in their group experience" (guideline 1f). If group practitioners intend to write journal articles or books, it is essential that they take measures to safeguard the confidentiality of material explored in their groups. The same care should be taken to disguise identities if the leaders talk with colleagues about their groups. Those who do group work in institutions, such as community mental-health clinics and schools, usually prepare reports for the institution. Group members have a right to know what kinds of information will appear in an institutional report.

Equitable Treatment of Members

"Group counselors make every reasonable effort to treat each member individually and equally" (guideline 8). Leaders sometimes burden themselves with the unrealistic expectation that they should be absolutely impartial at all times to all members. They may think that they should like each member to the same degree, give each member equal time, and be equally interested in each. If they do not feel this universal caring, some leaders develop guilt feelings.

What seems most important in reference to this guideline is that leaders do not cling to initial impressions of a member and that they keep themselves open to changing their reactions. Although it is true that some members may present themselves in ways that make it difficult to like them or find them interesting, a leader who hopes to have a therapeutic effect on these members should give each an equal chance of participating in the group.

It is the leader's responsibility to help members use the resources within the group to an optimal degree. At times certain members may display problematic behaviors such as monopolizing time, storytelling, asking many questions, making interpretations for others, and chronically jumping in to give advice or reassurance when it is not appropriate. The group leader does not have to take full responsibility for these interventions with difficult members, for the group also has a share of the responsibility. But it is the leader's task to make interventions so that some members do not sap the energy of the group and make it difficult for others to do productive work.

Personal Relationships

"Group counselors avoid dual relationships with group members that might impair their objectivity and professional judgment, as well as those which are likely to compromise a group member's ability to participate fully in the group" (guideline 9). As a part of this guideline, group leaders are cautioned not to misuse their professional role and power to promote personal or social contacts with group members. Nor should they use their professional relationship with group members to further their personal interests. Sexual intimacies between counselors and group members are unethical.

Although some behaviors may appear clearly unethical (such as sexual misconduct), certain other forms of nonsexual dual relationships may be less clear-cut. What criteria can a group leader use to determine the degree of appropriateness of personal and social relationships with group members? A key question is whether the social relationship is interfering with the therapeutic relationship. The crux of the matter is to avoid abusing one's power and misusing one's professional role to make personal or social contacts.

In the process of being honest about one's motivations, a group leader needs to keep in mind that there is a tendency on the part of some members to glorify the group leader and, in doing so, to lessen their own power. Ethical group leaders do not take advantage of this tendency, nor do they exploit group members in the service of their ego needs.

Promoting the Autonomy of Members

"Depending upon the purpose of participation in the group, counselors promote termination of members from the group in the most efficient period of time" (guideline 13). Ultimately, the goal of group participation is helping members make their own decisions and function autonomously. However, some group leaders actually promote the dependence of their members. They may need to be needed, may depend on their work as a confirmation of their worth, or may simply need to make money. Whatever their reasons for keeping members dependent, group leaders need to look continuously at their practices to determine whether they are fostering the growth of their clients.

Alcohol and Drugs

Group counselors emphasize the need to promote full psychological functioning and presence among group members. They inquire from prospective group members whether they are using any kind of drug or medication that may affect functioning in the group. They do not permit any use of alcohol and/or illegal drugs during group sessions and they discourage the use of alcohol and/or drugs (legal or illegal) prior to group meetings which may affect the physical or emotional presence of the member or other group members [guideline 1h].

Although many group leaders agree that using alcohol or drugs before or during group sessions is not productive and do not condone such practices, they may have some difficulty in dealing with members who come to a session under the influence. It is possible that leaders may not take a stand out of the fear of being seen as authoritarian. Or they may simply decide to tolerate members who come to sessions under the influence of drugs or alcohol because they feel powerless to change the situation. It is important that group leaders be prepared to give a rationale for any "no-drugs-or-alcohol" rule, rather than simply laying it down as an edict. Members might be testing the limits of the leader by coming to a session somewhat inebriated or stoned. If leaders give in to the pressure and do not challenge this testing, they are likely to lose the respect of the members. The setting of realistic limits by leaders can be a way to gain the respect that is necessary to conduct an effective group.

Values in Group Counseling

Group counselors are sometimes timid about making their values known, lest they influence the direction that the members are likely to take. Practitioners are not value-neutral, however, for the interventions they use are based on values. What is critical is an awareness of how values operate and influence strategies.

The ASGW's ethical guideline states "Group counselors develop an awareness of their own values and needs and the potential impact they have on the interventions likely to be made" (guideline 7). Although guideline 7a cautions group workers to avoid imposing their values on members, it does suggest that leaders consider situations when it might be appropriate to expose their own beliefs, decisions, needs, and values. The key issue is that leaders should not short-circuit the members' exploration. Rather, the leader's central function is to help members find answers that are congruent with their own values. The leader's role is to provide a context in which members can examine their feelings and values and arrive at solutions that are best for them.

From our perspective, the leader's function is to challenge members to evaluate their behavior to determine how it is working for them, not to advise them on the proper course to adopt. If members come to the realization that what they are doing is not serving them well, it is appropriate for the leader to challenge them to develop alternative ways of behaving that will enable them to reach their goals.

An area of particular importance is awareness of cultural diversity. The ASGW specifies that "group counselors are aware of their own values and assumptions and how these apply in a multicultural context" (guideline 7e). In working with groups characterized by a diverse membership, counselors need to be aware of the assumptions they make about ethnic and cultural groups, and they should adapt their practices to the needs of the members. They need to be watchful of tendencies to treat people on the basis of stereotypes. It is critical that leaders become aware of their biases based on age, disability, ethnicity, gender, race, religion, or sexual preference (guideline 7f).

We suggest that you refer to the discussion of value conflicts in Chapter 3 and consider specific areas in which you might be inclined to impose your values in the groups you lead. In an article on the role of group leaders' values, we describe a number of issues that are likely to surface in a group, such as gay and lesbian preferences, divorce, religion, cultural issues, abortion, and extramarital affairs (Corey, Corey, & Callanan, 1990). It would be good to reflect on any tendencies to lead your clients in a certain direction and to think about ways of minimizing the chances of imposing your values on them.

The Consultation and Referral Process

Group counselors need to be aware of their limitations in working with certain types of clients. The willingness to consult with other professionals demonstrates good faith on the practitioner's part. It is a good practice for leaders to explain to members their policies about consultation. When are they likely to consult? When they do consult, what measures do they take to protect confidentiality? Are they willing to have between-session consultations with group members? When and how might they refer?

Below are a few of the ASGW's guidelines pertaining to the consultation and referral process:

- Leaders should inform members of their policies about between-session consultations.
- It is a good idea for members to bring the issues discussed during between-session consultations into the group if appropriate.
- Group counselors should seek consultation and supervision when they are faced with ethical concerns or difficulties that interfere with the carrying out of leadership functions.
- Leaders should develop a sensitivity to making appropriate referrals.
- Leaders should learn the resources within the community and should help members make use of professional assistance, when required.

As we discussed earlier, one measure of protection against a malpractice suit is to demonstrate that consultation procedures were used in dealing with ethical dilemmas. If group leaders consult a supervisor or other professional, they are demonstrating good clinical practice, adhering to ethical guidelines, and minimizing their chances of malpractice.

Chapter Summary

Along with the growing popularity of group approaches to counseling and therapy comes a need for ethical and professional guidelines for those who lead groups.

There are many types of groups, and there are many possible uses of groups in various settings. Our attempt has been to select the issues that are related to most groups. Some of these questions are: How does a leader's theoretical view of groups influence the way that a group is structured? What are some key elements in recruiting, screening, selecting, and preparing group members? What ethical, professional, legal, and practical issues concerning confidentiality are involved in any type of group? To what degree should participants be prepared for a group before the group begins? What are some ethical issues in the selection and training of group leaders? In what ways can group techniques be used or abused? What responsibility do group leaders have in terms of follow-up and evaluation? With respect to these and other issues, we have stressed the importance of formulating your own views on ethical practice in leading groups.

Suggested Activities

1. Replicate the initial session of a group. Two students can volunteer to be co-leaders, and approximately ten other students can become group members. Assume that the group is a personal-growth group that will meet for a predetermined number of weeks. The co-leaders' job is to orient and prepare the members by describing the group's purpose, by giving an overview of group-process concepts, and by talking about ground rules for effective group participation. If time allows, members can express any fears and expectations they have about being involved in the group, and they can also raise questions they would like to explore. This exercise is designed to give you practice in dealing with concerns that both group leaders and members often have at the beginning of a group.

2. Practice conducting screening interviews for potential group members. One person volunteers to conduct interviews, and another student can role-play a potential group member. Allow about ten minutes for the interview. Afterward, the prospective client can talk about what it was like to be interviewed, and the group leader can share his or her experience. This exercise can be done with the entire class watching, in small groups, or in dyads.

3. Suppose you're expected as part of your job to lead a group composed of people who are *required* to be part of the group and who really don't want to be there. How will the nature of the group affect your approach? What might you do differently with this group, compared with a group of people who want the experience? This is a good situation to role-play in class, with several students playing the reluctant members while others practice dealing with them.

4. You're leading a counseling group with high school students on their campus. One day a member comes to the group obviously under the influence of drugs. He is incoherent and disruptive. How do you deal with him? What might you

say or do? Discuss in class how you would deal with this situation, or demonstrate how you might respond by having a fellow student role-play the part of the adolescent.

5. Again, assume that you're leading a high school counseling group. An angry father who gave written permission for his son's participation comes to your office and demands to know what's going on in your group. He is convinced that his son's participation in the group is an invasion of family privacy. As a group leader, how would you deal with his anger? To make the situation more real and interesting, someone can role-play the father.

6. The issue of selecting a co-leader for a group is an important one, for not all matches of co-leaders are productive. For this exercise form dyads and negotiate with your partner to determine whether the two of you would be effective if you were to lead a group together. You might discuss matters such as potential power struggles, competitiveness, compatibility of views and philosophy, your differing styles and how they might complement or interfere with each other, and other issues that you think would have a bearing on your ability to work as a team.

7. Form a panel in class to explore the uses and abuses of group techniques. The panel can look at specific ways in which group techniques can be used to enhance learning, as well as ways in which they can be misused.

8. Review the excerpts from *Ethical Guidelines for Group Counselors* (ASGW, 1989) that are listed in this chapter. Which of these guidelines do you consider to be most important? Are there any guidelines with which you do not agree? Form small groups in your class to discuss specific guidelines that stimulate the greatest controversy.

Suggested Readings

For a more detailed description of the various groups and the differences among them, see M. Corey and G. Corey (1992) and Gazda (1989). For training standards for group workers see ASGW (1991). For ethical guidelines for group counselors see ASGW (1989). On ethical and professional issues in screening and preparation of group members, see Yalom (1985); Corey et al. (1992); and M. Corey and G. Corey (1992). On training group leaders in ethical decision making, see Gumaer and Scott (1985). On the role of the group leader's values in group work, see Corey et al. (1990). For a discussion of ethical issues in outpatient group therapy with sex offenders see Aubrey and Dougher (1990). For a discussion of dual-relationship issues in the training of group counselors see Lloyd (1990), Forester-Miller and Duncan (1990), Gumaer and Martin (1990), Williams (1990), Merta and Sisson (1991), and Herlihy and Corey (1992). For a discussion of legal issues in group work see Paradise and Kirby (1990).

CHAPTER FOURTEEN

The Counselor in the Community

Pre-Chapter Self-Inventory

Directions: For each statement, indicate the response that most closely identifies your beliefs and attitudes. Use the following code:

5 = I *strongly agree* with this statement.
4 = I *agree* with this statement.
3 = I am *undecided* about this statement.
2 = I *disagree* with this statement.
1 = I *strongly disagree* with this statement.

____ 1. In general, it's important to include members of the client's environment in his or her treatment.

____ 2. Counselors ought to take an active role in dealing with the social and political conditions that are related to human suffering.

____ 3. Mental-health experts should devote more of their energies to preventing emotional and behavioral disorders, rather than treating them.

____ 4. With increasing attention being paid to the community mental-health approach, the role of the professional must be expanded to include a variety of indirect services to clients as well as direct clinical services.

____ 5. The use of paraprofessionals is a valuable and effective way of dealing with the shortage of professional help.

____ 6. Paraprofessionals who receive adequate training and close supervision are capable of providing most of the direct services that professionals now provide.

____ 7. In working with minority groups in the community, counselors must be skilled in out-of-office strategies such as outreach, consulting, and working as an agent for change.

____ 8. I generally don't like to challenge the people I work for.

____ 9. It's possible to work within the framework of a system and still do the things I'm convinced are most important to do.

____ 10. When I think of working in some agency or institution, I feel a sense of powerlessness about initiating any real change in that organization.

____ 11. I frequently have good ideas and proposals, and I see myself as willing to do the work necessary to translate these plans into actual programs.

____ 12. If I'm honest with myself, I can see that I might have a tendency to blame external sources for a failure on my part to do more professionally.

____ 13. I see myself as a fighter in a system, in the sense that I'll work to change things I don't approve of.

____ 14. Although I might be unable to bring about drastic changes in an institution or system, I do feel confident that I can make changes within the boundaries of my own position.

____ 15. I can see that I might fall into complacency and rarely question what I'm doing or how I could do my work more effectively.

____ 16. Counselors who no longer raise questions or struggle with ethical concerns have stopped growing professionally.

____ 17. It would be unethical to accept a position with an agency whose central aims I disagreed with philosophically.

___ 18. Ethical concerns are not simply answered once and for all; to become an ethical practitioner, I must be willing to continually raise questions about what I'm doing.

___ 19. As a counselor I'm part of a system, and I have a responsibility to work toward changing those aspects of the system that I think need changing.

___ 20. I feel a personal need for meaningful contact with colleagues so that I don't become excessively narrow in my thinking.

Introduction

Working with people who come for counseling is only one way in which professionals can use their skills to promote mental and emotional health. Many people would argue that professional helpers can foster real and lasting changes only if they have an impact on the total milieu of people's lives. The aspirations and difficulties of clients intertwine with those of many other people and, ultimately, with those of the community at large. For example, Herr (1991) advocates an active role for mental-health counselors in social planning and politics. Because neither individual behavior nor the counseling process occurs in a political, economic, or social vacuum, he sees a need for a broadened view of counseling as a sociopolitical instrument designed to bridge the gap between an individual and the environment.

In this chapter we focus on some special responsibilities of counselors. Do counselors see themselves as working with individuals in a community as though they were in private practice? Or do they see themselves as *community* counselors, with a broader responsibility to address the conditions that create problems for individuals who come to see them? Although some of the issues we present pertain mainly to counselors employed by a community agency, no professional can work in isolation, and all can benefit by knowing how to work with community resources.

We begin by looking at the community mental-health movement, an approach that emphasizes understanding clients by examining their social setting. The movement focuses on ways of changing the environment, rather than merely helping people adapt to their circumstances. Then we take up an issue of particular importance to the community mental-health worker—namely, how the system affects the counselor.

The Community Mental-Health Orientation

Many therapists see a need for new approaches to augment the process of individual therapy. Because only a relatively small number of people can be reached effectively by traditional therapeutic approaches, these practitioners support the idea of innovative measures to make maximum use of the professional resources available. The need for diverse and readily accessible treatment programs has been a key factor in the development of the community mental-health orientation.

The practice of counseling does not take place in a vacuum isolated from the larger social and political influences of society (Dinkmeyer, 1991; Herr, 1991; Ivey & Rigazio-DiGilio, 1991; & D. W. Sue & D. Sue, 1990). It is not a matter of whether to focus on the individual's dynamics or the environmental factors that are causing or contributing to the problems of many groups in society. A process that considers both aspects is often most beneficial to clients.

Herr (1991) clearly presents a case for developing broader strategies that do not ignore sociopolitical factors. Changing client populations, society's pressing problems, and the impact of advanced technology challenge mental-health counselors to develop problem-solving techniques that draw from various disciplines (Brooks & Gerstein, 1990; Gerstein & Brooks, 1990; Ivey & Rigazio-DiGilio, 1991). Herr's comments reflect the traditional social-work perspective of working with the "person in the environment." The mental-health professions are converging in their views of conditions that have multiple causes.

According to D. W. Sue and D. Sue (1990), it is wrong to assume that counseling is morally, ethically, and politically neutral. Sue and Sue maintain that people are thinking, feeling, behaving, social, cultural, and political beings and that counselors should recognize the totality of human experience. From their perspective, ignoring the ethical and social dimensions of counseling has resulted in (1) the subjugation of the culturally different, (2) a perpetuation of the view that minorities are inherently pathological, (3) a furthering of racist practices in counseling, and (4) a failure to accept responsibility for avoiding social action to rectify inequities in the system. Sue and Sue call for developing intervention strategies that deal with the societal factors that adversely affect the lives of many members of minority groups. Rather than focusing primarily on the problems within the individual, they suggest, counselors should actively intervene to attack environmental stressors. This approach calls for counselors to take on various roles, including consultant, outreach worker, ombudsman, and facilitator of indigenous support systems.

Lewis and Lewis (1989) define *community counseling* as "a multifaceted approach combining direct and indirect services to help community members live more effectively and to prevent the problems most frequently faced by those who use the services" (p. 10). They describe the activities that make up a comprehensive community-counseling program as having the following four distinct facets:

1. Direct community services in the form of *preventive education* are geared to the population at large. Examples of these programs include life-planning workshops, value-clarification seminars, and interpersonal-skills training. Because the emphasis is on prevention, these programs help people develop a wider range of competencies.

2. Indirect community services are attempts to change the social environment to meet the needs of the population as a whole and are carried out by influencing social policy. Community counseling deals with the victims of poverty, sexism, and racism, which typically leave people feeling powerless. The emphasis is on *influencing policymakers* and bringing about positive changes within the community.

3. Direct client services focus on *outreach activities* to a population that might be at risk for developing mental-health problems. Community counselors provide help to clients either facing crises or dealing with ongoing stressors that impair their coping ability. According to Herr (1991), one of the future challenges for the mental-health counselor will be to work with schools, churches, and employers in developing programs for employee assistance, substance-abuse treatment, and stress management for a variety of at-risk groups.

4. Indirect client services consist of *client advocacy* involving active intervention for an individual or a group. The community counselor works to empower disenfranchised groups that have become split off from the mainstream community; these include the unemployed, the homeless, the handicapped, and AIDS victims. In writing about challenges for the future, Herr (1991) predicts increased opportunities for mental-health counselors to play an advocacy role for individuals at risk. He believes that counselors need to work for effective day-care programs, interventions to deal with child abuse or spouse abuse, strategies for early identification and treatment, parent education, and formal programs to develop self-esteem and coping skills.

Educating the Community

There will always be room for individual services and private practices in counseling, but these in themselves are not sufficient, because there are systemic problems that private practitioners are not reaching. As a consequence, the helping professions need to think of the special needs of a larger community that are not being addressed.

There are many reasons why people do not make use of available resources: they may not be aware of their existence; they may not be able to afford these services; they may have misconceptions about the nature and purpose of counseling; they may be reluctant to recognize their problems; they may harbor the attitude that they should be able to take charge of their lives on their own; or they may perceive that these resources are not intended for them because the services are administered in a culturally insensitive way.

One goal of the community approach is to educate the public and attempt to change the attitudes of the community about mental health. Perhaps the most important task in this area is to demystify the notion of mental illness. Many people still cling to archaic notions of emotional disturbance. They may make a clear demarcation between people whom they perceive as "crazy" and those whom they perceive as "normal." Misconceptions that are still widespread include the notion that once people suffer from mental illness, they can never be cured; the idea that people with emotional or behavioral disorders are merely deficient in "willpower"; and the belief that the mentally ill are always dangerous and should be separated from the community lest they "contaminate" or harm others. Professionals face real challenges in combating these myths.

Psychotherapy is another area that needs to be demystified. Some of the misconceptions about psychotherapy include the beliefs that it is some form of magic, that it is only for people with extreme problems, that therapists provide clients with answers, that therapy is only for weak people, and that people should be able to solve their problems without professional help. These misconceptions often reinforce the resistance that people already have toward seeking professional help. Unless professionals actively work on presenting counseling services in a way that is understandable to the community at large, many people who could benefit from professional help may not seek it out.

Influencing Policymakers

The need for community programs is compounded by societal problems such as poverty, the plight of the homeless, AIDS, absent parents, child abuse, unemployment, tension and stress, alienation, addictions to drugs and alcohol, delinquency, and neglect of the elderly. These are merely a few of the formidable challenges that communities face in preventing and treating human problems.

At times, it seems that these challenges facing community workers are overwhelming, especially with current constraints on funding. An overriding ethical issue is the continual whittling away of state and federal financing for educational and social programs. How can even those most dedicated community workers continue to develop and maintain social programs if they are constantly faced with the likelihood that their programs will be cut back or canceled? In community agencies that are facing elimination, there is little room for the staff members to come up with innovative programs when they are concerned with mere survival. The real challenge is to persuade those who control funding to spend at least as much of the federal budget on prevention of human misery as they spend on military programs.

○ ***A case of funding and political pressure.***   Susan is the director of a community clinic in an inner-city neighborhood. Her agency provides birth-control counseling and funding for abortion for low-income women. As the time is approaching for her to submit her request for financing to the state government, she is contacted by a local politician who is adamantly opposed to the provision of these services. He informs her that if she requests funding for them, he will do everything in his power not only to deny the money but also to reduce the overall funding for the agency. He further says that if she informs anyone of his intent, he will deny it. Faced with this prospect of radically reduced funds, Susan omits her request for money for birth-control and abortion services.

- In light of the threats that were made, did Susan act in the best interest of her community? Can you see any justification for her action? Was her decision ethical?
- Would it be ethical for Susan to go along with the politician's request but later on, when the funding for the other programs was acquired, to divert some of the money for abortion and birth-control services?
- How ethically bound was Susan to disclose the coercive attempts of the influential politician, even though it was only her word against his?
- What other strategies might Susan have used? (One example is getting in touch with similar agencies.)

○ *A case of a community agency with a hidden agenda.*   The Family Wellness Clinic advertises a list of services pertaining to family well-being. Among the services is pregnancy counseling for unwed mothers. What it does not advertise is that all the pregnancy counselors are instructed to promote maintaining the pregnancy with the option of adoption. Clients are not informed that no other options will be suggested.

- Is the Family Wellness Clinic guilty of unethical practice?
- Do consumers have a right before they seek the services of an agency to know its orientation? Does an absence of information constitute a lack of informed consent? Does it promote the self-determination of clients?
- If the clinic was funded and staffed by a local church whose stance on birth control and abortion was well known, would that make a difference from an ethical standpoint?

The Outreach Approach

Effective outreach strategies are particularly important in reaching ethnic minorities because of their traditional mistrust of primarily white mental-health professionals who have often mislabeled minorities and excluded them from services. The complex issues involved in working with minority groups within the framework of the majority community have been well documented in the literature (Atkinson, Morten, & Sue, 1989; Levine & Padilla, 1980; Pedersen, 1988; Pedersen, Draguns, Lonner, & Trimble, 1989; D. W. Sue & D. Sue, 1990). If practitioners hope to reach a cultural group different from their own, they must acquire a broad understanding of diverse client populations.

Community counselors might imagine themselves doing more outreach work in the environment of their clients. They might function in a public-housing tract, at a hospital bedside, at a place of work, or in other places where clients conduct their lives. The outreach approach could include developmental and educational efforts such as skills training, stress management, and consultation in a variety of settings. This shift in the therapist's role truly involves a challenge, for the *community* counselor must see beyond the individual's problems and look for the factors that contribute to these problems. The traditional approach tends to treat dysfunctions as belonging to the individual with a corresponding tendency to teach people how to adjust to the "realities" of living in a society. In contrast, the community-counseling approach assesses the dysfunctions of the larger system and teaches individuals ways of empowering themselves so that they can change some of the inequities in society (Lewis & Lewis, 1989).

Client Advocacy

It is our view that an increasing number of people, unable to cope with the demands of their environment, are becoming receptive to the idea of professional assistance. As more people overcome the stigma attached to seeking psychological help, the demand for community services increases. In this climate, it is important that counselors demonstrate a willingness to deal with clients' economic survival from the outset. Too often, counselors ignore the fact that before people can move toward growth and actualization, their basic needs must be met. Psychotherapy can no longer afford to be tailor-made for the upper middle class. People who are unable to afford the services of professionals in private practice are entitled to adequate treatment. Consequently, a community-counseling approach is needed to serve people of all ages and backgrounds and with all types and degrees of problems.

It is clear that taking a community approach to mental health involves abandoning the view that the role of practitioners is to sit back and wait for change to occur. The community-counseling model challenges practitioners to find new ways of organizing and delivering services. A broader conception of the practitioner's role might include the following:

- developing abilities that help one support the needs of minority groups in the community
- actively reaching out to people with special needs
- initiating programs aimed at preventing problems rather than merely treating them
- drawing on and improving the skills of paraprofessionals and laypeople to meet the many different needs of clients
- developing strategies to deal effectively with problems such as drug and alcohol abuse, child sexual and physical abuse, and domestic violence
- attempting to develop strategies that will empower the disenfranchised in the community
- consulting with a variety of social agencies about programs in gerontology, welfare, child care, and rehabilitation and helping community workers apply psychological knowledge in their work
- evaluating human-services programs to assess agencies' intervention efforts
- advocating public and private initiatives that promote the total well-being of clients

How You Can Become Involved in the Community

It is easy for counselors to believe that they can effectively meet the needs of their clients through one-to-one sessions in an office, but many clients' needs are not met that way. We suggest that you consider your responsibility to teach clients to use the resources available to them in their communities. What follows is a list of things you might do to link your clients to the environment in which they live. Rate each of these activities, using the following code:

A = I would do this routinely.
B = I would do this occasionally.
C = I would do this rarely.

___ 1. I would familiarize myself with available community resources so that I could refer my clients to appropriate sources of further help. I would follow up to see whether clients had been helped.

_____ 2. With my clients' permission, I would contact people who had a direct influence on their lives.

_____ 3. I would try to arrange sessions with clients and loved ones so that we could explore ways of changing certain relationships.

_____ 4. As a part of the counseling process, I would teach my clients how to take advantage of the support systems in the community.

_____ 5. I would get involved in community action and work to influence public policy as a way of dealing with forces that limit the competence of community members.

_____ 6. I would work actively with groups that were trying to help themselves by sharing my human-relations skills.

_____ 7. I would help coordinate groups working to bring about change.

_____ 8. After observing a variety of informal groups to learn about the values and beliefs of a given culture, I would design outreach programs that were a natural extension of these informal helping networks.

_____ 9. I would fight against dehumanization, mainly by working to eliminate constraints in the social environment and to create opportunities.

_____ 10. I would encourage self-help and voluntary efforts while working to make the community's helping network more responsive.

_____ 11. I would suggest homework assignments or use other techniques to get clients thinking about ways to apply what they had learned in individual sessions to their everyday lives.

_____ 12. I would use community leaders in setting up liaisons with other professional practitioners and agencies.

_____ 13. I would train key people of various cultural groups in peer-counseling skills so that they could work with groups that might resist seeking professional services from an agency.

_____ 14. I would consider joining some type of informal group of another culture so that I could better understand a different world (examples: a church group, a community group, a social group).

_____ 15. I would actively support and campaign for politicians who promoted mental-health programs.

Now think of other options for encouraging your clients to find ways of meeting their needs besides the traditional approaches of individual and group counseling.

The Use of Paraprofessionals

The question of how best to deliver psychological services to the people who are most in need of them is a controversial one. It is clear that there are not enough professionally licensed practitioners to meet the demand for psychological assistance. Moreover, mental-health services have not always been available to those unable to pay. Faced with these realities, many in the mental-health field have concluded that nonprofessionals should be given the training and supervision they need to provide some psychological services. There has therefore been a trend toward the use of paraprofessionals in counseling and related fields. Service agencies have discovered that paraprofessionals can indeed provide some services as effectively as full professionals, for much lower salaries.

Not all mental-health professionals are enthusiastic about the paraprofessional movement. Some point to the danger that inadequately trained people might do more harm than good; others contend that the poor will receive inferior service; still others fear that more and more paraprofessionals will be allowed to practice without the close supervision and intensive training they need.

There are three general types of nontraditional mental-health workers:

1. Many community colleges offer two-year programs in the human services. Students in these programs receive specialized training that is aimed at preparing them to work in community mental-health centers, hospitals, and other human-service agencies. In addition, many colleges and universities have established four-year undergraduate programs in human services that stress practical experience, training, and supervision in mental-health work.

2. Lay volunteers from the community are also receiving training and supervision in therapeutic intervention with a wide range of clients. These volunteers work on hot lines, co-lead groups, and engage in other supportive activities.

3. The use of former patients is another way of meeting the increasing demand for mental-health services. Former addicts play a role through substance-abuse programs in rehabilitating others who are addicted to drugs. Besides helping alleviate the shortage of personnel, these nonprofessionals may actually be more effective in reaching certain people, because they have experienced similar problems and learned to deal with them successfully.

A large part of the success of community mental-health programs will depend on these nontraditional workers' receiving the training and supervision they need to develop the skills for effective intervention. Although practitioners are often trained in psychotherapeutic techniques, they may not have sufficient experience or training in working with various racial, ethnic, and socioeconomic groups.

The trend toward the increased use of paraprofessionals means that professionals will have to assume new and expanding roles. Mental-health professionals can be expected to spend less time in providing direct services to clients so that they will have time for teaching and consulting with community workers. Rather than devoting the bulk of their time to one-to-one counseling, they may need to offer in-service workshops for paraprofessionals and volunteer workers. Other activities could include educating the public about the nature of mental health, consulting, working as agents for change in the community, designing new programs, conducting research, and evaluating existing programs.

Consultation is an approach that allows mental-health professionals to offer a wide array of assistance on the individual, group, institutional, and community levels. Much of the work of consulting in agencies deals with training paraprofessionals and even lay volunteer workers. For example, Marianne Corey provided training for lay helpers in a church group who did grief counseling. This consulting took the form of teaching volunteers basic listening and attending skills, as well as ways to assess their limitations and to make appropriate referrals.

Working within a System

One of the major challenges of counselors who work in the community is to learn how to make the system work both for themselves as professionals and for the clients they serve. One of the reasons that working in a system can put an added strain on the counselor is that those providing financing may require monumental amounts of paperwork to justify continued funding. Another source of strain is the counselor's relationships with those who administer the agency or institution, who may have long forgotten the practicalities involved in providing direct services to clients. On the other hand, practitioners who deal with clients directly may have little appreciation for the intricacies with which administrators must contend in managing their programs. Thus, if communication is inadequate, as it often is, tension is inevitable.

Many professionals struggle with the issue of how to work within a system while retaining their dignity, vitality, and convictions. The most important component in any effort to bring about change is the attitude one takes. When people focus on what cannot be changed, they promote powerlessness and helplessness. When they focus, instead, on the things that can be changed, they foster a sense of power that allows for progress. Although working in any organization can be frustrating, we've observed a tendency of some counselors to put the blame too readily on institutions when their efforts to help others don't succeed. Although bureaucratic obstacles can certainly make it difficult to carry out sound ideas, it is possible to learn ways of working within an institution with dignity and self-respect. Consequently, we emphasize the need for honest self-examination in determining the degree to which the "system" is actually hindering you as you try to put your ideas into practice.

Relationships between the Counselor and the Agency

In addition to their degrees, training, and professional competencies, counselors working in the community must also have the ability to deal with the rules and regulations of agencies. In speaking about agencies and organizations, we are referring to resources such as these:

- an AIDS hospice
- a city or county mental-health agency
- a free clinic
- a church counseling agency
- a school system (elementary or secondary)
- a college counseling center
- a health-promotion program
- a state mental hospital
- a community halfway house

Counselors typically have little say in the formulation of agency policies. In comparison with counseling in private practice, they must mediate not only with clients but also with the system and are limited by what they can do because of the agency's rules and regulations. The system may be so cumbersome and difficult for clients to work with that the counselor has to assist them in obtaining resources through lobbying, advocacy, referrals, and networking.

As a counselor, you need to decide how you will work within a system and how you can be most effective. It is imperative that you investigate an agency's philosophy before you accept a position, to determine whether the agency's norms, values, and expectations coincide with what you expect from a position. If there is not a general congruence of values, you are almost certain to experience conflicts. Some counselors who are dissatisfied with an agency or the system decide to subvert it in as many ways as they can. Others conform to institutional policies for fear of losing their positions. Some find ways of making compromises between institutional demands and their personal requirements; others find it impossible to retain their personal and professional dignity and still work within an institutional framework. It will be up to you to find your own answers to questions such as these:

- To what degree is my philosophy of helping compatible with the agency where I work?
- How can I meet the requirements of an institution and at the same time do what I most believe in?
- What stance will I take in dealing with a system?
- In what ways can I work to change a particular system?
- At what point does the price of attempting to work within an organized structure become too high? Can I work within an institutional framework and still retain my dignity?
- What special ethical obligations am I likely to face in working in a system?
- Am I serving my clients in the best way possible in private practice if I do not develop community contacts?

○ *A case of racism and ignoring the problem.* Ronnie, an African-American student, moves with his family into a mostly white community and attends high school there. Almost immediately, he becomes the butt of racial jokes and social isolation. A teacher notices his isolation and sends him to the school counselor for remedial attention. It is evident to the counselor that he is being discriminated against, not only by many of the students but also by some of the faculty. The counselor has no reason to doubt the information provided by Ronnie, because she is aware of racism in the school and the community. She determines that it would be much more practical to help him ignore the prejudice and tolerate it, rather than to change the racist attitudes of the school and community. Her goal is to get him to adjust, rather than to try to correct a social ill.

- What do you think of the counselor's decision? What are its ethical ramifications? Does she have an ethical obligation to change community attitudes?
- What other courses of action could she have taken? What would you do in this situation?

- Does a school system have an ethical obligation to attempt to change attitudes of the community that discriminate against some of its citizens?

In this case, the counselor may be experiencing a conflict of values and may fear reprisals if she acts on values that are not shared by many in the community. She may want to do what is needed to promote the well-being of clients, yet she may be struggling with self-doubts and with her anxiety about not being accepted by the faculty. If you were consulting with this counselor, what might you say to her?

The Tendency to Avoid Responsibility

We've alluded to the tendency to blame institutions for failing to implement effective programs. So often we hear the "If only it weren't for —" argument, which absolves the speaker of responsibility and diminishes his or her personal power at the same time. Take a moment now to reflect on some typical statements of this kind, and apply them to yourself. How likely are you to resort to these statements as a way of deflecting responsibility to external sources? Rate each one, using the following code:

A = I feel this way often, and I can hear myself making this statement frequently.
B = I feel this way at times, and I might be inclined to say this occasionally.
C = I rarely feel this way.
D = I can't see myself using this statement as a way of absolving myself of personal responsibility.

___ 1. You have to play politics if you want to get your programs through.
___ 2. I can't do what I really want to do, because my director or supervisor wouldn't allow it.
___ 3. If the community were more receptive to mental-health programs, my projects would be far more successful than they are.
___ 4. I'm not succeeding because my clients aren't motivated.
___ 5. I can't really say what I think, because I'd lose my job.
___ 6. The bureaucratic system makes it almost impossible to develop innovative and meaningful programs.
___ 7. If I were given more time off, I could develop exciting projects; as it is now, all my time is consumed by busywork.
___ 8. I'm not free to pursue my own interests in my job, because the institution dictates what my interests will be.
___ 9. The system makes it difficult to engage in the kind of counseling that would produce real change.
___ 10. My own individuality and professional identity must be subordinate to the policies of the institution if I expect to survive in the system.

What other statements might you make about your difficulties as a professional working in a system?

Counselors who put the blame on the system when they fail to act in accordance with their beliefs are bound to experience a growing sense of powerlessness. This feeling is sometimes expressed in words such as these: "I really can't change anything at all. I may as well just do what's expected and play the game." The temptation to submit to this stance of professional impotence constitutes a real ethical concern. It is an attitude that feeds on itself, to the detriment of clients.

Another way of evading personal responsibility is to settle into a soft rut. We've seen many counselors who have found a niche in the system and who have learned to survive with a minimum of effort. In order to remain comfortable, they continue to do the same thing over and over for weeks, months, and years. They rarely question the effectiveness of their efforts or give much thought to ways of reaching a greater number of people more effectively. They neither question the system in which they're involved nor develop new projects that would give them a change of pace. Although we appreciate their difficulties, we think that this complacency is just as deadly a form of powerlessness as the defeated feeling of those who decide they can't really change things.

Defeatism and complacency both cheat clients. For this reason, we ask you to examine the ethics of counselors who become infected by these attitudes. And we encourage you to think about the following questions to clarify your position on ways in which you could increase your chances of assuming power within the system:

- What questions would you want to raise in a job interview?
- What ideas that you have wanted to put into practice have been resisted?
- What would you do if the organization for which you worked instituted a policy to which you were strongly opposed?
- What would you do if you strongly believed that some fundamental changes needed to be made in your institution but your colleagues disagreed?
- What would you do if your supervisor continually blocked most of your activities, despite your efforts to keep him or her informed of the reasons for them?
- How would you attempt to make contact with your colleagues if members of your staff seemed to work largely in isolation from one another?
- If your staff seemed to be divided by jealousies, hostilities, or unspoken conflicts, what do you think you would do?
- What do you consider to be the ethics involved in staying with a job after you've done everything you can to bring about change, but to no avail? (Consider that you have been asked to do things that are against your basic philosophy.)

Two Case Examples

The following two cases are designed to illustrate some of the issues we've discussed in this chapter. Try to imagine yourself in each of these situations, and ask yourself how you would deal with them.

○ *A case of a community mental-health worker.*   Sarah works in a community clinic, and most of her time is devoted to dealing with immediate crises. The more she works with people in crisis, the more she is convinced that the focus of her work should be on preventive programs designed to educate the public. Sarah comes to believe strongly that there would be far fewer clients in distress if people were effectively contacted and motivated to participate in growth-oriented educational programs. She develops detailed, logical, and convincing proposals for programs she would like to implement in the community, but they are consistently rejected by the director of her center. Because the clinic is partially funded by the government for the express purpose of crisis intervention, the director feels uneasy about approving any program that doesn't relate directly to this objective.

If you were in Sarah's place, what do you think you would do? Which of the following courses of action would you be likely to take?

___ I'd probably do what the director expected and complain that the bureaucratic structure inhibited imaginative programs.

___ Rather than taking the director's no as a final answer, I'd work toward a compromise. I'd do what was expected of me while finding some way to make room for my special project. I'd work with the director until I convinced her to permit me to launch my program in some form.

___ If I couldn't do what I deemed important, I'd look for another job.

___ I'd get several other staff members together in order to pool our resources and look for ways to implement our program as a group.

○ *A case of a school social worker.* George is a social worker in a school district. He is expected to devote most of his time to checking on children who are habitually truant and to do social-welfare work with dependent families. Although he knew his job description before he accepted the position, he now feels that his talents could be put to better use if he were allowed to do intensive counseling with families as units. Referral sources in the area are meager, and the families he works for cannot afford private treatment. Although he has the training to do the type of family counseling that he thinks is sorely needed, his school administrator makes it clear that any kind of therapy is outside the province of the school's responsibility. George is told to confine himself to tracking down truant children, doing legal work, and processing forms.

If you were in George's position, what do you think you would do?

___ I'd present a written plan to the local school board, showing that family counseling was needed and that public facilities were inadequate to meet this need.

___ I'd go ahead and do the family counseling without telling my administrator.

___ I wouldn't make waves, because I wouldn't want to lose my job.

Chapter Summary

The primary focus of this chapter has been on the importance of going beyond the limitations of one-to-one counseling. Counselors not only need to get involved in the community but also need to find ways of helping their clients make the transition from individual counseling to their everyday lives. The community mental-health orientation is an example of one way to meet the increasing demand for psychological services. Too often mental-health professionals have been denied the opportunity to devise programs addressed to the diverse needs of the community. For this reason some alternatives to conventional therapy have arisen, creating new roles for counselors and therapists.

You may be looking forward to a full-time career in a system. We think it is essential to consider how to make the system work *for* you, rather than *against* you. We challenge you to think of ways to accept the responsibility of surviving and working effectively in an organization and thus increasing your power as a person. Finally, we ask you to reflect on the major causes of the disillusionment that often accompanies working in a system and to find creative ways to remain vital as a person and as a professional.

Suggested Activities

1. In small groups explore specific ways of becoming involved in the community or using community resources to assist you in working with your clients. After you've explored these issues, the class can reconvene to pool ideas.
2. Several students who are interested in the use of paraprofessionals in the human-services field can investigate the issue and present their results in the form of a panel discussion. The discussion can focus on the advantages and disadvantages of the use of paraprofessionals, current trends, and other issues the panel deems important.
3. An issue you may well face in your practice is how to get through the resistance that people have toward asking for psychological assistance. Ask yourself how you should respond to clients who have questions such as "What will people think if they find out that I'm coming for professional help?" "Shouldn't I really be able to solve my problems on my own? Isn't it a sign of weakness that I need others to help me?" "Aren't most people who come to a community clinic really sick?" "Will I really be able to resolve my problems by consulting you?" After you've thought through your own responses, you can share them in dyads or in small groups.
4. For this exercise, begin by working in dyads. One student assumes the role of a person in some type of crisis. The student who will role-play the client should be able to identify in some way with the crisis situation. The other student becomes the crisis counselor and conducts an intake interview that does not exceed 30 minutes. Alternatively, a crisis situation can be presented to the entire class, and several students can show what immediate interventions they would make. Students who participate as counselors should be given feedback, and alternative intervention techniques should be discussed.
5. How aware are you of the resources that exist in your community? Would you know where to refer clients for special help? How aware are you of the support systems that exist in your community? Individually or with other students, investigate a comprehensive community mental-health center in your area. In doing so, find the answers to questions such as these:

- Where would you send a family who needed help?
- What facilities are available to treat drug and alcohol abuse?
- What kinds of crisis intervention are available? What are some common crises?
- Are health and medical services available at the center?
- What groups are offered?
- Is individual counseling available? For whom? At what fee? Long-term? Short-term?
- Where would you refer a couple seeking marital counseling?
- Are hot-line services available?
- What provisions are there for emergency situations?
- What do people have to do to qualify for help at the center?

6. As a small-group discussion activity, explore the topic of how you see yourself in relation to the educational system of which you are a part. Discuss the implications your style as a learner may have for the style you'll develop when you work for some institution or agency. Some questions for exploration are "How active am I in the process of my own education? What specific things do I do to make my education more meaningful? Am I willing to talk with instructors if I feel that they aren't offering me a valuable course? Am I willing to suggest constructive alternatives if I'm dissatisfied with a class or with my program? Do I often feel powerless as a student and thus assume the stance that there's nothing I can do to really change the things I think most need changing?" After you've had enough time to discuss this issue in small groups, the class can reconvene and compare results. Are there any common characteristics in the learning styles of the class members? How might these characteristics affect the way you work in a system as a professional?

7. With another student, role-play a job interview. One person is the director of a counseling center, and the other is the applicant. After 10 to 15 minutes, switch roles. Discuss how you felt in each position, and get feedback from your partner after both of you have had a chance to play each role. Questions the interviewer might ask include:
- Why are you applying for this job?
- What are your expectations if you get the position?
- Since there are many applicants and only a few positions, tell me why we should select you for the job. What do you have to offer that is unique?
- Could you briefly describe your philosophy of counseling?
- What do you most hope to accomplish as a counselor, and how would you evaluate whether you were accomplishing your goals?
- What kinds of clients could you *least* effectively counsel? What kinds of clients would you be *most* effective with?

8. Several students can interview a variety of professionals in the mental-health field about the major problems they encounter in their institution. What barriers do they meet when they attempt to implement programs? How do they deal with obstacles or red tape? How does the system affect them? You can divide this task up so that a wide range of professionals and paraprofessionals

are interviewed, including some who have been in the same job for a number of years and others who are just beginning. It would be interesting to compare the responses of experienced and inexperienced personnel. The students who do the interviewing can share their impressions and reactions without revealing the identities of the persons interviewed.

Suggested Readings

For a discussion of challenges for mental-health counselors in dealing with social-action issues, see Herr (1991), Ivey and Rigazio-DiGilio (1991), Dinkmeyer (1991), and D. W. Sue and D. Sue (1990). For community counseling strategies see Lewis and Lewis (1989). For outreach strategies in reaching ethnic groups in the community, see Atkinson et al. (1989) and Pedersen et al. (1989).

Some Concluding Ideas

In these chapters we've raised some of the ethical and professional issues that you will be most likely to encounter in your counseling practice. Instead of providing answers, we've tried to stimulate you to think about your own guidelines for professional practice and to initiate a process of reflection that you can apply to the many other issues you will face as a counselor.

If there is one fundamental question that can serve to tie together all the issues we've discussed, it is this: *Who has the right to counsel another person?* This question can be the focal point of your reflection on ethical and professional issues. It can also be the basis of your self-examination each day you meet with clients. You can continue to ask yourself: "What makes me think I have a right to counsel others? What do I have to offer the people I'm counseling? Am I doing in my own life what I'm encouraging my clients to do?" At times, if you answer these questions honestly, you may be troubled. There may be times when you feel that you have no ethical right to counsel others, perhaps because your own life isn't always the model you would like it to be for your clients. Yet this occasional self-doubt is far less damaging, in our view, than a failure to examine these questions. Complacency will stifle your growth as a counselor; honest self-examination, though more difficult, will make you a more effective helper.

We want to close our discussion by returning to the theme that has guided us throughout this book—namely, that developing a sense of professional and ethical responsibility is a task that is never really finished. There are no final or universal answers to many of the questions we have posed. For ourselves, we hope we never fall into the deadening trap of thinking that we "have it made" and no longer need to reexamine our assumptions and practices. We've found that the issues raised in this book have demanded periodic reflection and an openness to change. Thus, although we hope you've given careful thought to your own ethical and professional guidelines, we also hope you'll be willing to rethink your positions as you gain more experience.

Refer to the multiple-choice survey at the end of Chapter 1 on attitudes and beliefs about ethical and professional issues. We suggest that you cover your initial answers and retake the inventory now that you've come to the end of the course. Then you can compare your responses to see whether your thinking has changed. In addition, we suggest that you circle the ten questions that are most significant to you or that you're most interested in pursuing further. Bring these to class, and discuss them in small groups. Afterward, a survey can be conducted to get some idea of the issues that were most important to the students in your class.

As a way to review this book and the course you are completing, write down a few of the most important things you have learned. You might also write down some of the questions that this book and your course have left unanswered for you. After you've made your two lists, form small groups and exchange ideas with other students. This can be an excellent way to get some sense of the most crucial areas and topics that were explored by your fellow students and a fine way to wrap up the course.

Once the course is over, where can you go from here? How can you maintain the process of reflection that you've begun in this course? One excellent way to keep yourself alive intellectually is to develop a reading program. We suggest that you begin by selecting some of the books that we've listed in the References and Reading List. We'd also like to suggest that you dip into this book again from time to time. It can be valuable to reread various chapters as you take different courses that deal with the issues we've considered. In addition, periodically reexamining your responses can stimulate your thinking and provide a measure of your professional and intellectual growth. We hope you'll find other ways to make this book meaningful for yourself as you continue your search for your own direction.

References and Reading List*

Adair, J. G., Dushenko, T. W., & Lindsay, R. C. L. (1985). Ethical regulations and their impact on research practice. *American Psychologist, 40*(1), 59–72.

Akamatsu, T. J. (1988). Intimate relationships with former clients: National survey of attitudes and behavior among practitioners. *Professional Psychology: Research and Practice, 19*(4), 454–458.

Alvarez, P. A. (1990, May/June). Psychotherapy or spirituality. *The California Therapist,* pp. 58–59.

American Association for Counseling and Development. *Ethical Standards* (rev. ed.). (1988). Alexandria, VA: Author.

American Association for Marriage and Family Therapy. (1991). *AAMFT code of ethics.* Washington, DC: Author.

American Mental Health Counselors Association. (1987). *Code of ethics for mental health counselors.* Alexandria, VA: Author.

American Psychiatric Association. (1987). *Diagnostic and statistical manual of mental disorders* (3rd ed.). Washington, DC: Author.

American Psychiatric Association. (1989). *The principles of medical ethics, with annotations especially applicable to psychiatry.* Washington, DC: Author.

American Psychoanalytic Association. (1983). *Principles of ethics for psychoanalysts and provisions for implementation of the principles of ethics for psychoanalysts.* New York: Author.

American Psychological Association. (1981a). Specialty guidelines for the delivery of services. *American Psychologist, 36*(6), 639–681.

American Psychological Association. (1981b). *Specialty guidelines for the delivery of services by clinical psychologists.* Washington, DC: Author.

American Psychological Association. (1985). *White paper on duty to protect.* Washington, DC: Author.

*American Psychological Association. (1987). *Casebook on ethical principles of psychologists.* Washington, DC: Author.

American Psychological Association. (1988). Special issue: Psychology and AIDS. *American Psychologist, 43*(11).

American Psychological Association. (1989). *Ethical principles of psychologists.* Washington, DC: Author.

American Psychological Association. (1991a). Draft of APA ethics code. *APA Monitor, 22*(6), 30–35.

American Psychological Association. (1991b). *Draft of guidelines for providers of psychological services to ethnic, linguistic, and culturally diverse populations.* Washington, DC: Author.

*Books and articles marked with an asterisk are suggested for further study.

American Rehabilitation Counseling Association. (1987). *Code of professional ethics for rehabilitation counselors.* Arlington Heights, IL: Author.

American School Counselor Association. (1984). *Ethical standards for school counselors.* Alexandria, VA: Author.

Anderson, D. J., & Cranston-Gingras, A. (1991). Sensitizing counselors and educators to multicultural issues: An interactive approach. *Journal of Counseling and Development, 70*(1), 91–98.

Anderson, W. (1986). Stages of therapist comfort with sexual concerns of clients. *Professional Psychology: Research and Practice, 17*(4), 352–356.

Andrews, J. D. W. (1989). Integrating visions of reality: Interpersonal diagnosis and the existential vision. *American Psychologist, 44*(5), 803–817.

Anonymous. (1991). Sexual harassment: A female counseling student's experience. *Journal of Counseling and Development, 69*(6), 502–506.

Applebaum, P. (1981). *Tarasoff*: An update on the duty to warn. *Hospital and Community Psychiatry, 32,* 14–15.

Applebaum, P. S., & Rosenbaum, A. (1989). *Tarasoff* and the researcher: Does the duty to protect apply in the research setting? *American Psychologist 44*(6), 885–894.

Arredondo, P. (1985). Cross-cultural counselor education and training. In P. Pedersen (Ed.), *Handbook of cross-cultural counseling and therapy* (pp. 281–289). Westport, CT: Greenwood Press.

Association for Counselor Education and Supervision. (1990). Standards for counseling supervisors. *Journal of Counseling and Development, 69*(1), 30–32.

Association for Specialists in Group Work. (1989). *Ethical guidelines for group counselors.* Alexandria, VA: Author.

Association for Specialists in Group Work. (1991, Fall). Professional standards for the training of group workers. *Together: Association for Specialists in Group Work, 20,* 9–14. Alexandria, VA: Author.

*Atkinson, D. R., Morten, G., & Sue, D. W. (Eds.). (1989). *Counseling American minorities: A cross-cultural perspective* (3rd ed.). Dubuque, IA: William C. Brown.

Attneave, C. L. (1985). Practical counseling with American Indian and Alaska native clients. In P. Pedersen (Ed.), *Handbook of cross-cultural counseling and therapy* (pp. 135–140). Westport, CT: Greenwood Press.

Aubrey, M., & Dougher, M. J. (1990). Ethical issues in outpatient group therapy with sex offenders. *Journal for Specialists in Group Work, 15*(2), 75–82.

Aust, C. F. (1990). Using the client's religious values to aid progress in therapy. *Counseling and Values, 34*(2), 125–129.

Austin, K. M., Moline, M. M., & Williams, G. T. (1990). *Confronting malpractice: Legal and ethical dilemmas in psychotherapy.* Newbury Park, CA: Sage.

*Axelson, J. A. (1985). *Counseling and development in a multicultural society.* Pacific Grove, CA: Brooks/Cole.

Backer, T. E., Batchelor, W. F., Jones, J. M., & Mays, V. M. (1988). Introduction to the special issue: Psychology and AIDS. *American Psychologist, 43*(11), 835–836.

Baird, K. A., & Rupert, P. A. (1987). Clinical management of confidentiality: A survey of psychologists in seven states. *Professional Psychology: Research and Practice, 18*(4), 347–352.

Bajt, T. R., & Pope, K. S. (1989). Therapist-patient sexual intimacy involving children and adolescents. *American Psychologist, 44*(2), 455.

Baldick, T. (1980). Ethical discrimination ability of intern psychologists: A function of training in ethics. *Professional Psychology, 11,* 276–282.

Barak, A., & Fisher, W. A. (1989). Counselor and therapist gender bias? More questions than answers. *Professional Psychology: Research and Practice, 20*(6), 377–383.

*Barrows, P. A., & Halgin, R. P. (1988). Current issues in psychotherapy with gay men: Impact of the AIDS phenomenon. *Professional Psychology: Research and Practice, 19*(4), 395–402.

Bartell, P. A., & Rubin, L. J. (1990). Dangerous liaisons: Sexual intimacies in supervision. *Professional Psychology: Research and Practice, 21*(6), 442–450.

Baruth, L. G., & Manning, M. L. (1991). *Multicultural counseling and psychotherapy: A lifespan perspective.* New York: Macmillan.

*Bates, C. M., & Brodsky, A. M. (1989). *Sex in the therapy hour: A case of professional incest.* New York: Guilford Press.

Baumrind, D. (1985). Research using intentional deception. *American Psychologist, 40*(2), 165–174.

Bednar, R. L., Bednar, S. C., Lambert, M. J., & Waite, D. R. (1991). *Psychotherapy with high-risk clients: Legal and professional standards.* Pacific Grove, CA: Brooks/Cole.

*Beeman, D. G., & Scott, N. A. (1991). Therapists' attitudes toward psychotherapy: Informed consent with adolescents. *Professional Psychology: Research and Practice, 22*(3), 230–234.

*Benesch, K. F., & Ponterotto, J. G. (1989). East and West: Transpersonal psychology and cross-cultural counseling. *Counseling and Values, 33,* 121–131.

Bennett, B. E., Bryant, B. K., VandenBos, G. R., & Greenwood, A. (1990). *Professional liability and risk management.* Washington, DC: American Psychological Association.

Berger, Milton. (1982). Ethics and the therapeutic relationship: Patient rights and therapist responsibilities. In M. Rosenbaum (Ed.), *Ethics and values in psychotherapy: A guidebook.* New York: Free Press.

Berger, Morton. (1982). Ethical problems in the use of videotape. In M. Rosenbaum (Ed.), *Ethics and values in psychotherapy: A guidebook.* New York: Free Press.

Bergin, A. E. (1980). Psychotherapy and religious values. *Journal of Counseling and Clinical Psychology, 48*(1), 95–105.

Bergin, A. E. (1988, October). Three contributions of a spiritual perspective to counseling, psychotherapy, and behavior change. *Counseling and Values, 33,* 21–31.

Bergin, A. E. (1989). Religious faith and counseling: A commentary on Worthington. *The Counseling Psychologist, 17*(4), 621–623.

Bergin, A. E. (1991). Values and religious issues in psychotherapy and mental health. *American Psychology, 46*(4), 393–403.

Bergin, A. E., & Jensen, J. P. (1990). Religiosity of psychotherapists: A national survey. *Psychotherapy, 27*(1), 3–7.

Berman, A. L., & Jobes, D. A. (1991). *Adolescent suicide: Assessment and intervention.* Washington, DC: American Psychological Association.

Bernard, J. L., & Jara, C. S. (1986). The failure of clinical psychology graduate students to apply understood ethical principles. *Professional Psychology: Research and Practice, 17*(4), 313–315.

Bernard, J. L., Murphy, M., & Little, M. (1987). The failure of clinical psychologists to apply understood ethical principles. *Professional Psychology: Research and Practice, 18*(5), 489–491.

Bernot, D. J. (1983). Ethical and professional considerations in psychological assessment. *Professional Psychology: Research and Practice, 14*(5), 580–587.

Bernstein, B. L., & Lecomte, C. (1981). Licensure in psychology: Alternative direction. *Professional Psychology, 12*(2), 200–208.

Berven, N. L., & Scofield, M. E. (1987). Ethical responsibility in establishing and maintaining professional competence. *Journal of Applied Rehabilitation Counseling, 18*(4), 41–44.

Board of Behavioral Science Examiners. (1989, November/December). Sex should never be a part of therapy. *The California Therapist,* pp. 21–28.

Board of Behavioral Science Examiners. (1990). *Informal public hearing for discussion of the development of regulatory language addressing the issue of dual relationships.* Sacramento, CA: Author.

Board of Behavioral Science Examiners and Psychology Examining Committee. (1989, March/April). BBSE and PEC disciplinary actions. *The California Therapist,* p. 37.

Board of Medical Quality Assurance, Psychology Examining Committee, State of California Department of Consumer Affairs. (1980). *Newsletter.* Sacramento, CA: Author.

Bonger, B. (1991). *The suicidal patient: Clinical and legal standards of care.* Washington, DC: American Psychological Association.

Borders, L. D. (1991). A systematic approach to peer group supervision. *Journal of Counseling and Development, 69*(3), 248–252.

Borders, L. D., & Leddick, G. R. (1987). *Handbook of counseling supervision.* Alexandria, VA: Association for Counselor Education and Supervision.

Borders, L. D., & Leddick, G. R. (1988). A nationwide survey of supervision training. *Counselor Education and Supervision, 27*(3), 271–283.

Borys, D. S., (1988). *Dual relationships between therapist and client: A national survey of clinicians' attitudes and practices.* Unpublished doctoral dissertation, University of California, Los Angeles.

Borys, D. S., & Pope, K. S. (1989). Dual relationships between therapist and client: A national study of psychologists, psychiatrists, and social workers. *Professional Psychology: Research and Practice, 20*(5), 283–293.

Botkin, D. J., & Nietzel, M. T. (1987). How therapists manage potentially dangerous clients: Toward a standard of care for psychotherapists. *Professional Psychology: Research and Practice, 18*(1), 84–86.

Bouhoutsos, J., Holroyd, J., Lerman, H., Forer, B. R., & Greenberg, M. (1983). Sexual intimacy between psychotherapists and patients. *Professional Psychology: Research and Practice, 14*(2), 185–196.

Bowen, N. H., Bahrick, A. S., & Enns, C. Z. (1991). A feminist response to empowerment. *Journal of Counseling and Development, 69*(3), 228.

Brammer, L. M. (1985). Nonformal support in cross-cultural counseling and therapy. In P. Pedersen (Ed.), *Handbook of cross-cultural counseling and therapy* (pp. 87–92). Westport, CT: Greenwood Press.

Brammer, L. M. (1986). Needed: A paradigm shift in counseling theory. *The Counseling Psychologist, 14*(3), 443–447.

Brammer, L. M., Shostrom, E. L., & Abrego, P. J. (1989). *Therapeutic psychology: Fundamentals of counseling and psychotherapy* (5th ed.). Englewood Cliffs, NJ: Prentice-Hall.

Bray, J. H., Shepherd, J. N., & Hays, J. R. (1985). Legal and ethical issues in informed consent to psychotherapy. *American Journal of Family Therapy, 13*(2), 50–60.

Brewer, T., & Faitak, M. T. (1989). Ethical guidelines for the inpatient psychiatric care of children. *Professional Psychology: Research and Practice, 20*(3), 142–147.

Brickman, P., Rabinowitz, V., Karuza, J., Coates, D., Cohn, E., & Kidder, L. (1982). Models of helping and coping. *American Psychologist, 37*(4), 368–384.

*Brodsky, A. M. (1986). The distressed psychologist: Sexual intimacies and exploitation. In R. R. Kilburg, P. E. Nathan, & R. W. Thoreson (Eds.), *Professionals in distress: Issues, syndromes, and solutions in psychology* (pp. 153–172). Washington, DC: American Psychological Association.

Brody, E. M., & Farber, B. A. (1989). Effects of psychotherapy on significant others. *Professional Psychology: Research and Practice, 20*(2), 116–122.

Brooks, D. K., & Gerstein, L. H. (1990). Counselor credentialing and interprofessional collaboration. *Journal of Counseling and Development, 68*(5), 477–484.

Brown, J. H., & Christensen, D. N. (1986). *Family therapy: Theory and practice.* Pacific Grove, CA: Brooks/Cole.

Brown, L. S. (1990). Taking account of gender in the clinical assessment interview. *Professional Psychology: Research and Practice, 21*(1), 12–17.

Browning, C., Reynolds, A. L., & Dworkin, S. (1991). Affirmative psychotherapy for lesbian women. *The Counseling Psychologist, 19*(2), 177–196.

Bugental, J. F. T. (1987). *The art of the psychotherapist.* New York: Norton.

Buhrke, R. A. (1989a). Female student perspectives on training in lesbian and gay issues. *The Counseling Psychologist, 17*(4), 629–636.

Buhrke, R. A. (1989b). Incorporating lesbian and gay issues into counselor training: A resource guide. *Journal of Counseling and Development, 68*(1), 77–80.

Buhrke, R. A., & Douce, L. A. (1991). Training issues for counseling psychologists in working with lesbian women and gay men. *The Counseling Psychologist, 19*(2), 216–234.

California Department of Consumer Affairs. (undated). *Professional therapy never includes sex* (pamphlet). Sacramento: Author.

Campos, P. E., Brasfield, T. L., & Kelly, J. A. (1989). Psychology training related to AIDS: Survey of doctoral graduate programs and predoctoral internship programs. *Professional Psychology: Research and Practice, 20*(4), 214–220.

Carballo-Dieguez, A. (1989). Hispanic culture, gay male culture, and AIDS: Counseling implications. *Journal of Counseling and Development, 68*(1), 26–30.

Casas, J. M., & Thompson, C. E. (1991). Ethical principles and standards: A racial-ethnic minority research perspective. *Counseling and Values, 35*(3), 186–195.

Castronovo, N. R. (1990). Acquired immune deficiency syndrome education on the college campus: The mandate and the challenge. *Journal of Counseling and Development, 68*(5), 578–581.

Cavell, T. A., Frentz, C. E., & Kelley, M. L. (1986). Acceptability of paradoxical interventions: Some nonparadoxical findings. *Professional Psychology: Research and Practice, 17*(6), 519–523.

Cayleff, S. E. (1986). Ethical issues in counseling gender, race, and culturally distinct groups. *Journal of Counseling and Development, 64*(5), 345–347.

Cerney, M. S. (1985). Countertransference revisited. *Journal of Counseling and Development, 63*(6), 362–364.

Chamow, L. (1990, May/June). What to look for in a clinical supervisor. *The California Therapist*, p. 60.

Chan, C. S. (1989). Issues of identity development among Asian-American lesbians and gay men. *Journal of Counseling and Development, 68*(1), 16–20.

Chemtob, C. M., Bauer, G. B., Hamada, R. S., Pelowski, S. R., & Muraoka, M. Y. (1989). Patient suicide: Occupational hazard for psychologists and psychiatrists. *Professional Psychology: Research and Practice, 20*(5), 294–300.

Chemtob, C. M., Hamada, R. S., Bauer, G., & Torigoe, R. Y. (1988). Patient suicide: Frequency and impact on psychologists. *Professional Psychology: Research and Practice, 19*(4), 416–420.

Christensen, C. P. (1989). Cross-cultural awareness development: A conceptual model. *Counselor Education and Supervision, 28*(4), 270–289.

Claiborn, C. D. (1985). The counselor and physical attractiveness: A response. *Journal of Counseling and Development, 63*(8), 486–487.

Clark, M. M. (1986). Personal therapy: A review of empirical research. *Professional Psychology: Research and Practice, 17*(6), 541–543.

Coburn, W. J., II. (1990, May/June). Countertransference with couples and families. *The California Therapist*, p. 54.

Cohen, E. D. (1990). Confidentiality, counseling, and clients who have AIDS: Ethical foundations of a model rule. *Journal of Counseling and Development, 68*(3), 282–286.

Coleman, E., & Ramafedi, G. (1989). Gay, lesbian, and bisexual adolescents: A critical challenge to counselors. *Journal of Counseling and Development, 68*(1), 36–40.

*Coleman, E., & Schaefer, S. (1986). Boundaries of sex and intimacy between client and counselor. *Journal of Counseling and Development, 64*(5), 341–344.

Commission on Rehabilitation Counselor Certification. (1987). *Code of ethics.* Arlington Heights, IL: Author.

Committee on Women in Psychology, American Psychology Association. (1989). If sex enters into the psychotherapy relationship. *Professional Psychology: Research and Practice, 20*(2), 112–115.

Conway, C. G. (1989). The relevance of religious issues in counseling. *The Counseling Psychologist, 17*(4), 624–628.

Cook, E. P. (1990). Gender and psychological distress. *Journal of Counseling and Development, 68*(4), 371–374.

Corey, G. (1981). Description of a practicum course in group leadership. *Journal for Specialists in Group Work, 6*(2), 100–108.

Corey, G. (1982). Practical strategies for planning therapy groups. In P. Keller (Ed.), *Innovations in clinical practice: A sourcebook.* Sarasota, FL: Professional Resource Exchange.

Corey, G. (1983). An introduction to group counseling. In J. Brown & B. Pate (Eds.), *Being a counselor: Directions and challenges.* Pacific Grove, CA: Brooks/Cole.

Corey, G. (1984). Ethical issues in group therapy. In P. Keller, (Ed.), *Innovations in clinical practice: A sourcebook.* Sarasota, FL: Professional Resource Exchange.

Corey, G. (1989a). Commentary on Leonid Gozman's article "Ethical aspects of psychological therapy." *Journal of Counseling and Human Service Professions, 3*(3), 8–10.

Corey, G. (1989b). Invited commentary: "Values in counseling and psychotherapy" (C. H. Patterson). *Counseling and Values, 33,* 177–178.

Corey, G. (1990). *Theory and practice of group counseling* and *Manual* (3rd ed.). Pacific Grove, CA: Brooks/Cole.

Corey, G. (1991a). *Case approach to counseling and psychotherapy* (3rd ed.). Pacific Grove, CA: Brooks/Cole.

Corey, G. (1991b). *Theory and practice of counseling and psychotherapy* and *Manual.* (4th ed.). Pacific Grove, CA: Brooks/Cole.

Corey, G., & Corey, M. (1990). *I never knew I had a choice* (4th ed.). Pacific Grove, CA: Brooks/Cole.

Corey, G., Corey, M., & Callanan, P. (1990). Role of group leader's values in group counseling. *Journal for Specialists in Group Work, 15*(2), 68–74.

Corey, G., Corey, M., Callanan, P., & Russell, J. M. (1992). *Group techniques* (2nd ed.). Pacific Grove, CA: Brooks/Cole.

Corey, M., & Corey, G. (1986). Experiential/didactic training and supervision workshop for group leaders. *Journal of Counseling and Human Service Professions, 1*(1), 18–26.

Corey, M., & Corey, G. (1992). *Groups: Process and Practice* (4th ed.). Pacific Grove, CA: Brooks/Cole.

*Corey, M., & Corey, G. (1993). *Becoming a helper* (2nd ed.). Pacific Grove, CA: Brooks/Cole.

Cormier, L. S., & Bernard, J. M. (1982). Ethical and legal responsibilities of clinical supervisors. *Personnel and Guidance Journal, 60*(8), 486–490.

Corsini, R., & Wedding, D. (1989). *Current Psychotherapies* (4th ed.). Itasca, IL: F. E. Peacock.

Cramer, D. (1986). Gay parents and their children: A review of research and practical implications. *Journal of Counseling and Development, 64*(8), 504–507.

Crawford, I., Humfleet, G., Ribordy, S. C., Ho, F. C., & Vickers, V. L. (1991). Stigmatization of AIDS patients by mental health professionals. *Professional Psychology: Research and Practice, 22*(5), 357–361.

Crawford, I., & Jason, L. A. (1990). Strategies for implementing a media-based AIDS prevention program. *Professional Psychology: Research and Practice, 21*(3), 219–221.

Crego, C. A. (1985). Ethics: The need for improved consultation training. *The Counseling Psychologist, 13*(3), 473–476.

Crime Prevention Center, California Office of the Attorney General. (1988). *Child abuse prevention handbook.* Sacramento: Author.

Croteau, J. M., & Morgan, S. (1989). Combating homophobia in AIDS education. *Journal of Counseling and Development, 68*(1), 86–91.

Cummings, N. A. (1990). The credentialing of professional psychologists and its implication for the other mental health disciplines. *Journal of Counseling and Development, 68*(5), 485–490.

Davis, A. H., Savicki, V., Cooley, E. J., & Firth, J. L. (1989). Burnout and counselor practitioner expectations of supervision. *Counselor Education and Supervision, 28*(3), 234–241.

Davis, J. W. (1981). Counselor licensure: Overskill? *Personnel and Guidance Journal, 60*(2), 83–85.

Deardorff, W. W., Cross, H. J., & Hupprich, W. R. (1984). Malpractice liability in psychotherapy: Client and practitioner perspectives. *Professional Psychology: Research and Practice, 15*(4), 590–600.

DeBord, J. B. (1989). Paradoxical interventions: A review of the recent literature. *Journal of Counseling and Development, 67,* 394–398.

Deffenbacher, J. L. (1985). A cognitive-behavioral response and a modest proposal. *The Counseling Psychologist, 13*(2), 261–269.

DeKraai, M. B., & Sales, B. D. (1982). Privileged communications of psychologists. *Professional Psychology, 13*(3), 372–388.

Denkowski, K. M., & Denkowski, G. C. (1982). Client-counselor confidentiality: An update of rationale, legal status, and implications. *Personnel and Guidance Journal, 60*(6), 371–375.

Denton, W. H. (1989). DSM-III-R and the family therapist: Ethical considerations. *Journal of Marital and Family Therapy, 15*(4), 367–378.

Department of Consumer Affairs. (1990). *Professional therapy never includes sex.* Sacramento, CA: Author.

DePauw, M. E. (1986). Avoiding ethical violations: A timeline perspective for individual counseling. *Journal of Counseling and Development, 64*(5), 303–305.

Deutsch, C. J. (1984). Self-reported sources of stress among psychotherapists. *Professional Psychology: Research and Practice, 15*(6), 833–845.

Deutsch, C. J. (1985). A survey of therapists' personal problems and treatment. *Professional Psychology: Research and Practice, 16*(2), 305–315.

DeVoe, D. (1990). Feminist and nonsexist counseling: Implications for the male counselor. *Journal of Counseling and Development, 69*(1), 33–36.

Devore, W. (1985). Developing ethnic sensitivity for the counseling process: A social-work perspective. In P. Pedersen (Ed.), *Handbook of cross-cultural counseling and therapy* (pp. 93–98). Westport, CT: Greenwood Press.

Dinkmeyer, D. (1991). Mental health counseling: A psychoeducational approach. *Journal of Mental Health Counseling, 13*(1), 37–42.

Donigian, J. (1991). Dual relationships: An ethical issue. *Together, 19*(2), 6–7.

Dougherty, A. M. (1990). *Consultation: Practice and perspectives.* Pacific Grove, CA: Brooks/Cole.

Dougherty, A. M. (in press). Ethical issues in consultation. *Elementary School Guidance and Counseling.*

Dowd, E. T., & Milne, C. R. (1986). Paradoxical interventions in counseling psychology. *The Counseling Psychologist, 14*(2), 237–282.

Downing, N. E., & Roush, K. L. (1985). From passive acceptance to active commitment: A model of feminist identity development for women. *The Counseling Psychologist, 13*(4), 695–709.

Draguns, J. G. (1989). Dilemmas and choices in cross-cultural counseling: The universal versus the culturally distinctive. In P. Pedersen, J. Draguns, W. Lonner, and J. Trimble (Eds.), *Counseling across cultures* (3rd ed.) (pp. 3–22). Honolulu: University of Hawaii Press.

Duckworth, J. (1990). The counseling approach in the use of testing. *The Counseling Psychologist, 18*(2), 198–204.

Dye, H. A., & Borders, L. D. (1990). Counseling supervisors: Standards for preparation and practice. *Journal of Counseling and Development, 69*(1), 30–32.

Eberlein, L. (1987). Introducing ethics to beginning psychologists: A problem-solving approach. *Professional Psychology: Research and Practice, 18*(4), 353–359.

Edelwich, J., with Brodsky, A. (1980). *Burn-out: Stages of disillusionment in the helping professions.* New York: Human Sciences Press.

Edelwich, J., with Brodsky, A. (1982). *Sexual dilemmas for the helping professional.* New York: Brunner/Mazel.

Egan, G. (1990). *The skilled helper: A systematic approach to effective helping* (4th ed.). Pacific Grove, CA: Brooks/Cole.

Emener, W. G. (1987). Ethical standards for rehabilitation counseling: A brief review of critical historical developments. *Journal of Applied Rehabilitation Counseling, 18*(4), 5–8.

Emery, R. E. (1989). Family violence. *American Psychologist, 44*(2), 321–328.

Engels, D., Wilborn, B. L., & Schneider, L. J. (1990). Ethics curricula for counselor preparation programs. In B. Herlihy and B. Golden (Eds.), *AACD ethical standards casebook* (4th ed.) (pp. 111–126). Alexandria, VA: American Association for Counseling and Development.

Enns, C. Z. (1991). The "new" relationship models of women's identity: A review and critique for counselors. *Journal of Counseling and Development, 69*(3), 209–217.

Erickson, S. H. (1990). Counseling the irresponsible AIDS client: Guidelines for decision making. *Journal of Counseling and Development, 68*(4), 454–455.

Ethics Committee, American Psychological Association. (1987). Report of the ethics committee: 1986. *American Psychologist, 42*(7), 730–734.

Ethics Committee, American Psychological Association. (1988). Trends in ethics cases, common pitfalls, and published resources. *American Psychologist, 43*(7), 564–572.

Everett, C. A. (1990). The field of marital and family therapy. *Journal of Counseling and Development, 68*(5), 498–502.

Everstine, L., Everstine, D. S., Heymann, G. M., True, R. H., Frey, D. H., Johnson, H. G., & Seiden, R. H. (1980). Privacy and confidentiality in psychotherapy. *American Psychologist, 35*(9), 828–840.

Falk, P. J. (1989). Lesbian mothers: Psychosocial assumptions in family law. *American Psychologist, 44*(6), 941–947.

Farber, B. A. (1983a). Psychotherapists' perceptions of stressful patient behavior. *Professional Psychology: Research and Practice, 14*(5), 697–705.

Farber, B. A. (1983b). *Stress and burnout in the human service professions.* New York: Pergamon Press.

Farber, B. A., & Heifetz, L. J. (1982). The process and dimensions of burnout in psychotherapists. *Professional Psychology, 13*(2), 293–301.

Fassinger, R. E. (1991a). Counseling lesbian women and gay men. *The Counseling Psychologist, 19*(2), 156.

Fassinger, R. E. (1991b). The hidden minority: Issues and challenges in working with lesbian women and gay men. *The Counseling Psychologist, 19*(2), 157–176.

Fieldsteel, N. (1982). Ethical issues in family therapy. In M. Rosenbaum (Ed.), *Ethics and values in psychotherapy: A guidebook.* New York: Free Press.

Fischer, L., & Sorenson, G. P. (1991). *School law for counselors, psychologists, and social workers* (2nd ed.). New York: Longman.

Fitting, M. D. (1986). Ethical dilemmas in counseling elderly adults. *Journal of Counseling and Development, 64*(5), 325–327.

Fitzgerald, L. F., & Nutt, R. (1986). The Division 17 principles concerning the counseling/psychotherapy of women: Rationale and implementation. *The Counseling Psychologist, 14*(1), 180–216.

*Flora, J. A., & Thoresen, C. E. (1988). Reducing the risk of AIDS in adolescents. *American Psychologist, 43*(11), 965–970.

Fogel, M. S. (1990, May/June). Supervisors should not dominate but doubt, reflect, innovate. *Family Therapy News,* pp. 5–6.

Foltz, M. L., Kirby, P. C., & Paradise, L. V. (1989). The influence of empathy and negative consequences on ethical decisions in counseling situations. *Counselor Education and Supervision, 28*(3), 219–228.

Forester-Miller, H. (1990a). Ethics: The unmet challenge. *Journal for Specialists in Group Work, 15*(2), 66–67.

Forester-Miller, H. (Ed.) (1990b). Special issue: Ethical and legal issues in group work. *Journal for Specialists in Group Work, 15*(2). Alexandria, VA: American Association for Counseling and Development.

Forester-Miller, H., & Duncan, J. A. (1990). The ethics of dual relationships in the training of group counselors. *Journal for Specialists in Group Work, 15*(2), 88–93.

Fouad, N. A., Hains, A. A., & Davis, J. L. (1990). Factors in students' endorsement of counseling as a requirement for graduation from a counseling program. *Counselor Education and Supervision, 29*(4), 268–274.

Fremon, C. (1991, January 27). Love and death. *Los Angeles Times Magazine,* pp. 17–35.

*Fretz, B. R., & Mills, D. H. (1980). *Licensing and certification of psychologists and counselors.* San Francisco: Jossey-Bass.

Freudenberger, H. J. (1986). The health professional in treatment: Symptoms, dynamics, and treatment issues. In C. D. Scott & J. Hawk (Eds.), *Heal thyself: The health of health care professionals.* New York: Brunner/Mazel.

*Fujimura, L. E., Weis, D. M., & Cochran, J. R. (1985). Suicide: Dynamics and implications for counseling. *Journal of Counseling and Development, 63*(10), 612–615.

Fukuyama, M. A. (1990). Taking a universal approach to multicultural counseling. *Counselor Education and Supervision, 30*(1), 6–17.

*Fulero, S. M. (1988). *Tarasoff:* 10 years later. *Professional Psychology: Research and Practice, 19*(2), 184–190.

*Fulero, S. M., & Wilbert, J. R. (1988). Record-keeping practices of clinical and counseling psychologists: A survey of practitioners. *Professional Psychology: Research and Practice, 19*(6), 658–660.

Fuqua, D. R., & Newman, J. L. (1989). Research issues in the study of professional ethics. *Counselor Education and Supervision, 29*(2), 84–93.

Gabbard, G., & Pope, K. (1988). Sexual intimacies after termination: Clinical, ethical, and legal aspects. *The Independent Practitioner, 8*(2), 21–26.

Gallessich, J. (1982). *The profession and practice of consultation.* San Francisco: Jossey-Bass.

Garcia, A. (1990). An examination of the social work profession's efforts to achieve legal regulation. *Journal of Counseling and Development, 68*(5), 491–497.

Garcia, M. H., Wright, J. W., & Corey, G. (1991). A multicultural perspective in an undergraduate human services program. *Journal of Counseling and Development, 70*(1), 86–90.

Gard, L. H. (1990). Patient disclosure of human immunodeficiency virus (HIV) status to parents: Clinical considerations. *Professional Psychology: Research and Practice, 21*(4), 252–256.

Garfield, S. L. (1987). Ethical issues in research and psychotherapy. *Counseling and Values, 31*(2), 115–125.

Garnets, L., Hancock, K. A., Cochran, S. D., Goodchilds, J., & Peplau, L. A. (1991). Issues in psychotherapy with lesbians and gay men. *American Psychologist, 46*(9), 964–972.

Gazda, G. M. (1989). *Group counseling: A developmental approach* (4th ed.). Boston: Allyn & Bacon.

Gelso, C. J., & Carter, J. A. (1985). The relationship in counseling and psychotherapy: Components, consequences, and theoretical antecedents. *The Counseling Psychologist, 13*(2), 155–243.

Gendlin, E. T. (1986). What comes after traditional psychotherapy research? *American Psychologist, 41*(2), 131–136.

Gerstein, L. H., & Brooks, D. K. (1990). Introduction for a special feature. The helping professions' challenge: Credentialing and interdisciplinary collaboration. *Journal of Counseling and Development, 68*(5), 475–476.

Gilbert, L. A. (1980). Feminist therapy. In A. M. Brodsky & R. T. Hare-Mustin (Eds.), *Women and psychotherapy: An assessment of research and practice.* New York: Guilford Press.

Glaser, R. D., & Thorpe, J. S. (1986). Unethical intimacy: A survey of sexual contact and advances between psychology educators and female graduate students. *American Psychologist, 41*(1), 42–51.

Glenn, C. M. (1980). Ethical issues in the practice of child psychotherapy. *Professional Psychology, 11*(4), 613–619.

Goldenberg, H., & Goldenberg, I. (1990). *Counseling today's families.* Pacific Grove, CA: Brooks/Cole.

Goldenberg, I., & Goldenberg, H. (1991). *Family therapy: An overview* (3rd. ed.). Pacific Grove, CA: Brooks/Cole.

Good, G. E., Gilbert, L. A., & Scher, M. (1990). Gender aware therapy: A synthesis of feminist therapy and knowledge about gender. *Journal of Counseling and Development, 68*(4), 376–380.

Gordon, J., & Shontz, F. C. (1990). Living with the AIDS virus: A representative case. *Journal of Counseling and Development, 68*(3), 287–292.

Gottlieb, M. C. (1990). Accusations of sexual misconduct: Assisting in the complaint process. *Professional Psychology: Research and Practice, 21*(6), 455–461.

Gottlieb, M. C., Sell, J. M., & Schoenfeld, L. S. (1988). Social/romantic relationships with present and former clients: State licensing board actions. *Professional Psychology: Research and Practice, 19*(4), 459–462.

Goud, N. (1990). Spiritual and ethical beliefs of humanists in the counseling profession. *Journal of Counseling and Development, 68*(5), 571–574.

Gozman, L. (1989). Ethical aspects of psychological therapy. *Journal of Counseling and Human Service Professions, 3*(3), 3–7.

Graham, D. L. R., Rawlings, E. I., Halpern, H. S., & Hermes, J. (1984). Therapists' need for training in counseling lesbians and gay men. *Professional Psychology: Research and Practice, 15*(4), 482–496.

*Gray, L. A., & Harding, A. I. (1988). Confidentiality limits with clients who have the AIDS virus. *Journal of Counseling and Development, 66*(5), 219–223.

Gray, L. A., & Saracino, M. (1989). AIDS on campus: A preliminary study of college students' knowledge and behaviors. *Journal of Counseling and Development, 68*, 199–202.

Grayson, H. (1982). Ethical issues in the training of psychotherapists. In M. Rosenbaum (Ed.), *Ethics and values in psychotherapy: A guidebook*. New York: Free Press.

Green, S. L., & Hansen, J. C. (1986). Ethical dilemmas in family therapy. *Journal of Marital and Family Therapy, 12*(3), 225–230.

Green, S. L., & Hansen, J. C. (1989). Ethical dilemmas faced by family therapists. *Journal of Marital and Family Therapy, 15*(2), 149–158.

Greenberg, L. S., & Safran, J. D. (1989). Emotion in psychotherapy. *American Psychologist, 44*(1), 19–29.

Greenburg, S. L., Lewis, G. J., & Johnson, J. (1985). Peer consultation groups for private practitioners. *Professional Psychology: Research and Practice, 16*(3), 437–447.

Greenhut, M. (1991, May/June). Professional networking: The downward spiral to "health." *The California Therapist,* pp. 47–48.

Gross, D. R., & Robinson, S. E. (1987). Ethics, violence, and counseling: Hear no evil, see no evil, speak no evil? *Journal of Counseling and Development, 65*, 340–344.

Group for the Advancement of Psychiatry, Committee on Medical Education. (1990). *A casebook in psychiatric ethics.* New York: Brunner/Mazel.

Gumaer, J. (1987). Understanding and counseling gay men: A developmental perspective. *Journal of Counseling and Development, 66*, 144–146.

Gumaer, J., & Martin, D. (1990). Group ethics: A multicultural model for training knowledge and skill competencies. *Journal for Specialists in Group Work, 15*(2), 94–103.

Gumaer, J., & Scott, L. (1985). Training group leaders in ethical decision making. *Journal for Specialists in Group Work, 10*(4), 198–204.

Gumaer, J., & Scott, L. (1986). Group workers' perceptions of ethical and unethical behavior of group leaders. *Journal for Specialists in Group Work, 11*(3), 139–150.

Gustafson, K. E., & McNamara, J. R. (1987). Confidentiality with minor clients: Issues and guidelines for therapists. *Professional Psychology: Research and Practice, 17*(2), 111–114.

Gutheil, T. G. (1989, November/December). Patient-therapist sexual relations. *The California Therapist,* pp. 29–31.

Guy, J. D. (1987). *The personal life of the psychotherapists.* New York: Wiley.

Guy, J. D., & Liaboe, G. P. (1986a). The impact of conducting psychotherapy upon the interpersonal relationships of the psychotherapist. *Professional Psychology: Research and Practice, 17*(2), 111–114.

Guy, J. D., & Liaboe, G. P. (1986b). Personal therapy for the experienced psycho-therapist: A discussion of its usefulness and utilization. *The Clinical Psychologist, 39*(1), 20–23.

Guy, J. D., Poelstra, P. L., & Stark, M. J. (1989). Personal distress and therapeutic effectiveness: National survey of psychologists practicing psychotherapy. *Professional Psychology: Research and Practice, 20*(1), 48–50.

Guy, J. D., & Sauder, J. K. (1986). Impact of therapist's illness or accident on psychotherapeutic practice: Review and discussion. *Professional Psychology: Research and Practice, 17*(6), 509–513.

*Guy, J. D., Stark, M. J., & Poelstra, P. L. (1988). Personal therapy for psychotherapists before and after entering professional practice. *Professional Psychology: Research and Practice, 19*(4), 474–476.

Guy, K. C. (1987). Touch: An exploration of its role in the counseling process. *Journal of Mental Health Counseling, 9*(3), 142–149.

Haas, L. J., & Alexander, J. R. (1981). *Ethical and legal issues in family therapy.* Paper presented at the meeting of the American Psychological Association, Los Angeles.

*Haas, L. J., Malouf, J. L., & Mayerson, N. H. (1986). Ethical dilemmas in psychological practice: Results of a national survey. *Professional Psychology: Research and Practice, 17*(4), 316–321.

Haas, L. J., Malouf, J. L., & Mayerson, N. H. (1988). Personal and professional characteristics as factors in psychologists' ethical decision making. *Professional Psychology: Research and Practice, 19*(1), 35–42.

Hall, J. E. (1987). Gender-related ethical dilemmas and ethics education. *Professional Psychology: Research and Practice, 18*(6), 573–579.

Handelsman, M. M. (1986a). Ethics training at the master's level: A national survey. *Professional Psychology: Research and Practice, 17*(1), 24–26.

Handelsman, M. M. (1986b). Problems with ethics training by "osmosis." *Professional Psychology: Research and Practice, 17*(4), 371–372.

Handelsman, M. M. (1987). Confidentiality: The ethical baby in the legal bathwater. *Journal of Applied Rehabilitation Counseling, 18*(4), 33–34.

Handelsman, M. M. (1990). Do written consent forms influence clients' first impressions of therapists? *Professional Psychology: Research and Practice, 21*(6), 451–454.

Handelsman, M. M., & Galvin, M. D. (1988). Facilitating informed consent for outpatient psychotherapy: A suggested written format. *Professional Psychology: Research and Practice, 19*(2), 223–225.

Handelsman, M. M., Kemper, M. B., Kesson-Craig, P., McLain, J., & Johnsrud, C. (1986). Use, content, and readability of written informed consent forms for treatment. *Professional Psychology: Research and Practice, 17*(6), 514–518.

Hansen, J. C. (Ed.). (1982). *Values, ethics, legalities and the family therapist.* Rockville, MD: Aspen.

Hare-Mustin, R. T. (1979). Family therapy and sex role stereotypes. *The Counseling Psychologist, 8*(1), 31–32.

Hare-Mustin, R. T. (1980). Family therapy may be dangerous to your health. *Professional Psychology, 11*(6), 935–938.

Hare-Mustin, R. T., Marecek, J., Kaplan, A. G., & Liss-Levinson, N. (1979). Rights of clients, responsibilities of therapists. *American Psychologist, 34*(1), 3–16.

Hargrove, D. S. (1986). Ethical issues in rural mental health practice. *Professional Psychology: Research and Practice, 17*(1), 20–23.

Harrar, W. R., VandeCreek, L., & Knapp, S. (1990). Ethical and legal aspects of clinical supervision. *Professional Psychology: Research and Practice, 21*(1), 37–41.

Hayman, P. M., & Covert, J. A. (1986). Ethical dilemmas in college counseling centers. *Journal of Counseling and Development, 64*(5), 318–320.

Heinrich, R. K., Corbine, J. L., & Thomas, K. R. (1990). Counseling Native Americans. *Journal of Counseling and Development, 69*(2), 128–133.

Hendrix, D. H. (1991). Ethics and intrafamily confidentiality in counseling with children. *Journal of Mental Health Counseling, 13*(3), 323–333.

Henkin, W. A. (1985). Toward counseling the Japanese in America: A cross-cultural primer. *Journal of Counseling and Development, 63*(8), 500–503.

Hennessey, E. F. (1989). The family, the courts, and mental health professionals. *American Psychologist, 44*(9), 1223–1224.

Herek, G. M. (1989). Hate crimes against lesbians and gay men: Issues for research and policy. *American Psychologist, 44*(6), 948–955.

Herink, R. (Ed.). (1980). *The psychotherapy handbook.* New York: New American Library.

Herlihy, B., & Corey, G. (1992). *Dual relationships in counseling,* Alexandria, VA: American Association for Counseling and Development.

*Herlihy, B., & Golden, L. B. (1990). *AACD ethical standards casebook* (4th ed.). Alexandria, VA: American Association for Counseling and Development.

Herlihy, B., Healy, M., Cook, E. P., & Hudson, P. (1987). Ethical practices of licensed professional counselors: A survey of state licensing boards. *Counselor Education and Supervision, 27*(1), 69–76.

Herlihy, B., & Sheeley, V. L. (1988). Counselor liability and the duty to warn: Selected cases, statutory trends, and implications for practice. *Counselor Education and Supervision, 27*(3), 203–215.

Herr, E. L. (1991). Challenges to mental health counselors in a dynamic society: Macrostrategies in the profession. *Journal of Mental Health Counseling, 13*(1), 6–20.

Herr, E. L., & Niles, S. (1988). The values of counseling: Three domains. *Counseling and Values, 33,* 4–17.

Herring, R. D. (1990). Understanding Native-American values: Process and content concerns for counselors. *Counseling and Values, 34*(2), 134–137.

Herron, W. G., & Sitkowski, S. (1986). Effect of fees on psychotherapy: What is the evidence? *Professional Psychology: Research and Practice, 17*(4), 347–351.

Hillerbrand, E. T., & Claiborn, C. D. (1988). Ethical knowledge exhibited by clients and nonclients. *Professional Psychology: Research and Practice, 19*(5), 527–531.

Hillerbrand, E., & Stone, G. L. (1986). Ethics and clients: A challenging mixture for counselors. *Journal of Counseling and Development, 64*(7), 240–245.

Hines, P. M., & Hare-Mustin, R. T. (1978). Ethical concerns in family therapy. *Professional Psychology, 9,* 165–171.

Hinkeldey, N. S., & Spokane, A. R. (1985). Effects of pressure and legal guideline clarity on counselor decision making in legal and ethical conflict situations. *Journal of Counseling and Development, 64*(4), 240–245.

Ho, D. Y. F. (1985). Cultural values and professional issues in clinical psychology: Implications from the Hong Kong experience. *American Psychologist, 40*(11), 1212–1218.

Ho, D. Y. F. (1988). Asian psychology: A dialog on indigenization and beyond. In A. C. Paranjpe, D. Y. F. Ho, and R. W. Rieber (Eds.), *Asian contributions to psychology,* (pp. 53–78). New York: Praeger.

Hoffman, M. A. (1991a). Counseling the HIV-infected client: A psychosocial model for assessment and intervention. *The Counseling Psychologist, 19*(4), 467–542.

Hoffman, M. A. (1991b). Training mental health counselors for the AIDS crisis. *Journal of Mental Health Counseling, 13*(2), 264–269.

Hokenstad, M. C. (1987, October). Major challenges to social work education: Teaching practitioners ethical judgment. *NASW News,* p. 4.

Hollis, J. W., & Wantz, R. A. (1990). *Counselor preparation 1990–1992: Programs, personnel, trends* (7th ed.). Muncie, IN: Accelerated Development.

Holroyd, J. (1983). Erotic contact as an instance of sex-biased therapy. In J. Murray & P. Abramson (Eds.), *Bias in psychotherapy* (pp. 285–308). New York: Praeger.

Holroyd, J., & Bouhoutsos, J. C. (1985). Sources of bias in reporting effects of sexual contact with patients. *Professional Psychology: Research and Practice, 16*(5), 701–709.

Holroyd, J., & Brodsky, A. (1977). Psychologists' attitudes and practices regarding erotic and nonerotic physical contact with patients. *American Psychologist, 32*(10), 843–849.

Holroyd, J. C., & Brodsky, A. (1980). Does touching patients lead to sexual intercourse? *Professional Psychology, 11*(5), 807–811.

Holub, E. A., & Lee, S. S. (1990). Therapists' use of nonerotic physical contact: Ethical concerns. *Professional Psychology: Research and Practice, 21*(2), 115–117.

*Hopkins, B. R., & Anderson, B. S. (1990). *The counselor and the law* (3rd ed.). Alexandria, VA: AACD Press.

Horne, A. M., & Passmore, J. L. (1991). *Family counseling and therapy* (2nd ed.). Itasca, IL: F. E. Peacock.

*Hotelling, K. (1988). Ethical, legal, and administrative options to address sexual relationships between counselor and client. *Journal of Counseling and Development, 67*(4), 233–237.

Hotelling, K. (1991). Sexual harassment: A problem shielded by silence. *Journal of Counseling and Development, 69*(6), 497–501.

Howard, S. (1991). Organizational resources for addressing sexual harassment. *Journal of Counseling and Development, 69*(6), 507–511.

Huber, C. H., & Baruth, L. G. (1987). *Ethical, legal, and professional issues in the practice of marriage and family therapy.* Columbus, OH: Merrill.

Huddleston, J. E., & Engels, D. W. (1986). Issues related to the use of paradoxical techniques in counseling. *Journal of Counseling and Human Service Professions, 1*(1), 127–133.

Huey, W. C. (1986). Ethical concerns in school counseling. *Journal of Counseling and Development, 64*(5), 318–320.

Huey, W. C. (1987, May). Ethical standards for school counselors: Test your knowledge. *The School Counselor,* pp. 331–335.

Huey, W. C., & Remley, T. P., Jr. (1989). *Ethical issues in school counseling.* Alexandria, VA: American Association for Counseling and Development.

Humphrey, F. G. (1983). *Marital therapy.* Englewood Cliffs, NJ: Prentice-Hall.

Ibrahim, F. A. (1986). *Cultural encapsulation of the APA ethical principles.* Unpublished manuscript, University of Connecticut, Storrs.

*Ibrahim, F. A., & Arredondo, P. M. (1986). Ethical standards for cross-cultural counseling: Counselor preparation, practice, assessment, and research. *Journal of Counseling and Development, 64*(5), 349–352.

*Ibrahim, F. A., & Arredondo, P. M. (1990). Ethical issues in multicultural counseling. In B. Herlihy and L. B. Golden (Eds.), *AACD ethical standards casebook* (4th ed.) (pp. 137–145). Alexandria, VA: American Association for Counseling and Development.

Imber, S. D., Glanz, L. M., Elkin, I., Sotsky, S. M., Boyer, J. L., & Leber, W. R. (1986). Ethical issues in psychotherapy research: Problems in a collaborative clinical trials study. *American Psychologist, 41*(2), 137–146.

Ivey, A. E. (1990). *Developmental strategies for helpers: Individual, family, and network interventions.* Pacific Grove, CA: Brooks/Cole.

Ivey, A. E., & Rigazio-DiGilio, S. A. (1991). Toward a developmental practice of mental health counseling: Strategies for training, practice, and political unity. *Journal of Mental Health Counseling, 13*(1), 21–36.

Jacklin, C. N. (1989). Female and male: Issues of gender. *American Psychologist, 44*(2), 127–133.

Jaffe, D. T. (1986). The inner strains of healing work: Therapy and self-renewal for health professionals. In C. D. Scott and J. Hawk (Eds.), *Heal thyself: The health of health care professionals.* New York: Brunner/Mazel.

*Jensen, J. P., & Bergin, A. E. (1988). Mental health values of professional therapists: A national interdisciplinary survey. *Professional Psychology: Research and Practice, 19*(3), 290–297.

Johnson, W. B., & Ridley, C. R. (in press). Sources of gain in Christian counseling and psychotherapy. *The Counseling Psychologist.*

Jones, E. E. (1985). Psychotherapy and counseling with black clients. In P. Pedersen (Ed.), *Handbook of cross-cultural counseling and therapy* (pp. 173–179). Westport, CT: Greenwood Press.

Jordan, A. E., & Meara, N. M. (1990). Ethics and the professional practice of psychologists: The role of virtues and principles. *Professional Psychology: Research and Practice, 21*(2), 107–114.

Jourard, S. (1968). *Disclosing man to himself.* Princeton, NJ: Van Nostrand.

Jourard, S. (1971). *The transparent self* (rev. ed.). New York: Van Nostrand.

*Kain, C. D. (1988). To breach or not to breach: Is that the question? A response to Gray and Harding. *Journal of Counseling and Development, 66*(5), 224–225.

Kalichman, S. C., & Craig, M. E. (1991). Professional psychologists' decisions to report suspected child abuse: Clinician and situation influences. *Professional Psychology: Research and Practice, 22*(1), 84–89.

Kaser-Boyd, N., Adelman, H. S., & Taylor, L. (1985). Minors' ability to identify risks and benefits of therapy. *Professional Psychology: Research and Practice, 16*(3), 411–417.

Kaslow, F. W. (1991). The art and science of family psychology. *American Psychologist, 46*(6), 621–626.

Katz, J. H. (1985). The sociopolitical nature of counseling. *The Counseling Psychologist, 13*(4), 615–624.

*Keith-Spiegel, P., & Koocher, G. (1985). *Ethics in psychology: Professional standards and cases.* New York: Random House.

Kilburg, R. R., Nathan, P. E., & Thoreson, R. W. (Eds.). (1986). *Professionals in distress: Issues, syndromes, and solutions in psychology.* Washington, DC: American Psychological Association.

Kimmel, A. J. (1991). Predictable biases in the ethical decision making of American psychologists. *American Psychologist, 46*(7), 786–788.

Kinnier, R. T. (1986). The need for psychosocial research on AIDS and counseling interventions for AIDS victims. *Journal of Counseling and Development, 64*, 472–474.

Kitchener, K. S. (1984). Intuition, critical evaluation and ethical principles: The foundation for ethical decisions in counseling psychology. *The Counseling Psychologist, 12*(3), 43–55.

Kitchener, K. S. (1986). Teaching applied ethics in counselor education: An integration of psychological processes and philosophical analysis. *Journal of Counseling and Development, 64*(5), 306–310.

Kitchener, K. S., & Harding, S. S. (1990). Dual role relationships. In B. Herlihy and L. B. Golden (Eds.), *AACD ethical standards casebook* (4th ed.) (pp. 146–154). Alexandria, VA: American Association for Counseling and Development.

Klagsbrun, S. C. (1982). Ethics in hospice care. *American Psychologist, 37*(11), 1263–1265.

Knapp, S. (1980). A primer on malpractice for psychologists. *Professional Psychology, 11*(4), 606–612.

Knapp, S., & VandeCreek, L. (1982). *Tarasoff:* Five years later. *Professional Psychology, 13*(4), 511–516.

Knapp, S. J., & VandeCreek, L. (1985). Psychotherapy and privileged communication in child custody cases. *Professional Psychology: Research and Practice, 16*(3), 398–410.

Knapp, S., & VandeCreek, L. (1990). Application of the duty to protect to HIV-positive patients. *Professional Psychology: Research and Practice, 21*(3), 161–166.

Knapp, S., VandeCreek, L., & Herzog, C. (1986). The duty to protect: Legal principles and guidelines. In P. Keller & L. Ritt (Eds.), *Innovations in clinical practice: A source book* (pp. 383–389). Sarasota, FL: Professional Resource Exchange.

Knapp, S. J., VandeCreek, L., & Zirkel, P. A. (1985). Legal research techniques: What the psychologist needs to know. *Professional Psychology: Research and Practice, 16*(3), 363–372.

Koltko, M. E. (1990). How religious beliefs affect psychotherapy: The example of Mormonism. *Psychotherapy, 27*(1), 132–141.

Koocher, G. P. (1976). A bill of rights for children in psychotherapy. In G. P. Koocher (Ed.), *Children's rights and the mental health professions.* New York: Wiley.

Koocher, G. P. (1989). Screening licensing examinations for accuracy. *Professional Psychology: Research and Practice, 20*(4), 269–271.

Koss, M. P. (1990). The women's mental health research agenda: Violence against women. *American Psychologist, 45*(3), 374–380.

Kottler, J. A. (1986). *On being a therapist.* San Francisco: Jossey-Bass.

Kottler, J. A. (1991). *The compleat therapist.* San Francisco: Jossey-Bass.

Kottler, J. A., & Blau, D. S. (1989). *The imperfect therapist: Learning from failure in therapeutic practice.* San Francisco: Jossey-Bass.

Kramer, S. A. (1990). *Positive endings in psychotherapy: Bringing meaningful closure to therapeutic relationships.* San Francisco: Jossey-Bass.

Kurpius, D. J. (1986). Consultation: An important human and organizational intervention. *Journal of Counseling and Human Service Professions, 1*(1), 58–66.

Kurpius, D., Gibson, G., Lewis, J., & Corbet, M. (1991). Ethical issues in supervising counseling practitioners. *Counselor Education and Supervision, 31*(1), 48–57.

La Forge, J., & Henderson, P. (1990). Counselor competency in the courtroom. *Journal of Counseling and Development, 68*(4), 456–459.

LaFromboise, T. D. (1985). The role of cultural diversity in counseling psychology. *The Counseling Psychologist, 13*(4), 649–655.

*LaFromboise, T. D., & Foster, S. L. (1989). Ethics in multicultural counseling. In P. Pedersen, J. Draguns, W. Lonner, and J. Trimble (Eds.), *Counseling across cultures* (3rd ed.) (pp. 115–136). Honolulu: University of Hawaii Press.

LaFromboise, T. D., Trimble, J. E., & Mohatt, G. V. (1990). Counseling interventiona nd American Indian tradition: An integrative approach. *The Counseling Psychologist, 18*(4), 628–654.

Laliotis, D. A., & Grayson, J. H. (1985). Psychologist heal thyself: What is available for the impaired psychologist? *American Psychologist, 40*(1), 84–96.

Lamb, D. H., Clark, C., Drumheller, P., Frizzell, K., & Surrey, L. (1989). Applying *Tarasoff* to AIDS-related psychotherapy issues. *Professional Psychology: Research and Practice, 20*(1), 37–43.

Lasenza, S. (1989). Some challenges of integrating sexual orientations into counselor training and research. *Journal of Counseling and Development, 68*(1), 73–76.

Laughran, W., & Bakken, G. M. (1984). The psychotherapist's responsibility toward third parties under current California law. *Western State University Law Review, 12*(1), 1–33.

Lazarus, A. A. (1990). Can psychotherapists transcend the shackles of their training and superstitions? *Journal of Clinical Psychology, 46*(3), 351–358.

Leafgren, F. (1990). Men on a journey. In D. Moore and F. Leafgren (Eds.), *Problem solving strategies and interventions for men in conflict* (pp. 3–10). Alexandria, VA: American Association for Counseling and Development.

Lee, C. C. (1991a). Cultural dynamics: Their importance in multicultural counseling. In C. C. Lee & B. L. Richardson (Eds.), *Multicultural issues in counseling: New approaches to diversity* (pp. 11–17). Alexandria, VA: American Association for Counseling and Development.

Lee, C. C. (1991b). New approaches to diversity: Implications for multicultural counselor training and research. In C. C. Lee & B. L. Richardson (Eds.), *Multicultural issues in counseling: New approaches to diversity* (pp. 209–214). Alexandria, VA: American Association for Counseling and Development.

Lee, C. C., & Richardson, B. L. (1991a). *Multicultural issues in counseling: New approaches to diversity.* Alexandria, VA: American Association for Counseling and Development.

Lee, C. C., & Richardson, B. L. (1991b). Problems and pitfalls of multicultural counseling. In C. C. Lee & B. L. Richardson (Eds.), *Multicultural issues in counseling: New approaches to diversity* (pp. 3–9). Alexandria, VA: American Association for Counseling and Development.

Lee, L. A., & Heppner, P. P. (1991). The development and evaluation of a sexual harassment inventory. *Journal of Counseling and Development, 69*(6), 512–517.

Lefley, H. P., & Pedersen, P. (Eds.). (1986). *Cross-cultural training for mental health professionals.* Springfield, IL: Charles C Thomas.

Leininger, M. M. (1985). Transcultural caring: A different way to help people. In P. Pedersen (Ed.), *Handbook of cross-cultural counseling and therapy* (pp. 107–115). Westport, CT: Greenwood Press.

Leslie, R. (1989a, July/August). Confidentiality. *The California Therapist,* pp. 9–13.

Leslie, R. (1989b, November/December). Dual relationships: The legal view. *The California Therapist*, pp. 9–13.

Leslie, R. (1989c, March/April). Treatment of minors without parental consent. *The California Therapist*, p. 7.

Leslie, R. (1990, March/April). The dangerous patient: *Tarasoff* revisited. *The California Therapist*, pp. 11–14.

Leslie, R. (1991a, January/February). Dual relationships hearing held. *The California Therapist*, pp. 18–19.

Leslie, R. (1991b, July/August). Psychotherapist-patient privilege clarified. *The California Therapist*, pp. 11–19.

*Levenson, J. L. (1986). When a colleague practices unethically: Guidelines for intervention. *Journal of Counseling and Development, 64*(5), 315–317.

Levine, C. (1987). *Taking sides: Clashing views on controversial bioethical issues* (2nd ed.). Guilford, CT: Dushkin Publishing Group.

Levine, E. S., & Padilla, A. M. (1980). *Crossing cultures in therapy: Pluralistic counseling for the Hispanic.* Pacific Grove, CA: Brooks/Cole.

Lewis, G. J., Greenburg, S. L., & Hatch, D. B. (1988). Peer consultation groups for psychologists in private practice: A national survey. *Professional Psychology: Research and Practice, 19*(1), 81–86.

Lewis, J. A., & Lewis, M. D. (1989). *Community counseling.* Pacific Grove, CA: Brooks/Cole.

Lewis, R. E. (1985). *Educating effective counselors for women clients: A survey of training practices.* Paper presented at the annual meeting of the American Psychological Association, Los Angeles.

Lief, H. (1982). Ethical problems in sex therapy. In M. Rosenbaum (Ed.), *Ethics and values in psychotherapy: A guidebook.* New York: Free Press.

Lindsey, R. T. (1984). Informed consent and deception in psychotherapy research: An ethical analysis. *The Counseling Psychologist, 12*(3), 79–86.

Linzer, N. (1990). Ethics and human service practice. *Human Service Education, 10*(1), 15–22.

Lipsitz, N. E. (1985). *The relationship between ethics training and ethical discrimination ability.* Paper presented at the annual meeting of the American Psychological Association, Los Angeles.

Liss-Levinson, N. (1979). Women with sexual concerns. *The Counseling Psychologist, 8*(1), 36–37.

Lloyd, A. P. (1990). Dual relationships in group activities: A counselor education accreditation dilemma. *Journal for Specialists in Group Work, 15*(2), 83–87.

Loewenberg, F., & Dolgoff, R. (1988). *Ethical decisions for social work practice* (3rd ed.). Itasca, IL: F. E. Peacock.

Locke, D. C. (1990). A not so provincial view of multicultural counseling. *Counselor Education and Supervision, 30*(1), 18–25.

Loiacano, D. K. (1989). Gay identity issues among black Americans: Racism, homophobia, and the need for validation. *Journal of Counseling and Development, 68*(1), 21–25.

Lonner, W. J., & Ibrahim, F. A. (1989). Assessment in cross-cultural counseling. In P. Pedersen, J. Draguns, W. Lonner, and J. Trimble (Eds.), *Counseling across cultures* (pp. 299–333). Honolulu: University of Hawaii Press.

Lonner, W. J., & Sundberg, N. D. (1985). Assessment in cross-cultural counseling and therapy. In P. Pedersen (Ed.), *Handbook of cross-cultural counseling and therapy* (pp. 199–205). Westport, CT: Greenwood Press.

Lopez, S. R., Grover, K. P., Holland, D., Johnson, M. J., Kain, C. D., Kanel, K., Mellins, C. A., & Rhyne, M. C. (1989). Development of culturally sensitive psychotherapists. *Professional Psychology: Research and Practice, 20*(6), 369–376.

Lorion, R. P., & Parron, D. L. (1985). Countering the countertransference: A strategy for treating the untreatable. In P. Pedersen (Ed.), *Handbook of cross-cultural counseling and therapy* (pp. 79–86). Westport, CT: Greenwood Press.

Lovett, T., & Lovett, C. J. (1988). *Suggestions for continuing legal education units in counselor training.* Paper presented at the annual meeting of the American Association for Counseling and Development, Chicago.

Lowman, R. L. (1985). Ethical practice of psychological consultation: Not an impossible dream. *The Counseling Psychologist, 13*(3), 466–472.

Luken, D. (1990, May/June). An empowerment model of supervision: A guide to the therapist within. *The California Therapist,* pp. 42–46.

Lum, D. (1992). *Social work practice and people of color: A process-stage approach* (2nd ed.). Pacific Grove, CA: Brooks/Cole.

Mabe, A. R., & Rollin, S. A. (1986). The role of a code of ethical standards in counseling. *Journal of Counseling and Development, 64*(5), 294–297.

Mahalik, J. R. (1990). Systematic eclectic models. *The Counseling Psychologist, 18*(4), 655–679.

Mahoney, M. J. (1986). Paradoxical intention, symptom prescription, and principles of therapeutic change. *The Counseling Psychologist, 14*(2), 283–290.

*Mappes, D. C., Robb, G. P., & Engels, D. W. (1985). Conflicts between ethics and law in counseling and psychotherapy. *Journal of Counseling and Development, 64*(4), 246–252.

Margolin, G. (1982). Ethical and legal considerations in marital and family therapy. *American Psychologist, 37*(7), 788–801.

Martin, D. J. (1989). Human immunodeficiency virus infection and the gay community: Counseling and clinical issues. *Journal of Counseling and Development, 68*(1), 67–72.

Maslach, C. (1982). *Burnout: The cost of caring.* Englewood Cliffs, NJ: Prentice-Hall (Spectrum).

McBride, A. B. (1990). Mental health effects of women's multiple roles. *American Psychologist, 45*(3), 381–384.

McBride, M. C. (1990). Autonomy and the struggle for female identity: Implications for counseling women. *Journal of Counseling and Development, 69*(1), 22–26.

McDermott, D., Tyndall, L., & Lichtenberg, J. W. (1989). Factors related to counselor preference among gays and lesbians. *Journal of Counseling and Development,68*(1), 31–35.

McGoldrick, M., Pearce, J. K., & Giordano, J. (Eds.). (1982). *Ethnicity and family therapy.* New York: Guilford Press.

McGowen, K. R., & Hart, L. E. (1990). Still different after all these years: Gender differences in professional identity formation. *Professional Psychology: Research and Practice, 21*(2), 118–123.

McGuire, J. M., Toal, P., & Blau, B. (1985). The adult client's conception of confidentiality in the therapeutic relationship. *Professional Psychology: Research and Practice, 16*(3), 375–384.

McNamara, K., & Richard, K. M. (1989). Feminist identity development: Implications for feminist therapy with women. *Journal of Counseling and Development, 68*(2), 184–189.

McRae, M. B., & Johnson, S. D. (1991). Toward training for competence in multicultural counselor education. *Journal of Counseling and Development, 70*(1), 131–135.

McWhirter, E. H. (1991). Empowerment in counseling. *Journal of Counseling and Development, 69*(3), 222–227.

McWhirter, J. J. (1989). Religion and the practice of counseling psychology. *The Counseling Psychologist, 17*(4), 613–616.

McWhirter, J. J., & Okey, J. L. (1990). Ethical conflicts in cases of suspected child abuse. In B. Herlihy and L. B. Golden (Eds.), *AACD ethical standards casebook* (4th ed.) (pp. 155–161). Alexandria, VA: American Association for Counseling and Development.

Medeiros, M. E., & Prochaska, J. O. (1988). Coping strategies that psychotherapists use in working with stressful clients. *Professional Psychology: Research and Practice, 19*(1), 112–114.

Melton, G. B. (1981a). Children's participation in treatment planning: Psychological and legal issues. *Professional Psychology, 12*(2), 246–252.

Melton, G. B. (1981b). Effects of a state law permitting minors to consent to psychotherapy. *Professional Psychology, 12*(5), 647–654.

Melton, G. B. (1988). Ethical and legal issues in AIDS-related practice. *American Psychologist, 43*(11), 941–947.

Melton, G. B. (1991). Ethical judgments amid uncertainty. *The Counseling Psychologist,* 19(4), 561–565.

Melton, G. B., & Limber, S. (1989). Psychologists' involvement in cases of child maltreatment: Limits of role and expertise. *American Psychologist,* 44(9), 1225–1233.

Melton, G. B., & Wilcox, B. L. (1989). Changes in family law and family life: Challenges for psychology. *American Psychologist,* 44(9), 1213–1216.

Merta, R. J., & Sisson, J. A. (1991). The experiential group: An ethical and professional dilemma. *Journal for Specialists in Group Work,* 16(4), 236–245.

*Miller, D. J., & Thelen, M. H. (1986). Knowledge and beliefs about confidentiality in psychotherapy. *Professional Psychology: Research and Practice,* 17(1), 15–19.

Miller, W. R. (1988). Including clients' spiritual perspectives in cognitive-behavior therapy. In W. R. Miller & J. E. Martin (Eds.), *Behavior therapy and religion: Integrating spiritual and behavioral approaches to change* (pp. 43–56). Newbury Park, CA: Sage.

Miller, W. R., & Martin, J. E. (Eds.). (1988a). *Behavior therapy and religion: Integrating spiritual and behavioral approaches to change.* Newbury Park, CA: Sage.

Miller, W. R., & Martin, J. E. (1988b). Spirituality and behavioral psychology: Toward integration. In W. R. Miller & J. E. Martin (Eds.), *Behavior therapy and religion: Integrating spiritual and behavioral approaches to change* (pp. 13–24). Newbury Park, CA: Sage.

Mills, D. H. (1984). Ethics education and adjudication within psychology. *American Psychologist,* 39(6), 669–675.

Mintz, L. B., & O'Neil, J. M. (1990). Gender roles, sex and the process of psychotherapy: Many questions and few answers. *Journal of Counseling and Development,* 68(4), 381–387.

Minuchin, S. (1974). *Families and family therapy.* Cambridge, MA: Harvard University Press.

Mio, J. S., & Morris, D. R. (1990). Cross-cultural issues in psychology training programs: An invitation for discussion. *Professional Psychology: Research and Practice,* 21(6), 434–441.

Miranda, J., & Storms, M. (1989). Psychological adjustment of lesbians and gay men. *Journal of Counseling and Development,* 68(1), 41–45.

*Morin, S. F. (1988). AIDS: The challenge to psychology. *American Psychologist,* 43(11), 838–842.

Morrison, C. F. (1989). AIDS: Ethical implications for psychological intervention. *Professional Psychology: Research and Practice,* 20(3), 166–171.

Morrison, J., Layton, B., & Newman, J. (1982). Ethical conflict in clinical decision making: A challenge for family therapists. In J. Hansen (Ed.), *Values, ethics, legalities and the family therapist.* Rockville, MD: Aspen.

Morrow, S. L., & Hawxhurst, D. M. (1989). Lesbian partner abuse: Implications for therapists. *Journal of Counseling and Development,* 68(1), 58–62.

Moses, A. E., & Hawkins, R. O. (1982). *Counseling lesbian women and gay men: A life issues approach.* St. Louis: C. V. Mosby.

Moyers, J. C. (1990). Religious issues in the psychotherapy of former fundamentalists. *Psychotherapy,* 27(1), 42–45.

Muehleman, T., Kimmons, C. (1981). Psychologists' views on child abuse reporting, confidentiality, life, and the law: An exploratory study. *Professional Psychology,* 12(5), 631–638.

*Muehleman, T., Pickens, B. K., & Robinson, F. (1985). Informing clients about the limits to confidentiality, risks, and their rights: Is self-disclosure inhibited? *Professional Psychology: Research and Practice,* 16(3), 385–397.

Mulvey, E. P., Geller, J. L., & Roth, L. H. (1987). The promise and peril of involuntary outpatient commitment. *American Psychologist,* 42(6), 571–584.

Murphy, B. C. (1989). Lesbian couples and their parents: The effects of perceived parental attitudes on the couple. *Journal of Counseling and Development,* 68(1), 46–51.

National Association of Social Workers. (1989). *Standards for the private practice of clinical social work.* Washington, DC: Author.

National Association of Social Workers. (1990). *Code of ethics* (rev. ed.). Silver Springs, MD: Author.

National Board for Certified Counselors. (1989). *National Board for Certified Counselors: Code of ethics.* Alexandria, VA: Author.

National Federation of Societies for Clinical Social Work. (1985). *Code of ethics.* Silver Springs, MD: Author.

Neukrug, E. S., Healy, M., & Herlihy, B. (undated). *Ethical practices of licensed professional counselors: An updated survey of state licensing boards.* Unpublished manuscript.

Neukrug, E. S., & Williams, G. T. (undated). *The counselor's counselor: Type and frequency of attendance in therapy.* Unpublished manuscript.

Newman, A. S. (1981). Ethical issues in the supervision of psychotherapy. *Professional Psychology, 12*(6), 690–695.

Nichols, M. P., & Schwartz, R. C. (1991). *Family therapy: Concepts and methods* (2nd ed.). Boston: Allyn & Bacon.

Nishio, K., & Bilmes, M. (1987). Psychotherapy with Southeast Asian American clients. *Professional Psychology: Research and Practice, 18*(4), 342–346.

Nutt, R. L. (1979). Review and preview of attitudes and values of counselors of women. *The Counseling Psychologist, 8*(1), 18–20.

O'Neil, J. M. (1990). Assessing men's gender role conflict. In D. Moore and F. Leafgren (Eds.), *Problem solving strategies and interventions for men in conflict* (pp. 23–38). Alexandria, VA: American Association for Counseling and Development.

O'Neill, C., & Ritter, K. (1992). *Coming out within: Stages of spiritual awakening for lesbians and gay men.* San Francisco: Harper San Francisco.

O'Shea, M., & Jessee, E. (1982). Ethical, value, and professional conflicts in systems therapy. In J. Hansen (Ed.), *Values, ethics, legalities and the family therapist.* Rockville, MD: Aspen.

Overholser, J. C. (1991). The Socratic method as a technique in psychotherapy supervision. *Professional Psychology: Research and Practice, 22*(1), 68–74.

Overholser, J. C., & Fine, M. A. (1990). Defining the boundaries of professional competence: Managing subtle cases of clinical incompetence. *Professional Psychology: Research and Practice, 21*(6), 462–469.

Pape, D. A. (1987). A code of ethics as a working document. *Journal of Applied Rehabilitation Counseling, 18*(4), 48–49.

Paradise, L. V., & Kirby, P. C. (1990). Some perspectives on the legal liability of group counseling in private practice. *Journal for Specialists in Group Work, 15*(2), 114–118.

Paradise, L., & Siegelwaks, B. (1982). Ethical training for group leaders. *Journal for Specialists in Group Work, 7*(3), 162–166.

Paranjpe, A. C., Ho, D. Y. F., & Rieber, R. W. (Eds.). (1988). *Asian contributions to psychology.* New York: Praeger.

Patrick, K. D. (1989). Unique ethical dilemmas in counselor training. *Counselor Education and Supervision, 28*(4), 337–341.

Patten, C., Barnett, T., & Houlihan, D. (1991). Ethics in marital and family therapy: A review of the literature. *Professional Psychology: Research and Practice, 22*(2), 171–175.

Patterson, C. H. (1985a). New light for counseling theory. *Journal of Counseling and Development, 63*(6), 349–350.

Patterson, C. H. (1985b). *The therapeutic relationship: Foundations for an eclectic psychotherapy.* Pacific Grove, CA: Brooks/Cole.

Patterson, C. H. (1989). Values in counseling and psychotherapy. *Counseling and values, 33*, 164–176.

Patterson, G. R., DeBarsyshe, B. D., & Ramsey, E. (1989). A developmental perspective on antisocial behavior. *American Psychologist, 44*(2), 329–335.

Pedersen, P. (1981). Triad counseling. In R. Corsini (Ed.), *Innovative psychotherapies* (pp. 840–855). New York: Wiley Interscience.

*Pedersen, P. (Ed.). (1985a). *Handbook of cross-cultural counseling and therapy.* Westport, CT: Greenwood Press.

*Pedersen, P. (1985b). Intercultural criteria for mental-health training. In P. Pedersen (Ed.), *Handbook of cross-cultural counseling and therapy* (pp. 315–321). Westport, CT: Greenwood Press.

Pedersen, P. (1987). Ten frequent assumptions of cultural bias in counseling. *Journal of Multicultural Counseling and Development, 15*, 16–24.

Pedersen, P. (1988). *A handbook for developing multicultural awareness*. Alexandria, VA: American Association for Counseling and Development.

Pedersen, P. (1989). Developing multicultural ethical guidelines for psychology. *International Journal of Psychology, 24*, 643–652.

Pedersen, P. (1990a). The constructs of complexity and balance in multicultural counseling theory and practice. *Journal of Counseling and Development, 68*(5), 550–554.

Pedersen, P. (1990b). The multicultural perspective as a fourth force in counseling. *Journal of Mental Health Counselors, 12*(1), 93–94.

Pedersen, P. (1991). Multiculturalism as a generic approach to counseling. *Journal of Counseling and Development, 70*(1), 6–12.

Pedersen, P. B. (in press). The culture bound counselor. *Journal of Counseling and Development*.

Pedersen, P., Avelondo, P. M., Lefly, H. P., Johnson, S. E., Trimble, J. E., & Murase, K. (1983, August). *Symposium: Cross-cultural training programs for counselor education*. Paper presented at the annual meeting of the American Psychological Association, Anaheim, CA.

Pedersen, P. B., Draguns, J., Lonner, W., & Trimble, J. (Eds.). (1989). *Counseling across cultures* (3rd. ed.). Honolulu: University of Hawaii Press.

Pedersen, P. B., Fukuyama, M., & Heath, A. (1989). Client, counselor, and contextual variables in multicultural counseling. In P. B. Pedersen, J. Draguns, W. Lonner, & J. Trimble (Eds.), *Counseling across cultures* (3rd ed.) (pp. 23–52). Honolulu: University of Hawaii Press.

Pedersen, P. B., & Marsella, A. J. (1982). The ethical crisis for cross-cultural counseling and therapy. *Professional Psychology, 13*(4), 492–500.

Pelsma, D. M., & Borgers, S. G. (1986). Experience-based ethics: A developmental model of learning ethical reasoning. *Journal of Counseling and Development, 64*(5), 311–314.

Piazza, N. J., & Baruth, N. E. (1990). Client record guidelines. *Journal of Counseling and Development, 68*(3), 313–316.

Pincu, L. (1989). Sexual compulsivity in gay men: Controversy and treatment. *Journal of Counseling and Development, 68*(1), 63–66.

Pines, A. (1986). Who is to blame for helpers' burnout? Environmental impact. In C. D. Scott & J. Hawk (Eds.), *Heal thyself: The health of health care professionals*. New York: Brunner/Mazel.

Pines, A., & Aronson, E., with Kafry, D. (1981). *Burnout: From tedium to personal growth*. New York: Free Press.

Pinney, E. L. (1983). Ethical and legal issues in group psychotherapy. In H. Kaplan & B. Sadock (Eds.), *Comprehensive group psychotherapy* (2nd ed.). Baltimore: Williams & Wilkins.

Plotkin, R. (1978, March). Confidentiality in group counseling. *APA Monitor*, p. 14.

Ponzo, Z. (1985). The counselor and physical attractiveness. *Journal of Counseling and Development, 63*(8), 482–485.

Pope, K. S. (1985a, April). Dual relationships: A violation of ethical, legal, and clinical standards. *California State Psychologist, 20*(3), 3–5.

Pope, K. S. (1985b, July/August). The suicidal client: Guidelines for assessment and treatment. *California State Psychologist, 20*(5), 3–7.

Pope, K. S. (1986). New trends in malpractice cases and changes in APA's liability insurance. *Independent Practitioner, 6*(4), 23–26.

Pope, K. S. (1987). Preventing therapist-patient sexual intimacy: Therapy for a therapist at risk. *Professional Psychology: Research and Practice, 18*(6), 624–628.

*Pope, K. S. (1988). How clients are harmed by sexual contact with mental health professionals: The syndrome and its prevalence. *Journal of Counseling and Development, 67*(4), 222–226.

Pope, K. S. (1990a). Ethical and malpractice issues in hospital practice. *American Psychologist, 45*(9), 1066–1070.

Pope, K. S. (1990b). Therapist-patient sex as sex abuse: Six scientific, professional, and practical dilemmas in addressing victimization and rehabilitation. *Professional Psychology: Research and Practice, 21*(4), 227–239.

*Pope, K. S., & Bouhoutsos, J. C. (1986). *Sexual intimacy between therapists and patients.* New York: Praeger.

*Pope, K. S., Keith-Spiegel, P., & Tabachnick, B. G. (1986). Sexual attraction to clients: The human therapist and the (sometimes) inhuman training system. *American Psychologist, 41*(2), 147–158.

Pope, K. S., Levenson, H., & Schover, L. R. (1979). Sexual intimacy in psychology training: Results and implications of a national survey. *American Psychologist, 34*(8), 682–689.

Pope, K. S., Schover, L. R., Levenson, H. (1980). Sexual behavior between clinical supervisors and trainees: Implications for professional standards. *Professional Psychology, 10,* 157–162.

*Pope, K. S., Tabachnick, B. G., & Keith-Spiegel, P. (1987). Ethics of practice: The beliefs and behaviors of psychologists as therapists. *American Psychologist, 42*(11), 993–1006.

Pope, K. S., Tabachnick, B. G., & Keith-Spiegel, P. (1988). Good and poor practices in psychotherapy: National survey of beliefs of psychologists. *Professional Psychology: Research and Practice, 19*(5), 547–552.

Pope, K. S., & Vasquez, M. J. T. (1991). *Ethics in psychotherapy and counseling: A practical guide for psychologists.* San Francisco: Jossey-Bass.

Posey, E. C. (1988). Confidentiality in an AIDS support group. *Journal of Counseling and Development, 66*(5), 226–227.

Post, P. (1989). The use of the ethical judgment scale in counselor education. *Counselor Education and Supervision, 28*(3), 229–233.

Powell, C. (1982, August). *Adolescence and the right to die: Issues of autonomy, competence and paternalism.* Paper presented at the meeting of the American Psychological Association, Washington, DC.

Powell, C. (1984). Ethical principles and issues of competence in counseling adolescents. *The Counseling Psychologist, 12*(3), 57–68.

Quackenbos, S., Privette, G., & Klentz, B. (1986). Psychotherapy and religion: Rapprochment or antithesis? *Journal of Counseling and Development, 65*(2), 82–85.

Rabinowitz, F. E. (1991). The male-to-male embrace: Breaking the touch taboo in a men's therapy group. *Journal of Counseling and Development, 69*(6), 574–576.

Raquepaw, J. M., Miller, R. W. (1989). Psychotherapist burnout: A componential analysis. *Professional Psychology: Research and Practice, 20*(1), 32–36.

Raup, J. L., & Myers, J. E. (1989). The empty nest syndrome: Myth or reality? *Journal of Counseling and Development, 68*(2), 180–183.

Ray, L. Y., & Johnson, N. (1983). Adolescent suicide. *Personnel and Guidance Journal, 62*(3), 131–135.

Reaves, R. P. (1986). Legal liability and psychologists. In R. R. Kilburg, P. E. Nathan, & R. W. Thoreson (Eds.), *Professionals in distress: Issues, syndromes and solutions in psychology* (pp. 173–184). Washington, DC: American Psychological Association.

Remley, T. P. (1990). Counseling records: Legal and ethical issues. In B. Herlihy and L. B. Golden (Eds.), *AACD ethical standards casebook* (4th ed.) (pp. 162–169). Alexandria, VA: American Association for Counseling and Development.

Remley, T. P. (1991). *Preparing for court appearances.* Alexandria, VA: American Association for Counseling and Development.

Remley, T. P., & Reeves, T. G. (1990, March 17). *Counselor educator/graduate student relationships: Views from the literature.* Unpublished manuscript presented at the annual convention of the AACD, Cincinnati.

Reppucci, N. D., & Haugaard, J. J. (1989). Prevention of child sexual abuse: Myth or reality? *American Psychologist, 44*(10), 1266–1275.

Richards, D. L. (1990). *Building and managing your private practice.* Alexandria, VA: American Association for Counseling and Development.

Ridley, C. (1989). Racism in counseling as an aversive behavioral process. In P. Pedersen, J. Draguns, W. Lonner, and J. Trimble (Eds.), *Counseling across cultures* (3rd ed.) (pp. 55–79). Honolulu: University of Hawaii Press.

Ridley, C. R. (1984). Clinical treatment of the nondisclosing black client: A therapeutic paradox. *American Psychologist, 39*(11), 1234–1244.

Ridley, C. R. (1985). Imperatives for ethnic and cultural relevance in psychology training programs. *Professional Psychology: Research and Practice, 16*(5), 611–622.

Ridley, C. R. (1989). Racism in counseling as an adversive behavioral process. In P. Pedersen, J. Draguns, W. Lonner, & J. Trimble (Eds.), *Counseling across cultures* (3rd ed.) (pp. 55–77). Honolulu: University of Hawaii Press.

Riger, S. (1991). Gender dilemmas in sexual harassment: Policies and procedures. *American Psychologist, 46*(5), 497–505.

Ritter, K. Y., & O'Neill, C. W. (1989). Moving through loss: The spiritual journey of gay men and lesbian women. *Journal of Counseling and Development, 68*(1), 9–15.

Roan, S. (1991, July 17). Effectiveness of making therapists report all child abuse questioned. *Los Angeles Times.*

Roberts, G. T., Murrell, P. H., Thomas, R. E., & Claxton, C. S. (1982). Ethical concerns for counselor educators. *Counselor Education and Supervision, 22,* 8–14.

Robiner, W. N., & Schofield, W. (1990). References on supervision in clinical and counseling psychology. *Professional Psychology: Research and Practice, 21*(4), 297–312.

Robinson, S. E., & Gross, D. R. (1985). Ethics of consultation: The Canterville ghost. *The Counseling Psychologist, 13*(3), 444–465.

Robinson, W. L., & Reid, P. T. (1985). Sexual intimacies in psychology revisited. *Professional Psychology: Research and Practice, 16*(4), 512–520.

Robison, F. F., & Ward, D. (1990). Research activities and attitudes among ASGW members. *Journal for Specialists in Group Work, 19*(4), 215–224.

Rodolfa, E. R., Kitzrow, M., Vohra, S., & Wilson, B. (1990). Training interns to respond to sexual dilemmas. *Professional Psychology: Research and Practice, 21*(4), 313–315.

Rogers, C. (1942). *Counseling and psychotherapy.* Boston: Houghton Mifflin.

Rogers, C. (1951). *Client-centered therapy.* Boston: Houghton Mifflin.

Rogers, C. (1961). *On becoming a person.* Boston: Houghton Mifflin.

Rogers, C. (1980). *A way of being.* Boston: Houghton Mifflin.

Rogers, J. R. (1990). Female suicide: The trend toward increased lethality in method of choice and its implications. *Journal of Counseling and Development, 69*(1), 37–38.

Rogler, L. H., Malgady, R. G., Costantino, G., & Blumenthal, R. (1987, June). What do culturally sensitive mental health services mean? *American Psychologist, 42*(6), 565–570.

Rokeach, M., & Ball-Rokeach, S. J. (1989). Stability and change in American value priorities, 1968–1981. *American Psychologist, 44*(5), 775–784.

Rosenbaum, M. (1982a). Ethical problems of group psychotherapy. In M. Rosenbaum (Ed.), *Ethics and values in psychotherapy: A guidebook.* New York: Free Press.

Rosenbaum, M. (Ed.). (1982b). *Ethics and values in psychotherapy: A guidebook.* New York: Free Press.

*Rubanowitz, D. E. (1987). Public attitudes toward psychotherapist-client confidentiality. *Professional Psychology: Research and Practice, 18*(6), 613–618.

Rudolph, J. (1989a). Effects of a workshop on mental health practitioners' attitudes toward homosexuality and counseling effectiveness. *Journal of Counseling and Development, 68*(1), 81–85.

Rudolph, J. (1989b). The impact of contemporary ideology and AIDS on the counseling of gay clients. *Counseling and Values, 33,* 96–108.

Russo, F. (1990). Overview: Forging research priorities for women's mental health. *American Psychologist, 45*(3), 368–373.

Rutter, P. (1989). *Sex in the forbidden zone.* Los Angeles: J. P. Tarcher.

Ryder, R. & Hepworth, J. (1990). AAMFT ethical code: "Dual relationships." *Journal of Marital and Family Therapy, 16*(2), 127–132.

Saeki, C., & Borow, H. (1985). Counseling and psychotherapy: East and West. In P. Pedersen (Ed.), *Handbook of cross-cultural counseling and therapy* (pp. 223–229). Westport, CT: Greenwood Press.

Sampson, D. E., & Liberty, L. H. (1989). Textbooks used in counselor education programs. *Counselor Education and Supervision, 29*(2), 111–121.

Sampson, J. P. (1990). Ethical use of computer applications in counseling: Past, present and future perspectives. In B. Herlihy and L. Golden (Eds.), *AACD ethical standards casebook* (4th ed.) (pp. 170–176). Alexandria, VA: American Association for Counseling and Development.

Sanders, J. R., & Keith-Spiegel, P. (1980). Formal and informal adjudication of ethics complaints against psychologists. *American Psychologist, 3*(12), 1096–1105.

Sang, B. E. (1989). New directions in lesbian research, theory, and education. *Journal of Counseling and Development, 68*(1), 92–96.

Saper, B. (1987). Humor in psychotherapy: Is it good or bad for the client? *Professional Psychology: Research and Practice, 18*(4), 360–367.

Scarato, A. M., & Sigall, B. A. (1979). Multiple role women. *The Counseling Psychologist, 8*(1), 26–27.

Schaecher, R. M. (1988). Working with lesbian and gay youth. *Carrera/Spain, Adolescent Sexuality Report, 1*(4), 7–9.

Schafer, C. (1990). Ethics: Dual relationships come under scrutiny. *Guidepost* (AACD), 32(12).

Scher, M., & Good, G. E. (1990a). Gender and counseling in the twenty-first century: What does the future hold? *Journal of Counseling and Development, 68*(4), 388–391.

Scher, M., & Good, G. E. (1990b). Introduction: Special feature on gender issues in counseling. *Journal of Counseling and Development, 68*(4), 370.

Schmidt, L. D. (1986). Some questions about paradoxical interventions. *The Counseling Psychologist, 14*(2), 309–312.

Schneider, M. S., & Tremble, B. (1986). Training service providers to work with gay or lesbian adolescents: A workshop. *Journal of Counseling and Development, 65*(2), 98–99.

Schoener, G. R., & Gonsiorek, J. (1988). Assessment and development of rehabilitation plans for counselors who have sexually exploited their clients. *Journal of Counseling and Development, 67*(4), 227–232.

Schoener, G. R., & Gonsiorek, J. (1989, November/December). Assessment and development of rehabilitation plans for counselors who have sexually exploited their clients. *The California Therapist,* pp. 32–39.

Schoener, G. R., Milgrom, J. H., Gonsiorek, J. C., Luepker, E. T., & Conroe, R. M. (1989). *Psychotherapists' involvement with clients: Intervention and prevention.* Minneapolis: Walk-In Counseling Center.

Schulte, J. M. (1990). The morality of influencing in counseling. *Counseling and Values, 34*(2), 103–118.

*Schutz, B. (1982). *Legal liability in psychotherapy.* San Francisco: Jossey-Bass.

Scott, C. D., & Hawk, J. (Eds.). (1986). *Heal thyself: The health of health care professionals.* New York: Brunner/Mazel.

Scott, N. E., & Borodowsky, L. G. (1990). Effective use of cultural role taking. *Professional Psychology: Research and Practice, 21*(3), 167–170.

Scott, N. S. (1985, December). Counseling prisoners: Ethical issues, dilemmas, and cautions. *Journal of Counseling and Development, 64,* 272–273.

*Sell, J. M., Gottlieb, M. C., & Schoenfeld, L. (1986). Ethical considerations of social/romantic relationships with present and former clients. *Professional Psychology: Research and Practice, 17*(6), 504–508.

Seymour, W. (1982). Counselor/therapist values and therapeutic style. In J. Hansen (Ed.), *Values, ethics, legalities and the family therapist.* Rockville, MD: Aspen.

Shabahangi, N. R. (1990, May/June). Psychotherapy and the art of being humble. *The California Therapist*, p. 56.

Shafranske, E. P., & Malony, H. N. (1990). Clinical psychologists' religious and spiritual orientations and their practice of psychotherapy. *Psychotherapy, 27*(1), 72–78.

Shah, S. (1969). Privileged communications, confidentiality, and privacy: Privileged communications. *Professional Psychology, 1*(1), 56–69.

Shah, S. (1970a). Privileged communications, confidentiality, and privacy: Confidentiality. *Professional Psychology, 1*(2), 159–164.

Shah, S. (1970b). Privileged communications, confidentiality, and privacy: Privacy. *Professional Psychology, 1*(3), 243–252.

Shannon, J. W., & Woods, W. J. (1991). Affirmative psychotherapy for gay men. *The Counseling Psychologist, 19*(2), 197–215.

Shapiro, J. L., & Grandin, D. A. (1985). A comparative investigation of the effects of encounter groups on Japanese and Caucasian American counselors in training. *Psychotherapy, 22,* 451–452.

*Sheeley, V. L., & Herlihy, B. (1986). The ethics of confidentiality and privileged communication. *Journal of Counseling and Human Service Professions, 1*(1), 141–148.

Sheeley, V. L., & Herlihy, B. (1987, March). Privileged communication in school counseling: Status update. *The School Counselor,* pp. 268–272.

Sheinberg, M., & Penn, P. (1991). Gender dilemmas, gender questions, and gender mantra. *Journal of Marital and Family Therapy, 17*(1), 33–44.

Sherry, P. (1991). Ethical issues in the conduct of supervision. *The Counseling Psychologist, 19*(4), 566–584.

Siegel, M. (1979). Privacy, ethics, and confidentiality. *Professional Psychology, 10*(2), 249–258.

Skorina, J. K., Bissell, L., & De Soto, C. B. (1990). Alcoholic psychologists: Routes to recovery. *Professional Psychology: Research and Practice, 21*(4), 248–251.

Slater, B. R. (1988). Essential issues in working with lesbian and gay male youths. *Professional Psychology: Research and Practice, 19*(2), 226–235.

Smith, D. (1981). Unfinished business with informed consent procedures. *American Psychologist, 36*(1), 220–226.

Smith, D. (1982). Trends in counseling and psychotherapy. *American Psychologist, 37*(7), 802–809.

Smith, E. M. J. (1985a). Counseling black women. In P. Pedersen (Ed.), *Handbook of cross-cultural counseling and therapy* (pp. 181–187). Westport, CT: Greenwood Press.

Smith, E. M. J. (1985b). Ethnic minorities: Life stress, social support, and mental health issues. *The Counseling Psychologist, 13*(4), 537–579.

Smith, T. S., McGuire, J. M., Abbott, D. W., & Blau, B. I. (1991). Clinical ethical decision making: An investigation of the rationales used to justify doing less than one believes one should. *Professional Psychology: Research and Practice, 22*(3), 235–239.

Snipe, R. M. (1988). Ethical issues in the assessment and treatment of a rational suicidal client. *The Counseling Psychologist, 16*(1), 128–138.

Snowden, L. R., & Cheung, F. K. (1990). Use of inpatient mental health services by members of ethnic minority groups. *American Psychologist, 45*(3), 347–355.

Sobocinski, M. R. (1990). Ethical principles in the counseling of gay and lesbian adolescents: Issues of autonomy, competence, and confidentiality. *Professional Psychology: Research and Practice, 21*(4), 240–247.

*Sociological Practice Association (1987). *Ethical standards of sociological practitioners* (rev. ed.). Chester, NY: Author.

*Soisson, E. L., VandeCreek, L., & Knapp, S. (1987). Thorough record keeping: A good defense in a litigious era. *Professional Psychology: Research and Practice, 18*(5), 498–502.

Spiegel, S. B. (1979). Separate principles for counselors of women: A new form of sexism. *The Counseling Psychologist, 8*(1), 49–50.

Sporakowski, M. J. (1982). The regulation of marital and family therapy. In J. Hansen (Ed.), *Values, ethics, legalities and the family therapist.* Rockville, MD: Aspen.

Spruill, D. A., Fong, M. A. (1990). Defining the domain of mental health counseling: From identity confusion to consensus. *Journal of Mental Health Counseling, 12*(1), 17–23.

Stadler, H. A. (1986a). Making hard choices: Clarifying controversial ethical issues. *Counseling and Human Development, 19*(1), 1–10.

*Stadler, H. A. (1986b). To counsel or not to counsel: The ethical dilemma of dual relationships. *Journal of Counseling and Human Service Professions, 1*(1), 134–140.

Stadler, H. A. (1990a). Confidentiality. In B. Herlihy and L. B. Golden (Eds.), *AACD ethical standards casebook* (4th ed.) (pp. 102–110). Alexandria, VA: American Association for Counseling and Development.

Stadler, H. A. (1990b). Counselor impairment. In B. Herlihy and L. B. Golden (Eds.), *AACD ethical standards casebook* (4th ed.) (pp. 177–187). Alexandria, VA: American Association for Counseling and Development.

Stadler, H., & Paul, R. D. (1986). Counselor educators' preparations in ethics. *Journal of Counseling and Development, 64*(5), 328–330.

Stake, J. E., & Oliver, J. (1991). Sexual contact and touching between therapist and client: A survey of psychologists' attitudes and behavior. *Professional Psychology: Research and Practice, 22*(4), 297–307.

Stanley, B., Sieber, J. E., & Melton, G. B. (1987). Empirical studies of ethical issues in research. *American Psychologist, 42*(7), 735–741.

Steenbarger, B. N. (1990). Toward a development understanding of the counseling specialty: Lessons from our students. *Journal of Counseling and Development, 68*(4), 434–437.

Steinberg, J. L. (1980). Towards an interdisciplinary commitment: A divorce lawyer proposes attorney-therapist marriages or, at the least, an affair. *Journal of Marital and Family Therapy, 6*(3), 259–268.

Steindler, E. M. (1986). The role of professional organizations in developing support. In C. D. Scott and J. Hawk (Eds.), *Heal thyself: The health of health care professionals.* New York: Brunner/Mazel.

Stensrud, R., & Stensrud, K. (1981). Counseling may be hazardous to your health: How we teach people to feel powerless. *Personnel and Guidance Journal, 59*(5), 300–304.

Stern, S. (1984). Professional training and professional competence: A critique of current thinking. *Professional Psychology: Research and Practice, 1*(2), 230–243.

Stevens, M. J., Pfost, K. S., & Potts, M. K. (1990). Sex-role orientation and the willingness to confront existential issues. *Journal of Counseling and Development, 68*(4), 414–416.

Stiles, W. B., Shapiro, D. A., & Elliott, R. (1986). "Are all psychotherapies equivalent?" *American Psychologist, 41*(2), 165–180.

Stoltenberg, C. D., & Delworth, U. (1987). *Supervising counselors and therapists: A developmental approach.* San Francisco: Jossey-Bass.

Storm, C. L. (1991). Placing gender in the heart of MFT master's programs: Teaching a gender sensitive systematic view. *Journal of Marital and Family Therapy, 17*(1), 45–52.

Stricker, G. (1982). Ethical issues in psychotherapy research. In M. Rosenbaum (Ed.), *Ethics and values in psychotherapy: A guidebook.* New York: Free Press.

Stricker, G., Claiborn, W. L., & Bent, R. J. (1982). Peer review: An overview. *Professional Psychology, 13*(1), 5–8.

Strupp, H. H. (1986). Psychotherapy: Research, practice, and public policy (How to avoid dead ends). *American Psychologist, 41*(2), 120–130.

Stude, E. W., & McKelvey, J. (1979). Ethics and the law: Friend or foe? *Personnel and Guidance Journal, 57*(9), 453–456.

Suan, L. V., & Tyler, J. D. (1990). Mental health values and preference for mental health resources of Japanese-American and Caucasian-American students. *Professional Psychology: Research and Practice, 21*(4), 291–296.

Sue, D. (1990). Culture in transition: Counseling Asian-American men. In D. Moore and F. Leafgren (Eds.), *Problem solving strategies and interventions for men in conflict* (pp. 153–168). Alexandria, VA: American Association for Counseling and Development.

Sue, D., & Sue, D. W. (1991). Counseling strategies for Chinese Americans. In C. C. Lee & B. L. Richardson (Eds.), *Multicultural issues in counseling: New approaches to diversity* (pp. 79–90). Alexandria, VA: American Association for Counseling and Development.

*Sue, D. W. (1981a). *Counseling the culturally different: Theory and practice.* New York: Wiley.

Sue, D. W. (1981b, January). *Position paper on cross-cultural counseling competencies.* Education and Training Committee report delivered to the American Psychological Association's Division 17 Executive Committee.

Sue, D. W. (1990). Culture-specific strategies in counseling: A conceptual framework. *Professional Psychology: Research and Practice, 21*(6), 424–433.

Sue, D. W., Bernier, J. E., Durran, A., Feinberg, L., Pedersen, P., Smith, E. J., & Nuttall, E. V. (1982). Position paper: Cross-cultural counseling competencies. *The Counseling Psychologist, 10*(2), 45–52.

Sue, D. W., & Sue, D. (1985). Asian Americans and Pacific Islanders. In P. Pedersen (Ed.), *Handbook of cross-cultural counseling and therapy* (pp. 141–146). Westport, CT: Greenwood Press.

Sue, D. W., & Sue, D. (1990). *Counseling the culturally different: Theory and practice* (2nd ed.). New York: Wiley.

Sue, S. (1983). Ethnic minority issues in psychology. *American Psychologist, 38*(5), 583–592.

*Sue, S. (1988). Psychotherapeutic services for ethnic minorities: Two decades of research findings. *American Psychologist, 43*(4), 301–308.

Sue, S., Akutsu, P. D., & Higashi, C. (1985). Training issues in conducting therapy with ethnic-minority-group clients. In P. Pedersen (Ed.), *Handbook of cross-cultural counseling and therapy* (pp. 275–280). Westport, CT: Greenwood Press.

Suinn, R. M. (1985). Research and practice in cross-cultural counseling. *The Counseling Psychologist, 13*(4), 673–684.

Sundal-Hansen, L. S. (1985). Sex-role issues in counseling women and men. In P. Pedersen (Ed.), *Handbook of cross-cultural counseling and therapy* (pp. 213–222). Westport, CT: Greenwood Press.

Swanson, C. (1983). The law and the counselor. In J. Brown & B. Pate (Eds.), *Being a counselor: Directions and challenges.* Pacific Grove, CA: Brooks/Cole.

Szasz, T. (1974). *The myth of mental illness: Foundations of a theory of personal conduct* (rev. ed.). New York: Harper & Row.

*Szasz, T. (1986). The case against suicide prevention. *American Psychologist, 41*(7), 806–812.

Tabachnick, B. G., Keith-Spiegel, P., & Pope, K. S. (1991). Ethics of teaching: Beliefs and behaviors of psychologists as educators. *American Psychologist, 46*(5), 506–515.

Talbutt, L. C. (1981). Ethical standards: Assets and limitations. *Personnel and Guidance Journal, 60*(2), 110–112.

Tarvydas, V. M. (1987). Decision-making models in ethics: Models for increased clarity and wisdom. *Journal of Applied Rehabilitation Counseling, 18*(4), 50–52.

Taylor, L., & Adelman, H. S. (1989). Reframing the confidentiality dilemma to work in children's best interests. *Professional Psychology: Research and Practice, 20*(2), 79–83.

Taylor, L., Adelman, H. S., & Kaser-Boyd, N. (1985). Exploring minors' reluctance and dissatisfaction with psychotherapy. *Professional Psychology: Research and Practice, 16*(3), 418–425.

Tennyson, W. W., & Strom, S. A. (1986). Beyond professional standards: Developing responsibleness. *Journal of Counseling and Development, 64*(5), 298–302.

Theaman, M. (1984). The impact of peer review on professional practice. *American Psychologist, 39*(4), 406–414.

Thiers, N. (1987). AIDS: Counselors called to the front lines. *Guidepost* (AACD), 30(4).

Thomas, C. W. (1985). Counseling in a cultural context. *The Counseling Psychologist, 13*(4), 657–663.

Thoreson, R. W., Budd, F. C., & Kruskopf, C. J. (1986a). Alcoholism among psychologists: Factors in relapse and recovery. *Professional Psychology: Research and Practice, 17*(6), 497–503.

Thoreson, R. W., Budd, F. C., & Krauskopf, C. J. (1986b). Perceptions of alcohol misuse and work behavior among professionals: Identification and intervention. *Professional Psychology: Research and Practice, 17*(3), 210–216.

Thoreson, R. W., Miller, M., & Krauskopf, C. J. (1989). The distressed psychologist: Prevalence and treatment consideration. *Professional Psychology: Research and Practice, 20*(3), 153–158.

Tjeltveit, A. C. (1986). The ethics of value conversion in psychotherapy: Appropriate and inappropriate therapist influence on client values. *Clinical Psychology Review, 6,* 515–537.

Tokunaga, H. T. (1984). Ethical issues in consultation: An evaluative review. *Professional Psychology: Research and Practice, 15*(6), 811–821.

Totten, G., Lamb, D. H., & Reeder, G. D. (1990). *Tarasoff* and confidentiality in AIDS-related psychotherapy. *Professional Psychology: Research and Practice, 21*(3), 155–160.

Traver, L. B., & Cooksey, D. R. (1988). Featured debate: Psychotherapist responsibility in notifying individuals at risk for exposure to HIV. *Journal of Sex Research, 25*(1), 1–27.

Tremblay, J. M., Herron, W. G., & Schultz, C. L. (1986). Relation between therapeutic orientation and personality in psychotherapists. *Professional Psychology: Research and Practice, 17*(2), 106–110.

Triandis, H. (1985). Some major dimensions of cultural variation in client populations. In P. Pedersen (Ed.), *Handbook of cross-cultural counseling and therapy* (pp. 21–28). Westport, CT: Greenwood Press.

Triandis, H. C., & Brislin, R. W. (1984). Cross cultural psychology. *American Psychologist, 39*(9), 1006–1016.

Tryon, G. W. (1986). Abuse of therapists by patients: A national survey. *Professional Psychology: Research and Practice, 17*(4), 357–363.

Tymchuk, A. J. (1981). Ethical decision making and psychological treatment. *Journal of Psychiatric Treatment and Evaluation, 3,* 507–513.

Tymchuk, A. J., & Associates. (1979). Survey of training in ethics in APA-approved clinical psychology programs. *American Psychologist, 34*(12), 1168–1170.

Tymchuk, A. J., Drapkin, R., Major-Kinsley, S., Ackerman, A. B., Coffman, E. W., & Baum, M. S. (1982). Ethical decision making and psychologists' attitudes toward training in ethics. *Professional Psychology, 13*(3), 412–421.

Upchurch, D. W. (1985). Ethical standards and the supervisory process. *Counselor Education and Supervision, 25*(2), 90–98.

Vacc, N. A., Wittmer, J., & De Vaney, S. B. (1988). *Experiencing and counseling multicultural populations* (2nd ed.). Muncie, IN: Accelerated Development.

VandeCreek, L., Knapp, S., & Brace, K. (1990). Mandatory continuing education for licensed psychologists: Its rationale and current implementation. *Professional Psychology: Research and Practice, 21*(2), 135–140.

VandeCreek, L., Knapp, S., & Herzog, C. (1987). Malpractice risks in the treatment of dangerous patients. *Psychotherapy, 24*(2), 145–153.

VandeCreek, L., Knapp, S., & Herzog, C. (1988). Privileged communications for social workers. *Social Casework: The Journal of Contemporary Social Work, 69,* 28–34.

VandeCreek, L., Miars, R. D., & Herzog, C. (1987). Client anticipations and preferences for confidentiality of records. *Journal of Counseling Psychology, 34*(1), 62–67.

*Van Hoose, W. H., & Kottler, J. A. (1985). *Ethical and legal issues in counseling and psychotherapy* (2nd ed.). San Francisco: Jossey-Bass.

VanZandt, C. E. (1990). Professionalism: A matter of personal initiatives. *Journal of Counseling and Development, 68*(3), 243–245.

Vash, C. (1987). Fighting another's battles: When is it helpful? professional? ethical? *Journal of Applied Rehabilitation Counseling, 18*(4), 15–16.

*Vasquez, M. J. T. (1988). Counselor-client sexual contact: Implications for ethics training. *Journal of Counseling and Development, 67*(4), 238–241.

*Vasquez, M. J. T., & Kitchener, K. S. (1988). Introduction to special feature. *Journal of Counseling and Development, 67*(4), 214–216.

Vinson, J. (1989, November/December). Reflecting on dual relationships: Therapist-patient sex. *The California Therapist,* p. 41.

Ward, D. (1990, March 16). *Theoretical orientations of counselors: A national survey of AACD members.* Manuscript presented at the convention of the AACD, Cincinnati.

Watkins, C. E. (1983). Transference phenomena in the counseling situation. *Personnel and Guidance Journal, 62*(4), 206–210.

Watkins, C. E. (1985). Countertransference: Its impact on the counseling situation. *Journal of Counseling and Development, 63*(6), 356–359.

Watkins, C. E. (1990). The effects of counselor self-disclosure: A research review. *The Counseling Psychologist, 18*(3), 477–500.

Watkins, C. E., & Campbell, V. L. (1990). Contemporary developments and issues. *The Counseling Psychologist, 18*(2), 189–197.

Watkins, C. E., Jr., Schneider, L. J., Manus, M., & Hunton-Shoup, J. (1990). Terminal master's-level training in counseling psychology: Skills, competencies, and student interests. *Professional Psychology: Research and Practice, 21*(3), 216–218.

Weeks, G. R., & L'Abate, L. (1982). *Paradoxical psychotherapy: Theory and practice with individuals, couples, and families.* New York: Brunner/Mazel.

Weikel, W. J., & Palmo, A. J. (1989). The evolution and practice of mental health counseling. *Journal of Mental Health Counseling, 11*(1), 7–25.

Welfel, E. R. (1987). A new code of ethics for rehabilitation counselors: An achievement or a constraint? *Journal of Applied Rehabilitation Counseling, 18*(4), 9–11.

Welfel, E. R., & Lipsitz, N. E. (1983). Wanted: A comprehensive approach to ethics research and education. *Counselor Education and Supervision, 23,* 320–332.

Welfel, E. R., & Lipsitz, N. E. (1984). The ethical behavior of professional psychologists: A critical analysis of the research. *The Counseling Psychologist, 12*(3), 31–42.

Wellner, A. M. (1990). Some thoughts on the future of the professional practice of psychology. *Professional Psychology: Research and Practice, 21*(2), 141–143.

Westefeld, J. S., Whitchard, K. A., & Range, L. M. (1990). College and university student suicide: Trends and implications. *The Counseling Psychologist, 18*(3), 464–476.

Whiston, S. C., & Emerson, S. (1989). Ethical implications for supervisors in counseling of trainees. *Counselor Education and Supervision, 28*(4), 318–325.

White, M. D., & White, C. A. (1981). Involuntary committed patients' constitutional right to refuse treatment. *American Psychologist, 36*(9), 953–962.

*Wilbert, J. R., & Fulero, S. M. (1988). Impact of malpractice litigation on professional psychology: Survey of practitioners. *Professional Psychology: Research and Practice, 19*(4), 379–382.

Wilcox-Matthew, L., & Minor, C. W. (1989). The dual career couple: Concerns, benefits, and counseling implications. *Journal of Counseling and Development, 68*(2), 194–198.

Wilcoxon, S. A. (1986). Engaging non-attending family members in marital and family counseling: Ethical issues. *Journal of Counseling and Development, 64*(5), 323–324.

Wilcoxon, S. A., & Comas, R. E. (1986). Contemporary issues in family counseling: Implications for counselors. *Journal of Counseling and Human Service Professions, 1*(1), 118–126.

Willbach, D. (1989). Ethics and family therapy: The case management of family violence. *Journal of Marital and Family Therapy, 15*(1), 43–52.

Williams, G. T. (1990). Ethical dilemmas in teaching a group leadership course. *Journal for Specialists in Group Work, 15*(2), 104–113.

*Willison, B. G., & Masson, R. L. (1986). The role of touch in therapy: An adjunct to communication. *Journal of Counseling and Development, 64*(8), 497–500.

Winkelpleck, J. M., & Westfeld, J. S. (1982). Counseling considerations with gay couples. *Personnel and Guidance Journal, 60*(5), 294–345.

Wise, P. S., Lowery, S., & Silverglade, L. (1989). Personal counseling for counselors in training: Guidelines for supervisors. *Counselor Education and Supervision, 28*(4), 326–336.

Wolfgang, A. (1985). The function and importance of nonverbal behavior in intercultural counseling. In P. Pedersen, (Ed.), *Handbook of cross-cultural counseling and therapy.* (pp. 99–105). Westport, CT: Greenwood Press.

Wolman, B. (1982). Ethical problems in termination of psychotherapy. In M. Rosenbaum (Ed.), *Ethics and values in psychotherapy: A guidebook.* New York: Free Press.

Wood, P. S., & Mallinckrodt, B. (1990). Culturally sensitive assertiveness training for ethnic minority clients. *Professional Psychology: Research and Practice, 21*(1), 5–11.

Woodman, N. J., & Lenna, H. R. (1980). *Counseling with gay men and women.* San Francisco: Jossey-Bass.

Woody, J. D. (1990). Resolving ethical concerns in clinical practice: Toward a pragmatic model. *Journal of Marital and Family Therapy, 16*(2), 133–150.

*Woody, R. (1984). Professional responsibilities and liabilities. In R. Woody (Ed.), *The law and the practice of human services.* San Francisco: Jossey-Bass.

Woody, R. H. (1988). *Protecting your mental health practice: How to minimize legal and financial risk.* San Francisco: Jossey-Bass.

*Woody, R. H., & Associates. (1984). *The law and the practice of human services.* San Francisco: Jossey-Bass.

Worthington, E. L. (1989). Religious faith across the life span: Implications for counseling and research. *The Counseling Psychologist, 17*(4), 555–612.

Wrenn, C. G. (1962). The culturally encapsulated counselor. *Harvard Educational Review, 32,* 444–449.

Wrenn, C. G. (1985). Afterword: The culturally encapsulated counselor revisited. In P. Pedersen (Ed.), *Handbook of cross-cultural counseling and therapy* (pp. 323–329). Westport, CT: Greenwood Press.

Wright, B. A. (1987). Human dignity and professional self-monitoring. *Journal of Applied Rehabilitation Counseling, 18*(4), 12–14.

Wright, J., Coley, S., & Corey, G. (1989, May). Challenges facing human services education today. *Journal of Counseling and Human Service Professions, 3*(2), 3–11.

Wright, R. H. (1981). What to do until the malpractice lawyer comes: A survivor's manual. *American Psychologist, 36*(12), 1535–1541.

Wrightsman, L. S. (1991). *Psychology and the legal system* (2nd ed.). Pacific Grove, CA: Brooks/Cole.

Wubbolding, R. E. (1987). Professional ethics: Handling suicidal threats in the counseling session. *Journal of Reality Therapy. 7*(1), 12–15.

Wubbolding, R. E. (1988a). Intervention in suiciding behaviors. *Journal of Reality Therapy, 7*(2), 13–17.

Wubbolding, R. E. (1988b). Signs and myths surrounding suiciding behaviors. *Journal of Reality Therapy, 8*(1), 18–21.

Wubbolding, R. E. (1989). Professional issues: Four stages of decision making in suicidal client recovery. *Journal of Reality Therapy, 8*(2), 57–61.

Wubbolding, R. E. (1991). Professional issues: Consultation and ethics Part II. *Journal of Reality Therapy, 10*(2), 55–59.

Wyman, E., & McLaughlin, M. E. (1979). Traditional wives and mothers. *The Counseling Psychologist, 8*(1), 24–25.

Yalom, I. (1985). *The theory and practice of group psychotherapy* (3rd ed.). New York: Basic Books.

Youngstrom, N. (1991a, July). Lesbians and gay men still find bias in therapy. *APA Monitor,* pp. 24–25.

Youngstrom, N. (1991b, July). Mandatory reporting deters sex treatment. *APA Monitor,* p. 35.

Ziegler, J. L., & Kanas, N. (1986). Coping with stress during internship. In C. D. Scott & J. Hawk (Eds.), *Heal thyself: The health of health care professionals.* New York: Brunner/Mazel.

Zimpfer, D. G., & DeTrude, J. C. (1990). Follow-up of doctoral graduates in counseling. *Journal of Counseling and Development, 69*(1), 51–56.

Appendix

A. Ethical Standards
American Association for Counseling and Development

PREAMBLE

The Association is an educational, scientific, and professional organization whose members are dedicated to the enhancement of the worth, dignity, potential, and uniqueness of each individual and thus to the service of society.

The Association recognizes that the role definitions and work settings of its members include a wide variety of academic disciplines, levels of academic preparation, and agency services. This diversity reflects the breadth of the Association's interest and influence. It also poses challenging complexities in efforts to set standards for the performance of members, desired requisite preparation or practice, and supporting social, legal, and ethical controls.

The specification of ethical standards enables the Association to clarify to present and future members and to those served by members the nature of ethical responsibilities held in common by its members.

The existence of such standards serves to stimulate greater concern by members for their own professional functioning and for the conduct of fellow professionals such as counselors, guidance and student personnel workers, and others in the helping professions. As the ethical code of the Association, this document establishes principles that define the ethical behavior of Association members. Additional ethical guidelines developed by the Association's Divisions for their specialty areas may further define a member's ethical behavior.

Section A: General

1. The member influences the development of the profession by continuous efforts to improve professional practices, teaching, services, and research. Professional growth is continuous throughout the member's career and is exemplified by the development of a philosophy that explains why and how a member functions in the helping relationship. Members must gather data on their effectiveness and be guided by the findings. Members recognize the need for continuing education to ensure competent service.

2. The member has a responsibility both to the individual who is served and to the institution within which the service is performed to maintain high standards of professional conduct. The member strives to maintain the highest levels of professional services offered to the individuals to be served. The member also strives to assist the agency, organization, or institution in providing the highest caliber of professional services. The acceptance of employment in an institution implies that the member is in agreement with the general policies and principles of the institution. Therefore the professional activities of the member are also in accord with the objectives of the institution. If, despite concerted efforts, the member cannot reach agreement with the employer as to acceptable standards of conduct that allow for changes in institutional policy conducive to the positive growth and development

of clients, then terminating the affiliation should be seriously considered.

3. Ethical behavior among professional associates, both members and nonmembers, must be expected at all times. When information is possessed that raises doubt as to the ethical behavior of professional colleagues, whether Association members or not, the member must take action to attempt to rectify such a condition. Such action shall use the institution's channels first and then use procedures established by the Association.

4. The member neither claims nor implies professional qualifications exceeding those possessed and is responsible for correcting any misrepresentations of these qualifications by others.

5. In establishing fees for professional counseling services, members must consider the financial status of clients and locality. In the event that the established fee structure is inappropriate for a client, assistance must be provided in finding comparable services of acceptable cost.

6. When members provide information to the public or to subordinates, peers, or supervisors, they have a responsibility to ensure that the content is general, unidentified client information that is accurate, unbiased, and consists of objective, factual data.

7. Members recognize their boundaries of competence and provide only those services and use only those techniques for which they are qualified by training or experience. Members should only accept those positions for which they are professionally qualified.

8. In the counseling relationship, the counselor is aware of the intimacy of the relationship and maintains respect for the client and avoids engaging in activities that seek to meet the counselor's personal needs at the expense of that client.

9. Members do not condone or engage in sexual harassment which is defined as deliberate or repeated comments, gestures, or physical contacts of a sexual nature.

10. The member avoids bringing personal issues into the counseling relationship, especially if the potential for harm is present. Through awareness of the negative impact of both racial and sexual stereotyping and discrimination, the counselor guards the individual rights and personal dignity of the client in the counseling relationship.

11. Products or services provided by the member by means of classroom instruction, public lectures, demonstrations, written articles, radio or television programs, or other types of media must meet the criteria cited in these Standards.

Section B: Counseling Relationship

This section refers to practices and procedures of individual and/or group counseling relationships.

The member must recognize the need for client freedom of choice. Under those circumstances where this is not possible, the member must apprise clients of restrictions that may limit their freedom of choice.

1. The member's primary obligation is to respect the integrity and promote the welfare of the client(s), whether the client(s) is (are) assisted individually or in a group relationship. In a group setting, the member is also responsible for taking reasonable precautions to protect individuals from physical and/or psychological trauma resulting from interaction within the group.

2. Members make provisions for maintaining confidentiality in the storage and disposal of records and follow an established record retention and disposition policy. The counseling relationship and information resulting therefrom must be kept confidential, consistent with the obligations of the member as a professional person. In a group counseling setting, the counselor must set a norm of confidentiality regarding all group participants' disclosures.

3. If an individual is already in a counseling relationship with another professional person, the member does not enter into a counseling relationship without first contacting and receiving the approval of that other professional. If the member discovers that the client is in another counseling relationship after the counseling relationship begins, the member must gain the consent of the other professional or terminate the relationship, unless the client elects to terminate the other relationship.

4. When the client's condition indicates that there is clear and imminent danger to the client or others, the member must take reasonable personal action or inform responsible authorities. Consultation with other professionals must be used where possible. The assumption of responsibility for the client's(s') behavior must be taken

only after careful deliberation. The client must be involved in the resumption of responsibility as quickly as possible.

5. Records of the counseling relationship, including interview notes, test data, correspondence, tape recordings, electronic data storage, and other documents are to be considered professional information for use in counseling, and they should not be considered a part of the records of the institution or agency in which the counselor is employed unless specified by state statute or regulation. Revelation to others of counseling material must occur only upon the expressed consent of the client.

6. In view of the extensive data storage and processing capacities of the computer, the member must ensure that data maintained on a computer is: (a) limited to information that is appropriate and necessary for the services being provided; (b) destroyed after it is determined that the information is no longer of any value in providing services; and (c) restricted in terms of access to appropriate staff members involved in the provision of services by using the best computer security methods available.

7. Use of data derived from a counseling relationship for purposes of counselor training or research shall be confined to content that can be disguised to ensure full protection of the identity of the subject client.

8. The member must inform the client of the purposes, goals, techniques, rules of procedure, and limitations that may affect the relationship at or before the time that the counseling relationship is entered. When working with minors or persons who are unable to give consent, the member protects these clients' best interests.

9. In view of common misconceptions related to the perceived inherent validity of computer generated data and narrative reports, the member must ensure that the client is provided with information as part of the counseling relationship that adequately explains the limitations of computer technology.

10. The member must screen prospective group participants, especially when the emphasis is on self-understanding and growth through self-disclosure. The member must maintain an awareness of the group participants' compatibility throughout the life of the group.

11. The member may choose to consult with any other professionally competent person about a client. In choosing a consultant, the member must avoid placing the consultant in a conflict of interest situation that would preclude the consultant's being a proper party to the member's efforts to help the client.

12. If the member determines an inability to be of professional assistance to the client, the member must either avoid initiating the counseling relationship or immediately terminate that relationship. In either event, the member must suggest appropriate alternatives. (The member must be knowledgeable about referral resources so that a satisfactory referral can be initiated.) In the event the client declines the suggested referral, the member is not obligated to continue the relationship.

13. When the member has other relationships, particularly of an administrative, supervisory, and/or evaluative nature with an individual seeking counseling services, the member must not serve as the counselor but should refer the individual to another professional. Only in instances where such an alternative is unavailable and where the individual's situation warrants counseling intervention should the member enter into and/or maintain a counseling relationship. Dual relationships with clients that might impair the member's objectivity and professional judgment (e.g., as with close friends or relatives) must be avoided and/or the counseling relationship terminated through referral to another competent professional.

14. The member will avoid any type of sexual intimacies with clients. Sexual relationships with clients are unethical.

15. All experimental methods of treatment must be clearly indicated to prospective recipients, and safety precautions are to be adhered to by the member.

16. When computer applications are used as a component of counseling services, the member must ensure that: (a) the client is intellectually, emotionally, and physically capable of using the computer application; (b) the computer application is appropriate for the needs of the client; (c) the client understands the purpose and operation of the computer application; and (d) that a follow-up of client use of a computer application

is provided to both correct possible problems (misconceptions or inappropriate use) and assess subsequent needs.

17. When the member is engaged in short-term group treatment/training programs (e.g., marathons and other encounter-type or growth groups), the member ensures that there is professional assistance available during and following the group experience.

18. Should the member be engaged in a work setting that calls for any variation from the above statements, the member is obligated to consult with other professionals whenever possible to consider justifiable alternatives.

19. The member must ensure that members of various ethnic, racial, religious, disability, and socioeconomic groups have equal access to computer applications used to support counseling services and that the content of available computer applications does not discriminate against the groups described above.

20. When computer applications are developed by the member for use by the general public as self-help stand-alone computer software, the member must ensure that: (a) self-help computer applications are designed from the beginning to function in a stand-alone manner, as opposed to modifying software that was originally designed to require support from a counselor; (b) self-help computer applications will include within the program statements regarding intended user outcomes, suggestions for using the software, a description of the conditions under which self-help computer applications might not be appropriate, and a description of when and how counseling services might be beneficial; and (c) the manual for such applications will include the qualifications of the developer, the development process, validation data, and operating procedures.

Section C: Measurement and Evaluation

The primary purpose of educational and psychological testing is to provide descriptive measures that are objective and interpretable in either comparable or absolute terms. The member must recognize the need to interpret the statements that follow as applying to the whole range of appraisal techniques including test and nontest data. Test results constitute only one of a variety of pertinent sources of information for personnel, guidance, and counseling decisions.

1. The member must provide specific orientation or information to the examinee(s) prior to and following the test administration so that the results of testing may be placed in proper perspective with other relevant factors. In so doing, the member must recognize the effects of socioeconomic, ethnic, and cultural factors on test scores. It is the member's professional responsibility to use additional unvalidated information carefully in modifying interpretation of the test results.

2. In selecting tests for use in a given situation or with a particular client, the member must consider carefully the specific validity, reliability, and appropriateness of the test(s). General validity, reliability, and related issues may be questioned legally as well as ethically when tests are used for vocational and educational selection, placement, or counseling.

3. When making any statements to the public about tests and testing, the member must give accurate information and avoid false claims or misconceptions. Special efforts are often required to avoid unwarranted connotations of such terms as IQ and grade equivalent scores.

4. Different tests demand different levels of competence for administration, scoring, and interpretation. Members must recognize the limits of their competence and perform only those functions for which they are prepared. In particular, members using computer-based test interpretations must be trained in the construct being measured and the specific instrument being used prior to using this type of computer application.

5. In situations where a computer is used for test administration and scoring, the member is responsible for ensuring that administration and scoring programs function properly to provide clients with accurate test results.

6. Tests must be administered under the same conditions that were established in their standardization. When tests are not administered under standard conditions or when unusual behavior or irregularities occur during the testing session, those conditions must be noted and the results designated as invalid or of questionable validity.

Unsupervised or inadequately supervised test-taking, such as the use of tests through the mails, is considered unethical. On the other hand, the use of instruments that are so designed or standardized to be self-administered and self-scored, such as interest inventories, is to be encouraged.

7. The meaningfulness of test results used in personnel, guidance, and counseling functions generally depends on the examinee's unfamiliarity with the specific items on the test. Any prior coaching or dissemination of the test materials can invalidate test results. Therefore, test security is one of the professional obligations of the member. Conditions that produce most favorable test results must be made known to the examinee.

8. The purpose of testing and the explicit use of the results must be made known to the examinee prior to testing. The counselor must ensure that instrument limitations are not exceeded and that periodic review and/or retesting are made to prevent client stereotyping.

9. The examinee's welfare and explicit prior understanding must be the criteria for determining the recipients of the test results. The member must see that specific interpretation accompanies any release of individual or group test data. The interpretation of test data must be related to the examinee's particular concerns.

10. Members responsible for making decisions based on test results have an understanding of educational and psychological measurement, validation criteria, and test research.

11. The member must be cautious when interpreting the results of research instruments possessing insufficient technical data. The specific purposes for the use of such instruments must be stated explicitly to examinees.

12. The member must proceed with caution when attempting to evaluate and interpret the performance of minority group members or other persons who are not represented in the norm group on which the instrument was standardized.

13. When computer-based interpretations are developed by the member to support the assessment process, the member must ensure that the validity of such interpretations is established prior to the commercial distribution of such a computer application.

14. The member recognizes that test results may become obsolete. The member will avoid and prevent the misuse of obsolete test results.

15. The member must guard against the appropriation, reproduction, or modification of published tests or parts thereof without acknowledgment and permission from the previous publisher.

Section D: Research and Publication

1. Guidelines on research with human subjects shall be adhered to, such as:
   a. Ethical Principles in the Conduct of Research with Human Participants, Washington, D.C.: American Psychological Association, Inc., 1982.
   b. Code of Federal Regulations, Title 45, Subtitle A, Part 46, as currently issued.
   c. *Ethical Principles of Psychologists*, American Psychological Association, Principle #9: Research with Human Participants.
   d. Family Educational Rights and Privacy Act (the "Buckley Amendment").
   e. Current federal regulations and various state rights privacy acts.

2. In planning any research activity dealing with human subjects, the member must be aware of and responsive to all pertinent ethical principles and ensure that the research problem, design, and execution are in full compliance with them.

3. Responsibility for ethical research practice lies with the principal researcher, while others involved in the research activities share ethical obligation and full responsibility for their own actions.

4. In research with human subjects, researchers are responsible for the subjects' welfare throughout the experiment, and they must take all reasonable precautions to avoid causing injurious psychological, physical, or social effects on their subjects.

5. All research subjects must be informed of the purpose of the study except when withholding information or providing misinformation to them is essential to the investigation. In such research the member must be responsible for corrective action as soon as possible following completion of the research.

6. Participation in research must be voluntary. Involuntary participation is appropriate only when it can be demonstrated that participation will

have no harmful effects on subjects and is essential to the investigation.

7. When reporting research results, explicit mention must be made of all variables and conditions known to the investigator that might affect the outcome of the investigation or the interpretation of the data.

8. The member must be responsible for conducting and reporting investigations in a manner that minimizes the possibility that results will be misleading.

9. The member has an obligation to make available sufficient original research data to qualified others who may wish to replicate the study.

10. When supplying data, aiding in the research of another person, reporting research results, or in making original data available, due care must be taken to disguise the identity of the subjects in the absence of specific authorization from such subjects to do otherwise.

11. When conducting and reporting research, the member must be familiar with and give recognition to previous work on the topic, as well as to observe all copyright laws and follow the principles of giving full credit to all to whom credit is due.

12. The member must give due credit through joint authorship, acknowledgment, footnote statements, or other appropriate means to those who have contributed significantly to the research and/or publication, in accordance with such contributions.

13. The member must communicate to other members the results of any research judged to be of professional or scientific value. Results reflecting unfavorably on institutions, programs, services, or vested interests must not be withheld for such reasons.

14. If members agree to cooperate with another individual in research and/or publication, they incur an obligation to cooperate as promised in terms of punctuality of performance and with full regard to the completeness and accuracy of the information required.

15. Ethical practice requires that authors not submit the same manuscript or one essentially similar in content for simultaneous publication consideration by two or more journals. In addition, manuscripts published in whole or in substantial part in another journal or published work should not be submitted for publication without acknowledgment and permission from the previous publication.

Section E: Consulting

Consultation refers to a voluntary relationship between a professional helper and help-needing individual, group, or social unit in which the consultant is providing help to the client(s) in defining and solving a work-related problem or potential problem with a client or client system.

1. The member acting as a consultant must have a high degree of self-awareness of his/her own values, knowledge, skills, limitations, and needs in entering a helping relationship that involves human and/or organizational change and that the focus of the relationship be on the issues to be resolved and not on the person(s) presenting the problem.

2. There must be understanding and agreement between member and client for the problem definition, change of goals, and prediction of consequences of interventions selected.

3. The member must be reasonably certain that she/he or the organization represented has the necessary competencies and resources for giving the kind of help that is needed now or may be needed later and that appropriate referral resources are available to the consultant.

4. The consulting relationship must be one in which client adaptability and growth toward self-direction are encouraged and cultivated. The member must maintain this role consistently and not become a decision maker for the client or create a future dependency on the consultant.

5. When announcing consultant availability for services, the member conscientiously adheres to the Association's Ethical Standards.

6. The member must refuse a private fee or other remuneration for consultation with persons who are entitled to these services through the member's employing institution or agency. The policies of a particular agency may make explicit provisions for private practice with agency clients by members of its staff. In such instances, the clients must be apprised of other options open to them should they seek private counseling services.

Section F: Private Practice

1. The member should assist the profession by facilitating the availability of counseling services in private as well as public settings.

2. In advertising services as a private practitioner, the member must advertise the services in a manner that accurately informs the public of professional services, expertise, and techniques of counseling available. A member who assumes an executive leadership role in the organization shall not permit his/her name to be used in professional notices during periods when he/she is not actively engaged in the private practice of counseling.

3. The member may list the following: highest relevant degree, type and level of certification and/or license, address, telephone number, office hours, type and/or description of services, and other relevant information. Such information must not contain false, inaccurate, misleading, partial, out-of-context, or deceptive material or statements.

4. Members do not present their affiliation with any organization in such a way that would imply inaccurate sponsorship or certification by that organization.

5. Members may join in partnership/corporation with other members and/or other professionals provided that each member of the partnership or corporation makes clear the separate specialties by name in compliance with the regulations of the locality.

6. A member has an obligation to withdraw from a counseling relationship if it is believed that employment will result in violation of the Ethical Standards. If the mental or physical condition of the member renders it difficult to carry out an effective professional relationship or if the member is discharged by the client because the counseling relationship is no longer productive for the client, then the member is obligated to terminate the counseling relationship.

7. A member must adhere to the regulations for private practice of the locality where the services are offered.

8. It is unethical to use one's institutional affiliation to recruit clients for one's private practice.

Section G: Personnel Administration

It is recognized that most members are employed in public or quasi-public institutions. The functioning of a member within an institution must contribute to the goals of the institution and vice versa if either is to accomplish their respective goals or objectives. It is therefore essential that the member and the institution function in ways to: (a) make the institution's goals explicit and public; (b) make the member's contribution to institutional goals specific; and (c) foster mutual accountability for goal achievement.

To accomplish these objectives, it is recognized that the member and the employer must share responsibilities in the formulation and implementation of personnel policies.

1. Members must define and describe the parameters and levels of their professional competency.

2. Members must establish interpersonal relations and working agreements with supervisors and subordinates regarding counseling or clinical relationships, confidentiality, distinction between public and private material, maintenance and dissemination of recorded information, work load, and accountability. Working agreements in each instance must be specified and made known to those concerned.

3. Members must alert their employers to conditions that may be potentially disruptive or damaging.

4. Members must inform employers of conditions that may limit their effectiveness.

5. Members must submit regularly to professional review and evaluation.

6. Members must be responsible for in-service development of self and/or staff.

7. Members must inform their staff of goals and programs.

8. Members must provide personnel practices that guarantee and enhance the rights and welfare of each recipient of their service.

9. Members must select competent persons and assign responsibilities compatible with their skills and experiences.

10. The member, at the onset of a counseling relationship, will inform the client of the member's intended use of supervisors regarding the disclosure of information concerning this case. The member will clearly inform the client of the limits of confidentiality in the relationship.

11. Members, as either employers or employees, do not engage in or condone practices that are in-

humane, illegal, or unjustifiable (such as considerations based on sex, handicap, age, race) in hiring, promotion, or training.

Section H: Preparation Standards

Members who are responsible for training others must be guided by the preparation standards of the Association and relevant Division(s). The member who functions in the capacity of trainer assumes unique ethical responsibilities that frequently go beyond that of the member who does not function in a training capacity. These ethical responsibilities are outlined as follows:

1. Members must orient students to program expectations, basic skills development, and employment prospects prior to admission to the program.
2. Members in charge of learning experiences must establish programs that integrate academic study and supervised practice.
3. Members must establish a program directed toward developing students' skills, knowledge, and self-understanding, stated whenever possible in competency or performance terms.
4. Members must identify the levels of competencies of their students in compliance with relevant Division standards. These competencies must accommodate the paraprofessional as well as the professional.
5. Members, through continual student evaluation and appraisal, must be aware of the personal limitations of the learner that might impede future performance. The instructor must not only assist the learner in securing remedial assistance but also screen from the program those individuals who are unable to provide competent services.
6. Members must provide a program that includes training in research commensurate with levels of role functioning. Paraprofessional and technician-level personnel must be trained as consumers of research. In addition, personnel must learn how to evaluate their own and their program's effectiveness. Graduate training, especially at the doctoral level, would include preparation for original research by the member.
7. Members must make students aware of the ethical responsibilities and standards of the profession.
8. Preparatory programs must encourage students to value the ideals of service to individuals and to society. In this regard, direct financial remuneration or lack thereof must not influence the quality of service rendered. Monetary considerations must not be allowed to overshadow professional and humanitarian needs.
9. Members responsible for educational programs must be skilled as teachers and practitioners.
10. Members must present thoroughly varied theoretical positions so that students may make comparisons and have the opportunity to select a position.
11. Members must develop clear policies within their educational institutions regarding field placement and the roles of the student and the instructor in such placement.
12. Members must ensure that forms of learning focusing on self-understanding or growth are voluntary, or if required as part of the educational program, are made known to prospective students prior to entering the program. When the educational program offers a growth experience with an emphasis on self-disclosure or other relatively intimate or personal involvement, the member must have no administrative, supervisory, or evaluating authority regarding the participant.
13. The member will at all times provide students with clear and equally acceptable alternatives for self-understanding or growth experiences. The member will assure students that they have a right to accept these alternatives without prejudice or penalty.
14. Members must conduct an educational program in keeping with the current relevant guidelines of the Association.

B. AAMFT Code of Ethics
American Association for Marriage and Family Therapy

The Board of Directors of the American Association for Marriage and Family Therapy (AAMFT) hereby promulgates, pursuant to Article 2, Section 2.013 of the Association's By-laws, the Revised AAMFT Code of Ethics, effective August 1, 1991.

The AAMFT Code of Ethics is binding on Members of AAMFT in all membership categories, AAMFT Approved Supervisors, and applicants for membership and the Approved Supervisor designation (hereafter, AAMFT Member).

If an AAMFT Member resigns in anticipation of, or during the course of an ethics investigation, the Ethics Committee will complete its investigation. Any publication of action taken by the Association will include the fact that the Member attempted to resign during the investigation.

Marriage and family therapists are strongly encouraged to report alleged unethical behavior of colleagues to appropriate professional associations and state regulatory bodies.

1. Responsibility to Clients

Marriage and family therapists advance the welfare of families and individuals. They respect the rights of those persons seeking their assistance, and make reasonable efforts to ensure that their services are used appropriately.

1.1 Marriage and family therapists do not discriminate against or refuse professional service to anyone on the basis of race, gender, religion, national origin, or sexual orientation.

1.2 Marriage and family therapists are aware of their influential position with respect to clients, and they avoid exploiting the trust and dependency of such persons. Therapists, therefore, make every effort to avoid dual relationships with clients that could impair professional judgment or increase the risk of exploitation. When a dual relationship cannot be avoided, therapists take appropriate professional precautions to ensure judgment is not impaired and no exploitation occurs. Examples of such dual relationships include, but are not limited to, business or close personal relationships with clients. Sexual intimacy with clients is prohibited. Sexual intimacy with former clients for two years following the termination of therapy is prohibited.

1.3 Marriage and family therapists do not use their professional relationships with clients to further their own interests.

1.4 Marriage and family therapists respect the right of clients to make decisions and help them to understand the consequences of these decisions. Therapists clearly advise a client that a decision on marital status is the responsibility of the client.

1.5 Marriage and family therapists continue therapeutic relationships only so long as it is reasonably clear that clients are benefiting from the relationship.

1.6 Marriage and family therapists assist persons in obtaining other therapeutic services if the therapist is unable or unwilling, for appropriate reasons, to provide professional help.

1.7 Marriage and family therapists do not abandon or neglect clients in treatment without making reasonable arrangements for the continuation of such treatment.

1.8 Marriage and family therapists obtain written informed consent from clients before videotaping, audiorecording, or permitting third party observation.

2. Confidentiality

Marriage and family therapists have unique confidentiality concerns because the client in a therapeutic relationship may be more than one person. Therapists respect and guard confidences of each individual client.

2.1 Marriage and family therapists may not disclose client confidences except: (a) as mandated by law; (b) to prevent a clear and immediate danger to a person or persons; (c) where the therapist is a defendant in a civil, criminal, or disciplinary action arising from the therapy (in which case client confidences may be disclosed only in the course of that action); or (d) if there is a waiver previously obtained in writing, and then such information may be revealed only in accordance with the terms of the waiver. In circumstances where more than one person in a family receives therapy, each such family member who is legally competent to execute a waiver must agree to the waiver required by subparagraph (d). Without such a waiver from each family member legally competent to execute a waiver, a therapist cannot disclose information received from any family member.

2.2 Marriage and family therapists use client and/or clinical materials in teaching, writing, and public presentations only if a written waiver has been obtained in accordance with Subprinciple 2.1(d), or when appropriate steps have been taken to protect client identity and confidentiality.

2.3 Marriage and family therapists store or dispose of client records in ways that maintain confidentiality.

3. Professional Competence and Integrity

Marriage and family therapists maintain high standards of professional competence and integrity.

3.1 Marriage and family therapists are in violation of this Code and subject to termination of membership or other appropriate action if they: (a) are convicted of any felony; (b) are convicted of a misdemeanor related to their qualifications or functions; (c) engage in conduct which could lead to conviction of a felony, or a misdemeanor related to their qualifications or functions; (d) are expelled from or disciplined by other professional organizations; (e) have their licenses or certificates suspended or revoked or are otherwise disciplined by regulatory bodies; (f) are no longer competent to practice marriage and family therapy because they are impaired due to physical or mental causes or the abuse of alcohol or other substances; or (g) fail to cooperate with the Association at any point from the inception of an ethical complaint through the completion of all proceedings regarding that complaint.

3.2 Marriage and family therapists seek appropriate professional assistance for their personal problems or conflicts that may impair work performance or clinical judgment.

3.3 Marriage and family therapists, as teachers, supervisors, and researchers, are dedicated to high standards of scholarship and present accurate information.

3.4 Marriage and family therapists remain abreast of new developments in family therapy knowledge and practice through educational activities.

3.5 Marriage and family therapists do not engage in sexual or other harassment or exploitation of clients, students, trainees, supervisees, employees, colleagues, research subjects, or actual or potential witnesses or complainants in investigations and ethical proceedings.

3.6 Marriage and family therapists do not diagnose, treat, or advise on problems outside the recognized boundaries of their competence.

3.7 Marriage and family therapists make efforts to prevent the distortion or misuse of their clinical and research findings.

3.8 Marriage and family therapists, because of their ability to influence and alter the lives of others, exercise special care when making public their professional recommendations and opinions through testimony or other public statements.

4. Responsibility to Students, Employees, and Supervisees

Marriage and family therapists do not exploit the trust and dependency of students, employees, and supervisees.

4.1 Marriage and family therapists are aware of their influential position with respect to students, employees, and supervisees, and they avoid exploiting the trust and dependency of such persons. Therapists, therefore, make every effort to avoid dual relationships that could impair professional judgment or increase the risk of exploitation. When a dual relationship cannot be avoided, therapists take appropriate professional precautions to ensure judgment is not impaired and no exploitation occurs. Examples of such dual relationships include, but are not limited to, business or close personal relationships with students, employees, or supervisees. Provision of therapy to students, employees, or supervisees is prohibited. Sexual intimacy with students or supervisees is prohibited.

4.2 Marriage and family therapists do not permit students, employees, or suprvisees to perform or to hold themselves out as competent to perform professional services beyond their training, level of experience, and competence.

4.3 Marriage and family therapists do not disclose supervisee confidences except: (a) as mandated by law; (b) to prevent a clear and immediate danger to a person or persons; (c) where the therapist is a defendant in a civil, criminal, or disciplinary action arising from the supervision (in which case supervisee confidences may be disclosed only in the course of that action); (d) in educational or training settings where there are multiple supervisors, and then only to other professional colleagues who share responsibility for the training of the supervisee; or (e) if there is a waiver previously obtained in writing, and then such information may be revealed only in accordance with the terms of the waiver.

5. Responsibility to Research Participants

Investigators respect the dignity and protect the welfare of participants in research and are aware of federal and state laws and regulations and professional standards governing the conduct of research.

5.1 Investigators are responsible for making careful examinations of ethical acceptability in planning studies. To the extent that services to research participants may be compromiscd by participation in research, investigators seek the ethical advice of qualified professionals not directly involved in the investigation and observe safeguards to protect the rights of research participants.

5.2 Investigators requesting participants' involvement in research inform them of all aspects of the research that might reasonably be expected to influence willingness to participate. Investigators are especially sensitive to the possibility of diminished consent when participants are also receiving clinical services, have impairments which limit understanding and/or communication, or when participants are children.

5.3 Investigators respect participants' freedom to decline participation in or to withdraw from a research study at any time. This obligation requires special thought and consideration when investigators or other members of the research team are in positions of authority or influence over participants. Marriage and family therapists, therefore, make every effort to avoid dual relationships with research participants that could impair professional judgments or increase the risk of exploitation.

5.4 Information obtained about a research participant during the course of an investigation is confidential unless there is a waiver previously obtained in writing. When the possibility exists that others, including family members, may obtain access to such information, this possibility, together with the plan for protecting confidentiality, is explained as part of the procedure for obtaining informed consent.

6. Responsibility to the Profession

Marriage and family therapists respect the rights and responsibilities of professional colleagues and participate in activities which advance the goals of the profession.

6.1 Marriage and family therapists remain accountable to the standards of the profession when acting as members or employees of organizations.

6.2 Marriage and family therapists assign publication credit to those who have contributed to a publication in proportion to their contributions and in accordance with customary professional publication practices.

6.3 Marriage and family therapists who are the authors of books or other materials that are published or distributed cite persons to whom credit for original ideas is due.

6.4 Marriage and family therapists who are the authors of books or other materials published or distributed by an organization take reasonable precautions to ensure that the organization promotes and advertises the materials accurately and factually.

6.5 Marriage and family therapists participate in activities that contribute to a better community and society, including devoting a portion of their professional activity to services for which there is little or no financial return.

6.6 Marriage and family therapists are concerned with developing laws and regulations pertaining to marriage and family therapy that serve the public interest, and with altering such laws and regulations that are not in the public interest.

6.7 Marriage and family therapists encourage public participation in the design and delivery of professional services and in the regulation of practitioners.

7. Financial Arrangements

Marriage and family therapists make financial arrangements with clients, third party payors, and supervisees that are reasonably understandable and conform to accepted professional practices.

7.1 Marriage and family therapists do not offer or accept payment for referrals.

7.2 Marriage and family therapists do not charge excessive fees for services.

7.3 Marriage and family therapists disclose their fees to clients and supervisees at the beginning of services.

7.4 Marriage and family therapists represent facts truthfully to clients, third party payors, and supervisees regarding services rendered.

8. Advertising

Marriage and family therapists engage in appropriate informational activities, including those that enable laypersons to choose professional services on an informed basis.

General advertising

8.1 Marriage and family therapists accurately represent their competence, education, training, and experience relevant to their practice of marriage and family therapy.

8.2 Marriage and family therapists assure that advertisements and publications in any media (such as directories, announcements, business cards, newspapers, radio, television, and facsimiles) convey information that is necessary for the public to make an appropriate selection of professional services. Information could include: (a) office information, such as name, address, telephone number, credit card acceptability, fees, languages spoken, and office hours; (b) appropriate degrees, state licensure and/or certification, and AAMFT Clinical Member status; and (c) description of practice. (For requirements for advertising under the AAMFT name, logo, and/or the abbreviated initials AAMFT, see Subprinciple 8.15, below.)

8.3 Marriage and family therapists do not use a name which could mislead the public concerning the identity, responsibility, source, and status of those practicing under that name and do not hold themselves out as being partners or associates of a firm if they are not.

8.4 Marriage and family therapists do not use any professional identification (such as a business card, office sign, letterhead, or telephone or association directory listing) if it includes a statement or claim that is false, fraudulent, misleading, or deceptive. A statement is false, fraudulent, misleading, or deceptive if it (a) contains a material misrepresentation of fact; (b) fails to state any material fact necessary to make the statement, in light of all circumstances, not misleading; or (c) is intended to or is likely to create an unjustified expectation.

8.5 Marriage and family therapists correct, wherever possible, false, misleading, or inaccurate information and representations made by others concerning the therapist's qualifications, services, or products.

8.6 Marriage and family therapists make certain that the qualifications of persons in their employ are represented in a manner that is not false, misleading, or deceptive.

8.7 Marriage and family therapists may represent themselves as specializing within a limited area of marriage and family therapy, but only if they have the education and supervised experience in settings which meet recognized professional standards to practice in that specialty area.

Advertising using AAMFT designations

8.8 The AAMFT designations of Clinical Member, Approved Supervisor, and Fellow may be used in public information or advertising materials only by persons holding such designations. Persons holding such designations may, for example, advertise in the following manner:

- *Jane Doe, Ph.D., a Clinical Member of the American Association for Marriage and Family Therapy.*

   Alternately, the advertisement could read:

- *Jane Doe, Ph.D., AAMFT Clinical Member.*
- *John Doe, Ph.D., an Approved Supervisor of the American Association for Marriage and Family Therapy.*

   Alternately, the advertisement could read:

- *John Doe, Ph.D., AAMFT Approved Supervisor.*
- *Jane Doe, Ph.D., a Fellow of the American Association for Marriage and Family Therapy.*

   Alternately, the advertisement could read:

- *Jane Doe, Ph.D., AAMFT Fellow.*

   More than one designation may be used if held by the AAMFT Member.

8.9 Marriage and family therapists who hold the AAMFT Approved Supervisor or the Fellow designation may not represent the designation as an advanced clinical status.

8.10 Student, Associate, and Affiliate Members may not use their AAMFT membership status in public information or advertising materials. Such listings on professional resumes are not considered advertisements.

8.11 Persons applying for AAMFT membership may not list their application status on any resume or advertisement.

8.12 In conjunction with their AAMFT membership, marriage and family therapists claim as evidence of educational qualifications only those degrees (a) from regionally accredited institutions or (b) from institutions recognized by states which license or certify marriage and family therapists, but only if such state regulation is recognized by AAMFT.

8.13 Marriage and family therapists may not use the initials AAMFT following their name in the manner of an academic degree.

8.14 Marriage and family therapists may not use the AAMFT name, logo, and/or the abbreviated initials AAMFT or make any other such representation which would imply that they speak for or represent the Association. The Association is the sole owner of its name, logo, and the abbreviated initials AAMFT. Its committees and divisions, operating as such, may use the name, logo, and/or the abbreviated initials AAMFT in accordance with AAMFT policies.

8.15 Authorized advertisements of Clinical Members under the AAMFT name, log, and/or the abbreviated initials AAMFT may include the following: the Clinical Member's name, degree, license or certificate held when required by state law, name of business, address, and telephone number. If a business is listed, it must follow, not precede the Clinical Member's name. Such listings may not include AAMFT offices held by the Clinical Member, nor any specializations, since such a listing under the AAMFT name, logo, and/or the abbreviated initials, AAMFT, would imply that this specialization has been credentialed by AAMFT.

8.16 Marriage and family therapists use their membership in AAMFT only in connection with their clinical and professional activities.

8.17 Only AAMFT divisions and programs accredited by the AAMFT Commission on Accreditation for Marriage and Family Therapy Education, not businesses nor organizations, may use any AAMFT-related designation or affiliation in public information or advertising materials, and then only in accordance with AAMFT policies.

8.18 Programs accredited by the AAMFT Commission on Accreditation for Marriage and Family Therapy Education may not use the AAMFT name, logo, and/or the abbreviated initials AAMFT. Instead, they may have printed on their stationery and other appropriate materials a statement such as:

The (name of program) of the (name of institution) is accredited by the AAMFT Commission on Accreditation for Marriage and Family Therapy Education.

8.19 Programs not accredited by the AAMFT Commission on Accreditation for Marriage and Family Therapy Education may not use the AAMFT name, logo, and/or the abbreviated initials AAMFT. They may not state in printed program materials, program advertisements, and student advisement that their courses and training opportunities are accepted by AAMFT to meet AAMFT membership requirements.

C. Ethical Principles of Psychologists, *American Psychological Association*

PREAMBLE

Psychologists respect the dignity and worth of the individual and strive for the preservation and protection of fundamental human rights. They are committed to increasing the knowledge of human behavior and of people's understanding of themselves and others and to the utilization of such knowledge for the promotion of human welfare. While pursuing these objectives, they make every effort to protect the welfare of those who seek their services and of the research participants that may be the object of study. They use their skills only for purposes consistent with these values and do not knowingly permit their misuse by others. While demanding for themselves freedom of inquiry and communication, psychologists accept the responsibility this freedom requires: competence, objectivity in the application of skills, and concern for the best interests of clients, colleagues, students, research participants, and society. In the pursuit of these ideals, psychologists subscribe to principles in the following areas: 1. Responsibility, 2. Competence, 3. Moral and Legal Standards, 4. Public Statements, 5. Confidentiality, 6. Welfare of the Consumer, 7. Professional Relationship, 8. Assessment Techniques, 9. Research with Human Participants, and 10. Care and Use of Animals.

Acceptance of membership in the American Psychological Association commits the member to adherence to these principles.

Psychologists cooperate with duly constituted committees of the American Psychological Association, in particular, the Committee on Scientific and Professional Ethics and Conduct, by responding to inquiries promptly and completely. Members also respond promptly and completely to inquiries from duly constituted state association ethics committees and professional standards review committees.

Principle 1: Responsibility

In providing services, psychologists maintain the highest standards of their profession. They accept responsibility for the consequences of their acts and make every effort to ensure that their services are used appropriately.

a. As scientists, psychologists accept responsibility for the selection of their research topics and the methods used in investigation, analysis, and reporting. They plan their research in ways to minimize the possibility that their findings will be misleading. They provide thorough discussion of the limitations of their data, especially where their work touches on social policy or might be construed to the detriment of persons in specific age, sex, ethnic, socioeconomic, or other social groups. In publishing reports of their work, they never suppress disconfirming data, and they acknowledge the existence of alternative hypotheses and explanations of their findings. Psychologists take credit only for work they have actually done.

b. Psychologists clarify in advance with all appropriate persons and agencies the expectations for sharing and utilizing research data. They avoid relationships that may limit their objectivity or create a conflict of interest. Interference with the milieu in which data are collected is kept to a minimum.

c. Psychologists have the responsibility to attempt to prevent distortion, misuse, or suppression of psychological findings by the institution or agency of which they are employees.

d. As members of governmental or other organizational bodies, psychologists remain accountable as individuals to the highest standards of their profession.

e. As teachers, psychologists recognize their primary obligation to help others acquire knowledge and skill. They maintain high standards of scholarship by presenting psychological information objectively, fully, and accurately.

f. As practitioners, psychologists know that they bear a heavy social responsibility because their recommendations and professional actions may alter the lives of others. They are alert to personal, social, organizational, financial, or political situations and pressures that might lead to misuse of their influence.

a. Psychologists accurately represent their competence, education, training, and experience. They claim as evidence of education qualifications only those degrees obtained from institutions acceptable under the Bylaws and Rules of Council of the American Psychological Association.

b. As teachers, psychologists perform their duties on the basis of careful preparation so that their instruction is accurate, current, and scholarly.

c. Psychologists recognize the need for continuing education and are open to new procedures and changes in expectations and values over time.

d. Psychologists recognize differences among people, such as those that may be associated with age, sex, socioeconomic, and ethnic backgrounds. When necessary, they obtain training, experience, or counsel to assure competent service or research relating to such persons.

e. Psychologists responsible for decisions involving individuals or policies based on test results have an understanding of psychological or educational measurement, validation problems, and test research.

f. Psychologists recognize that personal problems and conflicts may interfere with professional effectiveness. Accordingly, they refrain from undertaking any activity in which their personal problems are likely to lead to inadequate performance or harm to a client, colleague, student, or research participant. If engaged in such activity when they become aware of their personal problems, they seek competent professional assistance to determine whether they should suspend, terminate, or limit the scope of their professional and/or scientific activities.

Principle 2: Competence

The maintenance of high standards of competence is a responsibility shared by all psychologists in the interest of the public and the profession as a whole. Psychologists recognize the boundaries of their competence and the limitations of their techniques. They only provide services and only use techniques for which they are qualified by training and experience. In those areas in which recognized standards do not yet exist, psychologists take whatever precautions are necessary to protect the welfare of their clients. They maintain knowledge of current scientific and professional information related to the services they render.

Principle 3: Moral and Legal Standards

Psychologists' moral and ethical standards of behavior are a personal matter to the same degree as they are for any other citizen, except as these may compromise the fulfillment of their professional responsibilities or reduce the public trust in psychology and psychologists. Regarding their own behavior, psychologists are sensitive to prevailing community standards and to the possible impact that conformity to or deviation from these standards may have upon the quality of their performance as psychologists. Psychologists are also aware of the possible impact of their public behavior upon the ability of colleagues to perform their professional duties.

a. As teachers, psychologists are aware of the fact that their personal values may affect the selection and presentation of instructional materials. When dealing with topics that may give offense, they recognize and respect the diverse attitudes that students may have toward such materials.

b. As employees or employers, psychologists do not engage in or condone practices that are inhumane or that result in illegal or unjustifiable actions. Such practices include, but are not limited to, those based on considerations of race, handicap, age, gender, sexual preference, religion, or national origin in hiring, promotion, or training.

c. In their professional roles, psychologists avoid any action that will violate or diminish the legal and civil rights of clients or of others who may be affected by their actions.

d. As practitioners and researchers, psychologists act in accord with Association standards and guidelines related to practice and to the conduct of research with human beings and animals. In the ordinary course of events, psychologists adhere to relevant governmental laws and institutional regulations. When federal, state, provincial, organizational, or institutional laws, regulations, or practices are in conflict with Association standards and guidelines, psychologists make known their commitment to Association standards and guidelines and, wherever possible, work toward a resolution of the conflict. Both practitioners and researchers are concerned with the development of such legal and quasilegal regulations as best serve the public interest, and they work toward changing existing regulations that are not beneficial to the public interest.

Principle 4: Public Statements

Public statements, announcements of services, advertising, and promotional activities of psychologists serve the purpose of helping the public make informed judgments and choices. Psychologists represent accurately and objectively their professional qualifications, affiliations, and functions, as well as those of the institutions or organizations with which they or the statements may be associated. In public statements providing psychological information or professional opinions or providing information about the availability of psychological products, publications, and services, psychologists base their statements on scientifically acceptable psychological findings and techniques with full recognition of the limits and uncertainties of such evidence.

a. When announcing or advertising professional services, psychologists may list the following information to describe the provider and services provided: name, highest relevant academic degree earned from a regionally accredited institution, date, type, and level of certification or licensure, diplomate status, APA membership status, address, telephone number, office hours, a brief listing of the type of psychological services offered, an appropriate presentation of fee information, foreign languages spoken, and policy with regard to third-party payments. Additional relevant or important consumer information may be included if not prohibited by other sections of these Ethical Principles.

b. In announcing or advertising the availability of psychological products, publications, or services, psychologists do not present their affiliation with any organization in a manner that falsely implies sponsorship or certification by that organization. In particular and for example, psychologists do not state APA membership or fellow status in a way to suggest that such status implies specialized professional competence or qualifications. Public statements include, but are not limited to, communication by means of periodical, book, list, directory, television, radio, or motion picture. They do not contain (i) a false, fraudulent, misleading, deceptive, or unfair statement; (ii) a misinterpretation of fact or a statement likely to mislead or deceive because in context it makes only a partial disclosure of relevant facts; (iii) a statement intended or likely to create false or unjustified expectations of favorable results.

c. Psychologists do not compensate or give anything of value to a representative of the press, radio, television, or other communication medium in anticipation of or in return for professional publicity in a news item. A paid advertisement must be identified as such, unless it is apparent from the context that it is a paid advertisement. If communicated to the public by use of radio or television, an advertisement is prerecorded and approved for broadcast by the psychologist, and a recording of the actual transmission is retained by the psychologist.

d. Announcements or advertisements of "personal growth groups," clinics and agencies give a clear statement of purpose and a clear description of the experience to be provided. The education, training, and experience of the staff members are appropriately specified.

e. Psychologists associated with the development or promotion of psychological devices, books, or other products offered for commercial sale make reasonable efforts to ensure that announcements and advertisements are presented in a professional, scientifically acceptable, and factually informative manner.

f. Psychologists do not participate for personal gain in commercial announcements or advertisements recommending to the public the purchase or use of proprietary or single-source products or services when that participation is based solely upon their identification as psychologists.

g. Psychologists present the science of psychology and offer their services, products, and publications fairly and accurately, avoiding misrepresentation through sensationalism, exaggeration, or superficiality. Psychologists are guided by the primary obligation to aid the public in developing informed judgments, opinions, and choices.

h. As teachers, psychologists ensure that statements in catalogs and course outlines are accurate and not misleading, particularly in terms of subject matter to be covered, bases for evaluating progress, and the nature of course experiences. Announcements, brochures, or advertisements describing workshops, seminars, or other educational programs accurately describe the audience for which the program is intended as well as eligibility requirements, educational objectives, and nature of the materials to be covered. These announcements also accurately represent the education, training, and experience of the psychologists representing the programs and any fees involved.

i. Public announcements or advertisements soliciting research participants in which clinical services or other professional services are offered as an inducement make clear the nature of the services as well as the costs and other obligations to be accepted by participants in the research.

j. A psychologist accepts the obligation to correct others who represent the psychologist's professional qualifications, or associations with products or services, in a manner incompatible with these guidelines.

k. Individual diagnostic and therapeutic services are provided only in the context of a professional psychological relationship. When personal advice is given by means of public lectures or demonstrations, newspaper or magazine articles, radio or television programs, mail, or similar media, the psychologist utilizes the most current relevant data and exercises the highest level of professional judgment.

l. Products that are described or presented by means of public lectures or demonstrations, newspaper or magazine articles, radio or television programs, or similar media meet the same recognized standards as exist for products used in the context of a professional relationship.

Principle 5: Confidentiality

Psychologists have a primary obligation to respect the confidentiality of information obtained from persons in the course of their work as psychologists. They reveal such information to others only with the consent of the person or the person's legal representative, except in those unusual circumstances in which not to do so would result in clear danger to the person or to others. Where appropriate, psychologists inform their clients of the legal limits of confidentiality.

a. Information obtained in clinical or consulting relationships, or evaluative data concerning children, students, employees, and others, is discussed only for professional purposes and only with persons clearly concerned with the case. Written and oral reports present only data germane to the purposes of the evaluation, and every effort is made to avoid undue invasion of privacy.

b. Psychologists who present personal information obtained during the course of professional work in writings, lectures, or other public forums either obtain adequate prior consent to do so or adequately disguise all identifying information.

c. Psychologists make provisions for maintaining confidentiality in the storage and disposal of records.

d. When working with minors or other persons who are unable to give voluntary, informed consent, psychologists take special care to protect these persons' best interests.

Principle 6: Welfare of the Consumer

Psychologists respect the integrity and protect the welfare of the people and groups with whom they work. When conflicts of interest arise between clients and psychologists' employing institutions, psychologists calrify the nature and direction of their loyalties and responsibilities and keep all parties informed of their commitments. Psychologists fully inform consumers as to the purpose and nature of an evaluative, treatment, educational, or training procedure, and they freely acknowledge that clients, students, or participants in research have freedom of choice with regard to participation.

a. Psychologists are continually cognizant of their own needs and of their potentially influential position vis-á-vis persons such as clients, students, and subordinates. They avoid exploiting the trust and dependency of such persons. Psychologists make every effort to avoid dual relationships that could impair their professional judgment or increase the risk of exploitation. Examples of such dual relationships include, but are not limited to, research with and treatment of employees, students, supervisees, close friends, or relatives. Sexual intimacies with clients are unethical.

b. When a psychologist agrees to provide services to a client at the request of a third party, the psychologist assumes the responsibility of clarifying the nature of the relationships to all parties concerned.

c. Where the demands of an organization require psychologists to violate these Ethical Principles, psychologists clarify the nature of the conflict between the demands and these principles. They inform all parties of psychologists' ethical responsibilities and take appropriate action.

d. Psychologists make advance financial arrangements that safeguard the best interests of and are clearly understood by their clients. They contribute a portion of their services to work for which they receive little or no financial return.

e. Psychologists terminate a clinical or consulting relationship when it is reasonably clear that the consumer is not benefiting from it. They offer to help the consumer locate alternative sources of assistance.

Principle 7: Professional Relationships

Psychologists act with due regard for the needs, special competencies, and obligations of their colleagues in psychology and other professions. They respect the prerogatives and obligations of the institutions or organizations with which these other colleagues are associated.

a. Psychologists understand the areas of competence of related professions. They make full use of all the professional, technical, and administrative resources that serve the best interests of consumers. The absence of formal relationships with other professional workers does not relieve psychologists of the responsibility of securing for their clients the best possible professional service, nor does it relieve them of the obligation to exercise foresight, diligence, and tact in obtaining the complementary or alternative assistance needed by clients.

b. Psychologists know and take into account the traditions and practices of other professional groups with whom they work and cooperate fully with such groups. If a psychologist is contacted by a person who is already receiving similar services from another professional, the psychologist carefully considers that professional relationship and proceeds with caution and sensitivity to the therapeutic issues as well as the client's welfare. The psychologist discusses these issues with the client so as to minimize the risk of confusion and conflict.

c. Psychologists who employ or supervise other professionals or professionals in training accept the obligation to facilitate the further professional development of these individuals. They provide appropriate working conditions, timely evaluations, constructive consultation and experience opportunities.

d. Psychologists do not exploit their professional relationships with clients, supervisees, students, employees, or research participants sexually or otherwise. Psychologists do not condone or engage in sexual harassment. Sexual harassment is defined as deliberate or repeated comments, gestures, or physical contacts of a sexual nature that are unwanted by the recipient.

e. In conducting research in institutions or organizations, psychologists secure appropriate authorization to conduct such research. They are aware of their obligations to future research workers and ensure that host institutions receive adequate information about the research and proper acknowledgment of their contributions.

f. Publication credit is assigned to those who have contributed to a publication in proportion to their professional contributions. Major contributions of a professional character made by several persons to a common project are recognized by joint authorship, with the individual who made the principal contribution listed first. Minor contributions of a professional character and extensive clerical or similar nonprofessional assistance may be acknowledged in footnotes or in an introductory statement. Acknowledgment through specific citations is made for unpublished as well as published material that has directly influenced the research or writing. Psychologists who compile and edit material of others for publication publish the material in the name of the originating group, if appropriate, with their own name appearing as chairperson or editor. All contributors are to be acknowledged and named.

Principle 8: Assessment Techniques

In the development, publication, and utilization of psychological assessment techniques, psychologists make every effort to promote the welfare and best interests of the client. They guard against the misuse of assessment results. They respect the client's right to know the results, the interpretations made, and the bases for their conclusions and recommendations. Psychologists make every effort to maintain the security of tests and other assessment techniques within limits of legal mandates. They strive to ensure the appropriate use of assessment techniques by others.

a. In using assessment techniques, psychologists respect the right of clients to have full explanations of the nature and purpose of the techniques in language the clients can understand, unless an explicit exception to this right has been agreed upon in advance. When the explanations are to be provided by others, psychologists establish procedures for ensuring the adequacy of these explanations.
b. Psychologists responsible for the development and standardization of psychological tests and other assessment techniques utilize established scientific procedures and observe the relevant APA standards.
c. In reporting assessment results, psychologists indicate any reservations that exist regarding validity or reliability because of the circumstances of the assessment or the inappropriateness of the norms for the person tested. Psychologists strive to en-

sure that the results of assessments and their interpretations are not misused by others.
d. Psychologists recognize that assessment results may become obsolete. They make every effort to avoid and prevent the misuse of obsolete measures.
e. Psychologists offering scoring and interpretation services are able to produce appropriate evidence for the validity of the programs and procedures used in arriving at interpretations. The public offering of an automated interpretation service is considered a professional-to-professional consultation. Psychologists make every effort to avoid misuse of assessment reports.
f. Psychologists do not encourage or promote the use of psychological assessment techniques by inappropriately trained or otherwise unqualified persons through teaching, sponsorship, or supervision.

Principle 9: Research with Human Participants

The decision to undertake research rests upon a considered judgment by the individual psychologist about how best to contribute to psychological science and human welfare. Having made the decision to conduct research, the psychologist considers alternative directions in which research energies and resources might be invested. On the basis of this consideration, the psychologist carries out the investigation with respect and concern for the dignity and welfare of the people who participate and with cognizance of federal and state regulations and professional standards governing the conduct of research with human participants.

a. In planning a study, the investigator has the responsibility to make a careful evaluation of its ethical acceptability. To the extent that the weighing of scientific and human values suggests a compromise of any principle, the investigator incurs a correspondingly serious obligation to seek ethical advice and to observe stringent safeguards to protect the rights of human participants.
b. Considering whether a participant in a planned study will be a "subject at risk" or a "subject at minimal risk," according to recognized standards, is of primary ethical concern to the investigator.
c. The investigator always retains the responsibility for ensuring ethical practice in research. The investigator is also responsible for the ethical treatment of research participants by collaborators, assistants, students, and employees, all of whom, however, incur similar obligations.

d. Except in minimal-risk research, the investigator establishes a clear and fair agreement with research participants, prior to their participation, that clarifies the obligations and responsibilities of each. The investigator has the obligation to honor all promises and commitments included in that agreement. The investigator informs the participants of all aspects of the research that might reasonably be expected to influence willingness to participate and explains all other aspects of the research about which the participants inquire. Failure to make full disclosure prior to obtaining informed consent requires additional safeguards to protect the welfare and dignity of the research participants. Research with children or with participants who have impairments that would limit understanding and/or communication requires special safeguarding procedures.

e. Methodological requirements of study may make the use of concealment or deception necessary. Before conducting such a study, the investigator has a special responsibility to (i) determine whether the use of such techniques is justified by the study's prospective scientific, educational, or applied value; (ii) determine whether alternative procedures are available that do not use concealment or deception; and (iii) ensure that the participants are provided with sufficient explanation as soon as possible.

f. The investigator respects the individual's freedom to decline to participate in or to withdraw from the research at any time. The obligation to protect this freedom requires careful thought and consideration when the investigator is in a position of authority or influence over the participant. Such positions of authority include, but are not limited to, situations in which research participation is required as part of employment or in which the participant is a student, client, or employee of the investigator.

g. The investigator protects the participant from physical and mental discomfort, harm, and danger that may arise from research procedures. If risks of such consequences exist, the investigator informs the participant of that fact. Research procedures likely to cause serious or lasting harm to a participant are not used unless the failure to use these procedures might expose the participant to risk of greater harm, or unless the research has great potential benefit and fully informed voluntary consent is obtained from each participant. The participant should be informed of procedures for contacting the investigator within a reasonable time period following participation should stress, potential harm, or related questions or concerns arise.

h. After the data are collected, the investigator provides the participant with information about the nature of the study and attempts to remove any misconceptions that may have arisen. Where scientific or human values justify delaying or withholding this information, the investigator incurs a special responsibility to monitor the research and to ensure that there are no damaging consequences for the participant.

i. Where research procedures result in undesirable consequences for the individual participant, the investigator has the responsibility to detect and remove or correct these consequences, including long-term effects.

j. Information obtained about a research participant during the course of an investigation is confidential unless otherwise agreed upon in advance. When the possibility exists that others may obtain access to such information, this possibility, together with the plans for protecting confidentiality, is explained to the participant as part of the procedure for obtaining informed consent.

Principle 10: Care and Use of Animals

An investigator of animal behavior strives to advance understanding of basic behavioral principles and/or to contribute to the improvement of human health and welfare. In seeking these ends, the investigator ensures the welfare of animals and treats them humanely. Laws and regulations notwithstanding, an animal's immediate protection depends upon the scientist's own conscience.

a. The acquisition, care, use, and disposal of all animals are in compliance with current federal, state or provincial, and local laws and regulations.

b. A psychologist trained in research methods and experienced in the care of laboratory animals closely supervises all procedures involving animals and is responsible for ensuring appropriate consideration of their comfort, health, and humane treatment.

c. Psychologists ensure that all individuals using animals under their supervision have received explicit instruction in experimental methods and in the care, maintenance, and handling of the species being used. Responsibilities and activities of individuals participating in a research project are consistent with their respective competencies.

d. Psychologists make every effort to minimize discomfort, illness, and pain of animals. A procedure subjecting animals to pain, stress, or privation is used only when an alternative procedure is unavailable and the goal is justified by its prospective scientific, educational, or applied value. Surgical procedures are performed under appropriate anesthesia; techniques to avoid infection and minimize pain are followed during and after surgery.

e. When it is appropriate that the animal's life be terminated, it is done rapidly and painlessly.

D. Code of Ethics, *National Association of Social Workers*

PREAMBLE

This code is intended to serve as a guide to the everyday conduct of members of the social work profession and as a basis for the adjudication of issues in ethics when the conduct of social workers is alleged to deviate from the standards expressed or implied in this code. It represents standards of ethical behavior for social workers in professional relationships with those served, with colleagues, with employers, with other individuals and professions, and with the community and society as a whole. It also embodies standards of ethical behavior governing individual conduct to the extent that such conduct is associated with an individual's status and identity as a social worker.

This code is based on the fundamental values of the social work profession that include the worth, dignity, and uniqueness of all persons as well as their rights and opportunities. It is also based on the nature of social work, which fosters conditions that promote these values.

In subscribing to and abiding by this code, the social worker is expected to view ethical responsibility in as inclusive a context as each situation demands and within which ethical judgement is required. The social worker is expected to take into consideration all the principles in this code that have a bearing upon any situation in which ethical judgement is to be exercised and professional intervention or conduct is planned. The course of action that the social worker chooses is expected to be consistent with the spirit as well as the letter of this code.

In itself, this code does not represent a set of rules that will prescribe all the behaviors of social workers in all the complexities of professional life. Rather, it offers general principles to guide conduct, and the judicious appraisal of conduct, in situations that have ethical implications. It provides the basis for making judgements about ethical actions before and after they occur. Frequently, the particular situation determines the ethical principles that apply and the manner of their application. In such cases, not only the particular ethical principles are taken into immediate consideration, but also the entire code and its spirit. Specific applications of ethical principles must be judged within the context in which they are being considered. Ethical behavior in a given situation must satisfy not only the judgement of the individual social worker, but also the judgement of an unbiased jury of professional peers.

This code should not be used as an instrument to deprive any social worker of the opportunity or freedom to practice with complete professional integrity; nor should any disciplinary action be taken on the basis of this code without maximum provision for safeguarding the rights of the social worker affected.

The ethical behavior of social workers results not from edict, but from a personal commitment of the individual. This code is offered to affirm the will and zeal of all social workers to be ethical and to act ethicallly in all that they do as social workers.

The following codified ethical principles should guide social workers in the various roles and relationships and at the various levels of responsibility in which

This *Code of Ethics* was adopted by the 1979 NASW Delegate Assembly and revised by the 1990 NASW Delegate Assembly. Reprinted with the permission of the National Association of Social Workers.

they function professionally. These principles also serve as a basis for the adjudication by the National Association of Social Workers of issues in ethics.

In subscribing to this code, social workers are required to cooperate in its implementation and abide by any disciplinary rulings based on it. They should also take adequate measures to discourage, prevent, expose, and correct the unethical conduct of colleagues. Finally, social workers should be equally ready to defend and assist colleagues unjustly charged with unethical conduct.

SUMMARY OF MAJOR PRINCIPLES

I. The Social Worker's Conduct and Comportment as a Social Worker

A. *Propriety.* The Social worker should maintain high standards of personal conduct in the capacity or identity as social worker.

B. *Competence and professional development.* The social worker should strive to become and remain proficient in professional practice and the performance of professional functions.

C. *Service.* The social worker should regard as primary the service obligation of the social work profession.

D. *Integrity.* The social worker should act in accordance with the highest standards of professional integrity.

E. *Scholarship and research.* The social worker engaged in study and research should be guided by the conventions of scholarly inquiry.

II. The Social Worker's Ethical Responsibility to Clients

F. *Primacy of clients' interests.* The social worker's primary responsibility is to clients.

G. *Rights and prerogatives of clients.* The social worker should make every effort to foster maximum self-determination on the part of clients.

H. *Confidentiality and privacy.* The social worker should respect the privacy of clients and hold in confidence all information obtained in the course of professional service.

I. *Fees.* When setting fees, the social worker should ensure that they are fair, reasonable, considerate, and commensurate with the service performed and with due regard for the clients' ability to pay.

III. The Social Worker's Ethical Responsibility to Colleagues

J. *Respect, fairness, and courtesy.* The social worker should treat colleagues with respect, courtesy, fairness, and good faith.

K. *Dealing with colleagues' clients.* The social worker has the responsibility to relate to the clients of colleagues with full professional consideration.

IV. The Social Worker's Ethical Responsibility to Employers and Employing Organizations

L. *Commitments to employing organizations.* The social worker should adhere to commitments made to the employing organizations.

V. The Social Worker's Ethical Responsibility to the Social Work Profession

M. *Maintaining the integrity of the profession.* The social worker should uphold and advance the values, ethics, knowledge, and mission of the profession.

N. *Community service.* The social worker should assist the profession in making social services available to the general public.

O. *Development of knowledge.* The social worker should take responsibility for identifying, developing, and fully utilizing knowledge for professional practice.

VI. The Social Worker's Ethical Responsibility to Society

P. *Promoting the general welfare.* The social worker should promote the general welfare of society.

THE NASW CODE OF ETHICS

I. The Social Worker's Conduct and Comportment as a Social Worker

A. *Propriety.* The social worker should maintain high standards of personal conduct in the capacity or identity as social worker.

   1. The private conduct of the social worker is a personal matter to the same degree as is any other person's, except when such conduct compromises the fulfillment of professional responsibilities.

2. The social worker should not participate in, condone, or be associated with dishonesty, fraud, deceit, or misrepresentation.

3. The social worker should distinguish clearly between statements and actions made as a private individual and as a representative of the social work profession or an organization or group.

B. *Competence and professional development.* The social worker should strive to become and remain proficient in professional practice and the performance of professional functions.

1. The social worker should accept responsibility or employment only on the basis of existing competence or the intention to acquire the necessary competence.

2. The social worker should not misrepresent professional qualifications, education, experience, or affiliations.

C. *Service.* The social worker should regard as primary the service obligation of the social work profession.

1. The social worker should retain ultimate responsibility for the quality and extent of the service that individual assumes, assigns, or performs.

2. The social worker should act to prevent practices that are inhumane or discriminatory against any person or group of persons.

D. *Integrity.* The social worker should act in accordance with the highest standards of professional integrity and impartiality.

1. The social worker should be alert to and resist the influences and pressures that interfere with the exercise of professional discretion and impartial judgement required for the performance of professional functions.

2. The social worker should not exploit professional relationships for personal gain.

E. *Scholarship and research.* The social worker engaged in study and research should be guided by the conventions of scholarly inquiry.

1. The social worker engaged in research should consider carefully its possible consequences for human beings.

2. The social worker engaged in research should ascertain that the consent of participants in the research is voluntary and informed, without any implied deprivation or penalty for refusal to participate, and with due regard for participants' privacy and dignity.

3. The social worker engaged in research should protect participants from unwarranted physical or mental discomfort, distress, harm, danger, or deprivation.

4. The social worker who engages in the evaluation of services or cases should discuss them only for the professional purposes and only with persons directly and professionally concerned with them.

5. Information obtained about participants in research should be treated as confidential.

6. The social worker should take credit only for work actually done in connection with scholarly and research endeavors and credit contributions made by others.

II. The Social Worker's Ethical Responsibility to Clients

F. *Primacy of clients' interest.* The social worker's primary responibility is to clients.

1. The social worker should serve clients with devotion, loyalty, determination, and the maximum application of professional skill and competence.

2. The social worker should not exploit relationships with clients for personal advantage.

3. The social worker should not practice, condone, facilitate or collaborate with any form of discrimination on the basis of race, color, sex, sexual orientation, age, religion, national origin, marital status, political belief, mental or physical handicap, or any other preference or personal characteristic, condition or status.

4. The social worker should avoid relationships or commitments that conflict with the interests of clients.

5. The social worker should under no circumstances engage in sexual activities with clients.

6. The social worker should provide clients with accurate and complete information regarding the extent and nature of the services available to them.

7. The social worker should apprise clients of their risks, rights, opportunities, and obligations associated with social service to them.

8. The social worker should seek advice and counsel of colleagues and supervisors whenever such consultation is in the best interest of clients.

9. The social worker should terminate service to clients, and professional relationships with them, when such service and relationships are no longer required or no longer serve the clients' needs or interests.

10. The social worker should withdraw services precipitously only under unusual circumstances, giving careful consideration to all factors in the situation and taking care to minimize possible adverse effects.

11. The social worker who anticipates the termination or interruption of service to clients should notify clients promptly and seek the transfer, referral, or continuation of service in relation to the clients' needs and preferences.

G. *Rights and prerogatives of clients.* The social worker should make every effort to foster maximum self-determination on the part of clients.

 1. When the social worker must act on behalf of a client who has been adjudged legally incompetent, the social worker should safeguard the interests and rights of that client.

 2. When another individual has been legally authorized to act in behalf of a client, the social worker should deal with that person always with the client's best interest in mind.

 3. The social worker should not engage in any action that violates or diminishes the civil or legal rights of clients.

H. *Confidentiality and privacy.* The social worker should respect the privacy of clients and hold in confidence all information obtained in the course of professional service.

 1. The social worker should share with others confidences revealed by clients, without their consent, only for compelling professional reasons.

 2. The social worker should inform clients fully about the limits of confidentiality in a given situation, the purposes for which information is obtained, and how it may be used.

 3. The social worker should afford clients reasonable access to any official social work records concerning them.

 4. When providing clients with access to records, the social worker should take due care to protect the confidences of others contained in those records.

5. The social worker should obtain informed consent of clients before taping, recording, or permitting third party observation of their activities.

I. *Fees.* When setting fees, the social worker should ensure that they are fair, reasonable, considerate, and commensurate with the service performed and with due regard for the clients' ability to pay.

 1. The social worker should not accept anything of value for making a referral.

III. The Social Worker's Ethical Responsibility to Colleagues

J. *Respect, fairness, and courtesy.* The social worker should treat colleagues with respect courtesy, fairness, and good faith.

 1. The social worker should cooperate with colleagues to promote professional interests and concerns.

 2. The social worker should respect confidences shared by colleagues in the course of their professional relationships and transactions.

 3. The social worker should create and maintain conditions of practice that facilitate ethical and competent professional performance by colleagues.

 4. The social worker should treat with respect, and represent accurately and fairly, the qualifications, views, and findings of colleagues and use appropriate channels to express judgements on these matters.

 5. The social worker who replaces or is replaced by a colleague in professional practice should act with consideration for the interest, character, and reputation of that colleague.

 6. The social worker should not exploit a dispute between a colleague and employers to obtain a position or otherwise advance the social worker's interest.

 7. The social worker should seek arbitration or mediation when conflicts with colleagues require resolution for compelling professional reasons.

 8. The social worker should extend to colleagues of other professions the same respect and cooperation that is extended to social work colleagues.

9. The social worker who serves as an employer, supervisor, or mentor to collegues should make orderly and explicit arrangements regarding the conditions of their continuing professional relationship.

10. The social worker who has the responsibility for employing and evaluating the performance of other staff members, should fulfill such responsibility in a fair, considerate, and equitable manner, on the basis of clearly enunciated criteria.

11. The social worker who has the responsibility for evaluating the performance of employees, supervisees, or students should share evaluations with them.

K. *Dealing with colleagues' clients.* The social worker has the responsibility to relate to the clients of colleagues with full professional consideration.

1. The social worker should not assume professional responsibility for the clients of another agency or a colleague without appropriate communication with that agency or colleague.

2. The social worker who serves the clients of colleagues, during a temporary absence or emergency, should serve those clients with the same consideration as that afforded any client.

IV. The Social Worker's Ethical Responsibility to Employers and Employing Organizations.

L. *Commitments to employing organization.* The social worker should adhere to commitments made to the employing organization.

1. The social worker should work to improve the employing agency's policies and procedures, and the efficiency and effectiveness of its services.

2. The social worker should not accept employment or arrange student field placements in an organization which is currently under public sanction by NASW for violating personnel standards, or imposing limitations on or penalties for professional actions on behalf of clients.

3. The social worker should act to prevent and eliminate discrimination in the employing organization's work assignments and in its employment policies and practices.

4. The social worker should use with scrupulous regard, and only for the purpose for which they are intended, the resources of the employing organization.

V. The Social Worker's Ethical Responsibility to the Social Work Profession

M. *Maintaining the integrity of the profession.* The social worker should uphold and advance the values, ethics, knowledge, and mission of the profession.

1. The social worker should protect and enhance the dignity and integrity of the profession and should be responsible and vigorous in discussion and criticism of the profession.

2. The social worker should take action through appropriate channels against unethical conduct by any other member of the profession.

3. The social worker should act to prevent the unauthorized and unqualified practice of social work.

4. The social worker should make no misrepresentation in advertising as to qualifications, competence, service, or results to be achieved.

N. *Community service.* The social worker should assist the profession in making social services available to the general public.

1. The social worker should contribute time and professional expertise to activities that promote respect for the utility, the integrity, and the competence of the social work profession.

2. The social worker should support the formulation, development, enactment and implementation of social policies of concern to the profession.

O. *Development of knowledge.* The social worker should take responsibility for identifying, developing, and fully utilizing knowledge for professional practice.

1. The social worker should base practice upon recognized knowledge relevant to social work.

2. The social worker should critically examine, and keep current with emerging knowledge relevant to social work.

3. The social worker should contribute to the knowledge base of social work and share research knowledge and practice wisdom with colleagues.

VI. The Social Worker's Ethical Responsibility to Society

P. *Promoting the general welfare.* The social worker should promote the general welfare of society.

1. The social worker should act to prevent and eliminate discrimination against any person or group on the basis of race, color, sex, sexual orientation, age, religion, national origin, marital status, political belief, mental or physical handicap, or any other preference or personal characteristic, condition, or status.

2. The social worker should act to ensure that all persons have access to the resources, services, and opportunities which they require.

3. The social worker should act to expand choice and opportunity for all persons, with special regard for disadvantaged or oppressed groups and persons.

4. The social worker should promote conditions that encourage respect for the diversity of cultures which constitute American society.

5. The social worker should provide appropriate professional services in public emergencies.

6. The social worker should advocate changes in policy and legislation to improve social conditions and to promote social justice.

7. The social worker should encourage informed participation by the public in shaping social policies and institutions.

E. Other Ethical Codes

- *Principles of Medical Ethics, with Annotations Especially Applicable to Psychiatry,* American Psychiatric Association (1989)
- *Ethical Standards for School Counselors,* American School Counselors Associatoin (1984)
- *Code of Ethics for Mental Health Counselors,* National Academy of Certified Clinical Mental Health Counselors (1987)
- *Code of Ethics,* Commission on Rehabilitation Counselor Certification (1987)
- *Ethical Standards for Rehabilitation Counselors,* National Rehabilitation Counseling Association
- *Code of Ethics,* National Board for Certified Counselors (1989)
- *Standards for Counseling Supervisors,* Association for Counselor Education and Supervision (1990)
- *Ethical Guidelines for Group Counselors,* Association for Specialists in Group Work (1989)
- Standards for the Practice of Clinical Social Work, National Association of Social Workers (1989)
- *Code of Ethics,* National Federation of Societies for Clinical Social Work (1985)

F. A Guide to Professional Organizations

It is a good idea while a student to begin your identification with state, regional, and national professional associations. To assist you in learning about student memberships, we list some of the major national professional organizations, along with a summary of student-membership benefits, if applicable.

American Association for Counseling and Development

The AACD has 56 state branches and four regional branch assemblies. Students qualify for a special annual membership rate of $32 and half-price membership in any of the 14 divisions. AACD membership provides a subscription to the *Journal of Counseling and Development* and eligibility for professional liability-insurance programs, legal-defense services, and professional development through workshops and conventions. For further information contact:

American Association for Counseling and
  Development
5999 Stevenson Avenue
Alexandria, VA 22304
(703) 823-9800

National Board for Certified Counselors

The NBCC offers a certification program for counselors. National Certified Counselors meet the generic professional standards established by the board and agree to abide by the NBCC *Code of Ethics* (amended in 1989). NCCs work in a variety of educational and social-service settings, such as schools, private practice, mental-health agencies, correctional facilities, community agencies, rehabilitation agencies, and business and industry. To qualify to be an NCC, candidates must meet the minimum requirements for both education and professional-counseling experience established by the NBCC. For a copy of the *Code of Ethics* and further information about becoming a National Certified Counselor, contact:

National Board for Certified Counselors
P. O. Box 5406
Greensboro, NC 27435

American Association for Marriage and Family Therapy

The AAMFT has a student-membership category. You must obtain an official application, including the names of at least two Clinical Members from whom the association can request official endorsements. You also need a statement, signed by the coordinator or director of a graduate program in marital and family therapy in a regionally accredited educational institution, verifying your current enrollment. Student membership may be held until receipt of a qualifying graduate degree or for a maximum of five years. Members receive the *Journal of Marital and Family Therapy*, which is published four times a year, and a subscription to six issues yearly of *Family Therapy News*. For an application and further information write to:

American Association for Marriage and Family
  Therapy
1100 17th Street, NW, 10th Floor
Washington, DC 20036-4601
(202) 452-0109

National Association of Social Workers

NASW membership is open to all professional social workers. The NASW Press produces *Social Work* and the *NASW News* as membrhsip benefits. The association offers a number of pamphlets. Regarding practice standards, the following publications are available by contacting the association:

- *Standards and Guidelines for Social Work Case Management for the Functionally Impaired*
- *Standards for the Practice of Clinical Social Work*
- *Standards for Social Work in Health Care Settings*
- *Standards for Social Work Practice in Child Protection*
- *Standards for Social Work Services in Long-Term Care Facilities*
- *Standards for Social Work Services in Schools*

For a copy of any of the above pamphlets, for a copy of the NASW *Code of Ethics*, or for information on membership categories and benefits, write to:

National Association of Social Workers
7981 Eastern Avenue
Silver Spring, MD 20910
(301) 565-0333

National Organization for Human Services Education

Human-service educators will find the National Organization for Human Service Education of use. Members are drawn from diverse disciplines—mental health, child care, social services, gerontology, recreation, corrections, and developmental disabilities. Membership is open to human-service educators, students, fieldwork supervisors, and direct-care professionals. For further information, write to:

National Organization for Human Service Education
c/o Robert Heasley
Department of Human Services
University of Alaska, Anchorage
3211 Providence Drive
Anchorage, AK 99508

American Psychological Association

The APA has a Student Affiliates category rather than student membership. Journals and subscriptions are extra. Each year in mid- or late August the APA holds a national convention. For further information, or for a copy of the *Ethical Principles of Psychologists,* write to:

American Psychological Association
1200 17th Street, NW
Washington, DC 20036
(202) 955-7600

In addition to the national organization there are seven regional divisions, each of which has an annual convention. For addresses or information about student membership in any of them, contact the main office of the APA or see a copy of the association's monthly journal, *American Psychologist:*

- New England Psychological Association
- Southeastern Psychological Association
- Eastern Psychological Association
- Southwestern Psychological Association
- Western Psychological Association
- Midwestern Psychological Association
- Rocky Mountain Psychological Association

The APA has a number of publications that may be of interest to you. The following can be ordered from:

American Psychological Association, Order Department
P. O. Box 2710
Hyattsville, MD 20784-0710
(703) 247-7705

1. *Specialty Guidelines for Delivery of Services by Psychologists*
   - "Delivery of Services by Clinical Psychologists"
   - "Delivery of Services by Counseling Psychologists"
   - "Delivery of Services by School Psychologists"
   - "Delivery of Services by Industrial/Organizational Psychologists"
2. *Careers in Psychology* (pamphlet)
3. *How to Manage Your Career in Psychology*
4. *Is Psychology the Major for You? Planning for Your Undergraduate Years*
5. *Graduate Study in Psychology and Associated Fields.* Information on graduate programs in the United States and Canada, including staff/student statistics, financial aid deadlines, tuition, teaching opportunities, housing, degree requirements, and program goals.

6. *Preparing for Graduate Study: Not for Seniors Only!*
7. *Ethnic Minority Perspectives on Clinical Training and Services in Psychology*
8. *Toward Ethnic Diversification in Psychology Education and Training*
9. *Ethical Principles in the Conduct of Research with Human Participants*
10. *Standards for Educational and Psychological Testing.* Revised standards for evaluating the quality of tests, testing practices, and the effects of test use. There are also chapters on licensure and certification and program evaluation. New in this edition are chapters on testing linguistic minorities and the rights of test takers.

American Psychoanalytic Association

The American Psychoanalytic Association approved a code of ethics in 1975 and revised it in 1983. Some of its sections deal with relationships with patients and colleagues, protection of confidentiality, fees, dispensing of drugs, consultation, sexual misconduct, remedial measures for the psychoanalyst, and safeguarding the public and the profession. These principles of ethics can be secured by writing to:

American Psychoanalytic Association
309 East 49th Street
New York, NY 10017

American Psychiatric Association

The American Psychiatric Association has a code of ethics entitled *Principles of Medical Ethics, with Annotations Especially Applicable to Psychiatry.* The address of this organization is:

1400 K Street, NW
Washington, DC 20005
(202) 682-6000

Sociological Practice Association

The Sociological Practice Association is the professional organization of clinical and applied sociologists. Clinical sociology is sociological intervention. Clinical sociologists have speciality areas such as organizations, health and illness, forensic sociology, aging, and comparative social systems. They work as action researchers, organizational-development specialists, socio-therapists, conflict interventionists, social-policy implementers, and consultants. For information regarding certification instructions and for a copy of the *Ethical Standards of Sociological Practitioners,* contact:

Sociological Practice Association
RD2, Box 141A
Chester, NY 10918

Name Index

Subject Index